THE ENLIGHTENMENT:

An Interpretation

The Rise of Modern Paganism

THE
Enlightenment:
AN
INTERPRETATION

The Rise of
Modern Paganism

by PETER GAY

VINTAGE BOOKS
A Division of Random House
New York

FOR RUTHIE

Boerhave utilior Hippocrate,
Newton totâ antiquitate,
Tassus Homero;
　　　　sed gloria primis.

VOLTAIRE,
Notebook entry, around 1750

Preface

THIS ESSAY is the first of two related but independent volumes which together will offer a comprehensive interpretation of the Enlightenment. For the last half century or more, intellectual historians, students of literature, and political theorists have worked to restore the Enlightenment to its true stature, to rescue it from its admirers nearly as much as from its detractors. They have published authoritative editions of major texts, discovered new documents, and compiled exhaustive, accurate, often supremely revealing collections of the philosophes' correspondence. And they have not rested content with this essential but technical labor; they have been angry. Ever since the fulminations of Burke and the denunciations of the German Romantics, the Enlightenment has been held responsible for the evils of the modern age, and much scorn has been directed at its supposed superficial rationalism, foolish optimism, and irresponsible Utopianism. Compared to these distortions, more superficial, foolish, and irresponsible than the failings they claim to castigate, the amiable caricature drawn by liberal and radical admirers of the Enlightenment has been innocuous: the naïveté of the Left has been far outweighed by the malice of the Right. Still, like the conservative view, the liberal view of the Enlightenment remains unsatisfactory and calls for revision. And so scholars have turned to polemics. I have had my share in these polemics, especially against the Right, and I must confess that I have enjoyed them. But the time is ready and the demand urgent to move from polemics to synthesis.

Synthesis demands regard for complexity: the men of the Enlightenment were divided by doctrine, temperament, environment, and generations. And in fact the spectrum of their ideas, their sometimes acrimonious disputes, have tempted many historians to abandon the search for a single Enlightenment. What, after all, does Hume, who was a conservative, have in common with Condorcet, who was a democrat? Holbach, who ridiculed all religion, with Lessing, who practically tried to invent one? Diderot, who envied and despised antiquaries, with Gibbon, who admired and emulated them? Rousseau, who worshipped Plato, with Jefferson, who could not bring himself to finish the *Republic*? But I decided that to yield to the force of these questions would be to fall into a despairing nominalism, to reduce history to biography, and thus to sacrifice unity to variety. These questions have their uses, but mainly as a corrective: they keep historians from sacrificing variety to unity and help to free them from simplistic interpretations that have served them for so long and so badly—interpretations that treat the Enlightenment as a compact body of doctrine, an Age of Reason, and then take the vitalism of Diderot, the passion of Rousseau, or the skepticism of Hume, as foreign bodies, as harbingers of Romanticism. This is definition by larceny; it is to strip the Enlightenment of its wealth and then complain about its poverty. I shall follow neither of these methods in these volumes. I shall respect the differences among the philosophes which, after all, supplied the Enlightenment with much of its vigor, generated much of its inner history. Yet, mindful that general names are not Platonic ideas but baskets collecting significant similarities, I shall speak throughout of *the* philosophes, and call the totality of their ideas, their strategies, and their careers, *the* Enlightenment, and I shall use these terms to refer to what I shall call a family, a family of intellectuals united by a single style of thinking.

While the Enlightenment was a family of philosophes, it was something more as well: it was a cultural climate, a world in which the philosophes acted, from which they noisily rebelled and quietly drew many of their ideas, and on which they attempted to impose their program. But the philosophes' world, *their* eighteenth century, was at least in part an ideological construct; their passionate engagement with their time gave them access to some of its deepest currents, but it also closed their eyes to some inconvenient realities. I found it essential therefore to account not merely for the philosophes' ideas and for the interplay of these ideas with their world but also to judge the adequacy or inadequacy of their perceptions. Is Jefferson's virtuous Roman Republic the Roman Republic of twentieth-century scholarship? Is Hume's Cicero our Cicero? Is the philosophes' "revival of letters" our Renaissance? It was questions like these that led me from intellectual to social history, to inquire whether and to what extent the Enlightenment which the philosophes constructed and experienced was the Enlightenment we now observe as a historical event.

Since I found myself primarily interested in the encounter of ideas with reality, I quite naturally made the experience of the philosophes the central concern and the organizing principle of my interpretation. The philosophes' experience, I discovered, was a dialectical struggle for autonomy, an attempt to assimilate the two pasts they had inherited—Christian and pagan—to pit them against one another and thus to secure their independence. The Enlightenment may be summed up in two words: criticism and power. Voltaire once wrote in a private letter that he knew how to hate because he knew how to love, and the other philosophes too employed destructive criticism to clear the ground for construction, so that criticism itself achieved a creative role. The Enlightenment, as Ernst Cassirer felicitously expresses it, "joined, to a degree scarcely ever achieved before, the critical with the productive function and converted the one directly into the other."

As the subtitle of this book makes plain, I see the philosophes' rebellion succeeding in both of its aims: theirs was a paganism directed against their Christian inheritance and dependent upon the paganism of classical antiquity, but it was also a *modern* paganism, emancipated from classical thought as much as from Christian dogma. The ancients taught the philosophes the uses of criticism, but it was modern philosophers who taught them the possibilities of power. In this book, I study the philosophes' education: I trace the fortunes of criticism from its prosperity in pagan antiquity and its decline in the Christian millennium to its recovery in both Renaissance and sixteenth and seventeenth centuries. What I call in this volume "The Appeal to Antiquity" and

"The Tension with Christianity" represents two essential elements in the dialectical progression from which the Enlightenment's radical program developed. The second volume will deal with that program, the synthesis of the struggle—with "The Pursuit of Modernity." Both volumes, then, are two aspects of a single interpretation, separable mainly for purposes of analysis, but united by an inner necessity. In this book I report on how the philosophes won their freedom; in its successor, which will, I trust, follow shortly, I shall report what they did with it.

I have been working on this essay since 1959 and, in a sense, since 1944, when as an undergraduate at the University of Denver I discovered David Hume. Much that I wrote before 1959, when I published my *Voltaire's Politics: The Poet as Realist*, and most that I have written since then has led up to this volume and the volume that will follow it. I have therefore accumulated many debts, including some debts to myself: if a reader should find here a phrase or an argument that strikes him as familiar, he may be right. Whenever I found it impossible to improve on an earlier formulation and essential to include it here, I have borrowed from myself.

My greatest debt is to my wife, to whom these two volumes are dedicated. She is not a professional historian and has an aversion to the kind of effusive acknowledgment that ascribes all the inspiration, all the merit, to the writer's wife. I appreciate this sentiment and indeed share it; but as a professional historian, I find myself obliged to record the plain truth: while I could have written this book without my wife, I could not have written it so soon, so well, or with so much pleasure; she has carefully read and perceptively criticized every part of it, from the title to the bibliography, often several times, and made invaluable suggestions. Arthur Wilson and Robert K. Webb gave each of the chapters a painstaking reading that was thoughtful and immensely helpful. Charles and Hanna Gray read the early chapters and offered some far-reaching suggestions that supplied clarity badly needed at a critical point. William Bouwsma helped me to revise Chapter IV and much of the rest of the book in long discussions on the relation of religion to criticism. Helen Bacon went over the early chapters with her trained classicist's eye. R. R. Palmer, to whom I have long been in debt, compelled me to think carefully about the relation of the philosophes to their Christian environment; the fruit of his criticism, at once severe and constructive, appears mainly in Chapter VI. For more than fifteen years, Richard Hofstadter has read nearly everything I have written, to my enduring advantage; he has read earlier drafts of this book, in a form now often unrecognizable. That they should now be unrecognizable is due in no small part to him.

Through the last few years, I have talked about this book to other friends. Henry Roberts in particular has been patient with my ideas, generous with my "inspirations," and unstinting in his encouragement. I must thank the nominalist criticism of Rudolf Binion offered at an early stage; it forced me to make my case for a unified Enlightenment as invulnerable as I could. My discovery of the central part played by classical antiquity came partly as the result of some stimulating conversations I had in 1959 and 1960 with the late Walter Dorn. In addition, I am grateful to discussions with Crane Brinton, Leo Gershoy, Beatrice Hofstadter, Irving Kristol, Gertrude Himmelfarb Kristol, Herbert Marcuse, Orest Ranum, Fritz Stern, and John William Ward, all of which, I think, I have turned to account. Raymond Grew and Richard Webster gave me welcome advice on the Italian Enlightenment.

I have been fortunate to be a member of a University Seminar at Columbia University on European Culture in the Eighteenth Century; in the fall of 1962, when it was founded, I presented to it the central argument of these two volumes—the dialectic of the Enlightenment—and had that argument examined, criticized, modified, and strengthened in two years of stimulating debate. I particularly thank my fellow Seminarians James Clifford, Otis Fellows, Allan Hazen, H. Jean Hecht, Albert Hofstadter, Paul Henry Lang, and Rudolf Wittkower. Some of my students have supplied me with some striking quotations and helpful criticisms; I am grateful especially to Gerald Cavanaugh, Stephen Kern, and Victor Wexler. While I did nearly all the research myself, two research assistants, Mrs. Patricia Lavendel and Mr. Augustus Pallotta, did some very useful digging into Italian materials.

In the course of writing this book, I have been able to test out some of its ideas through lectures; both the experience of preparing the lecture and that of rewriting it after discussion have been of great help to me. I am grateful to my gracious hosts and my alert listeners here at home, at Columbia University, Princeton University, Brandeis University, the University of California at Santa Barbara, Vassar College, the University of Minnesota, New York University, Amherst College, and the University of Virginia. In addition, I had some stimulating criticisms of papers I read to the American Historical Association at Chicago and to the French Historical Society at the University of Rochester.

I also gratefully acknowledge aid of a more tangible sort. The Council for Research in the Social Sciences at Columbia University and the Dunning Fund of the History Department at Columbia University gave me welcome funds for research and some indispensable books. I could not have begun to write this ambitious work without a timely and generous Fellowship from the American Council of Learned Societies in 1959–60 (my undertaking, which was to study the victory of modernity in the eighteenth century, will only be fully discharged after I have completed Volume II); I could not have written so much of the manuscript nearly so pleasantly without a Fellowship at the Center for Advanced Study in the Behavioral Sciences in 1963–4. The Center is a splendid refuge from ordinary duties that has been warmly celebrated in many Acknowledgments; let me only add that all the lyrical words spoken about the Center, all the affectionate jokes, are true. I am deeply grateful to Ralph Tyler, Preston Cutler, and Jane Kielsmeier, for making my year there truly productive; I am equally grateful to my secretary at the Center, Joan Warmbrunn. Among those who have patiently typed and retyped this book, Ene Sirvet deserves special thanks for her interest, her care, and her supervision of others. Finally, I want to express my pleasure at being able to complete this book in the fiftieth year of the career of Alfred Knopf, a great publisher with whom it is an honor to be associated; and my gratitude to my editor, Patrick Gregory, for not butchering my prose. Would there were others like him.

PETER GAY

New York City,
November 1965

ABBREVIATIONS USED IN THIS BOOK

AHR: American Historical Review (1895–   )

JHI: Journal of the History of Ideas (1940–   )

PMLA: Publications of the Modern Language Association of America (1884–   )

VS: Studies on Voltaire and the Eighteenth Century, ed. Theodore Besterman (1955–   ). Vol. I appeared under the title *Travaux sur Voltaire et le dix-huitième siècle.*

Warburg Journal: Journal of the Warburg Institute (1937–9); after April 1939 the title changed to *Journal of the Warburg and Courtauld Institute.*

Warburg Vorträge: Vorträge der Bibliothek Warburg, 1921–1922 (1923) to *1930–1931* (1932).

CONTENTS

OVERTURE: The Enlightenment in Its World

  1. *The Little Flock of Philosophes*   3
  2. *Appearances and Realities*   20

BOOK ONE: THE APPEAL TO ANTIQUITY

CHAPTER ONE: The Useful and Beloved Past
  1. *Hebrews and Hellenes*   31
  2. *A Congenial Sense and Spirit*   39
  3. *The Search for Paganism: From Identification to Identity*   59

CHAPTER TWO: The First Enlightenment
  1. *Greece: From Myth to Reason*   72
  2. *The Roman Enlightenment*   94

CHAPTER THREE: The Climate of Criticism
  1. *Criticism as Philosophy*   127
  2. *The Hospitable Pantheon*   160
  3. *The Primacy of Moral Realism*   178
  4. *Candide: The Epicurean as Stoic*   197

BOOK TWO: THE TENSION WITH CHRISTIANITY

CHAPTER FOUR: The Retreat from Reason
  1. *The Adulteration of Antiquity*   212
  2. *The Betrayal of Criticism*   226
  3. *The Rehabilitation of Myth*   236

CHAPTER FIVE: The Era of Pagan Christianity
1. *The Purification of the Sources* 257
2. *Ancients and Moderns: The Ancients* 279
3. *Ancients and Moderns: The Moderns* 308

CHAPTER SIX: In Dubious Battle
1. *The Christian Component* 323
2. *The Treason of the Clerks* 336

CHAPTER SEVEN: Beyond the Holy Circle
1. *The Abuse of Learning* 359
2. *The Mission of Lucretius* 371
3. *David Hume: The Complete Modern Pagan* 401

BIBLIOGRAPHICAL ESSAY

OVERTURE: The Enlightenment in Its World 423
CHAPTER ONE: The Useful and Beloved Past 451
CHAPTER TWO: The First Enlightenment 464
CHAPTER THREE: The Climate of Criticism 482
CHAPTER FOUR: The Retreat from Reason 489
CHAPTER FIVE: The Era of Pagan Christianity 505
CHAPTER SIX: In Dubious Battle 535
CHAPTER SEVEN: Beyond the Holy Circle 547
BIBLIOGRAPHY 553
INDEX *follows page* 556

THE ENLIGHTENMENT:

An Interpretation

The Rise of Modern Paganism

OVERTURE

The Enlightenment in Its World

I. THE LITTLE FLOCK OF PHILOSOPHES

I

THERE WERE MANY philosophes in the eighteenth century, but there was only one Enlightenment. A loose, informal, wholly unorganized coalition of cultural critics, religious skeptics, and political reformers from Edinburgh to Naples, Paris to Berlin, Boston to Philadelphia, the philosophes made up a clamorous chorus, and there were some discordant voices among them, but what is striking is their general harmony, not their occasional discord. The men of the Enlightenment united on a vastly ambitious program, a program of secularism, humanity, cosmopolitanism, and freedom, above all, freedom in its many forms— freedom from arbitrary power, freedom of speech, freedom of trade, freedom to realize one's talents, freedom of aesthetic response, freedom, in a word, of moral man to make his own way in the world. In 1784, when the Enlightenment had done most of its work, Kant defined it as man's emergence from his self-imposed tutelage, and offered as its motto *Sapere aude*—"Dare to know": take the risk of discovery, exercise the right of unfettered criticism, accept the loneliness of autonomy.[1] Like the other philosophes—for Kant only articulated what the others had long suggested in their polemics—Kant saw the Enlightenment as man's claim to be recognized as an adult, responsible being. It is the concord of the philosophes in staking this claim, as much as the

---

[1] "Beantwortung der Frage: Was Ist Aufklärung?" *Werke,* IV, 169.

claim itself, that makes the Enlightenment such a momentous event in the history of the Western mind.

Unity did not mean unanimity. The philosophic coalition was marked, and sometimes endangered, by disparities of philosophical and political convictions. A few—a very few—of the philosophes held tenaciously to vestiges of their Christian schooling, while others ventured into atheism and materialism; a handful remained loyal to dynastic authority, while radicals developed democratic ideas. The French took perverse pleasure in the opposition of church and state to their campaigns for free speech and a humane penal code, and to their polemics against "superstition." British men of letters, on the other hand, were relatively content with their political and social institutions. The German *Aufklärer* were isolated, impotent, and almost wholly unpolitical. As Georg Christoph Lichtenberg, essayist, wit, physicist, and skeptic, wrote in the privacy of his notebooks: "A heavy tax rests, at least in Germany, on the windows of the Enlightenment."[2] In those Italian states that were touched by the new ideas, chiefly Lombardy and Tuscany, the reformers had an appreciative public and found a sympathetic hearing from the authorities. The British had had their revolution, the French were creating conditions for a revolution, the Germans did not permit themselves to dream of a revolution, and the Italians were making a quiet revolution with the aid of the state. Thus the variety of political experience produced an Enlightenment with distinct branches; the philosophes were neither a disciplined phalanx nor a rigid school of thought. If they composed anything at all, it was something rather looser than that: a family.[3]

But while the philosophes were a family, they were a stormy one. They were allies and often friends, but second only to their pleasure in promoting the common cause was the pleasure in criticizing a comrade-in-arms. They carried on an unending debate with one another, and some of their exchanges were any-

---

[2] Aphorism L 88. *Aphorismen, 1793–1799*, ed. Albert Leitzmann (1908), 26.

[3] Since I have already used, and shall continue to use, the word "philosophe" as a synonym for the men of the Enlightenment all over the Western world, I have naturalized it and dropped the awkward italics.

thing but polite. Many of the charges later leveled against the Enlightenment—naïve optimism, pretentious rationalism, unphilosophical philosophizing—were first made by one philosophe against another. Even some of the misinterpretations that have become commonplace since their time were originated by philosophes: Voltaire launched the canard about Rousseau's primitivism, Diderot and Wieland repeated it; Hume was among the first to misread Voltaire's elegant wit as sprightly irresponsibility.

To the delight of their enemies, the philosophes generated a highly charged atmosphere in which friendships were emotional, quarrels noisy, reconciliations tearful, and private affairs public. Diderot, generous to everyone's faults except Rousseau's, found it hard to forgive d'Alembert's prudent desertion of the *Encyclopédie*. Voltaire, fondest of those who did not threaten him with their talent, gave Diderot uneasy and uncomprehending respect, and collaborated on an *Encyclopédie* in which he never really believed; in return, Diderot paid awkward tributes to the literary dictator of the age. He honored Voltaire, he told Sophie Volland, despite his bizarre behavior: "Someone gives him a shocking page which Rousseau, citizen of Geneva, has just scribbled against him. He gets furious, he loses his temper, he calls him villain, he foams with rage; he wants to have the miserable fellow beaten to death. 'Look,' says someone there, 'I have it on good authority that he's going to ask you for asylum, today, tomorrow, perhaps the day after tomorrow. What would you do?' 'What would I do?' replies Voltaire, gnashing his teeth, 'What would I do? I'd take him by the hand, lead him to my room, and say to him, 'Look, here's my bed, the best in the house, sleep there, sleep there for the rest of your life, and be happy.' "[4] There is something a little uneasy beneath this charming fable: Diderot thought well of Voltaire's writings and Voltaire's humane generosity, but he somehow never quite trusted him, and the two men did not meet until 1778, when Voltaire came back to Paris to die. For their part, the Germans, like Lessing, had distant, correct, or faintly unpleasant relations with the French: they admired them judiciously and from afar. Rousseau, at first indulged by all, came to reject and to be rejected by all, even by David Hume. Only

---

[4] January 27, 1766. *Correspondance*, VI, 34.

Hume, corpulent, free from envy and, in society, cheerfully un-skeptical, seems to have been universally popular, a favorite uncle in the philosophic family.

The metaphor of a philosophic family is not my invention. The philosophes used it themselves. They thought of themselves as a *petite troupe,* with common loyalties and a common world view. This sense survived all their high-spirited quarrels: the philosophes did not have a party line, but they were a party. Some of the harshest recriminations remained in the family, and when they did become public, they were usually sweetened by large doses of polite appreciation. Moreover, harassment or the fear of harassment drove the philosophes to remember what they had in common and forget what divided them. The report of a book burned, a radical writer imprisoned, a heterodox passage censured, was enough. Then, quarrelsome officers faced with sudden battle, they closed ranks: the tempest that burst over Helvétius's *De l'esprit* in 1758 and the prohibition issued against Diderot's *Encyclopédie* in the following year did more to weld the philosophes into a party than Voltaire's most hysterical calls for unity. Critics trying to destroy the movement only strength-ened it. In 1757 the journalist Fréron denounced Diderot to the chief censor, Malesherbes, as the "ringleader of a large company; he is at the head of a numerous society which pullulates, and multiplies itself every day by means of intrigues,"[5] but Malesherbes continued to protect the philosophes to the best of his considerable ability. In 1760, Palissot, a clever journalist with good political sense but doubtful taste, wrote a meager comedy entitled *Les philosophes,* in which he lampooned Rousseau as an apelike savage and brutally satirized Helvétius, Diderot, and Duclos as an un-principled gang of hypocrites who exploit idle, gullible society ladies with pretentious schemes. Palissot took it for granted that "everybody knows that there is an offensive and defensive league among these *philosophic* potentates."[6] Obviously, the potentates survived this assault: Horace Walpole, who did not like them, had no hesitation in identifying the little flock when he reached Paris in 1765. "The *philosophes,*" he wrote to Thomas Gray, "are in-

---

[5] March 21, 1757. Quoted in Diderot: *Correspondance,* I, 239.
[6] Quoted in F. C. Green: *Jean-Jacques Rousseau: A Study of His Life and Writings* (1955), 115.

supportable, superficial, overbearing, and fanatic: they preach
incessantly. . . ."[7]

Walpole's characterization is too bilious to be just. In fact,
the philosophes tolerated a wider range of opinions than fanatical
preachers could have: Voltaire was happy to admit that while
atheism is misguided and potentially dangerous, a world filled with
Holbachs would be palatable, far more palatable than a world
filled with Christians, and Holbach, who thought little of deism,
returned the compliment. There was one case, to be sure, that
seems to shatter the unity of the movement: the philosophes'
persecution of Rousseau. But the persecutors did not see it that
way. They rationalized their ruthlessness by arguing that Rousseau
had read himself out of the family to become that most despicable
of beings, an ex-philosophe. "No, my dear," wrote Diderot re-
assuringly to his Sophie Volland in July 1762, shortly after
Rousseau's *Émile* had been condemned and burned, "no, the
Rousseau business will have no consequences. He has the devout
party on his side. He owes their interest in him to the bad things
he says about philosophes. Since they hate us a thousand times
more than they love their God, it matters little to them that he has
dragged Christ in the mud—as long as he is not one of us. They
keep hoping that he will be converted; they're sure that a deserter
from our camp must sooner or later pass over into theirs."[8] While,
in general, arguments among philosophes were conducted in the
tones Voltaire used about Holbach rather than the tones used by
Diderot about Rousseau, Diderot's rhetoric in this letter—"we"
against "they," the military metaphors, and the virulent hatred of
the opposition—reveals at once the anxiety concealed behind the
confident façade and the cohesion achieved by the men of the
Enlightenment by the 1760's.

The Enlightenment, then, was a single army with a single

---

[7] November 19, 1765. *Letters,* ed. Mrs. Paget Toynbee, 16 vols.
(1904–5), VI, 352.
[8] July 18, 1762. *Correspondance,* IV, 55. Another, rather less
tragic case involved Beccaria. After he had acquired a European
reputation in the mid-1760's with his treatise *Dei Delitti e Delle
Pene,* his good friends the Verri brothers, who had encouraged
Beccaria (often indolent and depressed) to write it, began to
gossip about him from sheer envy. But later there was a re-
conciliation.

banner, with a large central corps, a right and left wing, daring scouts, and lame stragglers. And it enlisted soldiers who did not call themselves philosophes but who were their teachers, intimates, or disciples. The philosophic family was drawn together by the demands of political strategy, by the hostility of church and state, and by the struggle to enhance the prestige and increase the income of literary men. But the cohesion among the philosophes went deeper than this: behind their tactical alliances and personal fellowship there stood a common experience from which they constructed a coherent philosophy. This experience—which marked each of the philosophes with greater or lesser intensity, but which marked them all—was the dialectical interplay of their appeal to antiquity, their tension with Christianity, and their pursuit of modernity. This dialectic defines the philosophes and sets them apart from other enlightened men of their age: they, unlike the others, used their classical learning to free themselves from their Christian heritage, and then, having done with the ancients, turned their face toward a modern world view. The Enlightenment was a volatile mixture of classicism, impiety, and science; the philosophes, in a phrase, were modern pagans.

II

To call the Enlightenment pagan is to conjure up the most delightfully irresponsible sexual license: a lazy, sun-drenched summer afternoon, fauns and nymphs cavorting to sensual music, and lascivious paintings, preferably by Boucher. There is some reality in this fantasy: the philosophes argued for a positive appreciation of sensuality and despised asceticism. But these preachers of libertinism were far less self-indulgent, far more restrained in their habits, than their pronouncements would lead us to believe. Rousseau had masochistic tastes which he apparently never gratified; Hume had an affair in France; young Benjamin Franklin "fell into intrigues with low women" and fathered an illegitimate son; Diderot wrote a pornographic novel to keep a mistress in the style to which she hoped to become accustomed; La Mettrie, a glutton, died at the Prussian court shortly after eating a spoiled game pie, thus giving rise to the delicious rumor that

he had eaten himself to death; Voltaire had a passionate, prolonged affair with his niece—one of the few well-kept secrets of
the eighteenth century. But this rather scanty list almost exhausts
salacious gossip about the Enlightenment. Generally, the philosophes worked hard—made, in fact, a cult of work—ate moderately, and knew the joys of faithful affection, although rarely
with their wives. When Diderot found his Sophie Volland in
middle age, he found the passion of his life. His disdain of prostitutes or "loose women," which is such a curious theme in his
correspondence, was not motivated by mean fear of venereal
disease: it was the cheerful acceptance of obligation, the self-
imposed bond of the free man. David Hume testified in 1763 that
the French "Men of Letters" were all "Men of the World, living
in entire or almost entire Harmony among themselves, and quite
irreproachable in their Morals."[9] As a group, the philosophes were
a solid, respectable clan of revolutionaries, with their mission
continually before them.

In speaking of the Enlightenment as pagan, therefore, I am
referring not to sensuality but to the affinity of the Enlightenment to classical thought.[1] Words other than pagan—Augustan,
Classical, Humanist—have served as epithets to capture this
affinity, but they are all circumscribed by specific associations:
they illuminate segments of the Enlightenment but not the whole.
"Augustan" suggests the link between the first and eighteenth
centuries, the parallel between two ages of literary excellence,
mannered refinement, and political corruption. "Classical" brings
to mind Roman temples, Ciceronian gravity, and Greek myths
translated into French couplets. "Humanist" recalls the debt of
the Enlightenment to Renaissance scholarship, and a philosophy

---

[9] Hume to Hugh Blair (? December 1763). *Letters*, I, 419.
[1] It is worth emphasizing that the philosophes did not lay claim
to all possible varieties of paganism. Before the eighteenth century was over, the philosophes were under severe pressure from
a Germanic ideology, a strange mixture of Roman Catholic,
primitive Greek, and folkish Germanic notions—a kind of
Teutonic paganism. Its inspiration was the *Nibelungenlied*, not
Vergil's *Aeneid;* German folk songs, not Horace's *Odes.* Sometimes the benevolent critic, more often the implacable adversary
of the Enlightenment, this Teutonic paganism (quite as much
as traditional Christian doctrine) was to become a formidable
rival to the Mediterranean paganism of the philosophes.

that places man in the center of things. Yet I do not think that any of these terms makes, as it were, enough demands on the Enlightenment; they have about them subtle suggestions of parochialism and anemia of the emotions: "Augustan" properly applies to Great Britain in the first half of the eighteenth century; "Classical" is the name for a noble, artificial literary style and for a preference for antique subject matter; "Humanism" in all its confusing history has come to include an educated piety. The Enlightenment was richer and more radical than any of these terms can suggest: Diderot's plays, Voltaire's stories, Hume's epistemology, Lessing's polemics, Kant's Critiques—which all belong to the core of the Enlightenment—escape through their meshes.

III

For Walpole or Palissot, as for most historians since their time, a philosophe was a Frenchman. But *philosophe* is a French word for an international type, and that is how I shall use it in these pages. To be sure, it is right that the word should be French, for in France the encounter of the Enlightenment with the Establishment was the most dramatic: in eighteenth-century France, abuses were glaring enough to invite the most scathing criticism, while the machinery of repression was inefficient enough to permit critics adequate room for maneuver. France therefore fostered the type that has ever since been taken as *the* philosophe: the facile, articulate, doctrinaire, sociable, secular man of letters. The French philosophe, being the most belligerent, was the purest specimen.

Besides, Paris was the headquarters and French the lingua franca of European intellectuals, and philosophes of all nations were the declared disciples of French writers. In Naples, Gaetano Filangieri, the radical legal reformer, acknowledged that he had received the impetus for writing his *Scienza della Legislazione* from Montesquieu. Beccaria, Filangieri's Milanese counterpart, told his French translator, Morellet, that he owed his "conversion to philosophy" to Montesquieu's *Lettres persanes,* and that d'Alembert, Diderot, Helvétius, Buffon—and Hume—were his "constant reading matter," every day and "in the silence of night."[2] Hume and Gibbon attributed much of their historical consciousness, Adam Ferguson and Jean-Jacques Rousseau, most of their sociological understanding, to their delighted discovery and avid reading of Montesquieu's works. D'Alembert's *Discours préliminaire* to the *Encyclopédie* was widely read in Scotland and on the Continent. Adam Smith, without being a physiocrat himself, learned much from the physiocrats during his French visit from 1764 to 1766. Bentham derived his utilitarianism partly from Helvétius; Kant discovered his respect for the common man by reading Rousseau; while Voltaire's campaigns against *l'infâme* and on behalf of the victims of the French legal system had echoes all over Europe. Even Lessing, in rebellion against the French neo-classical drama of Corneille, Racine, and Voltaire, assailed it with weapons supplied to him by Diderot. And it is significant that monarchs like Catherine of Russia and Frederick of Prussia, who forced themselves on a movement to whose ideals their policies owed little, incessantly proclaimed their indebtedness to French models.

But while Paris was the modern Athens, the preceptor of Europe, it was the pupil as well. French philosophes were the great popularizers, transmitting in graceful language the discoveries of English natural philosophers and Dutch physicians. As early as 1706, Lord Shaftesbury wrote to Jean Le Clerc: "There is a mighty light which spreads itself over the world, especially in those two free nations of England and Holland, on whom the affairs of all Europe now turn."[3] Shaftesbury himself, with his optimistic, worldly, aesthetic, almost feminine Platonism, exercised immense power over his readers: over the young Diderot; over Moses Mendelssohn, Wieland, and Kant; over Thomas Jefferson; all in search of a philosophy of nature less hostile to the things of this world than traditional Christian doctrine. The propagandists of the Enlightenment were French, but its patron saints and pioneers were British: Bacon, Newton, and Locke had such

---

[2] Beccaria to Morellet (January 26, 1766). *Illuministi Italiani,* ed. Franco Venturi (1958), III, 203. In return, the young Montesquieu had greatly admired, and hoped to emulate, the Neapolitan historian Pietro Giannone.

[3] March 6, 1706. *Life, Unpublished Letters, and Philosophical Regimen,* ed. Benjamin Rand (1900), 353.

splendid reputations on the Continent that they quite over-
shadowed the revolutionary ideas of a Descartes or a Fontenelle,
and it became not only tactically useful but intellectually respectable in eighteenth-century France to attribute to British
savants ideas they may well have learned from Frenchmen. In an
Essai sur les études en Russie, probably by Grimm, we are told
that ever since the revival of letters, enlightenment had been
generated in Protestant rather than Catholic countries: "Without
the English, reason and philosophy would still be in the most
despicable infancy in France," and Montesquieu and Voltaire, the
two French pioneers, "were the pupils and followers of England's
philosophers and great men."[4]

Among scientists, poets, and philosophers on the Continent,
this admiration for England became so fashionable that its detractors coined a derisive epithet—Anglomania—which its devotees applied, a little self-consciously, to themselves. Skeptics like
Diderot and Holbach, who ventured at mid-century to find some
fault with British institutions, were in a distinct minority: in the
German-speaking world the poets Hagedorn and Klopstock and
the physicist Lichtenberg confessed to *Englandsehnsucht*, while
Lessing discovered Shakespeare and patterned his first bourgeois
tragedy, *Miss Sara Sampson*, on an English model. In the Italian
states, reformers idealized the English constitution and the English
genius for philosophy: Beccaria's friends could think of no more
affectionate and admiring nickname for him than *Newtoncino*—
little Newton. But *Anglomanie* was practiced most persistently
and most systematically in France: Montesquieu constructed a
fanciful but influential model of the British government for other,
less favored nations to imitate; Voltaire, well prepared by his early
reading, came back in 1728 from his long English visit a serious
deist and firm Newtonian and in general a lifelong worshipper of
England: "A thousand people," he wrote in 1764, "rise up and
declaim against 'Anglomania.' . . . If, by chance, these orators
want to make the desire to study, observe, philosophize like the
English into a crime, they would be very much in the wrong."[5]

---

[4] In Diderot: *Œuvres*, III, 416.
[5] "To the *Gazette littéraire*" (November 14, 1764). *Œuvres*,
XXV, 219–20.

For all of Voltaire's earnest claims, it must be admitted that this cosmopolitan dialogue was not always conducted on the highest level. Hume's influence on the French and the Germans is a study in missed opportunities: Kant, for all his much-advertised debt to Hume, seems never to have read the *Treatise of Human Nature;* except perhaps for d'Alembert and Turgot, the Parisian philosophes, whom Hume greatly liked and who gave him a rousing reception during his stay in the 1760's, neither shared nor fully understood his skepticism; Voltaire, who told an English visitor in his quaint accent that "I am hees great admeerer; he is a very great onor to Ingland, and abofe all to Ecosse,"[6] appears to have been as ignorant of Hume's epistemology as he was amused by Hume's quarrel with Rousseau. Still, not all philosophic intercourse was gossip and triviality. British empiricism transformed French rationalism; French scientific and political propaganda transformed Europe.

The philosophe was a cosmopolitan by conviction as well as by training. Like the ancient Stoic, he would exalt the interest of mankind above the interest of country or clan: as Diderot told Hume in an outburst of spontaneous good feeling, "My dear David, you belong to all nations, and you'll never ask an unhappy man for his birth-certificate. I flatter myself that I am, like you, citizen of the great city of the world."[7] Rousseau's intense patriotism was exceptional. Wieland, with all his pessimism, still thought *Weltbürgertum* a noble ideal: "Only the true cosmopolitan can be a good citizen"; only he can "do the great work to which we have been called: to cultivate, enlighten, and ennoble the human race."[8] Gibbon explained in his magisterial tones that "it is the duty of a patriot to prefer and promote the exclusive interest and glory of his native country; but a philosopher may be permitted to enlarge his views, and to consider Europe as a great republic, whose various inhabitants have attained almost the same level of politeness and cultivation."[9] As products of the best schools, with a solid grip on classical culture, the philosophes, the

---

[6] Ernest C. Mossner: *The Life of David Hume* (1954), 487.

[7] February 22, 1768. *Correspondance*, VIII, 16.

[8] *Gespräche unter vier Augen*, in *Werke*, XLII, 127–8.

[9] *Decline and Fall of the Roman Empire*, IV, 163.

most privileged citizens in Gibbon's great republic, spoke the
same language—literally and figuratively.

The typical philosophe, then, was a cultivated man, a respectable scholar and scientific amateur. The most distinguished
among the little flock were academics like Kant, Lichtenberg,
and Adam Smith, or men of letters like Diderot and Lessing and
Galiani, who possessed an erudition a professor might envy. Some
of the philosophes were in fact more than amateurs in natural
philosophy. Franklin, D'Alembert, Maupertuis, Lichtenberg, and
Buffon first achieved reputations as scientists before they acquired
notoriety as philosophes. Others, like Voltaire, advanced the cause
of scientific civilization with their skillful popularizations of
Newton's discoveries.

At the same time, learned as they were, the philosophes were
rarely ponderous and generally superbly articulate. It was the
philosophe Buffon who coined the celebrated maxim, *Le style est
l'homme même;* the philosophe Lessing who helped to make German into a literary language; the philosophe Hume who wrote the
most elegant of essays as well as the most technical of epistemological treatises. Rigorous Christians found it a source of chagrin
that practically all of the best writers belonged to the philosophic
family. Even men who detested Voltaire's opinions rushed to the
bookseller for his latest production. This concern with style was
linked to an old-fashioned versatility. The philosophes remained
men of letters, at times playwrights, at times journalists, at times
scholars, always wits. Adam Smith was not merely an economist,
but a moralist and political theorist—a philosopher in the most
comprehensive sense. Diderot was, with almost equal competence,
translator, editor, playwright, psychologist, art critic and theorist,
novelist, classical scholar, and educational and ethical reformer.
David Hume has often been accused of betraying his philosophical
vocation for turning in his later years from epistemology to
history and polite essays. But this accusation mistakes Hume's
conception of his place in the world: he was exercising his
prerogative as a man of letters qualified to pronounce on most
aspects of human experience, and writing for a cultivated public
in which he was consumer as well as producer.

Such a type could flourish only in the city, and in fact the
typical philosophe was eminently, defiantly, incurably urban. The

city was his soil; it nourished his mind and transmitted his message. His well-publicized visits to monarchs were more glittering than the life of the coffeehouse, the editor's office, or the salon, which was often little more than a gathering of congenial intellectuals. But they were also less productive. The philosophe belonged to the city, by birth or adoption: if he was born in the country he drifted to the city as his proper habitat. "The Town," observed David Hume in his autobiography, is "the true Scene for a man of Letters."[1] What would Kant have been without Königsberg, Franklin without Philadelphia, Rousseau without Geneva, Beccaria without Milan, Diderot without Paris, or for that matter, Gibbon without Rome? When the philosophe traveled, he moved from urban society to urban society in a pleasant glow of cosmopolitan communication. When he retired to the country, as he often did with protestations of his love for the simple life, he took the city with him: he invited like-minded men of letters to share his solitude, he escaped rural boredom by producing plays, he lined his walls with books, and he kept up with literary gossip through his correspondents in town—his letters were almost like little newspapers. For many years Holbach gathered an international company around his dinner table: Diderot and Raynal were regular visitors, joined from time to time by Horace Walpole, David Hume, the abbé Galiani, and other distinguished foreigners who would sit and talk endlessly about religion, about politics, about all the great forbidden subjects. In Milan, Beccaria, the Verri brothers, and other like-minded *illuministi* founded a newspaper, *Il Caffé*; it was short-lived, but its very existence documents the alliance of sociability and reformism in the Enlightenment everywhere. The leaders of the Scottish Enlightenment—a most distinguished society—were personal as well as intellectual intimates: Adam Smith, David Hume, Adam Ferguson, William Robertson, Lord Home—political economists, aestheticians, moralists, historians, philosophers and philosophes all—held continuous convivial discussions during the day and often through the night in libraries, clubs, coffeehouses, and when these closed, in taverns. Voltaire presided over a literary government-in-exile at Ferney. He stayed away from Paris for

---

[1] *My Own Life*, in *Works*, III, 4.

twenty-eight years in succession, but that did not matter: where
he was, *there* was Paris. The best of the urban spirit—experimental, mobile, irreverent—was in the philosophes' bones.

But this urbanity was colored and sometimes marred by a
sense of mission. The philosophes were threatening the most
powerful institutions of their day, and they were troubled by the
nagging anxiety that they were battling resourceful enemies—
for one, a church (as Voltaire said ruefully) that was truly built
on a rock. That is why the philosophes were both witty and
humorless: the wit was demanded by their profession, the humorlessness imposed on them by their belligerent status. Obsessed by
enemies, not all of whom were imaginary, they were likely to
treat criticism as libel and jokes as blasphemy. They were touchy
in the extreme; Diderot's correspondence and Rousseau's *Confessions* record bickerings over matters not worth a moment of a
grown man's attention. David Hume, who saw through the press
a polemical pamphlet directed against himself, was quite uncharacteristic; far more typical were d'Alembert, who petitioned the
censors to stifle his critics, or Lessing, who pursued scholars of
opposing views and inferior capacities with his relentless, savage
learning. This is what Goethe had in mind when he called the
Berlin *Aufklärer* Nicolai a "Jesuitenfresser"; and this is why
Horace Walpole observed in 1779 that "the *philosophes*, except
Buffon, are solemn, arrogant, dictatorial coxcombs—I need not
say superlatively disagreeable."[2] No doubt Walpole, the fastidious
spectator of life, saw the philosophes clearly, but what he did not
see is that this intensity and self-assurance (which often make men
disagreeable) are occupational hazards which reformers find hard
to avoid.

IV

In drawing this collective portrait, I have indiscriminately
taken evidence from the entire eighteenth century, from Montesquieu to Kant. This procedure has its advantages: it underlines
the family resemblance among the little flock. But it may obscure

---

[2] Walpole to Horace Mann (July 7, 1779). *Letters*, X, 441.

the fact that the Enlightenment had a history. Its end was not like
its beginning precisely because the last generation of philosophes
could draw on the work of its predecessors.

It has been traditional to delimit the Enlightenment within
a hundred-year span beginning with the English Revolution and
ending with the French Revolution. These are convenient and
evocative dates: Montesquieu was born in 1689 and Holbach died
in 1789. To be sure, these limits are not absolute, and there have
been repeated attempts to move the boundaries, to demote the
Enlightenment by calling it the last act of the Renaissance, or to
expand it by including Bayle, or even Descartes, among the philosophes. But while these attempts have thrown much light on the
prehistory of eighteenth-century polemics, I intend to stay with
the traditional dates: I shall argue that while characteristic Enlightenment ideas existed long before, they achieved their revolutionary force only in the eighteenth century. Hobbes, and even
Bayle, lived and wrote in a world markedly different from the
world of Holbach or Hume.

The Enlightenment, then, was the work of three overlapping,
closely associated generations. The first of these, dominated by 1)
Montesquieu and the long-lived Voltaire, long set the tone for
the other two; it grew up while the writings of Locke and Newton were still fresh and controversial, and did most of its great
work before 1750. The second generation reached maturity in 2)
mid-century: Franklin was born in 1706, Buffon in 1707, Hume
in 1711, Rousseau in 1712, Diderot in 1713, Condillac in 1714,
Helvétius in 1715, and d'Alembert in 1717. It was these writers
who fused the fashionable anticlericalism and scientific speculations of the first generation into a coherent modern view of the
world. The third generation, the generation of Holbach and 3)
Beccaria, of Lessing and Jefferson, of Wieland, Kant, and Turgot,
was close enough to the second, and to the survivors of the first,
to be applauded, encouraged, and irritated by both. It moved
into scientific mythology and materialist metaphysics, political
economy, legal reform, and practical politics. Criticism progressed by criticizing itself and its own works.

So the Enlightenment displays not merely coherence but a
distinct evolution, a continuity in styles of thinking as well as a
growing radicalism. The foundations of the philosophes' ideas did

not change significantly: between the young Montesquieu's essay
on ancient Rome and the aging Diderot's defense of Seneca there
is a lapse of half a century, and interest in ancient architecture
and sculpture had risen markedly during the interval; yet for the
two philosophes, the uses of antiquity remained the same. Similarly, the devotion to modern science and the hostility to Christianity that were characteristic of the late Enlightenment had
been characteristic of the early Enlightenment as well. The dialectic which defined the philosophes did not change; what
changed was the balance of forces within the philosophic coalition: as writer succeeded writer and polemic succeeded polemic,
criticism became deeper and wider, more far-reaching, more
uncompromising. In the first half of the century, the leading
philosophes had been deists and had used the vocabulary of natural law; in the second half, the leaders were atheists and used
the vocabulary of utility. In Enlightenment aesthetics, in close
conjunction with the decay of natural law, the neoclassical search
for the objective laws of beauty gave way to subjectivity and
the exaltation of taste, and especially in France, timid and often
trivial political ideas were shouldered aside by an aggressive
radicalism. Yet the scandal the later books caused was no greater
than that caused by the pioneering efforts: had Montesquieu's
Lettres persanes been published in 1770, the year of Holbach's
Système de la nature, rather than in 1721, it would have seemed
tame beside that materialist tract, and would have offered nothing
new to a world long since hardened to cultural criticism.

One reason the educated world of eighteenth-century Europe
and America had come to accept these polemics, or at least to
read them without flinching, was that the hard core of the Enlightenment was surrounded by an ever-growing penumbra of
associates. The dozen-odd captains of the movement, whose names
must bulk large in any history of the European mind, were
abetted by a host of lieutenants. Some of these, little read today,
had a considerable reputation in their time. They were men like
the abbé de Mably, precursor of socialism and propagandist of the
American cause in France; Jean-François Marmontel, fashionable,
mediocre playwright, careerist protégé of Voltaire and d'Alembert elected to the Académie française and chosen Royal Historiographer despite his participation in the *Encyclopédie* and his

pronounced views in favor of toleration; Charles Duclos, brilliant
and widely respected observer of the social scene, novelist, and
historian; the abbé Raynal, ex-priest turned radical historian,
whose *Histoire philosophique et politique des établissements et du
commerce des Européens dans les deux Indes,* first published in
1770, and immediately proscribed, went through several editions,
each more radical than its predecessor; the abbé Galiani, a Neapolitan wit who became an ornament of the Parisian salons and a
serious political economist; Moses Mendelssohn, Lessing's friend
and Kant's correspondent, aesthetician, epistemologist, and advocate of Jewish emancipation; Baron Grimm, who made a good
living purveying the new ideas to monarchs and aristocrats rich
enough to afford his private news service; Louis-Jean-Marie
Daubenton, a distinguished naturalist whose contributions to
science were eclipsed by Buffon, with whom he collaborated;
Freiherr von Sonnenfels, a humane political economist, professor
at the University of Vienna and, for all his advanced ideas, advisor to the Hapsburgs; Nicolas-Antoine Boulanger, who died
young, but left behind him two unorthodox scientific treatises on
the origins of religion for his friend Holbach to publish. These
men were philosophes of the second rank. Beyond them were the
privates of the movement, the hangers-on, consumers and dis-
tributors rather than producers of ideas: men like Étienne-Noël
Damilaville, Voltaire's correspondent in Paris, who basked in
borrowed prestige or secondhand notoriety by running humanitarian errands, smuggling subversive literature through the mails,
hiring theatrical claques, or offering disinterested friendship in a
harsh world. As the century progressed, these aides grew in number and influence: to embattled Christians, they appeared to be
everywhere, in strategic positions—in publishers' offices, in government posts, in exclusive salons, in influential university chairs,
near royal persons, and even in the august Académie française.
By the 1770's and 1780's, precisely when the philosophes had
grown intensely radical in their program, they had also achieved
a respectable place in their society.

2. APPEARANCES AND REALITIES

I

IN 1784, in the essay in which he tried to define the Enlightenment, Kant expressed some skepticism about his century. "If
someone asks," he observed, "are we living in an enlightened age
today? the answer would be, No." But, he immediately added,
"we are living in an Age of Enlightenment."[3]

Kant's observation is penetrating and important. Even late
in the eighteenth century, for all their influence and palpable
successes, the philosophes had reasons for uncertainty and occasional gloom. Voltaire, down to his last days, insisted that his age
was an age of cultural decline, and other philosophes deplored
what they considered the public's willful resistance to them, its
greatest benefactors. "People talk a lot about Enlightenment and
ask for more light," Lichtenberg wrote. "But my God, what good
is all that light, if people either have no eyes, or if those who do
have eyes, resolutely keep them shut?"[4] Diderot, in a moment of
depression, exclaimed to Hume: "Ah, my dear philosopher! Let
us weep and wail over the lot of philosophy. We preach wisdom
to the deaf, and we are still far indeed from the age of reason."[5]
And David Hume himself thought that beyond the world of Enlightenment and its cultivated supporters, there lay a large desert
of darkness; of stubborn indifference, of illiteracy and superstition, a realm he described with obvious distaste as the realm of
"Stupidity, Christianity & Ignorance."[6]

But then—and this was the other side of Kant's Delphic pronouncement—in their optimistic moods the philosophes liked to
think of themselves as the potential masters of Europe. Surveying
the cultural scene from Königsberg, Kant discerned a "revolt

---

[3] "Beantwortung der Frage: Was Ist Aufklärung?" *Werke*, IV,
174.
[4] Aphorism L 469. *Aphorismen, 1793–1799*, 90.
[5] March 17, 1769. *Correspondance*, IX, 40.
[6] Hume to Hugh Blair and others (April 6, 1765). *Letters*,
I, 498.

against superstition" among the civilized countries and civilized classes, and called this revolt the *Aufklärung* and its leaders the *Aufklärer*. The British did not naturalize the name "Enlightenment" until the nineteenth century, but even in the eighteenth, British philosophes thought that they were living in, and dominating, a civilized, philosophical age. The French philosophes liked to speak of a *siècle des lumières* and were sure that they were the men who were bringing light to others; with sublime self-satisfaction (for what can be more self-satisfied than to name a century after yourself?) they praised their age as an Age of Philosophy.

Both of these moods were grounded in reality, but there was more ground for hope than for despair. The Enlightenment of the philosophes was embedded in an enlightened atmosphere, a pervasive and congenial cultural style which supplied them with some of their ideas and much of their vocabulary. At once the gadflies and the representatives of their age, the philosophes preached to a Europe half prepared to listen to them.

Evidence for this enlightened climate is profuse. In 1759— to offer but one instance—Samuel Johnson's *Rasselas* appeared nearly simultaneously with Voltaire's *Candide*, and Johnson himself, Boswell reports, remarked on the resemblance between these two Stoic tracts: had they "not been published so closely one after the other that there was not time for imitation, it would have been in vain to deny that the scheme of that which came latest was taken from the other."[7] Boswell insisted, sensibly enough, that the intentions of the two authors had not been the same, but the crosscurrents of the eighteenth century made this famous conjunction into something more than a coincidence. Samuel Johnson called Voltaire a villain, Voltaire called Samuel Johnson a superstitious dog, but the political, literary, and even philosophical ideas of these two bore a striking resemblance. Voltaire took pride in the culture he was trying in his witty way to improve out of all recognition, while Johnson, who detested the philosophes as unprincipled infidels, accepted much of their program: he had the Enlightenment style. Antiphilosophe and archphilosophe were yoked together as improbable and unwitting allies. All

---

[7] *Life of Johnson* (under 1759), I, 342.

manner of men—even clergymen—claimed to possess light. Even Berkeley, it seems, advanced his outrageous epistemological paradoxes in the name of good sense. William Magee, archbishop of Dublin, voiced his concern over the pernicious influence of Hume's writings on even "the most enlightened"—that is, on modern Christians like himself.[8] And when Johnson and Boswell visited the Hebrides, a Scottish divine proudly told his visitors that the world was wrong to take the local clergy to be "credulous men in a remote corner. We'll show them that we are more enlightened than they think."[9] It is in this sense that the age of Montesquieu was also the age of Pope, the age of Hume also the age of Mozart.

The philosophes discovered influential friends everywhere. A king who tried to abolish the financial privileges of the clergy, a duke who expelled the Jesuits, a censor who winked at materialist tracts, an Anglican bishop who taught that good will was enough to get a Christian into heaven or a Tuscan bishop who prohibited pilgrimages and closed roadside shrines, an aristocrat who protected a proscribed atheist, a scrupulous or sensitive believer (like Albrecht von Haller, say, or Samuel Johnson) who was haunted by religious doubts, and perhaps best of all, a devout scholar who discredited religious mysteries with his philological or historical criticisms—none of these accepted all of the philosophes' program, or even much of it, but each of them was doing the philosophes' work. One of the most significant social facts of the eighteenth century, a priceless gift from the enlightened style to the Enlightenment of the philosophes, was the invasion of theology by rationalism: Jesuits gave fair and even generous hearing to scientific ideas, Protestant divines threw doubt upon the miraculous foundations of their creed, and churches everywhere tepidly resisted the philosophy of the philosophes with their own bland version of modern theology.

This treason of the clerks had its secular counterparts. Revolutionary innovations in science, psychology, economic and social ideas, education, and politics, most of them produced by serious

---

[8] John Rae: *The Life of Adam Smith* (1895), 429.
[9] James Boswell: *Journal of a Tour to the Hebrides with Samuel Johnson, 1773*, ed. Frederick A. Pottle and Charles H. Bennett (1961), 189.

and often by devout Christians, by men like Haller and Euler and Hartley and Priestley, aided the efforts, and consolidated the advanced positions, of the radical Enlightenment. So did the activities—the very mental style—of solid citizens who endowed schools and hospitals, supported humane causes, railed against superstition, and denounced enthusiasm. As I shall show over and over again in these pages, ideas and attitudes generally associated with subversive, atheistic philosophes—the disdain for Gothic architecture and for Dante, the condemnation of feudal institutions, the rejection of metaphysics and of Scholasticism—were the common property of most educated men in the eighteenth century. The philosophes did not lack courage, and their place in history is secure, but the war they fought was half won before they joined it.

II

These brilliant prospects, linked to their belligerent status and bellicose ideology—their uneasy coexistence with their world —obscured for the philosophes the complexity of their situation. Much like other combatants before and after them, the philosophes found it convenient to simplify the welter of their experience, to see their adversaries too starkly, and to dramatize their age as an age of unremitting warfare between the forces of unbelief and the forces of credulity—that is, between good and evil. Diderot's facile separation of the men of his century into philosophers and "enemies of philosophy"[1] was characteristic, but, in truth, both parties were made up of coalitions, both had affectionate ties with their adversary—the course of battle was beclouded by unstable treaties, cowardly retreats, inadequate intelligence of the enemy's strength and movements, moments of low morale, and treason within the ranks. The philosophes themselves were divided by differences over modes of religious thought and political tactics; there was never an end to debate within the little flock, and the triumph of the materialists and utilitarians

---

[1] Diderot to d'Alembert (c. May 10, 1765). *Correspondance*, V, 32.

was never complete. And on the other side, Anglicans, Lutherans, Catholics, were often hostile to one another. And so at times the philosophes, linked to their culture by their cultivation, were friendlier with Christians than with one another.

In their moments of calm reflection, when they discarded the naïve dichotomies that usually served them so admirably, the philosophes did recognize their age as something other than a perpetual bout between critics and Christians. Diderot amicably corresponded with père Berthier, the editor of the Jesuit *Journal de Trévoux;* Hume noted that Bishop Butler, the formidable apologist of Anglican Christianity, had recommended his essays; and even Voltaire, who publicly denounced the Jesuits as power-mad, sly, and as a lot, revolting pederasts, privately conceded that his old Jesuit teachers had been decent men and respectable scholars. But such moments were rare, partly because there were many times of real crisis when the philosophes stood against the rest, when the faithful squared off against unbelievers; besides, in the long run the issues between the secular world the philosophes wanted and the religious world in which they lived could not be compromised. But for all that, the philosophes were tied to their civilization—at least to the enlightened segment of it—by subtle, fine-spun ties. It is ironic to see the philosophes, as overworked ideologists, reluctant to acknowledge these ties: devoted though they were to piercing the veils of appearance, they often took appearances for realities. They were right to think of themselves as modern, secular philosophers, wrong to claim that they owed their Christian culture nothing.

In politics, their false consciousness took rather a different form. Far from dividing their age into two hostile camps, the philosophes cultivated their connections with power, and their cozy fraternizing with the enemy cost them heavily. It distorted their tactics, long circumscribed their freedom of action, some-times seduced them into intellectual dishonesty, and blurred their radicalism, not only for others but for themselves as well. True, not all their protestations of innocuousness need be taken seri-ously: they knew they were more subversive than they admitted to being—their constant evasions testify to that. They were too familiar with the history of martyrs to wish to join them. At the same time, it is clear that the philosophes often misread the drift of their age and the consequences of their ideas. Voltaire's insensitive reading of Rousseau's *Contrat social* and Diderot's equally insensitive reading of Rousseau's *Émile* are symptomatic: here are two of the most intelligent men of the century face to face with two of its prophetic masterpieces—books that came out of the philosophes' world and took some of the philosophes' ideas to their logical conclusion. The intellectual revolution over which the Enlightenment presided pointed to the abolition of hierarchy as much as to the abolition of God. But most of the philosophes found much to cherish in the existing order. It is revealing that Rousseau (and we must always come back to Rousseau when we wish to emphasize the complexity of the Enlightenment), perhaps the only Encyclopedist with moods in which he totally rejected his civilization, was treated as a madman by other philosophes long before his clinical symptoms became obtrusive.

All this does not mean that the philosophes were merely opportunists. They were radicals, even if they were not nihilists: for all the pretentious philosophizing the marquis de Sade injected into his tedious novels, he was never more than a caricature of the Enlightenment whose heir he claimed to be. The philosophes' comfortable sense that they belonged to the Establishment and the Enlightenment at the same time was not solely a symptom of self-deception: there was no conflict in their dual allegiance—not even in France, where the tension was strongest and the rhetoric most extreme. The philosophe Voltaire was royal historiographer and was succeeded in that post by the philosophe Duclos. The philosophe Buffon, aristocratic and self-protective, was the distinguished curator of the *Jardin du Roi*. Turgot cut short his career by preaching toleration of Protestants and by infuriating vested interests with his free-trade policies, but he always considered himself a conscientious servant of the French state. Even d'Alembert, who lived modestly and gave away half he earned, was not wholly detached from the old order: in a letter in which Hume praises his independence he adds that d'Alembert "has five pensions: one from the King of Prussia, one from the French King, one as member of the Academy of Sciences, one as member of the French Academy, and one from his

own family."[2] Such a man, and others like him, were hardly
alienated revolutionaries. After all, they prized wit, admired elegance, and craved the leisure essential to the cultivated life. When
they denounced civilization, they did so urbanely: even Rousseau
confessed that he had adopted his bearish mode of conduct only
because he was too awkward to practice the manners of good
society. Seeking to distinguish themselves, the philosophes had
little desire to level all distinctions; seeking to be respected, they
had no intention of destroying respectability. Their gingerly
treatment of the masses, which became less patronizing as the
century went on, reveals their attachment to the old order and
their fear of too drastic an upheaval.

In this fluid situation, in which neither collaboration nor
enmity appeared irrevocable, philosophes and the forces in power
made frequent alliances. Montesquieu defended the French
parlements against the king; Voltaire later defended the king
against the *parlements*. This forced Montesquieu into a common
front with the Jansenists, who deplored his deism, and Voltaire
into a common front with chancellor Maupeou, who hated all
philosophes. On the other side, Malesherbes, in charge of censorship from 1750 to 1763, often acted like an agent of the little
flock rather than like a repressive government official; and the
Parisian attorney and diarist Barbier, who was no philosophe, was
still anticlerical enough to seek out prohibited secular propaganda
and applaud Voltaire's efforts in behalf of Louis XV's program
to tax the clergy. Barbier, as his intelligent diary shows, was more
articulate than many of his fellow attorneys, but he was typical
of educated men all over Western Europe, alert and critical
beneficiaries of their social order, ready to be titillated and half
converted by radical propaganda. There were many men like
Barbier, nominal Christians who quoted the *Dictionnaire philosophique*, cried over the *Nouvelle Héloïse*, objected to the im-
prisonment of Diderot, welcomed Lessing's Masonic writings,
applauded the banishment of the Jesuits, practiced the new empiricism, embraced the new critical spirit, and in general found
something attractive in the philosophes' paganism and something

---

[2] Hume to Horace Walpole (November 20, 1766). *Letters*,
II, 110.

exciting in the philosophes' hopes. Thus, the philosophes were simultaneously at peace and at war with their civilization, and much of their revolutionary ideology was pushed forward by men who were hostile to its spokesmen and blind to its implications.

The philosophes, then, lived in a world at once exhilarating and bewildering, and they moved in it with a mixture of confidence and apprehensiveness, of shrewd understanding and ideological myopia. They never wholly discarded that final, most stubborn illusion that bedevils realists—the illusion that they were free from illusions. This distorted their perception and gave many of their judgments a certain shallowness. But it also lent them the aggressor's *élan* at a time when the defense was paralyzed by self-doubt, inner divisions, and costly concessions: as usual, the price the defense paid for misreading its situation was far greater than the price paid by its radical adversaries. Kant had admitted that his was not an enlightened age, but he could claim, after all, and with justice, that his was an age of Enlightenment. History was on the philosophes' side: it was a good thing to know.

BOOK ONE

The Appeal
to
Antiquity

If the Antients, in their Purity, are as yet out of your Reach; search the Moderns, that are nearest to them. If you cannot converse with the most Antient, use the most Modern. For the Authors of the middle Age, and all that sort of Philosophy, as well as Divinity, will be of little advantage to you.

Lord Shaftesbury
to Michael Ainsworth,
May 5, 1709

Lassen Sie uns bei den Alten in die Schule gehen. Was können wir nach der Natur für bessere Lehrer wählen?

Lessing
to Moses Mendelssohn,
1756

Lecteur éclairé et judicieux . . . de grâce apprenez à vos amis quelle est l'énorme distance des Offices de Cicéron, du Manuel d'Epictète, des Maximes de l'empereur Antonin, à tous les plats ouvrages de morale écrits dans nos jargons du Nord. Avons-nous seulement, dans tous les livres faits depuis six cents ans, rien de comparable à une page de Sénèque? Non, nous n'avons rien qui en approche, et nous osons nous élever contre nos maîtres!

Voltaire,
Note of 1769, to the poem *Les trois empereurs en Sorbonne*

CHAPTER ONE

The Useful and Beloved Past

1. HEBREWS AND HELLENES

I

As cultivated men in a cultivated age, the philosophes loved classical antiquity and took pure pleasure in it; as reformers, they did not hesitate to exploit, shrewdly and unscrupulously, the classics they loved. They could exploit them because, though their affection was authentic, they confronted the ancients with the self-confidence of men who had become their own masters. "*Boerhave utilior Hippocrate, Newton totà antiquitate, Tassus Homero; sed gloria primis,*" Voltaire jotted down in one of his notebooks: "Boerhaave is worth more than Hippocrates, Newton more than all antiquity, Tasso more than Homer; but glory to the first."[1]

For the men of the Enlightenment, glory to the first ancestors implied disrespect for the second. All men have a single past with many facets, but the philosophes divided their past into two sectors and put both to work. The Christian sector gave them an adversary worthy of their hostility: when the philosophes proclaimed that it was their mission to eradicate bigotry and superstition, they meant that it was a historic mission. At this point, on this issue, history became not past, but present politics: the philosophes never tired of pointing to the record Christians had compiled through the ages as evidence confirming the need for drastic remedial action in their own time. In the same manner, the pagan sector had its uses: it supplied them with illustrious

[1] *Notebooks,* 409.

models and a respectable ancestry. The philosophes liked to visualize themselves reenacting historic battles, to denounce religious fanaticism and popularize Newton wrapped in the toga of Cicero or Lucretius. This is how they gave their polemics the dignity of an age-old struggle between reason and unreason, a struggle that had been fought and lost in the ancient world and was now being fought again, this time with good prospects of success.

The historical writings of the Enlightenment are more than special pleading; they are comprehensive, critical, often brilliant —they are true history. Reversing Tacitus' famous precept, the philosophes wrote history with rage and partisanship, and their very passion often allowed them to penetrate into regions hitherto inaccessible to historical explorers. Yet it also made them condescending and oddly parochial: their sense of the past merged all too readily with their sense of the present. Whether they were imitating Lucretius, maligning St. Augustine, or flattering Catherine the Great, they were the same men facing different quarters of their intellectual horizon. Even more often than they intended, Enlightenment historians advanced the mission and buoyed up the missionaries; they looked into the past as into a mirror and extracted from their history the past they could use. This limits the range of philosophic history but enhances its value as a clue: it permits us to look over the philosophes' shoulders to discover in their historical portraits a portrait of themselves, and to read in their accounts of Seneca's heroism, or the iniquities of the Inquisition, the mind of the Enlightenment.

II

With all their passion for history, the philosophes' vision of the past was remarkably pessimistic. History was a register of crimes, a tale of cruelty and cunning, at best the record of unremitting conflict. All was not black: each age, each civilization had its defenders of the oppressed, its champions of reason and humanity. Diderot's bleak *Essai sur les règnes de Claude et de Néron* pits courageous Stoics against superstitious tyrants; Hume finds a minority of sensible men in the midst of darkest medieval England. In general, barbarism and religion had dominated the past, but a few glorious ages testified to the possibility that reason might not merely be the critic but the master of civilization.

It is possible to explain this pessimism as a projection of the philosophes' own situation, as a mixture of self-pity and self-importance which exaggerates the difficulties of their position to enhance the significance of their achievement. But it was more than that: it was a coherent account of the motive power both within and among epochs. As the Enlightenment saw it, the world was, and had always been divided between ascetic, superstitious enemies of the flesh, and men who affirmed life, the body, knowledge, and generosity; between mythmakers and realists, priests and philosophers. Heinrich Heine, wayward son of the Enlightenment, would later call these parties, most suggestively, Hebrews and Hellenes.

This conflict between two irreconcilable patterns of life, thought and feeling, divided historical periods internally; it also divided them from one another. Each era had a dominant style, with either reason or superstition in control, but the philosophes insisted that this dominance was merely the temporary ascendancy of one combatant over the other: few periods in history were without their admixture of reason or superstition—the darkest, most primitive ages had their philosophers, the most brilliant ages of reason and cultivation were infected by the survivals of old, or the seeds of new superstitions. This is what Voltaire meant when he said that the eighteenth century was both the Age of Philosophy and the Age of Superstition; it gives new meaning to Kant's observation that his age was the Age of Enlightenment, but not an enlightened age. The conflict between Hebrews and Hellenes was at once the source of disaster and of progress.

This dualist view of history, rather than the celebrated theory of progress, characterizes the mind of the Enlightenment. The theory of progress was a special case of this dualism: it gave formal expression to the hope that the alternations between Ages of Philosophy and Ages of Belief were not inescapable, that man was not forever trapped on the treadmill of historical cycles. Philosophical sociology and philosophical history supported and confirmed each other: both studied the conflict between reason and unreason. The first sought laws that might decide the struggle; the second traced its course through the ages. In fact, the philosophes developed a kind of comparative history which they explicitly distinguished from the study of the past for its own sake. This history, first practiced by Montesquieu, later explored by Scottish sociologists like Adam Ferguson, and finally christened "Theoretical or Conjectural History," *was* sociology.[2] But whatever history the Enlightenment historians pursued, they focused their attention on the rise and decline of the philosophic party, on the fortunes of criticism.

The Enlightenment's conception of history as a continuing struggle between two types of mentality implies a general scheme of periodization. The philosophes divided the past, roughly, into four great epochs: the great river civilizations of the Near East; ancient Greece and Rome; the Christian millennium; and modern times, beginning with the "revival of letters." These four epochs were rhythmically related to each other: the first and third were paired off as ages of myth, belief, and superstition, while the second and fourth were ages of rationality, science, and enlightenment.

I should observe immediately that the philosophes did not propose this scheme as a rigid system. They recognized the stubborn individuality of cultures, and the continuities that link the most disparate ages. "The arts and sciences, indeed," David Hume remarked, "have flourished in one period, and have decayed in another; but we may observe, that at the time when they rose to greatest perfection among one people, they were perhaps totally unknown to all the neighboring nations."[3] Some philosophes called attention to the autonomous development of Eastern civilizations: Voltaire, partly in calculated rebellion against Bossuet's narrow vision of the past, partly in unfeigned awe of Oriental sagacity, opened his *Essai sur les mœurs et l'esprit des nations* with some appreciative passages on the civilizations of the Indians and the Chinese. Others, like Condorcet, musing on the uneven

---

[2] The phrase is by Ferguson's favorite pupil, Dugald Stewart. See Gladys Bryson: *Man and Society* (1945), 88.
[3] "Of the Populousness of Ancient Nations," *Works*, III, 382.

development of social classes and neighboring cultures in their own time, sympathetically described the plight of contemporary savages (who seemed to have undergone little significant historical development), and of the lower orders (which remained much like their ancestors in the darkest of dark ages). Besides, despite some extravagant epithets, the most fanatical anti-Christians among the philosophes did not claim that the two pairs of ages matched precisely; they conceded that the Christian millennium was more rational and more civilized than the early civilizations, just as they took pride in the superiority of their own time over Greece and Rome.

But while the philosophes themselves sensibly insisted on these variations, the exceptions they adduced did not invalidate their general scheme; they wrote the history of the human mind as the history of its rise from myth in classical antiquity, its disastrous decline under Christianity, and its glorious rebirth. In one manner or another, whether expressed in the prophetic fervor of Condorcet or the ironic detachment of Hume, the scheme dominates philosophical history. The famous first chapter of Voltaire's *Siècle de Louis XIV* specifies "four happy ages": the centuries of Pericles and Plato, and of Caesar and Cicero (which correspond to what I shall call the First Age of Criticism); and the ages of the Medicean Renaissance, and of Louis XIV (which constitute the prehistory of the Enlightenment).[4] These happy periods are embedded in two Ages of Belief, which Voltaire dismisses with superb disdain as miserable, vicious, and backward.

---

[4] This periodic scheme, interestingly enough, was first developed in the last two of these four happy ages. Renaissance historians like Giorgio Vasari periodized Italian art from its perfection in Greece and Rome, through its decay after Constantine, to its rebirth in the time of Giotto. And Francis Bacon wrote: "Only three revolutions and periods of learning can properly be reckoned; one among the Greeks, the second among the Romans, and the last among us, that is to say, the nations of Western Europe; and to each of these hardly two centuries can justly be assigned. The intervening ages of the world, in respect to any rich or flourishing growth of the sciences, were unprosperous. For neither the Arabians nor the Schoolmen need be mentioned; who in the intermediate times rather crushed the sciences with a multitude of treatises, that increased their weight." *The New Organon*, LXXVIII, in *Works*, IV, 77.

Other historians use a similar vocabulary, suggesting the rhythmic alternation of periods: "Mankind," writes Hume, "having at length thrown off this yoke [of Aristotelianism], affairs are now returned nearly to the same situation as before, and EUROPE is at present a copy at large, of what GREECE was formerly a pattern in miniature."[5] Rousseau, with all the extravagance of his early *Discours sur les sciences et les arts*, characterizes medieval history as a return to the grossest of antiquity: "Europe had relapsed into the barbarism of the earliest ages. The peoples of this part of the world, so enlightened today, lived some centuries ago in a condition worse than ignorance."[6] D'Alembert, too, speaks of the "revival of letters" as emerging from a long interval of ignorance which had been preceded by centuries of enlightenment, of the "regeneration of ideas," the "return to reason and good taste," the "revival of spirits," and the "rebirth of light."[7] Condorcet, finally, portrays early modern Europe smarting under medieval tyranny, awaiting the moment when a new enlightenment would allow it to be reborn a free civilization. Clichés, all of them, but therefore all the more eloquent witnesses to the mentality of the philosophes.

This historical scheme will find few defenders today. It bears all the stigmata usually imputed to Enlightenment historiography in general—inadequate grasp of development, deficient sympathy with cultures alien or hostile to the movement, assimilation of past events to polemical interests, smuggling in of moral judgments, and rationalistic interpretations. I have no intention of denying that these indictments, first presented by nineteenth-century historicists and current today, are weighty and valid, but they concentrate on the failings of philosophic history at the expense of its merits. In fact, the historical writings of the Enlightenment were part of a comprehensive effort—of physicists, epistemologists, and literary critics as much as of historians—to secure rational control of the world, reliable knowledge of the past, and freedom from the pervasive domination of myth.

---

[5] "Of the Rise and Progress of the Arts and Sciences," *Works*, III, 183.

[6] Rousseau: *Œuvres*, III, 6.

[7] *Discours préliminaire de l'Encyclopédie*, in *Mélanges*, I, 102–5.

In the midst of the struggle for objectivity they could not themselves be objective: myth could be sympathetically understood only after it had been fully conquered, but in the course of its conquest it had to be faced as the enemy. The "pure insight" characteristic of the Enlightenment, writes Hegel in some fine pages of his *Phenomenology*, "only appears in genuinely active form in so far as it enters into conflict with belief."[8] The Enlightenment had to treat religion as superstition and error in order to recognize itself. Worship of the Chosen People and submissive concentration on saints' lives could be overcome only by a violent, and hence one-sided reaction. Scholars could see the Christian millennium fairly only after polemicists had freed themselves from it by seeing it unfairly.

The historians of the Enlightenment, then, did much. They did not do everything because they could not do everything, but at least they freed history from the parochialism of Christian scholars and from theological presuppositions, secularized the idea of causation and opened vast new territories for historical inquiry. They went beyond tedious chronology, endless research into sacred documents, and single-minded hagiography, and imposed rational, critical methods of study on social, political, and intellectual developments. As the organizing principle of Enlightenment historiography, the fourfold periodic scheme therefore shares its excellences as much as its shortcomings. Its most glaring and most notorious defect was its unsympathetic, often brutal, estimate of Christianity; yet it achieved the rudimentary recognition that historical epochs have a prevailing mental style which informs their science, their morals, their whole way of seeing the world; that the spectrum of available styles may be divided into two kinds, the mythmaking or religious and the critical or scientific; and finally, that history has discontinuities as well as continuities, dramatic revolutions as well as slow changes.

Paradoxical as it may sound, then, Enlightenment historians, rationalist in sensibility, partisan in purpose, careless in detail,

---

[8] G. W. F. Hegel: *Phenomenology of Mind*, tr. J. B. Baillie (1955), 560.

hasty in judgment, unfair in characterization, and deficient in empathy, willful, sectarian, even vicious, still made a historical discovery of enduring validity. This emergence of truth from error is neither a dialectical miracle nor an instance of pre-established harmony. It is something far more modest. For all their misjudgments and prejudices—and sometimes because of them—the philosophes took first steps, no more, toward a scientific history of culture. Montesquieu's distinction between forms and principles of government; Turgot's ladder of theological, metaphysical, and positive forms of thought traversed by succeeding epochs; Hume's analysis of the religious impulse in primitive and civilized countries; Lessing's speculative account of the evolution of religious beliefs; even Gibbon's feline dissection of Christian meekness insinuating itself into the Roman mind —all these are attempts to grasp the deepest, and hence least visible, convictions that hold a culture together and give it its distinctive shape.

It is largely the philosophes' own fault if later writers rarely appreciated their contribution to historical understanding. The philosophes' perception of a distinction between mythmaking and scientific mentalities was the perception of a fact, but since they came to it first of all through their position as critics and belligerents, they almost inevitably converted the historical fact into a moral judgment, praising, indeed identifying themselves with, one mentality and denigrating the other. They translated their insight into an indictment, and this made it not only less valid, but also less palatable and less visible, to succeeding generations. It is hardly surprising that those who later rejected the philosophes' verdict failed to give them credit for their discovery. But whatever the ingratitude of a later time, the discovery was theirs, and it reassured them and gave them a place to stand. It must be a peculiar pleasure to be able to kill one's father and choose another.

2 . A CONGENIAL SENSE AND SPIRIT

I

NOT ALL of the philosophes' classicism aimed at anything so portentous and liberating as parricide. Precisely because they were above all men of their times, much of their classical erudition was politically innocuous. Instead of separating them from the established orthodoxy, it tied them to it. After all, in the Age of Enlightenment classical literature was the common possession of educated men, not the preserve of the specialist; to quote a line from Lucretius was to demonstrate one's respectability rather than one's radicalism. Samuel Johnson spoke for the republic of letters as a whole when he defended the practice as demonstrating "a community of mind." "Classical quotation," he said, "is the *parole* of literary men all over the world."[9]

In our time, when Latinity is dying and has retreated to the academy, it is hard to visualize the easy, intimate traffic between the eighteenth century and the ancients. Educated Christians never thought for a moment that their classicism might in any way interfere with their religious duties. Horace especially, Horace, the most pagan of poets, was the great favorite of the century: Swift tried his hand at translating him, and so did Turgot; Diderot imitated him, and so did Wieland. Horace supplied topics for Addison's *Spectator* and rationalizations for country squires enjoying rural contentment. When Oglethorpe's expedition set sail for Georgia, Charles Wesley, with no sense of incongruity, borrowed his pious benediction—*Christo duce et auspice Christo*—from a Horatian ode.[1] Even in East Prussia classical currency was valid coin: Kant did not find it necessary to identify the phrase *sapere aude*, which he had suggested as a motto for the Enlightenment, as a Horatian tag.[2] And so when Diderot quoted

---

[9] *Life of Johnson* (under May 8, 1781), IV, 102.
[1] *Epistles*, I, 7, 27: *nil desperandum Teucro duce et auspice.* See Richard M. Gummere: *The American Colonial Mind and the Classical Tradition* (1963), 17.
[2] See Horace: *Epistles*, I, 2, 40–1: "*Dimidium facti qui coepit habet: sapere aude: Incipe*"—"To have begun is to be half done; dare to know; start!"

Horace without identifying him—and that in the *Encyclopédie*, aimed at a wide public—he was flattering the public's learning, not subverting its faith.[3]

In such a cultural atmosphere classical epigraphs usually meant simply that the author had enjoyed a good education or owned a handbook of Latin quotations; paintings depicting scenes from Ovid certified their owner as a man of the world and the painter himself as an alert reader of mythological dictionaries. Operas and ballets drew freely on Greek myths, but this did not restrict their audiences. Even popular journalists, not only in Europe but also in the far-away American colonies, found it useful to lard their newspapers with high-flown classical tags. After he started the *New England Courant*—a Colonial *Spectator*—in 1721, Benjamin Franklin informed his "gentle readers" that he designed "never to let a paper pass without a Latin motto, which carries a charm in it to the Vulgar, and the Learned admire the pleasure of construing."[4] The fashion of imitating ancient poems testifies to the familiarity of ancient Rome, for the success of imitations depended on the readers' ability to catch allusions and to appreciate subtle departures from the model. It was with such expectations—wholly justified—that Samuel Johnson imitated Juvenal's third Satire in *London* and his tenth Satire in the moving *Vanity of Human Wishes*, while Pope, a master of the genre, scored off literary and political enemies in his biting imitations of Horace.

There was nothing strenuous about this classicism: when Middleton published his widely-read *Life of Cicero* in 1741, he said flatly that the scene of the book was "laid in a place and age which are familiar to us from our childhood: we learn the names of all the chief actors at school, and choose our several favourites according to our tempers or fancies."[5] Rome belonged to every

---

[3] The article "Cura" reads in its entirety: "*Cura*: inquietude: goddess who has created man, and since that time has never lost sight of her work; *post equitem sedet . . . .*" *Œuvres*, XIV, 252. Readers were expected to understand the allusion, remember the ode, and complete the line "*Post equitem sedet atra cura*" (III, 1, 40).

[4] Gummere: *The American Colonial Mind and the Classical Tradition*, 16.

[5] Conyers Middleton: *The History of the Life of Marcus Tullius Cicero* (1741, ed. 1839), ix.

educated man. So did its language: toward the end of the seventeenth century, Lord Shaftesbury had written to his father that Latin is "absolutely necessary to every considerable station and almost every office"; besides, it is an "easy, pleasant language."[6] This remained true half a century later: Horace Walpole fondly recalled Eton as a sort of Roman paradise, and Lord Chesterfield could confidently write to his eight-year-old boy: "I take it for granted, that, by your late care and attention, you are now perfect in Latin verses. . . . Your Greek, too, I dare say, keeps pace with your Latin."[7]

Men of fashion and grave statesmen agreed that to know the classics helped to know the eighteenth century: Addison introduced a member of his Spectator club as a man whose "familiarity with the customs, manners, actions, and writings of the ancients" made him "a very delicate observer of what occurs to him in the present world."[8] Much of this familiarity, of course, was trivial. Political speeches were thought incomplete without some allusion, more or less apt, to ancient commonwealths: Voltaire noted in his book on England that members of Parliament enjoyed comparing themselves to Roman Republicans, while a few years later d'Argenson suggested rather sarcastically: "The English think they have taken from the government of the Romans all that is best, and corrected its faults."[9] Still more innocent than this was the classicism of poets from England to the Italian states, poets who toyed with Stoic notions of universal harmonies and patterned their pastoral verse on Alexandrian models. Antiquity invaded even eighteenth-century landscaping and occasioned debates over funerary inscriptions. "While infidelity has expunged the Christian theology from our creed," the English journal *The Connoisseur* said in March 1756, "taste has introduced the heathen mythology into our gardens. If a pond is dug, Neptune, at the command of taste, emerges from the bason, and presides in the

---

[6] July 1689. *Life, Unpublished Letters, and Philosophical Regimen*, 283.

[7] June 9, 1740. *Lord Chesterfield's Letters to His Son* (Everyman edn., 1929), 6–7.

[8] *The Spectator*, No. 2.

[9] Marquis D'Argenson: *Considérations sur le gouvernement ancien et présent de la France* (1764, edn. 1765), 23.

middle; or if a vista is cut through a grove, it must be terminated by a Flora, or an Apollo."[1] And when Samuel Johnson wrote his epitaph for Oliver Goldsmith, that most English of writers, he composed it in Latin and refused to translate it: he would never consent, he said, *"to disgrace the walls of Westminster Abbey with an English inscription."*[2] Classical antiquity was anything but esoteric: it was inescapable.

II

Far from disdaining such horticultural or funerary classicism, the philosophes enjoyed and contributed to it. It could hardly be otherwise; after all, the philosophes acquired the classics precisely as their contemporaries did, in school and after. Like their fellows, they read the classics directly, sometimes perceptively, sometimes superficially; adopted, or adapted, some ancient ideas that had been handed on through the Christian tradition; copied sentences from epitomes of ancient thought; or borrowed from moderns like Montaigne, who had rifled classical treasures in their own individual fashion. When Voltaire celebrates worldliness in his poem *Le mondain*, he may be recalling Montaigne, who quotes the Epicureans with evident enjoyment, or some other writer once read and afterwards forgotten; he may be misreading Epicurus or paraphrasing Horace; he may be reporting his own spontaneous joy in life; or—and this is quite possible—he may be doing all these things at once. The channels through which classical ideas, images, or attitudes reached the philosophes were as circuitous and as interwoven as a network of canals. Their classical heritage cannot be separated out into discrete, neatly labeled packages; it remains a confused and confusing cluster, resembling nothing so much as a ball of twine collected by a compulsive string saver.

Hence, some of the philosophes' seemingly pagan ideas were simply the property of thinking men in their time, while others, which sound like classical reminiscences, were merely coinci-

---

[1] Quoted in James Sutherland: *A Preface to Eighteenth Century Poetry* (1948), 142.
[2] Sir William Forbes to James Boswell. Boswell: *Life of Johnson* (under 1776), III, 85.

dences, a response not to their reading but to their immediate experience. Yet often the philosophes are not less but more pagan than they appear to be: their writings swarm with invisible quotations. When Diderot praises Seneca for "reasoning with Socrates, doubting with Carneades, fighting against nature with Zeno, seeking to conform to it with Epicurus, or trying to raise himself above it with Diogenes," he is also obliquely praising the Enlightenment's own eclecticism, and he does both by slightly paraphrasing Seneca's treatise *On the Shortness of Life.*[3] When Voltaire ridicules baptism ("What a strange idea, that a pot of water should wash away all crimes—as though you were cleaning clothes!") he is doubtless recalling Ovid: *"A! nimium faciles, qui tristia crimina caedis fluminea tolli posse putatis aqua!"*—"O irresponsible men, who think that the grim crime of murder can be washed away by river water!"[4] Many of these antique conceits were conventional flourishes imposed by the taste of the philosophes' time and the pretensions of their readers. Allusions to the ancients flowed from their pens, lightly and without deep emotion: when Voltaire was pleased with Frederick, he compared Prussia to Athens, although usually he derided it as a modern Sparta; d'Alembert, in the same vein, urged Geneva to permit a theatre within its borders, for then it would "unite the wisdom of

baptism

---

[3] *Essai sur les règnes de Claude et de Néron,* in *Œuvres,* III, 28.
[4] Voltaire: "Baptism," *Philosophical Dictionary,* I, 110; Ovid: *Fasti,* II, 45–6. To make matters even more confusing, the philosophes did not always supply accurate accounts of their debts, although most of their intellectual reminiscences have such specificity, such vividness, that they command confidence. Still, some youthful enthusiasms, perhaps never very important and in any case long since outgrown, were given disproportionate weight in recollection; other influences, subtly resonating through all their writings, were slighted. But then, not all the philosophes' inaccurate reports were tricks of memory. Some were tricks of their trade. As good Aesopians and single-minded polemicists, they sometimes concealed or misrepresented the origins of their ideas. Some preceptors, like Hobbes, went largely unacknowledged because their reputation for impiety made them political liabilities; others, like Descartes, were underestimated because their reputation for piety made them rather awkward ancestors. This purposeful memory, as I shall show in chapter II, did its work on the ancients too.

Lacedaemon with the civility of Athens."[5] These were common, fashionable metaphors which claimed for the philosophes membership in the club of cultivated men, nothing more.

But though distinguished members of that club, the philosophes, intelligent and ruthless, were also unreliable: their encounter with the classics, often casual or insignificant, was also decisive for them as it was for few other men. It gave shape to their rebelliousness; it justified their radicalism. While a program of study is not normally a reliable intellectual pedigree, the philosophes' classical education had special, lifelong meaning for them: it offered them an alternative to Christianity. There were critical moments in their lives, in adolescence and later, when they appealed to the ancients not merely for entertainment but for models, not merely for decoration but for substance, and not for bland substance—such as the staples of Horatian satire: complaints about crowded city life, laments on the brevity of existence, or the menace of bores and bluestockings—but for a philosophical option. Books forced on reluctant schoolboys are rarely more than hateful exercises, laboriously mastered and quickly forgotten, but all over Europe and America, for all philosophes alike, the ancients were signposts to secularism.[6]

---

[5] "Genève," in volume VII of Diderot's *Encyclopédie*. *The Encyclopédie*, 90.

[6] To make *political* capital of the ancients was not an invention of the philosophes; it placed them in a tradition going back to Machiavelli and beyond—medieval political theorists had quoted Aristotle on forms of government. But in the sixteenth, and especially the seventeenth century, classical reminiscences had become the property of radicals bent on reforming corrupt present-day institutions by recalling the glories of Sparta or early Rome. In the midst of the English Civil War, Harrington urged Englishmen to establish a republic on the model of "ancient prudence," while Milton, as Aubrey reports, was moved to write against monarchy "being so conversant in Livy and the Roman authors, and the greatness he saw done by the Roman Commonwealth." (See Z. S. Fink: *The Classical Republicans* [2d edn., 1962], 53, 90). Thus modern republicans drew strength from antique republics and were rebuked for it by their royalist adversaries: "As to rebellion in particular against monarchy," Hobbes complained in a famous passage, "one of the most frequent causes of it, is the reading of the books of policy, and histories of the ancient Greeks, and Romans." Reading these books, young men "and all others that are

Kant disliked the pedantic philologists who had trained him at the Collegium Fridericianum in Königsberg, but he gratefully recognized that he owed them his first acquaintance with Latin, his enduring affection for Latin poetry and—more indirectly—his intimate and significant knowledge of Latin thought. Friedrich Nicolai discovered the classics with an unholy joy. His *Waisenschule* in Halle prescribed and enforced a grim regimen of monotonous prayers for grace and interminable pious exercises; even the ancient languages were taught from a dry, pedantic, deadly grammar, and solely for the sake of reading the New Testament: "We declined, conjugated, expounded, analyzed, phraseologized, and who knows what else!"[7] Then, in an unforgettable moment, at fifteen, Nicolai first glimpsed Homer, and from then on his distaste for religiosity was incurable. He was fortunate enough to be transferred to the newly established *Realschule* in Berlin, and there he learned to read the classics with competence and for pleasure. When he founded his publishing house some years later, he celebrated and symbolized his appeal to antiquity by using a head of Homer as his colophon.[8] D'Alem-

---

unprovided of the antidote of solid reason" come to think of the ancients as thoroughly delightful companions, successful in war and prosperous in peace, and they overlook "the frequent seditions and civil wars, produced by the imperfection of their policy." This sentimental antiquarianism has led callow modern men to preach civil war and public murder: "Men have undertaken to kill their kings, because the Greek and Latin writers, in their books, and discourses of policy, make it lawful, and laudable, for any man to do it; provided, before he do it, he call him tyrant." (Thomas Hobbes: *Leviathan*, part II, chapter 29.) This political classicism persisted into the eighteenth century, although in attenuated form. The age of tyrannicide seemed at an end; still, it remained fashionable to seek for modern equivalents of ancient heroes and to deplore the decay of modern institutions by pointing to antique virtue. The philosophes, too, played at this political classicism: Diderot ominously called for a modern Brutus; Rousseau spoke highly of Spartan bravery and frugality as models worth imitating. But more important than this: when the philosophes turned to the ancients for inspiration, they looked for philosophical rather than political models. They wanted evidence to be used not against kings but against clerics.

[7] Friedrich Nicolai: *Über meine gelehrte Bildung, über meine Kenntniss der kritischen Philosophie . . .* (1799), 9.

[8] Karl Aner: *Der Aufklärer Friedrich Nicolai* (1912), 9.

bert records in an autobiographical fragment that in the Collège des Quatre-Nations, one of his Jansenist teachers, who hoped to make his brilliant pupil into a "pillar of his party," advised him against reading Latin poetry and to "read no poem other than St. Prosper's on Grace." But, d'Alembert wrily adds, "the young man preferred Horace and Vergil."[9] In Winckelmann's Latin school at Stendal, the pupils studied everything, including Latin itself, to learn true fear of God, but Winckelmann, for one, learned precisely the opposite: he was inattentive during theology classes and was punished for it, but to no avail. He read the classics secretly and copied them down: "Using the books available to him," one of his schoolmates remembered, "he made himself familiar with Latin writers; and if he found something that, by his standards, was fine, he preserved it carefully and thought it such a treasure that he was happier with it than with all the Bibles and theological compendia put together."[1] Winckelmann, the greatest of eighteenth-century pagans, learned his paganism with much pain, deep secrecy, and inexpressible delight, in a Christian school. The philosophes did not merely quote antiquity, they earned it, and they experienced it.

The most familiar mode in which the Enlightenment experienced the classical past is also the least significant: identification. Everyone knows Rousseau's claim that he became proud, intractable, and impatient with servitude through his reading of Plutarch: "Ceaselessly occupied with Rome and Athens; living, one might say, with their great men, myself born Citizen of a Republic and son of a father whose patriotism was his strongest passion, I took fire from his example; I thought myself a Greek or a Roman." One evening, telling the famous story of Scaevola, he frightened his listeners by grasping a chafing dish, "to depict his act."[2]

Rousseau was not alone in this sort of adolescent hero-worship. Vauvenargues told Mirabeau in 1740 that he had found

---

[9] The best version of this fragment appears in *Œuvres posthumes de d'Alembert*, ed. C. Pougens, 2 vols. (1821). See Ronald Grimsley: *Jean d'Alembert, 1717–83* (1963), 3.
[1] Carl Justi: *Winckelmann und seine Zeitgenossen*, 3 vols. (1866–72; edn. 1956), I, 30–3.
[2] *Confessions*, Book I. *Œuvres*, I, 9.

Plutarch "enthralling" at sixteen. "I cried with joy when I read those lives. I never spent a night without talking to Alcibiades, Agesilas and others. I visited the Roman Forum to harangue with the Gracchi, to defend Cato when they threw rocks at him." The letters from Brutus to Cicero were "so filled with firmness, elevation, passion and courage," that he found it impossible to read them calmly but fell into a kind of manic fit, racing around the terrace of his château until he dropped from exhaustion.[3] Alfieri went through this stage a little later. As a young man of twenty he came upon Plutarch. It was a revelation. "Five or six times I perused the lives of Timoleon, Caesar, Brutus, Pelopidas, Cato and some others"—a rather catholic assortment, consisting mainly of dictators and assassins of dictators. "I wept, raved, and fell into such ecstasies that if anyone had been in the next room he would have called me insane. Every time I came to any of the great actions of these famous persons, my agitation was so extreme that I could not remain seated. I was like one beside myself."[4]

Such youthful enthusiasm rarely survived into maturity, but identification remained a convenient rhetorical device: Voltaire introduces Marcus Aurelius into some of his dialogues as his spokesman, but the admirable Stoic emperor is little more than a splendid stock figure of generosity, intelligence, and tolerance. The antique pagan becomes a character in a morality play in which Mr. Christian is Mr. Badman. Elsewhere Voltaire appears as a modern Lucretius or speaks through Cicero. This is not the cult but the exploitation of antiquity.

Apart from Rousseau, perhaps the only major philosophe to whom identification with the ancients was a sustained fantasy was Diderot, although with this adventurous genius it is never possible to be sure. A striking and appealing figure, learned, talkative, energetic, changeable, inventive, sensual, and elusive, Diderot embodies the dualism of the Enlightenment to perfection: a partisan of empiricism and scientific method, a skeptic, a tireless experimenter and innovator, Diderot was possessed by the restlessness of modern man. Our firmest opinions, he once said in a moment of

---

[3] March 22, 1740. *Œuvres*, ed. D. L. Gilbert, 2 vols. (1857), II, 193.

[4] *Vita, scritta de esso*, epoch III, chapter 7, ed. Luigi Fassó, 2 vols. (1951), I, 93.

unintentional self-revelation, are not those we have always held but those to which we have returned most often. At the same time, he belonged to antiquity. "In my early years," he told Catherine of Russia, "I sucked up the milk of Homer, Vergil, Horace, Terence, Anacreon, Plato and Euripides, diluted with that of Moses and the Prophets."[5] He stands in his century like a sturdy Roman who has stepped out from one of David's classical canvases. Either he, or the world, was out of joint. "People tell me," he wrote to Sophie Volland in 1760, "that I have the air of a man perpetually seeking something he lacks";[6] and he accepted his good friend Grimm's view of him as a stranger in his age: "My friend, you are right. This world was not made for me, nor I for it"; he thought himself "enough of a monster to coexist with it, ill at ease, and not enough of a monster to be exterminated."[7] His irrepressible originality made him modern, but he longed for the mantle of an ancient philosopher.

Over and over again, more in earnest than in jest, Diderot turned himself into a pagan sage, most notably Diogenes, the self-sufficient cynic, or into an admiring contemporary of other pagan philosophers, of Socrates or Seneca. They were his collective conscience, the invisible Pantheon whose imaginary approval he sought and whose censure he feared. "O sages of Greece and Rome," he once wrote, "when I encounter your statues at the bend of a solitary avenue, and they detain me; when I stand before them delirious with admiration; when I feel my heart shudder with joy at the sight of your august images; when I feel the divine enthusiasm escape from your cold marble and pass into me; when, remembering your great actions and the ingratitude of your contemporaries, tears of compassion fill my eyes, how sweet it would be for me to interrogate my conscience and obtain its testimony that I too have deserved well of my nation and my century!"[8] These are extravagant words and extravagant tears, but the identification is authentic.

---

[5] *Plan d'une université pour le gouvernement de Russie*, in *Œuvres*, III, 478.
[6] September 30, 1760. *Correspondance*, III, 108.
[7] Undated fragment. Ibid., III, 187-8 *n*.
[8] Diderot to Falconet (August 5, 1766). Ibid., VI, 261. All this earnestness did not go uncontested: Voltaire derisively used a pseudoclassical epithet, "Diogenes's dog," to vilify Rousseau,

It explains much that is otherwise puzzling. The gravest production of Diderot's life was also, significantly, his most Roman: his *Essai sur les règnes de Claude et de Néron*, composed in the 1770's at the instance of Holbach. The *Essai* is a curious work, in part a biography of Seneca, in part a polemic on behalf of virtue; it falls into no category and follows no formula. The admirer of Diderot's wit who remembers the *Supplément au voyage de Bougainville* or the unbuttoned *Rêve de d'Alembert* may be repelled by the sententious harshness of this *Essai*. But its tone is worth attention: closely and deliberately it imitates Tacitus's somber lament for a grim time in Roman history when melodramatic villains victimized statesmen and philosophers. In Tacitus, good confronts evil in stark, almost naïve, opposition, and the same psychological scheme governs Diderot's work. Yet we know that Diderot was anything but naïve about motives—he was the subtlest of psychologists. This is not a paradox: in this *Essai* he is not a psychologist; he is a moralist. His irritable defense of Seneca's conduct and doctrines make his *Essai* into a eulogy of antique greatness. "After reading Seneca, am I the same man I was before I read him? That's not so—it can't be so."[9] We can believe Diderot: reading Seneca somehow made him into a new man.

This passion, it is worth repeating, did not stamp Diderot an eccentric in his time. It is true that he was exceptionally well equipped to play the part of an ancient, for he knew antiquity exceptionally well. His friend Grimm thought that "no one has as thorough a command of ancient philosophy as he."[1] He wrote an essay on Terence and commentaries on the elusive poet Persius, studied Vergil all his life, offered erudite observations on Homer and Pausanias, and followed an antique form, the Epistle, in corresponding with his friend the abbé Galiani about two difficult lines in Horace. His strange masterpiece *Le neveu de Rameau* is an

---

and Grimm referred to d'Alembert in some irritation as a "Diogenes whom we should leave in his barrel." *Correspondance littéraire*, V, 198–9.

[9] Unpublished note, first printed by Herbert Dieckmann in his *Inventaire du fonds Vandeul* (1951), 257.

[1] *Correspondance littéraire*, IV, 120. See Jean Seznec: *Essais sur Diderot et l'antiquité* (1957), 9.

imitation of a Satire by Horace. Yet even those among the little flock who could not write such scholarly exercises could at least read them appreciatively, and there were other philosophes who matched Diderot's erudition.

Montesquieu, who preceded Diderot by a generation, would have appreciated, in fact largely shared, Diderot's classical tastes. He confessed his own "relish for the ancients." Antiquity, he noted, "enchants me."[2] Montesquieu acquired this relish at the Oratorian *collège* of Juilly and expressed it early. At twenty he wrote a eulogy of Cicero; seven years later he sent a shrewdly argued *Dissertation sur la politique des Romains dans la religion* to the Bordeaux Academy. For many years he contemplated a treatise on the Stoic idea of duty, a persistent interest that pervades all his later work. While the critical defects of his *Considérations sur les causes de la grandeur des Romains et de leur décadence* were evident even to his contemporaries, he acquired an extensive classical erudition to write it. And his masterpiece *De l'esprit des lois* is a massive tribute to antique thought and antique literary style—it borrows freely from Vergil, incorporates the Stoic ideals of tranquillity and moderation, and supports its generalizations with numberless allusions to ancient politics. Trying to convey his satisfaction with his treatise, Montesquieu chose an epigraph from the *Metamorphoses*: *prolem sine matre creatam*—"this offspring was begot without a mother." His choice of an elliptical Latin phrase, curtly identified as "Ovid," was neither academic nor affected. Montesquieu expected his readers to understand him.

Perhaps they understood him too well. Shortly after *L'esprit des lois* was published, the bishop of Soissons courteously inquired whether some of its chapters were not infected by a Stoicism incompatible with the True Faith. "About thirty years ago," Montesquieu replied to Monseigneur de Fitz-James, "I conceived the project of writing a book on duty. Cicero's treatise *On Duties* had delighted me, and I took it as my model. As you know, Cicero had, as it were, copied Panaetius, who was a Stoic, and the Stoics had treated this question most successfully. So I read the Stoics' principal works, among them the moral reflections of Marcus Aurelius, which struck me as the masterpiece of antiquity. I

---

[2] *Pensées*, in *Œuvres*, II, 37.

confess that I was impressed by its morality, and that I should have liked to make a saint of Marcus Aurelius, as M. Dacier had done. What impressed me most was to discover that this morality was practical and that the three or four emperors who followed it were admirable princes, while those who didn't were monsters. . . . Really, now, if I wanted to write my book in order to discredit the Christian religion, I would have to be a big fool."[3] Montesquieu was no fool, and not much of a Christian, but his reply to the worried bishop was not merely a piece of evasive hypocrisy; his generation still knew a neutral zone where pagan and Christian could meet on relatively friendly terms.

While there might have been some doubt about the purity of Montesquieu's paganism, there could be none about Voltaire's. Instances of pagan conduct, pointedly contrasted with Christianity, are scattered through his polemical writings: his pamphlets on legal reform, addressed to the largest possible public, compare French cruelty and illogic with the humanity of Roman procedure; his anticlerical diatribes compare Christian persecution with antique toleration. Voltaire's library was filled with ancient authors, and his private notebooks were filled with allusions to them; when he described his article "Superstition" in the *Dictionnaire philosophique* as a "chapter taken from Cicero, Seneca, and Plutarch,"[4] he was listing a substantial part of his intellectual ancestry.

Voltaire was only a passable classical scholar, inclined to quote from memory and relatively indifferent to the refinements of antique speculation, but his very misquotations and simplifications make him eminently useful to the historian in search of a characteristic specimen. Like others in the little flock, he used the ancients mechanically, making ritualistic bows to saintly pagans and casual allusions to familiar tags. Yet like the others, Voltaire experienced crises in his intellectual and moral life, and then his appeal to antiquity revealed the seriousness of his affinity.

One such crisis broke late in 1755, when Voltaire learned of the disastrous earthquake that had devastated Lisbon on November 1, 1755. In his *Poème sur le désastre de Lisbonne*, Voltaire tried to

---

[3] October 1, 1750. *Œuvres*, III, 1328.
[4] *Philosophical Dictionary*, II, 473.

come to terms with this irrational and inexplicable event. The earthquake did not ruin Voltaire's cosmic optimism overnight— for a dozen years or more he had doubted the doctrine that this was the best of all possible worlds. But the disaster, which gave rise to feverish scientific and anguished theological debates, dramatized Voltaire's disillusionment. He had long rejected the optimists, who could see a higher justice in the deaths of thousands of innocents; but he refused to join the atheists, who, having no God, did not need to justify him. His problem was to keep his intellectual balance in a vertiginous world. In his perplexity, Voltaire turned to the philosophers. Leibniz's optimistic metaphysics, he wrote in the *Poème*, was at once insulting and depressing: whatever is, is manifestly not right. Plato's myth of man's original greatness only calls attention to his present misery. Epicurus' gods are irrelevant to human suffering:

> J'abandonne Platon, je rejette Epicure.
> Bayle en sait plus qu'eux tous; je vais le consulter;
> La balance à la main, Bayle enseigne à douter,
> Assez sage, assez grand pour être sans système,
> Il les a tous détruits, et se combat lui-même.[5]

The poem ends on a more hopeful note, but except for its coda, its tone is dark, resigned pessimism.

It would be too easy to dismiss this philosophizing as mere talk: when men have a choice of models, the model they choose is significant. "I had to say what I thought," Voltaire wrote to his friend Cideville about the Lisbon poem, "and say it in a way that would revolt neither overly philosophical nor overly credulous spirits."[6] Voltaire usually remained the controlled artist with an eye on his public, but the earthquake gravely disturbed him: he had to say what he thought. And saying it, he turned his suffering over the world into a philosophers' debate.

The grim Pyrrhonism of the Lisbon poem was not Voltaire's final intellectual position: he moved beyond it, and as he had turned to the classics in critical moments, he turned to them in

---

[5] *Œuvres*, IX, 476–7.
[6] April 12, 1756. *Correspondance*, XXIX, 156.

happy moments, too. Late in life, he wrote an *Épitre à Horace* into which he poured his love of the world, and in which he saluted the urbane Roman poet as his true ancestor:

> Je t'écris aujourd'hui, voluptueux Horace,
> À toi qui respira la mollesse et la grâce;
> Qui, facile en tes vers, et gai dans tes discours,
> Chantas les doux loisirs, les vins, et les amours.
>
> Jouissons, écrivons, vivons, mon cher Horace.
>
> J'ai vécu plus que toi; mes vers dureront moins.
> Mais au bord du tombeau je mettrai tous mes soins
> À suivre les leçons de ta philosophie,
> À mépriser la mort en savorant la vie,
> À lire tes écrits pleins de grâce et de sens
>
> Avec toi l'on apprend à souffrir l'indigence,
> À jouir sagement d'une honnête opulence,
> À vivre avec soi-même, à servir ses amis,
> À se moquer un peu de ses sots ennemis,
> À sortir d'une vie ou triste ou fortunée,
> En rendant grâce au dieux de nous l'avoir donné.[7]

Here is the cheerful pendant to the brooding poem on Lisbon.

Nothing would be easier than to enlarge this catalogue. Fontenelle, whose writings represent the transition from seventeenth-century libertinism to eighteenth-century philosophy, imitated Lucian in his witty *Dialogues des morts* and dedicated the book to him, "in the Elysian Fields." In his famous *Entretiens sur la pluralité des mondes*, which was to become a model for the popular scientific expositions of the Enlightenment, he compared himself to Cicero. Jeremy Bentham, who had been drilled in the classics since his boyhood and preferred to study the moderns, read the ancients for sheer pleasure. Once, having lost his way and hungry for lack of dinner, "beginning to feel rather faint and weary I was tempted by the sight of a delicious Hay-rick not far

---

[7] *Œuvres*, X, 442–6.

from the water to sit and repose myself.—I staid there two hours, and dined upon Epictetus's Morals which I had in my pocket."[8] Helvétius put together (it is the kindest phrase I can find) a poem about *Le bonheur*, professedly Epicurean in tone and professedly following Lucretius. Young Holbach told his friend John Wilkes: "I go hunting, fishing, shooting, I take walks all day long, without forgetting the ever-captivating conversation of Horace, Vergil, Homer and all our noble friends of the Elysian Fields. They are always faithful to me."[9] It was the kind of avowal one might expect from a country gentleman of his time, but in later life, when Holbach's propaganda factory for atheism was operating at full capacity, these conventional imaginary conversations bore literary and philosophical fruit. It was Holbach who commissioned Lagrange to make translations of Lucretius and Seneca, and who drew on ancient materialists for his own modern materialism. Adam Ferguson, the son of a Presbyterian minister, obediently studied for the ministry and actually served for several years as a regimental chaplain, but his preference for classical studies was invincible. In 1754 he gave up his clerical profession and turned, as he told Adam Smith, "downright layman,"[1] and ten years later he was appointed to the chair of Pneumatics and Moral Philosophy at the University of Edinburgh. There, Dugald Stewart recalled, his lectures revealed a character that "conjoined the simplicity, elevation, and ethical hardihood of the early Roman with Grecian refinement and eloquence."[2] The preacher's son had turned into a Stoic. Ferguson's friend Adam Smith was a brilliant and passionate classicist; he read the ancients all his life, both for pleasure and "in conformity with his theory that the best amusement of age was to renew acquaintance with the writers who were the delight of one's youth."[3] And besides delight, the classics gave Adam Smith his philosophy: his lectures on rhetoric

---

[8] Jeremy Bentham to his father (July 1768). I owe this reference to Mrs. Mary P. Mack.

[9] December 3, 1746. Pierre Naville: *D'Holbach* (1943), 7.

[1] Henry Grey Graham: *Scottish Men of Letters in the Eighteenth Century* (1901), 108.

[2] Herta Helena Jogland: *Ursprünge und Grundlagen der Soziologie bei Adam Ferguson* (1959), 31 *n.*

[3] Adam Smith: *Lectures on Rhetoric and Belles Lettres*, ed. John M. Lothian (1963), xiv.

and literature and more significantly, his lectures on ethics, show him a Roman Eclectic in modern dress. The Italian *illuministi*, for their part, complained of their Jesuit education and generally picked up or reinforced their pagan indifference to Christian religion from their own Renaissance classics, above all from Machiavelli. Thomas Jefferson, too, was deeply indebted to Machiavelli for his youthful Epicureanism, but at the Reverend James Maury's school, which he attended between the ages of fifteen and seventeen, he also read the Greek and Latin classics directly and with fair competence. Machiavelli and Bolingbroke confirmed what he had learned in Cicero's *Tusculan Disputations:* contempt for the fear of death, contempt for "superstition," admiration for sturdy pagan self-reliance. It was from Bolingbroke that he copied this sentence: while the system of Christ is doubtful and incomplete, "A system thus collected from the writings of antient heathen moralists, of Tully, of Seneca, of Epictetus, and others, would be more full, more entire, more coherent, and more clearly deduced from unquestionable principles of knowledge."[4] Nothing displays the family resemblance among all branches of the Western Enlightenment more strikingly than this earnest entry in a young colonial's commonplace book; the heathen sentiment from Bolingbroke, intellectual parent to Voltaire as much as to Jefferson, went back, like many such sentiments, to a common root: classical Latinity.

The most lucid account of a philosophe's lifelong purposeful engagement with classical paganism was compiled by Gibbon; he recorded it—perhaps almost too lucidly—in his *Autobiography* and exemplified it in his writings. As a boy, sickly and precocious, he read prodigiously, both at home with a tutor and during a brief stint at Westminster. When he went up to Magdalen, he was an oddly specialized young man; he arrived, he tells us, "with a stock of erudition that might have puzzled a doctor and a degree of ignorance of which a school boy would have been ashamed."[5] Oxford taught him nothing; the idleness of the fellows, their indifference to their duties and their charges, which rankled all

---

[4] Thomas Jefferson: *Literary Bible*, ed. Gilbert Chinard (1928), 50.
[5] *Autobiography*, 68.

his life, had a catastrophic effect on this clever, bookish, argumentative young man. The university, Gibbon complains, "contrived to unite the opposite extremes of bigotry and indifference." It condemned heretics and did nothing for the faithful, and so it precipitated—or at least did nothing to prevent or mitigate—a crisis of faith in Gibbon: "Such almost incredible neglect was productive of the worst mischiefs." From his early boyhood, Gibbon had enjoyed religious disputations, to advance doubts and combat dogma. Now, "the blind activity of idleness urged me to advance without armour into the dangerous mazes of controversy, and at the age of sixteen I bewildered myself in the errors of the Church of Rome."[6] His father sent him into exile, to Lausanne, to regain his senses and restore his faith. The cure worked; early in 1755, after a year or more of intense debate with local pastors, intense study, and intense self-examination, Gibbon could write to his aunt, "I have at length good news to tell you; I am now good protestant & am extremely glad of it."[7]

In this period, its anguish concealed behind the balanced cadence of his prose, Gibbon studied French and Latin as well as Protestant apologists, but it was his reconversion to Protestantism that seems to have liberated his scholarly energies: "I am tempted," he recalled, "to distinguish the last eight months of the year 1755 as the period of the most extraordinary diligence and rapid progress." He devoured Cicero: "I read with application and pleasure *all* the epistles, *all* the orations, and the most important treatises of rhetoric and philosophy." His pleasure in the philosopher was voracious: "I tasted the beauty of the language; I breathed the spirit of freedom; and I imbibed from his precepts and examples the public and private sense of a man." Then, "after finishing this great author, a library of eloquence and reason, I formed a more extensive plan of reviewing the Latin classics under the four divisions of (1) historians, (2) poets, (3) orators, and (4) philosophers, in a chronological series from the days of Plautus and Sallust to the decline of the language and empire of Rome; and

---

[6] Ibid., 82.
[7] Gibbon to Catherine Porten (February 1755). Edward Gibbon: *Letters,* ed. J. E. Norton, 3 vols. (1956), I, 3. Unfortunately for the historian, most of Gibbon's letters from this crucial period have been lost.

this plan, in the last twenty-seven months of my residence at Lausanne (January 1756–April 1758), I *nearly* accomplished." Remembering it all later, Gibbon insisted that this review, "however rapid," was neither hasty nor superficial: "I indulged myself in a second and even a third perusal of Terence, Virgil, Horace, Tacitus, etc., and studied to imbibe the sense and spirit most congenial to my own."[8] And this was the point of his classicism: by the late 1750's it was Roman philosophers, not Protestant divines, who were most congenial to Gibbon's spirit.

Gibbon's later career testifies that the classics remained both congenial and important to him. His first book, the *Essai sur l'étude de la littérature,* is an erudite and elegant defense of classical learning and classical tastes. Then came his service with the militia; it was an exhilarating and instructive experience, and for a while, distracted by the pleasures and hampered by the inconveniences of a military life, Gibbon laid aside his beloved classics. But he soon repaired his neglect and resumed his reading with his characteristic gluttony: "After this long fast, the longest which I have ever known, I once more tasted at Dover the pleasures of reading and thinking; and the hungry appetite with which I opened a volume of Tully's philosophical works is still present to my memory."[9] This was the spirit that moved Gibbon to write his famous sentences about his personal discovery of Rome. They are worn smooth with repetition, these sentences, but they were written under the pressure of and were meant to evoke powerful feelings: "My temper," Gibbon confesses, "is not very susceptible of enthusiasm, and the enthusiasm which I do not feel I have ever scorned to affect. But at the distance of twenty-five years I can neither forget nor express the strong emotions which agitated my mind as I first approached and entered the *Eternal City.* After a sleepless night I trod, with a lofty step, the ruins of the Forum; each memorable spot where Romulus stood, or Tully spoke, or Caesar fell, was at once present to my eye, and several days of intoxication were lost or enjoyed before I could descend to a cool and minute investigation."[1] Gibbon's shock in

---

[8] *Autobiography*, 98–100.
[9] Ibid., 135. Gibbon's writings offer a splendid array of oral metaphors.
[1] Ibid., 152.

Rome—the worldly wit drunk with excitement, sleepless like a schoolboy, arriving in the city in what he called a *"songe d'antiquité"*[2]—was a shock of recognition. This was his world— pagan, not Christian, Rome—whose writers he knew by heart and whose streets and buildings were as vivid in his mind, before he had ever seen them, as those of London or Lausanne. Until his Italian journey he had hesitated over what he should turn to, but classical Rome imposed itself on him and determined his future in a moment. "It was at Rome, on the 15th of October 1764, as I sat musing amid the ruins of the Capitol, while the barefooted friars were singing vespers in the temple of Jupiter, that the idea of writing the decline and fall of the city first started to my mind."[3]

For all his emotions, the ironist did not lose sight of the irony that eighteenth-century Rome presented to a philosophic observer: the Christian intruders chanting their superstitious songs in the noble pagan temple were, with their very incongruity, a call to duty, to philosophical history. And so Gibbon resolved to study how that city, the home of the first Enlightenment, had fallen to the merchants of Belief. The dramatic moment on the Capitol confirmed for Gibbon what he, like the other philosophes, had always felt: that classicism was a bridge thrown across the swamp of the Christian millennium; with a bold stroke of the imagination, he, like they, repudiated the recent past to fashion his ideals from a past remote only in time. We no longer think of the Christian millennium as a swamp, but the philosophes' image of a bridge to antiquity has withstood two centuries of criticism: what the philosophes thought they found in the classical world, and had every right to think they found there, was the sense and spirit most congenial to their own.

---

[2] *Gibbon's Journey from Geneva to Rome,* ed. Georges A. Bonnard (1961), 235.
[3] *Autobiography,* 154.

3. THE SEARCH FOR PAGANISM: FROM IDENTIFICATION TO IDENTITY

I

For most of the philosophes, this discovery of their true ancestors was anything but easy. The anxious query of the existentialist, *Why should anything exist?*, runs like a muted but audible theme through their writings. The dialectic of their experience—the tense interplay of admired antiquity, hated Christianity, and emerging modernity—defines both their supreme crisis of identity and its resolution. After all, the most militant battle cry of the Enlightenment, *écrasez l'infâme*, was directed against Christianity itself, against Christian dogma in all its forms, Christian institutions, Christian ethics, and the Christian view of man, but the philosophes had been born into a Christian world and kept many of their Christian friends. Inevitably this produced conflicts, both conscious and unconscious: the philosophes boasted that they were making all things new, but far from wholly discarding their Christian inheritance, they repressed, and retained, more than they knew.

Their Christian inheritance sometimes lay heavily upon them. It was not merely that the philosophes were less cheerful than they appeared in public—most men are; nor that they experienced private upheavals—many philosophers, especially young philosophers, do. There was more to their moods of discontent than that. Christianity had dominated their childhood; its teachings had saturated their formative years and had been reinforced by glowing promises and grim warnings. Many philosophes had a brother who was a priest or a sister who was a nun; many philosophes had seriously weighed a clerical career. Christianity did not retain possession of their intellects, but often it haunted them. When they turned against religion, they did so not from ignorance or indifference: their anticlerical humor has all the bitter intimacy of a family joke; their anti-Christian passion has the specificity and precision available only to men of long, close experience. They knew their Bible, their catechism, their articles of faith, their apologetics; and they knew, too, because it had been drummed into them early and without pause, that heretics and unbelievers suffer in hell forever. "He had to change his religion," Voltaire writes about Henri IV before Paris; "that always costs an honest man something."[4] Henri's choice, as Voltaire knew, was partly a statesman's act, but if even a half-political conversion—and merely a conversion from one Christian sect to another—took its toll, how much more expensive a private conversion, and to paganism at that! To embrace materialism or even deism was to defy strong and persuasive pressures, to reject a rich, well-entrenched heritage, to make a deliberate choice—the choice of freedom.

Such existentialist language may seem a little portentous in view of the philosophes' sociability and urbanity, but it is never easy to establish one's own identity, especially if that identity is in direct conflict with time-honored cultural ideals. There was something exhilarating in choosing freedom; it opened glorious vistas of independence and vast opportunities for work. But at the same time, this freedom imposed its burdens on the philosophes, burdens obscurely felt rather than clearly articulated, burdens of guilt, of uncertainty, of sheer fright at the uncharted territory before them. Poised as they seemed, and confidently articulate, the men of the Enlightenment often looked back on the clear, simple verities of their childhood with a wistfulness amounting to nostalgia.

All this inner stress had its value: it restrained the philosophes' optimism, encouraged them to respect the giants of the past, and gave them at least a glimpse of the tragic aspect of life; even the mature, self-confident Gibbon was not without some anxiety as he wrote the notorious chapters on the origins of Christianity for his *Decline and Fall of the Roman Empire*. Whatever its consequences, the traces of this stress were visible in philosophe after philosophe. In his youth, Lessing experienced Christianity at its most appealing: at home he saw a Lutheranism at once traditional and humane, conservative, vigorous, and soundly informed. His father, a distinguished pastor who rejected the theological innovations of his time, was yet a learned man, tolerant on principle:

---

[4] *Essai sur les mœurs*, II, 537–8.

among his writings were translations from the latitudinarian Tillotson. Hence when young Lessing deserted the Lutheranism of his fathers, he did so with deliberate speed and recurrent twinges of regret: his lifelong religious speculations were a perpetual debate, not only with others, but also with himself. Repeatedly he wondered out loud whether in his critical impetuosity he had not discarded too much. Toward the end of his life, in the midst of his most intense religious speculations, he confessed that he was uncertain whether it was a good or a bad thing that he should have lived in a time when theological controversy was fashionable. He describes himself as swallowing one book after the other, astonished at the scorn of each cleric for the rest and the dogmatic certainty of all. "I was pulled from one side to the other; none wholly satisfied me." The latest polemicist was always the most insistent, the most sarcastic, and in consequence, all polemics had unintended effects: "The more conclusively the one tried to prove Christianity to me, the more doubtful I became. The more petulantly and triumphantly another tried to trample it into the ground, the more inclined I was to preserve it at least in my heart."[5] These are not the tones of an untroubled pagan.

In 1770, while he was at Hamburg, Lessing was granted access to an unpublished manuscript by Hermann Samuel Reimarus, a local professor. Reimarus had died two years before and left to the world his final word on religion, the *Apologie oder Schutzschrift für die vernünftigen Verehrer Gottes,* a vast, erudite deist manifesto. Ironically, this very work, which confirmed the direction of Lessing's own religious ideas and settled many of his doubts, was the outcome of a long, painful, secret struggle. From his youth, Reimarus had been tormented by the irreconcilable contradiction between the conclusions of reason and the demands of faith. If God had wanted to teach mankind by dictating the Holy Scriptures, why had He made them so obscure? If God was truly One in Three, why could he, Reimarus, never visualize the Trinity in any coherent image? If all who were damned were damned forever, why did the Christian religion ask its votaries to

---

[5] "Bibliolatrie" (some late unpublished fragments). *Schriften,* XVI, 475–6.

think of their God as the God of love, and of Jesus Christ as the bringer of salvation? How could God choose the Jews above all other nations, when they were so disagreeable, so stubborn in their wickedness? All the apologetics Reimarus read—and he read them with grim perseverance and ever weakening confidence—seemed illogical, sophisticated, wholly unconvincing. Bayle and Spinoza, on the other hand, offered light if, for many years, no comfort. Reimarus was driven forward by his fierce honesty, and when he gave up Christianity at last, he did so reluctantly, after long misery, compelled by reason.

Another prominent *Aufklärer*, the Swabian poet Wieland, rather neglected today but regarded in his own time as (in Goethe's words) a star of the first magnitude, struggled his way to a consistent Epicureanism; like the others, he found the road to his final philosophy arduous. He was well trained in the classics, read Cornelius Nepos at eight, Horace and Vergil at ten; and he was only a boy when he chose his favorite writers, Cicero and Lucian, who remained his favorites throughout his long life. He claims to have read at sixteen "nearly all the authors of the Golden and Silver Age"; and he had read most of the Greeks too. To be sure, born into a Pietist household and trained in Pietist schools, young Wieland, who had an abnormally developed need to please his elders by imitating them, began to read the classics as others read them: as literary exercises and delicious food for the imagination. But then at fifteen he secured a copy of Bayle's *Dictionnaire*, and soon after, philosophical writings by Voltaire and German *Aufklärer* like Wolff, and they gave his classical reading a subversive turn. An exhausting inner conflict followed, between theology and philosophy, Pietist enthusiasm and enlightened skepticism: "How often," he wrote shortly afterwards, "how often did I all but bathe in tears of pain, all but rub my hands raw!" He was irritable and sick; he fell into "a rage of religious piety" and into the "most horrifying pangs of conscience"; and for a time he indulged in an extravagant campaign against German Epicurean poets. Characteristically, as a true classicist he cast his inner struggles as a debate between two Greeks: Plato (the symbol of religious mysticism) and Xenophon (the representative of common sense and urbane irony).

Xenophon won out, and pagan worldly wisdom became the

intellectual foundation of Wieland's prose and poetry. His aristocratic affirmation of worldliness and cultivation, of rationalism and
social responsibility, his distrust of enthusiasm and Utopian
optimism, were all grounded in antique speculation, especially in
the refined, eclectic, suave writings of Hellenistic Greece and
late, sophisticated Rome: in Xenophon's common sense, Horace's
aurea mediocritas, Lucian's sardonic skepticism. It is significant
that Wieland should have spent a decade and more of his life
translating, from all the large corpus of classical literature, Cicero,
Horace, and Lucian. His use of Hellenistic Athens as the scene for
many of his novels and long poems is more than an elegant touch;
it openly testifies to a profound affinity. During his translation of
Horace, one of his friends reported, his *Schwärmerei* went so far,
"that he often seriously maintained that Horace's soul was dwelling within him."[6] In his autobiography, Goethe recalled that
Wieland's light-hearted philosophical poem of 1768, *Musarion*,
had made an enormous impression on him: "It was here that I
thought to see antiquity again, alive and new."[7] And in his eulogy
on Wieland, Goethe recognized Wieland's essential paganism:
Wieland, he said, had been related to Greece by inclination and
to Rome by disposition. Like Horace, he had been a true artist,
"a courtier and man of the world, a sensible critic of life and art";
like Cicero, he had been "philosopher, orator, statesman, active
citizen."[8] But he had become such a splendid pagan only after
much turmoil.

It is tempting to suggest that the German philosophes, innocent of practical life and somewhat distant from the new currents
of Western thought, were especially reluctant to abandon the
religion of the past, and especially given to self-torture. But the
French and British philosophes display the same symptoms. Some,
like Raynal and Marmontel, surrendered their religious convictions with ease, but many found it a grave and exhausting struggle.
Diderot, most ebullient of philosophes, the freest, most inventive
of spirits, was driven from position to position and harassed by
doubts. Born into a family abundantly supplied with priests, of

---

[6] See Friedrich Sengle: *Wieland* (1949), 22, 21, 86, 395.

[7] *Dichtung und Wahrheit*, in *Gedenkausgabe*, X, 299.

[8] "Zum brüderlichen Andenken Wielands," (1813). Ibid.,
XII, 704.

pious parents, with a pious brother and sister, he long toyed with entering the priesthood. When he lost his vocation and his faith, he adopted an aesthetic theism on the model of Shaftesbury, then moved, first to deism, then to skepticism, and finally came to rest in a highly individualistic atheism. But atheism, with its denial of free will, repelled him even though he accepted it as true; while Catholicism, with its colorful ceremonial, moved him even though he rejected it as false. He was driven, as his sister put it with unconscious insight in the midst of a family quarrel, by a "*démon philosophe*"—a philosophic devil.[9] Writing to Sophie Volland, he cursed the philosophy—his own—that reduced their love to a blind encounter of atoms. "I am furious at being entangled in a confounded philosophy which my mind cannot refrain from approving and my heart from denying." He vehemently defended the proposition that man is innately good, but his faith in humanity was often shaken by untoward events: to deny original sin and maintain optimism about human nature seemed a depressing business.

Even David Hume, whose good cheer was celebrated, had to brood and struggle his way into paganism. At eighteen, in rebellion against the dour Scottish Presbyterianism of his childhood, and elated by his discovery that he had a vocation—philosophy— he stuffed himself, feverishly, with "Cicero, Seneca & Plutarch,"[1] and was soon crippled by hysterical symptoms, loss of appetite, hypochondria, and melancholy. He was unable to study with concentration or pleasure. He continued to function: it was in the midst of his long breakdown and during his gradual recovery that he thought through the audacious epistemological arguments of his *Treatise of Human Nature*. By the middle 1730's, when he

---

[9] Denise Diderot to Denis Diderot (early June 1768). *Correspondance*, VIII, 53. At times a close association with pagan writings had a deleterious effect on Christian scholars: this was the philosophes' anguish in reverse. The abbé d'Olivet, Voltaire's teacher at Louis-le-Grand, left the Jesuit order to devote himself to a highly regarded edition of Cicero; the abbé Barthélemy, in the second half of the century, lost his religious vocation in his passionate preoccupation with classical Greece.
[1] Hume to Dr. George Cheyne (March or April 1734). *Letters*, I, 14. By an amusing and revealing coincidence, Hume's list is precisely the list Voltaire gives of his intellectual ancestry in the *Philosophical Dictionary* (see above, p. 51).

wrote them down, he was largely restored. He was confident that his reasoning was sound, but uncomfortable with his conclusions. "I wish from my Heart," he wrote to Francis Hutcheson in 1740, "I could avoid concluding, that since Morality, according to your Opinion as well as mine, is determin'd merely by Sentiment, it regards only human Nature & human Life."[2] The *Treatise* itself shows only a single trace of what he had been through, the touching if rather melodramatic autobiographical chapter that concludes Book One: "Methinks," he begins his confession, perhaps unconsciously employing a classical metaphor, "I am like a man, who having struck on many shoals, and having narrowly escap'd shipwreck in passing a small frith, has yet the temerity to put out to sea in the same leaky weather-beaten vessel, and even carries his ambition so far as to think of compassing the globe under these disadvantageous circumstances." His memory of past "errors and perplexities" makes him diffident; the weakness and disorder of his faculties and the "impossibility of amending or correcting" them reduces him to despair and induces wishes of self-destruction. "This sudden view of my danger" on the boundless ocean of lonely search "strikes me with melancholy; and as 'tis usual for that passion, above all others, to indulge itself; I cannot forbear feeding my despair, with all those desponding reflections, which the present subject furnishes me with in such abundance."

The modern reader who studies this self-revelation with sympathy is, I think, struck less by its rhetoric than by its grim sense of isolation, by a self-pity rising almost to paranoia. "I am first affrighted and confounded with that forelorn solitude, in which I am plac'd in my philosophy." To be sure, this isolation may be rationally explained, but the explanation has that strange, self-enclosed rationality characteristic of men in situations of extreme loneliness: "I have expos'd myself to the enmity of all metaphysicians, logicians, mathematicians, and even theologians; and can I wonder at the insults I must suffer? I have declar'd my dis-approbation of their systems; and can I be surpriz'd, if they shou'd express a hatred of mine and of my person?" Detachment from society is mirrored by private emptiness: "When I look abroad, I foresee on every side, dispute, contradiction, anger,

---

[2] March 16, 1740. *Letters*, I, 40.

calumny and detraction. When I turn my eye inward, I find
nothing but doubt and ignorance." The world is hostile and,
significantly, conspiratorial: "All the world conspires to oppose
and contradict me; tho' such is my weakness, that I feel all my
opinions loosen and fall of themselves, when unsupported by the
approbation of others. Every step I take is with hesitation, and
every new reflection makes me dread an error and absurdity in
my reasoning." In the end, Hume proclaims that he no longer
knows who he is; his stable self-image has dissolved in a sea of
doubt and despair: he fancied himself, much as Diderot did in a
similar predicament, "some strange uncouth monster, who not
being able to mingle and unite in society, has been expell'd all
human commerce, and left utterly abandon'd and disconsolate."
And he is driven to ask: "Where am I, or what? From what causes
do I derive my existence, and to what condition shall I return?
Whose favour shall I court, and whose anger must I dread? What
beings surround me? and on whom have I any influence, or who
have any influence on me?"[3] Such insistent questions are a
precious indication of the price that rebellion exacted from the
philosophes. "Where am I, or what?"—these are the characteristic
questions a young man asks as he is threatened with the loss of his
identity.

When Hume looked back on this period, he remembered it as
a time of internal debate, which ended with the victory of classical
philosophy: "Upon the whole," he wrote to Hutcheson in 1739,
shortly after he had finished the *Treatise*, "I desire to take my
Catalogue of Virtues from Cicero's *Offices*, not from the *Whole
Duty of Man*. I had, indeed, the former Book in my Eye in all my
Reasonings."[4] And in 1751 he told his friend Gilbert Elliot in a
revealing letter that the propensity to skepticism had "crept in
upon me against my Will: And tis not long ago that I burn'd an
old Manuscript Book, wrote before I was twenty; which contain'd, Page after Page, the gradual Progress of my Thoughts on
that head. It begun with an anxious Search after Arguments, to
confirm the Common Opinion: Doubts stole in, dissipated,
return'd, were again dissipated, return'd again; and it was a per-

---

[3] *A Treatise of Human Nature* (1739–40, edn. 1951), 263–9.
[4] September 17, 1739. *Letters*, I, 34.

petual Struggle of a restless Imagination against Inclination, perhaps against Reason."[5] It has been said that historical personages often show little regard for historians: that old Manuscript Book would have been a priceless document for Hume's intellectual development, and—since in this Hume was representative of the philosophes—for the Enlightenment's inner history.

With Hume, as with most other philosophes, the troubled search for identity ended happily. The tension once mastered, Hume could command the pagan past with supreme ease: his magnificent demographic essay, "Of the Populousness of Ancient Nations," ranges across all of ancient literature. Hume wrote the essay to overturn the nostalgic theories of population prevalent in his time. Since antiquity was manifestly superior to modern times (so ran the argument), and since greatness is accompanied by populousness, it follows that the ancient world was more heavily populated than modern Europe. In the course of demonstrating the absurdity of this syllogism and the error of its conclusion, Hume has occasion to cite more than fifty ancient writers, some of them famous, like Plutarch, Strabo, Tacitus, and Pliny; others more obscure, and likely to be known by specialists only, authors like Columella, who wrote a treatise on rural life in the time of Nero, or Aelius Lampridius, one of the authors of the *Historia Augusta*. We can credit Hume's casual remark that in preparing the essay he had "read over almost all the Classics, both Greek and Latin."[6] Hume's *Dialogues Concerning Natural Religion* is an even more direct testimonial to antiquity than this: it is an imitation of Cicero's *De Natura Deorum*, which it follows closely in argument, exposition of doctrines, number and disposition of speakers, and even anecdotes. In choosing Cicero, and especially *De Natura Deorum*, Hume was making an ambitious choice; and surely nothing would have gratified Hume more than the modern judgment that he had surpassed his admired "Tully" in the *Dialogues*. He was the modern pagan, secure and serene. When he went to Paris in 1763, he carried only four books with him: a Vergil, a Horace, a Tasso, and a Tacitus.

Rousseau's inner struggles did not have this cheerful out-

---

[5] March 10, 1751. Ibid., I, 154.
[6] Hume to Gilbert Elliott, February 18, 1751. Ibid., I, 152.

come. True, his malaise was perpetual and it isolated him among the philosophes. But he too, like the others, struggled his way into deism through the classics, and his strains mirror, in enlarged and distorted shape, the strains that plagued most of the other philosophes. In his twenties, making up for a wasted youth, he educated himself at Madame de Warens's expense, devoured Plato in Latin and bought Cicero's *Opera omnia* with his scarce funds. He became a deist, but stubbornly and pathetically he tried to save at least some comforting aspects of his universe from the icy blasts of Voltaire's cosmic pessimism. "All the subtleties of metaphysics," he told Voltaire in reply to the poem on the Lisbon earthquake, "will not make me doubt for a moment the immortality of the soul or a beneficent Providence. I feel it, I believe it, I want it, I hope for it, and I shall defend it to my last breath."[7] Here is a declaration of faith at once defensive and revealing; defensive in the emotional reiterations that conclude it, and revealing because it cannot be made congruent with Rousseau's normal religious position. As a deist, Rousseau was hardly entitled to call upon a beneficent Providence: Christianity, it seemed, was not true, but it *was* consoling.

II

I am not suggesting that the philosophes lived in a permanent state of crisis. They were rather like political refugees returning to view the ruins of a city where they had lived as children: they were elated at the opportunity for ambitious reconstruction, confident that they could build a new and fairer city, but faintly mournful at the spectacle and faintly guilty at having helped in the destruction of a place that had been ugly, unhealthy, inhospitable, but in some sense their own. The philosophes' sociability, their wit, their argumentative vigor, their humanitarian energy, and their hopes were not simply substitutes or masks for despair. They were real enough. The deists were sustained by their warm sense of man's fraternity in an orderly universe; the materialists claimed to be, and doubtless often were, defiantly happy at being cosmic

---

[7] August 18, 1756. *Correspondance générale*, ed. Théophile Dufour and Pierre-Paul Plan, 20 vols. (1924–34), II, 324.

orphans. Besides, much like other men, they escaped from depression and mastered doubts through friendship and work and through play. "Since reason is incapable of dispelling these clouds," Hume reported in the *Treatise*, "nature herself suffices to that purpose, and cures me of this philosophical melancholy and delirium, either by relaxing this bent of mind, or by some avocation, and lively impression of my senses, which obliterate all these chimera. I dine, I play a game of back-gammon, I converse, and am merry with my friends; and when after three or four hours' amusement, I wou'd return to these speculations, they appear so cold, and strain'd, and ridiculous, that I cannot find it in my heart to enter into them any farther."[8] Other philosophes adopted similar remedies. "To work and think of you, that's my life," wrote Voltaire to his niece and mistress Madame Denis after his disastrous sojourn at the Prussian court.[9] Love and work: here was an energetic program to make an unpalatable world less unpalatable, although often it was rage, not love, that saved the philosophes from philosophical melancholy. Lessing, who had devoured Cicero, Vergil, Horace, and Sophocles in his *Gymnasium* at Meissen, and read Theophrastus, Plautus, and Terence for pleasure as a young theology student, did combat for the ancients all his life. Polemics on classical subjects were the best substitute for politics available to him; nothing stirred him more than an incompetent translation of Horace: "When it comes to ancient writers," he said, "I am a veritable knight errant"[1]—a pronouncement in the approved militant style of the Enlightenment. Since Lessing was battling over questions as harmless as the correct reading of a Greek text, his language seems a little excessive, but it reminds us, once again, that the philosophes' classicism was intimate, passionate, and aggressive. For the men of the Enlightenment, the road to independence lay through the ancients.

For this, after all and above all—help toward independence—was what the philosophes wanted from their cherished classics. They were too tough-minded to yearn for the restoration of a Roman or Spartan Utopia, too active to fall into fussy or snobbish

---

[8] *Treatise of Human Nature*, 269.
[9] September 3, 1753. *Correspondence*, XXIII, 166.
[1] Quoted by Franz Bornmüller, ed.: *Lessings Werke*, 5 vols. (n.d.), IV, xii.

antiquarianism. Locke, early in the battle for modernity, had insisted that "antiquity and history" were obstacles to true knowledge, "designed only to furnish men with story and talk" rather than with instruction "in the art of living well" or with "wisdom and prudence."[2] The philosophes, rather more secure, were less severe with antiquity than that. Gibbon warned against a slavish, uncritical worship of the ancients, but could accept "nature and antiquity" as the "two great sources of knowledge."[3] Diderot put it even more precisely: "It seems to me that we must study antiquity in order to learn to see nature."[4] In fact, Diderot made his appeal against submissive antiquarianism by citing an ancient who had made a similar appeal: Horace. Horace, Diderot wrote to his friend Naigeon, "protested against anticomania, and Horace was right."[5] Evidently Diderot liked the word: he criticized antiquarians for using the "spectacles of anticomania";[6] such men, he complained, endlessly compare the best work of the ancients with the feeblest work of the moderns and admire the ancients solely because they were ancient. But in doing so they kill the very spirit that makes them so admirable. To sigh over fragments from Herculaneum and slight the achievements of the seventeenth and eighteenth centuries is to do an injustice not only to the moderns but to the ancients as well. As for himself, Diderot protested, "I certainly don't have anticomania."[7] The other philosophes, classicists though they were, were free from this disease as well: Wieland, whose imagination ceaselessly circled about the classical world, and whose scholarship kept pace with his imagination, had the intellectual courage to set himself up against an antiquarian cult among educated Germans: modern men, he urged, should imitate only what was worth imitating. This discontent with blind imitation invaded even the Italian *illuministi*, who, living on clas-

---

[2] "On Study," an early essay of 1677. Quoted by Hélaine Blumenfeld: "John Locke: A Theory of Ethics," unpubl. diss. (Columbia Univ., 1965), 88.

[3] "Outlines of the History of the World," *Miscellaneous Works*, III, 19.

[4] Salon of 1765, *Salons*, II, 207.

[5] Undated letter. Quoted by Ernst Robert Curtius: *European Literature and the Latin Middle Ages* (1953), 580.

[6] Seznec: *Diderot et l'Antiquité*, 85.

[7] Diderot to Falconet (June 15, 1766). *Correspondance*, VI, 217.

sical soil, knew the ancients most intimately. Italian playwrights and Italian political economists called for realism and criticism rather than ancestor worship: Alessandro Verri, novelist and philosophe, told his brother, with a self-assurance resembling Diderot's disdain for anticomania, that while he admired ancient Greece, he was not a pedant: "*Non sono pedante ben che grecista.*"[8]

The philosophes, then, were moderns. Their grandiose aim was stated with splendid conciseness by Diderot in his *Encyclopédie:* they wanted to "change the general way of thinking." But they were ancients too, if largely for the sake of modernity. Thus they belonged to two worlds, but this did not disconcert them, for despite their protestations, they were not at heart modest men. They merely asked for the best of both.

---

[8] Alessandro Verri to Pietro Verri (May 5, 1774). *Carteggio di Pietro e Alessandro Verri,* ed. Emanuele Greppi and Alessandro Giulini, 12 vols. (1910–42), VI, 228.

CHAPTER TWO

The First Enlightenment

1. GREECE: FROM MYTH TO REASON

I

THE IMPASSIONED PARTISAN SLOGANS of one age often become the commonplaces of the next, and they become commonplaces because they enshrine a large truth. Today, no one would be startled at the assertion that it was the ancient Ionians who first liberated man from the tyranny of myth and breathed the bracing air of reason; the competing claims recent scholars have made for Babylonian mathematics or Hebrew theology, far-reaching as they are, do not—and indeed cannot—challenge the primacy of Greek thinkers in the discovery of mind. But in the eighteenth century, when the philosophes constructed their fourfold historical scheme and asserted their kinship with the classical world, they were being radical and deeply offensive to Christian sensibilities. Their exaltation of Greece contradicted, boldly and deliberately, the traditional Christian view of history; it shifted attention away from one people to another—from the Jews to the Greeks—and elevated critical thinking into the distinctive mark of historical periods. To make the Greeks into the fathers of true civilization —the fathers, in a word, of the first Enlightenment—was to subvert the foundations of Christian historiography by treating man's past as a secular, not a sacred, record. The primacy of Greece meant the primacy of philosophy, and the primacy of philosophy made nonsense of the claim that religion was man's central concern.

There was, therefore, nothing merely academic about Diderot's observation that Thales had been the thinker who "intro-

duced the scientific method into philosophy, and the first to
deserve the name of philosopher." Thales's successors (like him,
Greeks), had extended his inquisitive enterprise into all areas of
human concern and had made thinking capable of accumulating
knowledge by making it self-critical. This, said Diderot, was the
contribution of Greek civilization to mankind, and its claim to
the gratitude of all posterity.[1]

The other philosophes, usually so argumentative over questions of scholarship, saw little reason to argue over a point so
damaging to a religious view of the world. They readily conceded
that to wonder at the unknown, to raise questions about one's
past and one's inner being, was probably a pervasive human trait,
but they also insisted that the Greeks had been the first to harness
wonder to the discipline of logic, folk memories to the criticism
of history, and inner turmoil to the rational study of human nature. Gibbon credited the Greeks with inventing "the spirit of
inquiry" which bore the precious fruit of humanism: "The philosophers of Greece deduced their morals from the nature of man
rather than from that of God";[2] Hume asserted that "the sciences
arose in GREECE."[3] The abbé Yvon explained the French Enlightenment's position in the *Encyclopédie:* the Greeks had "invented that critical philosophy which defies all authority, and
which, in its search for truth, wishes to be guided by the glimmer
of evidence alone."[4] Reflecting on the progress of the human
mind, Condorcet summed up the conviction of a century. The
Greeks had exercised "a powerful and fortunate influence over
the progress of mankind." Their "genius opened all the ways to
truth," and fate destined them "to be the benefactors and guides
of all nations, of all ages."[5] A few years before, Immanuel Kant
had called the Greeks "that admirable nation"[6] for inventing
mathematics; and Voltaire had listed the contributions of the
philosophes' first teachers: "Beautiful architecture, perfect sculp-

---

[1] Article "Grecs (philosophie des)," *Œuvres*, XV, 64.
[2] *Decline and Fall of the Roman Empire*, I, 30.
[3] "Of the Rise and Progress of the Arts and Sciences," *Works*,
III, 184.
[4] Article "Barbares." Quoted in René Hubert: *Les sciences
sociales dans l'Encyclopédie* (1923), 71.
[5] *Esquisse*, in *Œuvres*, VI, 59.
[6] *Critik der reinen Vernunft*, in *Werke*, III, 15.

ture, painting, good music, true poetry, true eloquence, the
method of writing good history, finally philosophy itself, however
incomplete and obscure—all these came to the nations from the
Greeks alone."[7]

Among the items in Voltaire's formidable catalogue, one of
the most prominent was the craft of history, to which the philosophes, as accomplished practitioners, were particularly sensitive.
Diderot paid Enlightenment historians his supreme compliment
when he compared them to Thucydides and Xenophon; while
David Hume, himself a master in the discipline, said flatly that
"the first page of THUCYDIDES is, in my opinion, the commence-
ment of real history. All preceding narrations are so intermixed
with fable, that philosophers ought to abandon them, in a great
measure, to the embellishments of poets and orators."[8] Thus Hume
rediscovered in the historical writings of antiquity the supreme
distinction between superstition and thought as the distinction
between fable and history.

In pressing these distinctions, the philosophes could draw on
some formidable ancestors; their historical thought was closely
tied and deeply, if largely unconsciously, indebted to the Renaissance. True, the Humanists were fascinated by what they thought
the wisdom of the East, the secret knowledge of Moses, of
Zoroaster, or of Egyptian priests, but Rome and, more than Rome,
Greece enlisted their true affections. When Petrarch removed
the label "Dark Ages" from classical, pre-Christian times and
fastened it instead on the Christian era, he made a tentative beginning toward the periodical scheme that would come to
dominate the Enlightenment. Petrarch's reasons for reversing the
accepted order of light and darkness were largely literary, but in
the later Renaissance, in the hands of such pagans as Machiavelli,
Petrarch's periodization was grounded in the very principles of
classical and medieval culture: the ancients had possessed light

---

[7] *Essai sur les mœurs*, I, 89.
[8] "Of the Populousness of Ancient Nations," *Works*, III, 414.
Kant quotes the first part of this dictum with approval in his
"Idee zu einer allgemeinen Geschichte in weltbürgerlicher
Absicht," *Werke*, IV, 164. Other philosophes preferred Herodotus to Thucydides as the father of history (following Newton),
but the disagreement matters little: both putative fathers, after
all, were Greeks.

because they had been tough-minded, worldly, philosophical; the Christian millennium had been dark because it was quarrelsome, querulous, and grossly superstitious. Much was at stake in this reversal: it was a prologue to the secularization of history. Pious historians in the Renaissance and later in the seventeenth century abetted this secularization in other ways: they refined techniques of research and threw doubt on extravagant tales of Hebrew Prophets or Christian saints. They did more: they separated the history of the church from the history of nations and came to stress the importance of the second at the expense of the first. By the early eighteenth century, Johann Jakob Brucker, a liberal Lutheran pastor, could write the first modern history of philosophy and begin it, appropriately enough, with the Greeks: it was from Brucker that Diderot borrowed his article on Greek philosophy. He could not have borrowed it from Bossuet.

But as Bossuet's lasting fame makes plain, while the philosophes' discovery of Greece was not new, it remained subversive and, as it were, necessary. The Christian periodical scheme was over a thousand years old when Montesquieu and Voltaire began to write their histories, and it had been severely shaken by several centuries of more or less pious criticism. But it had not been displaced: Bossuet's reaffirmation of the traditional view, made most forcefully in his celebrated *Discours sur l'histoire universelle* of 1681, retained its popularity for many decades. The *Discours* itself continued to find readers and followers, and Bossuet's disciples, Charles Rollin, Claude Fleury, and in his own way Jonathan Edwards, carried his message to the age of the Enlightenment in their expansive historical works: Fleury's vast *Histoire ecclésiastique* was reprinted down to the time of the French Revolution, and while it was marked by the stigmata of skepticism and heresy, it suggested, with Bossuet, that for a good Christian the history of philosophy was comprehended in the history of the Church.

Bossuet was a brilliant and triumphant anachronism. His historical work lies across the philosophes' path, an obstacle, a problem—and a stimulus—to their philosophy of history, as Pascal was to their philosophy of man. The *Discours* makes some significant concessions to modernity, and Voltaire gave it reluctant praise for its eloquence and for its attempt to see cultures as

a whole. It is true as well that Bossuet treated Providence as a
religious version of what less devout historians called historical
causation—as a divine agent working through men in history,
rather than appearing in the clouds with signs, portents, and
miracles. Yet as a latter-day Augustinian, Bossuet also insisted
that the fate of Empires is ruled by divine decree: their dreadful
fall is divine punishment, God's way of humbling man's pride.

Bossuet's concessions, then, were hardly impressive, but they
made the *Discours*, as it were, intellectually available to the philosophes, an object of much open scorn and some covert emulation.
In its essence, though, Bossuet's historical vision was traditional,
credulous, and—compared to the brilliant researches of French
Benedictines and Flemish Jesuits in his time—hopelessly reactionary. The *Discours* is pervaded by myth. Bossuet chose its subjects
on theological not on historical grounds; since history is the
unrolling of a mysterious Divine plan, the chronicler must seek
the traces of that plan in those aspects of the human experience
that God has singled out for special attention: the Jews, His
Chosen People, and the great Empires, His favored realms. Not
surprisingly, Bossuet's periodization has a mystical rather than a
historical rationale: the *Discours* divides the history of the world
from Creation to Charlemagne into twelve epochs and seven ages
—two sacred numbers—and grounds the epochs in religious
events: the Creation, the Deluge, the Birth of Christ, and the
establishment of peace in the Church by the Emperor Constantine. Bossuet finds certain secular events—the Fall of Troy, Romulus's founding of Rome—worthy of lending their names to epochs;
but they are nothing more than the tribute a credulous chronicler
with a classical education pays to pagan mythology. Pagan reality
was something else again: Thucydides may be a "very exact"
historian, but it is Moses who deserves the title of first historian,
sublime philosopher, and wisest of legislators.[9]

As these judgments show, Bossuet accepted both the Bible
and pagan myths as precise historical records: Noah preserved the
arts through the Deluge; Hercules founded the Olympic Games.
Xenophon is the best of secular historians because he, more than

---

[9] *Discours sur l'histoire universelle*, in *Œuvres*, ed. abbé Velat
and Yvonne Champailler (1961), 700.

any other Greek, conforms his history to Scripture—Scripture which, with its antiquity and its concentration on the Jewish people, "would deserve to be preferred to all the Greek histories, even if we did not know that it had been dictated by the Holy Spirit."[1] The Greeks cannot constitute an epoch, for their learning is borrowed and their wisdom inferior to that of sacred authors; but Cyrus dominates a historical epoch, for he rescued the Jews. Sacred history matters more than anything else, more, certainly, than philosophy: philosophy, Bossuet suggests, like ignorance, sensuality, misplaced respect for antiquity, heresy, and other human delusions, is merely a kind of idolatry.[2]

Bossuet's *Discours* was admittedly an extreme statement of Christian parochialism, but his contemporaries accepted at least this much: the Greeks, with their boasts of philosophy, built neither the first nor the greatest of early civilizations. It was the Egyptians, Bossuet thought, who first established orderly government, who, "grave and serious," had sought to make the people happy, cultivated virtue, studied the laws, and practiced wisdom.[3] Bossuet had been anticipated: the Jesuit Athanasius Kircher, the most famous Egyptologist of the seventeenth century, had asserted some decades before that the Egyptians had been the source of Plato's philosophy and Pythagoras's wisdom, and had possessed a

---

[1] Ibid., 691.

[2] Ibid., 901–15.

[3] Ibid., 956–7. With the coming of the Enlightenment, the rage for the Egyptians steadily declined. While Isaac Newton had still accepted much of Herodotus's testimony on Egyptian civilization, he also insisted that the "Priests of Egypt" had magnified the "stories & antiquity of their Gods" out of sheer vanity. (Frank Manuel: *Isaac Newton, Historian* [1963] 91.) In the middle of the eighteenth century, Winckelmann's disdain—the art of the Egyptians was hideous, their religion absurdly superstitious—became characteristic, and only eccentrics like Monboddo persisted in the traditional view. Still, the vitality of the older, Christian view in the eighteenth century is remarkable: while Voltaire explicitly rejects Bossuet's estimation of the Egyptians, there are traces of the old seventeenth-century appreciation in some passages of his *Essai sur les mœurs;* Turgot paid some circumspect tributes to Egyptian learning in his youthful address on progress to the Sorbonne; and Rousseau casually called Egypt "the first school of the universe," the "mother of philosophy and the fine arts." *Discours sur les sciences et les arts,* in *Œuvres,* III, 10.

type of religion that most nearly approached the divine dispensation later revealed to Christians. Their sublime hieroglyphs,
Kircher claimed, prove that the Egyptians had understood the
mysteries of the universe better than the Greeks had: each hiero-
glyph represented a deep philosophical truth. Other scholars put
forth similar claims for Egypt's neighbors: Thomas Burnet, whose
Sacred Theory of the Earth long enjoyed wide popularity, argued
that Greek wisdom had been borrowed from the East. Except
for some stubborn classicists, then, seventeenth-century historians generally held that what was worthy about Greek life had
not been originally theirs and that what was originally theirs—a
certain conceited, vain form of speculation—was merely a symptom of false pride among them and a cause of false pride in others.
It was against this prevailing view that the philosophes paraded
their admiration of Greece.

II

Beyond doubt, their admiration was genuine, but as skeptics
and secularists, the philosophes did not think of the Greek Miracle
as a miracle. They argued instead that the invention of philosophy
—man's greatest invention in his long history—had been a collab-
orative venture, a happy conjunction of a benign climate, a favorable political environment, a patient working out of earlier insights, and an adroit assimilation of foreign ideas. Condorcet
noted that either exiles from the East or Greek traders had
"brought to Greece the knowledge and the errors of Asia and
Egypt."[4] This did not deter Condorcet from arguing that these
borrowings in no way diminished the Greeks' title to originality:
as true eighteenth-century men, happily free from the rage for
uniqueness, the philosophes defined real originality as the intelligent use of existing ideas.

This was, to the philosophes, the originality of the Greeks:
the Greeks transformed what they learned into something new.
"Barbarians," Diderot noted, "threw into Greece the first seed
of philosophy. This seed could not have fallen on more fruitful

---

[4] *Esquisse*, in *Œuvres*, VI, 61.

soil," for the Greeks had a "turn of mind quite different from that of the Orientals." When the notions of another people passed through Greek hands, they "acquired a touch of their own way of thinking, and never entered their writings without undergoing great change."[5] Mythopoeic cultures were capable of logical thinking. The Persians had possessed political skills; the Chaldeans had founded astronomy; the Phoenicians had known enough navigation to carry on trade with the most distant nations; the Egyptians had studied nature. In short, all the nations around Greece were well versed in "theology, ethics, politics, war, agriculture, metallurgy, and most of the mechanical arts which necessity and industry bring forth among men assembled in towns and subjected to laws."[6] This generous catalogue fairly summarizes the Enlightenment's estimate of pre-Greek antiquity; it reappears in a number of articles in the *Encyclopédie* and in Voltaire's *Essai sur les mœurs*, which epitomizes advanced opinion at mid-century: the Chaldeans, Voltaire writes, were apt astronomers and even deep thinkers, advanced enough to go beyond mere sense knowledge to understand things which "contradicted what they saw."[7]

But while the Enlightenment was ready to offer handsome appreciations to pre-classical civilizations and while it sometimes strained to discover their similarity to Greece for the sake of anticlerical propaganda—the stereotype of a tight, rationalist priestly clique manipulating a large, superstitious populace was portable, applicable equally to the Egypt of the Pharaohs, the Greece of Solon, or the France of Louis XV—this was not the essence of the philosophes' view. The philosophes balanced the cultural and scientific inventions which they ascribed to the Egyptians and Phoenicians against the beliefs, practices, and possibilities of these civilizations as a whole, and these were always markedly inferior to Greek thought and action. Diderot's appreciation, which I have quoted before, appears in an article on Greek philosophy and was designed to emphasize not Greek

---

[5] "Grecs (philosophie des)," *Œuvres*, XV, 64. Condillac employs the same formula in his *Traité des systèmes*, in *Œuvres*, I, 138.
[6] "Grecs (philosophie des)," *Œuvres*, XV, 65.
[7] *Essai sur les mœurs*, I, 34.

dependence but Greek superiority. Other cultures, Diderot argued throughout the *Encyclopédie,* had no claim to systematic thought: the ancient Greeks were right to be contemptuous of what the Arabs liked to call their "philosophy." Egypt, for all the shrewdness of its priests and its instinct for preserving knowledge, remained a breeding ground for superstitions, an ideal country for magicians and fortune tellers and for the worship of cats and onions. The Chaldeans took pride in an astronomy that was little more than a pile of disconnected maxims, traditional dogmas, and misinterpreted observations—hence the Chaldean priests in no way deserved to be called philosophers. Voltaire took the same position: in the very pages in which he acknowledges the rational achievements of Babylonian, Phoenician, or Egyptian sages, he adds that Egyptian philosophy was chaos; the pyramids, for all their technical cleverness, were built by despotism, vanity, servitude, and superstition; the Chaldeans began with astronomical observations and ended up with astrology. There could be no doubt, for Voltaire as for the others: the supremacy of Greece was beyond question.

These are complex judgments. For the Enlightenment, these cultures were civilized but superstitious: they were capable of some scientific thinking, but their occasional attempts at rational thought never tore the web of myth—it was sporadic and fitful rather than organized, cumulative, and self-critical. The rational skill needed to build the pyramids was never directed against the irrational regime that ordered them built or the irrational religion they served and advertised. Pre-Greek rationality was, as it were, intransitive: whatever reasoning mathematics or astronomy could muster did not lead to reasoning in politics or religion. At its darkest, antique superstition was blind and horrifying, but even at its most enlightened, it never ceased turning experience into myths.

The Greeks, on the other hand, by that special *tour d'esprit* which Diderot so prized, learned to convert what they saw and heard into a rational whole. In a beautiful passage of the *Timaeus,* Plato had paid tribute to the sense of sight as the father of thought, and derived the celestial gift of philosophy—the greatest boon mankind has ever received—from man's observations of the sun, the sky, and the stars. As the philosophes were well aware, this

gift had not been granted in a single, dazzling moment of illumination, but represented, rather, a long, laborious conquest of
myth by reason. In his article on Greek philosophy in the *Encyclopédie,* Diderot distinguishes three periods of speculation: first,
antique times, when the Greeks lived on fables, adapted oriental
tales, and rationalized Homeric theology; in this period Greece
was much like, and in many respects inferior to, the great civilizations that surrounded it; but in this period, too, the Greeks
took the majestic and painful first step beyond myth. Then came
the epoch of great legislation, the founding of political philosophy. And finally, there came "the time of the schools," which
developed the permanently influential systems.[8]

If there was any one figure that dramatized what was best in
this long cultural evolution, it was Socrates. A folk hero to the
philosophes as he had been to antiquity, Socrates became the
subject, in the eighteenth century, of plays, paintings, apostrophes,
and slightly uneasy jokes by literary men who admired his irony
without wishing to share his fate. Rousseau singled out the
Delphic maxim, which Socrates had quoted and indeed lived by,
as "a precept more important and more difficult than all the fat
volumes of the moralists."[9] The precept "Know thyself" is an
overworked platitude today, but the philosophes read it as a
critical moment in the history of man's mind, a laconic invitation
to moral self-mastery. Socrates, as d'Alembert said in his influential *Discours préliminaire,* had been a pioneer in the difficult and
all-important search for man's nature.

Yet even Socrates, despite his heroic stature, could not fully
embody the Greek revolution for the Enlightenment. The Greek
intellect had looked in two directions—outward: to nature, objective universal law—in a word, to science; and inward: to self-
knowledge, inner clarity—in a word, to morality. Socrates had
repudiated the first in behalf of the second and proclaimed the
vanity of cosmology compared to the knowledge that leads men
to right action. The philosophes had much sympathy with this
point of view; it reappears, as we shall see, in their suspicion of

---

[8] "Grecs (philosophie des)," *Œuvres,* XV, 44–68 *passim.* In this
periodization, Diderot relies heavily on Brucker's Latin *Historia
critica philosophiae.*
[9] *Discours sur l'origine de l'inégalité,* in *Œuvres,* III, 122.

metaphysics and in their commitment to practicality. At the same time, they regarded the scientific revolution of their own age as more than a game or merely abstract knowledge—as is evident from their rather confused moral demands on science, they hoped it would become the prelude, and even the servant, of moral and political improvement. Hence Socrates could not become the complete symbol of the philosophes' aspirations: he had separated what they intended to join.

In fact, Socrates was a symbol for the Enlightenment more through his death than through his ideas. His fate was painful evidence that the First Age of Criticism had been all too human. Socrates's death, Condorcet pronounced, "was the first crime announcing the war between philosophy and superstition, which still continues today."[1] This fact, grim as it was, was yet another link between the ancients and the moderns: the Enlightenment, as I have said, saw its own time struggling between superstition and reason; ancient Greece, it seemed, had been enmeshed in the same conflict. The Greeks had given criticism its first martyr, but they had also given it its first practitioners—that is why the Greeks, for all their failings, were the true ancestors of the Enlightenment. This was, on the whole, an unsentimental and sober view: the philosophes saw the Greeks as pioneers who had had all the daring and made all the mistakes characteristic of bold innovators clearing new ground.

III

Unsentimental and sober as they were, it would be too much to claim that the philosophes treated the Greek phase of the first Enlightenment with even-handed impartiality or adequate sympathy. Political preoccupations kept breaking in. Thus the philosophes slighted whatever contribution Aristotle may have made to the scientific method; they saw him mainly as the favorite of the Scholastics—a pagan who had trafficked with the enemy. Their treatment of Plato, which has long perplexed and annoyed students of the eighteenth century, was equally shabby. Rousseau,

---

[1] *Esquisse,* in *Œuvres,* VI, 66.

who worshipped Plato's writings as *divin,* was a lonely voice in the Enlightenment. Rather more characteristically, Montesquieu described Plato as a fine poet; Voltaire, puzzled and impudent, called Plato eloquent and unintelligible, a clever fabulist with occasional insights; Wieland equated Plato's metaphysical vision with an otherworldly mysticism; while Jefferson could hardly get through the *Republic:* it seemed to him puerile, whimsical, full of unintelligible jargon and downright nonsense—he simply could not understand how the admirable Cicero could have eulogized Plato so extravagantly. Despite this condescension, the Enlightenment was permeated with Platonic ideas. The Stoics, who taught the philosophes a great deal, had studied Plato closely, and had adopted many of his teachings. The neoplatonists had adopted others, and their system was transmitted to posterity in large part by Augustine. Now the philosophes patronized Plato, ignored the neoplatonists, and ridiculed Augustine, but they inherited, despite themselves, a wide range of Platonic ideas, largely through the Stoics and such modern Platonists as Galileo. Traveling through the ages incognito, Plato found himself welcomed by philosophes who did not recognize him: they borrowed better than they knew.

Besides, their rationalistic myopia was incurable. The philosophes found it hard to believe that reasonable men, the fathers of science, ethics, and history, should have been "caught in superstitions." Voltaire, for one, insisted on interpreting the Orphic mystery religion as an advanced monotheistic cult which had surrounded itself with secrecy from fear of violence at the hands of a gross populace. Diderot, capable of giving a discriminating account of Orpheus' life and death, his cult and influence, could resist the lure of rationalism no better. After citing some ancient authors on Orpheus' magic powers, he quoted a more congenial passage from Horace's *Ars poetica* which implied that Orpheus was an adroit impostor who had claimed divine sanction for reasonable codes of conduct in order to prevent his savage followers from tearing each other to pieces. This mode of interpretation, which imported eighteenth-century concerns into a distant past, imputed to the early Greeks a political shrewdness and religious cynicism wholly alien to them. Doubtless, this unhistorical skepticism saved the philosophes from improbable tales and helped them to sort the fabulous from the historical, rhetoric from reality. But it also kept them from capturing the inner logic, the mood, of styles of thought distant from their own. Rationalism set the stage for discoveries and discriminations, but it placed wrong accents. The contemptuous word "superstition," a *Schimpfwort* disguised as an analytical term, was a vessel insufficient to contain the religious experience of the ancients.

The philosophes' inadequate sympathy for early antiquity was further narrowed by their partial failure to appreciate contemporary scholarship, although most of the scholarship available to the educated public in the eighteenth century was accessible to the philosophes, both physically and, as it were, emotionally.[2] Much of that scholarship, in fact, was of high caliber. By the time of Locke, the heroic age of the rediscovery and re-editing of classical manuscripts had passed, and methods for critical reading of documents had been firmly established. Now the opportunity for some large generalizations was at hand. In the middle of the eighteenth century, while the leading philosophes were publishing their major works and the younger philosophes were beginning to make their reputations, the abbé Barthélemy enthusiastically propagandized Hellenism and the incomparable Winckelmann revolutionized the study of Greek art, and of Greek remains in general, by the sheer intuitive force of his twisted genius. Digging and drawing went hand in hand with writing. In 1733 the Society of the Dilettanti was founded in England, and while Horace Walpole dismissed it with characteristic acerbity as "a club, for which the nominal qualification is having been in Italy, and the real one, being drunk,"[3] the Dilettanti did more than travel in Italy and drink: they sponsored valuable collections of drawings, such as Stuart and Revett's brilliant *Antiquity of Athens*, the first volume of which appeared in 1762—the year of the Calas Case and the *Contrat social*. At this time, too, the excavations at Herculaneum and Pompeii became public property, although as yet in an unsatisfactory and incomplete form. We need only read Lessing's *Laocoon* or

---

[2] For this conflict between scholars and philosophes, see below, pp. 360–1.
[3] Walpole to Horace Mann (April 14, 1743). *Letters*, I, 340.

Diderot's salons to see the impact of all this erudite archeology on the more perceptive of the philosophes.

While modern scholarship provided points of departure and correctives for haphazard speculation, the philosophes continued to use the ancients themselves as their favorite informants on antiquity. Fortunately for later ages, the ancients had been indefatigable compilers and controversialists, cheerfully disregarding Horace's ideal of brevity. Cicero had conducted a vast conversation with centuries of philosophical opinion and had thus preserved for posterity the principles of competing schools with lawyer-like thoroughness and precision. Pausanias and Pliny the Elder had circumstantially described antique paintings and statuary which later had fallen victim to time and neglect. Livy had preserved the myths of Republican Rome, and even Aristotle had not disdained the task of the encyclopedist.

The philosophes handled this accumulation of evidence with vigorous independence. The great scholar Nicolas Fréret, who dominated the French Academy of Inscriptions in the first half of the century, laid down careful rules for weighing the credibility of antique sources. Adam Ferguson, who published a popular *History of the Progress and Termination of the Roman Republic* in 1783, prefaced his work with a conscientious list of ancient authorities. Hume's and Gibbon's skepticism toward Greek and Latin writers was, and justly remains, celebrated. The philosophes' beloved ancients were in constant use and under suspicious surveillance; Herodotus and Plutarch, garrulous, curious, and therefore invaluable, were idolized and distrusted like beautiful mistresses. Voltaire, the Enlightenment's self-appointed watchdog, never tired of warning the little flock of the need for alert discrimination. "Don't believe everything Herodotus tells you"— that, he wrote, is the guiding principle. It was a sound principle, and in the philosophes' century perhaps an inescapable one, for excessive skepticism is the natural reaction to excessive credulity. But there were times when it had unfortunate consequences: it made the philosophes reluctant fully to accept, or fully to exploit, the evidence before them.

A map of the philosophes' ancient Greece, then, would look like an old-fashioned map of the world, strewn with empty tracts of *terra incognita* and drawn in somewhat warped outlines. Large areas which today's scholar takes for granted were treacherous or alien ground for the eighteenth century: Troy was a literary not an archeological monument; Mycenaean civilization, whose discovery greatly expanded our understanding of early Greek culture, was unknown; modern philology, with its subtle investigations moving from words to things, from linguistic usage to the migration of religious dogma, was in its infancy; and so was comparative anthropology, which illuminates the rituals of one culture by the rituals of another. There were many answers the philosophes could not get from the past because they did not know what questions they had to ask: economics, sociology, and psychology were not yet systematic disciplines. The philosophes had glimpses, no more, of the religious roots of Greek art, drama, and athletic games, and these glimpses appear as occasional but brilliant flashes of insight in the writings of Montesquieu or Fontenelle or Hume. Teutonic scholarly tenacity, refined scholarly techniques, and well-financed scholarly opportunities, which would dissolve Homer into a committee and then restore him to tenuous identity, unearth and decipher the Mycenaean script, discover the class structure of the Greek city-state, the ritual behind the chorus in the tragedy, and the distinction between the thinking of Greek medicine and Greek school philosophy—all this, the great period of *Altertumswissenschaft*, was to come after 1800. But while the philosophes lacked the logical vocabulary, the conceptual apparatus and, as I have said, adequate empathy to describe the Greek Miracle precisely and profoundly, their view of it stands as an accurate anticipation. This, considering their limitations, is an impressive achievement. It was made possible by what Wilhelm Dilthey has called the *Lebensgefühl* of the Enlightenment, its *göttliche Frechheit*—its divine nerve. We can sense its inner freedom: everything was subject to the sovereign power of criticism; nothing in the past was sacred, least of all sacred things. To say that the philosophes' freedom from orthodoxy itself became an orthodoxy is largely a play on words: their toleration was not complete, but their commitment to the inquiring mind which knew no boundaries made their most self-confident pronouncements open to correction. And if the philosophes were sometimes a little sluggish in correcting themselves, they could always count on a fellow-philosophe to correct them.

IV

While the eighteenth century found the remains of the classical age profuse and manageable, their evidence from earlier times, both from prehistory and antique civilizations, was far more intractable. Gibbon could say in his *Autobiography*, "the dynasties of Assyria and Egypt were my top and cricket ball; and my sleep has been disturbed by the difficulty of reconciling the Septuagint with the Hebrew computation."[4] Yet for Gibbon, too, the evidence was scanty in many areas, undecipherable or uncongenial in others. The Old Testament, which had served countless generations as an authoritative witness, was in decline: the philosophes used it neither as revealed truth nor as authentic history but as an incriminating document. It revealed, if it revealed anything, the vices of the Chosen People and the tainted sources of the Christian religion.

All through the century, the philosophes deplored the gaps in their information. At the beginning of the Enlightenment, Montesquieu complained of speculative scholars who tried to explain civilizations about which they knew nothing: "While we know barely anything of Greek philosophy, how much less do we know about the philosophy of the Egyptians, the Persians, and the Chaldeans!"[5] Similar regrets troubled the Encyclopedists and were still powerful in Kant, who warned that pre-Greek history was largely unknown territory. Reviewing the first part of Herder's masterpiece, *Ideen zur Philosophie der Geschichte der Menschheit*, Kant praised its bold, free imagination, but criticized Herder's attempt to explain unknown pre-history by equally unknown forces. This, said Kant severely, is mere metaphysics; it shows what happens when a scientist despairs of finding the truth by scientific means—he turns to poetry. The task of philosophy, he added a little sententiously, is to trim rather

---

[4] Gibbon: *Autobiography*, 68.
[5] *Pensées*, in *Œuvres*, II, 122.

than to cultivate the luxuriant tree of imagination.[6] The review is a touching moment in the history of the late Enlightenment: the representative of a great but aging movement faces the representative of a new dispensation, refusing to believe that change is progress, defending science against fancy, rigor against vagueness, and criticism against a resurgence of mythmaking.

The philosophes had even more reason to be modest than they could have imagined: they knew that they did not know much, but knew neither how much they did not know nor how much more would soon be known. Egyptian hieroglyphics, a heatedly debated mystery in the Enlightenment, were deciphered early in the nineteenth century. In the same decades, the great river civilizations, which most philosophes had dismissed with the few words about Chaldean astrology and Egyptian despotism which I have quoted, yielded their secrets: archeologists deciphered cuneiform writing and transformed the ruins of Nineveh and Babylon from misty biblical memories into mutely eloquent witnesses to vanished cultures. In the 1740's, Voltaire had confessed that he did not "know anything about the two empires of Babylon and Assyria";[7] a hundred years later the exploits of eccentric adventurers, unscrupulous grave robbers, and imaginative scholars told educated men a great deal about both. Prehistory, too, had been dim and shapeless to the Enlightenment, a rich soil for speculation and the exercise of ingenuity. Some of the philosophes, like Condillac and Rousseau, made inventive and remarkably prescient inquiries into the origins of language, seeking to clarify the history of civilization through the history of man's speech. But it was not until the nineteenth century, when Danish archeologists applied a periodic scheme to prehistoric remains, that prehistory became, if not precisely transparent, at least a subject of informed study. At the same time, modern techniques of field archeology that would have astounded a Buffon led to great discoveries and finer discriminations.

These spectacular advances were accompanied, and partly caused, by advances in geology and biology which ruined, for all but fundamentalists, the Christian view that the world had been

---

[6] *Werke*, IV, 179–90.
[7] *Essai sur les mœurs*, I, 37.

created six thousand years earlier. The intellectual atmosphere and even some of the scientific presuppositions that were to govern Lyell's and Darwin's work were the creation of the Enlightenment: returning to antique teachings of an eternal, or at least a very ancient, universe, philosophes like Buffon and Diderot, La Mettrie and Hume, Holbach and Kant, postulated a course of cosmic and terrestrial development wholly incompatible with Archbishop Ussher's date for the creation in 4004 B.C., or other, similar Christian dates.

In these speculative excursions into pre-history and even early history, the philosophes were guided less by information than by ideology, and persistently violated their cherished Newtonian precept against "system-making." Indeed, they did not all make the same system: Voltaire was so intent on discrediting the biblical deluge that he refused to accept fossils as genuine deposits left by some ancient flood; other philosophes, more adroit, used the very testimony of fossil remains to cast doubt on Christian chronology. But all agreed that the world was very old and that early civilizations like Egypt, Assyria, and Babylonia had grown over many thousands of years.

While these ruminations about antique times foreshadow the scientific temper with which we study these times today, they were based on such slight evidence and advanced with so much political passion that what interest they retain is mainly historical. Their scientific value is slight. Yet these speculations contain in substance what I have called the great discovery of Enlightenment historiography, a discovery for which writers of our time have found more precise language: that there are, generally speaking, two ways in which men confront themselves, their experience, and their fate, and that these are summed up in the mythopoeic and the critical mentality.

Now, mythical thinking is not necessarily primitive, monotonous, purely superstitious, or prelogical—something the philosophes recognized when they granted the Egyptians or Babylonians their share of curiosity and of mastery over the environment, and a variety of motives for inventing religion. Mythical thinking is true thinking; it reduces the world to order, but its categories are unsettled, alive. They shift under the potent pressure of immediate experience or become rigid under the equally overwhelming weight of tradition. Minds as complex as the Egyptian or Babylonian knew the category of causality, but they established or dissolved causal relations on grounds the scientific investigator would reject.

Mythical thinking is a collective term describing a wide variety of mental operations. It can be observed in all its purity among primitive peoples, while it was overlaid among advanced ancient civilizations by touches of rationality, beauty of expression, and complexity of institutions. Yet mythical thinking seems to crumble at the edges first; its basic logical operations remain intact long after civilizations have acquired large rational sectors. Even a Babylonian astronomer found it exceedingly hard to draw up working hypotheses or to make information cumulative, to control assumptions or to check conclusions. He had little if any knowledge of such logical categories as resemblance, subsumption, or representation, all of which are second nature to the scientific mind. Hence he never cleanly or clearly separated part from whole, reality from copy, word from thing, subjective from objective—all indispensable instruments of clarification, ordering, and prediction. In the mythmaking mind, state and universe, king and god, man and nature, stood for and melted into each other. Ancient man did not think that his king resembled divinity: he *was* divine, the true son and accredited representative of a god. Ritual did not recall a miraculous event, it *was* that event. The warrior who fashioned a little statue of an enemy and then pierced it with a dagger was not merely uttering a ceremonial wish to harm that enemy: the doll *was* the enemy, and the damage to the doll was identical with the damage done in combat —indeed, in a sense hard for the scientific mind to grasp, it *was* that combat. Since empirical verification was severely restricted to certain practical operations, the efficacy of the ceremony could not be rendered questionable by the continued good health of the enemy. Proof and disproof are categories in a matrix of thought alien to the mythopoeic mind.

The great religions of antiquity all bear this character: they were not reasoned about; they did not require proof and hence could not be disproved. They were lived out as part of a universe in which even the dead were alive, gods took many forms simultaneously, and things were powers. The mythopoeic mind could not achieve *Sachlichkeit*—objectivity—both because it was incapable of dealing with experiences coolly, quantitatively, and because it could not experience objects as objects.

In the mythopoeic universe, therefore, the most remarkable connections could be made with ease. "A man seems to be one thing," writes the Egyptologist John A. Wilson, "and the sky or a tree seems to be another. But to the ancient Egyptian such concepts had a protean and complementary nature. The sky might be thought of as a material vault above earth, or as a cow, or as a female. A tree might be a tree or the female who was the tree-goddess. Truth might be treated as an abstract concept, or as a goddess, or as a divine hero who once lived on earth. A god might be depicted as a man, or as a falcon, or as a falcon-headed man. In one context the king is described as the sun, a star, a bull, a crocodile, a lion, a falcon, a jackal, and the two tutelary gods of Egypt—not so much in simile as in vital essence."[8] The last phrase deserves emphasis: this colorful assortment of mutually exclusive descriptions is not poetic or allegorical; it is realistic. We have evidence that the ancient Egyptian consciously practiced eloquence and was not a stranger to the simile, but his prevailing mode of thinking was a directly experienced belief in the coexistence and even the identity of things that we should separate.

In large areas of thought, especially in magic, the most primitive cultures link up with the most advanced antique civilizations. In simple tribes as much as in ancient Egypt, to pronounce the name of a deity correctly is to participate in its power; to efface a name is to interfere with a man's career even beyond death. In at least one Egyptian system, the so-called Memphite Theology, the god Ptah creates the parts of his body, the other gods, and all that lives, merely by naming them. In the beginning was the Word: the Word has power because it is not merely a sign but partakes of the essence of the thing it names.

Similarly, number magic and a cavalier disregard of time pervade mythical thought. It was one of the great achievements and essential preconditions of scientific thinking to have abstracted time from living particular rhythms into an impartial measure. But in myth, quantitative precision or notions of chro-

---

[8] *The Intellectual Adventure of Ancient Man* (1946), 62.

nology are insignificant or wholly absent: the mythopoeic mind is, on the whole, hostile to history. "Even in the accounts of royal achievements which we should classify as historical texts," writes the Egyptologist Henri Frankfort, "we find, to our exasperation, that everything that is singular and historical is treated as of little account. For example, we find that King Pepi II depicted his victory over the Libyans with such apparent care that he even had the names of captured Libyan chiefs written beside their images in the reliefs of his temple. But we happen to know that captured Libyan chiefs with precisely the same names figure in the reliefs of King Sahure, two hundred years earlier! In the same way Ramses III enumerated his conquests in Asia by name, but in so doing copied a list of Ramses II, who, in his turn, had utilized a list of Tuthmosis III."[9] To consider this as boastful or mendacious is to miss the essence of the mythopoeic mind: where the category of verification is absent, there are no lies.

I am not suggesting that myth floated disembodied above reality, uncontaminated by life and untouched by change. Quite the contrary: the myths were grandiose projections of the ancients' experience—the blessings of irrigation, the calamity of drought. The Babylonians treated their cosmos as a vast state resembling their own, and their cosmologies reproduced what they saw daily: the rule of caprice, the subordination of slave to master, the living power of all things. In their rituals, Babylonian priests re-enacted and became the rebirth of Spring, identifying themselves with divine powers and thus compelling them to act appropriately. These were survivals from a more primitive age in which sympathetic magic had played a central role, but magic was never outgrown.

Indeed, for all these changes, the myths always retained their aversion to analysis and their anthropomorphism: they continued to explain the unknown by the known and to populate the universe with beings resembling the believers themselves. As Babylonia and Egypt experienced times of trouble, the myths began to express concerns that approach philosophical problems. We have texts voicing surfeit with life, broad jokes against divinities, demands for explanations beyond the gift of the myths.

---

[9] Henri Frankfort: *Ancient Egyptian Religion* (ed. 1961), 48.

But none of these texts, no matter how skeptical in tone, was truly philosophical: their distance from traditional beliefs and ruling deities only plunged their authors into helplessness before an inexplicable universe or drove them to resort feverishly to magical practices devised to compel the world to become something is was not and could not be.

The tenacity of mythopoeic habits of mind is evident in the evolution of Hebrew conceptions of the world. The Biblical Jews, whom the philosophes were in no position to appreciate and took every opportunity to defame, enlarged the boundaries of myth, especially in the Babylonian period of their existence: in their world view, myth and philosophy converge. Far more than any other ancient Near Eastern people, the Hebrews developed the habit of self-doubt, rose to an abstract conception of a single deity governing all nations, approached the idea of a moral law, and created at least the rudiments of a personal identity beyond magic and freed from the delirious terrors of idolatry. Ancient Judaism demonstrated one of the directions in which myth could evolve: into a higher myth with a grandiose vision of the eternal drama, a relatively rational appreciation of conduct, and a noble conception of man as individual sufferer. Unlike other ancient religions, Judaism incorporated rational, rather than mythical, elements from its neighbors. As Voltaire recognized, the bitter disillusionment expressed by the author of Ecclesiastes, now known to be a late writer, was a form of philosophy, not a form of mythology: he was, Voltaire wrote, "an epicurean philosopher," a "materialist, at once sensual and disgusted."[1] Yet this absorptive capacity of Judaism did not give it a philosophical world view; the Old Testament, even at its most rationalist, overwhelmed law by charisma, orderly cosmology by creation myths, moral injunctions by word and number magic, the conception of the ethical individual by the myth of the Chosen People and the Promised Land, history by eschatology. The path to the scientific mentality lay elsewhere.

The mythopoeic mind saw the world through the iridescent veil of immediate experience, things as living powers. Deeply, and usually passively, enmeshed in realities, it had no logic for

---

[1] "Solomon," *Philosophical Dictionary*, II, 459.

reality. As the philosophes saw rightly, if a little simplistically, the veil could be pierced only by the organized habit of asking questions, by systematic criticism. It was left to the Greeks to codify that habit, and to the Romans to impose it on the world.

2. THE ROMAN ENLIGHTENMENT

I

"The Greeks were the teachers of the Romans," Diderot remarked to Catherine the Great, "the Greeks and Romans have been ours."[2] The remark seems obvious, but it must be treated with some reserve. It applied squarely to erudite literary men like himself, to Hume or Gibbon or Lessing, but for the most part the philosophes, like the culture around them, drew their intellectual sustenance from Rome rather than from Greece—from Roman Stoics, Roman Epicureans, and Roman Eclectics.

Why Rome and not Greece? The question, natural as it is, sounds almost like an accusation, for the reputation of the Roman mind is not high. It is considered, and has long been considered, rustic, harsh, and supremely unoriginal. While Rome's legacy to the world—tales of virile, self-sacrificing heroism, legal codes and administrative devices, and a language at once economical and expressive—was by no means contemptible, its contributions were, on the whole, too prosaic, or too fabulous, to arouse the enthusiasm of anyone but schoolboys, lawyers, and classicists. Rome's ruthlessness in war, unscrupulousness in diplomacy, corruption in politics, and bestiality in entertainment were notorious in antiquity and tarnished its name in later ages. To posterity, the symbol of Greek civilization was the Parthenon; the symbols of Rome, the Colosseum and the Pont du Gard—a stadium for blood sports and an aqueduct.

---

[2] *Plan d'une université pour le gouvernement de Russie*, in *Œuvres*, III, 477. For the German Romantic Hellenists, it was, of course, Greece alone—and the Greece of their fond imagination—that shaped their philosophy of life.

It would be absurd to suggest that it was to this side of Rome that the philosophes responded. In fact, they deplored its brutal coarseness and deprecated its administrator's mentality. Philosophic historians of Rome—Montesquieu and Ferguson and Gibbon—laid bare its shortcomings even as they extolled its accomplishments; philosophes in search of telling instances found almost as much to deplore in Rome as to admire. Still, the philosophes' choice of Rome seems to reflect on their taste; it seems a choice of sturdiness over brilliance, of popularizers over genius, of common sense over depth—in a word, of the comfortable second-rate over the unsettling first-rate.

There is something in this, but not much. Brilliance and originality and depth exhilarated the philosophes, but with their love of practicality and good sense, these traits also made them a little uneasy. In large part, the Enlightenment's choice of Rome was fortuitous. Rome, after all, had conquered the world: the soldiers who settled the colonies and the proconsuls who governed them used Latin. For all the long-lived practice of displaying Greek learning—fashionable first in the Roman Republic, then in the Empire, and once again in the Renaissance—it was Roman not Greek law, Roman not Greek administration, that impressed itself upon Europe. By the end of the fourth century, the Catholic Church—the *Roman* Catholic Church—the most powerful civilizing force in Europe for many centuries, published its edicts, said its prayers, and argued out most of its theology in Latin. As a result, Latin invaded vernacular languages all over Europe and was used as the idiom of science, philosophy, diplomacy, and even private correspondence down to the seventeenth and into the eighteenth century. The philosophes were taught Greek in their schools, but only a few of them could handle it with any ease. Whether Latin was in fact easier to learn than Greek was irrelevant: Latin was the heart of the curriculum. Hence the Roman world was readily accessible to educated men of the eighteenth century. "Rome," said Gibbon, "is familiar to the schoolboy and the statesman."[3]

This is not all. Rome was saved from being a mere barracks society by its capacity to absorb Greek culture. The philosophes knew this, for Roman writers acknowledged their debts in lines

---

[3] *Autobiography*, 175.

most familiar to them. Gibbon, who liked to quote Horace, reminded his readers that "it is a just though trite observation that victorious Rome was herself subdued by the arts of Greece."[4] Quoting Horace once more, he reiterated that "it is scarcely possible for a mind endowed with any active curiosity to be long conversant with the Latin classics without aspiring to know the Greek originals, whom they celebrate as their masters, and of whom they so warmly recommend the study and imitation: 'Study day and night/Your examples of Greek literature.' "[5]

Horace's lines show admirable candor, but deception would have been pointless: nothing was more patent than the dependence of Romans on Greeks. By the time of Caesar, Roman education was impregnated with Greek methods and Roman thinking with Greek philosophy; Roman poets and playwrights had barely left off translating Greek poetry; Greek science and medicine remained supreme. Cicero, greatest of orators and popularizers, studied in Athens and Rhodes; secure in his fame, he not merely admitted, but boasted of, his foreign training. Horace was right: while the great Mediterranean Empire was held together by Roman soldiers, it was nourished by Greek ideas. The captive had overwhelmed the captor—and so what the philosophes admired about Rome was, for the most part, what was most Greek in it.

Yet it was Greek with a difference; it was Greek made plain. Much like the philosophes of the eighteenth century, Roman literati gave their best talents to explicating, disseminating, and in the process vulgarizing, difficult philosophical ideas. Cicero above all, wrote Montesquieu, had made Greek ideas "available to all men, like reason itself."[6] He had been "the first of the Romans to take philosophy out of the hands of the scholars and detach it from the encumbrance of a foreign language."[7]

This praise suggests that the affinity which the philosophes

---

[4] *Decline and Fall of the Roman Empire*, I, 39. Gibbon is quoting Horace's celebrated dictum, *Graecia capta ferum victorem cepit et artes / intulit agresti Latio* (Ep. II, 1, 156–7).
[5] *Autobiography*, 100. *Vos exemplaria Graeca / nocturna versate manu, versate diurna* (*Ars poetica*, 268–9).
[6] "Discours sur Cicéron," (*c.* 1709). *Œuvres*, III, 16.
[7] Ibid.

felt for Rome was more than nostalgia, historical accident, or intellectual laziness. It was the affinity of one literary elite for another. Despite the vast distance in time and the obvious difference in concerns and status, the two belonged to a single family, allied by their tastes, their strategies, their aims, their styles, and above all, their view of the world.

To say this is not to say that the philosophes and Roman literati were alike in all things. For all their intimate affinities, all their obvious resemblance, they lived in different worlds. The philosophes have often been compared to their Roman ancestors, especially to the Augustans, for their supposed servility to power —men of letters, it seems, are always under attack for trying to do their work in peace. But this criticism of the Augustans is as unjust as the parallel between the Augustans and the philosophes is inexact. It is true that Livy, Vergil, and Horace were intimately associated with Augustus and with Maecenas, whose patronage became proverbial even in antiquity. Only Ovid, an unlucky misfit too disrespectful to find a place in the new order, stood aside. It is true, too, that the Augustans would have glorified Augustus' reign simply by writing as they pleased, without glorifying it (in the unsavory sense of that word) by writing panegyrics. Their servility disfigured their works and tainted the regime that exacted it, yet the fear of being thought naïve should not make us cynical: tough-minded historians from Mommsen onward have agreed that, with the Augustans, interest and inclination went conveniently hand in hand. They supported Caesar Augustus because they wanted freedom to work and to enjoy a secure prosperity, but they were also animated by the conviction that the state needed a stable government after more than half a century of civil war. Horace or Vergil did not need to be intimidated or cajoled into writing what they believed; in their relief over the end of terror and proscription, they were ready to overlook the cruelty of Augustus' early career and the artful deceptions of his reign.

At the same time, they were lavish with their compliments to the powerful, and some of their more embarrassing prose bears an unfortunate resemblance to some of the philosophes' most blatant flattery, a resemblance of which the philosophes appear to have been unaware. Voltaire said of Vergil that "he had the weakness of paying Augustus a homage that no man should ever give to another man, no matter who he is,"[8] which only proves that the Socratic maxim "Know thyself" was imperfectly realized in the Enlightenment: Pliny's panegyrics on Trajan or Vergil's on Augustus read rather like early drafts of Grimm's letters to Catherine the Great or Voltaire's letters to Frederick. But the resemblances, though undeniable, conceal an essential difference. In ancient Rome, the man of letters had no escape from patronage; in the eighteenth century, he was detaching himself from aristocratic support and throwing himself more and more on the uncertain mercies of the general public. The Roman writer was far more helpless than his modern successors: like them, he was close to power, hoped for influence, and worked in groups. The little flock had its antique counterpart: Catullus belonged to a coterie of poets; the Augustans were in general intimately associated with each other; later, Martial and Juvenal, Pliny and Tacitus, were friends. But while the ancients were an interest group, the philosophes practically achieved the cohesion of a pressure group. The Roman could hope for a favorable atmosphere, for a pension or a villa or fashionable public readings, but he could not demand anything. He might educate emperors or magnates by his writings or his personal influence, but he was usually (if not always) at the mercy of the government of the day. The philosophes lived in a kindlier age, reached a larger and more significant public, and took advantage of royal decency and divisions among the powerful. They did not merely want to entertain or beautify the world; they wanted to change it.

II

The philosophes' two most reliable sources of inspiration in Roman literature, the two writers to whom they could turn with confidence, certain of finding in them support for their great enterprise, were the greatest poet and the greatest publicist of the late Republic: Lucretius and Cicero.

Titus Lucretius Carus is a mysterious and shadowy figure,

---

[8] *Essai sur la poésie épique*, in *Œuvres*, VIII, 326.

although the men of the Enlightenment found themselves completely at home in his *De rerum natura*—that poetic rendering of the most unpoetic of philosophies, Epicureanism. They read it often and quoted it to the purpose; Voltaire had at least six editions and translations in his library, and the other philosophes collected him just as assiduously. Yet they had no way of visualizing Lucretius the man: none of his letters have survived, and while his ideas and style pervade the writings of his contemporaries, they quoted him without acknowledgment and passed him over in silence.

There has been much puzzlement over this silence, and it is the other favorite of the philosophes—Cicero—who at least provides a clue: in a private letter written in 54 B.C., Cicero tells his brother that Lucretius's *De rerum natura* is constructed with craftsmanship and marked by flashes of genius. Ten years later, in a disingenuous aside in the *Tusculan Disputations*, Cicero implies that he does not know the poem. Since Cicero was a courageous man, his reason for the denial must reflect a political position. Lucretius was to the dying Roman Republic much what Hobbes was to the seventeenth century, a disturber of the peace whose work was too great to be ignored but whose name was too disreputable to be praised. A poet who uses the word *religio* in the pejorative sense in which others used the word *superstitio* was dangerous.

Whatever the circumstances of Lucretius's life, the meaning of his poem was as clear to his readers in Cicero's Rome as it was to his readers in Voltaire's France or Frederick's Prussia. One famous tribute from no less a man than Vergil makes this plain:

Felix, qui potuit rerum cognoscere causas,
atque metus omnes et inexorabile fatum,
subiecit pedibus strepitumque Acherontis avari—

"Happy the man who can know the causes of things, and has trampled underfoot all fears, inexorable fate, and the clamor of greedy hell."[9]

What makes this apostrophe significant is that Vergil links

---

[9] *Georgics*, II, 490–2.

knowledge of causes with the conquest of fear, a coupling which is the essence of the critical mentality at work. Science, and science alone, pitilessly destroying myths, brings the greatest of freedoms, inner peace—this is Lucretius's message and mission, and this is how the philosophes read him. *De rerum natura* is a fierce polemic animated by the fanatical single-mindedness of the man with a cause. No propagandist ever conducted the battle of science against religion more exuberantly than Lucretius, nor won it for science with such simple means. In all forms but one, he argues, religion is merely superstition based on ignorance and maintained by terror. Science, by contrast, is right reason offering a complete and coherent account of the universe. The one sensible religion, the Epicurean doctrine of the passionless gods dwelling in serene indifference in the heavens, does not interfere with true—that is, Epicurean—science. Men must banish fear, and they banish it by banishing religion, and they will banish religion once they understand science. Thus Lucretius admonishes Memmius, to whom he addresses the poem, urging him to listen to "true reason" and glimpse a natural order free from the terrors of religion.

Lucretius has often been called the poet of nature. It is true that *De rerum natura* celebrates the natural world for its own sake. Rarely has so much poetical power been expended on so improbable a collection of subjects: the relation of mind to body, the rise of civilization from primitive beginnings, the sexual urge, the weather, the growth and decay of the body; earthquakes, volcanoes, burial rites. But Lucretius's grasp on his single subject, his obsessive preoccupation with the enemy religion, never weakens. All this natural science, he announces near the beginning, is needed to free Memmius from the bloodthirsty fairy tales of the priests. Prophets, he writes, frighten believers with tales of eternal punishment; *therefore—quapropter*—men must learn the laws that govern the sky and the earth. This argument has a curiously modern sound: it anticipates the positivist view that the more physics, astronomy, geology, and anthropology we know, the smaller the swamp of unreason; it anticipates Diderot's assertion that the advance of philosophy entails the retreat of religion.

Lucretius is aware of the utilitarian direction that his

scientific exposition takes. To admire the heavens or to marvel at the rhythm of sexual appetite or the beauty of landscape is one thing; but to know nature—and he insists on this—is something more aggressive than the cultivation of aesthetic sensibilities. Knowledge is intellectual: it is rational, objective, scientific; and it is even more than this: it is an instrument of social reconstruction. This is the meaning of the verses which appear in Book One, and are repeated several times in the poem for emphasis, verses the philosophes liked to remember:

> Hunc igitur terrorem animi, tenebrasque necesse est
> non radii solis, neque lucida tela diei
> discutiant, sed Naturae species, ratioque—

"This dread and darkness of the mind therefore need not the rays of the sun, the bright darts of day; only knowledge of nature's forms dispels them."[1]

There is some incoherence in *De rerum natura*, especially in Books Four to Six, and some of the Church Fathers later seized on this to impute to Lucretius fits of insanity. But most of the time Lucretius is masterfully in control of his material, so that the incongruities of the later books suggest a corrupt manuscript and a poem left unrevised at the time of the poet's death. Lucretius resembles a composer enamored of a musical phrase, toying with it, concealing it, bringing it to prominence when he feels it is time to hear it again. *De rerum natura* is a set of variations on a theme congenial to the skeptical mind in all times and all places: *tantum religio potuit suadere malorum*—"Such are the heights of evil that religion can urge."[2] This motif dominates strategic places in the poem: it is first stated at the beginning of Book One, announcing the purpose of the work, and restated at the beginnings of the other five books. It appears as an invocation to Epicurus, the godlike Greek who first dared to defy the powers of superstition and to bring men the gift of freedom; it appears as a proud declaration of the poet, intoxicated with his task: "I continue to loosen the hold of religion on men's minds." In Book Three, the best known,

---

[1] *De rerum natura*, I, 146–8.
[2] Ibid., I, 101.

the assault on religion reaches a powerful crescendo—Voltaire promised to translate it but never kept this engagement; Frederick the Great took it to battle with him and, with his heavy-handed humor, liked to call it his breviary. Lucretius here gives a materialistic account of mind and body, continually interrupting his scientific exposition with programmatic declarations, and ending the book with the most celebrated passage in the whole epic, an exalted declamation against the fear of death.

Lucretius was awake to the paradox haunting his assault on all accepted forms of worship. If religion is so pernicious, if it drives men to greed and barbarous cruelty, why is it so widespread? If the Epicurean solution of the religious problem is man's only cure for this oppressive curse, why is it so unpopular? Rather grimly, Lucretius concedes that he is offering bitter medicine to a patient as unreasonable as grievously sick men often are. The resistance of his patient, however, only demonstrated the need for Lucretius's prescription: it was a function of ignorance. This is the conclusion to which he points his analysis of the origin of religion in Book Five: men had visions of deities and in their ignorance equipped them with all desirable characteristics lacking in poor mortal men. In ignorance men attributed the regularities observed in nature to the labor of gods; in ignorance men converted their own helplessness into religious awe. Only science can cure this pervasive disease—*De rerum natura* ends as it had begun. In Book Six, the last, Lucretius once again reminds his reader of his mission and repeats the familiar verses: "This dread and darkness of the mind therefore require not the rays of the sun, the bright darts of day; only knowledge of nature's form dispels them."

The appeal of such ideas and such rhetoric for the Enlightenment is easy to understand. It is hardly surprising that the *philosophes* liked to quote Lucretius's verses, invoke his support, and imagine themselves to be his reincarnation. The image of bringing light into darkness, which pervades *De rerum natura*, is aged, conventional, and by no means confined to antireligious propaganda: Plato was fond of it; primitive priests and Christian Church Fathers identified their cult with the luminosity of the sun, their ritual with the conquest of dark powers or the illumination of mystical insight. But Lucretius's version of the metaphor was particularly congenial to the philosophes: when Lucretius spoke of dispelling night, lifting shadows, or clarifying ideas, he meant the conquest of religion by science. That is precisely how the philosophes used the metaphor; in fact, they used it so freely that the metaphorical basis of their words was forgotten. They claimed to bring a *siècle des lumières*, they called their movement an *Aufklärung*, an *illuminismo*, an Enlightenment. Pope borrowed the image of light-bringing for his famous couplet about Newton; Diderot used it with casual familiarity in the *Encyclopédie* to claim the growth of light and the decrease of shadows for his century; while Voltaire made it serve for both illumination and warmth in a single complimentary phrase: "The light which illuminates his mind," he wrote about Diderot, "warms his heart."[3] The very triteness of the language is an index to the ease with which philosophes could associate themselves with Lucretius, another light-bringer.

Still, the real weight of Lucretius's popularity is hard to assess. It is a plausible reading of the Enlightenment to say that Lucretius had no real hold over it: deists and atheists alike repudiated his atomism and his teaching that the world arose by chance; no one, except perhaps La Mettrie, accepted his hedonism without modification. The occasional citations from his epic, therefore, are classical garnishes, decorative but empty.

But such a reading assumes, wrongly I think, that a writer can influence posterity only by compelling it to accept a specific doctrine. There are other influences, more elusive, perhaps, but equally far reaching: implicitly as much as explicitly, in his rhetoric and his unflagging zeal against what he considered the forces of obscurantism, Lucretius invited emulation. When Holbach quoted the famous line, *Hunc igitur terrorem*, he was ornamenting his antireligious campaign with a classical touch, but one gets the feeling that he was strengthened in his crusade by his antique model.

Voltaire, too, was touched by Lucretius's magic. His famous early poem *Épitre à Uranie* is far shorter and far more informal than Lucretius's expansive lecture; but like Lucretius, Voltaire

---

[3] Voltaire to Damilaville (November 19, 1760). *Correspondence*, XLIV, 166.

invokes Venus; and like Lucretius, Voltaire writes for a reader who is to be liberated from the fear of death. With characteristic economy, Voltaire combines his Venus with his Memmius: he addresses one Madame de Rupelmonde, who seems eager for entertainment and enlightenment in about equal proportions. While Voltaire's involvement with the lady was a cozy, light-hearted arrangement typical of polite society in his time, his *Épitre à Uranie* was anything but society verse. Voltaire's intentions are serious, if not with Madame de Rupelmonde, then in pillorying a religion that believes in a cruel God. The author introduces himself as a new Lucretius who will tear the mask from the face of religion, expose sacred lies, and teach his reader to despise the horrors of the tomb and the terrors of another life:

> Tu veux donc, charmante Uranie,
> Qu'érige, par ton ordre, en Lucrèce nouveau,
> Devant toi, d'une main hardie
> A la religion j'arrache le bandeau;
> Que j'expose à tes yeux le dangereux tableau
> Des mensonges sacrés dont la terre est remplie,
> Et qu'enfin la philosophie
> T'apprenne à mépriser les horreurs du tombeau,
> Et les terreurs de l'autre vie.[4]

This was a literary pose, but it was significant that Voltaire should have chosen the model he did. We are reading nothing into his words: it was Voltaire himself who strutted before his lady as the modern Epicurean, boldly unmasking religion with the aid of philosophy.

Certainly, eighteenth-century Christians combated Lucretius as though he were alive. In the first half of the century, Cardinal de Polignac, a cultivated classicist, found it necessary to malign Epicurus and to refute *De rerum natura* in an interminable didactic poem in Latin; while the Jesuit *Journal de Trévoux*, usually urbane and generous, especially toward the classics, took the time to denounce Lucretius for his impiety. When Lagrange's transla-

---

[4] *Épitre à Uranie*, ed. Ira O. Wade, *PMLA*, XLVII: 4 (December 1932), 1105.

tion appeared, Grimm reported in his newsletter that it was widely considered part of the philosophes' "favorite project of destroying religion";[5] and when Holbach's *Système de la nature* was condemned by the *parlement* of Paris in August 1770, the *parlement* accused the book of "reviving" and "expanding" the "system of Lucretius"[6]—all of which shows that the philosophes had no monopoly on exaggerating the influence of antiquity on modernity. With his usual felicity, Voltaire summed up the position of the movement: "Lucretius is admirable in his exordiums, in his descriptions, in his ethics, in everything he says against superstition. That beautiful line, *Tantum religio potuit suadere malorum*, will last as long as the world lasts. If he had not been as ridiculous as all the others as a physical scientist, he would have been a divine man."[7] The brooding Epicurean inspired the youthful Voltaire and the mature Holbach, and his memory sustained the dying David Hume.[8]

While Lucretius supplied the philosophes with passionate slogans and an attitude, their real favorite, Cicero, gave them even more—a philosophy. Montesquieu hailed Cicero as the noblest among the ancients, the man whom, more than anyone else, he wished to resemble. He was a young man when he expressed these extravagant views, but Montesquieu's taste for Cicero never changed. Diderot thought Cicero a "*prodigy* of eloquence and patriotism."[9] David Hume, who was as sensitive to philosophical currents of his day as he was well informed in the history of philosophy, observed that "the fame of Cicero flourishes at present, but that of Aristotle is utterly decayed"[1]—and Hume did not seem unhappy with this state of affairs.

---

[5] *Correspondance littéraire*, VIII, 152.

[6] Gustav R. Hocke: *Lukrez in Frankreich von der Renaissance bis zur Revolution* (1935), 155.

[7] *Lettres de Memmius à Cicéron*, in *Œuvres*, XXVIII, 439.

[8] Some philosophes, on the other hand, thought of Lucretius as a "mere" poet or as the representative of an untenable philosophy of nature. This was Jefferson's position even though he seems to have owned as many as eight copies of *De rerum natura*.

[9] Diderot to Falconet (? September 1766). *Correspondance*, VI, 297.

[1] *Enquiry Concerning Human Understanding*, in *Works*, IV, 5.

Cicero's reputation in the Enlightenment is hard to appreciate today: nothing illustrates our distance from the eighteenth century better than this. To us, Cicero is at best an interesting politician and a master of a certain Latin style; at worst he is a bore or an unknown. It was different in the eighteenth century: as *Tristram Shandy* testifies, even moderately well-educated men affectionately called him "Tully"; Hume borrowed ideas from him; and the others too never ceased to read him. When Conyers Middleton's adulatory *Life of Cicero* appeared in 1741, it sold well despite its length and high price. Horace Walpole confessed to a friend: "I wait with some impatience to see Dr. Middleton's Tully, as I read the greatest part of it in manuscript; though indeed that is rather a reason for my being impatient to read the rest. If Tully can receive any additional honor, Dr. Middleton is most capable of conferring it."[2] Gibbon's tribute to the biography was rather more grudging: upon first reading it, he appreciated it "above its true value."[3] His reservations were sound: Middleton had borrowed from others even more than was customary in his generous age. Yet Gibbon meant to criticize Middleton for his execution, not for his choice of subject: there could never be too much written on Tully.

At the same time, if we may judge from Voltaire's references to his favorite Roman, there was at least some danger that Cicero might be reduced to the status of a school classic—honored, invoked, and unread. In 1749 he sent *Rome sauvée, ou Catilina* to the rescue. One unavowed reason for the play was Voltaire's attempt to outdo a tragedy by Crébillon on the Catiline conspiracy; another, avowed, reason was to write a drama without a declaration of love. But his central motive was to remind the public of a great ancient, to "make young people who go to the theatre acquainted with Cicero." At some private performances in 1750, the author took the part of Cicero and played it with such fire that his delighted audience claimed to be in the presence of the great orator himself. In his preface to the play, Voltaire listed Cicero's virtues: he was a fine general, the complete master of Greek

---

[2] Walpole to Henry Seymour Conway (March 25, 1741). *Letters*, I, 96.
[3] *Autobiography*, 99.

Cicero

thought, the "greatest as well as the most eloquent of Roman philosophers," an unexcelled popularizer, a remarkable poet, a sincere friend and virtuous associate, a good governor and courageous public servant. Most astonishing of all was that Cicero found time to read, and write, so much philosophy "in the midst of the tumults and storms of his life, steadily engaged in affairs of state."[4] This is not quite accurate; it mistakes what Cicero had wished to be for what he actually was, but Voltaire's very misreading reveals what the philosophes thought a philosopher should be: the thinker in action.

Rome sauvée suffers from some political confusion, remarkable in view of Voltaire's usual clarity about political questions. It simultaneously praises popular sovereignty and dictatorship, the rule of law and executive action free from legal control. But in the first place, Voltaire's hero is anything but naïve—the play ends with a speech by Cicero filled with foreboding, expressing doubts whether Caesar, now generous and virtuous, will resist the lure of absolute power. And besides, the play is not political but moral. Cicero represents the philosopher as public servant; with a simplicity approaching the melodramatic, he embodies the qualities of the dutiful, upright citizen and that most elusive of antique philosophical ideals—humanism.

The ideal of *humanitas* was first brought to Rome by the philosophic circle around Scipio and developed further by Cicero. For Cicero, *humanitas* was a style of thought, not a formal doctrine. It asserted man's importance as a cultivated being, in control of his moral universe. The man who practiced *humanitas* was confident of his worth, courteous to others, decent in his social conduct, and active in his political role. He was a man, moreover, who faced life with courageous skepticism: he knows that the consolations of popular religion are for more credulous beings than himself, that life is uncertain, and that sturdy pessimism is superior to self-deceptive optimism. Man becomes man as he refines himself; he even becomes godlike: "*Deus est mortali iuvare mortalem*," wrote Pliny, translating a Greek Stoic: "To help man is man's true God."[5] Finally, the man who practiced *humanitas*

---

[4] *Œuvres*, V, 205–6. See below, p. 192.
[5] Gilbert Murray: *Stoic, Christian and Humanist* (edn. 1950), 107.

cultivated his aesthetic sensibilities as he listened to his reason: *"Cum musis,"* wrote Cicero, *"id est, cum humanitate et cum doctrina habere commercium."*[6] Virtue, Cicero insisted, is nothing but nature perfected and developed to its highest point, and there is therefore a resemblance between man and God: *Est autem virtus nihil aliud quam in se perfecta et ad summum perducta natura; est igitur homini cum deo similitudo.* As a modern Humanist, Holbach quoted this Ciceronian dictum with approval; as a good atheist, he omitted its reference to God.[7] In the Enlightenment, at least for some philosophes, humanism was the ground, and the fruit, of atheism.

Cicero's *humanitas* had its followers both in the first and in the second age of criticism. It reappeared in the first century in Seneca's claim—made in the midst of a lament over Roman bestiality—that man is a sacred thing to man: *"homo res sacra homini";* and it reappeared once more in the eighteenth century in Kant's call for human autonomy and in Voltaire's stern injunction: "Remember your dignity as a man."[8] In the beginning of his *Meditations,* the Emperor Marcus Aurelius elaborated a veritable catalogue of qualities which, all together, made up the virtues which Cicero had called *humanitas* and which the philosophes hoped they possessed in good measure: modesty, self-control, manliness, beneficence, practicality, generosity, rationality, tolerance, and obedience to the dictates of nature.[9]

In the decades following the Catiline conspiracy, Cicero had ample opportunity to display all, or most, of these qualities. The Roman republic was crumbling under the unrelenting pressure of civil war. Coarse demagogy, brutally competitive politics among the leading families, abrupt oscillations between "aristocratic" and "democratic" policies, and the ready use of military solutions for political problems were grim commentaries on the inadequacy of republican institutions. Catullus and Lucretius had died in the fifties, but Cicero survived Caesar's dictatorship, alternately sur-

---

[6] *Tusculan Disputations,* V, 66.

[7] *De legibus,* I, viii, 25; *Système de la nature,* 2 vols. (1770), I, 5 *n.*

[8] *Epistulae morales,* VC, 33; "Evil," *Philosophical Dictionary,* II, 378.

[9] This Stoic catalogue contains other elements, like *pietàs,* for which the philosophes naturally had rather less respect.

Cicero

rendering to despair and rallying to devise ingenious political combinations. While Julius Caesar, the most dramatic politician of the age, was already dominating the state, Cicero continued to idealize a dying political system in a futile attempt to preserve what had already decayed. In this dark time, he wrote a whole collection of philosophical works, above all, *De natura deorum*, *De divinatione*, and *De officiis*, three books that survived to shape, more than any other products of ancient thought, the mind of the Enlightenment. Voltaire thought *De natura deorum* "perhaps the best book of all antiquity"; his only other claimant to the title was Cicero's *De officiis*.[1] With rare unanimity, the philosophes endorsed Voltaire's claims for these works and accepted Diderot's estimate that Cicero was indeed "the first of the Roman philosophers."[2]

III

All their reforming zeal did not spoil the philosophes' appetite for Roman literature as a whole. True, they often made non-literary use of literary works—most Roman writers, it seemed, had said something telling, something that could be hurled against *l'infâme*—and so the Enlightenment's Rome was not identical with what we might call the Roman Enlightenment. The significance, and the impress, of some Roman writers on the eighteenth century was often rather different from the meaning they had had for their own time. But in general there is a notable convergence: the Roman writers most relevant to the philosophes fall within the period which the ancients themselves regarded as the glorious time of Latin literature—the two centuries, from the middle of the first century B.C. to the middle of the second century A.D., that stretch between Catullus and Marcus Aurelius.

Catullus was not the first to adapt Alexandrian models to Latin purposes, but he was the most successful. "Alexandrian" has become a handy word of abuse, characterizing literature specializing in the elegant, the empty, and the effeminate—it has been

---

[1] "Fin du monde," *Questions sur l'Encyclopédie*, in *Œuvres*, XIX, 142.
[2] *Essai sur les règnes de Claude et de Néron*, in *Œuvres*, III, 18.

defined as making much of little. This is doubtless too harsh, but whatever the merits of the Alexandrian poets, Latin men of letters had to rise up against their poetic preceptors before they could find their own characteristic strength. Their revolution (like the philosophes' revolution) was less complete than they imagined: Alexandrian trifles never disappeared from their poems. And like the philosophes, they did not deny all tradition but rather affirmed an older against a more recent tradition: antique Greek meters and subject matter reverberate through their work. Catullus, one among a group of young rakes devoted in equal parts to debauchery and poetry, was at once a traditionalist and a rebel, but with his superb control of colloquial Latin diction, his passion, and his fine ear, he wrote intensely personal poems about love and hate, conquest, jealousy, and loss, and made them unmistakably his own. "Each line," wrote Hume, "each word in Catullus, has its merit; and I am never tired with the perusal of him."[3]

Catullus died in 54 B.C. Lucretius had preceded him by a year and Cicero was to produce his influential philosophical dialogues about ten years later, shortly before he was murdered in the proscriptions that followed the assassination of Caesar in 44 B.C. Then came more than a decade of civil war, ended by the emergence of Caesar Augustus, who founded an empire in the name of restoring the republic and presided over a time of superb poetry and prose. For the philosophes, as for many men before, and for a dwindling number since their time, the reign of Augustus was truly a Golden Age—at least in literature—and there were no writers whom they enjoyed more thoroughly and quoted more disinterestedly—shall I say, more unpolitically?—than the great Augustans. They read Ovid for his gaiety, Livy for his entertaining mythical tales, Vergil for his music, and Horace for his felicitous, intelligent worldliness.

With the death of Augustus in 14 A.D., the new institutions he had founded with the rhetoric of the old underwent a prolonged period of testing. A succession of bizarre emperors who seem to have strayed into history from some Gothic tale of horror strained but did not substantially alter the shape of power and policy laid down by their wily predecessor. When Nerva was elected em-

---

[3] "Of Simplicity and Refinement in Writing," *Works*, III, 243.

peror in 96 A.D. after the melodrama of the Claudian and Flavian dynasties, the empire was intact: the history of a society (as the historians of the eighteenth century had discovered) is not the history of its rulers alone. While a Caligula capriciously ordered executions or a Nero minced on the stage, sensible bureaucrats and reliable officers consolidated and defended Roman power. The Rome of these years was not only the Rome of Messalina but also that of Frontinus, an able provincial administrator and engineer whose book on military stratagems survived to be quoted by the philosophes, or of Agricola, Frontinus's successor as governor of Britain, whose noble career was preserved for the ages by his son-in-law Tacitus. The rise of freed slaves and the increasing independence of women doubtless had their shady aspects, but the rantings of reactionary satirists, accusing both of all imaginable crimes, conceal that the first formed the core of an efficient imperial bureaucracy and that the second was a welcome sign that Roman manners were adapting themselves to the burdens of world empire. The sickness of the state was, at least in this time, on the surface, as Gibbon recognized with his customary shrewdness: "the conspirators against Caligula, Nero, and Domitian . . . attacked the person of the tyrant without aiming their blow at the authority of the emperor,"[4] and it was this authority, as embodied in the army and the bureaucracy, that was the basis of the new public order.

But while the insane antics of the emperors, handed down to posterity by Suetonius and Tacitus, did not ruin the state, the leading writers of the time were rarely so fortunate. Free speech had been severely restricted under Augustus and almost vanished in the decades after his death. The reasons for this decline were both institutional and personal. The anarchy of the civil wars had offered unmatched opportunities to orators, who produced a splendid outpouring of libelous vituperation, assassinating character and uncovering conspiracies in great speeches before the senate or in court. But even during the second Triumvirate, before Octavianus had made himself Caesar Augustus, it was evident that the price of peace was support of the government, or silence. Had there been talented writers besides the great Augustans, Maecenas would have captured the willing or Augustus exiled the

---

[4] *Decline and Fall of the Roman Empire*, I, 71.

reluctant. From its inception, the Empire manufactured consent, and intellect withdrew into the private sphere.

Under Augustus the process had been at least rational; under his successors it was as irrational as they. Seneca, the most prominent philosopher of the age, was nearly put to death by Caligula, narrowly escaped execution under Claudius, and then was in turn the preceptor, the advisor, and the victim of Nero. Before he opened his wrists at his emperor's orders, he had managed to become one of the richest men in Rome, proof that wealth and Stoicism were not invariably incompatible. His blood-curdling tragedies on Greek themes were to leave their impress on the Elizabethan and the neoclassical French theatre, while his Stoic tracts and epistles, humane, melancholy, and didactic, were first claimed by the early Christians and later reclaimed in the Enlightenment: Diderot's ethics and Rousseau's pedagogy are much in their debt. Seneca's nephew, Lucan, died like his uncle at Nero's command, before he had finished his ambitious epic on the Roman civil wars, the *Pharsalia*. It is a curious production; its heated rhetoric punctuated with energetic epigrams, its bombast and fantastic incidents, its audacious omission of the customary divine machinery—all this divided the critics from the beginning. In his *Essai sur la poésie épique*, Voltaire characterized Lucan as an original genius, in debt to no one either for his fine things or for his faults.[5] Marmontel, aware of Lucan's rant, thought enough of the *Pharsalia* to translate it into vigorous French prose in the early 1760's. But as Marmontel and Voltaire made plain, it was not just the music of the epic that attracted them. Here was a masterpiece of pathos, a challenge to Vergil, and thus in its very manner an opposition poem. More, here was a defiantly republican poem, glorifying Cato and Pompey, the losers, and doing so under the very eyes of Nero, then in his insane autocratic phase. "In the midst of Lucan's high-flown declamations," Voltaire remarked, "there are daring, manly thoughts";[6] in fact, Voltaire thought that with his "philosophical and sublime courage" Lucan was unique in antiquity.[7] This was less a response to Lucan's republicanism than to his outspoken pantheism. Marmontel, on the other hand, hinted

---

[5] *Œuvres*, VIII, 326.
[6] Ibid., 327.
[7] "Épopée," *Questions sur l'Encyclopédie*, in *Œuvres*, XVIII, 572.

at some rather far-reaching generalizations on the basis of Lucan's politics: "This audacious genius felt that it is natural for all men to love liberty, to detest him who crushes it, to admire him who defends it; he wrote for all ages."[8] A man who writes as Lucan did "under a tyrant like Nero can expect to die young."[9]

Nero, in fact, claimed still another illustrious literary victim, Petronius. His *Satyricon*, the picaresque Odyssey of a pair of homosexual beachcombers, has so much wit, invention, disenchanted wisdom, and command of both formal and colloquial manner, that we must curse the cruelty of time or the laziness of some monkish copyist for leaving us only a fragment. If we may trust and collate our scattered information, we can assume that Petronius was at once a cynical man about town and a conscientious provincial governor, an expert in the vices of the rich and wellborn, whose corruption he chronicled without sharing. For a time Nero's intimate friend, Petronius seems to have aroused his emperor's displeasure and was driven into suicide. It seemed, in those days, the only way for a respectable man of letters to end: perhaps Persius, whose difficult Stoic satires still baffle the modern reader—although they did not baffle Diderot—escaped the fate of his friends only by dying young, in A.D. 62, of a stomach ailment.

The assassination of Nero in A.D. 69 improved the life expectancy of literary men, but it did not end their time of troubles. Domitian, the last and most unpredictable of the Flavians, took some interest in literature and patronized leading writers, but ended his reign by expelling philosophers from Rome and putting to death writers for literary opinions which he twisted into political crimes. The Flavian decades were not barren, as Tacitus later conceded, but the work of the period is more notable for what it avoids than for what it expresses. Quintilian, who would be preceptor to generations of rhetoricians in the Renaissance, had a distinguished public career which included a post as professor of rhetoric and the consulship. Yet his *Institutio oratoria*, an impeccably Ciceronian treatise on education, eloquence, and gram-

---

[8] Walter Fischli: *Studien zum Fortleben der* Pharsalia *des M. Annaeus Lucanus* (1943–14), 86.

[9] "Préface," *La Pharsale de Lucain*, in *Œuvres complètes*, 19 vols. (1818–20), XI, xlvii.

judicious

nar, is politically innocuous. Gibbon called Quintilian "that judicious critic,"[1] and meant it as praise, but "judicious" may also be read as the deliberate refusal to run risks. Even Quintilian's laments over the decline, and warnings against the abuse, of rhetoric—well-worn but timely themes in a civilization for which oratory was not a luxury but a necessity—were aesthetic and technical. The *Institutio oratoria* is filled with sound advice, wide learning, and intelligent criticism, but it remains the work of a private man living in a world of private men. Similarly, the poet Statius moved among antique epic themes, doubly safe since they steered clear of contemporary issues and were Domitian's favorite form of verse. Critics have granted him vigor and feeling, but his poems rarely depart from the decorative and the verbose.

Far more interesting than Statius, both for himself and for the light he casts on his time, is Martial, his contemporary and antithesis, who put the mark of his wit on Pope, Lessing, and Voltaire. Martial's style is almost rhetorically unrhetorical, a reflection of his conviction that the proper study of mankind is man:

> Non hic Centauros, non Gorgonas Harpyasque
> Invenies; hominem pagina nostra sapit—

"You'll find no centaurs here, no gorgons or harpies; our page smacks of man."[2] He is a fine reporter, both of himself and his culture, and both are less than savory. Martial is a panderer giving his public the lubricity it craves; a parasite obsessed with his need to live without giving up poetry; and a flatterer adroitly embroidering the virtues of his aristocratic patrons and grossly inventing virtues for his emperor Domitian. But candid rascality, especially when accompanied by talent, is often disarming: the feeling that Martial and his age thoroughly deserved one another gives way to enjoyment of his wit and sadness for a regime that compelled him to waste so much of his gift. For while Martial has often been censured for his outspokenness, far more significant is his reserve. His *Epigrams*, when they are not obscene, moralize freely, but their targets are the safe butts of satire in all ages: the

---

[1] *Decline and Fall of the Roman Empire*, V, 455 *n.*
[2] *Epigrams*, X, iv, 9-10.

bore, the bluestocking, the social climber, the aging virgin, the professional guest, and most hilarious and most innocuous of all, the inept physician. The philosophes, though less cautious than he, would still make his jokes nearly two thousand years later. Martial, by his very talent and his very self-control, shows that the Claudian and Flavian decades were stepchildren of the First Age of Criticism—they were a little like the Prussia of Frederick the Great, which, Lessing observed sarcastically, was a free country: everyone was free to make anticlerical jokes.

The Flavian reign of terror came to an abrupt end in A.D. 96, with the assassination of Domitian, and with equal abruptness the last generations of the Roman Enlightenment found their voice. It was a final glorious flicker of the pagan spirit before its losing battle with Christianity, barbarism, and its own inner fatigue. Gibbon has celebrated these years with some famous words:

> If a man were called to fix the period in the history of the world during which the condition of the human race was most happy and prosperous, he would, without hesitation, name that which elapsed from the death of Domitian to the accession of Commodus. The vast extent of the Roman empire was governed by absolute power, under the guidance of virtue and wisdom. The armies were restrained by the firm but gentle hand of four successive emperors whose characters and authority commanded involuntary respect. The forms of the civil administration were carefully preserved by Nerva, Trajan, Hadrian, and the Antonines, who delighted in the image of liberty and were pleased with considering themselves as the accountable ministers of the law.[3]

While the decency and energy of the great emperors was not matched by the quantity or the quality of literary or philosophical production, it remained impressive enough to produce a handful of writers whose works reverberate in the writings of the philosophes. There was the younger Pliny, for one, who sought immortality with Latin poetry and speeches of merely mortal caliber, and achieved immortality with his letters written for

---

[3] *Decline and Fall of the Roman Empire*, I, 78.

private as well as for public consumption. Their digressions into telling detail and their conscientious name-dropping earned them the gratitude of eighteenth-century historians and the imitations of eighteenth-century letter writers. There was Pliny's contemporary Suetonius, for another, who continued to be read with much pleasure but also with some suspicion: while he was an able reporter with an accurate eye for the striking anecdote, Voltaire (who liked mainly his own anecdotes) warned that Suetonius sometimes destroyed reputations worth preserving.

Destructive as he was, Suetonius pales before Tacitus and Juvenal, the two most illustrious and most puzzling literary figures of the fading Roman Enlightenment. Both treated similar themes, were driven by the same indignation, and claimed the same moral purposes, but they are rather different from one another—the techniques of their respective crafts and the contours of their characters made them so. Juvenal, governed by the pleasure of denunciation, was the perfect satirist, who must tell one sort of truth by means of exaggeration; Tacitus, who visibly curbs his feelings, was properly the historian, who tells another sort of truth by means of exactitude. They may be read with equal enjoyment, but as a witness to Roman realities the historian is more trustworthy than the satirist—which is, I suppose, as it should be.

Juvenal's *Satires* were widely quoted and freely imitated in the eighteenth century, which appreciated Juvenal's fertile gift for epigram and his critical freedom. But if Juvenal's Rome had been all of Rome, the Empire would have collapsed three centuries before it did. His portraits are caricatures: his poems are dominated by conventional themes and his observations distorted by fierce prejudices. Juvenal is ridden by nostalgia; he is an ideologist for rural simplicity and antique toughness. The great *Third Satire* is a savage libel on urban life, a version of Vergil's *Georgics* in acid; the sixth, the longest, best known, and most vituperative, lavishes the most extravagant invective on the new woman, railing with as much venom against the female who aspires to culture as against the female who murders her husband for the sake of a lover; his other satires lament the disappearance of the old Rome: what, he asks rhetorically, what would the sturdy farmers, the brave soldiers who died at Cannae, have said to Imperial corruption, the influx of Orientals, perfumed perverts, insolent modish women?

Juvenal's outbursts make magnificent reading, but while it is hard to read them without pleasure, it is impossible to read them without disbelief. They are great literature and the material for social history, but they should not be taken for that history itself. A satirist is not on oath; a historian is. Even Roman historians, who looked upon their craft as a sister to rhetoric, and were often more concerned with eloquent effects than with impartial analysis, made much of their devotion to truth. Tacitus, himself a great orator, proclaimed in an immortal phrase that he tried to write history *sine ira et studio*, without anger or partisanship.

The admiration of his contemporaries, who knew the recent past well enough to catch Tacitus in some errors, and the awe of later centuries, who were detached enough to detect some of his biases, suggests that on the whole Tacitus succeeded in the severe program he had laid down for himself: to forego the easy popularity that comes to the flatterer of the tyrant, and the equally easy popularity of the slanderer, who gives his work a specious air of independence by clever malice. Those philosophes who were in the best position to know accepted the verdict of the ages: Tacitus is Montesquieu's most important source for Imperial affairs in his *Grandeur et décadence des Romains;* Diderot's study of Seneca depends on the *Historiae* and the *Annales* as his chief, often his sole, authorities; David Hume, not given to hyperbole, called Tacitus "that fine historian," noted for "candor and veracity," and indeed, "the greatest and most penetrating genius, perhaps, of all antiquity."[4] As for Gibbon—Suzanne Curchod, the girl whom Gibbon loved so tepidly and yielded up so readily, intelligently perceived that Tacitus was "the model and perhaps the source" of much in the *Decline and Fall of the Roman Empire*.[5]

The most conspicuous dissenter from the chorus of admirers was Voltaire, who had enough confidence in human nature, for all his pessimism, to regard Tacitus as a traducer of man, a brilliant fanatic who happened to be a great writer. Tacitus's histories,

[4] *Enquiry Concerning Human Understanding*, in *Works*, IV, 100.
[5] See G. M. Young: *Gibbon* (1932), 133. For an analysis of Gibbon's dependence on Tacitus, see below, pp. 156-9.

Voltaire wrote, violate what we know of man, and since evidence for the early Empire is scanty, we must go by probabilities. Tacitus's reports, especially those on Tiberius, are incredible because "they do too much dishonor to human nature."[6] We have come to learn that this argument cannot be sustained: men are capable of all the evil Tacitus reports of them, and more. But Voltaire's mistake, like most of his mistakes, is instructive: it points to a subtle distortion, not of fact but of tone, that pervades Tacitus's histories. It is a tone of dignified and terrible gloom, appropriate, to be sure, to a terrible time, but better equipped to catch the deceit and cruelty of men than their decency, and ideally equipped to portray the good as the victim of the bad.

The grim decades of the Flavian dynasty darkened the brighter age of the Antonines, and gave the last generations of the Roman Enlightenment a tone of rage, pessimism, and regret for the past which the eighteenth-century Enlightenment, fortunately for itself, was to know only in passing. As the second century went on, the rage abated, but regret swallowed creativity, and pessimism became the pervasive undertone in philosophy and poetry alike. This age, which Gibbon singled out as the happiest and most prosperous period in history, offers melancholy evidence that while freedom and security may be favorable preconditions for artistic vitality, they do not guarantee it: under the Antonines political stability and cultural weariness existed side by side.

There was nothing new about this lassitude, this gradual but irreversible return from thought to myth, from independence to nostalgia: symptoms of this "failure of nerve" (as Gilbert Murray has called it) were visible as early as the last years of the Republic. By the second century the symptoms were marked, and everywhere: the Roman Empire was swarming with oriental superstitions and elaborate mystery religions; the masses and even educated men were overwhelmed by a disturbing feeling of sinfulness and of dependence on inscrutable powers, a growing desire for immortality and an obsessive fear of demons, a curiosity about religion that moved from intellectual inquiry to the pathetic hope for salvation. It seemed as though the traditional choice offered by the great philosophers—the life of reason, responsibility, auton-

---

[6] "Pyrrhonisme de l'histoire," Œuvres, XXVII, 256–61.

omy, and freedom from dependence on myth—was too strenuous, or too frightening, for the world of the Roman Empire, a world marked by severe social dislocation, the disappearance of local loyalties, the devastating contrasts of shameless luxury with abject poverty, and perhaps worst of all, the insurmountable separation of a narrow elite from the masses, crude in their beliefs, brutal in their conduct of life, childlike in their dependence on irrational powers. The philosophers did not deign to educate the believers, and in time the believers overwhelmed the philosophers.

This formula, like all formulas, is too neat to account for the failure of nerve among the cultivated in the second and third centuries. There was much enterprise left, and some good thinking. Some philosophers proudly resisted the barbarization of their culture and the dilution of their rationalist heritage; but others converted their philosophy into authoritarian dogmas or ecstatic experiences, seeking in it certainty and salvation rather than intellectual clarity and the opportunity for continued questioning. This was, perhaps, the most threatening symptom of all: the blending of religion and philosophy.

The philosophes studied the decline of the critical mentality with some regret, but with little surprise. It seemed to them an inescapable end for an age that had wrested thought from myth so painfully and so incompletely. For them, the decline and fall of the Roman Empire was a political and moral question: Montesquieu considered the very size of the state as a major cause of its eventual collapse; William Robertson blamed the loss of political freedom, the reliance on wretched provincials and barbarians in the army, and the loss of military vigor through the growth of luxury and Eastern effeminacy among the leaders of the state;[7] Gibbon explained the readiness of the Empire for the Christian message and its defenselessness against barbarian incursions by the torpor of long peace, the decline of old families, and the disappearance of the traditional public spirit. And Gibbon shrewdly saw something else as well: a slavish antiquarianism.

---

[7] "A View of the Progress of Society in Europe," in *The History of the Reign of The Emperor Charles V*, in *Works*, 12 vols. (1820), IV, 7–10.

"The name of Poet was almost forgotten, that of Orator was usurped by the sophists. A cloud of critics, of compilers, of commentators, darkened the face of learning, and the decline of genius was soon followed by the corruption of taste."[8] Gibbon's measured alliterations should not obscure their historical validity: the reigning taste in the second century prostrated itself before Greek models, and educated Romans grew ecstatic over ruins like so many antique Winckelmanns. This indiscriminate antiquarianism was not so much a cause as a symptom—of exhaustion, of self-contempt. It had little in common with the healthy admiration of Greece characteristic of Augustans like Horace, or for that matter, of the philosophes.

Significantly, some of the best writers of the age fed the Greek revival. It is idle to object that they did so because they came from the Greek part of the Roman Empire: in the Augustan Age they would have learned to express themselves in the language of Vergil and Horace. The philosophes admired them as lonely giants in an age of epigones, sometimes with surprising extravagance. Plutarch, a truly pious man, receptive to foreign mysticism and worried over the threat of atheism, impressed the eighteenth century with his love of experience and his moral earnestness, with what we might call his responsible journalism. Hume praised him for his fairness: "Plutarch is no more cramped by systems in his philosophy than in history";[9] while Wieland singled him out as a writer who "is, or should be, in everyone's hands."[1] Lucian, whose pitiless dialogues persecute metaphysicians, social climbers, and religious believers with impartiality, was a model of wit and astringent common sense. And Epictetus touched minds as different as Frederick the Great, Immanuel Kant, and Jeremy Bentham. Yet they were writing in an aging, weary culture. When Marcus Aurelius, the philosophes' kingly ideal, the "philosopher," as Montesquieu wrote, "who better than any other made men feel the sweetness of virtue and the dignity

---

[8] *Decline and Fall of the Roman Empire*, I, 58.
[9] *Enquiry Concerning the Principles of Morals*, in *Works*, IV, 285.
[1] "Über das historische im Agathon," *Agathon*, in *Werke*, IX, 16.

of their being,"[2] who touched men's hearts, ennobled their souls, and elevated their spirit—when this most Roman of Roman emperors composed his noble, melancholy *Meditations* in Greek, he closed the glorious circle of independence begun in the time of Catullus and signed the death certificate of the Roman Enlightenment, and with it, that of the First Age of Criticism. The philosophes, in any event, lost interest at this point.

IV

For the Enlightenment, then, the organized habit of criticism was the most far-reaching invention of classical antiquity. A solvent of custom, accepted explanations, and traditional institutions, it had been, the philosophes knew, a potent agent of historical change. But as they also knew, it did not only make history; it had a history of its own. Unwittingly adopting a medieval metaphor, the philosophes were fond of saying that if they surpassed antiquity, they surpassed it because they were standing on the shoulders of ancient giants. As their distance from their ancient masters defined the amount of work they had done for themselves (or, they conceded, their seventeenth-century precursors had done for them), so their intimacy with them revealed how persistently and productively they were in touch with the best of Greek and Roman thought.

Not all their pride was warranted, but the philosophes were right to see their own, second age of criticism as something more than merely a repetition of the first. Montesquieu's sardonic notes on pagan customs, Hume's argument that modern Europe was not a decayed version of antique greatness, Turgot's and Condorcet's theories of historical development, d'Alembert's polemics against worshippers of the ancients who treated the "bold and romantic"[3] speculations of the Greeks as early anticipations of Newton's science—all these have a certain rough justice. While the philosophes' disdain for Plato tells us a good deal about their limitations, it also tells us something about their distance from the first age

---

[2] *Pensées*, in *Œuvres*, II, 192.
[3] *Discours préliminaire de l'Encyclopédie*, in *Mélanges*, I, 138.

of criticism: probably more than any other ancient philosopher, Plato embodied the concord of philosophy and theology, and indeed of philosophy and myth. There was nothing incongruous in the spectacle of positive conviction expressed by a critical thinker; the philosophes themselves were capable of glowing apostrophes to nature. Some of the more emotional deists, in fact, were not ashamed to exhibit their religious passions: early one morning in 1774 the aged Voltaire asked a visitor at Ferney to join him to see the sunrise. After a strenuous climb the two men rested on a hill to survey the magnificent panorama before them; Voltaire took off his hat, prostrated himself, and exclaimed: "I believe! I believe in you! Powerful God, I believe!" Then he rose and added drily: "As for monsieur the Son, and madame His Mother, that's a different story." At least the deist wing of the Enlightenment had every right to claim that its polemics were designed not to destroy, but to purify religion—it sounded in this precisely like Epicurus. The difference between the two ages was thus a difference in emphasis, in tone. Antiquity at its most philosophical retained a certain religious coloring. The philosophes, on the other hand, subdued or excised awe before Power or even before the grand regularity of nature. When they were animated by what Freud has called the "oceanic feeling"—that sense of oneness with the universe that is the ground of so much poetic religious feeling—it was marginal to their thought. Criticism kept breaking in.

In their attempt to find their place in history and in their own time, to determine at once their intellectual ancestry and their own unique qualities, the philosophes took a persistent interest in antique piety, especially in the religious revival inaugurated by Caesar Augustus. Augustus did not invent the religiosity over which he presided. It had always been there. True, the Roman Senate at the time of Caesar, as Voltaire put it with only mild exaggeration, "was composed almost entirely of theoretical and practical atheists, that is, of men who believed neither in Providence nor in a future life."[4] But it takes more than a handful of atheists to make a civilization secular. "LIVY," Hume writes, "acknowledges as frankly, as any divine would at present, the

---

[4] "Atheist, Atheism," *Philosophical Dictionary*, I, 103.

common incredulity of his age; but then he condemns it as severely. And who can imagine, that a national superstition, which could delude so ingenious a man, would not also impose on the generality of the people?"[5] Evidently the philosophes knew their favorite ancients to be exceptional men and their favorite classics to be exceptional books written under exceptional circumstances. They knew, too, that ancient philosophers did not eliminate mythical components from their thinking. It was not merely that sects like the Stoics believed in a divinity; many of the philosophes, after all, did so too. But the Stoics, or most Stoics, while they denounced crude superstitions, accepted the omens of birds, the prophetic value of dreams, and tales of gods active in human affairs: *primum docent esse deos;* Cicero tells us, *deinde quales sint; tum mundum ab iis administrari; postremo consulere eos rebus humanis*—"first they teach that gods exist; then what they are; then that the world is governed by them; finally that they care about human welfare."[6] Thus, Hume comments acidulously, "the STOICS join a philosophical enthusiasm to a religious superstition. The force of their mind, being all turned to the side of morals, unbent itself in that of religion."[7]

Antique speculation was enlivened by an unending debate over true religion. One man's philosophy was another man's superstition, and a single writer often offered a bundle of assertions that a later age would find hopelessly incongruous. Pliny the Elder, whose enormous compendium of *Natural History* is a monument to antique erudition, treats Homer as an authority in scientific matters but expresses skepticism concerning Herodotus's tales. He reports that a woman gave birth to an elephant but ridicules the credulity of the lower orders; he credits the story of the miraculous basilisk but subjects the machinations of priests to dry and detached analysis. Gibbon aptly called his work "that immense register where Pliny has deposited the discoveries, the arts and the errors of mankind."[8] Plutarch, the cool-headed student of religious credulity, insisted that there are demons who serve as intermediaries between men and the gods. Pliny the Younger

---

[5] "The Natural History of Religion," *Works*, IV, 350.
[6] *De natura deorum*, II, i, iii.
[7] "The Natural History of Religion," *Works*, IV, 351.
[8] *Decline and Fall of the Roman Empire*, I, 365.

castigated the Christians as stubborn fanatics but listened to the admonitions of dreams. Men of affairs who saw through the artifices of the clever and exploited the fears of the weak, secured themselves against the blows of fortune with some favorite superstition of their own. David Hume, who was as skeptical of pagan as he was of Christian witnesses, was ready to accept Pliny's and Suetonius's testimony that "Augustus was tainted with superstition of every kind," listening to dreams and being "extremely uneasy, when he happened to change his shoes, and put the right foot shoe on the left foot."[9] Even the Stoic Marcus Aurelius was not free from the hopes and fears of ordinary men: Hume calls attention to a passage in his *Meditations* in which the emperor speaks of the "admonitions from the gods in his sleep."[1] The world was a dark and mysterious place even for Romans who had gone to Athens to study philosophy.

It is worth noting that the coexistence of such mental habits, which later ages would call contradictory and separate into "scientific" and "superstitious" elements, defined a coherent style of thinking in antiquity. All styles of thinking are composite, but they appear congruent to those who live with them—that is why they live with them. It may seem surprising that astrology and astronomy cohabit peacefully in one thinker, ritual observance and detached skepticism in another. But it is not enough for the historian to record what he is pleased to call these contradictions. He must penetrate to the center that made them appear organic parts of a single way of thought in its time. In his *Quaestiones naturales*, Seneca advanced scientific propositions that seem a curiously heterogeneous collection today: some are the result of careful observation, others of enthusiastic musings, still others of improbable tales credulously repeated. But the point is that to Seneca all were equally scientific; if he had recognized some as irrelevant and others as superstitious, he would have discarded them. Seneca's scientific method was primitive, and his conception of science moralistic. But he stood, no matter how unsteadily, on the ground of science. So did Pliny the Elder: his basilisk, for all its marvelous qualities, was only an animal.

---

[9] "The Natural History of Religion," *Works*, IV, 347.
[1] Ibid., 350.

By participating in the religious revival which Caesar Augustus commanded, partly from policy, partly from conviction, the Augustans did not regress to wholesale, primitive mythmaking. They merely stressed what had lain dormant and brought back what had been unfashionable without surrendering the claims of reason. While some of them and some of their successors in the first century A.D. derided philosophy and philosophers, this did not particularly disturb the philosophes, for as far as they could see, even these antique critics of the schools had done the work of philosophy. Horace and Petronius ridiculed superstitions; Juvenal exposed private pretensions and social corruption; Quintilian applied critical canons to literature; and even Tacitus, unsmilingly contemptuous of philosophic learning, advanced the cause of criticism by penetrating arcane regions of statecraft and leaving behind exemplars of disenchanted political analysis. The Augustans and their successors wrote works of sufficient literary distinction and intellectual vigor to make the Enlightenment forgive them for their patriotic piety. They were not notably superstitious men—how, if they had been, could they have ranked among the philosophes' favorites?

The affinity of the philosophes and the ancients was thus a selective affinity. What Voltaire called "sound antiquity" had lasted a long time—at least seven centuries, from Socrates to Marcus Aurelius—and offered a wide spectrum of ideas: systems from the most doctrinaire to the most skeptical; scientific, ethical, and religious notions impossible to group into a single rubric. An eighteenth-century pagan could be almost anything but a good Christian. But the very wealth of ancient material was an asset; it turned antiquity into a well-stocked arsenal to be rifled at will. What Cicero had written against entrail-reading Stoics, the philosophes could use against modern believers in astrology or witches; Plutarch's denunciations of Jewish superstitions they could apply to Jansenist enthusiasts; the Roman policy of toleration was a weighty lesson to eighteenth-century monarchs; the scorn of Celsus for the vulgar, credulous Christians of the second century could be adapted with much loss in justice, but little loss of vigor, to criticism of Christians in the age of the Enlightenment.

From the distance of centuries some of the ancients appeared a little quaint, but the philosophes admired them for their realism, their impatience with obfuscation and mystery. While Gibbon's "sense and spirit most congenial to his own" was most marked among the Epicureans, Skeptics, and Academics, the more pious ancients—Tacitus, say, or Plutarch—displayed that spirit at least in many moods and in most areas of their interest. Through the noise of antique debates, the philosophes heard a certain ground tone, a tone of confidence in rational inquiry, of contempt for superstition or naïveté, in a word, of reliance on critical philosophy. "What a pleasure it is to see him," exclaims Montesquieu watching Cicero at work, "passing in review all the sects in his book *De natura deorum*, shaming all the philosophers and marking each prejudice with some stigma! Sometimes he battles against these monsters, sometimes he toys with philosophy. The champions he introduces destroy one another; one is confounded by a second, who finds himself beaten in his turn. All these systems fade, one before the other, and in the mind of the reader nothing remains but contempt for the philosophers and admiration for the critic."[2] Here, for the philosophes, was antiquity at its best, the source of its enduring power over them: *hybris* and credulity being routed by the spirit of criticism.

---

[2] "Discours sur Cicéron," *Œuvres*, III, 17.

CHAPTER THREE

The Climate of Criticism

1. CRITICISM AS PHILOSOPHY

I

SINCE THE EIGHTEENTH CENTURY there have been detractors who have denied to the philosophes the title of philosopher. But the philosophes thought they deserved it, and they justified it, often by appealing to their classical models: they liked to think of themselves as inhabiting a climate of criticism first inhabited by their favorite ancient philosophers and now purified, and constantly renewed—by them—with modern, enlightened methods. It was precisely this critical activity which, they thought, gave them the right to call themselves philosophers.

Perhaps the most vigorous, certainly a most characteristic justification of their philosophical vocation, was the anonymous essay, *Le philosophe*, first published in 1743. It had a remarkable career. Voltaire, who later published two versions of it, claimed that it had circulated in manuscript since 1730, and Diderot, to whom the essay has often been attributed, abridged it for the *Encyclopédie*. *Le philosophe* thus bears the Enlightenment's official stamp of approval.

It begins with the warning that the title of philosopher has become too cheap. Some men claim it as a reward for shunning polite society, others for displaying their hatred of religion. The true philosopher has an orderly view of the world, a "spirit of observation and exactitude." As a true empiricist, he respects the limits of knowledge but is determined to know what can be known. Precisely because he recognizes no deity other than human society, he is far better equipped than the orthodox believer to serve his fellow men. He is neither frantic about sociability nor churlish about solitude, but "knows how to divide himself between retreat and commerce with men." The philosopher (and here is the appeal to antiquity) is a true humanist: he is "the Chremes of Terence" who can apply to himself the famous line *homo sum, humani a me nihil alienum puto*—"I am a man, I think nothing human alien to me."[1]

This mode of argument and this quotation from Terence had been worn smooth long before; they were no longer new when Seneca used them in his ninety-fifth Epistle. But their very triteness confirms the continuity between classical and eighteenth-century modes of thought. The philosopher's sense of order and limits, his love of virtue, his obedience to the rhythms imposed by the examined life—these had been favorite themes in Cicero's Rome and became favorite themes in Voltaire's France.

Whether Diderot wrote *Le philosophe* remains uncertain; that he accepted its point is clear from his mature work, the *Essai sur les règnes de Claude et de Néron*. In this lawyer's plea for Seneca, Diderot also pleads for philosophy, with his customary lyricism. The philosopher, he writes, is "the preceptor of mankind," and Diderot offers his client as a worthy exemplar of the master profession.[2] In his analysis of Seneca's *Epistles*, Diderot merges into Seneca until we can no longer separate the ancient from the modern philosopher:

The magistrate deals out justice; the philosopher teaches the magistrate what is just and unjust. The soldier defends his country; the philosopher teaches the soldier what a fatherland is. The priest recommends to his people the love and respect of the gods; the philosopher teaches the priest what the gods are. The sovereign commands all; the philosopher teaches the sovereign the origins and limits of his authority. Every man

---

[1] *Le philosophe*, ed. Herbert Dieckmann (1948), *passim*. The line from Terence was quite popular in the Enlightenment: Diderot used it; Lord Kames used it as the epigraph to his *Sketches of the History of Man* (1774), and so did others.

[2] *Œuvres*, III, 176. Diderot here echoes both Rousseau and Seneca: Rousseau: *Discours sur les sciences et les arts*, in *Œuvres*, III, 29; Seneca: *Epistulae morales*, LXXXIX, 13.

has duties to his family and his society; the philosopher teaches everyone what these duties are. Man is exposed to misfortune and pain; the philosopher teaches man how to suffer.[3]

Diderot did not think of himself as godlike and knew himself to be anything but free from passion, but he made most of the claims, for himself as for the rest of the philosophes, that the Stoics had made for the Wise Man.

While the center of such confidence was France, its warmth radiated through Europe. In Great Britain, David Hume proclaimed philosophy the supreme, indeed the only, cure for superstition. "True philosophy," he wrote in his essay *On Suicide*, inspires "juster sentiments" than the passions, or even the "soundest reason" not guided by philosophy, and not unexpectedly he supported his argument by recalling Cicero's *De divinatione*.[4] Similarly, Adam Smith recommended the cultivation of philosophy as "the great antidote to the poison of enthusiasm and superstition."[5] In the Italian states, the writings of the *illuministi* show how deeply this missionary view of philosophy had penetrated. Beccaria claimed that mankind owed immeasurable gratitude to the philosopher, who bravely scatters broadcast the seeds of truth "from the obscurity of his study."[6] In 1780, Gaetano Filangieri published his ambitious treatise on the science of politics, *La scienza della legislazione*, in which he exalted the philosopher to heights undreamed-of even by Diderot. "The philosopher," he wrote, "should not be the inventor of systems but the apostle of truth." As long as evils afflict humanity and ignorance perpetuates suffering, "it will remain the philosopher's duty to preach the truth, to sustain it, to promote it, and to illustrate it." The philosopher is a "citizen of all places and ages," he has "the whole world for his country and earth itself for his school. Posterity will be his disciples." Then, appealing to pagan models, Filangieri ranks

---

[3] *Essai sur les règnes de Claude et de Néron*, in *Œuvres*, III, 248.
[4] *Works*, IV, 406-7.
[5] *An Inquiry into the Nature and Causes of the Wealth of Nations* (1776; ed. Edwin Cannan, 1937), 748. Adam Smith here uses the word "science" which he practically equates with philosophy.
[6] "Introduction," *Dei delitti e delle pene*, in *Illuministi Italiani*, III, 32.

the calling of the philosopher with the calling of those semi-mythical legislators Numa and Lycurgus.[7]

In soberer tones, Immanuel Kant made a similar case in his *Streit der Fakultäten;* with droll, somewhat ponderous sarcasm, he here vindicates the independence of the "lower" faculty of philosophy from the three "higher" faculties of theology, law, and medicine. This division into lower and higher, he writes, must have been invented by governments, not by scholars. The state, which must intimidate its subjects in order to govern them, uses the three higher faculties to instill obedience, and dictates to them what they must teach. They are all subject to authority and must blindly obey the rules laid down for their guidance. As soon as they begin to ask questions about these rules, they meddle with philosophy, the only faculty that follows the dictates of reason alone. Let the higher faculties look down on the philosopher: the philosopher is indifferent to such scorn, for he alone is truly free.

In insisting on the philosopher's autonomy, Kant was not merely arguing in behalf of his guild. It was clear to Kant—and his popular essays were designed to make it clear to a larger public—that the philosopher's freedom is the precondition for universal freedom. Man's search for autonomy is impeded by laziness, cowardice, all the accumulated weight of tradition, and it is the philosopher alone, reasoning without alien constraints and criticizing without fear, who initiates and leads the great struggle for liberation.

The Enlightenment's definition of philosophy—the organized habit of criticism—does not correspond to the traditional definition. On one side, it was latitudinarian. It promoted confidence that good will, clear thinking, and unremitting hostility to superstition were on the whole adequate equipment for the philosopher. On the other side, but for the same reason, the philosophes' definition was narrow in the extreme; it banished verbal play or system making from the true province of thought. We keep coming back to it: for the Enlightenment, the Age of Philosophy was also, and mainly, the Age of Criticism. These two names did not merely designate allied activities: they were synonyms, "different ex-

---

[7] *Scienzia della legislazione,* 5 vols. (edn. 1807), II, 174.

pressions," as Ernst Cassirer has said, "of the same situation, intended to characterize from diverse angles the fundamental intellectual energy which permeates the era and to which it owes its great trends of thought."[8] This energy was the drive for knowledge and control, a restless Faustian dissatisfaction with mere surfaces, or mere passivity. Its favorite instrument was analysis, its essential atmosphere freedom, its goal reality. For all their brave talk about their need to destroy the wild beasts of superstition, talk that soon gave rise to the charge that the Enlightenment was "merely negative," the philosophes did not sharply separate their work into tearing down and building up. Both were inescapably linked parts of the same activity. The Enlightenment "joined, to a degree scarcely ever achieved before, the critical with the productive function and converted the one directly into the other."[9] It is this exalted conception of criticism that led Lessing to prefer the *search* for truth—that is, the unremitting and unending exercise of criticism—to its possession; and this is why Gibbon could endow it with the most desirable qualities: "All that men have been," he wrote, "all that genius has created, all that reason has weighed, all that labor has gathered up—all this is the business of criticism. Intellectual precision, ingenuity, penetration, are all necessary to exercise it properly."[1] To be this kind of critic clearly made one into something more than a wrecker, something better than a complainer.

It is with such arguments that the philosophes tried to substantiate their claim that they were philosophers. Yet their reiterated, almost plaintive, self-defense suggests some uncertainty: established elites do not trouble to justify themselves. It also suggests that their claim did not go unchallenged. "Now and again," Kant noted in his *Critique of Pure Reason*, "we hear complaints about the shallowness of the mentality of our age and the decline of solid science." But, he rejoined, "I do not see that those sciences whose foundations are secure, like mathematics, physics, etc., in the least deserve this reproach; on the contrary, they retain their former repute for solidity, and, as far as physics

---

[8] *The Philosophy of the Enlightenment*, 275.
[9] Ibid., 278.
[1] *Essai sur l'étude de la littérature*, in *Miscellaneous Works*, IV, 38.

is concerned, they even surpass it." Our age, he emphatically
concluded, "is the very age of criticism."[2]

We may agree that Kant's defense is valid, but it remains true
that the philosophes invited skepticism by their manner. I have
already mentioned their touchiness, their lack of distance from
themselves; and indeed, their language was redolent with metaphors of battle and the physical act of penetration: they spoke
of the beam that pierces corners of darkness, the blow that levels
barriers of censorship, the fresh wind that lifts the veil of religious
authority, the surgical knife that cuts away the accumulation of
tradition, the eye that sees through the disguise of political mys-
terymongers. "To tear the mask from error is to establish truth,"
wrote Falconet, sculptor and philosophe, in the approved tone.[3]
"We must cut off by the roots a tree that has always borne
poisons," wrote Voltaire, who enjoyed the role of the embattled
champion.[4] "Obscurity, indeed, is painful to the mind as well as
to the eye; but to bring light from obscurity, by whatever labour,
must needs be delightful and rejoicing," wrote Hume in his more
moderate accents, turning from metaphors of aggression to another metaphor whose popularity in the Enlightenment I have
already noted, the metaphor of light.[5] The Age of Criticism was
not always criticizing.

II

By identifying philosophy with criticism, the Enlightenment
raised serious doubts about the value of metaphysics. As early as
the seventeenth century, Christian Thomasius had gravely warned
against "*Abstractiones Metaphysicas.*"[6] The more impetuous
among the philosophes degraded the term into an imprecise word

---

[2] "Vorrede," *Critik der reinen Vernunft*, in *Werke*, III, 7.
[3] See Anne Betty Weinshenker: "The Writings of Falconet,
Sculpteur-Philosophe," unpubl. diss. (Columbia Univ., 1962),
108.
[4] *Le dîner du comte de Boulainvilliers*, in *Œuvres*, XXVI, 550.
[5] *Enquiry Concerning Human Understanding*, in *Works*, IV, 8.
[6] Hans M. Wolff: *Die Weltanschauung der deutschen Aufklärung*, 27.

of abuse, a synonym for pretentious meddling with the unknowable. In fact, Enlightenment wits—and the Enlightenment was full of wits—denigrated metaphysics with such abandon that the more responsible members of the little flock gradually drew back from this reckless positivism. To be sure, a beefy sort of good sense was a common possession of the eighteenth century: it was not a philosophe who had invited Boswell to clear his mind of cant or refuted Berkeley by kicking a stone. Nor was it a philosophe who portrayed Gulliver's amazement with the "defective" learning of the inhabitants of Brobdingnag, learning which consisted "only in morality, history, poetry, and mathematics," the last of which was "wholly applied to what may be called useful in life, to the improvement of agriculture, and all mechanical arts; so that among us it would be little esteemed." And, added Gulliver, with the fine outrage of the incurable metaphysician, "as to ideas, entities, abstractions, and transcendentals, I could never drive the least conception into their heads." Goethe later recalled the lively unfolding of good sense—*Menschenverstand*—which Swift had prized: "People opened their eyes, looked straight ahead, were attentive, diligent, active, and believed that if they judged and acted soundly in their own circle they might venture to put in a word about more remote matters. According to such a view, everyone was entitled not merely to philosophize, but gradually to come to think of himself as a philosopher. Philosophy, then, was a more or less sound and applied good sense."[7] But while this attitude was quite general, the philosophes were especially addicted to it. In 1751 the classical scholars of the Academy of Belles Lettres at Paris found it necessary to warn against the widespread preoccupation with science; significantly enough, their pamphlet defended their non-utilitarian concerns with utilitarian language: it was entitled "General Reflections on the Utility of Belles Lettres, and On the Disadvantages of the Ex-

---

[7] *Dichtung und Wahrheit*, in *Gedenkausgabe*, X, 301–2. At least one philosophe, Voltaire, thought *sens commun* an unflattering epithet. In ancient Rome, he notes, *sensus communis* had meant good sense as well as humanity. But modern usage has cheapened the term and it now refers merely to elementary reasonableness. " 'That man has no common sense,' is a coarse insult. 'That man has common sense' is an insult too." "Common Sense," *Philosophical Dictionary*, II, 467.

clusive Inclination which Seems to Be Establishing Itself in Favor
of Mathematics and Physics."[8] There was some point to this
warning: the philosophes' urgent desire for tangible results opened
the way to a shallow, hasty empiricism, a cavalier treatment of
theory, a brash contempt for some of the world's best minds. The
Enlightenment wanted to conquer reality by thought, and conquer it did. But like all victors, the philosophes paid a price for
their victory. Most of them traded depth for effectiveness, most
of the time.

Yet, while the philosophes did not wholly escape the taint of
intellectual vulgarity, there were occasions—occasions worth
recording—when they rose to a dignified conception of philosophy. It is not surprising that Kant should give profound, and
witty, attention to the relation of theory and practice.[9] But it is
significant to find Adam Smith bringing to bear his appreciation
of theory on the advance of technology; to find d'Alembert, the
severe positivist, and David Hume, the destructive skeptic, treating philosophy as the free play of mind. "If I banish the mania
for explanations from the physical sciences," wrote d'Alembert in
the *Encyclopédie*, "I am very far from banishing that spirit of
conjecture which, at once timid and enlightened, sometimes leads
to discoveries . . . or that spirit of analogy whose wise boldness
penetrates beyond what nature seems willing to reveal, and foresees the facts before it has seen them."[1] And David Hume strenuously defended learning for its own sake. If man reaped no advantage from philosophizing "beyond the gratification of an
innocent curiosity, yet ought not even this to be despised, as
being an accession to those few safe and harmless pleasures, which

[8] See Seznec: *Diderot et l'antiquité*, 137.
[9] See Kant's essay "Über den Gemeinspruch: Das mag in der
Theorie richtig sein, taugt aber nicht für die Praxis," (*Werke*,
VI, 355–98) which should dispose, once and for all, of the absurd commonplace that something that works in theory may not
work in practice. In general, the philosophes were alert to the
function of theory and of hypotheses: in a characteristic passage
—to give only one instance—Adam Ferguson defines theoretical
thinking as "referring particular operations to the principles or
general laws, under which they are comprehended; or in referring particular effects to the causes from which they proceed." Bryson: *Man and Society*, 17.
[1] "Expérimental," *The Encyclopédie*, 80.

metaphysics

are bestowed on the human race."[2] In the midst of his troubled musings about what he considered his lonely, unprecedented enterprise, he found it within himself to call philosophizing a pleasure.[3] These remarks show a little known side of the Enlightenment: the philosophes enjoying peaceful, relaxed thinking in the midst of belligerent activity—officers playing chess in the front lines.

Even the wits were mainly trying to sort out pernicious from fruitful speculation. It is this serious intent that lurks behind Voltaire's jokes. Metaphysics, he once wrote, is like the minuet, in which the dancer displays much agility and grace but ends where he starts. Elsewhere, Voltaire compared all metaphysicians from Plato to Leibniz with travelers who have entered the anterooms of the Grand Turk's seraglio, observed a eunuch from afar, and conjecture on this evidence how many times His Highness has made love to his odalisque that night. "One traveler said three times, another four times, etc. The truth is that the sultan had slept soundly the night through."[4] There is a point to this persiflage: the great preceptors of the Enlightenment—Bacon, Newton, and Locke—had immeasurably advanced man's knowledge of the world by practicing experimental philosophy. Newton, Voltaire sagely advised a young man in 1741, had taught men to "examine, weigh, calculate, and measure, and never to conjecture." Newton had not been a system maker: "He saw and he made people see; but he did not put his fantasies in place of truth."[5] Lichtenberg, combining his own scientific knowledge with the rhetoric of Voltaire, told a correspondent in 1788 that "general natural hypotheses" had never been of any use in physics and that, on the contrary, scientists had usually begun their work by "despising those *novels*" and those "dreams" which other men prize so highly.[6]

Wieland, who claimed not to be a disciple of Voltaire's, and

---

[2] *Enquiry Concerning Human Understanding*, in *Works*, IV, 7.
[3] *Treatise of Human Nature*, 271.
[4] Voltaire to des Alleurs (November 26, 1738). *Correspondence*, VII, 462–3.
[5] Voltaire to Le Cati (April 15, 1741). Ibid., XI, 85.
[6] See J. P. Stern: *Lichtenberg: A Doctrine of Scattered Occasions* (1959), 45.

Diderot, whose intellectual development was in many respects different from Voltaire's, both sounded on this question, as on so much else, precisely like Voltaire. As a student Wieland rejected "metaphysical subtleties," and in 1764, having decisively outgrown his youthful *Schwärmerei*, he drew a brief outline of his convictions: "I think about Christianity as Montesquieu did on his death bed; about the false wisdom of sectarian spirits and the false virtues of knaves, as Lucian did; about speculative ethics, like Helvétius; of metaphysics—nothing at all; to me it's nothing but a joke."[7] And Diderot recounts a significant dream in his early novel *Les bijoux indiscrets:* the dreamer sees himself transported to an enormous building suspended in space, inhabited by feeble, aged, and deformed men. Then a small healthy child enters, grows into a colossus, and destroys the building. That building (as Diderot interprets the dream) is the land of hypotheses, the cripples are the makers of systems, the colossus is Experiment. To Voltaire, as to Diderot, the attack on metaphysics was not an attack on thinking but an attack on bad, in behalf of good thinking.

The philosophes protected this style of philosophizing so jealously that they would criticize one another for lapses from the true path. When the precocious Turgot—he was then twenty-one—encountered some of Buffon's speculative utterances on natural history, he wrote to Buffon with the severity of a sage reproving a hasty disciple: "I ask, first of all, why do you undertake to explain such phenomena? Do you want to rob Newton's philosophy of the simplicity, the prudent circumspection, that characterize it? Do you, by plunging us back into the night of hypotheses, want to justify the Cartesians . . . ?"[8] Philosophy as criticism demanded constant vigilance.

The trained philosophers among the philosophes—Kant, Hume, Condillac—shared this view but stated it more moderately and more precisely. In 1766, before he had worked out the principles of his Critical Philosophy, Immanuel Kant satirized metaphysicians in his brilliant essay *Träume eines Geistersehers erläutert durch Träume der Metaphysik:* sounding for all the

---

[7] Sengle: *Wieland*, 41, 168.
[8] Turgot to Buffon (October 1748). *Œuvres*, I, 111.

Swedenborg

world like a character from a Voltairian *conte*, he describes himself studying the work of Swedenborg, and there "he found—as usually happens when one searches where one has no business looking—he found nothing." And, he added, this religious enthusiast, this "dreamer of emotion," was much like metaphysical enthusiasts, those "dreamers of reason." If metaphysics is a science at all, writes the young Kant, it is a science of limits, and he ends his essay with an appeal to "honest Candide": "Let us provide for our happiness, let us go into the garden and work."[9] In his great *Critiques*, Kant held to the same position; he was aware of being a revolutionary, but he made his "Copernican revolution" quite deliberately with the methods of the century now on the wane: he was, and he always proclaimed himself to be, a good Newtonian, feigning no hypotheses. At the same time, his devastating critique of all previous attempts at metaphysics did not mean contempt for metaphysics as such; it expressed his dissatisfaction with all earlier efforts. If it was true of anyone in the Enlightenment that he destroyed only in order to build, criticized only in order to make construction possible, it was true of Kant.

David Hume was rather less concerned with positive results than the man whom he started off on the path to Critical Philosophy, but he too drew some important distinctions. One species of philosophy, "the easy and obvious," considers "man chiefly as born for action," offering useful observations on vice and virtue and furnishing precepts for conduct. The other, "abstruse philosophy," considers "man in the light of a reasonable rather than an active being." It does not improve man but seeks to understand him. Hume admits that the first, the "easy philosophy," is, and deserves to be, more popular than the "accurate and abstract philosophy." But since "the matter is often carried farther, even to the absolute rejecting of all profound reasonings," he proceeds to defend "what is commonly called *metaphysics*." His defense is as reasonable as it is obvious: good sense, whether in ethics or aesthetics, depends on rigorous reasoning on general principles. "Accuracy is, in every case, advantageous to beauty, and just reasoning to delicate sentiment. In vain would we exalt the one

---

[9] Kant: *Werke*, II, 332, 390.

by depreciating the other." The remoteness of theoretical speculations from practical life does not reduce their utility.

But, he adds, "this obscurity, in the profound and abstract
philosophy, is objected to, not only as painful and fatiguing, but
as the inevitable source of uncertainty and error." This is an objection that Hume, *en philosophe*, is happy to entertain: "Here
indeed lies the justest and most plausible objection against a considerable part of metaphysics, that they are not properly a science;
but arise either from the fruitless efforts of human vanity, which
would penetrate into subjects utterly inaccessible to the understanding, or from the craft of popular superstitions, which, being
unable to defend themselves on fair ground, raise these entangling
brambles to cover and protect their weakness." The philosopher
must therefore disentangle one sort of metaphysics from another:
"The only method of freeing learning, at once, from these abstruse
questions, is to inquire seriously into the nature of human understanding, and show, from an exact analysis of its powers and
capacity, that it is by no means fitted for such remote and abstruse
subjects. We must submit to this fatigue, in order to live at ease
ever after: And must cultivate true metaphysics with some care,
in order to destroy the false and adulterate." Good metaphysics
will drive out bad: "Accurate and just reasoning is the only
catholic remedy, fitted for all persons and all dispositions; and is
alone able to subvert that abstruse philosophy and metaphysical
jargon, which, being mixed up with popular superstition, renders
it in a manner impenetrable to careless reasoners, and gives it the
air of science and wisdom."[1]

Hume's two species of philosophy have thus become three:
popular philosophy, rigorous speculation, and "airy" metaphysics.
His defense of metaphysics has turned into a defense of epistemology: the rancor with which he pursues the devotees of "an
abstruse philosophy, which seems to have hitherto served only as
a shelter to superstition, and a cover to absurdity and error,"
allies him closely with his French brethren—with Voltaire's admiring comments on Locke, and with d'Alembert's *Discours*

---

[1] *Enquiry Concerning Human Understanding*, in *Works*, IV,
3–9. This is why Hume's loyal and perceptive reader Beccaria
could properly call him a "profound metaphysician."

préliminaire. If there are any doubts of this alliance, Hume removes them with the celebrated conclusion to his *Enquiry Concerning Human Understanding*, as violent in tone as anything a French *philosophe* ever wrote: "When we run over libraries, persuaded of these principles, what havoc must we make? If we take in our hand any volume; of divinity or school metaphysics, for instance; let us ask, *Does it contain any abstract reasoning concerning quantity or number?* No. *Does it contain any experimental reasoning concerning matter of fact and existence?* No. Commit it then to the flames: For it can contain nothing but sophistry and illusion."[2]

Hume's distinction between useful and pernicious metaphysics corresponds in all particulars to the distinction made by Condillac and d'Alembert between *l'esprit systématique* and *l'esprit de système*. The classic statement of this distinction, and therefore a classic document of the Enlightenment, is Condillac's *Traité des systèmes*, published in 1749. Not unexpectedly, the heroes of the *Traité* are Locke and Newton, the one for exposing the absurdity of building vast constructions on abstract principles —of building, we might say, the unknowable on the unknown, the other for modestly contenting himself with observing the world without trying to create one out of his head—"a project less handsome, or rather less daring, than Descartes', but wiser."[3] Locke, Newton, and their followers have relied on observation and experiment, on accumulating and testing the data of experience, on using abstract terms merely as instruments of classification. In contrast, Condillac argued, the great system makers of the seventeenth century, Descartes, Malebranche, Spinoza, and Leibniz, have either established metaphysical structures on general principles by a priori reasoning, or elaborated speculative hypotheses, stretching out vague "suspicions" far beyond permissible limits. Both kinds of systems are harmful: they mistake tautologies for chains of reasoning, claim that they have explained a phenomenon when they have found a metaphor for it, and persistently fall into vague language, a cardinal error that scientific method is correcting at last. "*The art of reasoning,*" wrote Con-

---

[2] Ibid., 135.
[3] *Traité des systèmes*, in *Œuvres*, I, 200.

dillac, considering this a great enough truth to underline it, *"reduces itself to a well constructed language."*[4]

Condillac did something unusual: he took his adversaries seriously; he examined their works with meticulous care, rather than with the supercilious disdain current among many of his friends. Moreover, he buttressed his refutation with a psychological analysis of the "mania for systems": the aberration, he suggests, is the offspring of impatience. Confronted by unsolved problems, troubled by mysteries, surrounded by interesting and unexplained phenomena, philosophers yield to temptation. They make conjectures drawn from fancy, not fact, and consult their imaginations instead of interrogating nature. Finally, Condillac offered a remedy—not a Utopian panacea but a realistic proposal that was proving its efficacy every day: the method of the natural sciences. This method was not merely observation and experimentation; the logician had his share in it: he taught the scientist the discriminating use of abstraction and hypotheses. What made the scientific method particularly attractive to Condillac was that it was, as it were, portable: carefully employed, it could be applied to man's benefit in the mechanical arts and in the arts of politics. Thus by the transformation of destructive into constructive analysis, so natural to the Age of Criticism, Condillac's *Traité des systèmes* turns from a critique into a prophecy.

The cogency of Condillac's argument impressed his contemporaries as compelling; his criticism of metaphysics, as devastating. Both reappear without significant change in several articles of the *Encyclopédie* and with full acknowledgment in d'Alembert's *Discours préliminaire*. It was Condillac, one of the best of contemporary philosophers, d'Alembert wrote, who had reminded philosophy that its task was not to please but to instruct. The spirit of hypothesis and conjecture may have been useful in the past, in fact, essential to the rebirth of philosophy. But now, he concluded, times have changed, and Condillac's work has made all eulogies of systems irrelevant. In view of the prevailing temper among the philosophic family, this tribute to Condillac hardly seems extravagant. By mid-century, the philosophes were trying to identify their procedures with the methods of the natural sci-

---

[4] Ibid., 131.

ences. They were, as Condillac put it, perhaps a little grandly, but not inappropriately, "explaining facts by facts."[5]

III

The philosophes' glorification of criticism and their qualified repudiation of metaphysics make it obvious that the Enlightenment was not an Age of Reason but a Revolt against Rationalism. This revolt took two closely related forms: it rejected the assertion that reason is the sole, or even the dominant, spring of action; and it denied that all mysteries in the world can be penetrated by inquiry. The claim for the omnicompetence of criticism was in no way a claim for the omnipotence of reason. It was a political demand for the right to question everything, rather than the assertion that all could be known or mastered by rationality. This demand is a pervasive theme in the philosophes' tactical statements. In 1758, Malesherbes, then chief French censor, who was trying to protect the new ideas without giving them the range the philosophes claimed for them, asked in some irritation whether "M. Diderot couldn't even write a poetics without mentioning religion and the government in two or three places."[6] Obviously the answer was "no." There were liberal Christians ready to allow the new philosophy wide elbowroom, provided it stopped short of holy matters. A typical discourse before the Academy of Angers, for one, graciously suggested that "the philosophic mind which respects the sacred barriers laid down by the wisdom of the Supreme Legislator, is not excluded from the sanctuary."[7] But this was not the sort of territorial division to satisfy the philosophes. To turn into "Christian philosophers," as they were often asked to do, struck them as irrational and self-contradictory. D'Alembert, Voltaire, Kant, and others, in the same words and with the same energy, reiterated that if critics

---

[5] Ibid., 211.
[6] Diderot, *Correspondance*, II, 67 *n*. This theme of the revolt against rationalism, which I regard as central to the Enlightenment, will be taken up again in detail in volume II of this essay.
[7] John McManners: *French Ecclesiastical Society under the Ancien Régime* (1960), 44.

could not criticize everything, they might as well criticize nothing; and they identified politics and religion (as Swift had identified them long before in *A Tale of a Tub*) as the two areas most sensitive to criticism and, for that very reason, most in need of it. Diderot insisted all his life that it was just the matters that had never been questioned before which must be questioned now, in this philosophic time: only "two matters deserve my attention," Diderot has his spokesman say in *La promenade du sceptique*, an early work, "and they are precisely the ones you forbid me to discuss. Impose on me silence concerning religion and government, and I'll have nothing more to say."[8] But silence was not merely undesirable; it was impossible: "Everything must be examined," Diderot reiterated in the *Encyclopédie*, "everything must be shaken up, without exception and without circumspection."[9] In his first book, Jeremy Bentham claimed that Blackstone's erroneous principles were so well established in England because criticism had been waved aside as "a kind of presumption and ingratitude, and rebellion, and cruelty." Such self-protection damaged all men: "Under a government of Laws, what is the motto of a good citizen? *To obey punctually; to censure freely*."[1] As an Anglomaniac, doubtless with pronouncements like Bentham's in mind, Lichtenberg put the demand for free criticism on the highest possible ground—man's dignity—and with an English metaphor: "Since, once and for all, we have seats in God's House of Commons, and He Himself has entrusted us with the vote, shall we not express our opinion?"[2]

As we know all too well from their voluminous writings, the philosophes rarely hesitated to express their opinion. Yet they did so with a healthy appreciation of their own ignorance. It was, in

---

[8] *Œuvres*, I, 183–4.

[9] "Encyclopédie," ibid., XIV, 474. In his essay on Seneca, as elsewhere, Diderot resorted to the by then well-worn philosophic device of calling for complete freedom of speech in matters of religion, politics, and "manners" and of claiming, at the same time, that true philosophers, members of the most dignified of professions, could never be subversive.

[1] *A Fragment on Government* (1776; ed. F. C. Montague, 1951), 101.

[2] In Franz Mautner and Henry Hatfield: *The Lichtenberg Reader* (1959), 15.

learned ignorance

fact, a central concern of their philosophizing to find and establish the limits of reason. Hume urged thinking men to "discover the proper province of human reason,"[3] implying that there were improper provinces. Kant rejected any notion of a fixed body of truth waiting to be known: philosophical thinking was at its best a reliable method of procedure, a compass for the wilderness. Voltaire gave this view of philosophy wide circulation with his philosophical tales. In *Micromégas*, Voltaire invented a giant from the planet Sirius who promises to give men—these "infinitely insignificant atoms"—the secrets of nature in a large volume of philosophy. When the Secretary of the Academy of Sciences opens the book, he finds nothing but blank pages. "Aha!" says the Secretary, "just as I expected."[4] And in *Memnon*, one of his most biting stories, Voltaire created a self-satisfied rationalist who conceives the foolish notions of being wholly wise and of establishing the supremacy of reason over passion. In his ludicrous quest, he loses an eye, his money, his property, and at last his presumptuousness. Memnon is the ideal representative of an age of reason, but he is an anti-Voltaire; he is the very type that the Enlightenment repudiated and that its critics later took as its embodiment. Wieland's novel *Agathon* reads like a German adaptation of *Memnon*—and of *Candide:* its hero learns worldly wisdom from a lovely hetaira, and abandons his vain rationalist philosophizing in favor of a moderate commonsensical sensuality. Cold rationalism, proud system making, Wieland seems to be saying, damages man on all levels, especially that of enjoyment.

Such lighthearted attacks on human pride were known among the philosophes as "philosophical modesty." Gibbon praised the quality of "modest and learned ignorance";[5] doubtless remembering Newton's famous saying, d'Alembert vividly described man's knowledge as a few disconnected islands in the vast ocean of the universe;[6] Wieland asked, with Pontius Pilate, What is Truth?— and replied that man saw a few glimmers in the dark of his

[3] *Enquiry Concerning Human Understanding*, in *Works*, IV, 8.
[4] *Œuvres*, XXI, 122.
[5] *Essai sur l'étude de la littérature*, in *Miscellaneous Works*, IV, 19.
[6] *Discours préliminaire de l'Encyclopédie*, in *Mélanges*, I, 81-2.

ignorance, nothing more: "Let man be modest!"[7] Most of the philosophes, in fact, liked to enliven their disquisitions on this theme by affectionate anecdotes about philosophers who had trumpeted their ignorance and disclaimed any sweeping knowledge of the universe. This sort of modesty went back to Plato's Socrates: in the *Theaetetus*, Socrates calls himself a midwife, skilled in bringing forth the children of others and recognizing their talents, but incapable of childbearing himself. Bacon and Locke brought this metaphor up to date and made it directly available to the Enlightenment. Bacon called himself a "bell-ringer which is first up to call others to church";[8] Locke described his *Essay Concerning Human Understanding* as merely a preface to philosophy, and himself as an "under-labourer in clearing the ground a little, and removing some of the rubbish that lies in the way to knowledge."[9]

Much of this talk, to be sure, was little more than a becoming pose. Voltaire did not really think that the pages of Nature's book are empty. He did think that useful knowledge is born from the concentration of inquiry. "Philosophy," he wrote, "does not explain everything."[1] Yet while it does not explain everything, other modes of inquiry explain nothing. Man is adrift on a sea of ignorance and uncertainty, and philosophy is the only seaworthy craft afloat. That is why the philosophes' modesty was expressed in the most confident of tones, and why there were those among them who preached it without practicing it. The ironic course of Holbach's reputation is an amusing illustration of this "modesty" that no one could recognize: Holbach's *Système de la nature* contains impassioned and sardonic exclamations against soaring claims to knowledge—"It is not given man to know everything;

---

[7] "Was Ist Wahrheit?" (1778), *Werke*, XXX, 192.
[8] Quoted by Hugh G. Dick: "Introduction," *Selected Writings of Francis Bacon* (1955), x.
[9] Shaftesbury, who had been Locke's pupil and always remained in his debt, turned this rhetoric on his old master: "As ill a builder as he is, and as little able to treat the home-points of philosophy, he is of admirable use against the rubbish of the schools in which most of us have been bred up." Shaftesbury to Stanhope, November 7, 1709. *Life, Unpublished Letters, and Philosophical Regimen*, 416.
[1] "Matter," *Philosophical Dictionary*, II, 376.

it is not given him to know his origins; it is not given him to penetrate to the essence of things or to go back to first principles."[2] But when Goethe read the book, he blamed its arrogance for turning him "against all philosophy, and especially metaphysics."[3] But at his best, even Holbach, the archmaterialist, conceded that there was much that man could never know. The philosophes, whether they were materialists or deists, were what we might call secular fideists. Like Christian fideists, they sought for the limits of reason, but their discoveries had opposite effects. The Christians translated man's invincible ignorance into the demand for unconditional obedience to God and into subjection to suprarational sources of information: revelation, mystical experience, or the tradition of the Church. The philosophes, on the other hand, while they might bring to the unknown some respect for its very vastness, treated it mainly as a warning against excessive pride and as a target for their derisive wit. The very titles of their books (as harmless today as they must have been offensive then) implicitly argue that it is precisely in the dim reaches of the unknown that crafty priests and clever princes have found their charms and enchanted the world. In 1691 the Dutch pastor Balthasar Bekker had attacked the widespread belief in the devil with his *De betooverte Wereld*—The Enchanted World, and five years later John Toland had published his first deist tract under the title *Christianity not Mysterious*. This tone echoes through the eighteenth century: Voltaire wrote a *philosophical* dictionary; Hume, a *natural* history of religion; Raynal, a *philosophical* history of European expansion in the Indies; Kant, an essay on religion *within the limits of reason alone;* Holbach, a whole *system of nature.* For all their philosophical modesty, the philosophes were confident that it was their calling to break the great spell.

IV

In proclaiming the omnipotence of criticism, the philosophes called, at the same time, for a disenchanted universe, an end to

---

[2] *Système de la nature*, I, 88.
[3] *Dichtung und Wahrheit*, in *Gedenkausgabe*, X, 538.

myth. Their program is hard to analyze precisely because it is so pervasive; it was the air the philosophes breathed, as indispensable and as invisible. The philosophes rarely troubled to articulate what was so natural to them, but since so much of it centers on the proud consciousness of incredulity, it appears most plainly in casual remarks in which a philosophe records what he will not believe. Thus Diderot writes in his *Pensées philosophiques:* "The less likely a fact, the more the testimony of history loses its weight. I should believe, without hesitation, a single honest man who announced that 'His Majesty has just won a complete victory over the allies'; but all Paris could assure me that a dead man had just been resurrected at Passy, and I would not believe a word of it."[4] In his "Essay on Miracles," which forms part of his *Enquiry Concerning Human Understanding,* David Hume takes the same position: Hume supposes that "all authors, in all languages" testify that there was a "total darkness over the whole earth for eight days" beginning on January 1, 1600. This must be conceded a most unlikely event, yet "our present philosophers, instead of doubting the fact, ought to receive it as certain, and ought to search for the causes whence it might be derived." Such an eclipse is within the reach of natural possibility; it should therefore be explained, and not explained away. But, Hume supposes further, what if all English historians should agree that on that same day Queen Elizabeth died, in public as befitted her rank; that she was buried, had lain buried for a month, and then had reappeared to govern her country for three more years. Should we credit such a report, even if delivered unanimously and by such respectable persons? Hume denies that we should: "I must confess that I should be surprized at the occurrence of so many odd circumstances, but should not have the least inclination to believe so miraculous an event." Most of the details—the queen's death, the proclamation of her successor—are credible enough, and the probity of the witnesses would not be in question. Still, Hume would reply, "that the knavery and folly of men are such common phenomena, that I should rather believe the most extraordinary events to arise from their concurrence, than admit of so signal a violation of the laws of nature."[5]

---

[4] *Œuvres,* I, 146.
[5] *Works,* IV, 106.

These two remarkable statements lay bare the presuppositions of the critical mind at work. They are declarations of disbelief which offer no proof; in fact, they need no proof, since they are the basis of all other proofs.[6] Neither Diderot nor Hume was a Pyrrhonist skeptic; both were empiricists, committed to weighing testimony and judging the truth of a proposition by the probability of the evidence. But Diderot is ready to question the report of a resurrection in the face of "all Paris," which presumably contains many trustworthy witnesses. Similarly, Hume is ready to pit his conviction that "so miraculous an event" as Queen Elizabeth's resurrection is impossible against "all the historians who treat of England," that is, historians on whom he has relied in most, if not all, other matters.

These assertions are not propositions: they cannot be disproved by any amount of evidence. If all France or all the world or a committee made up of Voltaire and d'Alembert reported a

---

[6] The naturalistic empiricism of the Enlightenment rests on what in logic is called "primitives," certain fundamental assumptions on which all other assertions depend. Empiricism which simply accepts evidence at face value often led in a contrary direction —to credulity. Witness this discussion, involving Samuel Johnson, not usually a credulous man: On his trip to the Hebrides with Boswell, the assembled company began to discuss witchcraft, and Mr. Crosbie "said he thought it the greatest blasphemy to suppose evil spirits counteracting the Deity, and raising storms, for instance, to destroy his creatures. JOHNSON. 'Why, Sir, if moral evil be consistent with the government of the Deity, why may not physical evil be also consistent with it? It is not more strange that there should be evil spirits than evil men; evil unembodied spirits than evil embodied spirits. And as to storms, we know there are such things, and it is no worse that evil spirits raise them than that they rise.' CROSBIE. 'But it is not credible that witches should have effected what they are said in stories to have done.' JOHNSON. 'Sir, I am not defending their credibility. I am only saying that your arguments are not good, and will not overturn the belief of witchcraft.' (Dr. Ferguson said to me aside, 'He is right.') 'And then, sir, you have all mankind, rude and civilized, agreeing in the belief of the agency of preternatural powers. You must take evidence; you must consider that wise and great men have condemned witches to die.' CROSBIE. 'But an Act of Parliament put an end to witchcraft.' JOHNSON. 'No, sir; witchcraft had ceased, and therefore an Act of Parliament was passed to prevent persecution for what was not witchcraft. Why it ceased, we cannot tell, as we cannot tell the reason of many other things.'" Boswell, *Journal of a Tour to the Hebrides*, 27–8.

resurrection at Passy, Diderot would remain incredulous: he would seek naturalistic reasons—a practical joke, a conspiracy, or perhaps his own madness—to explain so inexplicable an occurrence. Hume's position is the same: the world is orderly, subject to universal, irreversible laws. A miracle, as Hume defines it, is a violation of the laws of nature, and such a violation is by definition impossible. If a miracle seems to occur, it must be treated either as a mendacious report or as a natural event for which, at present, no scientific explanation is available. An eclipse that lasts a week is a strange event, but it should drive the philosopher neither to despair nor to a belief in miracles; it should impel him, instead, to "search for the causes whence it might be derived."

The philosophes, like Plato and Descartes before them, agreed that philosophizing begins in wonder. But the quality of their wonder was new. What Bacon had called idols had presented men with deceptive marvels, with seductive and dangerous mirages. A miracle, Voltaire wrote in the *Philosophical Dictionary*, originally meant "something admirable." Now if we take miracles to mean this, instead of those absurd tales which are the heart of religion, then the world is full of miracles. "The marvelous order of nature, the rotation of a hundred million globes around a million suns, the activity of light, the life of animals—these are perpetual miracles."[7] To be disenchanted is not to give way to jaded, supercilious skepticism, but to shift canons of proof and direction of worship. What is at work in the incredulity of the philosophes is not the shrinking of experience to the hard, the measurable, the prosaic, the surface of events; it is, on the contrary, an expansion of the natural. The disenchanted universe of the Enlightenment is a natural universe.

This naturalistic view of the world should not be equated with skepticism or atheism. These two modes of thought are the most extreme consequences to which the atrophy of mythical thinking can lead, and they dominated most of the philosophes in the second half of the eighteenth century, but the deists of the earlier generation were just as critical, just as disenchanted, as their radical successors. Seen from the outer end of the spectrum of disbelief and in its historical development, deism was in fact

---

[7] "Miracles," *Philosophical Dictionary*, II, 392.

a last compromise with religion. But it was not a compromise with mythopoeic thinking: the only "miracle" the deists were ready to concede was the marvelous orderliness of the universe with its unbreakable laws of nature. To devotees of revealed religion, miracles were irruptions of divine powers, the setting aside of ordinary proceedings; to the deists, the only miracle was the miracle not of irregularity but of regularity. The critical posture was not a specific doctrine but a general method of looking at the world.

Religion, to be sure, offered the most rewarding prospects for the exercise of the critical mentality. The higher criticism of the Bible, the widespread discussion of the origins of the gods in pagan religions (and, by implication, in Christianity) and even Lessing's Christianity of reason, which was (at least, to his mind) a philosophical faith reached by incessant questioning and rational inquiry—all these indicated the trophies which the critical mind might bring home from the battlefield of theology. Hume's dissertation, "The Natural History of Religion," which traces "the origin of religion in human nature," indicates that the claims of naturalism were unlimited. While Hume might shield himself by asserting that he was taking the truth of Christianity on faith, the tenor of his inquiry reveals his tough-minded conviction that religion is a cultural phenomenon like any other. Thus the philosophes chased the sacred from its privileged sanctuary and treated it as a fact—as a symptom in hysteria, a device of political management, a mark of illiteracy, or a stage in historical development.

But I cannot insist enough that to equate criticism with anticlericalism is to underestimate the Enlightenment. Criticism did its work everywhere. "Facts," Diderot wrote in the *Encyclopédie*, "may be distributed into three classes: the acts of divinity, the phenomena of nature, and the actions of men. The first belong to theology, the second to philosophy, and the last to history properly speaking. All are equally subject to criticism."[8] That

---

[8] "Fait," *Œuvres*, XV, 3. The objection has been raised, properly enough, that the philosophes did not criticize their own presuppositions as actively as they should have, and thus they remained enslaved to—or at least influenced by—remnants of mythical thinking. True. But at least their program, though imperfectly realized, was perfectly candid criticism, including self-criticism.

was precisely the point and it explains the philosophes' all-
pervasive curiosity, their insatiable thirst for clarity. It is at the
heart of Montesquieu's and Gibbon's analyses of the arcana of
government, of the deists' dissection of the priestcraft which had
converted the reasonable, plain religion of nature into a profitable
puzzle, of Rousseau's naturalistic account of the history of language, of Holbach's and Hume's psychological studies of religion,
and of the utilitarians' attacks on fictions. *All things are equally
subject to criticism;* to say this was to move confidently in a world
free—or rather, waiting to be freed—from enchantment.

V

The use of antiquity in shaping this bellicose naturalism was
twofold: ancient writers gave the philosophes models of analytical
penetration, and ancient life was a museum of striking examples.
As Shaftesbury wrote to a friend: the philosophy of men like
Cicero had been the enemy of "effeminacy and superstition," of
bigotry, affectation, bad habits, and belief in supernatural things:
"Here are rocks we often split upon, which the ancients (bold,
blind fellows) could sail through with all ease." Many of the
ancient philosophers were religious, but "their religion seldom
cost them their wits."[9] Clearly, there was much that moderns
could learn from such ancients.

Obviously, many antique rules of intellectual procedure were
largely rhetorical: educated Christians, too, liked to claim that
they were devoted to fact and opposed to superstition; they too
acknowledged no master but the truth. But it was only when
these pronouncements—the permanent clichés of philosophers,
religious and irreligious alike—were embedded in a disenchanted
world view and realized in the persistent, unsparing use of intellect that they achieved the status of usable truths for the
Enlightenment. Lucian could describe his "ideal historian" as
"fearless, incorruptible, independent, a believer in frankness and
veracity; one that will call a spade a spade, make no concession

---

[9] Shaftesbury to Lord Somers (October 20, 1705). *Life, Unpublished Letters, and Philosophical Regimen,* 337–9.

to likes and dislikes, nor spare any man for pity or respect or
propriety; an impartial judge, kind to all, but too kind to none; a
literary cosmopolite with neither suzerain nor king, never heeding
what this or that man may think, but setting down the thing that
befell."[1] What made these admirable rules meaningful canons of
conduct rather than empty boasts was the rest of Lucian's work,
work that was indeed fearless, incorruptible, and independent. In
their more pacific, generous moods, the philosophes conceded to
the pious man his share of honesty, but they considered him incapable of pursuing an inquiry to its end—the man caught in
myth must make the myth, not the truth, his final value. It was
reserved to men living in a climate of criticism to turn well-
meaning precepts into living principles, which is another way of
saying that to the philosophes only a pagan could be a genuine
philosopher.

Attractive as sounding generalities were to the Enlightenment, the antique temper perpetuated itself largely through specific applications; and it was these applications, in all their specificity, that reappear in eighteenth-century writings, often without
significant modification. Diderot pronounced Seneca the philosopher who had "struck the most violent blows at the two handles
by which the robust man and the adroit priest seize the weak to
lead them by the nose,"[2] and, to judge from some of his own
writings, he was content to strike the same blows in precisely the
same manner. When Diderot links tyranny with superstition,
uneasiness with credulity, the fear of death with submissiveness
to authority, he is merely paraphrasing his Seneca. In the same
fashion, Gibbon singled out Cicero and Lucian for "exposing the
idle tales of the poets and the incoherent traditions of antiquity";
Cicero "condescended to employ the arms of reason and eloquence," while Lucian used satire, "a much more adequate as
well as more efficacious weapon."[3] Then, in the *Decline and
Fall*, Gibbon takes Cicero's dignified republicanism as the yard-

---

[1] "The Way to Write History," *The Works of Lucian of Samo-
sata*, tr. H. W. and F. G. Fowler, 4 vols. (1905), II, 129.
[2] *Essai sur les règnes de Claude et de Néron*, in *Œuvres*, III, 189.
Diderot's image, which for some reason he thought "energetic,"
is borrowed from the Stoic Arrian.
[3] *Decline and Fall of the Roman Empire*, I, 30.

stick against which even the most glorious decades of the Empire fall short, and Lucian's wry, disrespectful mockery as the paradigm for many of his own thrusts at the human comedy.

David Hume's reliance on ancient criticism is just as extensive. In his "Natural History of Religion," he adopts Strabo's suggestion that superstition is strongest among the weak and timid, and hence most tenacious among women; he agrees with Longinus that anthropomorphic conceptions of deities are really a kind of atheism; he highly praises and cheerfully imitates "the learned, philosophical VARRO," who did not "deliver any thing beyond probabilities and appearances" in matters of religion;[4] he shares Lucian's amusement at the "most ridiculous fables" which the populace insisted on believing; and he concludes with a celebrated paragraph that reads like a mixture of Cicero's skepticism, Lucian's irony, and Lucretius's passion. "The whole is a riddle, an ænigma, an inexplicable mystery. Doubt, uncertainty, suspence of judgment appear the only result of our most accurate scrutiny, concerning this subject. But such is the frailty of human reason, and such the irresistible contagion of opinion, that even this deliberate doubt could scarcely be upheld; did we not enlarge our view, and opposing one species of superstition to another, set them a quarreling; while we ourselves, during their fury and contention, happily make our escape into the calm, though obscure regions of philosophy."[5]

A favorite companion in this escape was Plutarch's little essay *On Superstition*. Like his other moral writings, *On Superstition* has little claim to originality, and in many respects it reflects Cicero's treatment of the same question in *De divinatione*. Its chief merit is clarity and economy: Bayle quoted it, with only minor disagreements, in his *Pensées diverses sur la comète*, and through Bayle, the tract passed into the main stream of Enlightenment speculation. Its argument, briefly, is that superstition is a far greater calamity than atheism. Both are the fruit of ignorance, but atheism is merely reason deceived, while superstition is a passion which arises from false reasoning and gives birth to fear. Thus superstition adds cowardice to stupidity: it paralyzes the

---

4 *Works*, IV, 346.
5 Ibid., 363.

faithful; far from securing peace of mind, it creates perpetual anxiety. The man who is "afraid of the gods, is afraid of everything—the sea, the air, the sky, darkness, light, a call, silence, a dream." He is the most abject of creatures, enslaved in his very sleep, where he is victimized by an unending parade of nocturnal spectres, by "phantoms, monsters, apparitions, and tortures of all kinds." Plutarch finds most religions infested with this scourge: Judaism and Eastern idolatries are among the worst, but Greeks and Romans also suffer from superstition in one or another of its myriad manifestations. "The appointed end of life for all men is death; but for superstition not even death is the limit—it leaps over the boundaries of life into the other side, making fear longer-lived than life, and tacking on to death the imagination of never-ending troubles."[6] Bad as it is, atheism is better than this— it only harms a single person, the unbeliever himself, and does not insult divine dignity with ridiculous tales. In his portrait of the superstitious man—miserable everywhere, even in sleep, tormented by dreams and terrified by the thought of hell after death —David Hume quotes his beloved Tully, but in the background the voice of Plutarch is heard.

Plutarch's religious sociology reflects the political practice of antiquity, a practice that placed superstition into the service of mass manipulation. The philosophes could study this practice with so much care and sympathy precisely because they, like ancient politicians, were disenchanted. After all (it is worth remembering) the word *disenchantment* is endowed with a happy ambiguity. It suggests both freedom from superstition and a certain disappointment with the ways of the world. In experience if not in logic, these two meanings are often linked: both the philosophes and their classical masters season their analyses of religion and politics with touches of bitterness and cynicism. The irony of Hume, of Gibbon and Voltaire, is celebrated, and it, too, has its antique roots. It was, after all, Juvenal who coined the famous phrase *panem et circenses*[7] to stigmatize the cravings of the Roman populace and the bait held out to them by their masters; and it

---

[6] "On Superstition," in *Plutarch's Morals: Theosophical Essays,* tr. C. W. King (1908), 258–75.

[7] *Duas tantum res anxius optat / panem et circenses* ("Only two things it wants eagerly: bread and circuses"). *Satires,* X, 80–1.

was Ovid who recommended religious belief on grounds of convenience:

Expedit esse deos; et, ut expedit, esse putemus.

"It is convenient that there should be gods; and, since it is convenient, let us think they exist".[8] Polybius, Cicero, Sextus Empiricus, Varro, all agreed that false myths were socially useful. When Gibbon described Augustus as "sensible that mankind is governed by names,"[9] he was merely paraphrasing this antique cynicism.

Plutarch, the most curious and most candid of men, was ready to check his curiosity and rein in his candor for the sake of social stability. He was fascinated by the spectacle of religious variety, enjoyed comparing cults and analyzing rituals, but he took care to look at religion neither too deeply nor too publicly. He rejects as dangerous to public order Stoic theories that the gods are allegories, and dismisses as beneath notice Epicurean theories that the gods are the product of fear. It is "a very big and risky matter" to discuss religion: "When you question the opinion we hold about the gods, and ask reason and demonstration for everything, you are discussing what should not be discussed at all." The "ancient and ancestral faith is enough," a "common home and an established foundation for all piety." If its "stable and traditional character is shaken and disturbed in one point, it will be undermined and no one will trust it." Once men lay hands on sacred things and devise sophisms on each practice, "nothing will be free from quibble and cross-examination." To interpret Aphrodite as a personification of desire, Hermes as reason, the Muses as crafts, and Athene as thought is to open the door to the "abyss of atheism."[1]

The philosophes' historical writings reflect their enduring concern with these rationalizations. In his essay *Sur la politique des Romains dans la religion*, Montesquieu noted that from the very beginning the rulers of Rome had employed rational devices to govern irrational masses. They had established religion neither

---

[8] *Ars amatoria*, I, 637.
[9] *Decline and Fall of the Roman Empire*, I, 71.
[1] Quoted in T. R. Glover, *The Conflict of Religions in the Early Roman Empire* (edn. 1960), 76.

Cicero

from fear nor from piety, but simply because all societies need religion. It was the recognition of this need, Montesquieu observed, that made Roman statesmen unique: "They made a religion for the state while others had made the state for religion."[2] In his survey of Roman legislators, which closely follows ancient authorities, Montesquieu discovered a consistent policy from Romulus and Numa down to Augustus: ruling princes and ruling groups took advantage of popular credulity by perpetuating cults and manipulating myths, and attracted foreign subjects by tolerating their gods and assimilating their practices. One group of senators prudently destroyed a newly discovered document which would have revealed the gap between prevailing religious practices and the prescriptions attributed to the semi-divine founders of the city; another group of senators pressed for worldly policies by lending them the prestige of divine pronouncements. *Sur la politique des Romains* was an early work, but *L'Esprit des lois,* Montesquieu's masterpiece, shows his continuing concern with these ancient devices and his lifelong conviction that classical politics was the product of a disenchanted world view: men who invent gods no longer believe in them.

Cicero, too, disclosed by his conduct the gulf between a few philosophers and the mass of believers, between private disenchantment and public observance. He was a skeptic, yet precisely while he was writing against augury, he retained his membership on the Board of Augurs of the Republic. The very book that demonstrates the absurdity of divination presents Cicero's moving plea for time-honored religious practices: "It is wise and reasonable for us to preserve the institutions of our forefathers by retaining their rites and ceremonies."[3] This was a conscious compromise: Cicero was urging Romans to stand fast against new cults and oriental superstitions, but Cicero did not see, or did not say, that his policy sanctified practices which he scorned privately as vulgar and absurd. Whether a superstition was admissible or pernicious seemed to depend on whether it was domestic or foreign, old or new.

The philosophes reported this Aesopianism faithfully. Diderot

---

[2] *Œuvres,* III, 38.
[3] *De divinatione,* II, 77.

suggested that Cicero was irreligious, but then, in his time, "the people hardly read at all; they listened to the speeches of their orators, and these speeches were always filled with piety toward the gods; but they did not know what the orator thought and wrote about it in his study."[4] David Hume filled Diderot's brief observation with specific detail: "If there ever was a nation or a time in which the public religion lost all authority over mankind, we might expect, that infidelity in Rome, during the Ciceronian age, would openly have erected its throne, and that Cicero himself, in every speech and action, would have been its most declared abettor. But it appears, that, whatever sceptical liberties that great man might take, in his writings or in philosophical conversation, he yet avoided, in the common conduct of life, the imputation of deism and profaneness. Even in his own family, and to his wife Terentia, whom he highly trusted, he was willing to appear a devout religionist; and there remains a letter, addressed to her, in which he seriously desires her to offer sacrifices to Apollo and Aesculapius, in gratitude for the recovery of health."[5]

It was only natural that Gibbon, the most learned of the philosophic historians, would explore this political manipulation with the keenest delight and the most profitable results. Gibbon's Rome is pervaded with religious faith, and his *Decline and Fall*, rightly enough, treats the management of politics as practically synonymous with the management of religion: the rulers of Rome assign religion a leading part in the political comedy in order to keep the plebs docile and suitably uncurious about their activities. The philosophers were willing actors in this charade: "Both the interests of the priests and the credulity of the people were sufficiently respected. In their writings and conversation the philosophers of antiquity asserted the independent dignity of reason; but they resigned their actions to the commands of law and of custom. Viewing with a smile of pity and indulgence the various errors of the vulgar, they diligently practiced the ceremonies of their fathers, devoutly frequented the temples of the gods; and sometimes condescending to act a part on the theatre of superstition, they concealed the sentiments of an atheist under the

---

[4] "Aius-Locutius," *Encyclopédie*, in *Œuvres*, XIII, 268.
[5] "The Natural History of Religion," *Works*, IV, 347.

sacerdotal robes."[6] In the early Empire, Gibbon writes in a celebrated passage, "The policy of the emperors and the senate, as far as it concerned religion, was happily seconded by the reflections of the enlightened, and by the habits of the superstitious, part of their subjects. The various modes of worship which prevailed in the Roman world were all considered by the people as equally true, by the philosopher as equally false, and by the magistrate as equally useful."[7]

While the stately cadence, the rolling periods and balanced phrases of these passages are Ciceronian, their irony, the whole intellectual style, is a legacy from Tacitus. Gibbon was proud of his independence, steeped in the corpus of ancient literature and the researches of his contemporaries, discriminating in his use of authorities, and malicious about his forerunners; yet with all this Gibbon quotes Tacitus often, without dissent, and models himself after him.

The reason for this affinity is at once very obvious and very deep. David Hume, as I have said, called Tacitus a "penetrating genius," and that single adjective defines Gibbon's dependence on him. Tacitus was a psychologist who sought to understand the irrational by rational means; his theme is human nature in politics, and his universe is secular. Whatever the distant, indistinct rumblings of the gods in his work, the occasional obeisances to fate, his history is essentially the clash of men against men, motives against motives. And the political process, which is existence in its most intense form, is the collision of force and fraud, the arena of persuasion, enthusiasm, and violence, of the attempts by charismatic, clever, or unscrupulous leaders to control and exploit multitudes afraid of ghosts and greedy for food, shelter, and entertainment. Tacitus, the historian, not content with recording events, seeks to understand the conflicts that create them.

Tacitus, then, is, above all, *penetrating*. All the cutting, epigrammatic edge, all his psychological finesse, all his tight-lipped spleen are concentrated on a single task: to get behind surfaces; to strike through the mask of fair appearance and grasp the hidden

---

[6] *Decline and Fall of the Roman Empire*, I, 30–1.
[7] Ibid., I, 28.

reality. Gibbon, who was the most conscious of stylists, and who had laid it down in his *Autobiography* that "the style of an author should be the image of his mind,"[8] understood that Tacitus's style was more than a decoration; it was an expression and servant of his self-imposed, grave, and exalted calling. Tacitus's epigrams are like the thrust of a knife, clean and wounding; they imitate, in their very unadorned economy, the terrible times they describe. Tacitus's antitheses are never pretty; they are images which contrast appearance and reality with almost brutal concision, and always at the expense of reality. The Romans are elegant in the forum and ruthless in the field: *Solitudinem faciunt, pacem appellant*—"They make a desert, and call it peace."[9] The Britons mistake the trappings for the essence of culture: *Humanitas vocabantur, cum pars servitutis esset*—"They called it civilization, when it was part of servitude."[1] Such contradictions persist because men insist on giving fine justifications for ugly deeds, and are driven by irrational inner forces. *Proprium humani ingenii est odisse quem laeseris*—"It is characteristic of human nature to hate the man you have wronged."[2] Epigrams like these, which dot every page of Tacitus's writings, may be cynical, but they are not platitudes. They are the quintessence of disillusionment.

Gibbon's mood is lighter than this, and hence his style is more florid, more cheerful.[3] But Gibbon, too, lives in a disenchanted universe, and he too sees it as his task to penetrate beyond appearance. Hence he can borrow from Tacitus with complete freedom. His sly habit of coupling motives—"conviction or fear," "piety or prudence,"—which conveys the ambiguity of action and permits a charitable, while suggesting a cynical, appraisal of human behavior, is pure Tacitus. So is his survey of

---

[8] *Autobiography*, 173.
[9] *Agricola*, 30.
[1] Ibid., 21.
[2] Ibid., 42.
[3] As Sir Ronald Syme has shown, by the time Tacitus came to write his masterpiece, the *Annales,* he had eliminated most of his adjectives; Gibbon, in contrast, always reveled in them: Gibbon's Augustus is always "artful"—artful, with its nice ambiguity, its simultaneous suggestion of cultivation and fraud, is Gibbon's favorite adjective.

Augustus's position at his accession: the dictator's ambition; his military strength enhanced by the weakness of the constitution; the humiliation of the aristocracy coupled with the decay of old families and the decline of the senate; the war-weariness of the provinces; the readiness of the mob to be bribed by bread and circuses and the upper classes, by peace and quiet; the elimination of republicans by the proscriptions—the whole skillful, complex portrait is a slightly rearranged quotation from the *Annales*.[4]

All this explains why Gibbon can refer to Tacitus as "the first of the historians who applied the science of philosophy to the study of facts," perhaps the only ancient historian who was a true "philosophical historian"[5]—Tacitus, who treated philosophers with derision and who, to judge from his infrequent, inconsistent philosophical asides, was himself a hopeless amateur in philosophy. With nice precision, Gibbon here captures the real meaning of what the philosophes meant by philosophy: not so much a technical discipline as a stance toward the world, a critical freedom. Gibbon's many hidden quotations from Tacitus do not in themselves establish an intimate connection; they are the tribute a classicist pays to his classic. *The Decline and Fall of the Roman Empire* is an imitation in a larger sense than this: Tacitus is Gibbon's model not merely because Gibbon found in him valuable information, striking phrases, or imposing moral lessons. Far more than that, Gibbon found in Tacitus—as Diderot found in Seneca, Wieland in Lucian, and Hume in Cicero—his own mode of thinking; and in a very real sense, an aspect of himself. Men need not be twins to be brothers.

---

[4] This passage (*Decline and Fall of the Roman Empire*, I, 59–60) should be read side by side with Tacitus' *Annales*, I, 1–2: the dependence of the first on the second is striking.
[5] *Decline and Fall of the Roman Empire*, I, 213; *Essai sur l'étude de la littérature*, in *Miscellaneous Works*, IV, 66.

2. THE HOSPITABLE PANTHEON

I

R ECEPTIVE TO ANTIQUE WINDS of doctrine as they blew across
the centuries, yet resistant to any single school, the philosophes found eclecticism—the school that denied being a school
—the mode of thinking that gave their informality and their
desire for action the most generous room for play. They liked to
borrow from Eclectics above all, and they chose their models
eclectically: this, for the Enlightenment, was the triumph of
criticism over theory, the symbol of its intellectual independence.

Among all the aspects of the Enlightenment's eclecticism,
this is the most remarkable: it was not embarrassed but exultant;
it was exhibited, not as a last resort or as a declaration of intellectual bankruptcy, but as an appropriate, in fact the most
appropriate, style of philosophizing. Diderot expressed the convictions of all the philosophes when he denied that an eclectic is
merely a lazy syncretist who collects bits of philosophy from a
convenient assortment of ideas. Rather, the Eclectic preaches and
practices autonomy: he "is a philosopher who tramples underfoot
prejudices, tradition, antiquity, universal assent, authority, in a
word, everything that overawes the mass of minds, who dares to
think for himself, to go back to the clearest general principles,
examine them, discuss them, admit nothing save on the testimony
of his experience and his reasoning."[6] Here, in the guise of an
appreciative article on the Eclectics in the Roman Empire, is a
virtual self-portrait of the eighteenth-century philosophe.

Ironically, this declaration of philosophical independence was
largely a plagiarism: the article "Eclecticism" was freely adapted
from Brucker's history of philosophy. But since Diderot took
only what suited him, and added his characteristic touches, his
very borrowing becomes an exhibit in eclectic procedure. "From
all the philosophies he has analyzed . . ." Diderot writes, almost as

---

[6] "Éclectisme," Œuvres, XIV, 304.

though to disarm criticism of his own proceedings, the eclectic "makes a philosophy for himself, individual and personal, one that is his own." That is why modern eclectics, critical of all systems, are critical even of their intellectual ancestors.[7]

The philosophes agreed that the ancient philosophers, even at their best, had showed the way to the promised land without entering it themselves. "Consider," David Hume wrote,

> the blind submission of the ancient philosophers to the several masters in each school, and you will be convinced, that little good could be expected from a hundred centuries of such a servile philosophy. Even the Eclectics, who arose about the age of Augustus, notwithstanding their professing to chuse freely what pleased them from every different sect, were yet, in the main, as slavish and dependent as any of their brethren, since they sought for truth not in nature, but in the several schools, where they supposed they must necessarily be found, though not united in a body, yet dispersed in parts.[8]

The very "fall" of ancient systems during the "revival of learning" had taught modern philosophers the value of independence. To seek truth, not in nature, but in an antiquity of their own, as the Eclectics had done, violated Hume's sense of proper philosophic procedure as, of course, it violated that of the other philosophes.

Hume's strictures are far too sweeping; they even misrepresent his own manner of reading the ancients. As we well know, neither Hume nor any of the other philosophes learned from antiquity only what to avoid: his words are the words of an apt and ungrateful pupil. When it came to individual favorites,

---

[7] Ibid. Brucker himself distinguishes between the original "Alexandrian" school and their modern counterparts. The modern Eclectic, he suggests, rises above all prejudices, scrutinizes all systems, obeys rational principles, and listens to experience alone. Significantly, Brucker's list of notable modern Eclectics is itself an eclectic compilation: it includes such disparate names as Bruno, Bacon, Hobbes, and Leibniz, philosophers who had little in common save aversion to the system-making of the late Scholastics.

[8] "Of the Rise and Progress of the Arts and Sciences," *Works*, IV, 184.

Cicero

Hume, like the others, was inclined to discover a philosophical vigor denied to what he liked to call the "sects."

The most honored, and the most quoted, among the Eclectic company was, inevitably, Cicero. Cicero's dialogues allowed the philosophes to treat ancient doctrines as ideal types, sharply delineated, and to pit these types against each other in free and candid combat. "We love to read the books of the ancients," Montesquieu noted, "to see the prejudices of others."[9] The road to autonomy was lit by these debates, for the harsh light that the criticisms of each school cast upon the others, tested the strength and exposed the weaknesses of all. Seneca, too, was admired for rising above sectarian loyalties to philosophical autonomy. Diderot observed that while Seneca "valued the Stoic rigorists highly," he was himself only a "modified Stoic, and perhaps even an eclectic"; and, consequently, Diderot energetically rejected La Mettrie's description of Seneca as a rigid sectarian, with "all the asperities of Stoicism," as simply false.[1] Horace also was drawn into this select circle, although the philosophes treated him, properly enough, as an eclectic by instinct rather than by reflection. Much of Horace's influence on the eighteenth century was superficial: his poems were exploited as a fertile village commons; they were grazed freely, thoughtlessly, by everyone. His *curiosa felicitas*—his thoughtful felicity—had been praised as early as the first century, by Petronius, and his apt, terse sayings became the bromides of educated men. That is why Swift sardonically advised poets in 1733, to

> Get scraps of Horace from your friends,
> And have them at your fingers' ends.

But this was an aspect of Horace's legacy which the best-informed among the philosophes recognized and regretted: Diderot, whose knowledge of Horace was unsurpassed, prized him as "the most sensible and delicate author of antiquity"[2] and bitterly resented

---

[9] *Pensées*, in *Œuvres*, II, 399.
[1] *Essai sur les règnes de Claude et de Néron*, in *Œuvres*, III, 28, 217.
[2] Diderot to Sophie Volland (August 22, 1762). *Correspondance*, IV, 115.

those of his contemporaries who mouthed the famous phrase *ut pictura poesis* without knowing a single other line from Horace.[3] But after all it was hardly Horace's fault that his poetry had been despoiled to furnish copybook maxims for the trivial moralizing of the eighteenth century. And in fact, to the philosophes, Horace meant more than this: he was a master in the art of living; he was the urbane advocate of moderation, free alike from doctrine and fanaticism, a free spirit who took from the schools what he needed and tested his reading by his experience. He had described himself as "a hog from Epicurus' herd," but he was enough of a Stoic to detach himself from slavish dependence even on Epicurus. Being everyone's disciple, he was no one's; living in the interstices of doctrine, he achieved an ideal individuality that moved the philosophes to imitate not merely his writings, but his style of life as well.

II

It is appropriate that the Eclectics' appeal to experience should itself be the fruit of experience. Their teaching gave philosophical formulation to political imperatives; it systematized the relativism and tolerance essential to the management of the enormous empires founded in the Hellenistic age and after.

Relativism, Eclecticism, and toleration are so intimately related that they cannot be strictly separated even in thought. Relativism is a way of looking at the world, the recognition that no single set of convictions has absolute validity; Eclecticism is the philosophical method consequent on relativism—since no system has the whole truth, and most systems have some truth, discriminating selection among systems is the only valid procedure. Toleration, finally, is the political counterpart of this world view and this method: it is a policy for a large and varied society.

The ancients had experienced this sort of society as early as Alexander. The Macedonian triumph over the Greek city-states

---

[3] *Pensées détachées sur la peinture* (c. 1776–81), in *Œuvres esthétiques*, 828.

was a forceful, unanswerable critique of political parochialism, and Alexander's vastly ambitious project to marry East and West (literally and figuratively), partially realized by his succession states, envisaged peaceful rule over a diversified population. Aristotelian distinctions between natural masters and natural slaves could have been maintained only by a totalitarian regime far beyond the technical means, and wholly alien to the basic convictions, of ancient statesmen. Instead, the creation of empires brought in its train the cosmopolitan conception of man as such, equal, in fact identical, in essential nature and different only in the accidents of wealth, looks, or education. The Hellenistic states, and later the Roman Empire, destroyed traditional loyalties and social structures; they encouraged the migration of administrators and professors, gave opportunities to freed slaves, and evolved an antique version of what came to be known in modern times as the career open to talents, a doctrine at once the result, and the cause, of a relativist cast of mind. Literary men preached cosmopolitanism in two languages, and their very origins underscored the process of cultural fusion: Seneca, Quintilian, and Martial came from Spain; Cicero, Vergil, Livy, Horace, and Ovid, though all Italians, were all provincials; Apuleius was an African; Plutarch, a Greek; and Lucian, a Syrian. In such a cultural community, serious literature and popular fables traveled widely and strengthened the sense of uniformity by calling forth frequent imitations; philosophers exchanged ideas and rubbed off doctrinaire corners.

Even school philosophies officially hostile to eclecticism grew eclectic in this atmosphere. The long and somewhat devious history of Stoicism demonstrates the survival value of adaptability, the profits that can accrue to a sect ready to absorb new ideas. The founders of Stoicism prepared the ground for survival with their radical cosmopolitanism: they taught that all men are brothers, members of the great city, bound together by their possession of the spark that is part of divine reason. Diogenes the Cynic, Diderot's ideal, seems to have been the first to claim to be a citizen of the world—*cosmopolites*—and his followers Crates and Zeno converted this remark into dogma. At the same time, the early Stoics affronted many of their thoughtful listeners with their ethical rigidity, their demand that the wise man detach himself from public business, their doctrinaire theory of knowl-

Cicero

edge, their elaborate metaphysical system, and their mania for playing with etymologies and definitions. To these Stoics, all parts of the doctrine belonged together and explained one another, but many sympathizers found it possible to embrace the morals without accepting the theology or the logic, and this too helped Stoicism to survive.

The eclectic possibilities of Stoicism were exploited early, by Panaetius of Rhodes and his pupil Posidonius, who taught Cicero, and through Cicero, all of Europe. Posidonius retained the old Stoic teaching of the cosmos animated by a living force, governed by reason, and united in a rational order, but he stressed, far more than the early Stoics, man's duty to his community, the unity of ethics and politics, and the identity of theory and practice. Here was a philosophy that the Romans, as soldiers and administrators, could appreciate. It allowed politicians like Cicero and worldly poets like Horace to read Stoic writings with sympathy. What Stoicism lost in rigor, with its move to Rome, it gained in influence.

With the Stoicism of the Empire, with Seneca, Epictetus, and Marcus Aurelius, the reorientation toward practical ethics was completed: man must play his part as best he can; emperor or slave can still act well in his place; he must live, suffer, and die bravely; true freedom lies in discipline, the recognition of what is beyond our reach, and indifference to evils that we cannot avert. But this freedom from passion is accompanied by devotion to work, brotherhood, and above all, to self-respect. In late Stoicism, "Live according to nature," a favorite precept, came to be interpreted as a prescription for dignity, political service, egalitarianism, and a total independence which implies man's right to suicide.

In this fashion, Roman Stoicism established pacific relations with the Epicureans, and both collaborated with the Academics. Doctrine gave way to experience, and ambitious constructions faced the smiles of urbane skeptics. As Condorcet recognized, "The philosophy that claimed to elevate itself above nature, and the one that wanted only to obey it; the morality that recognized no good other than virtue, and the one that placed happiness in pleasure, led to the same practical consequences, even though they started from such contrary principles and used such opposite language."[4]

This eclecticism in philosophy was accompanied by syncretism in religion; for many educated people, in fact, the two were the same—a way of seeking truth by an appreciative study of divergent behavior and beliefs. It was easy to believe, as Plutarch did, that the most diverse mysteries were merely different versions of a single worship; or as the Stoics did, that tales of the gods told in different cultures were all stories of real heroes converted into deities. It was easy to arrive at such conclusions because ancient religions had no theology, required not beliefs but ritual acts, and were not evangelical. They had little organization; even cults with priestly castes, like the cults of Persia and Babylon, were tolerant of unbelievers. Worship was by no means casual, but it was subsumed under politics: Rousseau's idea that a community should exact a civil profession of faith as proof of loyal citizenship had ancient roots. Even the mystery religions, which imposed rigorous tests, conducted secret initiations, and transformed the initiate into a new man, had little imperialist zeal. The exclusiveness of the ancient Jews struck nearly all of their neighbors as eccentric and offensive—a devotee of the cult of Isis, or Mithras, might sneer at the ignorance of the outsider, but it would not occur to him to portray his own god as a jealous father, or to condemn the worship of other gods as idolatry or blasphemy.

As a consequence, ancient religious policy was tolerant, not from any philosophical conception of human brotherhood, which was preached by a few thinkers only, but rather because religion had a circumscribed role to play. It seemed logical that each nation or city or family should have its own gods who governed their own territory. When soldiers or settlers moved from one culture to another, they quite naturally worshipped the gods and used the liturgical forms of their new country without any sense of betraying their old loyalties. The opposite current, the importation of foreign gods, was less obvious, but with constant shifts of power in the Mediterranean region it became almost as

---

[4] *Esquisse*, in *Œuvres*, VI, 91–2.

casual. It was likely that strong and imaginative nations would impose their deities on weaker neighbors, but the imposition was almost always by persuasion. Missionary activity was practically unknown.

Voltaire described this attitude in words that recent scholarship has done nothing to supersede. "The Greeks recognized the gods of the Egyptians: I don't say the bull Apis or the dog Anubis, but Ammon and the twelve great gods. The Romans worshipped all the gods of the Greeks." And indeed, Roman receptivity was proverbial: it was the practice of the Romans to adopt the gods of other nations by law and thus to protect them. "This association of all the divinities of the world, this species of divine hospitality, was the international law of all antiquity." Toleration was not automatic: the authorities had to be satisfied that a foreign cult would not subvert public order before they placed it among the authorized religions. But since most were harmless and ancient religions were rites without dogmas, "there were no wars of religion."[5]

The educated Roman of Caesar's time was tolerant partly because he was a worldling who scoffed at religions and retained a few private superstitions of his own, partly because he was animated by a cosmopolitan curiosity—he was likely to be a collector of new worships and curious practices, seeking either for their underlying similarity or, in contrast, glorying in their colorful variety. His urbanity was supported by the separation between religion and philosophy: cult embodied political loyalties and family traditions, philosophy answered an educated man's questions about right conduct and the nature of the universe.

It was only to be expected that the policy of toleration and the associated idea of cultural relativism should have their opponents. The strains of social change and the swamping of old faiths brought protests from conservatives fearful of losing the world they had known. Juvenal's famous diatribe against Eastern immigrants, which conceals anxiety beneath its contempt, sounds like the last cry of aristocratic parochialism against a leveling cosmopolitanism:

---

[5] *Essai sur les mœurs*, I, 15, 182.

Fellow citizens, I cannot bear a Greek Rome. And yet
What part of our slum dwellers are Achaian?
Syrian Orontes flowed into the Tiber long ago,
Bringing its lingo and habits along.

Fortunately for the philosophes, there was abundant material in antiquity more generous, more relativistic, in a word, more tolerant, than this—much that they could quote for their own purposes.

III

The mixed motives that mark so much of the philosophes' historical research also mark their treatment of antique tolerance. It was useful in their prosecution of Christianity, but it also validated their affection. Its use was the use of all relativist techniques: like travel, it gave perspective on contemporary and familiar institutions. Voltaire properly grouped these devices together when he recommended that men discard their prejudices while "reading ancient authors, or traveling among faraway nations."[6] A critic who stays at home may note symptoms; the critic who travels, whether in reality or through books, may go to the roots of social ills at home from the distance of foreign ways. Montesquieu making cultivated Persians criticize French institutions, Diderot speaking through an idealized Tahitian who radically disapproves of Western sexual repressions, Voltaire assailing French bigotry by comparing it unfavorably to Chinese toleration, are all setting up cross-cultural dialogues in which primitive, or at least non-European, cultures pointed the way to a more rational civilization at home.

To study antiquity was to travel in time, to discover still another culture superior to Christian culture. Voltaire's chapters on ancient religion in his *Essai sur les mœurs* and in his *Dictionnaire philosophique* were written with a malicious glance at his own country. "The Romans permitted all cults, even that of the Jews, even that of the Egyptians, although they had so much

_____

[6] "Of Ezekiel," *Philosophical Dictionary*, I, 265.

contempt for both. Why did Rome tolerate these cults? Because neither the Egyptians nor even the Jews tried to exterminate the ancient religion of the Empire; they didn't cross land and sea to make proselytes, but thought only of making money."[7] Montesquieu, too, cited antique tolerance as a model for all posterity: "The spirit of toleration and kindness," he wrote in his essay on the *Politique des Romains*, "reigned in the pagan world."[8] And David Hume came to the startling and sardonic conclusion that polytheism, for all its vulgar absurdities, was by nature tolerant, while monotheism, with all its sublimity, gave rise to rancor and religious fury. It thus became possible to argue— and the philosophes did not hesitate to argue it—that pagan philosophers and statesmen had been tolerant, whether from conviction or policy, while Christians had been intolerant both from conviction and policy. The Roman Pantheon had been a hospitable Pantheon.

Addressing their propaganda to a largely Christian audience, the philosophes enjoyed quoting the founders of Christianity, including Christ himself, in support of their position. Diderot called the intolerant man not merely a bad citizen but a bad Christian as well; he argued that Jesus, Paul, Origen and other Church Fathers had preached peace, not a sword, and had taught pious Christians to win over their erring brothers by persuasion, not constraint. Voltaire took the same unexceptionable line in his polemics. But such adroit posturing barely concealed the philosophes' conviction that Christianity was the worst of fanaticisms. Writing to Voltaire in 1762, Diderot asked rhetorically, "Isn't this mania for granting probity only to the members of your own sect peculiar to Christianity?"[9] Voltaire knew the answer. The Church Fathers, he wrote, thought "that the whole world should be Christian. They were therefore necessarily the enemies of the whole world, until it was converted."[1] In one of his rare kindly observations about the Jews, prompted not by kind feelings toward the Jews but by hostility to the Christians,

---

[7] "Tolerance," ibid., II, 482.
[8] *Œuvres*, III, 45.
[9] September 29, 1762. *Correspondance*, IV, 177.
[1] "Tolerance," *Philosophical Dictionary*, II, 483.

Voltaire notes that "the Jews didn't want the statue of Jupiter in Jerusalem; but the Christians didn't want it in the Capitol."[2]

This is the kind of tendentious history we have come to expect from the philosophes: a mixture of malice and accuracy. Their distinction between relativist paganism and absolutist Christianity, which is central to their historical vision, had not merely value as propaganda but some merit as history too. Christianity gathered up functions that had long been separated: it offered to gratify curiosity about the nature of the world and history of the nations, to relieve moral incertitude by prescribing conduct, to satisfy men's need for community, and to fulfill the longing for some control over destiny by promising salvation. Mystery cult, social religion, ethical system, historical theory, and cosmology all at once, Christianity found toleration a luxury it could not afford. It had to be organized and to move from cult to church. In its own way, Christianity was cosmopolitan—or, as it came to say, catholic—but its universality depended on enforced consent: the threat of excommunication, damnation, and, later, the unanswerable argument of the secular arm. Even the most genial and civilized Christian had to regard his religion as absolutely true (and therefore all others as radically false) and heathens as unwitting precursors, unregenerate enemies, or miserable souls in need of light. This hostility to pagan culture was impossible to maintain in its pure form: Christian metaphysicians, Christian humanists, and Christian Stoics in succession tried to absorb the classical heritage and, at least in part, succeeded. But by the seventeenth century, and certainly in the Enlightenment, philosophical eclecticism was an instrument serving, not the integration, but the exclusion of Christianity. The philosophes' eclecticism was therefore a weapon. But it is not always possible, or even desirable, to separate instrument from ideal. "I should think myself a weak reasoner and a bad citizen," Jeremy Bentham wrote, "were I not, though a Royalist in London, a republican in Paris."[3] "If there were only one religion in England, one would have to fear despotism;" Voltaire wrote, "if there were two, they would cut each other's throats; but they have thirty, and they

---

[2] Ibid., 482–3.
[3] *Works*, X, 282.

live happy and in peace."[4] These expressions of political and religious relativism are critiques of contemporary political and
religious dogmas, but they also reveal the world in which Bentham, Voltaire, and indeed, the whole Enlightenment wanted to
live. It was a world united by its celebration of diversity, a cosmopolitan harmony orchestrated in free individuality; an open
world, not of absolutes or of persecution, but of pacific and continuous dialogue.

IV

A good deal of nonsense has been written about dialogue,
and I have no wish to add to it here. It has become fashionable
to see the dialogue as a prototype of modern man's dilemmas, to
visualize each protagonist as merely one facet of the author, and
the clash of opinion as symptomatic of some unresolved inner
conflict. In fact, the dialogue is a traditional and highly flexible
didactic device that has proved useful to most civilized ages and
in a wide variety of causes. Latin dialogues of Carolingian times
were mnemonic devices to improve the student's grasp of grammatical rules. In the dialectical writings of St. Anselm, St. Thomas
Aquinas, and Abelard, dialogues forcefully stated mistaken positions for the sake of clarifying the truth. Medieval inquiry,
especially in the universities, proceeded in an atmosphere of vigorous debate, and the clash of opinion was organized in disputations. The dialogue, therefore, is not the monopoly of Greek
irony, twentieth-century ambivalence, or even eighteenth-century
informality.

At the same time, the Christian millennium, for all its delight
in argument, did not provide a hospitable atmosphere for genuine
dialogue. The absolute claims of Christian revelation foreclosed
the questioning of fundamentals: all supposed similarities between
Socrates, the instigator of uncertainty, and Jesus Christ, who
brought the Word, break down here—one does not debate with
the son of God. The time for dialogue was a time of intellectual
ferment—Plato's Athens, Bruni's Florence, and Voltaire's Paris.

---

[4] *Lettres philosophiques*, I, 74.

The mood of the Enlightenment was favorable to dialogue, and dialogue was favorable to the Enlightenment. The Scholastics had been compelled to move within a relatively narrow range; the primary purpose of their debates had been to assimilate vast amounts of new ideas without bursting the bonds of their Christian universe. The philosophes, for their part, could exploit the potentialities of dialogue fully, to propound the most outrageous hypotheses for the sake, not of refutation, but of serious consideration, to dramatize the constructive role of criticism, to record their own education, their struggles and uncertainties, and by recording them, educate their readers.

An inventive company, the philosophes wrote dialogues in many forms. Some were explicit; others hovered directly beneath the surface of an essay. In his *Theory of Moral Sentiments*, Adam Smith constructed an ethical system out of a carefully modulated exchange among Stoics, Epicureans, Platonists, and some modern moralists. Voltaire, as I have said, tried to resolve the problem of evil in his poem on the Lisbon earthquake by staging a philosophers' debate. Imaginary voyages, like Montesquieu's *Lettres persanes* or Diderot's *Voyage de Bougainville*, which I have called cross-cultural dialogues, are dramatic confrontations in which the alien has by no means all the good lines.

Other dialogues were out in the open: Wieland was Lucian's disciple during his whole long literary career, and true to his model, cast some of his most attractive essays in dialogue form. Dialogue, Lucian says, passes for the son of philosophy and is the enemy of rhetoric; urbane, satirical, he is the nemesis of fanaticism, of dogmatism, of blind faith. This is precisely how Wieland used his dialogues: to defeat the claims of the absolute. Voltaire, the archsatirist of the century, used the dialogue for similar purposes: sometimes to ridicule an opponent, but more often to suggest the spectrum within which his own opinions moved. *L'A, B, C*, for one, has three speakers who agree on the need for toleration and the rule of law, but who dispute over forms of government and the question of a social religion within a range of opinions which had all been held by Voltaire himself. Lessing wrote *Freimaurergespräche*, and composed in *Nathan der Weise* a dialogue on toleration for the stage. The famous story of the three rings, which Nathan tells in the third act to demonstrate the equivalence of the three great religions, is, in its didactic way, a call for dialogue.

It was Hume and Diderot who explored the ironic and dra-matic possibilities of the form most effectively. Hume's *Dialogues Concerning Natural Religion* pits a deist, a skeptic, and a fideist against one another in a tense debate over proofs for the existence of God. The tension, palpable from the first confrontation, is heightened by an unexpected reversal of sides long after the lines of argument seem to be firmly set: for most of the work, deist and skeptic are allied against the fideist, but toward the end of the dialogue the skeptic rather suddenly discloses his sympathy for the intellectual modesty of the Orthodox position. As a result, both deist and Christian proofs are refuted in turn, and the skeptic remains triumphant. Or does he? For two centuries, readers of the *Dialogues* have argued over which of the speakers, if any, represents Hume—proof of how brilliantly Hume had mastered the art of disguise, how fully he had succeeded in establishing his characters as independent, completely realized dramatic beings.[5]

Diderot's dialogues are less formal than Hume's; they often sound like transcriptions of conversations held in Holbach's salon. Unquestionably, Diderot's masterpiece in the form is *Le Neveu de Rameau*. The Satire of Horace which it imitates is a long mono-logue by Horace's slave Davus, punctuated with a few interjec-tions by his master. Davus takes advantage of a slave's traditional right to speak his mind during the Saturnalia and accuses his master of irrational contradictions in his conduct: he derides Horace as a free man who is actually more of a slave than his slave; a hypocrite who cants about simplicity while living in luxury, and who deplores the disappearance of antique Roman honesty in the midst of an adulterous love affair. *Quisnam igitur liber?*—"Who is free?" Davus asks. Only the wise man, the man who fears neither death nor poverty nor chains, who cares not for honors but is all to himself, and against whom fortune con-tends in vain.

Diderot ends at the same point, but his conversation takes a more sinuous and more scenic course. The dissolute, amoral, and highly gifted Rameau is Davus, a penetrating, pitiless observer

---

[5] See below, pp. 413–18.

who lampoons the wealthy hosts whose parasite he is. But the other speaker, the virtuous, sensible, slightly sententious "I" of the dialogue, has more to say than Horace; in *Le Neveu de Rameau*, the two protagonists are rather more evenly matched than they are in its Latin prototype. Rameau, despite his legal freedom and verbal license, is more of a slave than Davus; while "I", for all his limitations, is invulnerable to really serious attack, since his own life is blameless. True dialogue thus becomes possible.

Diderot—that is, "I"—is ready to acknowledge that sensuality is almost irresistible: the hardest thing in the world is to live according to principle. "In the whole country," says Rameau, "only one man walks—the king. Everybody else takes a position." This, Diderot is almost willing to grant—the observation is, after all, an epigrammatic expression of the truth that freedom and power are conjoined. Diderot does not share Rameau's view of life, but he takes it seriously enough to present it at length: Rameau is worth debating with. Just as Voltaire has shrewdly recognized in Pascal the most formidable intellectual adversary of his hedonism, so Diderot recognizes that the most insidious opponent to his Stoicism is just this irresponsible, amoral sensuality:

I. . . . Still, there is one being exempt from pantomime. That is the philosopher who has nothing and who asks for nothing.

HE. And where is that animal? If he has nothing, he suffers; if he demands nothing, he will get nothing and will suffer forever.

I. No. Diogenes scoffed at want.

HE. But a man must be dressed.

I. No, he went naked.

HE. Sometimes it was cold in Athens.

I. Less than here.

HE. People ate there.

I. No doubt.

HE. At whose expense?

I. At nature's. To whom does the savage appeal? To the earth, the animals, the fish, the trees, the plants, the roots, the brooks.

HE. Poor fare.

I. It is abundant.

HE. But badly served.

I. Yet it's the one whose remains are used to set our tables.

HE. But you'll admit that the ingenuity of our chefs, pastry cooks, caterers, restaurateurs, and confectioners put something of their own into it. With that austere diet, your Diogenes must have had very tractable organs.

I. You're wrong. The Cynic's dress was once our monastic habit, and just as virtuous. The Cynics were the Carmelites and Cordeliers of Athens.

HE. I've got you then. Diogenes then danced the pantomime too, if not in front of Pericles, at least in front of Lais or Phryne?

I. You're wrong again; the others paid a good deal for the courtesan who gave herself to him for pleasure.

HE. But if the courtesan happened to be busy and the Cynic in a hurry?

I. He went back to his tub and did without her.

HE. And you advise me to imitate him?

I. I'll bet my life that it's better than crawling, debasing and prostituting yourself.

HE. I need a good bed, good fare, warm clothes in winter, cool clothes in summer, rest, money, and plenty of other things that I prefer owing to benevolence to acquiring by labor.

I. That's because you are a sluggard, a glutton, a coward, a mean soul.

HE. I believe I told you that.

I. No doubt, the things of life have a value, but you're unaware of the sacrifice you make in order to get them. You dance, you have danced, and you will keep on dancing the vile pantomime.[6]

I have quoted this passage at length even though it is not Diderot's final word about morality. He was too familiar with sensual passion, and valued it too highly, to regard ascetic Cynicism as a satisfactory ethical position. But it vividly evokes

---

[6] *Le Neveu de Rameau* (ed. Jean Fabre, 1950), 106–7.

the style of philosophizing typical of the Enlightenment: tentative and yet didactic, casual but pointed in its classical allusions, hospitable to the variety of experience, and in all respects close to life. The maker of systems lived alone: he was a Spinoza constructing geometric patterns while he ground his lenses. The philosophe thought in public and was in this, too, much like his beloved ancients, who had generally written "in a free and familiar style" and treated "their subjects in the way of dialogue and free debate."[7] Locke's *Essay Concerning Human Understanding*, as he himself tells us, was conceived and first talked out in a series of conversations among "five or six friends meeting at my chamber."[8] Voltaire began his great *Essai sur les mœurs* after discussions with his mistress Madame du Châtelet. Other works were outright collaborations: Lessing wrote essays with Moses Mendelssohn; Beccaria's *Dei delitti e delle pene* was a virtual group effort; Rousseau's *Discours sur l'origine de l'inégalité*, Holbach's *Système de la nature*, and Raynal's *Histoire des Deux Indes* are the offspring, and in many respects the imitations, of conversations—all three books contain unknown and undeterminable quantities of Diderot's prose. Raynal's *Histoire*, indeed, was the work of perhaps a dozen philosophes, among whom Diderot was merely the most prominent.

This collective thinking was not all pure gain, and the philosophes did much of their most serious work in monastic privacy. Yet even Kant experimented with technical ideas in his correspondence and was a popular wit and welcome dinner companion. True, sociable philosophizing created opportunities for gossip and lighthearted generalizations, but at the same time, it was part of an exhilarating intellectual atmosphere in which women were drawn into the circle of discussion, ideas counted more than family origins, and points of view were tested in free debate. "This, then, is our life," wrote Diderot to Sophie Volland, for whom

---

[7] Shaftesbury: "An Essay on the Freedom of Wit and Humor," in *Characteristics of Men, Manners, Opinions, Times etc.*, ed. John M. Robertson, 2 vols. (1900), I, 51.

[8] "Epistle to the Reader," *Essay Concerning Human Understanding*. Statements like these appear so often in the prefaces of seventeenth- and eighteenth-century books that one might suspect them of being simple conventional formulas. But with Locke as with other authors, they are also accurate reports of how books originated in the age of the Enlightenment.

he reproduced the ambiance of Holbach's salon with dramatic fidelity. "Conversations sometimes playful, sometimes serious; a little gambling; a little strolling, in groups or alone; much reading, meditation, silence, solitude, and rest."[9] We often hear regrets nowadays over the decline of conversation as an art; if it has declined, it is the eighteenth century it has declined from—Boswell's *Life of Johnson* testifies to that on every page. No doubt, decorum encouraged artificiality, and conversely, the rage to do verbal combat led to some absurd debates. Many a would-be wit entered society prepared with nothing more than scraps he had picked up from the *Tatler*. By the time Lord Chesterfield could instruct his son never to be caught laughing, the vice of superficial politeness had become glaring. Yet conversation always remained a civilizing agent. In Paris, art criticism was brought to a high pitch by continuous talk and by the lively exchange of brochures. In Weimar, Wieland, Goethe, and Herder were the nucleus of a dazzling company. In England, Lord Shaftesbury implicitly claimed general significance for conversation, that most aristocratic of arts, by defending it with mercantile metaphors. "All politeness is owing to liberty," he wrote. "We polish one another, and rub off our corners and rough sides by a sort of amicable collision. To restrain this, is inevitably to bring a rust upon men's understandings." For "wit is its own remedy. Liberty and commerce bring it to its true standard. The only danger is, the laying an embargo. The same thing happens here, as in the case of trade. Imposition and restriction reduce it to a low ebb. Nothing is so advantageous to it as a free port."[1] David Hume, himself a fine conversationalist, also saw society as a training ground for relativism. "Among the arts of conversation, no one pleases more than mutual deference or civility, which leads us to resign our own inclinations to those of our companion, and to curb and conceal that presumption and arrogance so natural to the human mind."[2] Conversation was the continuation of warfare by other means.

---

[9] Diderot to Sophie Volland (September 10, 1760). *Correspondance*, III, 61.
[1] "Essay on the Freedom of Wit and Humor," *Characteristics*, I, 45–6.
[2] "Of the Rise and Progress of the Arts and Sciences," *Works*, III, 187.

This may seem like a large claim to make for mere talk. But in fact conversation was an indispensable part of the Enlightenment's way of life. It expressed and utilized the philosophes' professions of ignorance, dislike for dogmatism, concern with practicality, and pleasure in dialogue and made their pleas for free speech more than abstract slogans. The salon and its counterpart, the letter, were the parliament of the philosophes, where witty talk and playful formulations were tested for action and directed to some higher aim beyond themselves and their immediate audience; an aim at once simple and obvious—beyond making effects to being effective.

3. THE PRIMACY OF MORAL REALISM

I

THE SPECTACLE of professional talkers expressing impatience with mere talk would smack of paradox were not such impatience the traditional tactics of rhetoric. When Cicero, whom admirers from Quintilian to the philosophes called the embodiment of eloquence, had professed to prefer *res* to *verba*, he was really pleading for talk that is to some purpose. The Enlightenment made the same plea, with its energetic, almost pious earnestness, its moral realism.

I call it *realism*, not because I think the Enlightenment lacked imagination: on the contrary, it exercised the moral imagination freely, even strenuously. The philosophes were realists in that they took the material for their activity from the concrete experience of daily existence and continually returned to that existence for refreshment and confirmation: the philosophes who founded the United States and wrote its great apologetic documents appealed to experience on almost every page, and their European brethren admired them for it. The Enlightenment's realism did not take the depressing form that marks so much later realism: the philosophes delighted too much in social and aesthetic refinement to equate reality with sordidness; the rich were as real to them as the poor. But, far from disdaining ordinary things, the philosophes found their world among them; they were not too fastidious to seek the laws of political economy, legal institutions, and human motivation, or to describe the travails of the unlettered and the careers of the middle orders. The mixture of styles that invaded their plays, stories, and novels cannot be exhaustively explained as a reflection of bourgeois values; it embodied the philosophes' conviction that reality must be sought in workshops as much as in salons, in introspection much more than in metaphysical ratiocination, and in the commercial relations of traders rather than in the imaginary history of the social contract. Some of the philosophes' most intense thinking and most passionate activity was occasioned by ordinary events: Voltaire converted himself into a tireless critic of the French legal system, when he was nearly seventy, as a result of hearing about the execution of Jean Calas. Their literature, too, is the imaginative transfiguration of the real—perhaps not more so than most other literature, but certainly not less so: Lessing's and Diderot's plays, Wieland's novels, attempt realistic, individualized, truthful, and morally relevant portraits. Wieland, as Goethe beautifully put it, "early educated himself in those ideal regions in which youth likes so much to dwell; but since they were spoiled for him by what is called experience, by encounters with world and women, he threw himself onto the side of the real, and pleased himself and others in the combat of the two worlds, where, in light skirmish, between jest and earnest, his talent showed itself at its finest."[3] The philosophes' attack on fancy was not an attack on imagination but on thought ungrounded in life.

I call the Enlightenment's realism *moral* because whatever channel of expression it used—anticlerical mockery or political polemics—its vital center was a moral vision of the world. "The truth I love," wrote Rousseau in 1761, in harmony on this point with all the other philosophes, "is not so much metaphysical as moral."[4] Most men of the Enlightenment had outgrown the naïve hope that the truth makes men free automatically. The pursuit and

---

[3] *Dichtung und Wahrheit*, in *Gedenkausgabe*, X, 298.
[4] Rousseau to du Parc, June 25, 1761. *Correspondance générale*, VI, 160.

conquest of truth had moral dimensions for them: Kant, who argued that any lie whatever is wrong, was not alone in holding that the truth by itself is a good; other philosophes, like Voltaire, who lied incessantly, agreed with him. Yet the philosophes were all too painfully aware that a man who knows the truth may not act on it, that inconvenient information is likely to be suppressed, that, in short, knowledge and morality are not always allies. As Diderot put it in one of his moments of moral ecstasy, if there is a God, "he cares a great deal more for the purity of our souls than for the truth of our opinions."[5] In fact, it was precisely their awareness of this disjunction—a disjunction often merely nasty but sometimes tragic—that made the philosophes preach so much. Their single-minded concern for morality was the source of most of their cant, anti-intellectualism, and intolerance of opposition. But it also gave their philosophizing vigor and point; they knew they were concentrating on what was important.

In the rhetoric of the Enlightenment, this concentration on essentials took the form of a rather complacent claim to practicality. Even Rousseau, whom all but his most infatuated disciples dismissed as an unworldly dreamer, insisted that true knowledge is practical knowledge: "It is not a question of knowing what is," he wrote in *Émile*, "but only what is useful,"[6] and he made young Émile grow up among things, not books.

This claim, coupled with the assertion that their thought was a form of action,[7] does the philosophes less than justice. Clearly, the sort of action congenial, or even possible, to each of them depended not only on his country and his generation, but on his character as well. Gibbon tried to do little more than to amuse and instruct a select circle of educated men and women,

---

[5] Diderot to Sophie Volland (August 17 or 18, 1759). *Correspondance*, II, 230.

[6] *Œuvres complètes*, ed. Hachette, 12 vols. (1871-7), II, 136-7.

[7] In their self-protective utterances, the philosophes, of course, claimed precisely the opposite: that their thought was harmless because it did not lead to action. But as the great book XII of Montesquieu's *Esprit des lois* makes plain, this separation of thought and action was more than a screen behind which the subversive men of letters might operate in safety; it was also a cogent argument in behalf of civil liberties, especially of free speech.

most of whom were probably unbelievers even before they read the *Decline and Fall of the Roman Empire*. Polemicists like Condorcet, on the other hand, tried to do nothing less than to make a revolution in politics, economics, and social relations. The philosophes' action ranged from Adam Smith's theoretical lectures on politics and Lessing's lyrical advocacy of toleration, to Holbach's fierce anti-Christianity and Voltaire's frenetic campaign against *l'infâme*.

Besides, practicality does not characterize all of the philosophes' activity. Not all philosophes were Encyclopedists trying to change the general way of thinking, and the Encyclopedists were not Encyclopedists all of the time. Many of Diderot's inventions, Hume's essays on taste, Lessing's philological controversies, Voltaire's neo-classical tragedies, were free from any conceivable utility except the important one of giving gratification to the writer and pleasure to the reader. After all, as I have said before, the philosophes even practiced certain forms of metaphysical speculation for pleasure. As stylists and classicists, as playwrights, art critics, and poets, they were saved from being Philistines by their very cultivation; they were far too much interested in letters and in art—and, indeed, in sheer thinking as such—to follow out their methodological prescriptions to their rather dreary conclusions.

On one side, then, the practical philosophes often took a holiday from practicality. On the other side, they practiced it in a special way. After all, in itself, the claim to practicality in no way differentiates the Enlightenment from other ages: while there have always been speculative minds happy to proclaim that their work had no relevance whatever to anything outside itself, in general philosophers have defined what they are doing as useful, and useful precisely because they are doing it. The claim to being practical is one of the traditional debating points in Western civilization. When the Church Fathers called their theology the only practical philosophy because pagans were too busy quibbling to attend to serious business, they were using a polemical device they had taken over from their classical opponents. When Bacon and Descartes, and later the philosophes, criticized the Scholastics for "contentious learning," they too were adopting the weapons of their enemies. As experienced polemicists, the philosophes, I

think, would not have been surprised had they known that their
successors would ridicule *them* as system makers, shallow rationalists, and impractical dreamers—for being, in a word, the very
Utopians they had taken care not to be.

When the philosophes indicted the Scholastics for logomachy,
then, this merely showed that what had mattered supremely to
the Scholastics had lost its significance for the Enlightenment; it
was only the definition of what is practical, not the claim to
practicality itself, that had changed. When in the thirteenth
century Vincent of Beauvais compiled a kind of *Encyclopédie*
designed to gather up all significant knowledge, insisting that
"the end of life is not to know but to act";[8] and when in the same
century St. Thomas Aquinas composed his *Summa theologiae*,
inveighing against useless speculation and "vain and evanescent
curiosity,"[9] these pious clerics talked much the way Voltaire did
when he said that his motto was *Au fait!* or Lessing did when he
said: "Man was made to act, not to split hairs."[1]

Yet this continuity of vocabulary conceals a crucial difference
of world view. Vincent's great compendium deals with human
and natural things under the eye of divinity; it directs man's
attention to his religious vocation and his dependence upon God.
And Aquinas's warning is accompanied by a revealing definition:
the vain and evanescent curiosity he decries is the "contemplation
of creatures," which ought to give way to the study of "immortal
and lasting things." In a culture in which men believed in God and
yearned for salvation, the study of His nature and of the road to
eternal blessedness were matters of intense daily concern. To the
Enlightenment, they seemed like verbal games. The philosophes'
practicality was worldly, designed to translate into reality Bacon's
and Descartes's grandiose vision of man controlling nature for his
profit and delight. It has sometimes been said that Diderot wasted
twenty years of his life and ruined his precious eyesight editing a
mere Encyclopedia. But except for moments of discouragement,
Diderot considered his editorship as much part of his philosophical vocation as anything else he ever did. As he put it in a

---

[8] Quoted by Emile Mâle: *The Gothic Image* (edn. 1958), 25.
[9] *Summa theologiae*, section II, question 7, article 1.
[1] "Gedanken über die Herrnhuter" (1750), *Schriften*, XIV, 155.

rather ominous sentence, man was learning to "torment nature" into yielding her secrets for man's benefit. The philosopher's new role as the guide to such torture was sending him from the study to the market place, from systems to reality. The Scholastics, d'Alembert wrote, going back to Cicero in his language, had "substituted words for things, and frivolous or ridiculous questions for the great objects of true philosophy."[2] This charge appeared in the *Encyclopédie*, which the philosophes liked to consider the living image of that true philosophy. Preparing his articles on crafts and industry, Diderot practiced his calling in workshops and on farms. "We addressed ourselves to the ablest craftsmen of Paris and the kingdom," he wrote in a well-known passage of his *Prospectus* for the *Encyclopédie*, "we took the trouble of going to their workshops, interrogating them, taking down their dictation, developing their thoughts, eliciting from them the terms appropriate to their profession, constructing lists from them, defining them, talking with those from whom we had obtained memoranda, and (an almost indispensable precaution) rectifying, in long and frequent conversations with some, what others had imperfectly, obscurely, and sometimes incorrectly expressed."[3] This striking passage is more a declaration of intent than an accurate description of Diderot's procedure, but it is significant that Diderot chose to write it. The philosopher in the factory was an analogue to the bourgeois drama, in which the rigid separation of styles was giving way to a kind of democracy of sentiment. Hand and intellect, technology and philosophy, separated since the Greeks, were now finding common ground in the utilization of science for the sake of improving man's lot.

II

This conversion of philosophy into disciplined aggression against concrete problems marks an epoch in the history of the human will. The mythopoeic mind is caught in a violent oscillation: it swings erratically from extreme confidence to extreme

---

[2] "École, philosophie de l'," *The Encyclopédie*, 40.
[3] *Œuvres*, XIII, 140.

despair. By ritual and magical practices, the man in the world of myth controls his environment with fantastic power. He kills enemies far beyond his reach, guarantees bountiful harvests, or secures a male succession. His faith moves mountains. But his glorious sense of mastery has its counterpart, the abject sense of impotence. Evil unseen forces or incomprehensible divine wrath destroy labor, thwart hopes, and nullify even the most meticulous religious observance. For such powers, the mythopoeic mind knows no sure remedy and has no rational explanation. It turns to surrender or propitiation: humble submission or grim sacrifice.

From the vantage point of the Enlightenment, unsympathetic as it was to the refinements of theology, it appeared as if the higher religions had done little to mitigate the swings of this pendulum of emotions. Some theologians seemed to claim that man could be certain of salvation or damnation, others, that he must remain forever uncertain—but all agreed on man's abject dependence. Even those who argued that man's conduct bore some relation to his fate did not liberate him from the grasp of superstitious elation or despair. In the same manner, the higher pseudo sciences left man as helpless as before: the vast aspirations of the alchemists, wholly unrelated to experience, and the ambitious predictions of the astrologers, offered dramatic instances of a fancied omnipotence which proved, again and again, to be a delusion. The philosophes were confident that their scientific empiricism alone could lead to a realistic appraisal of man's place and possibilities. "Man is unhappy only because he does not know nature"—this is the opening sentence of Holbach's *Système de la nature*. Man's mind, Holbach continues, is infected with prejudice; his intellect, crippled by false opinion. To make things worse, man tries to break out of his proper sphere and "rush beyond the visible world." Even repeated and cruel disasters have not cured him of his mad enterprise: "He despises realities to meditate on chimeras; neglects experience to indulge in systems and conjectures; dares not cultivate his reason"; and makes claims for knowing his way about the imaginary regions of another life instead of trying to make himself happy in his own dwelling place. "In a word, man disdains the study of nature to run after phantoms" and leaves the straight path of truth, which alone can make him happy. In this paragraph, the Enlightenment's moral

myth

realism is summed up in passionate words and workmanlike logic: only philosophical modesty brings intellectual results, only rational (that is, scientific) inquiry brings happiness.

Like the philosophers of antiquity, therefore, the philosophes found it impossible to separate their inquiries into nature from their inquiries into morality, and their inquiries into morality from their inquiries into human nature. Control of the outside world and the inner man depended on a rational understanding of both, and this understanding in turn depended on a clear definition of the sphere—in fact, of the very nature—of action. Whatever the universal, unchanging component of man's nature, that nature defined itself for its time and its culture through its particular activity. The philosophes, generally tied to the rhetoric of natural law, did not put it quite so simply, but they came to recognize that man is what he does, and comes to know what he is by discovering himself in action: "I love wisdom in evidence," wrote Diderot, "like the athlete in the arena: the strong man recognizes himself only on the occasions that he has to show his power."[4] In myth, man's ignorance of himself and his world is veiled by extravagance; man feigns self-knowledge by drawing plausible but false inferences. What the philosophes rather harshly called the "destruction of superstition" was the unmasking of these inferences—the critical mind took it upon itself to show that the course of the stars has no influence on human lives, or that a few words or gestures do not alter the regular rhythms of nature. In magical thinking, mind is inhabited by a demon and the world is constantly, bewilderingly, alive; in philosophy, the demon is exorcised and the confusion is reduced to law. Magical thinking is an ever-repeated yet ever-futile attempt to control anxiety-producing situations; the control exercised by scientific thinking acts to remove the very sources of the anxiety itself. The mythopoeic mind is crippled by what Freud has called the "omnipotence of thought" and by its opposite, wretched dependence. The critical mind, on the contrary, seeks to establish the supremacy of the ego against the blind drive of the id and the harsh denials of the superego: "The enhanced feeling of self which seems to express itself in the magical world view indicates actually that at

---

[4] *Essai sur les règnes de Claude et de Néron,* in *Œuvres,* III, 221.

this stage there is as yet no true self. Through the magical omnipotence of the will the I seeks to seize upon all things and bend
them to its purpose; but precisely in this attempt it shows itself
still totally dominated, totally 'possessed' by things." Science
escapes this projection of hopes and fears upon the world by its
controlled, methodical objectivity. It understands that "all true
freedom of action presupposes an inner limitation, a recognition of
certain objective limits of action."[5]

It was precisely the failure to seek these limits which proved
to the philosophes that most metaphysics was merely a higher
form of mythmaking. That was neither a generous nor even a
just appraisal, but it explains why the philosophes found it necessary to deride Descartes for boasting that he could construct the
universe with matter and movement, and similar claims by other
metaphysicians—these boasts struck them as fine specimens of the
omnipotence of thought. Paradoxically—and that is why the
Enlightenment is a stage in the history of the will—the philosophes' manner of philosophizing increased man's power by
mitigating his claims. This is what Bacon and, after him, the
Enlightenment meant by saying that we master nature by obeying
her.

III

"You'll find no centaurs here, no gorgons or harpies; our page
smacks of man"—thus Martial on his poetry, sounding like an
antique Pope. Antique realism was more constricted, more aristocratic, than the realism of the philosophes; the urge to test inquiry
in action or to reform society, was checked by the feeling of
impotence before nature and events and by the acceptance of a
hierarchical social structure. Yet Hellenistic and, later, Roman
thought, with its tendency to translate philosophical questions
into moral issues, to seek the definition of problems and, sometimes, their solution in the arena of daily life—in the law courts, in
friendship, and in politics—give ancient philosophy its family

---

[5] Ernst Cassirer: *The Philosophy of Symbolic Forms* (1955), II,
158.

resemblance to the philosophy of the Enlightenment. *Equidem beatos puto, quibus deorum munere datum est aut facere scribenda aut scribere legenda, beatissimos vero, quibus utrumque*—"For my part, I think happy those whom the gods have endowed either to do what must be written or to write what must be read; indeed, happiest those who have been endowed with both."[6] This epigram of the younger Pliny, felicitously putting the case for the committed man of letters, anticipates the philosophes discoursing on the effective life.

The philosophes, in fact, liked to take such dicta as their texts; none more earnestly than Diderot. I have suggested it before: Diderot the moralist was a Roman out of his time; his incessant and, to us, sometimes tiresome moralizing is the philosophe in Roman dress. It was a congenial pose, so natural that the word *pose* slights it: Diderot's excitable imagination made him a Roman censor, the scourge of vice and the celebrant of virtue. "Horace's tic is to make verses, mine is to moralize," he said of himself, shrewdly enough.[7] It was this tic that led him to remark —not once but twice—that he envied Voltaire his rehabilitation of the Calas family far more than his tragedy *Mahomet*, sublime work though that was.[8] The sight of goodness stirred him as deeply, and in the same manner, as a supreme work of art and, it would seem, as a satisfying sexual experience. "If," he wrote to Sophie Volland,

the spectacle of injustice sometimes rouses me to so much indignation that I lose my judgment over it, and that I'd kill, I'd destroy, during this delirium; so the spectacle of equity fills me with a sweetness, inflames me with such ardor and enthusiasm that life would mean nothing to me if I had to yield it up. Then it seems to me that my heart expands beyond me, that it swims; an indescribably delicious and subtle sensation runs through me; I have difficulty breathing; the whole surface of my body is animated by something like a shudder; it is

---

[6] Pliny the Younger: *Epistulae*, VI, 16, 3.
[7] *Satire I, sur les caractères et les mots de caractère de profession*, in *Œuvres*, VI, 315.
[8] *Le neveu de Rameau*, 42; *Essai sur les règnes de Claude et de Néron*, in *Œuvres*, III, 285.

marked above all on my forehead, at the hairline; and then the symptoms of admiration and pleasure come to mingle on my face with those of joy, and my eyes fill with tears.[9]

Diderot was a voyeur of virtue; but in general he put his moral appreciation with less orgastic force and more economy, rather more like the antique moralist he wanted to be. "I love the philosophy which exalts mankind," he wrote Sophie Volland;[1] and again, joining what he feared was all too often separated: "To do good, to know the true—that's what distinguishes one man from another. The rest is nothing."[2] All intelligent human effort, all art, literature, and even history, ought to be suffused with moral passion: "Other historians," he wrote to Voltaire, "tell us facts in order to teach us facts. You do it in order to excite in the depth of our souls a strong indignation against mendacity, ignorance, hypocrisy, superstition, fanaticism, tyranny; and that indignation remains when the memory of facts has gone."[3] It was a compliment Voltaire could appreciate, even if he did not quite deserve it.

He could appreciate it largely because he, like Diderot, idealized those ancients who had made ethics the core of philosophy and treated thinking as a preparation for action. Diderot's Seneca was such a man: a public servant who celebrated public duty but found room too for the cultivation of the inner life and the study of science; as a moderate eclectic Stoic, he was ready to admit the virtues of retirement and private life as long as it became neither permanent nor an end in itself: *Gloriari otio iners*

---

[9] Diderot to Sophie Volland (October 18, 1760). *Correspondance*, III, 156. This passage should be read in conjunction with the description of the irascible Mr. Bramble in Smollett's *Humphrey Clinker:* "His blood rises at every instance of insolence and cruelty, even where he himself is in no way concerned; and ingratitude makes his teeth chatter. On the other hand, the recital of a generous, humane, or grateful action, never fails to draw from him tears of approbation, which he is often greatly distressed to conceal." Mr. Bramble shares Diderot's humanitarian passion, but, unlike Diderot, he dare not show it: the *philosophe* glories in the conjunction of passion and morality which his rather more pious (or Protestant?) counterpart finds it necessary to hide.

[1] (August 17, 1759). Ibid., II, 225.

[2] (November 3, 1759). Ibid., II, 318.

[3] Diderot to Voltaire (November 28, 1760). Ibid., III, 275.

Cicero

ambitio est—"To boast about our retirement is indolent ambition."[4] Diderot thought Seneca's concessions to the "monastic"
spirit of Stoicism and to Epicurean indifference a little excessive:
the wise man, he warned, should "visit" the country of retirement but not live there: "to expatriate yourself like this is to be
neither kinsman, nor friend, nor citizen."[5] But these were differences of nuance, no more: Diderot welcomed Seneca's doctrine
of responsible, public-spirited philosophizing as an authoritative
endorsement of his own moral athleticism.

Like Seneca, Cicero had had a dazzling and well-documented
public career, and it was his total career, not his writings alone,
that made him a culture hero of the Enlightenment. "Cicero in
Latin and Xenophon in Greek," Gibbon wrote, "are indeed the
two ancients whom I would first propose to a liberal scholar, not
only for the merit of their style and sentiments, but for the
admirable lessons which may be applied almost to every situation of public and private life."[6] Cicero had acknowledged that
the search for wisdom might well be regarded as the highest of
human activities, but he was quick to warn that such preoccupation often seduced men to "treat the unknown as known," and to
"devote too much time and energy to matters that are obscure,
difficult, and useless as well." Purely intellectual effort, such as the
study of astronomy or civil law, is morally right and admirable,
yet "to be drawn away from active life by study is contrary to
moral duty." *Virtutis enim laus omnis in actione consistit*—"For
the whole glory of virtue lies in activity."[7] Here, the philosophes
said approvingly, here was a philosopher who understood the
interplay of theory and practice, word and act.

Such understanding was impressive enough, but even better,
Cicero could claim that he did not merely preach this philosophy
but embodied it. He had always, he wrote, *lived* his principles.
Now lived principles are ethics in action, and Cicero often reiterated that there is no phase of life, private or public, that cannot
be clarified and purified by persistent, self-critical moral reflec-

[4] *Epistulae morales*, LXVIII, 3.
[5] *Essai sur les règnes de Claude et de Néron*, in *Œuvres*, III, 221.
[6] *Autobiography*, 99.
[7] *De officiis*, I, 6.

tion. The one indispensable task of philosophy was to make right action possible: *Quis est enim, qui nullis officii praeceptis tradendis philosophum se audeat dicere?*—"Indeed, who would dare call himself a philosopher without teaching lessons in moral duties?"[8]

Cicero was a New Academic who took pride in his skeptical rejection of dogma and in the practicality of his thought. Yet on the primacy of ethics all Roman schools of thought converged: it was an expression of the prevailing eclectic mood to exalt the search for goodness over the investigation of nature, of right conduct over proficiency in logic. While the Roman Stoics did not rigidly insist on perpetual public service, the Epicureans, for their part, could see the uses of activity. It is true that Lucretius begins the second book of *De rerum natura* with the celebrated *Suave mari magno*, a magnificent paean to the happy man who watches a storm-tossed ship or a fierce battle from the distant fortress of indifference. Yet even Lucretius's poem is not the work of a detached spectator; it seethes with frustration at the course of political events and calls for strenuous intellectual activity in the moral sphere: there is nothing remote in the task of freeing men from the fears inculcated by religion. His indignation reminds us of Holbach, with his cold hatred for the enslavers of men's minds, and even of Hume, far too cheerful and corpulent to exhaust himself improving the world: when Hume excoriates the superstitions of most men in most ages ("sick men's dreams") his sentences tighten, his adjectives grow more biting, his urbane skepticism turns into anger—the anger of a moral philosopher surrounded by vicious fools. In the Enlightenment, as in Rome, the varieties of philosophy narrowed to the sharp point of the search for right thought that would support right action.

The link that made the relation of theory to practice rational rather than fortuitous was ethics; the link that made it generally available was rhetoric. This was true in the Enlightenment as it had been true in Rome, with one significant change: in antiquity, persuasion was largely verbal; a by-product of harangues in law courts or in the Senate. By the eighteenth century, for all the continuing importance of conversation, persuasion had shifted

---

[8] Ibid., I, 2.

rhetoric

largely to writing, and rhetoric had given way to style.[9] One consequence, on the whole a fortunate one for the Enlightenment, was that the philosophes were less obsessed by form than the ancients. Form remained almost as important as content; in fact, Buffon's famous remark that style is the man himself, shows that it remained an essential ingredient rather than something pasted on to substance; not a mere grace note employed to decorate a humdrum melody. But aware that they were competing for the attention of the elite and trying to capture the attention of a new, growing reading public, the philosophes did not disdain devices; without apologies, they tried to make their writings clear, specific, simple, and repetitious, to overwhelm their opponents with irony and dazzle their audience with wit. They had no intention of seeing their polemics go unheard in a desert of bored readers. But it will not do to make too much of this: the philosophes liked to write well for the same reason that men of letters have always liked to write well: it pleased craftsmen and audience alike; it involved a satisfying application of time-honored principles to their craft; it might bring applause and, at best, lasting fame. Hence for all its intensity, its rage, hidden and open, its straining for persuasiveness, there was something purely aesthetic in the philosophes' most didactic writings. Ancient orators had found it necessary to justify oratory before they discussed its techniques or displayed its possibilities. Since educated men in antiquity had studied rhetoric thoroughly in their schools, they were cynical, suspicious of clever tricks, appeals to emotion, striking images,

---

[9] But not entirely, as appears from the success of treatises on oratory in the eighteenth century and from articles on the subject by Voltaire, Marmontel, and others. Lord Chesterfield, writing to his son on November 1, 1739, sounds precisely like an antique Roman rhetorician: "Let us return to Oratory, or the art of speaking well; which should never be entirely out of your thoughts, since it is so useful in every part of life, and so absolutely necessary in most. A man can make no figure without it, in Parliament, in the Church, or in the law; and even in common conversation, a man that has acquired an easy and habitual eloquence, who speaks properly and accurately, will have a great advantage over those who speak incorrectly or inelegantly"— and Lord Chesterfield then proceeds to discourse to his son about persuasion, gaining attention, the proper uses of metaphor and wit, all in the manner of classical treatises.

and effective repetitions. In antiquity, we may say without undue paradox, the art of persuasion had first to persuade that it was not being artful. The philosophes took this more or less for granted. They were confident that the public needed to be educated and that it was their calling to educate it. Hume wrote an essay on the decline of eloquence without sounding very regretful: the philosophes agreed that they did not need to imitate the ancients in everything.

For all this independence, Cicero the thinker in action remained the Enlightenment's ideal, the man who more than anyone else embodied the *vita activa*. Voltaire found it astonishing that Cicero should find time to read and write so much philosophy "in the midst of the tumults and storms of his life, steadily engaged in affairs of state."[1] This idealization is an interesting specimen of the strategies of affinity. The picture of Cicero writing his *De officiis* deeply engaged in public life mistakes what Cicero had wished to be for what he actually was. A similar misreading, touching in its intensity, was Alfieri's bitter frustration at seeing his admired ancients at work in politics: "I shed tears of mingled grief and rage at having been born in Piedmont at a time, and under a government, that made it impossible to conceive or execute any great plan." All too often, antiquity was like Piedmont: ironically enough, philosophy was often the fruit of inaction. Philosophers from Plato to Seneca did much of their most influential work only after they had been forced out of public life, in retirement or in exile. Cicero conceded this candidly and sadly; for him, philosophy was a substitute for politics. If the Roman commonwealth had continued on its course, he observes in a noble passage, "I should be writing down, not these philosophical essays, but my public speeches, as I often did in earlier days."[2] The death of the republic and the rise of despotism had ruined his usefulness as a public orator, but in his inability to resign himself to grief and unwillingness to give himself to debauchery, he turned to philosophy.

Yet these biographical misinterpretations in no way invalidate

---

[1] "Preface," *Rome sauvée, ou Catilina*, in *Œuvres*, V, 205–6.
[2] *De officiis*, II, 1.

the philosophes' ideal of the *vita activa;* rather, they illustrate the curious chemistry we call *influence.* Cicero himself never questioned the virtue of action: *cum dignitate otium,* leisure with dignity, was at its best a second choice, acceptable only in times of settled peace, or for elderly statesmen. Scipio Africanus, Cicero reports a little wistfully, used to say of himself, *numquam se minus otiosum esse, quam cum otiosus, nec minus solum, quam cum solus esset*—"that he was never less idle than when he was idle, and never less alone than when he was alone." Retirement and leisure only served that great a man as breathing spaces, times in which to reflect on public business.[3]

In stating this ideal so eloquently and trying so earnestly to live it, Cicero was singling out one possible "way of life," which, shorn of some of its heroism and strenuous rhetoric, was to become the philosophes' ideal. From Plato onward, Greek philosophers had speculated on forms of human existence and had sorted out three archetypes: the contemplative, the lustful, and the active life. These types, like the three pure types of government, were severely simplified models. Each contained elements of the others; none was unambiguously defined. The inconclusiveness of the debate is illustrated by the conflicting allegorical interpretations given the two ancient tales of the Decision of Hercules and the Judgment of Paris. The relation of the life of virtue to the life of action, or the life of pleasure to the life of thought, could not be settled simply. Indeed, in the hands of the masters, complexity was, not a sign of unclarity or indecision, but of profound understanding of life's ambiguities. Plato, with his powerful vindication of philosophy against cynical rhetoricians and his great dialogues on political theory, glorified the happy union of the contemplative and active life: thought without serious moral purpose is frivolous; action without knowledge is criminal. Plato found room even for pleasure: his *Republic* is a grandiose allegory of the human soul finding inner peace through the just allocation of functions to each of its elements: the rational element, the head, governs the passionate element, the heart, and the lustful element, the belly, but it governs without suppressing them. *Governing* here has two

---

[3] Ibid., III, 1.

meanings: personal self-control and rational regulation of political
life. Thus Plato strove for a synthesis, for the life of rational
action filled with passion. His delicate balance was shifted but not
destroyed by Aristotle, whose ethical writings are a continuing
inquiry into these ways of life. Aristotle's changes of view make it
impossible to settle on a single, final Aristotelian position, but this
much is clear: even when he unambiguously exalts the life of
religious contemplation, he defines contemplation, not as with-
drawal or passivity, but as a noble form of activity which crowns,
without displacing, other forms: the philosopher is "an architect
with his thoughts."

These Platonic and Aristotelian syntheses were dissolved by
the harsh pressure of reality, by the destruction of civic life in the
Hellenistic period and the increasing separation of theoretical
from practical studies. In a world in which the individual's voice
was lost in the vastness of empire and talk seemed irrelevant to
politics—a world that Plato had not known and Aristotle had
refused to face—theory and action confronted each other as
simple antagonists: *sophia*, abstract contemplative wisdom, faced
phronesis, moral reason in society. Roman Stoics and some late
Peripatetics acknowledged the new situation by radically sim-
plifying the complexities of their revered teachers, although even
their hardheaded common sense continued to recognize that
thinking was indispensable to action. But once contemplation had
come to mean flight from life, total privacy, the only thinking
relevant to action was being done in ethics, politics, and applied
science. Cicero, who in this typified Roman tough-mindedness,
showed his dependence on Plato (but also his distance from him)
in his political writings, his *De republica* and *De legibus*. These
books are hymns to the founders of cities, to rational men "foolish"
enough to devote themselves to their commonwealth; the greatest
of men, Cicero wrote, those who most nearly approximate
divinity, are the men who had founded states or preserved them.
Thus the road from thinking to action had been straightened and
always remained open, if not in reality, then in wistful imagination. Writing in enforced retirement, Cicero continued to dwell
almost obsessively on the state and on public morality; his
thoughts fastened on the arena he had been forced to leave

behind, and his most theoretical speculations retain the savor of the marketplace.[4]

Just as Cicero had been unable to appreciate the sinuous evolution of the idea of "ways of life," so the philosophes were compelled by their situation to simplify their own commitment to practicality. Their experience of the Christian ideal, which had identified the contemplative with the monastic life, drove them to place *vita activa* and *vita contemplativa* in sharp opposition and to choose Cicero rather than Plato or Aristotle as a guide. This, as I have said, was not fatal to intellect; consider their idealization of Turgot, a statesman who was, significantly enough, neither a glib talker nor a clever politician. Turgot was a modern Cicero: the thinker in action, the right man in the right place, a trained political economist, experienced administrator, original philosopher of history, and proved humanitarian, doing his part in the alleviation of man's estate.

This surely was a worthy ideal, if a little thin. It was also under constant attack, and its patent incompatibility with the Christian ideal made the philosophes excessively sensitive to any attempt at restoring the old Platonic complexities. This, I suggest, is the real meaning of the famous quarrel between Diderot and Rousseau. In the mid-1750's Jean-Jacques Rousseau renounced the elegant society in whose midst he had lived, and as part of what he called his personal reform, he retreated to rural solitude. This retirement infuriated his acquaintances, and especially his old friend Diderot, who struck back with an unmistakable allusion to Rousseau's self-imposed isolation in his play *Le Fils Naturel*: "Interrogate your heart: it will tell you that the good man is in society, and that only the bad man is alone."[5] Wounded, Rousseau protested, and there ensued a long and increasingly acrimonious

---

[4] In this connection it is illuminating to think of Machiavelli, one of the first of modern pagans, whom the philosophes much appreciated. In his most celebrated letter, Machiavelli describes his life in exile: in the evening, when the day's conversation and trivial business are done, he changes his clothes to put on his robes of state and goes to his study to talk, once again, with the ancients, and to think and write about politics. Machiavelli's appeal to antiquity is therapeutic, but the ancients to whom he appeals are not distant from him: they lead him where he wants to be, in the midst of the activity of politics.

[5] Act IV, scene 3. *Œuvres*, VII, 66.

exchange resulting in a final breach. It was a personal quarrel, but it was much more than that: Diderot's intolerable officiousness and the unusual intensity of his rancor suggest that nothing less than a clash of ideals was at stake. Rousseau's act appeared like a stinging criticism of the philosophes' sociability and amiable philosophizing; but worse than that, it looked like a betrayal of the Enlightenment's cause, a rejection of effectiveness in behalf of an isolation reminiscent of Christian monasticism. Seneca had said the final word on such behavior—"to boast about our retirement is indolent ambition." What could be more boastful than Rousseau in his hermitage?

The quarrel has its ridiculous aspects—it escapes complete absurdity only when we realize the heavy weight the philosophes were willing to put on what we consider small things, the open-hearted simplicity with which they argued moral matters, and the importance they attached to that ancient problem, the way of life. Yet, while the quarrel may escape absurdity, it does not escape irony. Rousseau, one of the few philosophes who appreciated Plato, was not trying to shirk responsibility; his very retreat was a form of social criticism, and—as with Scipio Africanus—a preparation for social action. And his most determined adversaries were Platonists too, and Aristotelians as well, only without knowing it: they knew that Plato had called for the philosopher-king and that Marcus Aurelius had embodied this ideal; they knew that Aristotle had called man a political animal and they hoped that they were political men. Yet in their drive for action they were willing to settle for part of Plato's and Aristotle's ideal and persecuted the one philosophe among them who called upon them to ask for all of it.

The Enlightenment's moral realism, then, with all its vigor and well-meaning intelligence, had its limitations: it led the philosophes to show two faces to the world in their attitude toward mind. In this too they followed their ancient masters who had in one breath denounced useless erudition and in the other deplored vulgar resistance to philosophy, decried speculation and given room to their curiosity. We need only recall Diderot, slaving devotedly over his tiresome, commonplace editorial tasks—Diderot, the most inventive, versatile, and mercurial of literary men—to grasp the double nature of his movement. Yet this moral realism also (and this too at a price) suggested a manner of reconciling the love of play with didacticism, right action with beautiful talk: they could be reconciled by the ancient prescription of moralizing art, of literature that instructs and delights at the same time. The philosophes did not disdain pure art, as we know; and technical treatises like Kant's *Critiques* and Condillac's essays on linguistics are among its most enduring monuments. Yet the most characteristic mode of its expression was witty, informal, and didactic at once; it was Lichtenberg's aphorisms, Diderot's *Rêve de d'Alembert*, Lessing's *Nathan der Weise*, and Voltaire's *Candide*.

4. CANDIDE: THE EPICUREAN AS STOIC

I

CANDIDE IS INEXHAUSTIBLE. It repays many readings and survives prosaic analysis. It is as many-layered as the site of Troy and as rich in surprises. In a moment of creative mastery, Voltaire has matched manner and matter perfectly, and constructed a unified work of art which is flawless and complete. It must have been as much pleasure to write as it is to read, but only for a writer as talented and as knowledgeable as Voltaire. Talent—that is self-evident; but knowledge too was essential to Voltaire's wit. Diderot recognized this when he told Catherine of Russia: "What is it that particularly distinguishes Voltaire from all our young writers? Learning. Voltaire knows a great deal, and our young poets are ignorant. The work of Voltaire is full of matter, their works are empty."[6] *Candide* is a classic, in two senses of the term: it is a permanent possession of literate men, and it draws, with supreme ease, on classical antiquity.

As a classic of the Enlightenment at once extraordinary and representative, *Candide* epitomizes the appeal to antiquity. Its story is familiar to all: young Candide, innocent and naïve, is expelled

---

[6] *Essai sur les études en Russie*, in *Œuvres*, III, 444.

from a miserable chateau in Westphalia by the baron who owns it, and propelled into a series of grotesque adventures. Candide is imbued with love for Cunégonde, the baron's daughter, and with the fatuous optimistic metaphysics of Dr. Pangloss, the tutor of the house, a cruel caricature of Leibniz. In the end, Candide wins Cunégonde and loses his optimism; his adventures have taught him to see through the doctrine that all is for the best in the best of all possible worlds. Candide's experiences, which are the matter of the tale, are fantastic and horrible, but *Candide* is not simply a fable. The individual pieces of Voltaire's philosophic mosaic are painfully real. What Candide undergoes in his travels all too many people were undergoing in Voltaire's time—Voltaire could document most, perhaps all, of Candide's adventures from the journals of his day: real men were being tricked into joining armies, flogged mercilessly in the course of what was euphemistically called "military training," maltreated by the Inquisition, robbed by greedy merchants, fleeced by unscrupulous courtesans, maligned by venal scribblers, subjected to the grand, silent indifference of nature and the cruelty and selfishness of men. On occasion, Voltaire's realism is so pointedly topical that the modern reader needs a key to grasp the specificity of his allusion: when Candide is made to run the gauntlet in the Bulgarian army, Voltaire is reproducing, almost down to the last detail, a scene that he himself had witnessed at the court of Frederick of Prussia. When Voltaire makes Frederick appear briefly, as king of the Bulgarians—that is, of the *bougres*—his sardonic realism reaches the height of impudence: Voltaire is hinting that the great warrior-philosopher-king of the Prussians may not be a lover of women.

Obviously, Voltaire is not writing a realistic story but a morality tale, and he violates verisimilitude when it fits his didactic purposes. Candide's disasters occur at so rapid a speed—characters are hanged, stabbed, disembowelled so casually and healed so quickly—that no blood seems to flow and the reader has time neither to be horrified nor to be deeply sympathetic. This quality of *Candide*, far from being a flaw, is deliberate: Voltaire draws his characters as stick figures, presents them as marionettes to be manipulated, in order to keep the reader distant and thus alert and rational. *Candide* is not called a philosophical tale for nothing: the reader is purged, not through pity and terror, but through reason, and hence aroused to rational action. Thus the reality of detail is an essential quality of the fable: only the land of Eldorado, where men live in peace, despise riches, have no jails or priests, and are all deists, is obviously, ironically—alas, inevitably—a fiction.

Wherever Candide goes, he observes: he witnesses the Lisbon earthquake and the superstitious reactions of the Portuguese; he happens upon the execution of the British admiral Byng, shot by his fellow citizens in a solemn ceremony *pour encourager les autres;* he visits the Jesuit "kingdom" of Paraguay; he has a sympathetic conversation with a Negro slave from the Dutch sugar plantations who has been brutally mutilated by his owner. And wherever he goes, he argues: his thirst for conversation is never slaked.

All this talk (much like the philosophes' talk in the salons) is to some purpose. Voltaire transforms *Candide,* sprung from the genre of picaresque tales, into a *Bildungsroman,* the story of an education. Candide comes to reject the metaphysical system called "optimism," not by discovering an opposing metaphysical system, but by allowing life to act upon him. He moves from the greedy, heedless, childish pleasure principle to the acceptance of reality. He is slow to learn, and like the typical metaphysician in the Enlightenment's caricature, he continues to parrot "All is for the best" in the midst of rapine, shipwreck, and slaughter. But eventually experience conquers doctrine: in this sense, *Candide* is propaganda in behalf of empiricism, a dramatization of Newton's methods.

It is significant that Candide does not simply receive and record impressions, but talks them out. In this sense, *Candide* is a dialogue, and on several levels. There is Candide's unending debate with Pangloss, carried on whether Pangloss is present or absent. Each new horror is pitted against the doctrine that all is for the best: "O Pangloss," Candide will exclaim, "if you were only here . . ." or, after some light has broken through his blinders: "If this is the best of all possible worlds, what are the others like?" This central debate is surrounded by subsidiary dialogues. Everyone serves Candide as a foil, as a companion in the painful exploration of experience: Cunégonde; her maid; Martin, the coolheaded Manichean whom he meets on his travels and chooses as a friend because Martin is willing to talk philosophy with him; the disillusioned Venetian patrician Pococuranté, whom he seeks out to discover whether wealth and cultivation bring happiness. Even cannibals about to eat him are made to debate international law with him. Voltaire was aware of this aspect of his tale: the twenty-first chapter has what must be one of the most expressive chapter headings of the century—"Candide and Martin Approach the Coast of France and Argue." And, indeed, *Candide* is a dialogue in still another respect: it was part of Voltaire's own evolution into an aggressive social reformer. In the late 1750's when he wrote *Candide*, Voltaire still defined action as thoughtful resignation to reality; a few years later, after and partly through *Candide*, resignation gave way to tireless polemical action—just as the Enlightenment itself was moving toward overt and bellicose radicalism.

Like other dialogues of the Enlightenment, *Candide* is a lesson in eclecticism. Candide builds his world of experience from his visits to South America and the English coast, Paris and Venice, from talks with kings and prostitutes, savages and philosophers. Voltaire's immediate environment—the world of Christian Europe—is confronted from the critical perspective of the Utopia Eldorado, which lives happily without knowing much either of Christianity or of Europe. To draw the contrast as sharply as possible, Voltaire makes Europe's least prepossessing representatives its most prominent spokesmen: rapacious merchants, boorish Barons, worldly Jesuits with eyes for pretty boys, and fanatical Inquisitors are the instruments of Candide's education. By valuing each of them equally, Candide with his democratic curiosity is the very model of the tolerant cosmopolitan. By making him decent, eager for knowledge but a little slow, Voltaire was not merely trying to spin out his tale: he was wryly conceding that even the purest of men has only a precarious hold on reality.

This world in which Candide moves is wholly disenchanted. I have called *Candide* a morality tale; I should add that it is a secular morality tale. There are no harpies here, no gorgons: the causes that move the story are within nature. Some, like the earthquake, are inexplicable but no more miraculous for that. Others find their explanation in social institutions or in human nature as such. Candide leaves Eldorado, at least partly because it is human to boast at home of travels abroad, and also, quite simply, lovely as it is there, human life is not like that; innocent victims are burned at an auto-da-fé in Lisbon after the earthquake because superstitious men reason stupidly and give their hostile impulses free rein; the Westphalian chateau of Baron Thunder-ten-tronckh is razed, its residents are violated and disembowelled, because men at war are beasts; M. Vanderdendur tricks Candide out of his gold because men in general, and merchants in particular, trample on all moral scruples in their lust for gain. All this is so not because men are damned or God is harsh. Nor can it be changed through prayer, pilgrimages, or appeals to the world beyond nature. Change can come from recognition of limits and concentration on realities—this is the moral of the famous last sentence: *Cela est bien dit, mais il faut cultiver notre jardin.*

Candide has pointed to that conclusion from the beginning. The end of the tale, which portrays stability after long wandering, is happy—or at least not intolerably unhappy. Settled on a little farm with his wife Cunégonde, Dr. Pangloss, his philosophical friend Martin, and several other companions, Candide presides over a little society that works contentedly at farming, baking, and embroidery, watches the affairs of the great world with detachment, and whiles away its leisure hours with philosophical disputation. Cunégonde has grown ugly, but honest Candide has fulfilled his pledge and married her despite her looks—proving that it is possible for men to lose their illusions without losing their honor. Only Pangloss is incurable: the madness of metaphysics is too deeply ingrained to be exorcised by the realities around him, or by his own sufferings. But to his involved logical chains of argument in behalf of optimism, Candide opposes the brief, wise sentence, "That's well said, but we must cultivate our garden." Here, in that concluding sentence of the tale, Voltaire has fused the lessons of ancient philosophy into a prescription: Men are thrown into the world to suffer and to dominate their suffering. Life is a shipwreck, but we must not forget to sing in the lifeboats; life is a desert, but we can transform our corner into a garden. Talk is entertaining, but it is useful only when it directs us to our duties and possibilities, since action is irresponsible without a clear conception of duty and unrealistic without a fair appreciation of our possibilities. It is the task of philosophy to discover, as the Stoics said long ago, what is within our power and what is beyond it. *Candide* is thus a morality tale in the most concrete sense possible: it teaches, by example, the supremacy of realistic moral thinking.

II

This is the classicism of *Candide:* its wit is Voltaire's own, its message places it in the tradition of antique speculation. Voltaire greatly admired the Stoics but thought of himself largely as an Epicurean: "The only Stoic principles I have adopted," he wrote in 1755, about three years before he wrote *Candide*, "are the ones that grant the soul to be susceptible to the charms of friendship and pain to be an evil. To spend your life between calumny and colic is a little hard, but study and friendship are consoling."[7] Unlike the Stoics, the Epicureans give room to human nature. And yet, as a true eclectic, Voltaire in *Candide* is the Epicurean as Stoic. His fable enjoins men to cultivate their private selves, but the question remains: how large is our garden? Voltaire's specific answer to this question, as I have suggested, changed after he published *Candide:* if we take the last twenty-five years of Voltaire's life, busy, even frantic, with good causes, as a commentary on this question, the answer becomes that our garden is the world—or more realistically, whatever in the world is in our power. The very writing of *Candide* was therapeutic: it gave Voltaire a sense of control in a universe plagued by irrational disasters. But *Candide* pointed beyond self-mastery to moral action, action which is the only cure for the sense of impotence and the only justification for happiness. That is why *Candide* is so unsparing in its criticism—more than almost any other production of the Enlightenment, *Candide* embodies the philosophes' equation of criticism with philosophy. Its savage portrait of ecclesiastics, its pitiless lampoon of the Jesuits, its curt but bitingly effective delineation of military savagery and economic exploitation—all these suggest the same moral lesson: life is hard and will always be hard,

---

[7] Voltaire to Bertrand (September 30, 1755). *Correspondence*, XXVIII, 71.

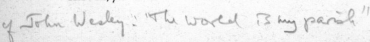 of John Wesley: "The world is my parish"

but in any case, men must uproot the noxious weeds of superstition, fanaticism, and cruelty before they can cultivate their garden with any prospect of a harvest.

This is uncompromising enough, but *Candide* is uncompromising in yet another and even more decisive respect. Its central target, after all, is Leibniz, and Leibniz was the great compromiser of the age. He was the accommodating metaphysician who sought to reconcile religion and philosophy, the principles of Christianity to the principles of rationalism, the theologian who attempted to justify God to men with arguments which a philosopher steeped in Cicero could respect. *Candide* denies that any such accommodation is possible; the book is like a slap in the face of an adroit and benevolent envoy, a firm rejection of negotiations on any basis, and hence, in essence, a declaration of war on Christianity.

BOOK TWO

The Tension
with
Christianity

Upon the whole, we may conclude, that the Christian Religion *not only was at first attended with miracles, but even at this day cannot be believed by any reasonable person without one.*

David Hume,
Enquiry Concerning
Human Understanding
(1748)

Notre devise est: Sans quartier pour les superstitieux, pour les fanatiques, pour les ignorants, pour les fous, pour les méchants et pour les tyrans. . . . Est-ce qu'on s'appelle philosophe pour rien? Quoi! le mensonge aura ses martyrs, et la vérité ne sera prêchée que par les lâches? Ce qui me plaît des frères, c'est de les voir presque tous moins unis par la haine et le mépris de celle que vous avez appelée l'infâme que par l'amour de la vertu, par le sentiment de la bienfaisance et par le goût du vrai, du bon et du beau, espèce de trinité qui vaut un peu mieux que la leur. Ce n'est pas assez que d'en sçavoir plus qu'eux; il faut leur montrer que nous sommes meilleurs, et que la philosophie fait plus de gens de bien que la grâce suffisante ou efficace.

Diderot to Voltaire,
September 29, 1762

Es gibt zwar viele rechtschaffende Christlichen, das ist gar keine Frage, so wie es überall und in allen Ständen gute Menschen gibt, allein so viel ist gewiss, 'in corpore,' und was sie als solches unternommen haben, ist nie viel wert gewesen.

Lichtenberg,
"Bemerkungen"
(ca. 1790)

CHAPTER FOUR

The Retreat from Reason

SOME TIME LATE IN THE FIRST CENTURY OF OUR ERA, an insidious force began to insinuate itself into the mentality of the Roman Empire. Slyly exploiting men's fears and anxieties and offering grandiose promises of eternal salvation, Christianity gradually subverted the self-reliant paganism that had sustained the ruling classes. The Roman state had been far from perfect—with all his contempt for its destroyers, Gibbon acknowledged that in chronicling its decline and fall, he was writing a tragedy. Rome's tragic flaws were at once deep-rooted and patent: its philosophy had never achieved authentic originality; its treatment of the lower orders had rarely risen above a clever mixture of pandering, bribery, and repression; the state itself had been victimized by a succession of debauched and callous emperors. Yet educated Romans had at least made a serious attempt to construct a civilization founded on reason, not myth. Then came Christianity, profiting, vulturelike, from decay, preserving ideas that deserved to perish, and stamping out ideas that deserved to survive.

In its early history, its very origins, there was something unsavory about Christianity. Significantly, it flourished in an age of decadence and among the lower orders, among men and women sunk in ignorance, vice, and despair. Significantly, too, it hammered out its doctrine, its discipline and organization, amidst undignified wranglings, inane debates in endless assemblies, angry conflicts over trivial matters, mutual slanders and persecutions. Christianity claimed to bring light, hope, and truth, but its central myth was incredible, its dogma a conflation of rustic superstitions, its sacred book an incoherent collection of primitive tales, its church a cohort of servile fanatics as long as they were out of power and of despotic fanatics once they had seized control. With its triumph in the fourth century, Christianity secured the victory of infantile credulity; one by one, the lamps of learning were put out, and for centuries darkness covered the earth.

These centuries of darkness were not simply a time of asceticism and persecution. Like other times, they had their hard-working peasants, proud aristocrats, and prudent merchants. But all alike were ruled by priests and ridden with superstition; the laborer carousing in the tavern, the knight performing his courtly ritual, and the philosopher speculating about essences might forget for a moment the burden of religion, but the childish hope of heaven and the equally childish fear of hell governed their lives. A small but influential elite of enlightened ancients had made man the proper study of mankind; in the Christian millennium, no matter what one's occupation, the proper study of mankind was God. In the distant classical past, the meeting place of the best minds had been the philosophical school or the political forum; in Christian times, it was the church—the church dominated the medieval landscape, literally and emotionally. "A revolution was necessary," wrote Rousseau, "to bring men back to common sense."[1]

There were some signs of that revolution during the Middle Ages themselves: it was not an epoch equally dark at all times. The Fathers of the Church, far from being all barbarians, had been influenced by Platonism; some of them had even exploited the classics for their own uses: they had claimed Vergil's Fourth Eclogue as a prediction of Christ's coming and claimed Seneca himself for Christianity. Then later, in the twelfth and thirteenth centuries, medieval culture underwent a transformation; a transformation more profound in appearance than in reality, to be sure, but still far-reaching in scope. Heretics questioned the reigning doctrine and, while they were not themselves committed to reason, furthered the cause of reason by reopening debate. In the same way, crusaders, fanatics though they were, served critical thought by opening men's eyes to other civilizations. Philosophy re-emerged, and while it was largely a specious substitute for thinking, a set of superstitious propositions decked out with pretentious logic and ludicrous metaphysics, it improved the tone, even if it

---

[1] *Discours sur les sciences et les arts*, in *Œuvres*, III, 6.

did not change the substance, of Christian civilization. Towns revived and wrested from princes charters of privilege that became the ancestors of modern declarations of rights. Trade improved standards of living and touched backward areas with cultivation; the sciences of jurisprudence, politics, and economics remained in naïve infancy, but at least they allowed themselves to learn from experience. Christians had plunged the world back into credulity, but their millennium was, at least after a dismal interlude, vastly superior to the first age of belief. It produced a few books worth reading and solved a few of its political problems. In its accumulation of material goods, its handful of great men, and even some of its intellectual performance, the Middle Ages offered rational men hope for better things to come—hope for a revival of learning.

This, with minor variations, is the Enlightenment's view of the Middle Ages. I need hardly say that it is a caricature, a tendentious misreading of massive evidence: two centuries of scholarship have exposed the philosophes' blindness to the beauty, the learning, and the variety of the Christian millennium. The *Encyclopédie* printed several relatively sympathetic articles about medieval customs; historians like Dubos, Turgot, and Voltaire carefully differentiated periods within the Middle Ages and brought themselves to say some good words for medieval institutions. They conceded that Christianity had triumphed because other cults had failed. They found exceptional personages, like Emperor Frederick II, whom they could praise for their learning and their tolerance—in a word, for anticipating the Enlightenment; Condorcet noted that Frederick—the very emperor whom Dante had placed into the sixth circle of hell—had been "suspected of being what the priests of our eighteenth century have come to call a 'philosophe.' "[2] And Condorcet, for all his fanatical deprecation of the Middle Ages, also conceded that the Scholastics had done much for "sound philosophy."[3] And so, with majestic condescension, Gibbon allowed that "the darkness of the middle ages exhibits some scenes not unworthy of our notice."[4]

---

[2] *Esquisse*, in *Œuvres*, VI, 127.
[3] *Vie de Turgot*, ibid., V, 11.
[4] *Decline and Fall of the Roman Empire*, VII, 210.

But asides like these were merely grudging concessions to objectivity. Long before he wrote his *Decline and Fall of the Roman Empire*, a book not noted for its generosity to Christians, Gibbon had laid it down that "the enemies of a religion never know it, because they hate it, and often they hate it because they do not know it."[5] But the philosophes did not observe the sound advice concealed in this dictum. It is not that they were wholly ignorant—Gibbon himself knew the history of the early church as well as anyone in the eighteenth century—but that they sought out what would discredit, and slighted what would exalt their Christian enemy.

Condorcet's hostile analysis of the expansion of Christianity, or Voltaire's sardonic treatment of early Councils overlooked that fourth-century Christianity was radical, offering a new dispensation to men weary of oriental superstitions or creaking doctrines whose main appeal was that they stood for the good old cause. The philosophies of the late Empire (if they deserve to be called philosophy) appealed in tones of tired, dignified snobbishness to a cultivated antiquarianism or dabbled in a gloomy version of astrology which only confirmed men's sense of impotence before inexorable fate. Christianity was more dramatic and less crude than the prevailing superstitions; more attractive and less pessimistic than the prevailing philosophies. In later centuries, too, Christianity was a far more constructive, far more civilizing, force than the philosophes were willing to admit. Gibbon's unmeasured contempt for the Byzantine Empire, Voltaire's rejection of medieval literature, Diderot's, Lessing's, Hume's insensitivity to Gothic architecture, and the ubiquitous Enlightenment cliché about clerics being all either fools or knaves, gluttons or perverts —all these are the unhappy consequences of the philosophes' political bias joined to a certain self-satisfaction. "A philosophic age has abolished with too liberal and indiscriminate disdain, the honours of these spiritual heroes"—thus Gibbon on saints like Bernard of Clairvaux. "The meanest among them are distinguished by some energies of the mind; they were at least superior to their votaries and disciples." St. Bernard, "in speech, in writing, in

---

[5] *Essai sur l'étude de la littérature*, in *Miscellaneous Works*, IV, 70.

action," stood "high above his rivals and contemporaries; his compositions are not devoid of wit and eloquence; and he seems to have preserved as much reason and humanity as may be reconciled with the character of a saint."[6] So meager, so ungracious a tribute explains the impatience of later critics with the Enlightenment's view of the Middle Ages: the philosophes seem more malicious when they praise medieval Christians than when they criticize them.

Yet in their impatience with the philosophes' injustice to a thousand years of history, critics of the Enlightenment have generally been as partisan as the partisanship they tried to eradicate; they have used the philosophes' prejudices as a target rather than as a clue. When literate and cultivated men make what seem to us Philistine judgments, their inconsistency—which was not an inconsistency to them—should provide historians with a window to the inner recesses of past convictions. It should remind us, first of all, that the pervasive attitude of eighteenth-century Christians gave the philosophes little encouragement to find anything valuable in the Middle Ages. Those ages, said Addison, were a period of "darkness and superstition," when men looked upon nature with "reverence and horror," and his opinion was too widely shared in his day to call for documentation or defense.[7] Isolated visionaries apart, pious men were as insensitive as atheists to the glories of Chartres or the *Divine Comedy* or Provençal poetry. The rage for modernity was general. But obviously—I have said it before—the philosophes brought a special zest to this rage: when Addison early in the century or Percy in the 1760's hinted at the glories of medieval romance, they refused to respond; they treated the past ideologically because they were engaged in an ideological battle that knew no quarter. The Christian millennium, whether it was the irrationalism of Augustine, the vaulting architectonics of Aquinas, or the pitiless legalism of Calvin, was part of their political present.

These cultural realities go far to explain the failures of the philosophes' historiography, even if they do not excuse them. But there is one critical point where their historiography needs no

---

[6] *Decline and Fall of the Roman Empire*, VI, 332–3.
[7] *Spectator*, No. 419.

palliations, where the philosophes' view of the Middle Ages, tendentious and narrow as it was, celebrated a paradoxical triumph of which I have spoken before: hidden behind a tissue of erroneous detail and prejudiced judgment stands a major historical truth, a truth that remains valid and becomes more obvious after its animus has been stripped away and its emotional terminology replaced by neutral language—the Middle Ages were different in vital essence from the ages that preceded and followed them. And they were different, above all, because they introduced—or rather, reinstated—religious myth as the deepest motive power and final purpose of civilization. The Christians' equivocal reception of classical learning and their demotion of philosophy, significant though they are as contributory causes, stand largely as signs or symptoms of that vast transvaluation of values.

1. THE ADULTERATION OF ANTIQUITY

I

As IRRITABLE LOVERS OF ANTIQUITY, the philosophes were exceedingly scornful toward the Christians' handling of their precious classical inheritance. "Contempt for the humanities—*sciences humaines*—" writes Condorcet, "was one of the principal characteristics of Christianity. It had to avenge itself against the insults offered by philosophy." The cause of this contempt, he thought, was evident: Christianity "feared that spirit of investigation and doubt, that confidence in one's own reason, which is the scourge of all religious beliefs. It found the very light of the natural sciences hateful and suspect, for it is extremely dangerous to the success of miracles; and there is not a single religion that does not force its devotees to swallow a few scientific absurdities. Thus the triumph of Christianity was the signal for the complete decay of the sciences and philosophy."[8] Christianity stood—and could only stand—on the ruins of ancient secular learning. Greek

---

[8] *Esquisse*, in *Œuvres*, VI, 103.

learning had suffered as much as Roman—perhaps more: the men of the Byzantine Empire, wrote Gibbon, whose relative ignorance of Byzantium did not cause him a moment's hesitation,

> held in their lifeless hands the riches of their fathers, without inheriting the spirit which had created and improved that sacred patrimony; they read, they praised, they compiled, but their languid souls seemed alike incapable of thought and action. In the revolution of ten centuries, not a single discovery was made to exalt the dignity or promote the happiness of mankind. Not a single idea has been added to the speculative systems of antiquity, and a succession of patient disciples became in their turn the dogmatic teachers of the next servile generation. Not a single composition of history, philosophy, or literature has been saved from oblivion by the intrinsic beauties of style, or sentiment, or original fancy, or even of successful imitation.

Even though twelfth-century Constantinople had been "enlightened by the genius of Homer and Demosthenes, of Aristotle and Plato," such an enlightenment was fleeting and superficial.[9] In the callous hands of Christians, Greek and Roman literature had survived, but barely, and at great cost.

The measure of this cost (both as it appeared to the philosophes and in actuality, for the two, while similar, are not the same) may perhaps best be taken through Dante, for Dante— on this much, at least, philosophes and modern critics agree— was the greatest poet of the Christian Middle Ages, and Dante demonstrated in his life's work what the marriage of classical poetry and Christian philosophy could produce in the hands of a genius. The philosophes acknowledged this marriage, if a little ungraciously: Voltaire called the *Inferno* a "bizarre mixture of Christianity and paganism,"[1] while in his acceptance speech to the Académie française, he praised Dante a little more generously for "expressing everything" freely, following "the example of the ancients."[2] It has often been said that Dante's encounter with

---

[9] *Decline and Fall of the Roman Empire*, VI, 106–7.
[1] Lettre XII, "Sur le Dante," *Lettre chinoises* (1776), in *Œuvres*, XXIX, 497.
[2] *Discours de réception* (1746), ibid., XXIII, 208.

Vergil was one of the great moments in European literature, and while the philosophes were skeptical, even sardonic, about it, they conceded that Dante had written imperishable poetry. It compelled Concorcet's admiration for its nobility, precision, and energy; it moved Voltaire, even though he could not suppress the witticism that if the Italians called Dante divine, he must be a hidden God: there are verses in the *Divine Comedy*, he allowed, so felicitous, so beautifully simple, that they have not grown stale in four centuries, and will never grow stale. Yet having paid this reluctant tribute, Voltaire insisted that as a whole the *Divine Comedy* was a "hodgepodge," a "bizarre" compilation of puerile tales and absurd allegories;[3] and while his obtuseness testifies to his distance from Dante, his critique, no matter how inept, also points to Dante's distance from Vergil.

For it is true that while, to Dante, Vergil was more alive, more intimate, more directly relevant, than he was to any of the philosophes, Dante's Vergil is largely a fictitious figure, a travesty of the pagan poet, while Lessing's or Diderot's Vergil, a popular, much-read but somewhat distant classic, was closer to the historical reality. Dante used Vergil as an allegory for reason and philosophy, a virtuous, courageous, and perceptive guide through the very depths of Inferno where Satan, the supreme rebel, stands forever frozen, beating his ghastly wings and chewing with his three mouths the three archtraitors of history, Judas, Brutus, and Cassius—three figures for whom the Enlightenment was to profess rather different feelings. And Vergil was more than that: Dante's poetic genius, and medieval sensibility at its best, fed on multiple visions and complex interpretations in which a commanding figure like Vergil could be many things.

Thus Dante's Vergil was first of all himself, his "master and author": Dante endows him with marked individuality, with Roman rectitude, love of his native city, hatred for evil, a capacity for all too human impatience and even fear. Beyond that, Vergil

---

[3] Condorcet: *Esquisse*, in *Œuvres*, VI, 135; Voltaire: "Dante (le)" (1765), *Œuvres*, XVIII, 312–13. Some Voltaire specialists have suggested that this short article should not be taken as a serious expression of Voltaire's taste, but such suggestions are wishful thinking: for all his occasional words of appreciation, Voltaire nowhere shows any real understanding of Dante's poetic achievement.

is an authority on ancient history, authoritative with almost Scriptural finality. Like other men of the Middle Ages, Dante did not think that Rome had ever fallen; it had been beset and corrupted, but its political mission was as alive as it had been in the days of Augustus. Vergil is a reminder of that eternal Rome to which Dante appealed in passionate political nostalgia. And then Vergil is a pagan prophet of Christian history: Dante accepted the common view that the fourth *Eclogue* had foretold the coming of Christ. Vergil (so speaks the Roman poet Statius in the *Purgatorio*) was like a man who bears a light behind him, illuminating the way for others while he himself walks in darkness. In the *Divine Comedy*, Vergil, condemned to limbo for eternity as a virtuous pagan, sounds like a shade who found Christianity after death: in the *Inferno*, he harshly berates sinners and conducts himself as one who fully accepts the Christian dispensation; in the *Purgatorio*, he even exhorts Dante to prayer. The *Divine Comedy* is filled with the most articulate admiration for pagan antiquity, but the highest use of that antiquity was to serve as the harbinger of Christian truth. This is the paradox of Dante's relation to antiquity. It is a commonplace that lovers reshape what they love nearer to their hearts' desire, and Dante, the Christian lover of the classics, was no exception, but to jaundiced philosophes it seemed as though Dante's reshaping resembled a drastic operation whose results were fatal.

The most discriminating of Enlightenment historians never escaped this partisan estimate of Dante—or of his age as a whole. In his analysis of Rome's decline and fall, Gibbon offers a whole list of causes and carefully differentiates the triumph of barbarism from the triumph of religion: one was a military invasion from without; the other, a spiritual inner cancer. Yet he implies again and again that barbarism and religion were interdependent: religion was as barbarizing an influence as the barbarians. The other philosophes agreed: the Fathers of the Church had secured the victory of the Faith by compromising the learning, the very spirit, of antiquity, and the Doctors of the Church had been no better —their assault on the ancients had been more subtle, but no less ruthless. In the fatal affection of Christians for pagans, the philosophes saw only the fatality, not the affection. They could not muster the historical sympathy that would have allowed them to see the pathos of the Christian love for the classics, or its felicities, and so they condemned it, sarcastically or indignantly, as a concentrated assault on a great past. They did not see the spiritual travail of the Church Fathers, themselves steeped in the classics, faced with powerful and appealing secular learning that stood as a competitor to their faith and a distraction from higher things; they did not see, ironically enough, that the Fathers of the Church could not deal generously with secular literature precisely for the reason that they, the philosophes, could not deal generously with religious literature: they were at war for a high cause. And they did not see the tortuous evolution of Christian policy. All they saw was the adulteration of antiquity in the Christian millennium.

II

It is possible, and even relatively easy, to find Christians hating pagan antiquity with all the passion the philosophes ascribed to them, but such ascetics were extremists. Suspicious of all worldly things, they feared pagan learning as the supreme, the most seductive, example of secular achievement. In the third century, Tertullian ("that African madman," as Voltaire called him) rhetorically inquired: "What has Athens to do with Jerusalem?" And again: "What is there in common between the philosopher and the Christian, the pupil of Hellas and the pupil of Heaven, the worker for reputation and for salvation, the manufacturer of words and of deeds, the builder and the destroyer, the interpolator of error and the artificer of truth, the thief of truth and its custodian?" Thales falling into the well while gazing at the stars is an appropriate warning to all who busy themselves with the "stupidities of philosophy"; nothing is more repugnant than learned attempts to patch up Christianity with Stoic or Platonic elements; in fact, since the advent of Jesus Christ and the Gospel there has been no need for curiosity, which is but brazen impiety.[4]

These outbursts are often quoted since they represent a prominent and persistent Christian attitude. This distrust of knowledge, of science and literature, had been implicit in St.

---

[4] See Charles N. Cochrane: *Christianity and Classical Culture* (edn. 1957), 222–3.

Paul's statement to the Corinthians that God will confound the wisdom of the wise by the "sheer folly" of his message, and it was echoed by Christian rigorists through the centuries: in the sixth century, as intelligent and learned a cleric as Pope Gregory could deplore the grammarians and glory in his own barbarisms. With the recrudescence of learning in the eleventh and twelfth centuries, the opposition to profane letters redoubled its vehemence. Around 1050, Peter Damian, chancellor to Pope Gregory VII, published a virulent tract against the grammarians, significantly entitled *De sancta simplicitate:* was not the Devil the father of grammar? Did not monkish grammarians tempt the good Christian to polytheistic heresies by teaching him to decline *deus* in the plural? A century later, St. Bernard of Clairvaux, whose own writings reverberate with antique memories, polemicized against Abelard's dialectical writings by disdainfully dismissing those who "call themselves philosophers": such men, he wrote, are no better than "slaves to curiosity and pride."[5] Pious and fearful clerks, from Tertullian to Bernard and after, looked upon the most innocuous of pagan writings as a temptation to sin, and on pagan philosophy in general as a diabolical temptation, luring weak men to teachings that extol pleasures, worldliness, and dignified self-sufficiency. The only teacher the true Christian needed was the Holy Spirit.

At least some of this uncompromising rejection of learning was a response to the vigorous polemics of an opposing party within Christendom, a long line of clerics who were reluctant to abandon the rich treasures of pagan antiquity. It was this party, above all, that was slighted by the silence, or the facile disdain, of Enlightenment historians. As articulate and civilized men who saw no need to abandon Vergil for the sake of Christ, these devout humanists defended some pagan writings as innocent, and others as prefigurations of sublime scriptural wisdom. A few of them, good scholars in their own right, held a sound knowledge of Latin and Greek indispensable for an understanding of the Holy Message and for the propagation of the faith among alien peoples.

In the centuries from Augustine to John of Salisbury, this

---

[5] See Étienne Gilson: *Reason and Revelation in the Middle Ages* (1938), 12.

erudite Christian band produced dozens of grammarians and commentators. Cultivated pedants preserved antiquity in its least impressive and least attractive form, but by their very diligence and earnestness, they prevented the destruction of Greek and Roman letters. They were supported by other clerics and exceptional laymen whose feeling for antiquity was one of sheer affection. Together, these humanists created some lively outbursts of literary enthusiasm. At the court of Charlemagne, the emperor's friends indulged in a fashionable classicism, imitated pagan poetry, and called one another by pagan nicknames; in the Greek East there were sporadic appeals to ancient Greece. But the Byzantine enlightenment was generally connected with the political needs of the ruling dynasty; it was an ideological weapon rather than a true cultural flowering, even though its contribution to the preservation of the ancients was greater than could be guessed from Gibbon's description. In the West, classical learning had an impressive efflorescence in the twelfth century. These revivals were not Renaissances but periodic injections that kept the classical heritage alive. When Dante hailed Vergil as the greatest of poets, Livy as an infallible historian, and Aristotle as the master of those who know, the way for such classicism had been thoroughly prepared.

The main stream of Christian policy toward antiquity ran somewhat unsteadily between these extremes. St. Jerome and St. Augustine laid down rules adapted to meet the exigencies of their times, rigid enough for severe piety, flexible enough to vary with the strength of the opposition, and ingenious enough to survive for centuries. Their very ingenuity reveals an incurable ambivalence toward pagan literature: Christians could not do without it, but they could not refrain from tampering with it. The great compromise, achieved in the fourth and fifth centuries, was to extract from paganism whatever could be adapted to religious purposes or enjoyed in wholesome innocence, and to throw the rest away. A celebrated incident in St. Jerome's life shows that this policy imposed a grave strain on some of the Fathers. Sometime around the year 374, Jerome had a vision at the height of a fever. He dreamt that he had been brought before the Eternal Judge and there condemned: *Ciceronianus es, non Christianus*—"You are a Ciceronian, not a Christian." Trembling at the justice of the indictment, he foreswore his beloved classics, did a long hard penance, and (as he recalled later) did not read a secular author for fifteen years. Then he resumed, slowly and carefully, and began his great Latin version of the Bible, a monument to Christian erudition.

Jerome's dream and subsequent vacillations—he refused to quote Varro on the ground that he did not want to bring uncircumcised men into the temple of God, but began his concentrated study of Cicero after he had received his fateful warning—dramatize the intensity with which early Christians confronted the classics: they invested their reading of Cicero or Ovid with all the sinfulness usually reserved for illicit sexual indulgence. And Jerome's dream became the model for others who could not resolve the same conflict; it was often quoted and sometimes imitated. Throughout the Middle Ages, pious Christians stopped reading their classics after being warned by hysterical symptoms of a kind we have learned to associate with frustrated erotic urges. Otloh of St. Emmeram, a German scholar of the eleventh century, reports that after reading Lucan he was attacked by skin rashes and nightmares; after he had recovered from his illness, he wrote an essay on pious erudition, in which he exclaimed: "What then were Socrates to me? Or Plato, Aristotle, or even Tullius the Orator?"

Early in his agitated reflections, Jerome had come upon a Scriptural text that was to provide him with a policy: "When thou goest forth to war against thine enemies, and the Lord thy God hath delivered them into thine hands, and thou hast taken them captive, And seest among the captives a beautiful woman, and hast a desire unto her, that thou wouldst have her to thy wife; Then thou shalt bring her home to thine house; and she shall shave her head, and pare her nails; And she shall put the raiment of her captivity from off her, and shall remain in thine house."[6] This passage had first been used by Origen, but Jerome made it famous. He liked it enough to quote it more than once, and so did later Christians unsettled by classical learning. St. Augustine lent it his enormous authority; Hrabanus Maurus, encyclopedist and archbishop of Mainz in the time of Charle-

---

[6] Deuteronomy, XXI, 11–13.

magne, quoted it in his influential treatise on the training of the clergy; and St. Peter Damian used it in the eleventh century to exorcise the perils of pagan thought. It was a hardy cliché that survived into the Renaissance, conclusive because it brought to bear the authority of the Bible on a question that no educated Christian could resolve with ease.

The allegory from Deuteronomy is a harsh one, and its harshness is telling; it leaves no uncertainty as to the conditions under which pagan thought could survive in a Christian atmosphere. Other metaphors, almost equally popular, were just as harsh. Church Fathers as different as Justin Martyr and St. Augustine justified pious borrowings from pagan literature on the ground that Christians were merely taking back what had originally been stolen from them. It was commonly accepted that Greek philosophers had leaned heavily on the wisdom of Moses —eighteenth-century philosophic polemicists still took the trouble to refute this legend. Thus one theft justified another. In his *De doctrina christiana*, St. Augustine alluded to still another theft: the children of Israel had left Egypt laden with the treasures of the country, and so ancient culture, a storehouse of the precious and the dangerous, should be looted of what was needed— rhetorical devices, above all, and ethical ideas. As late as the twelfth century, the Benedictine monk Conrad of Hirsau returned to this allegory and added a touch of his own: the treasures of Egypt, he wrote in his *Dialogus super auctores*, are pagan literature; they should be used as a cooking herb, to be thrown away after they have flavored the food. In the same century, around 1150, the abbot of Hildesheim energetically defended the study of the classics in similar language: "You go over to the camp of the enemy not as a deserter, but as a spy." Ironically, his very remark fulfilled his recommendation—he had taken his image from Seneca.[7] Pagan learning, then, was a slave, precious booty, or secret enemy information—all metaphors implying that it was invaluable and indispensable without being respectable. As antique a thinker as Augustine defended the use of the classics for

---

[7] *Epistulae morales*, II, 5. For Conrad of Hirsau see Ernst Robert Curtius: *European Literature and the Latin Middle Ages*, 466.

religious purposes only. No wonder that the philosophes, who liked their classics neat, could find no virtue in such procedures.

III

The rigorous prescription implied in Deuteronomy was sometimes ignored, sometimes evaded, and sometimes bent to the uses of an adventurous mind, but in general, pagan poets, pagan philosophers, and pagan gods were shaved, pared, and kept in the house of Christianity to serve a Christian master. The learned reinterpreted and the ignorant confused them. The pagan deities survived the Christian era largely by going underground; sometimes, in fact, when they re-emerged, they were quickly buried again. The great Florentine sculptor Ghiberti reports that sometime in the 1350's a statue of Venus, signed by Lysippus, was excavated in Siena and at first exhibited triumphantly as a glorious antique treasure. But then one of the citizens publicly blamed the disasters of the city on this sort of pagan idolatry, and in November 1357, the statue was removed from its prominent place of display and buried—in Florentine territory, to transfer the curse to Siena's fiercest enemy. Sir Kenneth Clark, who quotes Ghiberti's story, observes that it was not the nudity of the statue that was at issue —nudity could be reinterpreted as temperance or chastity, and thus find its place even on the porches of cathedrals—but its character as "a heathen idol."[8] Pagan gods could keep their form, no matter how pagan, if they surrendered their nature, or retain their nature if they gave up their form: the "Venus" illustrated in Hrabanus Maurus's Encyclopedia was clearly based on antique models but had lost her seductive charms and appeared heavy, clumsy, most un-Venuslike; on the other hand, in the *Roman de la rose*, Venus appears worldly and sensual, but dressed as a fourteenth-century lady. Other deities, like Fortuna, were saved in the same manner.

Classical poetry, too, although guardedly admired and widely read, was fitted into the Christian scheme of things. Dante's choice of Vergil as his guide in no way convicts Dante of heretical in-

---

[8] *The Nude* (1956), 94.

clinations: Vergil had been a favorite among Christians ever since
the Emperor Constantine had singled him out as a prophet of
Christ's incarnation. If his fourth *Eclogue*, Gibbon writes with
heavy but well-informed irony, "contributed to the conversion
of the first Christian emperor, Vergil may deserve to be ranked
among the most successful missionaries of the gospel."[9] In fact,
the Christian cult of Vergil was widespread and long-lived. He
was celebrated as a prophet and a sage, and almost became a saint.
The popular mind transformed the poet into a mysterious magician, and scholarly imagination invented and transmitted the most
remarkable legends. In Mantua, Vergil's birthplace, it was said
that St. Paul had made a pilgrimage to Vergil's tomb and had
wept that The Poet should have died before the Truth of Christ
had been made manifest—the same thought that made Dante
weep more than twelve centuries later. Stories about Vergil's
prowess spread through Europe and were repeated for centuries,
by word of mouth, in popular manuscripts, and after the invention
of printing, even in books. In the twelfth century, John of Salisbury recorded in his *Policraticus* that Vergil controlled a miraculous fly which rid the city of Naples of an unbearable invasion
of insects. Other stories made Vergil into an incomparable
necromancer: Voltaire reports that in Naples his reputation as a
sorcerer had survived into the eighteenth century.

The effect of these legends was to keep the work of Vergil
alive. Another, more deliberate way of preserving Vergil was to
convert his *Aeneid* into an edifying allegory. In the sixth century,
the Christian poet and grammarian Fulgentius reinterpreted the
Aeneid as the history of man's earthly pilgrimage: he read Book I
as an account of early childhood, complete with lullaby. In the
twelfth century, Bernard Silvestris, a leading figure in the erudite
school of Chartres, drew a similar but far subtler allegory from
the first six books and discovered, among other things, a treatment
of the seven liberal arts in Book VI. This unbuttoned allegorizing
could convert anything into anything else. But at least it kept the
classics from extinction, though at the price of covering them
with layers of pious legend.

Allegory even saved Ovid. For centuries he had served,

---

[9] *Decline and Fall of the Roman Empire*, II, 307–8.

appropriately enough, as little more than a terrible example of
lax pagan morals. But the rich culture of twelfth-century Europe,
starved for good stories and ready to mock its religion gently
and piously, found Ovid entertaining. The distaste of rigorists
was soothed, if not wholly overcome, by a generous reinterpretation of Ovid's life and work: Ovid was first cleared of the
charge of personal licentiousness and then converted by the kindly
hand of legend into another Vergil—into a magician, a philosopher, and on occasion even into a saint. From the moral Roman
to the Roman moralist, and from the moralist to the theologian,
was only two steps, easy for the nimble allegorizing mind of the
twelfth century. The popular *florilegia*, little "golden treasures"
of ancient sayings arranged according to topics, gave generous
space to excerpts from all of Ovid's writings, quoting him on
solemn themes like death, or *de mutabilitate rerum temporalium*,
the mutability of worldly things. In the twelfth century, too, full-
fledged allegory, so successful with Vergil, began to be applied
with great imaginative freedom to the *Ars amatoria* and other
Ovidian poems. The gods of the *Metamorphoses* were seen as
clerics, the goddesses as nuns, and their couplings as innocent
meetings—a metamorphosis perhaps more astounding than any
that Ovid himself had recorded. In the thirteenth century, the
Integumenta, a much-quoted poem, converted Venus into Spring,
Vulcan into Summer, and Mars into bristling Autumn. This conversion of Ovid, the most gaily lascivious and incurably pagan of
poets, into a servant of Christian civilization reached its climax
early in the fourteenth century with a gigantic allegory win-
ningly entitled *Ovide moralisé*, which transformed Diana into the
Trinity, Actaeon into Jesus Christ, Ceres searching for Proser-
pina into the True Church looking for strayed Christian sheep,
and as an ultimate refinement, Ceres's two torches into the Old
and New Testaments. This was not the Ovid whom Augustus had
banished, and whom the philosophes would later read with such
secular enjoyment.

Horace, the philosophes' favorite, was harder to deal with,
but he too found his place in the Christian universe. His verses
could not be made to yield prophecies of Christianity, and they
did not lend themselves to the mask of allegory. As the poet of

rural felicity, friendship, and that most irreligious of qualities, Epicurean moderation, Horace could be saved only by the most dramatic excisions. His popularity was never great; no legends formed around him. His Odes and Epodes were almost unknown, but the *Ars poetica,* with its sententious advice to poets and dramatists, and moral tags from the Epistles and Satires found their way into the *florilegia.*

Yet the truths which antique poetry was thought to conceal beneath its frivolity were always innocuous. In a famous scene of the *Inferno,* Dante is invited to join the immortal company of ancient poets: of Homer, Horace, Ovid, Lucan, and Vergil himself. Entering this timeless establishment, Dante is himself an ancient, but his use of antiquity is characteristically medieval: Homer was the sovereign poet of pagans and Christians alike, invoked but unknown; Dante's Ovid was the Ovid of Dante's time—the source of allegories and myths, the elegant stylist; Lucan was the master of pathos and hence a poetic model; Horace was the "satirist," author of moral tales and critic of his age; Vergil was the poet from whom alone Dante claims to have learned the *bello stilo* that has made him famous. There is nothing here to burst the bonds of the medieval world view.

The forcible assimilation that worked so well with the poets worked equally well with the philosophers. The clerks who guarded Christian culture, in fact, saw little difference between them: the threat of paganism to their world view was not contained in some specific philosophical doctrine, although it was most obvious there, but in the whole intellectual posture implicit in ancient writings; in the worldliness, the critical detachment from myth, the disenchantment that marked many works of antique imagination as strongly as it marked many works of antique philosophy. Like the poets, therefore, the ancient philosophers were ruthlessly culled, suppressed, and reinterpreted. Cicero, whose honored place in the Enlightenment we know, was admired as a great rhetor (that is to say, as a technician), and persistently misread down to the thirteenth century: his praise of Scipio's active leisure—*in otio de negotio cogitabat*—was taken by St. Ambrose as consonant with the monastic life, and by St. Jerome as an outright commendation of the philosophic life in preference to marriage. Thus the greatest antique advocate of the *vita activa* was enlisted under the banner of the *vita contemplativa*.

By the time of Albertus Magnus and St. Thomas Aquinas, there were scholars who dealt with ancient philosophers in a more straightforward manner. In the twelfth century, John of Salisbury and Abelard had still interpreted Cicero as the teacher of eloquence yearning for saintliness; in the thirteenth century, the great Scholastics interpreted him as the supreme advocate of the active life, but rejected his ideal in favor of another pagan ideal—Aristotle's theoretic life. This new capacity for reading the ancients sensibly, reflected the growing self-confidence of Christian philosophers and a century's experience of grappling with the commanding system of Aristotle. Awed as they were by the encyclopedic grasp and logical persuasiveness of The Philosopher, anxious as they were to shelter under his enormous authority, the Scholastics yet treated Aristotle as Jerome and Augustine had commanded good Christians to treat all of antiquity. Respectfully, almost timidly, Albertus Magnus and Thomas Aquinas sought ways of reconciling Aristotle's teachings with Christian dogma—and sometimes, as wary contemporaries charged, stretched Christian dogma to rescue Aristotle's teachings. But they had sufficient intellectual vigor to acknowledge that Aristotle's work contained heretical ideas, and to reject them; reluctantly but piously, they turned to Augustine and away from The Philosopher when serious points of doctrine were at stake. The philosophes' scornful characterization of the Scholastics as the slavish copyists of Aristotle is wide of the mark; ironically enough, a more accurate judgment would have served their cause better: the Scholastics were more independent than the Enlightenment knew, but their independence did not result in critical freedom. The Scholastics were the slaves, not of censors or Inquisitors, but of their ruling myth.

The philosophes' misreadings do not end here. As they overestimated the dependence of the Scholastics on Aristotle, so they underestimated the continuity between antique and medieval civilization. The Middle Ages was not merely an abyss, as the philosophes liked to charge, but also a transmission belt. Ancient metaphors, types of rhetoric, favorite literary topics, and mythological themes were all taken up by medieval writers and kept

alive for modern literature.[1] The survival of these forms carried
with it at least some vestiges of ancient thought. But—and this the
philosophes understood for all their partisanship and all their
simplistic interpretations—if we are to judge the shape of medieval
civilization it is not enough to document these survivals: what
matters most is the function of these survivals in the scheme of
medieval life. In accepting and handling antique forms of expression and antique ideas, medieval clerks were all too often like
couriers carrying a sealed message. Medieval Humanists fought
stout battles for classical letters, and won important skirmishes
against rigorists and mystics. But while they held grimly on to
the ramparts of antiquity, they surrendered its citadel—the autonomy of critical thought.

2. THE BETRAYAL OF CRITICISM

I

FROM THE VANTAGE POINT of the Enlightenment, this surrender
was nothing less than treason: the educated, whose very task
it was to guard the inviolability of criticism, had first led the
enemy into the fortress and then had made him feel thoroughly at
home. As the philosophes saw it, there are two ways of betraying
philosophy, and the Christians had followed each in turn. First
they had despised the resources of the mind; then, with the rise
of Scholasticism, they had abused them. In the thirteenth century,
Voltaire quipped, men had moved from "savage ignorance to

---

[1] As Ernst Robert Curtius has shown in his *European Literature
and the Latin Middle Ages,* ancient metaphors were widely used
by medieval writers. It is possible to show further that these
metaphors later found their way into the writings of the philosophes. The metaphor of the world as a stage, first used by
Plato and Horace, survived to be used by Diderot; the author's
conventional claim that he cannot express all that he feels, which
goes back to Homer, appears in a crucial paragraph of Rousseau's *Confessions;* and the antique metaphor which links the
profession of arms with the profession of literature, pen and
sword, was used dramatically by Voltaire.

scholastic ignorance" and had created "scholastic theology," the "bastard daughter of Aristotle's philosophy."[2] Diderot tried to match this sarcasm in the *Encyclopédie:* in his article "Logomachie," he records a controversy between two modern Scholastics over the question whether the whale that swallowed Jonah was male or female. A little more seriously—but with no better understanding—David Hume denounced Scholasticism as "false philosophy" and "spurious erudition"; the philosophers of the Middle Ages, he charged, "were universally infected with superstition and sophistry" worthy to stand side by side with poets and historians who for their part were infected with "barbarism."[3] Condillac, drawing up a course of historical studies for the prince of Parma, described medieval philosophers as arguing heatedly over trivial questions, piling subtlety on subtlety, and gravely abusing the dialectical method for theological purposes. Condorcet conceded with unwonted generosity that Scholasticism had improved precision of argumentation and whetted intellectual appetites, but he withdrew his concession almost as soon as he made it: these beneficial consequences had been unintended consequences. In general, Scholasticism had retarded man's enlightenment by retarding "the progress of the natural sciences."[4]

The most moderate Enlightenment historian of them all, William Robertson, found medieval philosophy rash and ridiculous. After some centuries of lethargy, he writes, Europe awoke in the twelfth century and turned its attention to new objects. Unfortunately, "the first literary efforts" of thoughtful Europeans "were extremely ill directed." It is natural for nations to cultivate their imagination before they develop their reason: "Men are poets before they are philosophers." But to their loss, medieval

---

[2] *Essai sur les mœurs*, I, 638, 767. It is worth noting once again that this sort of attack, this facile identification of scholasticism with all medieval philosophy, and misidentification of scholastic philosophy with scholastic theology, was characteristic of seventeenth- and eighteenth-century thought in general: the philosophes had read it all in Bacon, Descartes, and that most quotable of treatises, Brucker's *History of Philosophy*, which denigrates the dialectic of the Scholastics as the art of squabbling. All the philosophes added to this was malicious wit.

[3] *The History of England from the Invasion of Caesar to the Revolution of 1688*, 8 vols. (edn. 1770), II, 239, 87; III, 320.

[4] *Esquisse*, in *Œuvres*, VI, 133.

thinkers deviated from this natural progression, and "plunged at once into the depths of abstruse and metaphysical inquiry"—with disastrous consequences. Filled as they were with "the theories of a vain philosophy," they "attempted to penetrate into mysteries, and decide questions, which the limited faculties of the human mind are unable to comprehend or to resolve." The Scholastics, it must be said in their behalf, were animated by curiosity, that quality so essential to real philosophizing, but they indulged it without disciplining it. "Acute and inquisitive to excess," the Scholastics involved themselves "in a maze of intricate inquiries. Instead of allowing their fancy to take its natural range, and to produce such works of invention as might have improved their taste and refined their sentiments, instead of cultivating those arts which embellish human life, and render it comfortable, they were fettered by authority, they were led astray by example, and wasted the whole force of their genius in speculations as unavailing as they were difficult."[5] This *esprit de système* run riot, this misplaced rationalism, had some useful consequences: universities were founded, cathedral schools extended learning, and at least a few men began to exercise their minds. Still, real thinking could begin only with the advent of modern science. "True philosophy," wrote Voltaire, concurring with Robertson, "began to shine on men only with the end of the sixteenth century"—with Galileo.[6]

II

It is likely that medieval clerks would have greeted such disdain with disdain in their turn, but they would have agreed with the philosophes that the advent of Jesus had subordinated ratiocination to higher forms of insight and circumscribed the truths men could discover without divine aid. Medieval philosophers and theologians might debate the precise province of reason and the precise relation of metaphysics to theology, but these were merely jurisdictional disputes. For Christians, the demotion of

---

[5] "A View of the Progress of Society in Europe," *Works*, IV, 87–99.
[6] *Essai sur les mœurs*, II, 172.

philosophy was a cause for rejoicing: it signified the escape from
fruitless wrangling and the discovery of the saving Truth.

This demotion began early, with the Fathers of the Church.
Nor did it cease with the efflorescence of learning in the twelfth
century: it merely changed direction. Medieval encyclopedias,
which gathered up the sum of Christian knowledge, are proof of
this—they grow more pious, less encyclopedic, through the centuries. Unlike Diderot's *Encyclopédie*, these Christian compendia
were designed more and more openly to lead man toward God.
The seventh-century compiler Isidore of Seville still constructed
his *Etymologiae* on information drawn largely from the Roman
encyclopedist Varro: he starts with secular matters and describes
pagan gods and worldly diversions like the theatre. But he takes
good care to impart secular learning with pious warnings: his was
a Christian edifice built with pagan materials. Two centuries later,
in the *De rerum naturis* of Hrabanus Maurus, the emphasis has
shifted. While Hrabanus borrows heavily from Isidore and retains
much of the old pagan material, he begins with God and then
turns to the Church; his illustrations and descriptions of secular
matters appear almost as alien intrusions. By the early twelfth
century, this Christianization was complete. In Lambert's *Liber
floridus* of 1120, which extensively copies from its predecessors,
there are neither pagan nor secular matters; it is filled instead with
apocalyptic stories and symbolic interpretations of natural phenomena. Half a century later, with the *Hortus deliciarum* of
Herrad, abbess of Hohenburg in Alsace, the encyclopedia has
become a vehicle for religious edification: God holds pride of
place; the Fall of Man, the patriarchs and the prophets, the creation of the world and the course of history, all allow the compiler
to convey astronomical and geographical information. The stars
and the earth, philosophy itself, are in the encyclopedia to make
a religious point—to glorify God.

This retreat from secular philosophy was exactly analogous
to the Christian adulteration of antiquity: it too created two
parties of extremists and called forth a moderate compromise,
and again it was St. Augustine who early suggested a workable
policy. Augustine, after all, had come to Christianity through
pagan speculation, and he never quite surrendered his affection
for Plato, or for pagan literature in general. Even his late writings,

skeptical as they are about the uses of reason, are marked with the stamp of a vigorous philosophical mind: his history is philosophical history, his works on ecclesiastical institutions or Christian education are linked by a thousand threads to antique learning.

Yet just as Augustine recommended the gradual replacement of pagan by Christian classics, and the expurgation of all obnoxious passages from ancient literature, so his very commendation of the human understanding has a new and unclassical tone. *Ipsum credere nihil aliud est quam cum assensione cogitare*—"To believe is itself nothing but to cogitate with assent,"[7] might be read (and has been read by apologists) as the demand that religious faith be tested by rational investigation. But the statement is antithetical to antique—and to the philosophes'—conception of philosophy: it stresses, not the will to criticism, but the will to believe. Augustine sees man as unhappy; puzzled by himself, his world, and his destiny. All men want happiness, and all philosophers seek the way to it, but without divine aid all fail: "Thou hast made us for Thyself, and our heart is restless until it rest in Thee"—this famous exclamation in the *Confessions* is the exclamation of a tormented soul weary of mere thought, weary of autonomy, yearning for the sheltering security found in dependence on higher powers. When Augustine speaks of *understanding* or *reason*, these words have a religious admixture: philosophy to him is touched by the divine. And even that philosophy is not enough. "If God, through whom all things are made, is Wisdom, as the divine truth declares, the true philosopher is a lover of God."[8]

Verus philosophus est amator Dei—this affirmation sounds innocent enough at first glance: Plato and Aristotle had considered the love of God the culmination of philosophy. But Augustine's dictum stands the traditional method of classical philosophizing on its head: God, who to the ancients was the result of thought, now becomes its presupposition. Faith is not the reward of understanding; understanding is the reward of faith. Man may search for the explanation of his situation by his humble reason; he may

---

[7] *De praedestinatione sanctorum*, chapter 2, n. 5. Quoted by Martin Grabmann in his "Augustins Lehre vom Glauben und Wissen: ihr Einfluss auf das mittelalterliche Denken," *Mittelalterliches Geistesleben*, II (1936), 39.
[8] *The City of God Against the Pagans*, Book VIII, section 1.

even try to order his moral conduct through the understanding. But the explanation for the human condition is a myth—the Fall; the guide to his salvation is a supernatural being—Jesus Christ; the proof text for the primacy of faith over reason is a divinely inspired book—the Bible; the interpreter of this Book is an infallible authority—the Church. All four testify to the collapse of confidence in man's unaided intellect.

Hence, *nisi credideritis, non intelligetis:* unless you believe, you will not understand.[9] This injunction is the center of Augustine's doctrine on the relation of philosophy to theology, and through his enormous authority, it became the center of medieval speculation on the same subject, although the Scholastics, as the philosophes knew, provided intellect with much room for play. Late in the eleventh century, Anselm of Canterbury, pondering the same texts that his master Augustine had pondered long before, drew Augustine's conclusions with great dialectical subtlety: *credo ut intelligam*—"I believe so that I may understand." Anselm made it plain that his famous proof for the existence of God, which Kant was to criticize in the *Critique of Pure Reason*, was not designed to demonstrate God to unbelievers or to strengthen the faith of waverers. There could be no doubts of the fundamental Christian truths. But faith imposed on the believer the obligation to strive within his limited means to understand what he believes. True faith is a kind of love, the highest kind of love, and a true lover does not love ignorantly: like other medieval philosophers, Anselm accepted Aristotle's dictum that man naturally strives for knowledge. The career of the thoughtful Christian, therefore, is a pilgrimage, a *fides quaerens intellectum*—"a faith in search of understanding." It begins and ends with God; the search is imposed, and made possible, by the very mysterious Being who is its object. Anselm's dialectic, therefore, may be rationalist in form, but it is mystical in essence.

Anselm's theology was difficult but orthodox. Abelard's theology, which agitated Paris early in the twelfth century, was more dramatic, more inclined than Anselm's to grant philosoph-

---

[9] This much-quoted passage is from the Septuagint version of the Bible, from Isaiah, VII, 9. All other versions translate the Hebrew differently. The King James Version has, "If ye will not believe, surely ye shall not be established."

izing scope. Like other cultivated men of his time, Abelard was cast down at the thought that his favorite pagan philosophers were eternally damned in hell; he devoted much of his ethical and theological speculation to finding for these saintly thinkers, unlucky enough to have been born too early for Christ, a place in the Christian scheme of salvation. Yet even this master of dialectic, this brilliant teacher whom the timid feared as the sower of doubt, this admirer of the ancients who used the Socratic maxim, *Know thyself*, as the title for a treatise on ethics, this Christian rationalist, was drenched in the love for God. He firmly told Héloïse that he had no wish to be a philosopher if it meant resisting St. Paul, nor to be Aristotle if it meant separating himself from Christ.

The same spirit animated the remarkable group of clerics who composed the School of Chartres in the twelfth century. They were called Platonists, but the title is more courteous than precise: all they had of Plato was the diffuse speculations of a few Neoplatonists and a fragment of the *Timaeus* in Latin, elucidated by two mediocre commentaries. These Chartres Platonists meditated boldly on the Creation and sought to relate the Biblical account of the first Six Days to what little natural science they knew; they ventured into ontological arguments concerning the Divine Being. But their mathematical flights of fancy did not devalue the mystery of the Trinity, their classicism did not impair the authority of Scriptures or the Fathers: the most audacious among them died as Princes of the Church. The School of Chartres represents in all its purity the Christian curiosity that William Robertson had granted to the Scholastics, a curiosity which seeks for reasons, or for mystical experiences, not from a critical sense of philosophical doubt, but from a devout longing for closeness to the divine center.

III

Late in the twelfth and early in the thirteenth century, the Christian world was invaded by Aristotle, both directly and through the medium of Arabic and Jewish commentaries. This invasion accentuated the tension between philosophy and theology, and reinforced the need for a clear allocation of function.

The settlement was reached amid vigorous and often acrimonious debates: the Church first forbade and then reinstated the teachings of Aristotle; first frowned on the Latin Averroists and finally condemned them in 1277. Piety itself was not in question: with few and doubtful exceptions, the men who were driven from the universities were religious men; many, indeed, who were condemned as heretics were far more hostile to reason than were the orthodox. The battles of the thirteenth and fourteenth centuries were fought out over concrete, often narrowly defined status of propositions that were philosophically tenable but doctrinally unacceptable, the competence of logic in the realm of areas of controversy: the range of academic freedom, the precise mystery.

The ascendancy of theology over philosophy, therefore, was not the triumph of believers over unbelievers, but the reaffirmation of the order appropriate to a hierarchical universe. The Scholastics were neither the victims of intimidation nor manipulators of the double truth. Some must have regretted the curbs on their speculative flights, but all, or almost all, were men of unexceptionable piety who differed from the authorities only on the best road to God. The old saying that philosophy is the handmaiden of theology, which became a favorite cliché with philosophes writing on the Middle Ages, was merely the pithy expression of an accepted truth.

The first to pronounce the dictum, *philosophia ancilla theologiae*, was probably Peter Damian, whose suspicion of pagan learning was well known. But others repeated it. Roger Bacon firmly declared that knowledge which takes no account of Christian dogma leads men straight to hell, and he thought it the central task of philosophy to offer proofs for the truth of the Christian religion. Vincent of Beauvais, an erudite and ambitious encyclopedist of the thirteenth century, wrote in his *De eruditione filiorum regalum:* "Every art and all knowledge must serve divine science, which exists for edification, that is, for the sake of belief and right action. They must be related and directed toward it as its purpose and goal."

Thomas Aquinas's careful analysis of this question, strategically placed at the beginning of his *Summa theologiae*, makes it obvious that these elaborations of *philosophia ancilla theologiae* were not merely conventional flourishes or adroit mimicry. Philosophy, Thomas argues, cannot teach all that men must know: "In addition to the philosophical sciences investigated by reason, there should be a sacred science by way of revelation." This "sacred doctrine" is a science, since it proceeds "from principles made known by the light of a higher science, namely the science of God and the blessed." It is both speculative and practical, although more "speculative than practical, because it is more concerned with divine things than with human acts." It argues from authority, since its principles are derived from revelation, and is nobler than other sciences, because its proofs are more certain and its concerns more elevated than those of other sciences. "This science can draw upon the philosophical sciences, not as though it stood in need of them, but only in order to make its teaching clearer. For it accepts its principles, not from the other sciences, but immediately from God, by revelation. Therefore it does not draw upon the other sciences as upon its superiors, but uses them as its inferiors and handmaidens."[1]

Metaphors, especially familiar metaphors, mislead. To call philosophy the handmaiden of theology is to suggest a permanent, servile dependence which most medieval philosophers did not feel. The most effective limitation on them was neither fear nor deference but an inner check: some positions were simply inconceivable or conceivable only as debaters' points inviting immediate refutation. There were many subjects, especially in logic and ontology, which philosophers treated philosophically—that is by the sole light of reason. There were philosophical questions which did not touch on theology: by no means all philosophical activity was apologetic. There were even theological questions that philosophers could ponder without recourse to the Fathers or to revealed truth. Yet it remains true that philosophy, for all its independence, was embedded within a religious atmosphere. Neither ontology nor epistemology could long subsist without the fuel of religious concerns. Even the much discussed dispute between Realists and Nominalists over the status of universals was primarily a search for the right mode of faith; even Occam's severe Nominalism, which has often been taken as a precursor of

---

[1] See *Summa Theologiae*, part I, question 1.

scientific empiricism, was less an agent of modernity than a warning that the Scholastic synthesis was breaking down. If Occam was an ancestor of Locke's *Essay Concerning Human Understanding,* his paternity was remote and reluctant.

It is possible to abstract epistemological notions from the writings of Christian philosophers: mystics, rationalists, and fideists disputed over how best to know God, and in the course of their speculations they developed elaborate schemes for the status of concepts and the powers of the mind. But Christian philosophers from Augustine to Occam reflected on knowledge principally for religious reasons: the Bible abounded in dark sayings and the world in false prophets, hence clarity of perception was a prerequisite for right religious action. Epistemology achieved importance only so far as it helped to establish a right (that is to say, a pious) relation between the temporal and the eternal. No medieval thinker, no matter how adventurous, could have undertaken Kant's construction of a religion within the limits of reason alone—he could hardly have imagined it.

Dante's *Inferno* shows the fate reserved for those who did imagine it. The virtuous pagan thinkers are placed in limbo: they escape the torments of hell since they had at least groped dimly for the *logos* that is Christ, but they will never see God face to face. But there is one exception to Dante's Christian charity: Epicurus lies in the sixth circle of Hell, side by side with other heretics who had denied the immortality of the soul, in a vast cemetery of flaming tombs. It seemed a proper place for a philosopher who denied all religion.

Yet Dante loved philosophy. In his younger years, in his *Convivio,* he had represented it as a *donna gentile,* and pursued it with passionate, single-minded, almost blasphemous love. Still, even in that time—when he had found good words for Epicurus and considered rational thought an adequate guide to whatever earthly blessedness men might enjoy—even then Dante had experienced philosophy as a religious emotion, a charismatic infusion from a higher power. Like the ancients, Dante cherished ethical speculation, but unlike the ancients, he could couple a thinker like Boethius with Cicero and could prize Cicero's writings as sweet and consoling. In his most rationalist phase, Dante used philosophy as an exalted kind of therapy. But then in the *Divine*

Comedy he turned away even from this pious worldliness: philosophy retains its value as the purest form of merely human activity, a road sign pointing in the right direction, but it can never be the path to salvation, and it is salvation after all that must be man's central concern. I said before that Vergil was many things to Dante. So was Beatrice: to describe her merely as a symbol of religion or theology or the road to blessedness is to reduce a vivid poetical figure to a pale abstraction. Yet Beatrice is also a symbol: in the *Purgatorio* Vergil says explicitly that reason can go only so far; only Beatrice, faith, can penetrate the sacred reaches of paradise.

Dante's journey from the *Convivio* to the *Divine Comedy* mirrors the retreat from critical thinking that Christian civilization as a whole had undertaken through the centuries. Like Christianity at large, Dante did not surrender his love for thought and continued to use his reason, but he subordinated rationality to higher things. The philosophes could not understand this hierarchy of values, and refused to make any attempt to understand it. For the Enlightenment, as we know, philosophy was autonomous and omnipotent, or it was nothing.

3. THE REHABILITATION OF MYTH

I

THE RANK OF PHILOSOPHY was more than an academic matter for the philosophes; it involved their whole conception of man's relation to his experience, to say nothing of their self-esteem. Obviously, the Enlightenment had its own unexamined presuppositions, its notions taken—as the deceptive expression has it—"on faith." But in principle the philosophes regarded such dark corners of thought as blemishes: they were errors of method or flaws of personality to be exposed to the cleansing stream of public criticism. The autonomy of philosophy, of which the Enlightenment made so much, was like a passport valid in all countries. For the Christian, on the other hand, it was clear that nothing but the divine could penetrate everywhere. There were some medieval theologians, notably Thomas Aquinas, who professed to see no conflict between reason and revelation, and who negotiated a peaceful coexistence between philosophy and theology. Yet even the most pacific division of territory remains a division of territory; the most pugnacious of medieval thinkers conceded that there were sacred areas into which they must not, could not step, where faith, revelation, tradition, and ecclesiastical authority gave the orders and offered the answers, where speculation was irrelevant and curiosity an unwelcome intrusion into holy ground.

It is the indispensability of the sacred that differentiates the Middle Ages at its most scientific and skeptical from ages of criticism. The Christian feared the divine and desired it; to claim full knowledge of it was the sin of pride—had not the serpent seduced Adam and Eve into the supreme crime of disobedience by promising them the knowledge that would make them "as gods"? Some things were inaccessible, veiled—in believing this, as we know, the Christian was like the philosophe. But, unlike the philosophe, the Christian yearned for this unknown, tried to approach it through mystic experience, theological speculation, and sheer prayerful hope: somehow to share in the great myth was, after all, his destination.

To speak of the Christian millennium as a return to myth is not to accept the philosophes' bland identification of religion with superstition, but to recognize the family resemblance of religion and myth. The two doubtless have their origins in the same human needs and are indistinguishable in early cultures: there, religion *is* myth. But with the development of civilization, refined religious ideas and crude superstitions diverge. While primitive tribes outside the European pale and the illiterate within Europe itself attempted to control their destiny or lamented their impotence through age-old rites, educated Christians opposed to them a sublime history and a reasoned theology: far more than the philosophes admitted, Christianity was the enemy of superstition. In the Christian millennium, especially in the hands of philosophical theologians, myth was, in the threefold meaning of Hegel's famous pun, *aufgehoben*—it was preserved, transcended, and raised to a higher level.

This Christian myth, itself complex, dominated a richly articulated civilization, in which subtle ratiocination coexisted with the most primitive of beliefs, and saintly self-denial with vigorous gaiety. Incessant sermons against pride and greed are proof, if proof is needed, that worldliness had survived the strictures of priests, and that it sturdily contradicted monastic ideals. Joyousness and naturalism mark much of medieval art and literature: the smiling angel who adorns Rheims cathedral, and the shrewdly observed and exquisitely carved leaves, plants, and animals that decorate the capitals of columns in so many churches, are of a piece with the realistic images in the *Divine Comedy*, the exciting, almost tactile concreteness of Dante's adventures in the other world. The thirteenth-century architect Villard de Honnecourt, whose *Album*, a little book of miscellaneous sketches, gives valuable testimony to his age, liked to draw what he saw on his travels: the windows of Rheims cathedral, swans and parakeets, church towers, and a captive lion—the last drawn, as he insists, from life: *Eh bien sacies que cil lion fut contrefais al vif.*

This full-blooded worldliness was not merely a lapse from approved conduct or a failure to achieve the ideal of asceticism. Dante makes it clear that misery is a crime and joy a duty: the sullen are in the fifth circle of his Hell. The Christian ideal of love, both of God and man, was harmonious with the ideal of otherworldliness and in no way contradicted Christian duties. Monasticism was not an example that all should follow; it was a service to the Christian community at large. Profane activities had their own dignity: while religious matters, and hence priesthood, held preeminence, craftsmen and philosophers, peasants and soldiers, served the Divine purpose in their own way. Once the Church had discarded its apocalyptic expectations, it settled down to the business of organizing a Christian community, and in this enterprise secular works found a worthy place. The effigies of shoemakers, architects, and winegrowers appeared in churches side by side with portraits of saints.

When all this has been said, it must be added that unencumbered naturalism was exceptional: it was swamped in the general estrangement from the things of this world. Honnecourt's lion—*contrefais al vif*, after all—is a grotesque, looking a great deal like the caricature of a bearded man with pointed ears and claws instead of hands. And Honnecourt's nudes, drawn, as he claims, in the antique style, are strained, almost ludicrous, and thoroughly unnatural.

And even what realism there was, served, after all, as adornment to religious edifices: it was, in Erich Auerbach's phrase, a "figural realism." It was this figural realism that allowed Dante to endow his poetic characters with the wealth of meaning on which I have commented: God's creatures are real in themselves; they are truly historical, to be experienced in all their individuality, tangible beings with mobile features and private fates. Yet, and at the same time, they are also the bearers of political and religious symbolism, prefigurations of the divine plan for the universe.

With their disenchanted world view, the philosophes confronted figural realism with a kind of outraged incomprehension. They knew more or less clearly that the most unworldly mysticism and most tough-minded realism could coexist within the same civilization and sometimes within the same man: they were acquainted with such figures as Nicolas of Cusa, philosopher, theologian, scientist, bureaucrat, mystic, and ecclesiastical statesman. Their reading told them, too, that good Christians could treat the most sacred of themes in vulgar language: Dante's *Divine Comedy* is sprinkled with common metaphors and coarse words. But the inner connection between these extremes escaped them, and they misread medieval realism as a sign of religious skepticism. It is not so much that the philosophes despised fancy, but that in their scientific way of thinking, they sharply separated fancy from reality. In their literary writings, allegory had become a useful, transparent convention, and in their scientific writings, metaphor was being replaced by the severe, unpictorial language of mathematics. The modern analysis of language had to await the work of Humboldt, but the philosophes, in their own commonsensical way, had pierced the mystery of symbols: in their scientific empiricism, thought as it were looked itself full in the face, and stripped words and images of their substantial power.

It was different in the Christian millennium. Allegory, metaphor, figurative interpretations, retained their power precisely because they were never reduced to mere linguistic devices or literary frills. This was only reasonable: since God had scattered traces of His intent throughout creation, the man schooled in the ways of the divine language might read sacred meanings everywhere. Methods of allegorical interpretation and metaphorical devices had been handed down to the Middle Ages from antiquity, but in Christian hands they flowered beyond anything the ancients might have imagined. Allegoresis went back to the Greek sophists and the Stoics; it had been invented to elevate myth and rescue it from the assaults of total skepticism, and it developed into a vulgar reductionism that explained cults or deities as "mere" representations of natural forces or virtues and vices. In pious hands, allegoresis was turned on its inventors; it helped to discredit antique religions, to assimilate pagan literature, and to discover foreshadowings of Christian verities in the Old Testament or in classical writings. Christian allegoresis proved that history and nature were tales told by God to man. As the Scriptures were filled with parables, so the whole world was a parable, or set of parables, which devout reason must try to decipher. By the high Middle Ages, theologians had developed this deciphering into a system. Allegory, wrote the thirteenth-century liturgist Gulielmus Durandus, makes one visible fact intelligible by another; anagogy (the most exalted form allegory can take) leads man from the visible to the invisible: the presence of Christ in the sacraments is a real event, but it also turns man's mind to think on his redemption. A Voltaire might profess much amusement at a Church that could force sacred meanings on the erotic language of the Song of Songs, but to the medieval mind nothing could be more natural.

Metaphor, too, retained some of its primitive flavor. Medieval literature was laden with elaborate constructions and secular images. To compare life to a voyage on the stormy seas, or books to happy children, was to endow metaphor with a purely aesthetic dimension that cut it off from the sacredness of ritual. Yet metaphor also had a religious function: since God himself was incomprehensible and deigned to speak in language adapted to man's understanding darkened by the Fall, metaphors communicated mystical visions. Nicolas of Cusa sought to bring his readers to a true understanding of the divine by using a comparison: an "omnivoyant face," that seemed to have its eyes on everything and everyone at the same time. Thus man might feebly glimpse God through metaphor.

homo Dei

The Christian world, then, was tied together by symbols charged with sacred energies precisely because they were so concrete, so real. As Dante rather casually reminds his readers in the *Purgatorio*, that man is God's man—*homo Dei*—may be literally read in his face: it was generally agreed that the eyes make two Os, the eyebrows combined with the nose spell out the M, and since H is an aspirate, this gives us man—*homo*. Then the ear can be seen as a D, the nostrils and the mouth spell out respectively, an E and an I.—*Dei*.

This sort of divine speech was imitated in religious ceremony. Theologians might dispute over the finer points in Trinitarian doctrine, church administrators subject the Mass to minute regulations, and artists paint or carve the story of Christ's Passion. But the meaning of these debates, rules, and images was not exhausted in their forensic, bureaucratic, or artistic forms. Nothing was mere sign: each symbol participated in the myth it symbolized. Each crucifix rises beyond the material of which it is made—it participates, no matter how remotely, in the Passion of Christ. The Trinity is not a metaphor: One *is* Three and Three *is* One. The bread and wine of the Mass are not merely reminders of the Saviour: they are not *like*, but they miraculously *become* the flesh and blood of Christ. The Creation and the Fall are not mere stories, or allegories for birth and suffering; they were real events, and events of crucial importance in man's history. The same is true of the Resurrection. It is not an edifying tale; it happened, precisely in the miraculous way that the Gospel reports. Easter is not celebrated to symbolize the annual revival of nature in Spring; quite the contrary, Spring symbolizes the glorious Resurrection. To be sure, the naïve literal interpretation of the Bible had been discarded by Origen and Augustine, and the naïve worship of the unlettered was spiritualized by the Doctors of the Church, but the most philosophical reinterpretation of Christianity left its central mysteries intact. Anthropologists might point out that sacrificing the god and eating the divine body are familiar practices in many religions, including primitive ones; psychoanalysts might argue that the number three, so indispensable to medieval Christianity, has psychological undertones deeply buried in the unconscious; cultural historians might observe that medieval man's dependence on creation myths reflected his helpless acceptance of Augustine's dictum, *creatura non potest creare*—"the creature cannot create."[2] The medieval Christian would not have scorned this sort of analysis; he would simply not have understood it. He was willing to be analytical—but chiefly about the world of others; he could have written the natural history of every religion but his own. But there was no way for him to analyze the psychological or anthropological origins of his own faith, for analysis means separation and dissection, while faith strives for unity and life. Christian symbols, like Christian experience or Christian history, were alive because they were witnesses, testifying to God's work.

II

On the deepest possible level, this mystical life pervades the categories by which medieval man oriented himself in his world. Space, time, and purpose were all part of a gorgeous fabric spun by the divine artificer, and possessed qualities that made them resistant to quantitative determination or critical examination. They were felt, not measured; celebrated, not analyzed.

Space retained the magic characteristic of mythical thinking: medieval Christians translated mystical Neoplatonic speculations into terms appropriate to their theology and their society. Up was better than down; right better than left. These spatial intuitions were not trivial: they pointed to the master metaphor of the Middle Ages—the hierarchy. Reasoning from analogy, Christian philosophers and theologians established it as a universal principle that the higher governs the lower everywhere: thus the brute fact of social inequality was at once expressed and rationalized; thus the overwhelming need for peace, both political and psychological, was translated into the grand image of cosmic concord. The old Platonic principle that tranquillity results when each part of the soul occupies its appropriate place and performs its appropriate function became the vital center of spatial mysticism. The heavens were seen as a series of spheres ascending to God, and the

---

[2] Quoted by Erwin Panofsky: "Artist, Scientist, Genius: Notes on the 'Renaissance-Dämmerung,'" *The Renaissance: Six Essays* (edn. 1962), 171.

pride

stages of ascent were marked by carefully differentiated degrees of light. Motion was ranked by its celestial or terrestrial nature. Angels, devils, and (as the *Divine Comedy* makes clear) men after death, occupied their appointed place in an order of rank. Law descended from divine commandments to natural law to human legislation. Clerics and the secular orders of society were differentiated by degrees. The relation of ecclesiastics to laymen, the constitution by which the prince ruled his subjects, the obligations of a vassal in the feudal order, the organization through which the Pope shepherded his flock, the rules by which the *pater familias* superintended his family, and the scheme by which society regulated its social precedence and economic rewards—all these were perfect and perfectly analogous hierarchies.

The analogical relationship of these rank orders had the mystic reality of all such symbols; the argument from analogy was therefore far more than a convenient device. It was considered as conclusive proof: the precedence observed in one hierarchy confirmed the precedence to be observed in another. John of Salisbury revived Plutarch's image of the body politic to establish the proper political order: in a celebrated paragraph of his *Policraticus*, he assigned the soul to the church, the head to the prince, the heart to the senate, the hands to officials and soldiers, the sides to courtiers, the stomach and intestines to financial officers, and the feet to the peasants. His readers treated this oddly shaped centipede as anything but an amusing metaphor: it was a mirror of an ideal reality. A hundred years after John, Thomas Aquinas established by the same method that monarchy is the best form of government: Whatever most nearly approaches a natural process, he wrote, is best, and we can observe in nature that government is always entrusted to one—the bees have one queen and the universe has one Lord. Nothing could be more logical.

In a society ridden with ceremonial and obsessed with the rights of each rank, and in centuries that celebrated each event with scrupulous regard for precedence, clarity of hierarchical orders was a necessity and breach of hierarchy a threat. That is why the sin of pride, so endemic and so lamentable to the preachers, was so dangerous: *superbia*, from Lucifer's first rebellion down to the disobedience of some sixteenth-century princeling, was the subversion of the divinely ordained order of life. In Shakespeare's plays, which demonstrate the persistence of this medieval notion through the Renaissance, the shaking of degree, or the crimes of kings (which are violations of their divinely-appointed place) appear like enormous natural catastrophes, or like fearful diseases in the political body. It took the scientific revolution and the triumph of critical thinking to reduce the idea of hierarchy to a convenient metaphor or a sociological category describing patterns of domination, and to convert hierarchy from being the foundation of a rational social order into its enemy.

Like space, medieval time partook of the intense, personal, imprecise quality of myth. Historians, often remarkably shrewd, diligent, and discriminating, are yet desperately confused in their chronologies; chroniclers fail to supply the dates of important events, and sometimes the events themselves. Their conceptions of sequence and of precise temporal relation are at best rudimentary. Annalists endow kings separated by centuries with one another's adventures and attributes, and blend historical individuals into the hazy, mythical hero: toward the end of the ninth century, Asser's *Life of King Alfred* describes Alfred in circumstantial detail, but his king's characteristics are copied directly from Einhard's *Life of Charlemagne:* the parallel of this practice with the mythopoeic historiography of the ancient Egyptians is too obvious to be missed.

Vagueness was enhanced by ignorance and confirmed by piety: Italian chroniclers, who have forgotten the coronation of Charlemagne, make Louis the Pious into the first Carolingian king; Otto of Freising, perhaps the greatest of medieval historians, makes Aristotle as well as Plato into the pupil of Socrates. The Bible is used as a completely reliable historical source. Historical periods center around the prophecies in the Book of Daniel or around mystic numbers derived from Scriptures. Over and over again, historians look toward the end of time, to the apocalypse, and confess that the earthly city they chronicle is not the center of man's concerns.

Medieval historiography thus mirrors a pervasive "vast indifference to time."[3] Men do not know and do not care how old

---

[3] Marc Bloch: *La société féodale,* 2 vols. (1939–40), I, 119. Modern historians in search of reliable information are often reduced to invective born of frustration. Johan Huizinga gives the exam-

they are or when something happened. Until the fourteenth century or later, they were content with antique and cumbersome water clocks, and until the end of the sixteenth century, they were content with an inaccurate calendar. Marc Bloch recalls the difficulties in the path of precision: in the city of Mons a duellist presents himself at the appointed place to fight his adversary at the customary hour of nine. The day goes by and the opponent does not appear—has he forfeited? Clearly, but when? It takes a prolonged and painstaking consultation with the judges and the clerics of the town to determine precisely when the hour of nine had passed.[4]

Some sequences imposed themselves, as they had imposed themselves on more primitive cultures: the cycle of the seasons and the stages of life were inescapable marks of the passage of time. But in these recurrent events, intersected rather imprecisely by the celebration of holy days, time was not a neutral measure. It was a sacred rhythm. Double-entry bookkeeping, reliable statistics, and sensible chronologies had to wait until the late Renaissance: their invention reflects a growing appetite for exactitude. The absence of precision instruments was not the obstacle to precision—rather, indifference to precision was an obstacle to the invention of precision instruments.

The philosophes, weary of oppressive schedules, mechanical regularity, and hateful discipline, on occasion exalted imprecision into a virtue. In the winter of 1750, Jean-Jacques Rousseau threw away his watch. "Thank heavens," he remembered exclaiming after this sublime gesture, "I shall no longer need to know what time it is!"[5] With this single impulsive act Rousseau overthrew, for himself at least, the tyranny of absolute, objective Newtonian time. But his temper remains modern: Rousseau was rebelling against the rationalist allocation of moments in the name of an

---

ple of Olivier de la Marche, a fifteenth-century historiographer to the dukes of Burgundy, who "goes so far as to make the marriage of Charles with Margaret of York take place after the siege of Neuss in 1475, though he was present at the wedding festivities in 1468." The "lack of precision" of such famous chroniclers as Froissart, moreover, is "deplorable." *The Waning of the Middle Ages* (1924; edn. 1956), 236–7.

[4] Bloch: *La société féodale*, I, 119.
[5] *Confessions*, Book VIII, *Œuvres*, I, 363.

intensity that is beyond measurement. For all its spontaneity, Rousseau's gesture depended for its effect on his self-awareness, and his nostalgic protest failed to recapture primitive innocence toward time. Medieval man did not have to rebel against precision—one does not rebel against what one does not know.

Nostalgic moments apart, the philosophes liked to deride medieval categories as infantile or vicious. They were neither: they followed inevitably from the qualitative cast of the medieval mind, a mind bent on endowing the empty vessels of space and time with religious significance.

It is this style of thinking that explains the sterility of medieval science. Qualitative thinking is, in general, teleological thinking, and the history of scientific progress is the history of liberation from teleology. The philosophes were not themselves wholly free from the belief in final causes (Voltaire, for one, always held to some form of it), but they were distant enough from medieval modes of thinking to recognize and despise them. Condillac maintained that during the "centuries of ignorance" chemistry and astronomy alone were cultivated, and cultivated for unsavory reasons—impostors abused, and visionaries shared popular credulity.[6] Rousseau derided what he called the "scientific jargon" of the Middle Ages, "more contemptible even than ignorance," and an almost "invincible obstacle to the recovery of knowledge."[7] Condorcet granted to medieval scientists the invention of the compass and gunpowder, but beyond that, he wrote, medieval science amounted to "some anatomical research; some obscure works on chemistry, wholly taken up with the alchemist's search for gold; some studies in geometry and algebra, which rose neither to the knowledge of all the Arabs had discovered nor to an understanding of the works of the ancients; finally, some observations and astronomical calculations which limited themselves to making up and perfecting tables and were polluted by a ridiculous admixture of astrology."[8]

This is an uncharitable appraisal, but it is not far off the mark. Medieval scientists did some respectable work in technology,

---

[6] Condillac: "Cours d'Histoire" for the Prince of Parma, "Histoire moderne," books VIII and IX. Œuvres, II, 129–67 passim.
[7] Discours sur les sciences et les arts, in Œuvres, III, 6.
[8] Esquisse, in Œuvres, VI, 133.

optics, and medicine, and many of the methodological principles with which geniuses like Galileo made their scientific revolution were first enunciated by Grosseteste and Roger Bacon in the thirteenth century and by the faculty of the University of Padua in the fourteenth. There were significant threads of continuity between medieval scientific speculation and the great avalanche of discoveries that gives luster to the seventeenth century: the proud boast of the revolutionaries that they had learned nothing from the past is as untenable historically as it was psychologically profitable. The Middle Ages practiced rational science and, to a limited degree, sought power over nature, but it is significant that the pronouncements of Roger Bacon had to wait three centuries until they were fitted into a program for action. They sound impressive and astonishingly modern only if they are taken out of context. It is not merely that Bacon's advocacy of experimentation and mathematics coexisted with his conviction that the Bible, properly understood, contains practically all the truth worth knowing, that theology is superior to natural science, that the intuitions of the prophets outweigh the searchings of fallible clerics, and that astrology and alchemy enshrine vital scientific secrets. What matters more is that his pronouncements on method had no larger function: they fertilized neither his own researches nor the science of his civilization. They were, at best, trenchant criticisms of prevailing techniques, and in general, unintegrated, isolated forays. The primacy of theology—and Christian theology—was not in any way challenged by Roger Bacon's writings.

Yet there was a scientific ferment as well, stimulated largely by remnants of Platonism and by Averroist Aristotelians. That is why the medieval mind found the pseudo sciences of alchemy and astrology so congenial. With their division of knowledge into exoteric and esoteric, their obsessive procedures followed through most scrupulously, their refusal to check results or design experiments, their trust in number magic, and their violent oscillations from vast hopes to impotent despair, both alchemy and astrology were a mixture of primitive mythical intuitions and rational inquiries into natural laws. The Church vehemently opposed them, especially astrology, but largely in the spirit of a monopolist annoyed by shrewd competitors. Its objection was less to the astrological way of thinking than to its fatalist mood, which denied man's freedom of the will and thus his hope for redemption by good works. Pious princes and prelates employed necromancers to predict the future and find the philosopher's stone; Aquinas and Grosseteste employed arguments from astrology; Roger Bacon explained the rise of Christianity by a fortunate conjunction of the planets Mercury and Jupiter; while Dante elaborately connected the "seven planets" with the seven liberal arts in his *Convivio* and introduced astrological considerations into his *Purgatorio*. In the living universe of Christian belief, there were many ways to God.

Medieval science, then, like medieval philosophy, took its place, prominent but secondary, in the hierarchy of human activities: it was, like philosophy, guided by man's search for holiness and salvation. And like philosophy, it called forth two responses; a Christian could justify either neglect or cultivation of science on religious grounds. There were some Christians who abhorred the preoccupation with natural causes as an impudent invasion of Divine privacy and a diversion of energies from the truly important. These rigorists used the same arguments against science that they used against the cultivation of letters or of philosophy, and without any sense of strain; in their eyes these were all alike: why should man inquire into the shape of the earth or read Ovid or reason about angels, when it was his part to walk the earth in piety and humility? Yet in the end, it was the scientists who won, aided in part by a metaphor that gained wide popularity: Vincent of Beauvais was only one of many to call nature a "book written by the hand of God." The study of nature was rationalized as a perusal of the divine writing.

Medieval science was thus doubly teleological: its purpose was knowledge for the sake of God; and its discoveries were discoveries of purposes—God's intentions for His creation. The well-known insistence on the part of medieval scientists that the earth is the center of the universe and that the planetary orbits are circular are only the two most familiar symptoms of the crippling effect that the imposition of extraneous considerations had on scientific inquiry. But then, to put the matter this way is to impose modern criteria on medieval concerns: to the Christian of the Middle Ages, science, like ignorance, was part of a vast symbolic, holy tapestry.

III

The most substantial and accessible of Christian symbols was the church, awesome and homely, exalted and intimate. It was the place of religious festivals and prosaic fairs: at Chartres, the cathedral chapter had to request the wine merchants not to sell their products in the nave, but to confine their commercial activities to the crypt. With its cruciform shape and orientation toward the East, its stained-glass windows and carved choir screens, the building was designed to lead the worshipper beyond the world of sense and mortality. Medieval churches have been called silent sermons and religious dramas in stone. The names are apt: the foundations of the church bore more than a load of masonry. They groaned under symbolic meanings.

These meanings were often hard to interpret, for they required some learning; nor were they ever consistently or authoritatively settled. There was no handbook that codified images; styles of interpretation often depended on local custom or an imaginative bishop. There were fashions in saints; there was confusion over the significance of some figures. In one church, floral carvings recalled the Virgin; in another, they simply, joyously, meant themselves. But of course, since nature itself was part of a larger creation, the most homely representation was in a sense symbolic even if it had no explicit sacred significance.

On whatever level, this churchly symbolism, although usually planned with care, was not manipulative. The philosophes liked to draw disparaging portraits of unscrupulous clerics busy mystifying the faithful. But the truth is quite different. Merchants who sold devotional objects were not cynical atheists. They were not even cynical Christians—their profits and their faith were not in conflict. Theologians who employed symbols in their apologetics and architects who used them in their buildings were fully aware of their skills: they knew they were using linguistic or pictorial instruments. But they handled them with a delicacy appropriate to sacred objects. Even the most rationalist of Christians, the

Scholastics, who had moved far beyond primitive mythopoeic thinking, retained their awe before the power of the Word. God had pronounced and perpetually embodied the *logos*—did not the Gospel say that in the beginning was the Word? But the Christian *logos*, for all its debt and resemblance to the *logos* of the Greeks, was tinged with mystery where the boundaries between the sign and the thing signified, reality and ideal, were wiped away and the human and divine met. That is why the Scholastics filled the margins of their treatises with pious ejaculations and uttered fervent prayers that they might use their learning without presumption. Their most intellectual formulations were divine gifts: when Anselm had completed his proof for the existence of God, he noted that he took no credit for this achievement; and Thomas Aquinas scribbled *ave, ave Maria* on the margins of his *Summa contra gentiles*. Thus producers and consumers of symbols were joined in a harmonious religious fraternity.

The church edifice, which collected Christian symbols in one concentrated spot, even concealed that most elusive of symbolisms, number mysticism—it was on the rock of number that architects built their churches. Cathedrals, on which princes lavished their most precious resources, architects their finest talents, and ecclesiastics their keenest administrative attention, had divine ratios hidden in their ground plan or their spires: the mathematical-religious speculations of the subtlest theologians were translated into stone and glass to celebrate the system of numbers with which the Divine Musician had composed the world harmony.

Of all mythopoeic forms of thought, number mysticism seems to have influenced the most highly educated. It may be called the superstition of the intellectuals: it delighted Greek philosophers and Jewish sages, Persian kings and Christian theologians. Neoplatonists elaborated Pythagorean ratios, Biblical Jews stood in awe of the number forty; and this mystical mathematics did not loosen its hold through the Middle Ages. It remained to haunt scientists like Kepler and Galileo.

Numbers pervade Christianity, and they are not, as in modern mathematics, abstract signs expressing relationships; they are, in true mythopoeic fashion, symbols of transcendent truths or instruments with specific powers. St. Augustine, who taught that we "must not despise the science of numbers," had special regard for the number six, which suffers neither excess nor deficiency since its divisors add up to itself: six, he wrote, is perfect, but not because God created the world in six days. Rather, God chose that number because six is perfect.[9] This sounds like audaciously pagan doctrine, and its Neoplatonic and Neo-Pythagorean antecedents are plain, but it was perfectly orthodox in the Middle Ages, not only among the illiterate but also among the educated. Christians knew seven virtues, seven works of mercy, seven planets, seven sacraments, seven liberal arts, seven degrees of sanctity, seven deadly sins, seven ages of man; they knew twelve prophets, twelve patriarchs, twelve apostles, twelve months, twelve sacred jewels in the vision of John.

With wholly serious, wholly devout playfulness, medieval man contemplated these numbers as the visible mark of the structure of reality, and related them to one another—there are no coincidences in the world of myth. The conjunction of numbers points to the methods of divine creation: *omnia in mensura et numero et pondere disposuisti*—"you founded everything in measure, number, and weight"—so ran the much-quoted verse from the Wisdom of Solomon. Seven and twelve have mystical connections: seven is three plus four while twelve is three times four; now, three is sacred because it represents the Trinity—the world of spirit; while four is the number of the elements—the world of matter. The seven virtues dramatize this relationship; there are four cardinal and three revealed virtues, combining into a perfect mathematical whole. Seven and twelve, then, stand for the holy conjunction of three and four.

Examples of this mathematical mysticism can be multiplied almost without end. The number thirty-three is sacred because it represents the years Christ spend among men and is, in addition, a reminder of the Trinity. The number nine, as Dante tells his readers in his *Vita Nuova*, is sacred for a similar reason: the adored Beatrice is a number nine, a miracle whose root is the Trinity, a three which creates nine by means of itself. It is hardly necessary to observe that the *Divine Comedy* as a whole is a tissue of sacred numbers: it is made up of three parts with thirty-three

---

[9] *The City of God Against The Pagans*, Book XI, chapter 30.

cantos each, plus an introductory canto to make up another sacred number, one hundred. These large rhythms are echoed and reinforced by subsidiary proportions: there are nine circles in hell and the lower circles display their own mystic proportions: circle seven has three rounds; circle eight, ten ditches; circle nine, four rounds. In *Purgatorio*, Dante's forehead is marked with seven "P's," one for each of the deadly sins, and Purgatory is constructed of an ante-purgatory with four levels, and of purgatory proper, with seven levels. Add the island on which the whole structure stands and another sacred number, twelve, appears. The *Paradiso* yields similar results.

In constructing his masterpiece on numbers and hierarchies of numbers, Dante was working in a well-established literary tradition. But it was a theological tradition as well: it was a game that was more than a game, an image that was more than an image. It did not merely point to the sacred reality that is this universe but was itself an important aspect of that reality: God could not have constructed His creation in a nonmathematical way, for to have done so would have been to create disproportion, disharmony, and such creations were the work of the devil. The builders of cathedrals and the worshippers for whom they built them thought of their building as beautiful because it was "true," because it mirrored, as closely as man can mirror, the effortless labors of the Divine Architect. The musical-mathematical foundations of cathedral design lifted man to a religious experience beyond words and above logical examination; the church was not merely a reminder, but a copy and foretaste of heaven, the blessed Jerusalem.

There were dramatic moments when the reality of such symbolism came poignantly alive. In June 1194, a great fire ravaged most of the town of Chartres, and its new cathedral. The tunic worn by the Virgin Mary at the birth of Christ, the most cherished relic the cathedral possessed, disappeared during the conflagration. This calamity threw the people of Chartres, including its bishop, priests, and scholars, into profound dejection. The Virgin had withdrawn her protection, and there seemed little point to rebuilding her shrine. Divine wrath had descended on Chartres; the Virgin, who had made it her favorite dwelling place, had turned her back on it.

The clerks were the first to recover some perspective. Cardinal Melior of Pisa, then at Chartres, a clever diplomat, impressive orator, and ebullient organizer, persuaded the bishop and the cathedral chapter to make an attempt at rebuilding the church. A few days later he called an assembly of the townspeople, and as he urged them to support this holy enterprise, the bishop and priests appeared in procession, carrying the Sacred Tunic—it had survived the fire in the crypt. This miraculous recovery of what had been feared irretrievably lost made an overwhelming impression on the assembly. With tears in their eyes, the burghers pledged what they had saved from the fire to make the new cathedral even more glorious than the old. In their elation, they improvised an optimistic interpretation of the catastrophe: the Virgin had allowed the sanctuary to be destroyed because she wanted a new, beautiful church. With an impressive outpouring of money and energy, they began to construct a shrine worthy of its divine protector.

As we read this story today, we are struck by its all too human manifestations: the brilliant speaker playing on his audience, the dramatic reappearance of the relic at the right moment, and the notable conjunction of religious and commercial interests. Chartres heavily depended for its prosperity on festivals and pilgrimages, and a new cathedral might soon pay for itself. But there is more to the rebuilding of Chartres cathedral than this: for all its worldly ingredients, the initial distress and the subsequent elation were religious in character. For all the divisions between the lettered and unlettered, all had been at one in grief and happiness. The Virgin had appeared to be angry, but she was not. It was a cause for rejoicing.

By the middle of the eighteenth century, the mental universe in which this incident had occurred was under severe attack, and this unanimity of response had been destroyed. On February 8, and March 8, 1750, London underwent two slight earthquakes. No one was killed, but the peculiar conjunction of dates created considerable panic in the city. When a demented soldier went about London predicting a third and devastating earthquake on April 8, he found many who believed him. Horace Walpole wrote to Mann on April 4 that hundreds of Londoners were leaving town, and that others were surrendering to the most baleful speculations. Among the braver ladies, he reported, there were some who had made "earthquake gowns"—warm gowns to be worn outdoors at night. Hume sardonically informed his friend, the physician John Clephane, that the bishop of London had published a pastoral letter recommending such earthquake pills as "fasting, prayer, repentance, mortification, and other drugs, which are entirely to come from his own shop." The bishop's Letter had an enormous sale, while Hume's *Philosophical Essays Concerning Human Understanding* were an innocent victim of the panic. "You'll scarcely believe what I am going to tell you," he wrote Clephane, "but it is literally true. Millar had printed off some months ago a new Edition of certain philosophical Essays, but he tells me very gravely, that he has delay'd publishing because of the Earthquake."[1]

The terrified crowds, in miserable fear of their lives, who went to hear Wesley and Whitefield preach would have been at home in twelfth-century Chartres. The philosophers who commented so sardonically on their terror would have been strangers there: the enchantment of the supernatural had gone from their lives. All societies live in tension: medieval society too had rebellions of the poor, burghers struggling against wealthy bishops and noble landowners, and heretics questioning aspects of Catholic doctrine. But no one, not even the heretic, doubted the religious foundation of the world or the inferiority of the temporal in face of eternity. In the eighteenth century, the tension went deeper, and many of the men who used words for a living were estranged from the religious foundations of their society.

This estrangement stands before us with all its bold and pitiless aggressiveness in the philosophes' antireligious humor. Eighteenth-century Christians, like their medieval forebears, could gibe at priests and, on occasion, take their ritual with a certain casual gaiety. But at least they kept the sacraments sacred, and it was precisely the sacraments that the Enlightenment found least comprehensible and most laughable. Voltaire blandly reported that baptism could not be performed with sand, not even in the deserts of Arabia; and he dismissed centuries of bitter controversy over Transubstantiation by explaining that "those who are called

---

[1] April 18, 1750. *Letters*, I, 141-2.

Papists eat God without bread, the Lutherans eat bread and God, while the Calvinists, who came soon after them, eat bread without eating God."[2] Whatever one's response to such impudence, the historian must read such witticisms as proof of the enormous distance separating the philosophes from the medieval world view, proof that the Enlightenment was the terminal point of a long process of alienation that had begun centuries before, in the Renaissance.

---

[2] *Essai sur les mœurs,* II, 219.

CHAPTER FIVE

The Era of Pagan Christianity

T HE FOUR CENTURIES between 1300 and 1700 are the prehistory
of the Enlightenment. Obviously they were more than that;
obviously they existed in their own right, and they produced ideas
and styles to which the philosophes, if they knew them at all, were
quite indifferent. Besides, these centuries—the years between
Petrarch and Locke—were times of irrepressible conflicts, striking
regional variations, and irreversible changes, times that seemed to
have little in common beyond the prevalence of revolution on all
fronts. But from the vantage point of the Enlightenment, these
were the centuries of gradual renewal in the midst of civil war,
when the critical mind resumed its interrupted conversation with
classical antiquity and moved toward independence. These were
the centuries that supplied the Enlightenment with its image of
the past, both pagan and Christian, its vocabulary, its philosophical method, and much of its program. To be sure, these
centuries, for all their enormous contributions to a secular mode
of thought, were still overwhelmingly religious; they were still—
as the philosophes would have said—in the thrall of the great
myth. That is why they belong to the prehistory of the Enlightenment rather than to its history proper. But all the resistance of
Christian institutions and all the tenacious hold of religious belief
did not prevent the resurgence of an old, and eventually the
triumph of a new mode of thinking. These were centuries when
secular forces first expanded and then exploded whatever unity the
Christian millennium had possessed. It was the era of pagan
Christianity.

This name—pagan Christianity—may sound like a self-
conscious paradox. But it aptly describes a time when men held,
more or less comfortably, beliefs that the Enlightenment would
regard as wholly incompatible, when there was nothing incon-

gruous about the sight of a Christian Humanist, a Christian Stoic, a Christian Platonist, or even a Christian skeptic. Christian thought had proved flexible and remarkably absorptive, and Lorenzo de' Medici could say in all seriousness that one could not be either a good citizen or a good Christian without being a good Platonist. The rebellion against the Middle Ages was therefore not a rebellion against religion.

The philosophes, mystified by the coexistence of criticism and myth and eager to pit one against the other, were sometimes rather puzzled by this period. Still, they did not simply invent the turmoil they thought they saw among and within the men of that age. It is the fate of intellectuals in all ages to agonize over fundamentals; what makes the era of pagan Christianity special is that the dominant form of that agony was a struggle between Christian and classical modes of thought. The world that took shape in those four centuries was no longer medieval and not yet modern. It was not yet modern because it found ways of accommodating new situations and ideas to traditional responses. But it was no longer medieval because it also created new institutions, established new relations with antiquity, and gradually—slowly and uncertainly but manifestly—attenuated its religious fervor.

I. THE PURIFICATION OF THE SOURCES

I

THE RENAISSANCE and the Enlightenment were much alike. Both had a history, an intricate evolution, with its setbacks, its local variations, its factions and divisions, its radicals and nostalgic conservatives. The road from Petrarch to Erasmus was long—far longer, in physical and emotional distance, than the road from Locke to Condorcet. Giotto did not paint like Raphael, Boccaccio did not write like Machiavelli: with the passage of years, interests shifted, ideas and styles changed. A little superciliously, a little mechanically, the philosophes recognized it: the Humanists, d'Alembert wrote in his *Discours préliminaire*, began as erudite antiquarians, moved on to the study of literature, and ended up as philosophers. Yet beneath all this diversity there was a consensus of ideals and ways of thinking that calls for recognition.

One cause and sign of this consensus was the informal alliance among its spokesmen. Like the Enlightenment, the Renaissance was dominated by men of letters, an energetic brotherhood in which class counted less than talents. Much like the philosophes, the Humanists spoke for a movement wider than their immediate circle, and much like them, the Humanists occupied strategic posts and led an active existence. They were historians, antiquarians, moral philosophers, poets, scholars, and art critics, and many of them found the opportunity to be statesmen, propagandists, or professors. Again, much like the philosophes, the Humanists organized their friendships for the sake of their mission; they read one another's books, went on long journeys to debate with each other, and formed centers of study where they practiced and perfected the art of conversation; they spread their learning across Europe and handed it down to new generations. Many of them were patriots, by inclination or for profit, and placed their facile Latinity at the service of their cities, extolling Florence at the expense of Milan, or Milan at the expense of Florence. But in their philosophical style the Humanists were cosmopolitan men of letters; long before Voltaire or Kant, they taught that philosophers, no matter how much they disagree, must strive for universal solidarity, tolerate divergent opinions, and cooperate in the search for the truth. And like the philosophes, finally, the Humanists cultivated their ties to the rulers of states; they were their servants, correspondents, and friends, and on favorable occasions, their critics. As the philosophes flourished in a secular urban environment of intelligent aristocrats and merchants, so the Humanists were the products of vigorous cities governed by alert commercial plutocracies or enlivened by cultivated ecclesiastical dignitaries. "The progress of commerce," wrote William Robertson in praise of the Italian city-state, "had considerable influence in polishing the manners of European nations, and in establishing among them order, equal laws, and humanity."[1] The exhilarating intercourse between men of ideas and men of power that marks the Enlighten-

---

[1] "A View of the Progress of Society in Europe," *Works*, IV, 91.

Cicero

ment also marked the Renaissance, and with the same beneficial consequences to both: as society grew philosophical, the philosophers became social.

One obvious reason why the Renaissance and the Enlightenment seem, and are, so much alike is that both admired classical antiquity, especially ancient Rome. To be sure, antiquity appeared to them in rather different guises: the antiquity of the Enlightenment, classical, differentiated, and influential especially through its critical world view, did not confront the Humanists as a ready-made, finished product; it had to be discovered. Classical antiquity, as Aby Warburg once put it, lay hidden behind demonic antiquity, and for a long time logic and magic coexisted peacefully side by side: Athens had to be recovered from the hands of Alexandria.[2] The continuing debate over the outlines, the very nature of antiquity was not the least of the Humanists' concerns, and it created divisions as well as alliances; their serious efforts to recover it wholly and see it clearly, no matter how unsatisfactory the results often were, lends Renaissance scholarship so much point and so much poignance. It was Florence, the statesman and Humanist Leonardo Bruni boasted in 1428 with a characteristic metaphor, Florence alone that had restored Latin and even Greek learning and had allowed men "to see face to face, and no longer through the veil of absurd translations, the greatest philosophers and admirable orators and all those other men distinguished by their learning."[3] Such panegyrics testify that while the Humanists' antiquity and the philosophes' antiquity were not the same, they were kin: the first was to the second as an illuminated manuscript is to a printed book—an ancestor, a little archaic, but manifestly within the same family.

This family resemblance was confirmed by a common admiration for Cicero. For every Middleton, Montesquieu, or Voltaire who wrote biographies, eulogies, or plays in praise of Cicero, the

---

[2] Aby Warburg: "Heidnisch-antike Weissagung in Wort und Bild zu Luthers Zeiten" (1920), *Gesammelte Schriften*, 2 vols. continuously paginated (1932), II, 491–2, 534.

[3] Quoted in Hans Baron: *The Crisis of the Early Italian Renaissance: Civic Humanism and Republican Liberty in an Age of Classicism and Tyranny*, 2 vols. continuously paginated (1955), I, 362.

Renaissance had a Petrarch who studied Cicero with affectionate care, a Bruni who wrote Cicero's *Life*, and a Longolius who vowed to use only words found in Cicero's writings. Even Humanists like Erasmus who lampooned "Cicero's apes" did so out of respect for the real Cicero: to write like Cicero in the sixteenth century, said Erasmus, is not to possess but to travesty Cicero's spirit, for Cicero had always been himself.

The rediscovery of Cicero was a slow process rather than a single act. As we know, Christian readers down to the twelfth century had converted him into a great orator who had preached the virtues of the monastic life, while the Scholastics, still confined to fragments of his vast output, had glimpsed his advocacy of the active life and had rejected it. Then in 1345, Petrarch discovered Cicero's letters to Atticus with mingled excitement and regret. He found in this chatty, candid correspondence a statesman-lawyer, an ambitious man avid for applause and pathetically in need of reassurance. Here was a pagan thinker in action, without disguise or pretense. Petrarch's discovery dismayed him: Cicero's thirst for fame seemed to him a lamentable distraction from a philosopher's true occupation. Yet for Petrarch, tenderly and tentatively exploring the minds of the ancients he admired for the purity of their style, Cicero's conduct was both warning and guide. Petrarch himself sought solitude, dwelling on divine things in his retreat, but he came to see *otium* as an active condition; not monkish leisure but, like Scipio's withdrawals, a gathering of energies: it was the example of Cicero, more than anything else, that made Petrarch into the adviser of princes.

Petrarch's Ciceronianism is a beginning, both in its dawning appreciation for the man of action and in its diligent search for Cicero's words: in addition to Cicero's letters to Atticus, Petrarch found several of his speeches. Toward the end of the fourteenth century, Petrarch' loyal disciple Coluccio Salutati, a vigorous Humanist and pious Christian, discovered Cicero's important *Epistulae ad familiares;* and throughout his career—this was even more important than enlarging the corpus of Cicero's correspond-ence—Salutati embodied the Ciceronian ideal: around 1400, in the midst of a war with Milan and while he was chancellor of Flor-ence, he took the time to write *De Tyranno,* a treatise on political theory, on Dante and Caesarism; here was Renaissance man

Cicero

personified, a modern Cicero. A few years later, Poggio Bracciolini, the most assiduous and successful discoverer of classical texts in the Renaissance, found many of Cicero's legal speeches and in his last years achieved a sympathetic view of Cicero's philosophy, treating him not merely as a model of style but as a model of civic virtue as well. Finally, in 1421, Gerardo Landriani, bishop of Lodi, rounded out the corpus of Cicero's rhetorical writings with his discovery of the complete *Brutus*, *Orator*, and *De oratore*.

With these discoveries the physical restoration of Cicero had run its course; early in the fifteenth century, Florentine Humanists like Salutati and Bruni could portray a Cicero who was reasonably close to, if a little larger than life. Their Cicero was the great philosopher who is a family man, a splendid orator, and a statesman—or rather, the philosopher great precisely because he loved both his family and his republic.

Compared with the medieval version, this Renaissance Cicero was at once a nobler and a more plausible human being. Medieval scholars, too, had admired the rhetorician, but they had been hampered by their scanty knowledge of his technical treatises and forensic performances. The Humanists, professionally concerned with eloquence, were delighted to take Cicero as their model, for as they came to see him, Cicero had both preached and practiced the maxim that a good orator is a man of good character who employs his rhetorical resources in the public service. Seeing the orator more fully than their medieval predecessors, the Humanists also saw the philosopher-citizen, and it was this Cicero whom the philosophes inherited from the Renaissance.

The career of Cicero's reputation in the Renaissance underscores the radical consequences of the Humanists' rediscovery of antiquity. The title of discoverer has sometimes been denied them, but the Humanists deserved it, for while many ancient manuscripts had not been literally lost—they had been stored in monastery libraries and guarded by monks—most of them had lain unread; their impact on medieval culture had been for the most part negligible. If an antiquarian is a dry-as-dust pedant who worships the past because it is dead, then the Humanists were not antiquarians. The dust on their hands was a devastating indictment of monkish librarians who had allowed the classical heritage to decay: the Humanists' accounts of the libraries they ransacked are chilling in their clinical detail. When Boccaccio visited the great Benedictine library of Monte Cassino, he found it a room without a door, with grass growing on the window sills, and the manuscripts covered with dust, torn and mutilated. Profoundly dejected, and in tears, he asked one of the monks how such desecrations could have been permitted, and was told that the monks would tear off strips of parchment, to be made into psalters for boys or amulets for women, just to make a little money. From 1414 to 1418, Poggio Bracciolini found himself as Apostolic Secretary at the Council of Constance, a council which, fortunately for scholarship, rarely met. Happy to be relieved from clerical duties, Poggio made forays into monasteries in Switzerland, southern Germany, and eastern France and returned laden with invaluable manuscripts and reports of indescribable neglect. At St. Gallen, a monastery situated on a steep, almost inaccessible slope, Poggio found the first complete Quintilian and cared for it as a kindly samaritan cares for a sickly waif. If he had not come to the rescue, he told a friend, Quintilian must soon have perished: so elegant, urbane, and witty a man could not have endured much more of this sort of treatment, in his squalid, filthy prison, surrounded by barbarian jailers.

These devoted searches, which the Humanists undertook with no regard to their safety or comfort and no scruples against sharp practices, bribery, and even theft, brought to light many an ancient work that would later become a favorite in the Enlightenment. I have spoken of the recovery of Cicero; the recovery of Lucretius was even more dramatic: *De rerum natura* had been practically unknown for many centuries, and for a time its survival seems to have depended on a single manuscript. Then Poggio found it late in 1417 at St. Gallen. Whatever we have of Tacitus was first seriously studied by Boccaccio, who found him in—or stole him from—the library of Monte Cassino and left the manuscripts for Florentine Humanists to feed their debates on the respective merits of the Roman Republic or Roman Empire. Catullus, too, precariously survived the Middle Ages in a single manuscript that was recovered by the Humanists. In the light of such discoveries it was ungracious as well as unfair for d'Alembert to describe the Humanists as enthusiasts who indiscriminately devoured all the ancients had left, and who worshipped it all "without knowing very clearly what it was worth."[4]

To be sure, the uses of antiquity varied, just as they were to vary in the Enlightenment. As knowledge and intimacy grew, so did admiration: while Humanists of the late fourteenth century were still inclined to prefer Petrarch to Cicero, the generation that followed them reversed this order and found it hard to see much merit in the "vulgar" Italian language. But the charge that the Humanists incapacitated themselves for creativity with their indiscriminate antiquarianism—a charge first made in the Renaissance itself—applies only to a few of them and only in a few periods. At best, and in general, the Humanists' admiration for classical writings stimulated, rather than prevented, independence: Renaissance classicism was a great debate with antiquity. Even imitations were creative: Leonardo Bruni's *Dialogi ad Petrum Paulum Histrum*, a pair of dialogues pitting ancient against modern literature and Latin against Italian, imitates Cicero's *De oratore* in structure and dramatic action, but its ideas are vigorously independent of antique arguments and appropriate to the debates among Florentine Humanists at the beginning of the fifteenth century. The analogue to Hume's *Dialogues Concerning Natural Religion* is patent.

This imitation—and there were countless others—makes it plain that the Humanists' rediscovery of the ancients was more of an intellectual than a physical exploration. Their delight in antique manuscripts was not merely a collector's delight in a fine specimen, although it was that too; rather it was, in the full sense in which the philosophes understood this word, *philosophical*. Renaissance scholarship, like its rhetoric, had public purposes and political consequences. To reconstruct the real Plato or the real Aristotle, to rescue them from the incrustations of Christian interpretations, was to gain firm philosophical ground from which to criticize medieval systems of thought. To read Lucretius with care and appreciation was to discover a history of civilization at variance with the account given in *Genesis:* to read Vergil without pious allegorizing was to free a great pagan writer from Christian distortions and to recover the ideals of Augustan Rome. To re-

---

[4] *Discours préliminaire de l'Encyclopédie*, in *Mélanges*, I, 106.

cover the meaning of old symbols, of figures from classical mythology or ancient history, was to convert classicism into an instrument of subversion. Thus the Humanists restored Prometheus, creative man against the jealous gods, to his antique luster; and there were Florentine Humanists who in their political diatribes, much like Diderot over three centuries later, turned Brutus into the stock figure of a culture hero—Brutus, the rebellious son whom Dante had placed at the very bottom of Hell. Many of the Humanists approved of Dante's verdict: like the Enlightenment, the Renaissance never ceased arguing over forms of government. But even the scattered applause for Brutus was a drastic departure: the Middle Ages, which prized man's dependence, never celebrated parricide; now there were at least some men in the Renaissance, as there would be in the Enlightenment, who saw a point in it.

Gradually classic after classic reappeared as if reborn. Seneca, who was still called a Father of the Church at the Council of Trent, was restored to his pagan stature in two important editions of his works, one by Erasmus in 1515, the other by Justus Lipsius in 1605. Neither of these editors intended to stir up conflict between Stoicism and Christianity, but their scrupulous work on Seneca's text enabled later readers to understand his thought without any fictitious pieties. In the same manner, Humanist scholars from Niccolo Niccoli to Erasmus collated manuscripts and purified them of the corrupt accretions of centuries. Such labors permitted and almost compelled readers to see the ancient texts in their plain meaning. A transitional figure like Boccaccio could still tamper with Ovid in the approved medieval manner: his novel *Ameto,* Ovidian in tone and subject matter, begins as a sensual, even lascivious work, and ends up by explaining away its eroticism as an allegory on the Trinity and the seven virtues. Ovid's stories invited such treatment, and they continued to receive it well into the Renaissance, but the advances in critical scholarship made it nearly impossible to maintain that these allegories were in any way serious interpretations. In his Prologue to Book I of *Gargantua et Pantagruel,* Rabelais could ridicule the allegorical interpretation of the *Metamorphoses* as a foolish monk's trick. Clearly, the veil of pious interpretation, the figural world view, was being pierced, and Athens was being recon-

quered from the hands of Alexandria. The philosophes reported
and appreciated this Humanistic activity, if rather more tepidly
than was called for; but then, the philosophes did not know the
full story of the Humanists' dramatic searches and dramatic discoveries in monastic libraries. Had they known, they would, I
think, have been properly impressed and properly grateful: hard-
working men of letters, especially iconoclasts, were always among
the philosophes' favorite ancestors.

While the philosophes did not fully recognize the revolutionary implications of the Humanists' work, the Humanists did:
they claimed that they were witnessing and making a Renaissance.
It was early in the fourteenth century that Petrarch denounced
the preceding millennium as an age of darkness and hailed his
own time as a time of renewal. A century later, Lorenzo Valla
and Marsilio Ficino noted that literature and the arts, neglected
for so many centuries, had recovered and risen to new glories;
and a century after them, Rabelais and Vasari greeted all learning
and all art as friends who had returned from long and dismal
exile. As the Humanists saw it—and rightly—all aspects of life
were touched by new vigor, and if sometimes this vigor was
confined to boastful speech, the very form of the boasting was
new. The Renaissance passion for art was neither a phrase nor
mere aestheticism: artistic creation was taken as the model of all
creativity. As technical a subject as epistemology was drawn into
the erotic sphere: we know what we love; eros, the ground of all
action, underlies man's search for knowledge as surely as his
political activity or artistic expression. Cognition, in Francesco
Patrizzi's striking phrase, is coition—*cognitio nihil est aliud, quam
Coitio quaedam cum suo cognobili.*[5] In such speculations, the
fourfold historical scheme of the philosophes was clearly pre-
figured.

Medieval thought had assigned to man a dignified place in the
cosmic scheme. Was man not made in God's image? Had the son
of God not sacrificed himself for man's sins? Yet there is a new
tone in the anthropology of the Renaissance—more complex

---

[5] Patrizzi: *Panarchias*, quoted in Ernst Cassirer: *Individuum und
Kosmos in der Philosophie der Renaissance* (1927), 142.

perhaps than Burckhardt's famous formulations suggest, but no less confident. Some Renaissance philosophers taught that man is free, the master of his fortune, not chained to his place in a universal hierarchy but capable of all things. Even the pessimists, who saw Fortune as an unconquerable and capricious goddess, took pride in man's energetic, heroic combat with fate. Augustine's pious formula that the creature cannot create was now overcome; it was eroded, as it were, from within. Man remains God's creature—of that few Renaissance philosophers had any doubt. But he is a creative creature; he creates, in his art, his civic life, his scholarship, and his moral philosophizing, that noblest of creatures—himself.

The evidence for this new vigor, this new power, is abundant. It was a time, especially in the Italian cities, when old norms were shaken and when men were testing the limits of the permissible, a time at once heady and frightening. Voltaire shrewdly noted the extremes that mark the age: "Intelligence, superstition, atheism, masquerades, poetry, treason, devotion, poison, assassination, a few great men, an infinite number of clever and yet unfortunate rascals—that was Italy."[6] Burckhardt would not say it much better.

The Humanists, too, shared in that exuberance, if a little more sedately than some of the despots. They searched for manuscripts with unbounded energy. They polemicized; they were driven to communicate and persuade; hence, like the philosophes, they enjoyed writing dialogues and conducting disputations. Erasmus pressed his obsessive need for cleanliness into the service of scholarship; he must purify the sources of faith and cultivation and purify them as publicly as possible. And Erasmus was not alone: the Renaissance is pervaded with an urge to action, a philosophy that looks for results.

There were important exceptions to this utilitarianism: the circle of Florentine Neoplatonists around Marsilio Ficino extolled the contemplative life, and above all the contemplation of God, as man's proper work. But even this Platonic theology finds a place for practical activity; and besides, the unworldliness of Ficino's philosophizing is not so much a return to the monastic

---

[6] *Essai sur les mœurs*, II, 69.

ideal as it is the recognition of a political reality—by the second half of fifteenth century, the Medici had stifled all political action in Florence save that of conspiracy. Finally—and this is significant both for the contours of Renaissance thought and for its affinity with the Enlightenment—Ficino was enough in the main stream of Renaissance speculation to be an eclectic; he was ready to sacrifice system to effective thought. The most elegant of doctrines, Ficino argued, is inferior to the truths to be gathered from all teachings, philosophical and theological alike.

With this eclecticism, this urge toward practical philosophizing, we have penetrated to the core of the affinity between Renaissance and Enlightenment. The Humanists, like the philosophes after them, were moral realists: Petrarch preferred Cicero, Seneca, and Horace to Aristotle and the Scholastics, because the latter merely gave knowledge while the former set the reader afire with love of virtue: the object of the will, Petrarch wrote, "is to be good; that of the intellect is truth. It is better to will the good than to know the truth." Goodness is better than truth—we seem to be reading Diderot.[7]

The artists, who were in general intimately associated with the intellectuals, shared their ideas: art was a paradigm of fruitful philosophizing, for paintings, statues, and buildings demonstrated the uses of thought to action. "Understanding must grow together with practice," wrote Albrecht Dürer, speaking for generations of writers and painters, "so that the hand can do what the will in the understanding wants to be done. From this there results, in time, a certainty both in theory and practice. These two must go together, for the one without the other is of no avail"—again we seem to be hearing Diderot's voice.[8]

---

[7] "On His Own Ignorance and that of Many Others," tr. Hans Nachod, in *The Renaissance Philosophy of Man*, ed. Ernst Cassirer et al. (1948), 105.

[8] Quoted by Ernst Panofsky: "Artist, Scientist, Genius: Notes on the 'Renaissance-Dämmerung,'" *The Renaissance*, 131 *n.* For Diderot, see above, p. 180. The formal similarities of Petrarch's and Dürer's statements with that of Diderot illustrate some of the complexities of intellectual history. As I have said before, the claim to practicality was not the sole property of the philosophes; and in the same way, the argument that goodness is superior to truth was not confined to the Enlightenment:

In a sense, this sort of preachment, like similar preachments in the Enlightenment, made a virtue of limitations. Rigorous speculation was not to the Humanists' taste, although much of their philosophical work has a delightful freshness, a boldness of touch, alien to more academic minds. With the wealth of intellectual materials lying about—materials constantly enriched by the Humanists themselves—with Neoplatonic cosmology, Pythagorean mathematical theology, Orphic or Cabbalistic mysteries, Christian mysticism, various forms of astrology, Roman Stoicism, and Epicureanism all equally available to the insatiable scholars of the age, this was the time, not for discipline, but for adventure. A syncretic fusion of all thought and all theology—to the greater glory of man—was a tantalizing possibility; even Humanists less erudite and less ambitious than Pico della Mirandola hoped to channel all learning into a single philosophy of life.

Inevitably, much of this speculation was extravagant, and those who indulged in it built syntheses as unstable as radioactive atoms. Many of the Humanists were amateurs in philosophy; they might call themselves Aristotelians or Platonists, but the clarity of these labels hides an eclectic mixture of beliefs drawn from the widest variety of doctrines and periods. It is therefore not surprising that the accusation often made against the philosophes— that they were not philosophers—was made earlier against the Humanists, with equal plausibility and equal injustice. The Humanists saw themselves as men at work rescuing a maltreated past for the sake of perfecting their own civilization, and their metaphysical, psychological, aesthetic, and theological speculations stood in the service of their impatience. The affinity between Renaissance and Enlightenment, therefore, is quite fundamental: the same dialectic characterizes them both. Both appealed to antiquity, developed tensions with Christianity, and launched themselves on the sea of modernity.

---

good Augustinians held the same position. What makes the resemblances more than formal, however, is that despite all the differences in aim between the Humanist and the philosophe, both are here arguing against Scholasticism and the *vita contemplativa*. Petrarch and Dürer begin a development that is completed in Diderot.

II

But neither this affinity nor all the similarities, real and close as they were, amount to identity. Each movement had its own historic task, defined by its relative proximity to the Christian Middle Ages. The Enlightenment could look upon medieval civilization across the centuries through Humanist eyes. The Renaissance, on the other hand, while it could take some comfort from earlier classical revivals, had no Enlightenment in its past. If the philosophes knew more than the Humanists, they did so (we may say with T. S. Eliot) because the Humanists were what they knew. What I have called the dialectic of the Renaissance was ancestor and precondition to the dialectic of the Enlightenment; but while the tensions were similar, the resolution was not. The Renaissance could not take antiquity as casually as the Enlightenment would take it: precisely because it had to be wrested from medieval hands, it remained problematic; many of the Humanists therefore found their true eighteenth-century heirs not in the philosophes but in their opponents, the *érudits*. Again —with few exceptions the Humanists remained within the Christian fold; their affection for pagan works did not make them pagans. And finally, their sense of modernity had different origins and took different forms from that of the Enlightenment: while the philosophes reveled in their age because they were witnessing the triumphs of the scientific intellect, the Humanists, at least at the beginning, proclaimed a new world because they had come to see that the old was lost forever. Dante's *De monarchia* and Cola di Rienzi's quixotic attempt to restore the Roman Republic in 1347 were two final flickers of a fading ideal: by the time of Petrarch's death in 1374 it was clear to most educated Europeans that Rome was dead and that it had been succeeded by a barren age. Like the Enlightenment, the Renaissance turned to the distant past to conquer the recent past, but unlike it, the Renaissance founded its radicalism in despair. Indeed, one cannot read Erasmus or Machiavelli without feeling that it also ended in despair: neither of them shows much confidence in the eventual victory of reason and humanity.

These differences between the two ages are as far-reaching as their similarities: Nietzsche could enlist Petrarch, Erasmus, and Voltaire under the "flag of the Enlightenment,"[9] but these three and their cohorts belonged to different divisions even if they fought in the same cause. The central intellectual problem of the Renaissance was to find what Aby Warburg once called a compromise formula, an *Ausgleichsformel*,[1] that would enable men to live comfortably with classical forms and Christian convictions, trust in man and trust in God, vigorous secular energies and a tenacious ascetic ideal. There were many men in the Renaissance, men of action or uncomplicated views, who seemed, as it were, to be born with this compromise formula. Adventurous tradesmen or bellicose *condottieri* endowed chapels and rejoiced in pagan statuary, worshipped saints and held thoroughly unorthodox ideas about fate, all without any sign of inner conflict. A ruthless merchant prince like Cosimo de' Medici went on periodic monastic retreats for the good of his soul. But the artists, and even more the philosophers—who are rarely once-born men—bore the scars of their travail: articulate and self-critical, they sensed that their devotion to scholarship and their love of classical antiquity led them in new and dangerous paths.

The first of these radicals was doubtless Petrarch. He sought for *his* compromise formula with all the daring of the pioneer and all the hesitancy of a man lost in uncharted territory. His ambivalence was conscious and persistent: he desperately needed to please, and yet he espoused unpopular views; he longed for fame and for solitude, and when he achieved fame he remained restless, dissatisfied, and often depressed. He was vain, egotistical, selfish, and filled with self-doubt; he claimed the loyalty of others while freeing himself from all shackles of responsibility: his moods, like his philosophy, were in tense disequilibrium; the healthy alternations between action and leisure preached by Cicero and embodied by Scipio were distant, unachieved ideals for him.

Petrarch's private suffering has more than private significance:

---

[9] *Menschliches, Allzumenschliches*, I, 26.
[1] "Francesco Sassettis letztwillige Verfügung," *Gesammelte Schriften*, I, 151.

very much like Rousseau, Petrarch was a world-historical neurotic whose anguish mirrored a cultural situation and whose writings confronted problems other men failed to recognize. He idealized, almost idolized, pagan antiquity, but he remained a Catholic Christian. He celebrated individualism but cherished tradition. He read ancient poems as they had been read in antiquity, in all their sensual worldliness, but he inflicted allegorical interpretations on them. He was a republican enthusiast, nostalgically hoping for the restoration of the Roman Republic, but he also played the courtier to tyrants, and preached submission to authority in good medieval fashion. His life abounds with events that dramatize this ambivalence: in 1341, he was crowned in Rome with the poet's laurel, but nine years later, he went to the same city as a pious pilgrim to celebrate the Jubilee. The same duality haunts his famous climb of Mont Ventoux, which he ascended in the Spring of 1335 for the sake of the view: the book in his pocket was St. Augustine's *Confessions.*

This excursion later earned Petrarch the title of the first modern man, but there is something pathetic about his modernity: his masters were Cicero and Plato, but he could not wholly approve of Cicero's philosophy of life, and he could not read Plato in the original. And yet, it is easier to belittle revolutions than to make them: the Humanists, and the philosophes, too, quite rightly hailed Petrarch as the father of a great cultural revival. Gibbon called him "the eloquent Petrarch," the "first harbinger of day," and while he claimed to see little value in his writings, he professed gratitude to "the man, who by precept and example revived the spirit and study of the Augustan Age" and to the student of Greek who after hard labor "began to reach the sense, and to feel the spirit, of poets and philosophers whose minds were congenial to his own"—words that recall precisely Gibbon's own discovery of the Romans.[2] Even if we cannot applaud Gibbon's taste, we may applaud his penetration: with his customary keenness he has gone to the heart of the matter. However inconclusive

---

[2] *Decline and Fall of the Roman Empire,* VII, 117, 119, 256. Voltaire also thought that the reader could find in Dante and Petrarch, especially in Petrarch, virtues reminiscent of the "energy of the ancients and the freshness of the moderns." *Essai sur les mœurs,* I, 764.

and inconsistent his revolution, Petrarch placed many generations in his debt, and those who went beyond him merely continued what he had begun.

Yet this revolution did not directly aim at religion. Nicolas of Cusa, who has been called the greatest mind of the fifteenth century, read Plato intensively and penetrated the screen of medieval interpretation; he raised epistemological questions that sharply differentiate his work from medieval speculation and developed a philosophical physics that discarded the most fundamental of medieval metaphors, the hierarchy. Yet this informed classicist, adversary of medieval philosophizing, and father of modern philosophy was a subtle theologian, a mystic, and a cardinal. With Marsilio Ficino, head of the informal group known as the Platonic Academy of Florence, the compromise formula was less orthodox than it had been with Nicolas of Cusa, but it was no less religious. Ficino, a gentle and pious scholar, lived wholly in the Medici atmosphere; he had been tutor to Lorenzo the Magnificent and became his friend, and it was with Lorenzo and a select group that he formed a circle of poets and philosophers who, among other observances, celebrated Plato's supposed day of birth and death every year by re-enacting the Symposium. As a young man, Ficino had suffered a severe and prolonged religious crisis; he emerged to become a priest in his middle years, the editor of Plato, and a close student of Augustine and Plotinus. His best known work, the *Theologia Platonica*, an astounding book with an astounding title, claims divine inspiration for Platonism and places Plato's eros in the center of all living activity. God's love for His creation overflows and sanctifies all; in turn, man loves God because God loves him. This eclecticism is neither antique paganism nor modern metaphysics: Ficino's generous appreciation of non-Christian thought and wistful assimilation of classical ideas in no way interfered with his own religious vocation. It may be that Ficino's philosophical theology enjoyed such enormous popularity because it lent respectability to a sentimental eroticism, but in Ficino's own thought that secular element is muted.

Comprehensive as Ficino's synthesis attempted to be, it appears almost provincial compared to the bold syncretic structure erected by his brilliant disciple Pico Della Mirandola. Ficino's God spoke Greek as well as Hebrew; Pico's God was the Great Linguist: he was a divine projection of Pico's own uncanny erudition.[3] In his famous oration on the dignity of man he could quote the Bible and Lucan, appeal to Plato and St. Paul, Averroës and St. Thomas, to celebrate man's freedom and his possibilities. Yet this aggressive Humanist, whose writings fell under papal condemnation, was an ascetic and something of a mystic who turned to Christian apologetics toward the end of his short life and died a follower of Savonarola.

Pride in man, then, was not in itself irreligious. Giannozzo Manetti, the fifteenth-century Florentine Humanist and statesman, famous as much for his elegant handwriting as for his public service, composed a treatise in defense of man's dignity: it was explicitly directed against a work by Pope Innocent III and was filled in true Renaissance style with invectives against Churchmen. Yet even as it appealed to the authority of Cicero, it used arguments from Genesis and from Lactantius. Manetti preached and practiced the life of action: asked by King Alfonso of Naples about the proper duty of man, he replied: *agere et intelligere*— "to act and to understand." But he also took time to translate the Psalms from the Hebrew and the New Testament from the Greek.

In the same way, the widespread interest in textual criticism —a technical pursuit in which the critical mind did much destructive work—neither signified nor did it necessarily produce impiety. In the middle of the fifteenth century, Lorenzo Valla, advocate of the active life and virulent critic of Scholasticism, conclusively demonstrated that the so-called Donation of Constantine was a forgery. It was a brilliant piece of scholarly detection, and damaged papal claims to temporal authority, but Valla was a critical philologist, not a critical philosopher. It is true that

---

[3] Voltaire, who devotes a superficial but not uninformed chapter to Pico in his *Essai sur les mœurs* was, as a facile linguist, rather suspicious of Pico's reputed linguistic attainments: "He is reported to have known twenty-two languages at the age of eighteen. That is surely not within the ordinary course of nature. There is no language that does not require about a year before we can really know it. Whoever knows twenty-two of them at such a young age may be suspected of knowing them very badly; or rather, he will know their elements, which is to know nothing." *Essai*, II, 87.

his notorious *De voluptate*, which tried to reconcile Epicurean with Christian doctrine, is anything but orthodox and not notably pious, yet Valla ended his stormy career as papal secretary to Nicolas V, a stranger to doubts concerning the truth of Christian revelation.

Erasmus, the greatest of the critics and the giant among the late Humanists, had much in common with Valla and is even harder to estimate: like Nicolas of Cusa he escapes all labels. But no matter how cleverly he concealed himself from the world, it is certain that he was not a Voltaire before his time. What is at work in Erasmus is not the rejection of religion nor even the rejection of Christianity in behalf of some universal religion of humanity; it is, rather, the cumulative pressure exerted by two centuries of Renaissance scholarship and criticism, a pressure for the displacement of religious emotion from the center of life, accompanied by the intellectualization of theology. The Renaissance had come a long way from Petrarch, yet even Erasmus is not a modern secularist: antiquity and Christianity converge in him as the subjects—and almost the servants—of literary elegance and accurate scholarship. A publicist is known by the enemies he chooses, and Erasmus concentrated not merely on greedy monks, empty ritual, naïve superstitions, or corrupt texts—these were by his time traditional targets. He also criticized the Philistines who divorced sound learning from true piety, the fanatics who insisted on substituting their private fancies for the great treasures of Christian literature, the snobs who wanted to keep classical learning a monopoly in the hands of a restricted elite. As I have said, he wanted to possess antiquity in all its purity, but his antiquity embraced the New Testament and the Church Fathers, especially his beloved Jerome. Erasmus was a true classical spirit in his search for clarity and simplicity, a modern in his complexity, an ancestor of the Enlightenment in his critical temper and pacific cosmopolitanism. But above all he was a Christian intellectual, striving, as he himself said, to establish a *philosophia Christi*. It is ironic—a fate perhaps inevitable for intellectuals writing in a time of upheaval—that the Enlightenment should have used Erasmus's writings to separate what he had worked so diligently to keep united, and to pit, with his own words, philosophy against Christ. Voltaire's Erasmus was the supple man of letters perpetually threatened by fanatics, the pitiless adversary of monasticism; Wieland's Erasmus, the pacific Humanist who rightly refused to become a partisan in the stormy controversies of the Reformation; and the Erasmus of the *Encyclopédie*, the effective scholar who introduced "science, criticism, and the taste for antiquity" into the North and was "one of the first to have treated religious matters with the nobility and dignity becoming to our mysteries" —a compliment of truly Erasmian ambiguity.[4]

A wholly secular, wholly disenchanted world view, then, was a relative rarity among Renaissance men of letters; in that respect Machiavelli is more prophetic than characteristic. Far more typical was the painter Andrea Mantegna, a reliable scholar and assiduous antiquarian. One morning in September 1464 he went on a celebrated excursion—a fifteenth-century counterpart to Petrarch's climb of Mont Ventoux. With a small group of friends Mantegna set out to Toscolano to copy down antique inscriptions from the Roman ruins there. It was a busy and a playful day: the little society assumed ancient titles and played at being emperors and consuls. But they piously ended their day in a church not far from the ruins and fervently thanked the Virgin and her Son for the success of their expedition.

I have cited this incident not merely because it is charming and revealing but also because it serves as a reminder that in the course of two centuries Renaissance artists fully participated in the evolutions of Renaissance thought. Vasari notes that Brunelleschi rediscovered the ancients, Donatello equalled them, and Masaccio went beyond them to represent nature more perfectly than anyone before, but while they disagreed on how to solve the great question of antiquity versus nature, imitation versus individual talent, their classicism seems to have caused no religious turmoil within them.[5] The sacred remained a central theme for

---

[4] Article "Rotterdam," quoted by Werner Kaegi in his "Erasmus im achtzehnten Jahrhundert," *Gedenkschrift zum 400. Todestage des Erasmus von Rotterdam* (1936), 218.

[5] The Renaissance thus anticipates still another significant theme of Enlightenment speculation. Diderot, as we know, had laid it down that man should discover nature by studying the ancients. In the same way, the German poet Uz could think of no higher praise for Wieland than to call him one of the few men of his time to have "the good taste of nature and antiquity." (Sengle:

Renaissance sculptors, architects, and painters, an inspiration to most, a profitable commission to some, and a problem to a few. Still, there can be no doubt that the artists of the Renaissance were compelled to find their own compromise formulas, to accommodate secular and classical concerns with the prevailing, still religious culture of their day. Botticelli took his inspiration equally from Politian and the New Testament and painted the Birth of Venus and the Annunciation with equal devotion; he frequented the Neoplatonic circle of the Medici and ended up as a disciple of Savonarola. Ghirlandaio is celebrated for endowing his paintings with glowing vitality and sumptuous prettiness, but he concentrated on religious subjects and finally joined a religious brotherhood. In his *Adoration of the Shepherds* the Christ child lies in front of a classical sarcophagus, and the praying Virgin kneels in a landscape complete with a Roman arch of triumph and two antique columns. Donatello, Leonardo, Raphael, Michelangelo—the greatest of them, who had all absorbed the lessons of antiquity and the teachings of nature, lavished their genius on Madonnas, on Davids, on scenes from the Passion of Christ. As Rudolf Wittkower has said, the symbol of the Renaissance was a church—as it had been in the Middle Ages. But its form had changed, from cruciform to round or square, and this change of form signified a change of feeling, a shift from the literal mysticism of medieval allegoresis to the mysticism of Christian Neoplatonism. The cruciform church had been the symbol of the crucified Christ, the church based on geometric figures like the circle or the square symbolized God, the sublime mathematician —the god whom Plato had been the first to discover. This was not the time for deism—not yet. But it was no longer—for some at least—the time for orthodoxy or for subjection to an unquestioned hierarchical order of things.

But then nothing, not even the circular church, is a symbol adequate to so lively, so diverse, a time as the Renaissance. The irrational cruelty of the tyrants, the extravagance in dress and

---

Wieland, 253.) And d'Alembert singled out Malherbe for being "nourished by his reading of the excellent poets of antiquity and for taking, as they did, nature for his model." *Discours préliminaire de l'Encyclopédie, in Mélanges*, I, 113.

speculation, the mixture of artistic self-discipline and imaginative freedom, the new realism in political thought and historical writing—all this, as I suggested at the outset, is perhaps the central reality of the period. It was not yet an age of criticism but an age whose very chaos made criticism possible and even imperative.

III

Looking back upon these centuries with their disrespectful, disenchanted eyes, the philosophes saw a time of great beginnings. It has often been said, and it is true, that the Enlightenment lacked the intimate knowledge of local history, the generous appreciation of philosophical speculation, and the full understanding of international politics, on which the recognition of the Renaissance depends—it would have been interesting to see Gibbon's interpretation of Florence under the Medici, a history he planned but never wrote. Certainly the subtleties of nineteenth- and twentieth-century scholarship make the philosophes' pronouncements on the Renaissance often appear ignorant or naïve.[6] It is true, too, that the Enlightenment made no marked advance over Bayle's vigorous restatement of the Humanists' thesis that, beginning with Petrarch and ending with Erasmus, there had been a "revival of letters and the arts," first in Florence, then in other Italian cities, and finally in the northern countries of Europe.

This conception falls short of the grandiose "Renaissance" discovered by Michelet's febrile imagination and Burckhardt's synthetic scholarship. The philosophes simplified much in the Renaissance that was complicated, missed much that was interesting. But they seized on the essential thing: when men of letters single out a preceding age for reviving letters, this is weighty praise. The revival was not merely literary: the Humanists' pas-

---

[6] D'Alembert still held to the simplistic theory, doubtless taken from Bayle, that the Italian Renaissance was a direct consequence of the Fall of Constantinople. But this notion was decisively refuted in the Enlightenment itself, by Gibbon and by Voltaire, who said flatly: "In those days Florence was a new Athens. . . . It is not to the refugees from Constantinople that we owe the rebirth of the arts. Those Greeks could teach the Italians only Greek." *Essai sur les mœurs*, I, 766.

sion for form and their search for pure classical texts was the precondition for a change in styles of thinking. Imitation—on this Gibbon insisted with special firmness—imitation is the foundation for independence, the youthful acquisition of the materials for autonomy: "Genius may anticipate the season of maturity, but in the education of a people, as in that of an individual, memory must be exercised, before the powers of reason and fancy can be expanded; nor may the artist hope to equal or surpass, till he has learned to imitate, the works of his predecessors." Petrarch's revolt and the revolt of his immediate successors had been largely a call for good taste: the Scholastics were barbarians to them because they wrote barbarous Latin. But form has its content: the search for texts exercises the critical mentality not merely by what it finds but by the way it seeks. Hence the philological rebellion issued in a philosophical revolution: "The study and imitation of the writers of ancient Rome," Gibbon noted, brought in its train not merely a "purer style of composition" but also a "more generous and rational strain of sentiment." In short, "in Italy, as afterwards in France and England, the pleasing reign of poetry and fiction was succeeded by the light of speculative and experimental philosophy."[7] Petrarch, after all, as I have said, was admirable to Gibbon because he revived not merely the study but also the spirit of the Augustan Age; and, we may add, Petrarch revived that spirit precisely by reviving the study.

Since the Enlightenment saw the Renaissance as an evolution, with the light of philosophy succeeding the reign of fancy, it was only natural that the philosophes should feel the closest affinity with the writers of the late Renaissance. Boccaccio was amusing, but Vasari and Machiavelli and Guicciardini were immensely useful to them. And they were useful to them because they had drawn the consequences of the great revival of letters. The Humanists of the fourteenth and fifteenth centuries (so it seemed to the philosophes) had been adventurous archeologists who had stumbled on a neglected site; they had dug up remains whose existence had not been suspected, cleaned objects covered with the dust of centuries, restored their pristine meaning to inscriptions long misread, and invited later generations to draw

---

[7] *Decline and Fall of the Roman Empire*, VII, 130–1.

their own critical conclusions from this devoted and devout scholarship. Philosophers like Pico had been seduced by the very profusion of new ideas, but the hardheaded historians and political scientists of the early sixteenth century prepared the way to true philosophy. In short, the philosophes saw the Renaissance as the first act of a great drama in which the Enlightenment itself was the last—the great drama of the disenchantment of the European mind.

2. ANCIENTS AND MODERNS: THE ANCIENTS

I

WITH THE COMING of the sixteenth century, the prehistory of the Enlightenment enters its decisive phase. The accession of the Tudors, the unification of Spain, the French invasion of Italy in 1494, the loss of control suffered by papacy and empire—all were symptoms of disease in the traditional body politic and, with the writings of Machiavelli, heralds of the modern state system. The parochial world view that had made the Mediterranean area the center of the universe was discredited by spectacular voyages across the seas; strange cultures raised disturbing questions about the souls of heathens and the value of Christian civilization. The revolution in cosmology initiated by Copernicus was at first treated lightly, but its subversive implications began to reverberate among educated men long before Galileo was silenced. The European economy, with its lumbering communications and limited exchanges, was greatly expanded by the exploitation of new territories overseas and by technological improvements at home; economic power and the centers of prosperity shifted, slowly but decisively, to the north and west. Perhaps most important of all—at least for the career of the critical mind—the Protestant heresy persisted and thus stripped Christian Europe of one of its most tenacious myths, the myth of a Catholic commonwealth centered at Rome, which had so long covered over social cleavages, regional conflicts, struggles for power, and radical dissensions on religious and ecclesiastical matters: the success of Luther and Calvin and of Henry VIII called for new conceptions of political loyalty and social integration. Thus statesmen, adventurers, merchants, scholars, and religious reformers presented European intellectuals with new problems, new at least in intensity and range.

The great clashes of the sixteenth century were not so much clashes between innovation and tradition as between two incompatible traditions. Christian confronted Christian. The Protestant Reformation, partly the rival, partly the fruit of Humanism, sought to revive the intimate religious experience of primitive Christianity and to discard the ritualistic and institutional accretions indispensable to Catholicism. Yet the search for the old was an ally of the new: the Reformers were, in both senses of the word, radical—they penetrated to the roots of their religion and they presided over a movement that changed the face of Europe. Whatever form it took, Protestantism was the reverse of secularism or skepticism, but in the long run its embattled polemics won elbow room for both skeptics and secularists: political desperation, and in some places religious fervor, gave rise to the idea of toleration, while the Reformers' need to defend the antiquity of their doctrines sharpened the historical criticism first developed in the Renaissance. As Voltaire put it with a characteristic metaphor: when Luther, in 1517, attacked the selling of indulgences and questioned the authority of the Papacy, "a corner of the veil was lifted. The nations, aroused, wanted to judge what they had worshipped."[8] It was not the first or the last time that religious men advanced the cause of unbelief.

It was into this volatile world, torn by religious war, economic dislocation, political instability, and philosophical uncertainty, that the book trade threw its scrupulously edited and exquisitely printed editions of classical authors. The philosophes, whose own propaganda activities would have been unthinkable without it, hailed the invention of the printing press as a cultural revolution: Condorcet placed it at the beginning of the eighth phase of human history—the phase, that is, immediately preceding the era of the Enlightenment. Condorcet was right: printing

---

[8] *Essai sur les mœurs*, II, 217.

multiplied the hands of the Humanists, and while their fine hand-writing continued to find customers, the resistance to those ugly new things, printed books, dwindled rapidly as their uses became apparent. Between 1465 and 1470, in the first few years of book-making, most of Cicero and all of Horace were made available; Vergil, Ovid, Seneca, were printed in dozens of cities and dozens of editions before 1500. Humanists like Erasmus traveled to live with printers like Aldus Manutius; and the Aldine press was not alone in deluging Europe with editions, commentaries, and trans-lations.[9]

As printing was the essential element, translation was a pow-erful aid in the diffusion of the classics. By the middle of the sixteenth century, the educated man who had no Greek, and even the ordinary literate man who had no Latin, found most of Livy and Tacitus, Plato and Aristotle, accessible to him. Machia-velli relied on Latin translations of Polybius, Montaigne on Jacques Amyot's French version of Plutarch's *Lives;* the labors of Amyot, Sir Thomas North who Englished Plutarch, and other translators, opened new windows to the ancients. Thus the texture of sixteenth- and seventeenth-century civilization was enriched with a liberal admixture of classical culture.

The political significance of this classicism is hard to esti-mate. Much of it was absorbed in aesthetic expression or political cant—this was the unpolitical classicism that would later permit Rousseau to quote Caligula in the *Contrat social* or Voltaire to flatter Louis XV by comparing him to Trajan. Elizabethan dramatists adopted conventions from Seneca, borrowed plots from Plutarch, imitated Stoic sentences or Epicurean paeans to worldliness, all without incurring charges of impiety. Whatever was subversive in French neoclassicism was muted and subter-ranean. Molière was associated with an Epicurean circle; Racine, libertine, courtier, and late in life, austere Jansenist, wrote trag-edies electric with illicit passions and insoluble tensions; all the classicists, in their poems, essays, and dramas, restated the precepts of Aristotle and Horace and re-enacted the subjects of Greek and

---

[9] It is worth stressing—this, after all, is still the prehistory of the Enlightenment—that the classics were not alone in being printed: the Bible, the Church Fathers, pious commentaries, and saints' lives were more popular than pagan writings.

Roman playwrights. Yet, as Voltaire noted, "Louis XIV, Colbert, Sophocles, and Euripides all collaborated in shaping Racine"[1]— the French classicists concealed their radicalism, to themselves as much as to others, by their obedience to the rules, their search for decorum, balance, and purity of form, and placed their talents at the service of the French crown in its campaign for cultural hegemony in Europe. This classicism was rationalist without being irreligious.

Art, too, was rooted in this comprehensive Christianity: Poussin painted scenes from Ovid and, in his maturity, canvases illustrating Stoic virtues, but his customers included wealthy bourgeois, Roman cardinals, and the Most Christian King of France. During his stay in Paris, from 1640 to 1642, Poussin designed three frontispieces for books to be produced by the royal printed. One was a Bible, another a Horace, the third a Vergil— no one seems to have thought this an incongruous trio.

To the extent that classical ideas and themes were assimilated into the arts, their sting was drawn. And yet the new economic and political conditions, coupled with the new intellectual situation, exacerbated the malaise in Christian civilization first uncovered—or produced—by the Humanists. To many Christians, the religious crises of the sixteenth century were a conclusive refutation of Erasmus's Christian philosophy and of the great compromise that had taken the best efforts of Jerome and Augustine and Aquinas. In its panic, the Catholic leadership pursued two contradictory policies: it permitted the Jesuits to use suitably expurgated pagan writings and it launched an energetic attack on the classics. Seventeenth-century classicism is evidence that the association of antique with Christian culture could not be unraveled—at least not by Christians. But late in the sixteenth century the Council of Trent certainly made a serious effort; intent on reaffirming the mythical qualities of Christianity, the council put allegories like the *Ovide moralisé* on the Index, and purged art. The loincloths that made Michelangelo's *Last Judgment* presentable were symptoms of a great fear of paganism, and signs that the compromise formulas of the Renaissance were threatening to collapse.

---

[1] *Siècle de Louis XIV*, chapter 32. *Œuvres historiques*, 1011.

They did not collapse quickly and were not abandoned without protest: they had worked too well for that; their hold was too tenacious. But while the ancient heritage continued to be handled delicately by pious hands, there were enough tepid believers and downright unbelievers among sixteenth- and seventeenth-century historians, editors, translators, and philosophers, to make the classicism of that period intensely interesting, and supremely relevant, to the Enlightenment. We need only glance at Hume's essays, Rousseau's autobiographies, Voltaire's notebooks, Diderot's letters, Lessing's polemics, or Wieland's novels to see how much the philosophes took over from their immediate predecessors. Their libraries were filled with the books of Bodin and Pascal, Harrington and Spinoza, Dutch Arminians and Cambridge Platonists, minor Epicurean poets and earnest neo-Stoic commentators, and since the philosophes lived in a time when books were still expensive acquisitions and precious possessions and were bought, at least by men of letters, for their content rather than their binding, we can be confident that the books they owned give us a fair idea of the books they read, and the books they read a fair idea of the furniture of their minds.

Their very voracity, joined as it was to a brisk, independent stance toward congenial writers of the past, saved the philosophes from becoming mere disciples, either of ancient philosophers or of modern interpreters of classical thought. Their eclecticism was only partly an ethical or methodological ideal—it was also a recognition of their own intellectual wealth. In fact, one can make a good case for the argument that writers from Machiavelli to Bayle taught the philosophes mainly how to appropriate the past without losing their individuality.[2] After reading Machiavelli, they could appreciate him without becoming Machiavellians in the same way and for the same reason that Machiavelli had read the Romans without parroting them. Machiavelli, the philosophes knew, had written his *Discourses* and his *Prince* in continuous and intimate intercourse with Livy, with Tacitus and Polybius. At

---

[2] In the light of the philosophes' reputation as slavish followers of Bayle and irresponsible critics of Descartes, it is remarkable to read in Voltaire's notebooks: "Descartes and Bayle were the apostles of reason, but by teaching us to combat their errors." *Notebooks*, 220.

the same time, he had proudly proclaimed his originality: his *Discourses*, he said, had opened a "new route, which has not yet been followed by anyone." Similarly, reading Montaigne taught the philosophes not merely how to read Montaigne but how to read the ancients in his manner. Montaigne had lived with the classics as though they were contemporaries, friends more intimate than his neighbors. Yet he had insisted that he was above what he called "pedantry"; his discourse with his beloved Romans was a dialogue among equals, the path to self-reliance: "We take the opinions and the knowledge of others into our care, and that is all. We must make them ours." After all, "what good is it to us to have a belly full of meat if it is not digested? if it is not transformed in us? if it does not enlarge and strengthen us?" As long as we lean on the arms of others, we enfeeble our own powers; we may grow learned with other men's learning, but we can only be wise with our wisdom: "I have no love for this dependent and beggarly capacity."[3] This was precisely the sort of precept the philosophes could applaud and apply: "What a crying injustice to say that Montaigne did nothing but comment on the ancients," wrote Voltaire in 1746. "He quotes them to the point, which is precisely what the commentators have not done."[4] Bayle, too, another favorite with the philosophes, was steeped in the ancients, but manifestly Plutarch and Pyrrho had trained him to rely on his own judgment.

These were important lessons, but important as they were, Machiavelli and the others did more for the philosophes than to teach them how to read. They also transmitted, or at least confirmed, an attitude toward the world, a style of thinking. As the philosophes read their Montaigne and their Lipsius, they found in them the very qualities that had made antiquity so congenial: realism, detachment from myth, intimacy with the life of action, a tendency to prefer ethics to metaphysics, and a hardheaded eclecticism.

---

[3] "Du Pédantisme," *Essais*, I, 25. *Œuvres complètes* (ed. Pléiade, 1962), 136–7.
[4] Voltaire to comte de Tressan, August 21 (1746). *Correspondence*, XV, 119–20.

Machiavelli

II

Among the first rediscoverers of antique realism, one of the greatest, but also, for the Enlightenment, the most problematical, was Machiavelli. While the philosophes unanimously discarded the lurid caricature that had so long passed for his portrait, they could not be wholly at ease with the amoral precepts of the *Prince*. Hume, who thought Machiavelli "a great genius," a virtuous man, and among the finest historians of modern times, argued that the brutal, corrupt, and cynical age in which Machiavelli had lived had seduced him into an excessive pessimism and into giving some bad advice.[5] Montesquieu separated Machiavellianism from Machiavelli: he was too strongly imbued with Stoic ethics to approve of maxims inculcating lying, treachery, and assassination; still, he followed Machiavelli closely in his own analysis of the politics of religion and cherished him as a pioneer in political sociology: in Montesquieu's *Dissertation sur la politique des Romains dans la religion* and in his masterpiece, *L'Esprit des lois*, Machiavelli the tough-minded methodologist blots out the diabolical poisoner of men's minds—Shakespeare's "murderous Machiavel." In fact, Montesquieu adopted the view, advanced earlier by a few isolated thinkers like Spinoza, that the real Machiavelli was a lover of liberty, the Machiavelli of the *Discourses*, not of the *Prince*. It was this estimate of Machiavelli which Rousseau, so often Montesquieu's disciple, perpetuated in his writings: Machiavelli, Rousseau suggested, had been a republican—the satirist, not the theoretician, of tyranny: "He was an honorable man and a good citizen."[6] Voltaire, despite his facile moralizing, was an appreciative, careful, and lifelong reader of Machiavelli. He thought him a strange man, a versatile and talented writer, like Tacitus too pessimistic about human nature, but an advocate of virtue despite himself. There is deeper meaning in his celebrated witticism against Frederick the Great than is

---

[5] "Of Civil Liberty," *Works*, III, 156; "Of the Study of History," ibid., IV, 391.
[6] *Contrat social*, Book III, chapter 6, additional note. *Œuvres*, III, 1480.

commonly supposed: "If Machiavelli had had a prince as pupil, the first thing he would have recommended would have been that he write against him"—this malicious sentence in his *Mémoires* of 1759 suggests that Voltaire accepted the harsh necessities of power, the inescapable conflict between political rhetoric and political realities—and the need for such a ruthless realist as Machiavelli.[7]

It is with a short article by Diderot in the *Encyclopédie*, an article which ends with this Voltairian quip, that we penetrate to the heart of Machiavelli's meaning for the Enlightenment. "Machiavélisme" interprets the *Prince* as a vivid warning against tyranny misread by his contemporaries: "They took a satire for a eulogy." It sharply distinguishes Machiavellianism—"detestable politics"—from Machiavelli, who is described as an erudite man of genius, a cultivated man of letters who wrote some good dramas, hated the despotism of the Medici, survived torture through his courage, and died like a philosopher. If (the article notes a little disingenuously) the reports are to be believed, "he said that he preferred being in hell with Socrates, Alcibiades, Caesar, Pompey, and the other great men of antiquity, to being in heaven with the founders of Christianity."[8] This, for obvious reasons, was an attractive enough picture to Diderot—the modern pagan, brave to the end, joining the ancients whom he had always preferred to the preachers of meekness and superstition. But Diderot goes deeper than this; he quotes and accepts Bacon's famous verdict: *Est quod gratias agamus Machiavello et hujus modi scriptoribus, qui aperte et indissimulanter proferunt quod homines facere soleant, non quod debeant*—"We are much beholden to Machiavelli and other writers of that class, who openly and unfeignedly declare or describe what men do, and not what

---

[7] *Mémoires*, in *Œuvres*, I, 17.

[8] Diderot: *Œuvres*, XVI, 32. These last words sound too apt to be authentic; they sound more like the invention of an eighteenth-century propagandist than the pronouncement of the dying Florentine. But they were first reported in the sixteenth century, and today authoritative biographers like Ridolfi accept them. Diderot might have learned them either from Brucker's *History of Philosophy* or from Bayle's *Dictionnaire* (see Proust: *Diderot et l'Encyclopédie*, 552–3).

they ought to do."[9] The Enlightenment's Machiavelli, then, was Bacon's Machiavelli, the historian who had claimed to "open a new route" after "long experience and assiduous research";[1] the innovator who had invented the science of politics, a study that amalgamated contemporary affairs with ancient history. Only a man who has turned his back on myth, who gives his critical faculties full range, could convert politics and history into twin laboratories in which the raw materials of experience are transformed into valid generalizations about human action. But, Machiavelli insisted—and here too the philosophes found him most instructive—these lessons of experience can be understood and utilized only by an experienced man: the cloistered metaphysician is nearly always and at nearly all points inferior to the statesman, the practical thinker. Only a man firmly planted in the present can use the past as it deserves to be used: only he can exploit it as he explores it and can pit his *virtù*, unafraid and well-informed, against the merciless and unpredictable blows of *fortuna*. That Machiavelli should have been a virulent adversary of the Papacy and an astringent critic of Christian morality struck the philosophes as merely an added virtue, a sign of good sense, proof of his capacity to learn from his experience; it confirmed their view of him as an antique Humanist in the modern world.

III

Much as they appreciated his genius, the philosophes thought of Machiavelli largely as an ultimate failure, as a great historian whose realism had seized on a partial reality. Montaigne, on the other hand, was not vulnerable to this criticism, and the

---

[9] Diderot: "Machiavélisme," *Œuvres*, XVI, 33. Bacon's comment is in *De Augmentis Scientiarum*, Book VII, chapter 2. (Latin version, *Works*, I, 729; English version, ibid., V, 17.) Toward the end of the seventeenth century, the Epicurean essayist Saint Evremond took the same view: Machiavelli's "excellent" *Discourses*, he wrote to the maréchal de Créqui, like his other works, are marked by notable "penetration." *The Letters of Saint Evremond*, ed. John Hayward (1930), 128.
[1] "Introduction" to Book I, and "Dedication," *Discorsi sopra la prima deca di Tito Livio*.

philosophes could delight in him without reserve. They cherished
his informality, his open-minded and erudite relativism. In the
Encyclopédie, Diderot predicted that Montaigne's *Essais* would
last as long as there were men who loved truth, energy, and
simplicity, and added: "The contradictions in his work are the
faithful image of the contradictions in the human understanding.
He follows the thread of his ideas artlessly; he cares little where
he starts from, how he goes, or where he ends up."[2] To Diderot,
as to the other philosophes, the *Essais* splendidly embodied the
manner of a man whose doctrine it was to have no doctrine, but
to take the best from all the thought of past and present and to
test ideas in and by life.

Montaigne was in touch with the political realities of his
time; his writings disclose a deeply felt, if cautiously expressed,
anxiety over social struggles and religious controversy, and a
powerful urge toward self-expression, even self-creation. But for
Montaigne, as for other educated men, life was also a life of books;
the thoughts and actions of the ancients were as real as the events
around him. Hence, precisely as an empiricist, as an eclectic on
principle, Montaigne was an antiquarian. In fact, he was an exceptionally well-equipped and communicative antiquarian, as
garrulous and inescapable a conversationalist as Coleridge's
ancient mariner—and even more interesting. His *Essais* are sprinkled with quotations, often long quotations, chosen to embroider
an anecdote or prove a point. Several *Essais*, indeed, are little more
than commentaries on some ancient texts. Montaigne's baroque
indirections, his countless digressions, may disconcert the twentieth-century reader, who is a man in a hurry and used to leaner
prose. But they gave pleasure to the philosophes who enjoyed talk
and appreciated apt allusions. Epictetus, Horace, Cicero, Seneca,
Plutarch, speak in Montaigne's *Essais* many dozens of times, in
voices that are their own. Montaigne's Vergil is not the necromancer dear to the Middle Ages, but Homer's greatest descendant;
his Ovid is not the compiler of allegories for nuns, but the
imaginative poet of fascinating, often lascivious adventures.

This was attractive enough to the Enlightenment; what made
it still more attractive was that Montaigne's view of life had

---

[2] "Pyrrhonienne, ou sceptique," *Œuvres*, XVI, 485.

Montaigne

undergone marked changes and that these changes, which reflect the teachings of ancient schools, deposited their traces in the *Essais*. It would be unjust to Montaigne to divide his development into rigid stages; even as a young man he was not a doctrinaire. But in his youth, when he dwelled with Roman resignation on the idea that to philosophize is to learn how to die, he echoed the Stoic philosophy of Seneca and Marcus Aurelius. Later—as a vigorous skeptic who coined the motto *Que scais-je?*—he sounded much like the Pyrrhonists and like Cicero in his most skeptical phase. At last he grew to depend on himself and his experience alone, taking for his only master Socrates, who had taught the supreme virtue of self-knowledge. Montaigne's philosophical pilgrimage thus offered his readers a clear-eyed anthology of pagan thought and an impressive drama of self-liberation. "He bases his ideas on the ideas of great men," Voltaire noted. "He judges them, he fights them, he talks with them, with his reader, with himself. He is always original in his manner of presentation, always full of imagination, always a painter, and he always (and I love that!) he always knows how to doubt."[3]

It is evident that what the Enlightenment chose to learn from Montaigne was not precisely what he had meant to teach. Montaigne never abjured Catholicism; he lived and died a Christian—by his lights. But many of his eighteenth-century readers found it easy to put his tepid religiosity into the service of their secular world view. They appropriated Montaigne's preoccupation with himself, his unashamed pleasure in sensuality, his refusal to repent of his worldliness, his contempt for fanaticism, his humane views on education, and above all, his Pyrrhonist pronouncements derived so unmistakably from pagan authorities. The philosophes' Montaigne was the skeptical, humane explorer of human folly who could dwell with almost eighteenth-century relish on the crimes produced by religion and could quote with approval their favorite line from Lucretius, *Tantum religio potuit suadere malorum*.[4] His *Essais*, Diderot wrote, contain literally hundreds of quotable passages as beautiful as they are irreligious;

---

[3] Voltaire to comte de Tressan, August 21 (1746). *Correspondence*, XV, 119–20.
[4] "Apologie de Raimond Sebond," *Essais*, II, 12. *Œuvres complètes*, 502.

and his memorable device—*Que scais-je?*—had given the Pyrrhonists their battle cry.[5] Significantly, Diderot, who knew and loved his Montaigne better than most of the other philosophes —who indeed knew and loved him well enough—enlisted Montaigne himself among the followers of Pyrrho and placed him directly before Bayle: "But," he wrote, concluding his appreciative paragraph on Montaigne, "skepticism had no doughtier athlete, either among the ancients or the moderns, than Bayle."[6]

IV

In the even light of modern scholarship, Montaigne, the urbane aristocratic Catholic, and Bayle, the combative scholarly Protestant, make a somewhat incongruous pair. They were separated by their temperaments and their styles, by the sources, objects, and intended consequences of their skepticism. They were separated also by their life history: Montaigne, it is true, was spectator to a grim religious conflict, but it was comforting to be a wealthy seigneur and the intimate of the king of France; Bayle, for his part, was the victim of *his* king, a hounded Huguenot refugee, driven to make a scanty living by his talents. But for the philosophes, the line from Montaigne's to Bayle's skepticism was straight and unobstructed; they read his opacity and evasiveness, not as signs of inner combat, not as possible clues to a kind of wry fideism, but as tactical devices designed to spread a maximum of subversive information with a minimum of risk. He was, they said, beyond question or quibble, a trustworthy bridge to a much neglected branch of antique speculation; he was the wittiest, the most reliable, teacher of Pyrrhonist skepticism, so sensible that he did not practice what he preached: he knew too much, Diderot said, echoing Bayle himself, either to believe or to doubt everything. If there was one work in the large canon of his writings that all the Enlightenment appropriated, it was the article on Pyrrho in his *Dictionnaire historique et critique*: Pyrrho, Bayle there told his readers, had taught that all things are at bottom mysterious.

---

[5] *Œuvres*, I, 217.
[6] "Pyrrhonienne, ou sceptique," *Œuvres*, XVI, 486.

Since diligent, honest men can find reasons on all sides of every question, it is the part of wisdom to continue inquiry and suspend judgment. When Holbach called Bayle that celebrated man "who teaches so well how to doubt,"[7] he was uttering a firmly established platitude that testifies to the pervasiveness of Bayle's influence and to the single-minded uses to which his complex work was put.

That Bayle was a great teacher of doubt, an instigator of rebellion against Christian belief, is beyond question. The German *Aufklärer*, far less exposed to irreverent writings than the literary men of other countries, experienced his relentless scholarship and ruthless criticisms as a devastating solvent: it was through Bayle that the young Lessing freed himself from the strict Protestantism of his childhood, while the adolescent Wieland, as I have said before, broke loose from his Pietist upbringing after he managed to get hold of Bayle's *Dictionnaire*. As early as 1729, the *Bibliothèque germanique* had warned that "the works of M. Bayle have unsettled a large number of readers and have cast doubt on some of the most widely accepted principles of morality and religion."[8] To judge from his effect on the *Aufklärer*, Bayle's works continued to unsettle susceptible young men down through the century.

The French and British philosophes perhaps needed Bayle rather less; they were unsettled enough by other writings, open and clandestine. But they read him as eagerly as their German brethren. In 1737, Rousseau spent some of his scarce funds to buy Bayle's *Dictionnaire*, at a time when Voltaire and Montesquieu had already assimilated him. David Hume found Bayle congenial all his life. As a young rebel in search of an alternative to Presbyterianism, he discovered ancient atheists, skeptics, and rationalists through the writings of Bayle; this was the time when he noted with approval a maxim by the ancient Greek poet Epicharmus: "Keep sober and remember to be skeptical."[9] And as the full-

---

[7] *Système de la nature*, II, 356 n.

[8] Quoted in Paul Hazard: *The European Mind: 1680–1715* (1963), 114.

[9] Mossner: *Life of Hume*, 78. In the light of the Enlightenment's commitment to common sense and to action, Hume's rejection of Pyrrhonism is revealing: he thought it intellectually excessive, emotionally paralyzing, but in the long run, also ineffective.

fledged philosopher, in his *Enquiries* and his *Dialogues Concerning Natural Religion*, he followed Bayle's arguments and often accepted Bayle's conclusions—usually without mentioning Bayle's name. Gibbon acknowledged, with the elevated elegance of an eighteenth-century classicist, the merits of the seventeenth-century *érudit*, who had taught him respect for facts and the subversive possibilities of historical accuracy:

> A calm and lofty spectator of the religious tempest, the philosopher of Rotterdam condemned with equal firmness the persecution of Louis the Fourteenth, and the republican maxims of the Calvinists. . . . In reviewing the controversies of the times, he turned against each other the arguments of the disputants; successively wielding the arms of the Catholics and Protestants, he proves that neither the way of authority nor the way of examination can afford the multitude any test of religious truth; and dexterously concludes that custom and education must be the sole grounds of popular belief. The ancient paradox of Plutarch, that atheism is less pernicious than superstition, acquires a tenfold vigour when it is adorned with the colours of his wit, and pointed with the acuteness of his logic. His critical dictionary is a vast repository of facts and opinions; and he balances the *false* religions in his sceptical scales, till the opposite quantities (if I may use the language of algebra) annihilate each other.[1]

Gibbon's coy italicizing of "false," implying the existence of a true religion, is simply another legacy of Bayle's method.

"A Stoic or Epicurean displays principles, which may not only be durable, but which have an effect on conduct and behaviour. But a Pyrrhonian cannot expect, that his philosophy will have any constant influence on the mind: or if it had, that its influence would be beneficial to society." But then, men are rarely content to rest in Pyrrhonist principles; these are usually subverted by "action, and employment, and the occupations of common life." Like the other philosophes, Hume would not surrender the virtues of the *vita activa* for those of the *vita contemplativa*, no matter how attractively the latter might present themselves. (See Hume, *Enquiry Concerning Human Understanding*, in *Works*, IV, 130–1.)

[1] *Autobiography*, 89.

The great engine of skepticism was Bayle's celebrated *Dictionnaire historique et critique*, which expounded Pyrrhonism in several articles and exemplified it in many others. The *Dictionnaire* was first published in 1697 and was soon expanded and translated: in the early 1740's, Gottsched even supervised a translation into German, which was just beginning to become a literary language. He rather spoiled the effect with querulous, disparaging remarks in his notes designed to convict Bayle of impiety, but then, educated Germans could read the *Dictionnaire* in reliable French editions or an adequate English translation— and even his tepid German version, to judge by its impact on the young Winckelmann, had a more subversive effect than Gottsched had intended. Despite its awkward bulk and forbidding price, the *Dictionnaire* was one of the most frequently printed and widely used books in the eighteenth century; no self-respecting library was without it. American intellectuals like Thomas Jefferson and Benjamin Franklin read and warmly recommended it. Little wonder: it offered rich fare and not to skeptics alone; Samuel Johnson, who confessed that he loved "the biographical part of literature" most, told Boswell that he found Bayle's *Dictionnaire* very useful. It gave full critical accounts of Biblical figures, philosophical systems, saints, religious movements, and historical events and it larded its biographies with an admixture of salacious scandal, added to keep the reader alert and to help the sales. Many of its articles corrected earlier, less accurate dictionaries; many conveyed esoteric information or gave persuasive analyses of philosophical doctrines; some, like the celebrated article on Spinoza, misled a whole century.

For the philosophes, the *Dictionnaire* was an unsurpassed source of information, a delight, and a library of stratagems: it concealed so much so well that the author virtually disappears behind the elaborate duplicity of the arguments, the sly innuendos of the massive footnotes, and the deft cross references, while the message itself stands forth clearly. Frederick of Prussia, whose admiration for Bayle was unbounded, had two abridgments made of the *Dictionnaire*. Voltaire singled it out as the first dictionary that had taught men how to think and he recommended that it be reduced to one volume—to make it not less but more pointed. This was more than irresponsible Voltairian phrasemaking: his own *Dictionnaire philosophique* was partly a one-man *Encyclo-pédie*, partly a compact version of Bayle's ponderous machine of war. Still, these condensations and demands for condensation conceal the true nature of the Enlightenment's obligation to the *Dictionnaire:* it was precisely Bayle's deficient sense of form, his prolixity, of which his most uncritical admirers complained, that made the book so indispensable to the little flock: they pillaged no book more freely, more often.

The authorities of church and state, and men of business, testified to Bayle's pervasive influence in other ways. As late as 1754, his *Dictionnaire* was publicly burned at Colmar, and in the same period the Jesuit *Journal de Trévoux* showed its respect for Bayle's destructive philosophizing by analyzing his work at some length: he had been a writer of extraordinary talents, the Jesuits wrote, but he had chosen to abuse those talents and become a "great skeptic." Then, in the fall of 1764, Diderot discovered that Le Breton, the crafty publisher of the *Encyclopédie,* had made extensive cuts in several articles after Diderot had read the proofs. The article mutilated most severely was "*Pyrrhonienne ou sceptique philosophie,*" and the passages cut most drastically were those in which Diderot had eulogized Bayle's character, abused Bayle's clerical persecutors, and restated, in appreciative detail, Bayle's skeptical philosophy. Diderot burst out in impotent rage and could barely be persuaded to resume work on the remaining volumes of the *Encyclopédie;* still, while the experience was an infuriating setback for Diderot, it was also a wry tribute to Bayle's corrosive power.

But Bayle was as little the man of one idea as he was the man of one book, and the philosophes appreciated his versatility. They admired his campaign against superstition and shared his contempt for those timid Christians who had taken the comet of 1680 as a supernatural portent. They rejoiced in his polemics against Louis XIV's brutal attempt to make France "all Catholic" and advocated toleration for the reasons—and sometimes with the very words— they found in his pamphlets. They perfected his critical method of reading documents: their own cool appraisal of the Bible and of astounding historical narratives owes much to Bayle's procedures. Beyond that, the philosophes, who scanned history not for infallible authorities but for exemplars, liked to point to Bayle's life:

to his blameless, frugal scholar's existence, his courageous conduct under persecution at the hands of both Catholics and Protestants, his indefatigable polemicizing in behalf of the right causes. For them he was the first citizen in the republic of letters; in Diderot's words, a doughty athlete of skepticism.

A literary man of such range, a philosopher of such astringency, was more to the philosophes than a teacher of doubt or the author of a valuable work of reference. He embodied the principle, so important to the Enlightenment, that the destructive and constructive phases of criticism are two aspects of a single activity. Montesquieu could say, a little ungraciously, that Bayle had achieved glory with the easiest possible method, by destroying the views of others, but he nevertheless honored Bayle as the advocate of toleration. Lessing wrote his *Nathan der Weise* as Bayle's disciple. And Voltaire paid tribute to Bayle in words quoted so often that they have lost their original savor and appear as bland formulas of courtesy. But once they are read as they were meant, they regain their force and the sincerity of their intention. And read in this way, they illuminate the creative consequences of skepticism—at least of Bayle's skepticism. Voltaire called Bayle —Bayle, the supreme enemy of all confident dogmatism—"the eternal honor of human reason," proof, once again, that for the Enlightenment reason and rationalism were far from identical. He called him the "attorney general of philosophers," a responsible post in the eyes of one for whom philosophers occupied, or should occupy, the highest place in civilization. And most flattering of all, Voltaire compared Bayle to Cicero, reaffirming the bond between ancient Rome and modern Europe and placing Bayle where he belonged—in the ranks of the intellectual architects who were restoring the critical mentality.[2]

V

Realism, eclecticism, skepticism—these were not, strictly speaking, philosophies; they were intellectual positions that made

---

[2] "Note de M. Morza," variant reading, *Œuvres*, VIII, 477; "Poème sur le désastre de Lisbonne," ibid., IX, 476 *n*.

philosophy possible. But just as we cannot draw a clear distinction between the constructive and destructive aspects of the philosophes' thought, so we cannot draw a clear distinction between these positions and the philosophical principles toward which they were hospitable. In the great campaign against Christianity, all—Stoicism and Epicureanism as much as Skepticism, especially Stoicism—had their place.

Quite apart from its scholarly transmission of classical ideas to modern readers, Neo-Stoicism had an appeal of its own: it was a practical philosophy of life which had grown up as a response to social and political needs. Stoicism regained its distinct identity not because a few scholars had been impressed by Seneca or Marcus Aurelius. It was not an intellectual fad but a political program.

For many centuries there had been no room for specifically Stoic ideas. The affinity of Stoic and Christian teachings had enabled the Church Fathers to claim Stoicism as a groping precursor of the Truth and to incorporate much of it into the capacious amalgam of Christian philosophy. But the divergence of Stoic and Christian doctrine was as real as the affinities, and what man has joined together he can put asunder. Now in the time of Reformation and Counter-Reformation, when men of good will and pacific inclinations stood appalled at their world, the formulas of Stoic philosophy seemed a possible basis for the restoration of order. Slowly scholars began to disentangle Stoic doctrine from its Christian formulations. Stoicism remained Christian in temper for a hundred years, but at least the old pagan philosophy was made available in all its purity. Seneca's works and Cicero's most Stoical dialogues were responsibly edited and widely read; Epictetus's noble manual was translated into Latin and French: from 1567 on, Frenchmen could read *La doctrine d'Épictète philosophe, comme l'homme se peut rendre vertueus, libre, heureus, & sans passion.*

Obviously there was nothing new in the vicious recriminations of the sixteenth century, in the mutual persecutions and the indiscriminate slaughter. What was new was the apparent deadlock of hostile religious sects and the complete bankruptcy of traditional institutions and shibboleths. Quite early in its long life, the Council of Trent had ruled out all compromise with Lutherans and Calvinists, while Protestants for their part refused to negotiate with the Whore of Babylon. The Wars of Religion that bled

France in the second half of the sixteenth century and the Thirty Years' War that devastated central Europe in the first half of the seventeenth century were not merely religious wars. They were the military expressions of economic grievances, regional and provincial particularism, competing lusts for power, shifts in class structure, and high rational policy. But they were also the last Crusades, fought in defiance of the palpable reality that Protestantism had come to stay and that Catholicism would survive. Much of the savage perseverance with which Catholics prosecuted their cause came from their rage and frustration at the disappearance of an at least nominally united Europe; much of the Protestants' matching savagery was fed by their Utopian hope for a Europe purged of Antichrist.

While the extent of political dislocation was new, there was also a new possibility for a solution. The Humanists had prepared the way for that solution; their realism made possible a secular view of political power and a secular, or at least no longer specifically Christian, justification for political obligation; their critical philology, combined with their admiration for antiquity, prepared educated men to read Christian documents with skeptical detachment, and pagan philosophies with sympathy; their appeal to nature laid the foundations for what Wilhelm Dilthey has called the "natural system," a style of thought that ordered the world by natural law, natural morality, and natural theology. Sixteenth-century historians served the same cause indirectly, but they nevertheless served it: in fierce competition they gathered facts and piled up documents to demonstrate the antiquity of their particular persuasion, and to prove that their sect was in the apostolic succession. This was hardly irenic, but historical criticism corroded tradition, threw doubt on dogmatism, and encouraged a relativistic detachment from all sectarian arguments.

Thus, slowly and painfully, European intellectuals developed new instruments for understanding the world and reaching accommodations. Throughout Western civilization there were men —still in a minority, but vocal and often highly placed—who agreed that the road to peace lay in the discovery of a religion catholic in the true sense of that word, a religion anchored in the nature of man rather than in historical or geographic accident, rational in character, with a short catalogue of doctrines expressing universal truths which all sensible human beings could accept. Some men preached a mystical vision of a single Deity manifesting itself in many forms, some went back to Augustine for the great ideal of a Christian peace. Others revived the ideals of the Florentine Academy and drew an appealing portrait of a higher, all-embracing Neoplatonic unity, while still others, disgusted with special pleading, incomprehensible Scholasticism, or formalistic rituals, called with irritable common sense for a single reasonable faith. Jean Bodin is characteristic of this motley army of philosophical peacemakers: a believer in sorcery, witchcraft and number mysticism, he was also a pioneering economist and sociologist whose theories of climate and inflation lived to exert their influence on Montesquieu. He was another Pico in the uncanny breadth of his erudition, a typical Renaissance scholar with his profuse accumulation of miscellaneous facts and fanciful constructions, but he was also a modern in his careful reading of Polybius or Guicciardini, in his critical method for reading documents and testing historical assertions. He was a learned lawyer who tried to construct a universally valid legal theory from his comparative studies, but his political and social theory reflect his immediate experience as much as his technical learning: they are a response to the French Wars of Religion and of bloody St. Bartholomew's Night, when his own life had been in danger. He was anything but a modern rationalist, but his most remarkable efforts are among the early masterpieces of modern critical rationalism. His celebrated *Six livres de la république* attempts to establish a coherent theory of sovereignty on secular grounds—to discover, that is, a rational foundation for the state; its pendant, the *Colloquium heptaplomeres*, not published until the nineteenth century but widely distributed before then, depicts religion in debate—one might almost say, religion *as* debate. As Dilthey has observed, its sharply drawn, sympathetically perceived characters anticipate the protagonists of Lessing's *Nathan der Weise*: Jew and Lutheran, pagan and Catholic agree that all schools of belief are sisters, that all are the daughters of natural religion; the speakers conclude that dogmatism is absurd and suspension of judgment indispensable, that men must tolerate one another and seek the truth humbly in their own way. Thus political absolutism and religious toleration, the improbable twins of the modern state system, make their first appearance in the writings of this enigmatic sixteenth-century French lawyer.

Many tributaries, then, contributed to this pacific current, but as Wilhelm Dilthey showed half a century ago in a series of brilliant essays, its chief ingredient was Stoicism. Neo-Stoicism fertilized debate all through Western Europe, most fruitfully in the centers of internecine religious conflict. In the rebellious Netherlands, the center of learning and religious controversy, educated men turned to Stoicism as a cure for the disease of civil war. Dirck Coornhert, who witnessed the start of the Dutch rebellion against Spain, was the first in a distinguished line of Dutch Stoics to embody its ideal of public service and intellectual brotherhood: he was a statesman and theologian, Humanist and Christian. He knew the Romans well: he translated Seneca and Cicero's *De officiis* and drew from them the irenic message that all men are brothers. The warring sects, he wrote, are not so deeply divided as narrow passions have led them to believe; the true Word of God is the healing Word of Christ and that alone.

Coornhert's most important pupil was Jacobus Arminius, who came to preach against his heresies and stayed to preach for them. In Arminius's sermons, Calvinism is softened to gentle instruction designed to lead sinful men toward a reform of their lives. Through Dutch Arminianism, a growing and articulate minority in the seventeenth-century Netherlands despite its defeats at the hands of rigid Calvinists, Neo-Stoicism obtained a wide hearing. The Arminians argued that the truths by which men must live are Christian truths; they are found in the loving teachings of the New Testament, and they remain true outside and without revelation. It was with this group that Hugo Grotius, the founder of modern international law and an admirer of Galileo, associated himself, to his cost and his glory. Steeped in Seneca and Cicero, and explicitly their disciple, Grotius applied their philosophical method to impose order on a disordered world: there are certain ideas common to all rational men, and these ideas are discovered by reason; they do not depend on theology. "Natural law," he wrote in a famous passage, "is so unalterable that God himself cannot change it." Assuming that God did not exist, he wrote in another, equally famous passage, the rules of natural law would retain their validity. With these pronouncements, natural law, which had occupied a subordinate place in the Christian scheme of things, made its declaration of independence.

This hypothetical construction of a natural law without God was not meant in any way to throw doubt on God's existence: Grotius was an impressive historical critic of sacred texts, a great Erasmian, whose annotations on the Old and New Testaments long held the field and survived to become one of John Wesley's favorite books, while Samuel Johnson could recommend Grotius's religious writings to "every man whose faith is yet unsettled." Grotius reduced Christianity to a few central tenets, rationalized the doctrine, and championed freedom of the will against Calvinist Predestination, but the Resurrection of Jesus remained for him an undisputed, indisputable truth.

Grotius was a brilliant scholar who imposed himself on a whole discipline, international law; he was a Christian rationalist and, if not exactly a pacifist, a pacific man.[3] He was the sort of author, clear, vigorous, logical, and humane, whose writings easily achieve the status of prescribed textbooks, and his fame accordingly has lasted and grown. But in his own century and even in the eighteenth century, another Dutch Christian Stoic, Justus Lipsius, was a far more powerful cultural force than Grotius. Lipsius lived to see his Stoic tract *De constantia* reprinted in twenty-four Latin editions and translated into seven modern languages before his death in 1606. His compilation of antique political writings, the *Politicorum libri sex*, which gave wide circulation to Tacitus, and his introductions to Stoic philosophizing, which he published shortly before his death, found an enormous public. For a hundred and fifty years Lipsius sold more books than Bacon or Bodin, and he was probably better known than Montaigne. Gibbon delighted in his "vivacity";[4] Montesquieu owned Lipsius's edition of Tacitus,

---

[3] The philosophes were a little quizzical about him; their style of thinking was no longer his. But they took him seriously: Rousseau took considerable trouble to argue with him about the law of war, while Gibbon, always respectful to erudition, praised Grotius for "enlightening the world." "All antiquity showed itself unveiled to Grotius's eyes," Gibbon wrote; "he unraveled sacred oracles, combated ignorance and superstition, alleviated the horrors of war." *Essai sur l'étude de la littérature*, in *Miscellaneous Works*, IV, 21.

[4] Ibid., 22.

De constantia, the *Politicorum*, and other works; Voltaire had Lipsius's commentary on Polybius at Ferney; Diderot relied on his critical edition of Seneca in his *Essai sur les Règnes de Claude et de Néron;*[5] while the fathers of the German Enlightenment, the academic philosophers Thomasius and Wolff, recommended Lipsius to their students. Some writers—a very few—give their name to the age in which they live; most are its creatures: Lipsius achieved fame by giving people what they wanted. Stoicism was the fashion: when Du Vair's *Philosophie morale des stoïques* appeared in English in 1598, the translator put a significant epigraph on the title page: *Non quaero quodmihi utile est, sed quod multis*—"I do not look for what is useful to me, but to the many."[6]

Evidently what the many thought useful was a Stoicism a Christian could accept, and Lipsius, the most pliable of scholars, supplied it: his Stoicism adds up to a philosophy firmly grounded in erudition; it allowed men to feel some satisfaction in themselves, pointed toward a solution of confessional squabbles, and was at once new and acceptable. It was learned: Lipsius recapitulated in his personal history the history of Humanism, for, as he said, he had begun as a philologist and ended as a philosopher: *e philologia philosophiam feci.*[7] It anchored the ideal of social order in man's moral worth: its ethical rationalism taught men to be patient in the face of adversity and pious in the face of fanaticism. It offered an answer to the crisis of the age that had not been offered before: when David Chrytäus, a Protestant theologian, hailed *De constantia* as a work students must read, "for the like has not been seen or written in philosophy for a thousand years,"[8] he meant to

---

[5] It was with the aid of Lipsius that Diderot could summarily dismiss Seneca's supposititious correspondence with St. Paul as "either the work of a schoolboy trying out his Latin, or of a man who admired the philosopher's doctrines and was anxious to associate him with the disciples of Jesus Christ." *Essai sur les règnes de Claude et de Néron,* in *Œuvres,* III, 194.

[6] Justus Lipsius: *Two Bookes of Constancie,* first translated from the Latin in 1594 by Sir John Stradling (ed. Rudolf Kirk, 1939), 34 *n.*

[7] Max Pohlenz: *Die Stoa* (2nd edn., 1959), 469.

[8] Gerhard Oestreich: "Justus Lipsius als Theoretiker des neuzeitlichen Machtstaates," *Historische Zeitschrift,* CLXXXI (February 1956), 36. *De constantia* is a dialogue between Lipsius, who wishes to flee his war-ravaged country, and the wise Stoic

pay a hyperbolic compliment, but he was pronouncing a historic truth. Such secular morality had not been preached even in the Italian Renaissance. Its acceptance of power translated Machiavelli's disillusioned insights into a theory for the evolving modern state.

At the same time, Lipsius paraded his doctrine as safe to Christian consumers. He enjoyed enlisting the Church Fathers, whose affection for Stoicism was well known, in his campaign to keep Seneca respectable without making him into a Christian. He expounded Stoic ideas with precision and real zest, but when they conflicted with Christian doctrine, when they taught the supremacy of fate or man's right to suicide, he rejected them: Stoicism, he reiterated, was not the true philosophy, but of all untrue philosophies it came closest to the Revealed Faith.

I cannot insist enough that in Lipsius's age this procedure did not necessarily signify insincerity, although Lipsius's religious professions might well arouse some suspicion, timid as he was and supple, ridden with self-satisfaction, ambition, and a restless worldliness. His repeated, opportune shifts from one confession to another stirred up comment even in his own time, a time resigned to such oscillations. But then, whatever his real convictions, what matters in the history of the Enlightenment is that as the years passed and his writings went into edition after edition, Lipsius's Stoicism retained its vigor while his apologetic Christianity lost its relevance. The official ideology of Christian civilization had united ethics and politics and subjected both to theology. In Lipsius's writings these bonds were weakened: his *De constantia*, with its sympathetic exposition of Stoic ethics as the doctrine of the good life according to nature, was both cause and symptom of the separation of ethics from theology; his *Politicorum*, with its treatment of the state as a rational construct guided by realistic considerations of power, was both cause and symptom of the

Langius, who tells Lipsius that the only meaningful improvement he can make in his lot is through an inner reformation. Much of the dialogue takes place in Langius's lovely garden, which the owner cultivates in the manner of Scipio: he is idle that he may gather strength and steadfastness in the world. There is no proof, but it is at least possible that Voltaire derived the celebrated conclusion of his *Candide* from this Stoic dialogue.

separation of ethics from politics. The Christian tinges of his Stoicism were evidence of the tenacious hold of religion over men's minds, but his eighteenth-century readers treated Lipsius as the Church Fathers had treated Cicero: they kept what they found congenial and threw the rest away.

While the Christian Stoics were busy restoring the distinct content of ancient Stoicism, some of their contemporaries appropriated segments of Stoic doctrine and incorporated them into eclectic systems. Perhaps the most popular of these eclectics was Charron, whose *De la sagesse*, first published in 1601, was still widely read in the Enlightenment. When Charron quotes or paraphrases the moderns, as he does incessantly, he turns to his master Montaigne, to Bodin, Du Vair, and Lipsius; when he appeals to antiquity, he appeals to Cicero and Seneca. Charron's teaching was persuasively simple and courageously secular: man's highest good is wisdom, and conversely, it is wisdom that defines man's nature and guarantees man's dignity. Wisdom is not easy, for the senses are deceptive and reason is feeble, but if man eschews theological squabbling or metaphysical brooding, he may direct his will toward his supreme task, self-knowledge, and achieve his supreme purpose, which is to live according to nature. Charron's ideal is thus the Stoic sage humanized by a liberal dash of skeptical modesty. While Charron was not a philosophe before his time— he was a priest and a theologian—the values he celebrates, in open deference to his favorite Romans, are the values of the Enlightenment: the supremacy of philosophy and the autonomy of man; the superiority of eclecticism to dogma, of intelligent ignorance to grandiose rationalism, and of practical moral reflection to theoretical speculation. It seems as though Stoicism was detaching itself from Christianity only to be reabsorbed into the great philosophical reappraisal of the seventeenth century: in Charron, in Lord Herbert of Cherbury's famous deist tract *De veritate*, in Descartes or in Spinoza, whenever men are told to live according to nature, to acquire knowledge by discovering universal truths and the natural laws by which the physical and the moral world are governed—whenever we encounter such ideas, we are witnessing Stoicism lending strategic support to the campaign for the independence of philosophy. By the middle of the seventeenth century, and even more distinctly in the Enlightenment, Stoicism had become a part—an important part, but still only a part—of a comprehensive view of the world which men had come to call libertinism, or freethinking, and which I have called the autonomy of criticism.

VI

The career of Epicureanism has some superficial similarities with that of Stoicism—it too reappeared only to be absorbed into the new mentality—but its actual course was much more dramatic. Even in antiquity the Epicureans had been denounced as godless and socially irresponsible; their picturesque gods, immortal, serene, and detached from human concerns, had been taken as nothing better than a mask for atheism: Cicero's spokesman in *De natura deorum* accused the Epicureans of destroying religion in the name of destroying superstition and agreed with Posidonius that Epicurus was an atheist—and Cicero was more urbane than most. The Church Fathers had turned from Epicureanism with loathing, and as we know, Dante had placed Epicurus in Hell among the atheists. When Lucretius, the poet of Epicureanism, came to be printed late in the fifteenth and early in the sixteenth century, his great metaphysical poem was soon enmeshed in controversy. The scarcity of manuscripts and inevitable copying errors produced scholars' debates over the text, while Lucretius's materialism and polemics against *religio* called forth unmeasured attacks and subtle defenses. Piero di Cosimo could draw on the fifth book of *De rerum natura* to depict the evolution of civilization in a series of paintings, but around the same time, in 1500, Aldo Manuzzi edited that same poem with a pointed disclaimer: whatever was unacceptable to Catholic doctrine, he said in the preface, was unacceptable to publisher and editor alike. In 1563 the French Humanist Denis Lambin elaborated this line of defense: in his fine critical edition of *De rerum natura* (which silenced textual arguments for three centuries) he asserted that Lucretius's philosophical ideas are so patently absurd that they need no refutation and can do no harm. The ideas of a poet, Lambin suggested, matter little; even Homer is full of impieties and obscenities. What does matter is Lucretius's brilliant evocation

Gassendi

of nature, the beauty of his language, and the elevation of his moral sentiments—at least some of the time. This prudent divorce of despicable atheism from admirable poetry, blunted, without silencing, attacks on Lucretius and assured survival to a pagan writer whom pious men looked upon with unmitigated aversion and growing concern. Saved by the industry and adroitness of a late Humanist, Lucretius became a favorite with a small coterie of materialists, with the *libertins* in the late seventeenth century, and finally, with the philosophes.

The continuing popularity of Lucretius was buttressed by the rehabilitation of Lucretius' teacher, Epicurus, undertaken almost singlehanded by Pierre Gassendi, a priest of unimpeachable orthodoxy. Quite like medieval admirers of Ovid, Gassendi—"the best philosopher among literary men and the best literary man among philosophers,"[9]—began by clearing Epicurus's character and proceeded by defending his philosophy. Epicurus, he wrote, had neither lived viciously nor incited others to vice; he had been a model of sobriety, cheerfulness, and honesty. His advocacy of *voluptas* had been, not an advocacy of debauchery, but of mental calm; his materialism, although filled with error, was not on principle incompatible with Christian teachings: the atoms and the void were not eternal but products of Divine Providence.

Gassendi, who knew most leading intellectuals of his time, was neither a great scientist nor a great philosopher, but he powerfully influenced both great scientists and great philosophers: Leibniz thought that Locke was more deeply indebted to Gassendi than to anyone else, and Voltaire wrote in 1738 that Newton had admired Gassendi as a most intelligent man, entirely correct in his ideas on God, space, and time.[1] Of course, to claim that Gassendi's scholarly revival and Lucretius's poetic evocation of Epicureanism were the foundations of Newtonian science is to treat a compli-

---

[9] Gibbon: *Essai sur l'étude de la littérature,* in *Miscellaneous Works,* IV, 22. This *bon mot* reads like an unacknowledged reminiscence of Diderot's remark, published in 1755, that it could be said of Gassendi, "Never was a philosopher a better humanist, nor humanist such a good philosopher." "Epicuréisme," *Encyclopédie,* in *Œuvres,* XIV, 525.

[1] Leibniz: *Nouveaux essais sur l'entendement humain,* I, i (see Richard I. Aaron: *John Locke* [2nd edn., 1955], 31–2); Voltaire: *Éléments de la philosophie de Newton,* in *Œuvres,* XXII, 410.

cated interaction as a simple cause; it would be more accurate to say that the spectacular advances of Natural Philosophy revived serious interest in ancient materialism and atomistic theories. Still it is clear that Gassendi's corpuscular physics impressed Boyle, and through Boyle, Newton. Besides, while the Epicurean model of a world of atoms whirling in the void was crude and arbitrary, it was a useful corrective to the scientific world picture that had dominated Christian civilization for many centuries. A much-quoted piece of doggerel written in the 1660's makes this point neatly: the members of the Royal Society—"these collegiates"—were setting themselves up in opposition to the hidebound teachings of the universities:

> These collegiates do assure us,
> Aristotle's an ass to Epicurus.[2]

Thus the scientific battles of the seventeenth century were fought out with the vocabulary and the conceptions of pagan antiquity.

The philosophes appreciated Gassendi highly, as Bayle had appreciated him before them. La Mettrie, Holbach, and the other materialists quoted him little but used him often; Voltaire singled him out as a spectacular guesser, Diderot called him a philosopher of whom his nation could be proud, and Condillac, who praised few men, praised him warmly. Gassendi's scrupulous scholarship permitted the philosophes to see Epicureanism accurately, to despise the sensational popular allegations against it, and to set its ethical doctrines against Stoic severity.

But while the philosophes had a clear view of Epicureanism, they were amused and impressed by those *libertins* who misunderstood or deliberately misinterpreted it. It was this group, small but colorful, who sounded the note of infidelity in the seventeenth century. The philosophes greeted them with pleased recognition and, through their recognition, gave them an importance they do not deserve in their own right. Among them were wandering eccentrics who preached that life springs from matter alone, and learned physicians certain that reports of miracles were actually reports of hysterical seizures. There were a few aggressive atheists and there was La Mothe le Vayer who extolled the virtues of the

---

[2] Thomas F. Mayo: *Epicurus in England* (1934), 129.

pagans and placed Pyrrho next to Christ. The ideas of these *libertins* circulated by word of mouth or through clandestine manuscripts; many of their defiant jests against saints, scurrilous slanders of Moses or of the Saviour himself, were put into easily remembered rhymes. They were not representative of their time; they were rarely even accurate transmitters of ancient doctrine. But they survive in history because, in making piety ridiculous and freethinking amusing, they stimulated the philosophes.

For this erudite band of unbelievers, as for men and women of the world, Epicureanism was a respectable philosophical cloak to drape their witty impiety or lighthearted sensuality. In his article on "*Épicuréisme*" in the *Encyclopédie*, Diderot suggested that seventeenth-century France was filled with Epicureans of all sorts, and he listed among them both sober philosophers like Gassendi and intelligent courtesans like Ninon de l'Enclos. Among Gassendi's associates there had been some, like Molière and Cyrano de Bergerac, who admired Epicurus and Lucretius for their candor, their courage, and their sensible view of life. But there were others, mainly wealthy, idle aristocrats, who were Epicureans not in the technical but in the popular sense: they preached eroticism in fashionable salons and practiced it in transparent privacy. Baron Blot de l'Église, whose obscene poems fill the youthful Voltaire's private notebooks, was typical of a whole tribe of wits; in one of his *Chansons* he raised the question whether an Epicurean might be saved, and concluded that he was sure of one thing,

> on vit content
> En buvant, mangeant et f——[3]

And the abbé de Chaulieu, in whose house the young Voltaire was to meet the rakes of the Regency, confessed that while he found that theology of Epicurus and Lucretius indigestible, he was their disciple in one respect:

> je n'aime leur doctrine
> Que touchant la volupté.[4]

---

[3] J. S. Spink: *French Free-Thought From Gassendi to Voltaire* (1960), 136–7 *n.*
[4] Ibid., 167 *n.*

These pigs from Epicurus's sty had their talents. Ninon de
l'Enclos was more than a courtesan; she was a brilliant leader of
fashion and a sensualist almost from philosophic principle. Voltaire
was introduced to her when he was a boy and she an old lady—
too early for him and too late for her. Perhaps the most extraordinary member of her circle—one of her first lovers—was Saint
Evremond; a dashing French officer in his youth, he went into
exile in the middle of the seventeenth century, first to the Netherlands and then to London, where he formed an elegant Epicurean
coterie. A literary essayist of remarkable range and refined discriminations, an intelligent student of Gassendi, a perceptive judge
of literature, ancient and modern, he preferred sociability to work,
and the writing of charming letters to the writing of learned
books. Diderot was too much of a Stoic to forgive him his disdain
for Seneca, but the other philosophes, less censorious, enjoyed
Saint Evremond's work, chiefly for its good taste and urbane wit.
Saint Evremond was too lazy—or perhaps too sensible—to be
great, but he lived his philosophy, such as it was, and was therefore better than a gourmand of life. His devotion to pleasure,
although lightly expressed, was not merely playful—it was a
serious pagan position. And so Saint Evremond, like the Stoics and
Skeptics of his time, did his work for the Enlightenment.

3. ANCIENTS AND MODERNS: THE MODERNS

I

WHILE MANY of the philosophes' most respected seventeenth-
century preceptors rooted their radical philosophies in
classical doctrines, there were others, equally respected, who drew
their energies from the opposite procedure, the repudiation of
antiquity. Impelled by the imperatives of the scientific discipline,
excited by new discoveries, new instruments, and the free international commerce of information, the natural philosophers proclaimed themselves new men, pioneers without ancestors, superior
to all the ancients. They rejected the very idea of a classic.

Intellectual buccaneers who directed their eyes toward the future, toward conquest, they turned to the past only to pillage or to denigrate it.

It is easy to see now that their claims for themselves were excessive and their view of themselves a little naïve: while Bayle or Lipsius were modern men for all their antique rhetoric, so, conversely, the natural philosophers drew on the past they affected to despise. Often, indeed, it is impossible to determine whether a seventeenth-century philosopher should be called an ancient or a modern: like, say, Machiavelli before, and Diderot after him, he was both. The training, the concerns, and frequently the solutions of the scientists could not wholly escape the world into which they had been born: classical scientific notions and scholastic modes of argument continued to pervade their work. And yet the essence of their self-appraisal was sound enough: to read these natural philosophers is to enter a new world, a world far different from that of the antiquarian or the scholarly editor. It is a world of intense energy, of great hopes and great pride coupled with respect for rigor and passion for method. Rapidly and with accelerating pace, the study of nature, especially of astronomy and dynamics, grew into an autonomous pursuit, and by the time of Newton, science had triumphantly proved itself a progressive field of inquiry: each theory was a provisional statement inviting modification; each experiment was a threat—a welcome threat—to prevailing formulations. By the force of its logic, science began to cut its ties to philosophy and to assume a posture at first equal, and then hostile, to theology.

In the early stages of this revolution, it was still common practice to acknowledge antique inspiration. Gassendi, as we know, propagated the long-neglected atomic theories of the ancients, and before him, Galileo ruined the scholastic theory of a universe striving to realize religious purposes in the name of the Platonic vision of a universe composed in mathematical harmonies. But while Galileo was a fervent admirer of Plato's writings and pitted Plato against Aristotelian physics, he was a slavish disciple neither of the Plato of the *Timaeus* nor, for that matter, of the Plato of the Florentine Academy. Plato taught Galileo that man understands God only through His work, which is the universe; He had inscribed His revelation in the only book He had written

—the Book of Nature. This was a lesson of supreme importance; it lends support to Whitehead's well-known observation that all philosophy is a series of footnotes to Plato. But if Galileo was a Platonist, he was a modern Platonist: in his universe, celestial and terrestrial phenomena follow the same principles and possess the same worth; his inquiry into its constitution, its laws, yields to nothing, not even to theology, in its claim for dignity. Galileo's very excitement, his very scorn for the academic astronomers who refused to look through his telescope, is modern: it makes centuries of cosmological and philosophical wrangling appear simply irrelevant.

Galileo's Platonism, then, is witness both to the continuities and to the discontinuities of intellectual history. His appeal to antiquity is still vivid, but it is no longer decisive. As the century progressed, and partly in consequence of Galileo's own work, as the natural philosophers increasingly took their models from contemporary theories and concentrated on devising new experiments, this appeal faded. In the combat between the Ancients and the Moderns which agitated poets and philosophers at the end of the seventeenth century, the victory of the moderns was secured far less by literary than by scientific arguments.

The victory was won largely by practicing scientists—by Boyle and Newton—but it was prepared by the great propagandists of science early in the seventeenth century—by Bacon and Descartes—philosophers who, for all the antagonism of their later disciples and all the divergences in their temperament and method, were close allies. Both, as d'Alembert recognized, "introduced the spirit of experimental science."[5] Both were intellectual mavericks, developing their ideas outside and against the universities. Both carved out independent spheres for philosophical activity and stood the medieval rank order of philosophy and theology on its head. Both deplored the condition of knowledge in their own time and charged that philosophy was mired in vain imaginings or sterile verbal controversy. Mankind, as Bacon put it, must "commence a total reconstruction of sciences, arts, and all human knowledge, raised upon proper foundations,"[6] for "the knowledge

---

[5] "Expérimental," *The Encyclopédie,* 73.
[6] *The Great Instauration,* in *Works,* IV, 8.

whereof the world is now possessed, especially that of nature, extendeth not to magnitude and certainty of works. The Physician pronounceth many diseases incurable and faileth oft in the rest. The Alchemists wax old and die in hopes. The Magicians perform nothing that is permanent and profitable. The mechanics take small light from natural philosophy, and do but spin on their own little threads."[7] A few years later, Descartes expressed the same dissatisfaction in similar words. The methods of the Schools, the teachings of the ancients, and the pretensions of theology led only to confusion, and "as for the other sciences, since after all they borrow their principles from philosophy, I decided that nothing solid could have been built on such unstable foundations."[8] From this diagnosis, both drew the same prescription: what was needed was a proper method, the method of science. Bacon, the prophet of induction and collective research, has often been pitted against Descartes, the mathematician and advocate of clear and distinct ideas. But both recognized the complexity of scientific procedure: Descartes appreciated the uses of empirical research and collective experiments, while Bacon respected ratiocination. In one of his striking images, Bacon compared reasoners to spiders "who make cobwebs out of their own substance," and experimenters to ants who "only collect and use." His ideal natural philosopher was the bee, gathering "its material from the flowers of the garden and of the field" and digesting it "by a power of its own."[9] For his part, Descartes the rationalist knew that he could not do without a "store of experience to serve as matter for my reasonings," and he laid down as a rule that "observations" become "the more necessary the further we advance in knowledge."[1]

This convergence was of great strategic significance for the Enlightenment. Since Bacon's utilitarian empiricism did not essentially conflict with Descartes's severe mathematical intellectuality, it followed that in the sciences the most highly developed rationality was also the most useful. In fact, Bacon's and Descartes's

---

[7] *Filium Labyrinthi*, ibid., III, 496.

[8] *Discours de la méthode*, part I, *Œuvres*, ed. Charles Adam and Paul Tannery, 12 vols. (1897–1910), VI, 8–9.

[9] *The New Organon*, in *Works*, IV, 93.

[1] *Discours de la méthode*, parts II and VI, *Œuvres*, VI, 22, 63.

ideas on method converged because they agreed on the true purposes of philosophy: the end of true philosophizing was mastery
over nature. "The true and lawful goal of the sciences," wrote
Bacon, "is none other than this: that human life be endowed with
new discoveries and powers."[2] Once men understood that knowledge and power are the same, they would enter into their rightful
heritage. Bacon's writings, including his unfinished Utopia, the
New Atlantis, are filled with ringing calls to discard the idols of
faulty thinking, to enter into the "kingdom of man, founded on
the sciences,"[3] and to enlarge "the bounds of Human Empire, to
the effecting of all things possible."[4]

This eloquent rhetoric appears, at first glance, to lead away
from practicality rather than toward it, but to Bacon all things
possible did not mean all possible things, and while his hopes
are grandiose, they are weighted down with the ballast of quali-
fications: "sober" is one of his favorite adjectives. To Bacon, all
things possible meant better food, sounder health, greater kindness: science, rightly practiced, would produce "helps to man,
and a line and race of inventions that may in some degree subdue
and overcome the necessities and miseries of humanity."[5] So far,
men have shackled themselves with "too mean an estimate"[6] of
their powers: "By far the greatest obstacle to the progress of
science and to the undertaking of new tasks and provinces therein,
is found in this—that men despair and think things impossible."[7]
At the same time, Bacon warned against visionary Utopianism:
man must remember that he is "the servant and interpreter of
Nature." Mastery will come, but only through obedience—
"nature to be commanded must be obeyed"[8]—and this obedience
is equivalent to a declaration of independence from all authority,
including the classics. "That wisdom," Bacon wrote in a famous
passage, "which we have derived principally from the Greeks is
but like the boyhood of knowledge, and has the characteristic

---

[2] *The New Organon*, in *Works*, IV, 79.
[3] Ibid., 69.
[4] *The New Atlantis*, in *Works*, III, 156.
[5] *The Great Instauration*, in *Works*, IV, 27.
[6] Ibid., 13.
[7] *The New Organon*, ibid., IV, 90.
[8] Ibid., 47.

property of boys: it can talk, but it cannot generate; for it is fruitful of controversies but barren of works."[9] It was this judicious mixture of confidence and caution, trust in human power and call for modesty, that shaped the rhetoric and excited the admiration of the philosophes; its firm, pragmatic concentration on work explains Bacon's hold on the Enlightenment's imagination, which equals that of Cicero.

Descartes's vision was just as breathtaking, just as practical, just as disciplined—and just as modern. Mankind, Descartes predicted in a powerful paragraph of his *Discours de la méthode*, may "render themselves the masters and possessors of nature";[1] they can abolish labor, improve health, lengthen life, and banish the terrors of old age. But they will do all this only if they find their powers and their limits and repudiate the past: Descartes begins the great work of his maturity, *Les passions de l'âme*, with the observation that "in nothing do the sciences we have inherited from the ancients appear more defective than in what they have written on the passions." Their work is so slight and so untrustworthy that a total revolution is necessary: "I feel myself obliged to write as if I were treating of a matter to which no one before me had ever paid due attention."[2] This was strong talk, especially in a book filled with reminiscences from Stoic philosophy, but it was obviously essential to the morale of the innovators of the age. It there were a debtor's prison for intellectuals who have failed to acknowledge their obligations, it would be filled with the natural philosophers of the scientific revolution.

II

"Classicism plus science"—these, I suggested at the beginning of this book, were prominent ingredients in the Enlightenment. It is a definition supported by the philosophes' own slogan, "Nature and the ancients," and it is supported further by their prehistory: both the classical and scientific modes of thought,

---

[9] *The Great Instauration*, ibid., 14.
[1] *Discours de la méthode*, part VI, *Œuvres*, VI, 61-2.
[2] *Les passions de l'âme*, ibid., XI, 327-8.

which converged in the eighteenth century to produce the peculiar amalgam that is the Enlightenment, acquired powerful impetus and achieved limpid clarity in the seventeenth century.

This very power and clarity has tempted many historians to join the seventeenth and eighteenth centuries into a single period. It is evident that they had much in common; yet the seventeenth century had a physiognomy of its own: with refined methods and with anxious care, it continued the search for a compromise formula between worldliness and piety, classicism and Christianity, that had begun many centuries before. While its Christianity was no longer quite the Christianity of the Renaissance, its worldliness was not yet the secularism of the Enlightenment. A philosopher like Hobbes, whom his contemporaries tirelessly denounced as an atheist and Epicurean, was isolated and disreputable; he was as notorious in his time as it was possible for a philosopher to be and still escape hanging. Far more characteristic of this period than Hobbes were thinkers like Pascal, who was first a great scientist and then a great Christian, and the Cambridge Platonists, who studied Plato with almost mystical devotion, vehemently criticized Biblical literalism, and contemptuously decried fanatical enthusiasm, but who were Christians to their very bones.

Even the revolutionary discoveries of seventeenth-century scientists were not in general regarded as subversive: many warm supporters of the "new learning" greeted the writings of Galileo, and later those of Newton, as evidence for the faith rather than as a threat to it. It is true that there were poets and scholars steeped in Renaissance conceptions of the world, in correspondences and hierarchies and microcosms, who were troubled by the new science. John Donne, as everyone knows, lamented that the "new philosophy" called "all in doubt," and that the cosmos, once stable and comprehensible, was now "all in pieces, all coherence gone." But this plaint, which is always quoted, formed part of a searching self-examination, and in any event, it represents the exceptional response of an exceptional man, speaking for a small and dwindling group of select spirits. In Great Britain, Humanists associated science with Puritanism and both with Philistinism, but the point of their assault was a defense of culture, not of religion; and it was blunted by the utter respectability of the Royal Society, which was, after all, patronized by King Charles

II—who was manifestly no Puritan, and graced by Boyle and Newton—who were manifestly not atheists. For the most part, the seventeenth-century imagination exuberantly expanded with each new discovery. Abraham Cowley wrote an ode "To the Royal Society" and hailed Bacon with an image that anticipated d'Alembert's and Voltaire's view of Bacon as a Moses who had led humanity to the promised land. Pious churchmen dabbled in experiments and took commanding parts in the new scientific societies. Early in the Restoration, in 1662, Simon Patrick, who would later become bishop of Ely, defended Latitudinarian religion and the "new and free philosophy" in the same pamphlet. This new philosophy, Patrick wrote, showed that "the theatre of nature is much enlarged since Aristotle's time, and there is no part of the world wherein there are not some notable new phenomena lately discovered."[3] Five years later, Thomas Sprat, who was to become bishop of Rochester, published a *History of the Royal Society* which was a vigorous, partisan defense of the new learning. In the same period, Dryden, a fideist but not an irreligious skeptic, celebrated the Royal Society as a great and diligent searcher for God and His works and extolled the moderns at the expense of the ancients: "Is it not evident in these last hundred years (when the study of philosophy has been the business of all the Virtuosi in Christendom), that almost a new Nature has been revealed to us?—that more errors of the School have been detected, more useful experiments in philosophy have been made, more noble secrets in optics, medicine, anatomy, astronomy, discovered, than in all those credulous and doting ages from Aristotle to us?"[4]

Nothing is easier than to amass evidence for this continuing association of science and religion, both in Britain and on the Continent.[5] The scientists themselves sounded precisely like their

---

[3] Norman Sykes: *From Sheldon to Secker: Aspects of English Church History* (1959), 148.

[4] *An Essay of Dramatic Poesy* (1668), in *Essays*, ed. W. P. Ker, 2 vols. (1900), I, 36–7.

[5] The coexistence of science and religion was accompanied by that of science and classicism. As a Christian, Dryden neatly shows both in a remarkable passage; the compromise I have called "pagan Christianity" continued to flourish in the second half of the seventeenth century.

poetic supporters. Van Helmont, the versatile Flemish scientist who greatly advanced medicine, chemistry, and biology, neatly reversed the argument against the New Philosophy by accusing the Scholastics of advocating an "atheist" physics, and by holding up his own scientific inquiries as religious in nature and purpose. Robert Boyle, the most famous chemist of the age, wrote tracts on the religious value of scientific research and left £350 in his will for lectures that would demonstrate the truth of Christianity. Joseph Glanvill, Fellow of the Royal Society and valorous champion of modern learning, piously believed in witches. Isaac Newton himself—Newton, whom the philosophes unanimously and categorically called the greatest man who ever lived—was a passionately religious man; he expressed that passion in his scientific speculations, his profound preoccupation with theology and Biblical chronology, and his private correspondence. After the classicist Richard Bentley had delivered his Boyle lectures, assailing Hobbes for his atheism and using arguments from Newton in behalf of Christian theism, Newton wrote him with warm approval, weighing his words: "When I wrote my treatise about our system, I had an eye upon such principles as might work with considering men for the belief of a Deity, and nothing can rejoice me more than to find it useful for that purpose."[6] When Leibniz later accused Newton of weakening the cause of natural religion with his cosmology, Newton and his faithful supporters were sincerely outraged: if they were confident of anything, it was that they were laboring in behalf of Christianity. When Voltaire was in England in 1726, a year before Newton's death, he had several conversations with Samuel Clarke, Newton's devoted philosophical friend, and he later recalled that "this philosopher

---

Accused of having been dogmatic in his *Essay of Dramatic Poesy,* Dryden replied in self-defense: ". . . my whole discourse was sceptical, according to that way of reasoning which was used by Socrates, Plato, and all the Academics of old, which Tully and the best of the Ancients followed, and which is imitated by the modest inquisitions of the Royal Society." *Defense of an Essay of Dramatic Poesy* (1668), in *Essays,* I, 124. It took the Enlightenment to sort out the various elements and make the compromise untenable.

[6] Newton to Richard Bentley (December 10, 1962). *Newton's Philosophy of Nature,* ed. H. S. Thayer (1953), 46.

always pronounced the name of God with an air of contemplation and extreme respect. I acknowledged the impression this made on me; he told me that he had insensibly acquired this habit from Newton."[7] Nor, as Voltaire also knew, was Newton merely a pallid theist. He was a Christian; a Socinian, Voltaire wrote, who refused to reduce his system to deism, as other Socinians had done: "He differed from the Anglican Church only on the matter of consubstantiation, and believed all the rest."[8] The Christian convictions of Newton—the greatest man who ever lived—were too strong to escape even the philosophes.

It is Fontenelle, therefore, who best exhibits the tenacity of pagan Christianity in its decline, for while the philosophes did not claim Newton, they almost claimed Fontenelle as one of their own: "The *esprit philosophique*, so widespread today," wrote Grimm shortly after his death, "owes its beginnings to Fontenelle."[9] Fontenelle spans two ages; he was born in 1657 in the minority of Louis XIV and died in 1757, a month before his hundredth birthday, outliving Montesquieu. In the quarrel between the ancients and the moderns, he was an unabashed modern: we might stand on the shoulders of giants, he wrote, but whatever the reasons, the moderns saw further than the greatest of the ancients ever had—not in morals or in literature, which are not progressive disciplines, but in the knowledge of nature. A firm supporter, Fontenelle was also a superlative popularizer of the new science; he wrote with equal competence about its results, its methods, and its philosophy. As Cicero had naturalized Greek philosophy among the Romans, Fontenelle spread Cartesian—and, be it remembered, Baconian—ideas among civilized men and women in elegant and eloquent prose. Through his celebrated *éloges*, which he delivered as Secretary of the Paris Academy of Sciences, he did much to enhance the social position and cultural influence of leading scientists. As a moralist, he gracefully and persuasively modernized classical ideas: like the Stoics, he urged men to live according to nature; and like the Epicureans, he

---

[7] *Éléments de la philosophie de Newton*, in *Œuvres*, XXII, 403.
[8] See *Lettres philosophiques*, II, 74. (This passage appeared in the editions from 1756 to 1775).
[9] Quoted by Leonard M. Marsak: *Bernard de Fontenelle: The Idea of Science in the French Enlightenment* (1959), 6.

defined that nature as filled with passions which need to be gratified for the sake of inner peace. He sounded like Hume in his skepticism toward miracles and in his conviction that man's strongest and most unfortunate inclination was the love of mystery. Decades before Voltaire, he advocated philosophical modesty, criticized metaphysics as a vain enterprise, valued common sense above dogma and moderation above rigor, and recommended activity as a cure for philosophical melancholy. Like the philosophes, he preferred witty expression to clumsy erudition, although, also like them, he was a versatile and intelligent scholar: he taught educated men, as the grateful d'Alembert later put it, "to shake off the yoke of pedantry." And yet this urbane literary man, this admirer of modernity, who anticipated the philosophes in so much of his work, was not a philosophe in his heart: he never made the leap to naturalism, whether it be the deism of Voltaire, the atheism of Holbach, or the skepticism of Hume; he remained, with the century in which he was born, a tolerant, cultivated, firmly committed Christian.

At the same time, Fontenelle stands at the transitional point where one historical period shades off into another: his religiosity was so bland that it offered little resistance to, and even welcomed, subversive ideas. While the seventeenth century was still an age of peace between science and religion, that peace grew more and more unstable as devout natural philosophers piled discovery on discovery. There were some ominous rumblings quite early—when in 1633 Galileo was compelled to retract what he had always believed and would continue to believe, the maladroit handling of his case by the Holy Office crippled scientific research in Italy, intimidated Descartes, and proclaimed to the world that conflict between science and theology was at least possible. The rash of pamphlets proclaiming their conformity only revealed the growing tension. Boyle, offering the public "Some Considerations about the Reconcileableness of Reason and Religion" only suggested that arguments about their irreconcilability were current and persuasive enough to deserve refutation; Boyle, again, writing the "Christian Virtuoso, Shewing that by being addicted to Experimental Philosophy, a man is rather assisted than indisposed to be a good Christian," only conceded that preoccupation with scientific matters might be dangerous to piety. At the same time in Germany, Leibniz published a "Dissertation on the Conformity of Faith with Reason," because (he wrote) he was living in an age "when there is only too much tendency to overthrow natural religion to its very foundations."[1] And this, of course—to overthrow natural religion—was the historic mission of the Enlightenment. But it worked with the materials handed it by the seventeenth century: "Once the foundations of a revolution have been laid down," d'Alembert said, "it is almost always the succeeding generation which completes that revolution."[2]

III

D'Alembert's attitude toward the seventeenth century—a curious mixture of diffidence and pride—will surprise only those who have imagined the philosophes as unbounded in their vanity and self-satisfaction. In fact, confident as they were, the philosophes displayed enormous, perhaps even excessive, esteem for the Age of Genius: it is not a small thing to pronounce what others have only implied, to finish what others have started. D'Alembert was convinced that his own time was, in many respects, inferior to the age that had preceded it; as the century of Lucan and Seneca, estimable but not quite first-rate, had followed the century of Cicero and Vergil, so the eighteenth century had followed the age of Louis XIV. Even the philosophical spirit, he thought, the special mark of the eighteenth century, the best of instruments, was in constant danger of degenerating into a dry, cold rationalism.

This philosophical modesty was in no way weakened by the philosophes' unblinking recognition that the natural philosophers they admired so much had been religious men; contrary to their reputation, the philosophes did not write off all Christians as knaves, fools, or secret atheists. David Hume, who despised the religious impulse and distrusted religious behavior more than most other philosophes, did not hesitate on this point: "I maintain," he

---

[1] *Theodicy,* ed. Austin Farrer (1951), 80.
[2] D'Alembert: "Expérimental," *The Encyclopédie,* 74.

wrote in the "Natural History of Religion," "that Newton, Locke, Clarke, etc., being Arians or Socinians, were very sincere in the creed they professed: and I always oppose this argument to some libertines, who will needs have it, that it was impossible but that these philosophers must have been hypocrites."[3] Even Voltaire, be it remembered, Voltaire the great scoffer, reiterated that Newton had been a good Christian. The philosophes may have been Whigs, but they were not naïve.

Yet it is precisely at this point, at the point of understanding their distance from their preceptors, that their modesty turned into confidence: the philosophes could recognize the religious basis of the seventeenth century, but they could not suppress their surprise, their slightly amused disdain. Gibbon pointed out that revelation had "even in an enlightened age, satisfied or subdued the reason of a Grotius, a Pascal, or a Locke," but it never occurred to him that this was anything but a regrettable lapse, proof of the weakness of man's intellect. When the abbé de la Bletterie, the pious and therefore hostile biographer of the Emperor Julian, called for a "philosophical theologian," Gibbon could think of such a being only as a "strange centaur."[4] Neither Gibbon nor the other philosophes could ever grant that philosophical Christians or Stoic Christians were men with a coherent world view, and it was precisely this failure that freed the Enlightenment from diffidence and made it revolutionary.

Not even Locke, who left his mark on the Enlightenment as much as any man, more perhaps even than Newton—not even Locke escaped the criticism of his disciples. In his own time, and to polemical Christians, Locke had been a radical, although some of his radicalism—such as his casual and tentative remark that there might be such a thing as thinking matter—appeared more uncompromising in the hands of eighteenth-century propagandists than in his own writings. Locke worked out the empiricism of Bacon, codified the universe of the natural scientists, offered rational foundations for religious toleration and political liberalism, modernized ideas of education, and defined the function of phi-

---

[3] *Works*, IV, 351 *n.*
[4] Shelby T. McCloy: *Gibbon's Hostility to Christianity* (1933), 37.

losophy as criticism. He repudiated the self-denying ordinances of Christian ethics, and like Bacon and Descartes, called for liberation from the shackles of antique and medieval rules of thought. As a result, his impact on the Enlightenment was so pervasive that to analyze it fully would be to write another book: when Condillac wrote his treatises on method, on epistemology and psychology, he quoted Locke's *Essay Concerning Human Understanding* on page after page, and simply referred to it on other pages, confident that the book was in everybody's hands.[5]

Still, while churchmen denounced him as a deist or Hobbesian in disguise, Locke was to the Enlightenment what Cowley had said Bacon was to the Royal Society: a Moses, writing the law, showing the way, dominating the scene, exacting gratitude, but stopping short of the promised land. Locke had begun his philosophical career studying Scholasticism, and much of his philosophizing continued to revolve around scholastic problems. It was his decisive repudiation of the Scholastics that allowed the philosophes to malign them in their turn without troubling to study them. Locke remained a mediator, the last in the long line of pagan Christians. His book on religion, characteristically entitled *The Reasonableness of Christianity*, was not yet, not wholly, a naturalistic work. The book did not please the pious, who thought it scandalous that Christianity could be summed up by the Divinity of Christ, and revelation be reduced to an exalted form of reason. But it did not satisfy the philosophes either: the title of Locke's book struck them as a contradiction in terms, and, largely on Lockean grounds, they repudiated any possibility of a reasonable revelation. It was a sign of their distance from Locke that while they quoted his other writings with delight, they generally passed over his *Reasonableness of Christianity* with respectful silence. Voltaire summed it all up rather curtly with an entry into his English notebook: "Mr. Lock's reasonableness of Christian relligion is really a new relligion."[6] And that was that.

---

[5] Condillac's English readers knew this: when his *An Essay On the Origin of Human Knowledge* of 1746 was translated into English ten years later, it was announced in its subtitle as "A Supplement to Mr. *Locke's* Essay on the Human Understanding."

[6] *Notebooks*, 45.

CHAPTER SIX

In Dubious Battle

THE PHILOSOPHES' CLAIM to distance from their Christian world has rarely been fully honored. Instead the philosophes have been sarcastically commended for "merely" secularizing religious ideas and caricatured as medieval clerks in modern dress, ungrateful and forgetful heirs of the Christian tradition who combated the pious wish for salvation in the name of a secular salvation disguised as progress; who denied the immortality of the soul only to substitute the immortality of reputation; who laughed at religious idolatry but had their own saints—Bacon, Newton, and Locke; who excommunicated their heretics—Rousseau; and even made pilgrimages—to Ferney.

Such analogies are seductive and even telling: they draw attention to origins the philosophes did not like to remember. There was some point after all in the derisive observation that the Enlightenment was a derivative, vulgarized restatement of traditional Christian values: the new philosophy a secularized faith, optimism a secularized hope, humanitarianism a secularized charity. For this much of course is true: pious Christians from Luther and Calvin down to the eloquent Arminian publicists and learned Catholic scholars of the early eighteenth century built a bridge between modern religion and modern philosophy, a bridge of reason and good sense on which Christian ideals and Christian scholarship traveled to receptive audiences in the age of the Enlightenment.

But from the vantage point of each camp the same set of facts takes on two very different shapes. What Christians saw, with some justice, as an act of imitation, the philosophes saw, with greater justice, as an act of repudiation or, at best, of exploitation. The image of a bridge is helpful but incomplete; it fails to evoke the essential hostility between eighteenth-century religion and

eighteenth-century secularism: the philosophes rudely treated the
Christian past rather as Voltaire treated the plays of Shakespeare
—as a dunghill strewn with diamonds, crying out to be pillaged
and badly needing to be cleaned out. For even when the philosophes openly sought a secular equivalent for a Christian idea,
they were engaged in revolutionary activity: it makes a difference
whether a man is terrified of hell or concerned for his posthumous
reputation, makes God or a historical hero into a father figure,
admires a universe that allows the invasions of Providence or one
that persists in unalterable, lawful regularity. The origins of ideas
may be a clue to their function, they do not determine it.
Christianity made a substantial contribution to the philosophes'
education, but of the definition of the Enlightenment it forms
no part.

1. THE CHRISTIAN COMPONENT

I

WHILE THE PHILOSOPHES acknowledged that there were
Christians who sounded like decent and sensible men,
they hedged even this grudging concession with reservations:
David Hume slyly suggested that the Roman Emperor Julian had
conceded "the great Charity of the Christians, which they extended, he says, even sometimes to Heathens: But he asserts, like
a Rogue as he is, that they borrow'd that Virtue from the writings
of Homer & other heathen Poets."[1] The clandestine anonymous
pamphlet *Le militaire philosophe* made the obverse of this point a
little less elegantly: "There is not a single impertinence in the
most extravagant paganism which has not been faithfully copied

---

[1] Hume to Sir David Dalrymple, April 3, 1754. *Letters*, I, 188–9.
In his short article on "Origine" in the *Encyclopédie* Diderot
suggests that "the religious practices of our time almost all
have their origins in paganism" (*Œuvres*, XVI, 179). This observation was, of course, a thrust at contemporary Christianity.

in our Religion."[2] While the Christians, in other words, had incorporated and intensified pagan vices, they had incorporated and debased pagan virtues. Hence the philosophes—rogues that they were—could claim that they were doing to the Christians what the Church Fathers had claimed they had done to the Greeks and Romans: they were merely taking back what had originally belonged to them.

This philosophic estimate is uncharitable, positively un-Christian; still, here as so often before, we encounter the curious duality of the Enlightenment's historical verdicts: the philosophes were ungenerous and prejudiced and still right in substance. What the philosophes took over from Christian theologians and Christian philosophers were the least distinctively Christian, the least religious, parts of their teachings—they were usually ideas that had come to the Church Fathers from the Stoics. Moreover the philosophes rarely left these semipagan borrowings untouched—as the ancient Greeks unmistakably made their own what they took from their neighbors, so the philosophes emptied what they borrowed of its religious content.

This freedom permitted the philosophes to be condescendingly tolerant of at least some Christians and to discriminate among individuals and denominations: they agreed that Christian rationalists were more sensible than Scholastics, moderate Calvinists more tolerant than Puritan enthusiasts, Protestants in general less superstitious than Catholics. These distinctions were neither fixed nor absolute: usually, and not unexpectedly, the philosophes were more indulgent with sects other than those into which they had been born. D'Alembert was delighted to find Genevan pastors sociable, intelligent, and humane; Voltaire held up the humanity of English Quakers for imitation; David Hume, who had grown up among Scottish Presbyterians, therefore enjoyed the company of cultivated French Catholics.

And just as they reluctantly recognized that the opposition had its virtues, the philosophes also recognized, quite as reluctantly, that they had a debt to the era of pagan Christianity—and not to its pagans alone. They knew that the dunghill of

---

[2] Ira O. Wade: *The Clandestine Organization and Diffusion of Philosophic Ideas in France from 1700 to 1750* (1938), 50.

superstition displayed diamonds of rationality. They did well to recognize this, for their debt in fact was sizable. The culture of the sixteenth and seventeenth centuries, divided and enriched by acrimonious controversies, had thrown up rationalist versions of Protestantism and philosophical interpretations of Roman Catholicism which the philosophes could read without hostility and absorb without embarrassment, if with some rather drastic amendments. Socinians, Cambridge Platonists, advocates of a universal religion, Christian pacifists—all could be put to use. They could be exploited, of course; nothing was easier than to harness their learned and vitriolic polemics against other believers to the Enlightenment's campaign against all organized religion. But these modern Christians had other uses as well; they found their natural heirs among British deists and German *Aufklärer*. There were scores of theologians and scholars—most of them unknown to the Enlightenment, many of them treated with contempt, and only a few of them honored—who embodied qualities and advocated ideals echoed in the philosophes' philosophy and who had these qualities and ideals, I must emphasize, not because they were Christian Stoics or Christian Skeptics but simply because they were Christians. Much of the decency in seventeenth-century civilization, much of its intelligence and critical acumen, was exercised by Christians for Christian purposes. And it was largely these Christians who created the atmosphere of the late seventeenth and early eighteenth century into which the philosophes were born, when manners were beginning to be polished, toleration became fashionable, and pulpits filled with Latitudinarians, Arminians, and rational Catholics.

In these modern believers reason and religion were firmly yoked together. "The denial of reason in religion," Joseph Glanvill laid down late in the seventeenth century, "hath been the principal engine, that heretics and enthusiasts have used against the Faith."[3] A little later, Swift offered his savage clinical analysis of those very enthusiasts in the name of a reasonable Christianity. The philosophes were grateful for all such opinions, even if they strove to separate the two things, reason and religion, which these

---

[3] Quoted in Roland Stromberg: *Religious Liberalism in Eighteenth-Century England* (1954), 13.

Christians had tried so valiantly to keep united. They were grateful especially to Archbishop Tillotson, the most eloquent of Latitudinarians, whose optimism and reasonableness delighted his
Anglican listeners and later delighted deists and skeptics. Hume
used Tillotson's argument against the Real Presence, Voltaire
called him the best preacher in Europe, while the deist Anthony
Collins acknowledged him as the divine "whom all English freethinkers own as their head."[4] Meanwhile Dutch Arminians and
French Jesuits offered similar doctrine on the Continent, and even
the German Pietists thought it right to stress a certain worldliness
in their academies: Francke's school in Halle trained its pupils not
merely in true piety and the essentials of science but also in eloquence and good manners. For some Christians—all too many,
the rigorists feared—the essence of Christianity was summed up,
blandly, in Young's *Night Thoughts:* What is religion? the poet
asks, and answers, "Religion *what?*—the Proof of Common
Sense."[5] Anthony Collins's well-known witticism against the
learned Dr. Samuel Clarke—that no one had doubted the existence
of God until Dr. Clarke tried to prove it—may well be extended:
no one had thought that Christianity might give way to rationalism until Christians tried to prove that Christianity was reasonable.

II

The French philosophes and British infidels like Hume or
Gibbon rejected revealed religion so vehemently and so completely that the Christian contribution to their ideas was modest
and subterranean; they were usually unaware of it. It reinforced
their Stoicism and contributed—when it contributed anything at
all—to the general benevolent climate of opinion in which
heathens could publish their polemics with relative impunity. But
among the deists and even more the *Aufklärer* the Christian component was more overt and more important, and left its traces
in their autobiographical utterances and theological controversies.

---

[4] See Ernest C. Mossner: *Bishop Butler and the Age of Reason*
(1936), 23.
[5] *Night Thoughts*, IX, 2050.

There are moments in intellectual history when a small change in quantity induces a change in quality, when the addition of a new shade to a seemingly continuous spectrum produces a new color. Such a moment occurred in England shortly before 1700. Locke published his *Reasonableness of Christianity* in 1695; it was followed the next year by Toland's *Christianity Not Mysterious,* and nothing could demonstrate more forcibly than these two books the strange illogic that governs the history of ideas. Toland claimed to be a disciple of Locke, and he was right; Locke repudiated Toland, and he too was right. Liberal Anglicanism and the dawning deist Enlightenment were connected by a thousand threads: both saw the universe as rational and God as beneficent, both despised enthusiasm and mysticism, both were critical of the written tradition and long catalogs of dogma. Yet they were separated by a chasm as impassable as it was narrow. In 1706 a critic charged that Locke was responsible not merely for the deism of Toland, but that of Tindal as well: "*The Reasonableness of Christianity:* and *Christianity not Mysterious,*" he wrote. "Those two Titles are different in Sound, but agree in Sense." And now "another Book is lately publish'd, Intituled, *The Rights of the Christian Church,*" which has been "writ by a Gentleman"—that is, by Matthew Tindal—"mislead by the Principles establish'd in the *Essay of Human Understanding.*"[6] Three years later Locke's perceptive disciple Shaftesbury recognized the poignancy of the situation: "Mr. Locke," he wrote in 1709, "as much as I honour him on account of other writings (viz., on government, policy, trade, coin, education, toleration &c.), and as well as I knew him, and can answer for his sincerity as a most zealous *Christian* and believer, did, however, go in the self-same tract, and is followed by the Tindals, and all the other ingenious free authors of our time."[7] Locke had tried to prove that Christianity was acceptable to reasonable men; Toland, that what was mysterious and miraculous about Christianity must be discarded —and in that single amendment the essence of revealed, dogmatic religion evaporated.

---

[6] William Carroll, quoted in John W. Yolton: *John Locke and the Way of Ideas* (1956), 178.

[7] Shaftesbury to Michael Ainsworth, June 3, 1709. *Life, Unpublished Letters, and Philosophical Regimen,* 403.

III

While we can date the birth of full-fledged deism with spectacular precision, the growth of the Enlightenment in Lutheran and Calvinist soil was a rather subtler affair. Both sects, born in revolution, never wholly lost their capacity for inner renewal. Therefore the gradual elaboration of the naturalist *Aufklärung* strains the definition of a single Enlightenment, a single philosophic family, to the utmost.

Beginning late in the seventeenth century, Protestant theology, especially the Lutheran theology of the North German states, enjoyed a slow but distinct revival of energies. Lutheranism had long lost the crusading fervor and intellectual vigor of its founder and settled down into a rigid, obtuse, authoritarian clerical hierarchy more interested in the minutiae of observance and quibbles on dogma than the great tenets of faith. When it came, the revolt against this torpid autocracy went in two opposed directions: the anti-intellectualism of the Pietists and the intellectualism of religious metaphysicians like Christian Thomasius and Christian Wolff. Pietism, with its democratic confidence in religious experience, its impatience with doctrine and ratiocination, secured wide support, but it gradually hardened into an orthodoxy of its own: at the University of Halle the Pietists drove Wolff from his chair into exile. Its extravagant demands for visible conversion and effusions of religious feeling gave birth to scenes of revivalist enthusiasm and to sentimental poetry of embarrassing banality. By the middle of the eighteenth century, after the death of its leading representatives, it declined, but its echoes reverberated long after, even in rationalists who were its declared opponents. Kant, born into a Pietist household and instructed by some admirable Pietist teachers, testified that at its best Pietism gave its serious adherents "that calm, that cheerfulness, that inner peace that is disturbed by no passion."[8] As a consequence even Kant—who repudiated all but the most abstract religion, who condemned enthusiasm and refused to engage in any religious

---

[8] Cassirer: *Kants Leben und Lehre*, 15.

observance—even Kant himself paid Pietism the unconscious
tribute of incorporating some of its teachings into his work: its
love of peace both in public and domestic life, its inner sweetness,
and its conviction that religion depends not on dogma or ritual
or prayer but on experience.

While the young Kant constructed a peculiar alliance between rationalist religious proofs and Pietist religious sensibility,
most educated Lutherans repelled by orthodoxy bypassed Pietism
altogether. They studied the Socinians and, after the 1720's, the
English deists. But for some decades they found a haven in the
less agitated waters of Wolff's comfortable Christian rationalism.
Christian Wolff is a philosopher who seems to invite caricature—
certainly Voltaire found the urge to lampoon him irresistible. But
in his lifetime his popularity was immense and his influence in-
calculable: he was the Locke of Germany, on a lower level. A
facile popularizer, he vulgarized Leibniz's complicated thought
and made that great compromise between modern science and
Christian faith available to all who found Leibniz's own writings
too demanding. Wolff had a genius for taming rebellious ideas
and grouping them under clear, memorable rubrics; he was a
systematizer of military thoroughness, assigning a firm place to
the most exalted of spiritual problems and the most trivial of
mundane details. He was, we might say, an extreme moderate who
allowed men to enjoy the security of religious tradition as they
ventured into the excitement of modernity. Revelation, he taught,
transcends reason but never contradicts it; there are a few—only
a few—mysteries reserved to the sphere of the supernatural, but,
Wolff assured his readers, men, preserving their awe before
Christian marvels, could discover religious truth by their reason.
When Kant said, in his much-quoted remark, that Hume had
awakened him from his dogmatic slumbers, he meant that it was
Wolff who had put him to sleep.

Intellectual revolutions rarely proceed by enormous leaps;
certainly in the German states the Enlightenment emerged not
through sudden mutations but through gradual, minute variations.
Wolff's philosophy gently modernized Protestant orthodoxy; it
was a perfect compromise for literate Christians anxious to justify
nonrational beliefs with rational proofs. Like most such compro-
mises, it did not last: by mid-century advanced Lutherans had

moved a step, but only a step, beyond Wolff into the rationalist theological position of Neology. The leading Neologians were all prominent pastors and ecclesiastical statesmen: Sack was court preacher in Berlin, Jerusalem court preacher in Brunswick, and Spalding, after a distinguished career in Berlin, confessor to the queen of Prussia. All three had made similar religious pilgrimages: educated in strict Lutheranism, they had first embraced Wolff's system and then moved to a liberal Christianity which retained the idea of revelation but emptied it of all meaning: "All revealed religion," thus Lessing summarized their position, "is nothing but a reconfirmation of the religion of reason. Either it has no mysteries, or, if it does, it is indifferent whether the Christian combines them with one idea or another, or with none at all."[9] The Neologians' theological empiricism, which allowed revelation to reveal only what experience would find reasonable, showed the traces of their extensive reading in Dutch and English radical theology: their writings reverberate with arguments from Locke, from Boerhaave, and from Shaftesbury. Thus without being Machiavellians the Neologians acted on a trusted Machiavellian principle: they kept the word but destroyed the substance. "What is a revelation that reveals nothing?" Lessing asked angrily and rhetorically.[1] Just as Hume turned on the deists, his obvious allies against Christian orthodoxy, so the aging Lessing repudiated the Neologians, although he had earlier shared many of their views. As he admitted in his private letters, he polemicized against shallow theological liberalism in order to isolate orthodoxy, which he intended to attack in its turn. But his opposition to the Neologians was more than tactical: he came to see them, he wrote to his brother, as cowardly rationalists who aimed at making reasonable Christians and only succeeded in making unreasonable philosophers.[2]

Whatever Lessing's irritation with the liberals, to the historian their indecisiveness is most illuminating; it documents the desiccation of Christian mysteries after a century of criticism, a hollowing out of faith concealed behind surviving Christian

---

[9] "Gegensätze des Herausgebers" (Comments on the first of the Wolfenbüttel Fragments), *Schriften*, XII, 431.

[1] Ibid., 432.

[2] To Karl Lessing, February 2, 1774. Ibid., XVIII, 101.

rhetoric and a few remaining Christian tenets. Looking back on
the eighteenth century, the liberal church historian Gottlieb Jakob
Planck said that Socinianism should be considered the ladder on
which the "new theology climbed to its present height, and on
which alone it could climb."[3] His metaphor is apt: while French
philosophes leaped into unbelief, their German brethren were
seduced into it, step by reluctant step.

Lessing's poignant pioneer's life strikingly recapitulates this
evolution: his religious development may be read as the painful
but decisive abandonment of specifically Christian theology, the
dwindling of the Christian component. After Lessing, nourished
on Bayle and the classics, gave up orthodox Lutheranism, he
managed to touch nearly all the positions held by Protestant
theologians in his lifetime. In his first theological writings and
his early plays Lessing appears as a rather conventional adherent
of Wolff's Christian rationalism; his brief collection of aphorisms,
"The Christianity of Reason," compiled in his early twenties,
offers a symbolical interpretation of the Trinity and sounds the
unmistakable note of natural theology: "Act in accord with your
individual perfections," that is the supreme moral law.[4] A decade
later, in the 1750's, as a young litterateur and book reviewer busy
mastering the vast literature of theological controversy, he showed
marked sympathy with the Neologians, with their assiduous
scholarship, their smart hits at ossified orthodoxy, their open-
mindedness. Then in the 1760's he read philosophy and theology
really seriously for the first time; he studied the Fathers of the
Church, and he took the trouble to discover Leibniz and Spinoza
not through Wolff or Bayle but fully and for himself. As a result
he rejected liberal theology as altogether too bland and too easy,
and he sought for a wholly individual religious position.

His final position, incompletely revealed in his *Erziehung des
Menschengeschlechts* and *Nathan der Weise*, remains the subject
of debate, and for good reasons. Almost literally Lessing had to
create his public and build his stage, for in his time there was
practically no German literature, little literary criticism, and no

---

[3] Quoted in Karl Aner: *Die Theologie der Lessingzeit*
(1929), 34.
[4] "Das Christenthum der Vernunft," *Schriften*, XIV, 178.

theological controversy intelligible outside the academy. Lessing made himself into an educator who must achieve clarity that he may disseminate it among his German readers; he wrote about aesthetics or the theatre precisely in the same manner and for the same reason that he wrote about religion: his theological writings are the counterpart of his *Laokoon*. But, not being God, Lessing never fully succeeded in bringing order out of chaos, and besides he was despite all his natural talent not a constructive philosopher or trained theologian: it is significant that he made his most pregnant religious pronouncements in a play. The stage was more than a refuge from prying censors, although it was that too; it was, as he himself said, his natural pulpit, an ideal forum for preaching the religion of humanity.

It is true that Lessing cherished the gravity of the Christian vision, but he denied it both supernatural character and supernatural justification; it was its philosophical seriousness, not its theological content, that interested him. When J. A. Eberhard, a leading Neologian, suggested on humane and scholarly grounds that hell for heathens was not eternal, Lessing objected, paradoxically but consequently: "The hell which Mr. Eberhard does not want to be eternal does not exist at all, but the hell that does exist is eternal."[5] It is true also that Lessing valued the lessons of Christian history, but he denied that it enshrined some absolute, exclusive truth withheld from other religions. Jesus was a sublime human teacher, and the religion of Christ was distinct in essence from the Christian religion. In his famous *Erziehung des Menschengeschlechts*, that gnomic, inspired, not wholly translucent product of his last years, Lessing recognizes the history of Christianity as a stage in the development of mankind, an essential and temporary stage, like adolescence in the cycle of life. History, Lessing argues, is the record of man's moral and intellectual growth; revelation is collective education, part of God's pedagogic program. Like mundane education, divine education, too, proceeds on a deliberate plan; it pursues byways of error to discover truth by indirection, rather as a child indulges its infantile caprices to find its true vocation. The Old Testament is the primer of humanity, containing one great truth, the unity of God, and

---

[5] To Karl Lessing, July 14, 1773. Ibid., XVIII, 86.

hints and anticipations of truths reserved for later years. Then Christ appeared, a better pedagogue, bringing the second dispensation, teaching immortality, original sin, and justification. But this, even at its purest, is not man's goal. When mankind is ready and the time is ripe, a third dispensation will come forth, the third gospel predicted by medieval enthusiasts. "Is mankind never to reach this highest step of enlightenment and purity? Never?" Lessing throws out this passionate question only to offer the equally passionate reply: "It will come, it will surely come. . . . It will surely come, the time of a new eternal gospel!"[6]

Whatever the philosophical imperfections of the *Erziehung* —and it is less a triumph of logic than of sweeping rhetoric, the distillation of a poetic, hard-won optimism—its vision is that of a noble rationalism. For all its concern with religious figures and religious experience, it foresees a time when men will act morally not from hope of reward or fear of retribution, not in obedience to higher commands, but from an inner freedom, as autonomous, self-directed ethical beings. The *Erziehung* confirms the scanty reports of Lessing's friends, who testified that he felt bound to no sect, no creed; it makes explicit what he had implied in his other theological writings: the heart of religion is ethics. Christian mysteries are symbols and allegories, aids to understanding. In 1777, when he had completed most of the *Erziehung*, he published his moving short dialogue *Das Testament Johannis*, which reiterates this lesson over and over again, like a litany: "Little children, love each other." That is the beginning and the end. It is "enough if men hold on to Christian love; what happens to the Christian religion does not matter."[7] It is here that Lessing, for all his stress on *Christian* love, openly joins the deists of the British and French Enlightenments: the love he calls for is universal, it is the love human beings feel for each other not as children of God, not as brothers in Christ, but as fellow men; a love implicit in Stoic cosmopolitanism, achieved only after man has liberated himself from all sects, including Christianity.

This is the gospel of fraternal love, born in religious emotion but emancipated from all sectarian loyalties, that Lessing preaches

---

[6] Ibid., XIII, 433.
[7] Ibid., 13–15.

in his finest work, *Nathan der Weise*, the masterpiece in the didactic theatre of the Enlightenment. *Nathan* is a dramatized lesson in rationalism, cosmopolitanism, and brotherhood. Except for Nathan himself, who is Lessing personified and whose task it is to educate the others, each of the characters begins as a partial, parochial being: as a Jew, a Muslim, a Christian. And each learns, in dialogue and through crisis, what Nathan, the patient sufferer and victim of bestial persecution, has learned long before: that men are different, should remain different, and should prize one another through and for their differences. Each religion, at its best, is the incomplete incarnation of a larger truth, the truth of the *Testament Johannis:* "Little children, love one another." Let every man cherish his father's house, but without pride and without contempt for his neighbors, and may every man recognize in his neighbor what is essential—his humanity. The ideal society is not a choir singing in unison but a symphony playing in harmony; Saladin, the sultan, after he has absorbed Nathan's teachings, says: "I have never asked that all trees have one bark"—

> Ich habe nie verlangt,
> Dass allen Bäumen eine Rinde wachse.[8]

It requires a powerful effort of the historical imagination to recognize the freshness and the boldness of these sentiments; for a century, they have been an inescapable part of liberal rhetoric and have lost their value through debasement. But in Lessing's time they were serious, and they were radical. Their links to the Christian past were obvious: Lessing himself liked to describe his religious thought as the renewal of the Lutheran spirit. And in fact in its firm, earnest constructiveness, its enthusiasm for goodness, and its acceptance of the positive contribution of all major religions to man's evolving ethical consciousness, Lessing's mature religious thought lacks the polemical edge of his earlier writings and the acidulous negations of the French philosophes. It constitutes an acceptance of history, an attempt to solve the great philosophical conundrum posed by Leibniz: how, Leibniz had

---

[8] Act IV, Scene 4, ibid., III, 123.

asked, can we reconcile truths of history with truths of reason? Lessing now asked the same question. His *Erziehung des Menschengeschlechts*, the education *of* humanity, was one part of the answer: it describes the career of all men through the analogy of the education of individuals. His *Nathan der Weise* was the other part: it prescribes the career of a few characteristic individuals as a model for the education of all men; it is, we might say, Lessing's essay on education *for* humanity. For in Lessing's religious philosophy "humanity" has its characteristic double meaning, and it is from this ambiguity that it derives its strength: only when men can love all men as men can they become truly human themselves.

It is in this dual humanism that Lessing's radicalism resides: it is a philosophical religion which uses tradition only to transcend it. Its vocabulary retains the flavor of Christian expressions; it echoes the apocalyptic vision of Joachim of Floris and takes Leibniz's speculations seriously. And yet all these traces are like haunting memories which recede before its daylight reality. Lessing's God is immanent in the world: He realizes Himself as men realize themselves; revelation is a grand metaphor with purely naturalistic significance: it is an intuitive insight into supreme moral truths. And however enthusiastic his sensibilities, however warm his religious passion, the critical method with which Lessing analyzed existing creeds and constructed his own position was the disenchanted secular method of the Enlightenment.

It is therefore not so ironic after all that Lessing, who had such disdain for Voltaire's devious tactics, should resort to Voltairian subterfuges in his last years and gravest writings: this similarity in tactics points to a larger and more significant affinity. To remove Lessing from the gallery of philosophes would be another instance of what I have earlier called definition by larceny. For this much, I think, is clear: while Lessing outgrew what German historians like to call *Populärphilosophie* or *seichte Aufklärung*, he was at the end the true disciple of his beloved classics, the son of Bayle, and—faint though the family resemblance might at first appear—quite as much as d'Alembert, the brother of Voltaire.

2 . THE TREASON OF THE CLERKS

I

IN AUGUST 1756 d'Alembert came to *Les Délices* to see Voltaire. It was a true eighteenth-century visit, long and leisurely, enriched by sociability: it mixed work and urbane talk in about equal doses. At the time Voltaire was on excellent terms with the Genevan patriciate—that tight oligarchy of Calvinist pastors, bankers, and physicians who dominated the little republic—and he invited leading citizens to meet his distinguished guest. They came, ate Voltaire's fine food, and talked to his agreeable, celebrated visitor. D'Alembert turned out to be a good listener, apparently interested in Geneva, and so the patricians told him much. A year later, when d'Alembert published his article on Geneva in the *Encyclopédie*, they regretted their candor.

The article "Genève" was a grave blunder in taste and tactics. It occupied four pages while articles on other, larger countries took up as many paragraphs; its very length stamped it as a weighty ideological pronouncement. Hence it was read widely and with care, and, as its message penetrated, with shock: "Genève" lavishly praised d'Alembert's recent acquaintances and offered them some unsolicited advice. The Genevans resented both. D'Alembert suggested that the Genevans give up their traditional opposition to a theatre within their borders and allow the drama to educate their sensibilities. This gratuitous remark struck Diderot, and later Rousseau, as a touch added, or at least suggested, by Voltaire: it was well known that Voltaire liked nothing better than to put on private theatricals and that the Genevan Consistory had prevented him from mounting such entertainments on Genevan territory. This was bad enough, but d'Alembert's praise was if anything more unwelcome than this piece of advice. "*Genève*" singled out the Genevan pastors for the profundity of their learning and the purity of their morals, for their fraternal concord and advanced religious views. "Some of them no longer believe in the divinity of Jesus Christ," d'Alembert wrote.[9] In fact, some pastors did not condone Calvin's burning of Servetus and interpreted the Bible in purely rationalist fashion. "In a word"—and this was d'Alembert's supreme compliment—"some Genevan pastors have no religion other than a perfect Socinianism."[1]

The article caused considerable comment among Encyclopedists and Christians alike. Devout critics in France redoubled their attacks on the *Encyclopédie*, censors asked some uncomfortable questions, and in January 1758 d'Alembert resigned from his editorial post: "He deserted," Diderot bluntly said a month later. The next year, after vehement public controversy and private maneuvering, the French government withdrew its royal privilege from the *Encyclopédie*. The reverberations in Geneva were just as violent. Genevan pastors were incensed at the epithet "Socinian" and disavowed it with horror: it might be a term of praise among philosophes, but for Christians it was a *Schimpfwort*, hinting darkly at deism or, even worse, atheism. The Genevan government appointed a committee to refute d'Alembert's description of Geneva's religiosity and made Dr. Théodore Tronchin, Voltaire's physician and friend, its chairman. In letters and manifestos Genevans told the world that they neither deserved nor wanted d'Alembert's good opinion.

Voltaire played a characteristic role through it all. He tried to pacify the patricians with whom he was living so comfortably, but he urged d'Alembert not to retract: "Genève," as far as he could tell, had revealed a truth everybody had long known; a truth, moreover, of which Genevans should be proud. Several months before d'Alembert's visit Voltaire had written to a good friend that in Geneva "the reasonable Christianity of Locke is the religion of all the ministers";[2] now, some months after it, and in the midst of the uproar, he held to his position: in January 1758 he pointedly told Théodore Tronchin, "M. d'Alembert has the courage to tell you that you approach this simple and divine cult, and you are cowardly enough to take it in bad part!"[3]

---

[9] "Genève," in *The Encyclopédie*, 94.
[1] Ibid., 95.
[2] Voltaire to Cideville, April 12, 1756. *Correspondence*, XXIX, 156-7.
[3] January 15 (1758). Ibid., XXXIII, 49.

D'Alembert's article on Geneva, with its drastic consequences, lays bare the tensions within the philosophic family and their disagreement on tactics—the united front of the Enlightenment covered over a well-stocked fund of irritability. But by disclosing the touchiness of the authorities and the nervousness of the pious the incident also points to the vulnerability of Christian orthodoxy at mid-century. Secularization was making inroads.

Secularization is a word easy to use and therefore easy to misuse. To speak of the secularization of life in the eighteenth century is not to speak of the collapse of clerical establishments or the decay of religious concerns. The age of the Enlightenment, as the philosophes were among the first to note, was still a religious age; the old association of Christianity and science, symbolized clearly, indeed strikingly, by the clerical members of the Royal Society—no one ever accused Cotton Mather of betraying Christ to the Enlightenment—was shaken in the eighteenth century but not dissolved: for every infidel mathematician there was a pious one, for every d'Alembert there was an Euler. The religious revival that gripped the educated and the intellectuals in the wake of the French Revolution testifies to the vitality of the Christian persuasion in the midst of and after a century of philosophic propaganda. The most vehement critics of enthusiasm retained a genuine and often exalted piety—after all, even the Genevan pastors whom Voltaire had singled out for praise had only "approached" the religion of nature. Not only the poor, not only ignorant country clerics, but also professors and even bishops continued to believe in the Christian God. Thoughtful laymen like Samuel Johnson prayed, fasted, took communion with humility, and daily made earnest endeavors to be good, and become better, servants of Christ. In country after country social and political conflicts were still fought out on religious issues, and there were many thousands of educated Europeans, Protestant and Catholic alike, who believed in the efficacy of prayer, the blessings of the monastic life, or the Thirty-Nine Articles. Theological debates retained much of their old vigor and much of their popularity. To speak of secularization, therefore, is to speak of a subtle shift of attention: religious institutions and religious explanations of events were slowly being displaced from the center of life to its periphery.

The evidence for a growing disenchantment, a growing component of critical rationalism in the minds of educated Christians, is overwhelming. For religious men sensitive or learned enough to participate in the currents of their century this was a time of trouble. The dangers of atheism and materialism, the threat of secularism, had been cried up for centuries; the decay of true religion had been a steady theme for lament since the Church Fathers. But in the age of the Enlightenment realities seemed to bear out the predictions of the most pessimistic Christians. Cardinal de Bernis noted in his *Memoirs* that by 1720 it "was no longer considered well-bred to believe in the gospels,"[4] and only a few years later, in 1736, Bishop Butler sardonically reported, "It is come, I know not how, to be taken for granted by many persons that Christianity is not so much as a subject of enquiry; but that it is now at length discovered to be fictitious. And accordingly they treat it as if in the present age this were an agreed point among all people of discernment; and nothing remained but to set it up as a principal subject of mirth and ridicule, as it were by way of reprisals for its having so long interrupted the pleasures of the world."[5]

These are strong words, but they are more than the professional complaints of clerics keeping their missionary zeal alive by denouncing the irreligiosity of their flock. The decline in religious fervor and even interest was palpable in Britain as in Geneva, in Paris as in Vienna. Polite literature, serious music, and political controversy all grew more secular in subject matter and forms of expression. A polemicist like Swift might indulge in pardonable exaggerations—it is doubtful that he was reporting the situation accurately when he estimated that "hardly one in a hundred among our people of quality or gentry appears to act by any principle of religion" and that "the vulgar, especially in great towns," were equally irreligious[6]—and yet there is good evidence

---

[4] *Mémoires et lettres*, 2 vols. (1878), I, 41. Quoted in René Pomeau: *La religion de Voltaire*, 90..
[5] *The Analogy of Religion, Natural and Revealed, to the Constitution and Course of Nature* (1736), "Advertisement."
[6] "A Project for the Advancement of Religion and for the Reformation of Manners," *Bickerstaff Papers and Pamphlets on the Church*, ed. Herbert Davis (1957), 45.

that his laments had some substance. They were reiterated in 1749 by David Hartley in his great treatise on psychology, *Observations on Man*. There are six things, he wrote, that threaten "ruin and dissolution" to the states of Christendom: the lewdness of the upper classes, the contempt of authority in the "inferior ranks," the corruption of the younger generation through bad education, the prevalence of self-interest among the governors, "the great worldly-mindedness of the clergy, and the gross neglects in the discharge of their proper functions," and (in fact Hartley had listed this first) "the great growth of atheism and infidelity, particularly amongst the governing part of these states."[7] Thousands of Europeans were torn between inherited beliefs and fashionable unbelief and thus open to the seductions of antireligious propaganda. When the distinguished French scientist La Condamine was in London in 1763, he told Boswell that "Helvétius's *De l'esprit* was a dangerous book for women and young people whose principles were unfixed,"[8] but he might easily have extended his list. Other thousands were pagans simply from indifference, without polemical intentions or philosophical interests. "It is a strange thing that the Bible is so little read," young Boswell ingenuously confided to his journal in February 1763. "I dare say there are many people of distinction in London who know Nothing about it."[9] These people were like Samuel Foote, the London actor and wit, of whom Samuel Johnson said to Boswell, "I do not know, Sir, that the fellow is an infidel; but if he be an infidel, he is an infidel as a dog is an infidel; that is to say, he has never thought upon the subject."[1]

Philosophes could pour ridicule upon theological disputes and blaspheme the sacred precisely because Samuel Foote was not an isolated figure. Writing to Sophie Volland from Langres in August 1759, Diderot reported that he had met "several men here firmly decided and quite frank about the Great Prejudice, and what has given me special pleasure is that they hold a place among

---

[7] David Hartley: *Observations on Man, His Frame, His Duty and His Expectations*, 2 vols. (1749; edn. 1791), II, 441.

[8] James Boswell: *London Journal, 1762-1763*, ed. Frederick A. Pottle (1950), 278 (under June 12, 1763).

[9] Ibid., 196 (under February 20, 1763).

[1] Boswell: *Life of Johnson* (under October 19, 1769), II, 95.

the most respected of men."[2] And these *honnêtes hommes* were far from being philosophes; they were *Chrétiens honnêtes hommes*, solid, respectable, often influential citizens. One of them—and there were many like him—was M. de Montamy, a competent chemist and steward to the duc d'Orléans, whom Diderot rather liked: "No one," Diderot told Sophie Volland, "is better informed than he is. No one behaves with better judgment or more moderation than he does. He is attached to his duties, to which he subordinates everything else in his mind. . . . He goes to mass without believing in it too much; respects religion and laughs up his sleeve at the jokes made against it; hopes for resurrection without being too sure about the nature of the soul. In general he is a large heap of contradictory ideas which make his conversation a complete pleasure."[3] It was precisely the contradictions which made M. de Montamy so charming a companion that also made him an uncertain defender of the faith.

Philosophes living in Protestant countries found similar acquaintances. David Hume, hardly a disinterested but still a responsible witness, noted in his private correspondence the progress of the tolerant mood which is the brother to religious indifference. When in 1737 he had completed his scandalous essay on miracles, he would not publish it because it would "give too much offense, even as the world is disposed at present."[4] Ten years later he resolved to bring out his *Enquiry Concerning Human Understanding* over the objections of his friend Henry Home: "In the first place, I think I am too deep engaged to think of a retreat. In the second place, I see not what bad consequences follow, in the present age, from the character of an infidel."[5] In an essay first published in 1742 Hume claimed that "there has been a sudden and sensible change in the opinions of men within these last fifty years, by the progress of learning and of liberty. Most people, in this island, have divested themselves of all superstitious reverence to names and authority: The Clergy have entirely lost their credit: Their pretensions and doctrines have been ridiculed; and even

---

[2] *Correspondance*, II, 202.
[3] September 26, 1762. Ibid., IV, 169–70.
[4] Hume to Henry Home, December 2, 1737. *Letters*, I, 24.
[5] See Hume to James Oswald of Dunnikier, October 2, 1747. Ibid., I, 106.

religion can scarcely support itself in the world." Beginning with the editions of 1748, Hume replaced "entirely lost" with "much lost"—whether from prudence or a more moderate estimate of the situation it is impossible to say.[6] Doubtless even the claim that the British clergy had "much lost their credit" was an exaggeration— wishful thinking, or the report of an infidel giving excessive weight to the opinions of like-minded friends. But it remains a clue to the temper of his times: the philosophes' receptive public was increasing year by year. In 1765, during his French visit, Hume observed that France differed from Britain in its "almost universal Contempt of all Religion, among both Sexes, and among all Ranks of Men,"[7] but his own correspondence suggests that this difference, though noticeable, was hardly decisive. After all, as Hume well knew, the modern wing of his own Scottish clergy was propagating an emancipated theology strikingly similar to the enlightened religion of the Genevan pastorate. "They taught," Elizabeth Mure said of them, "that whoever could please God must resemble him in goodness and benevolence, and those who had it not must affect it by politeness and good manners."[8] This was not a strenuous faith.

II

The malaise in eighteenth-century Christianity which Hume and Diderot recorded with such malicious pleasure was less a response to philosophic propaganda—although that had its part to play—than the reflection of a crisis in religious confidence. The internecine squabbles, so rewarding for the philosophes, were symptoms rather than causes of that crisis. Nor was it primarily the result of malfeasance in clerical office: there was laziness, corruption, family pride in the eighteenth-century churches as there had always been, but in fact clerics in the age of the Enlightenment were probably less vulnerable to criticism on this score

---

[6] "Whether the British Government inclines more to Absolute Monarchy, or to a Republic," *Works*, III, 125, 125n.
[7] Hume to Rev. Hugh Blair and others, April 6, 1765. *Letters*, I, 497.
[8] Bryson: *Man and Society*, 6.

than their predecessors. The real source of trouble, hard to diagnose and almost impossible to eradicate, was a bland piety, a self-satisfied and prosperous reasonableness, the honest conviction that churches must, after all, move with the times. This—the concessions to modernity, to criticism, science, and philosophy, and to good tone—this was the treason of the clerks.

In Great Britain the Anglican church had been deprived of most of its power after the Restoration, even over its own affairs: Convocation, its constituted legislature, rarely met, and when it did meet, its two houses rarely agreed. As early as 1664 the House of Commons had arrogated the all-important privilege of taxing the clergy; Parliament took control over all new canons; and the courts assumed the traditional right of Convocation to censor heterodox writings. A church as impotent as this could not avoid becoming involved in politics: significantly enough, when leading Anglicans refused to countenance the deposition of King James II, all they could do was to leave their posts quietly.

Guided by supple politicians, the Hanoverians used the Anglican church as a reliable political adjunct. The twenty-six bishops, who sat in the House of Lords, could be counted on to vote as they were told: in 1733, in some crucial divisions, Walpole was saved by twenty-four episcopal votes. The government's favorite device was known as "translation"; it was nearly infallible. A promising cleric, usually a complaisant and articulate orator, would be first appointed to one of the least desirable bishoprics— to Bristol (worth £450 a year) or Llandaff (worth £500). Then, if he had behaved himself by voting right and talking well, he could move up to middle-range sees like Lincoln or Exeter, which carried between £1,000 and £1,400 a year. Finally he might aspire to one of the sees endowed with great prestige, munificent funds, and lucrative patronage: the archbishop of Canterbury drew £7,000 and the bishop of Durham £5,000 a year, to say nothing of the clerical sinecures in their gift.

This ladder, the target of much cynical comment by the opposition and much amused remark by unbelievers, was not merely the device of a Walpole anxious to stabilize a new dynasty and secure his Protestant policy. It predates Walpole by half a century, and it survived him: political preferment was the rule throughout the eighteenth century. As late as Good Friday of

1775 Samuel Johnson complained that no one "can now be made a bishop for his learning and piety; his only chance for promotion is his being connected with somebody who has parliamentary interest."[9] In such a system the duty—or at least the advantage— of a clergyman eager for preferment was plain: Benjamin Hoadly's brilliant career was one that others despised and imitated. Hoadly was a fervent Whig who as a young man attained some notoriety as a liberal pamphleteer; he was a disciple of Locke who fitted smoothly into the Hanoverian regime. By 1715, a year after the accession of George I, Hoadly was bishop of Bangor, a Welsh see he never visited—it was too far from the centers of politics. Six years later, in 1721, after a lengthy and not very edifying controversy over the status of the sacraments and the powers of the clergy, he was made bishop of Hereford. As Whiggish as Walpole, more Latitudinarian than Tillotson, he could be stopped by nothing, not even the charge of deism: he was made bishop of Salisbury in 1723, and in 1734, at the height of Walpole's power, he was appointed bishop of Winchester, which brought him £5,000 a year. There he resided for many years in his splendid episcopal palace, proof that a man of liberal sentiments and servile temper might go far in the eighteenth-century Church of England.[1]

Hoadly, of course, was an extreme instance: he was subject to criticism in his own day and in his own ranks. High Churchmen and men of latitude often disagreed. There were pockets of severity in the Established Church as much as among Scottish Presbyterians; most of the bishops were men of impressive rectitude, some of them men of learning and true, if rather abstract, piety. Yet most leaders of the Church occupied themselves with politics and the cure of wealthy souls, while many country curates lived in poverty and abject dependence on local gentry. When Sir Roger de Coverley, *Spectator*'s benign country squire, looked for a parson, he asked for a "clergyman rather of plain sense than

---

[9] Boswell: *Life of Johnson* (under April 14, 1775), II, 352–3.
[1] Hoadly has had such a bad press that the epithet "egregious" is almost invariably applied to him. But the American colonists in search of arguments for disobedience thought rather better of him and admired his writing for its unexceptional liberal doctrine. Thus Hoadly may claim to have advanced the cause of Enlightenment, if not in religion precisely, then at least in politics.

much learning, of a good aspect, a clear voice, a sociable temper, and, if possible, a man that understood a little of backgammon." He was successful: the parson he found was beloved by his parishioners, kept peace in the village, and was "a good scholar, though he does not show it."[2] The Englishman's need for peace after a century of upheaval and the revulsion of educated and respectable men against religious enthusiasm coalesced with the growing authority of naturalism to produce a torpid church and a tepid religion. The Church of England, one good Anglican said, was an admirable institution because "it is fit for the people, subject to the laws, and most suitable to the clergy. For here, without care, without thought, and without trouble, honour and ease are enjoyed at once, which is a state that most men wish for."[3] These were the professional soldiers of Christianity, living without care, without thought, and without trouble—asleep at their posts while philosophes quietly invaded their domains.

The main reason why in Britain the treason of the clerks was such a danger to religion was precisely that the church's pursuit of social acceptability and political advantage pointed in the same direction as the drift of the times, and all were supported by the intellectual temper prevalent among many respected theologians. Not even the Dissenters could maintain the high moral temperature and ascetic earnestness of their Puritan ancestors, while the rational theology of the mid-seventeenth century ripened into a relaxed, mellow Latitudinarianism in the time of Locke. There was much comfort and little anxiety in sermons purporting to prove that the course of a Christian life was easy, that reward for good conduct was sure and glorious, that God had commanded men nothing "either unsuitable to our reason or prejudicial to our interest; nay, nothing that is severe and against the grain of our nature," and that, on the contrary, "the laws of God are reasonable, that is suited to our nature and advantageous to our interest."[4] Early in the eighteenth century Archbishop Sharp of

---

[2] *Spectator,* No. 106.

[3] Sir Godfrey Copley, quoted in James Sutherland: *A Preface to Eighteenth Century Poetry* (1948), 13.

[4] Archbishop John Tillotson, sermon on the text "His commandments are not grievous," quoted in Norman Sykes: *Church and State in England in the XVIIIth Century* (1934), 258–9. This bland theology was restated, often in just these words, throughout the eighteenth century.

York signalized the victory of this reasonable, urbane religion with his self-satisfied claim that "the Church of England is undoubtedly both as to doctrine and worship the purest church that is at this day in the world: the most orthodox in faith, the freest on the one hand from idolatry and superstition, and on the other hand from freakishness and enthusiasm, of any now extant."[5] Candidly translated, Archbishop Sharp's definition of religion amounted to a faith singularly devoid of religious content: it is little wonder that Charles Leslie, the nonjuring High Church Anglican, could define Whigs as atheists and deists—it was a charge partisan in purpose and violent in tone but by no means extravagant.

The rise of Methodism in this environment must be taken as a devastating criticism of the Anglican clergy, as proof that Christians were aware of the treason of the clerks while philosophes were taking advantage of it. Samuel Johnson, the apostle of good sense and a loyal Anglican, conceded that the established clergy "in general did not preach plain enough"; that the common people were "sunk in languor and lethargy," unimpressed by the "polished periods and glittering sentences" which "flew over their heads"; and that Methodists therefore had their useful place in religious life.[6] The Methodists themselves, who long remained within the Anglican church, regarded philosophical, liberal religion as their worst enemy; they were convinced that it was the desiccated theology of *The Whole Duty of Man*, first published in 1658 but a perennial favorite among modern Christians through the eighteenth century, and the Latitudinarianism of Tillotson, that seduced men away from true religion: George Whitefield, Wesley's stout companion in arms, denounced the author of *The Whole Duty of Man* together with Tillotson as men who knew "no more about true Christianity than Mahomet."[7]

In the light of such denunciations it is ironic that pagan classicism should touch even the Methodists—but it did. John Wesley, as we know, studied his ancients as assiduously as his

[5] Quoted in ibid., 427.
[6] Boswell: *Life of Johnson* (under 1770), II, 123.
[7] Norman Sykes: *From Sheldon to Secker*, 187.

Bible; he had to be recalled from his "philosophy" by a stern Moravian. And when his brother Charles learned of John's marriage, a marriage which he rightly feared would be a disaster, he took from his shelf a volume of Marcus Aurelius's *Meditations* to learn patience in affliction. But then not all treason is the fruit of conscious policy.

<h1 style="text-align:center">III</h1>

In the German states the religious situation was rather less parlous than in Britain but more complicated. The Settlement of Westphalia had left the Germanies with three major sects, Roman Catholic, Lutheran, and Calvinist. In some delicately balanced territories peace was enforced by religious parity, which often led to ludicrous incidents: in the Free City of Augsburg the city fathers maintained parity by separating the confessions, and built in front of the city gates two pigsties, one for Catholics, the other for Protestants. But in most lands the traditional prescription *cuius regio, eius religio* prevailed. The Roman Catholic family that controlled the dukedom of Hohenlohe forced its sizable Protestant population to celebrate Easter in accord with the Gregorian calendar rather than the old Julian calendar which it had followed in the past. Whenever the ruling house was inclined to bigotry, the minorities in its territory were subjected to harassment or outright persecution. In the Palatinate, which was declared to be Roman Catholic by the Peace of Ryswick in 1687, public posts were reserved to Catholics, while Protestants, who made up four-fifths of the population, were fined for minor or imaginary infractions and compelled to celebrate Catholic holidays. The consequence was large-scale emigration. Persecution was a religious instrument of assured efficacy: a prince who wanted his territories pure of heresy could simply drive the heretics out.

This intolerance of Christian for Christian, held in check only by occasional threats of military intervention by neighboring powers, was not confined to the unappeasable conflict between Catholic and Protestant. Calvinists vigorously persecuted Lutherans, Lutherans retaliated against Calvinists, and both proceeded in concert against minor sects.[8] The Pietists, usually the victims of persecution, persecuted others whenever they got the opportunity; Lutheran Neologians publicly despised pious enthusiasts and treated them as barbarians sunk in the darkest of superstition. This fratricidal warfare veiled the real enemy confronting eighteenth-century Christians in the German states and compelled them to expend their most concentrated venom against other Christians.

It was not merely intolerance that did damage to the Christian cause: the version of political tolerance that grew up in German states like Prussia did the same damage in a different way. A tolerance based on indifference or on calculation only encouraged indifference or calculation in turn. Prussia, a Lutheran country governed by a House that had turned Calvinist early in the seventeenth century, was led into toleration by a sequence of adroit rulers. As good mercantilists the Great Elector and his successors sought the services of trained craftsmen or learned professors, no matter what their religious persuasion. Thus French Huguenots and German Pietists flocked to Berlin, to enrich the state and confuse the religious situation. In June 1740, when Frederick II came to the throne as Voltaire's declared disciple, he proclaimed toleration in two celebrated pronouncements. When the General Directory inquired whether a Roman Catholic might become a citizen of Frankfurt an der Oder, he wrote in vigorous if rather uncertain German: *Alle Religionen seindt gleich und guht, wan nuhr die leute so sie profesieren Erlige leute seindt und wenn Türken und Heiden kähmen und wollten das Land pöpliren so wollen wir sie Mosqueen und Kirchen bauen*—"All religions are equal and good, if only those people who profess them are honest people; and if Turks and heathens came and wanted to populate the country, we would build them mosques and churches." Again, asked whether the Roman Catholic schools for soldiers should remain open, he replied: *Die Religionen müssen alle tolleriret*

---

[8] History records—of course—numerous instances of Christian forbearance as well. Young Handel was allowed to play the organ in a Calvinist church even though he was a Lutheran; the region in which Lessing grew up had several towns in which Roman Catholics and Lutherans used the same church building for their services. But then, as I have said, the German situation was highly complicated.

werden und mus der Fiscal nuhr das Auge darauf haben, dass keine der anderen Abbruch tuhe, denn hier mus ein jeder nach seiner Fasson selich werden—"Religions must all be tolerated; only the Attorney General should see to it that none of them injures any other, for here everyone must be saved in his own fashion."[9]

Frederick—Epicurean, atheist, and cynical exploiter of the human animal—was an exception in his House. But the outline of his religious policy was much the same as that of his predecessors in his own state and that of his contemporaries elsewhere. The territorial churches—*Landeskirchen*—of the German states were more dependent on the secular power than the Anglican church under Walpole, and to say that is to say a good deal. Germany was a conglomeration of Erastian states: Hobbes, had he lived to see it, would have approved. Neither political nor theological vigor could persist in such an atmosphere. Lutheran and Calvinist pastors and Catholic priests all preached humble submission to the worldly power and practiced it. Church affairs were under strict and often petty control; sermons were written with an eye to the authorities. Pastors were employed as civil servants, teachers, promoters of patriotic morale, and, as Herder complained in a celebrated outburst, as government spies. Clerical appointments depended on political favor or private patronage. Some posts were for sale, others were auctioned off, but few were desirable: the pay of the clergy was almost invariably small, their social status low, and their life dreary. Lessing's father, although a *pastor primarius*, lived in extreme poverty most of his life, despite all his learning and all his vigor, and wrote pathetic poems on hunger and destitution drawn from his own experience. He was typical, not exceptional.

The results were predictable. The elder Lessing reported that in his youth learned theologians had battled bigotry, but now, in the eighteenth century, it was "godless deism" and that "horrible monster atheism" that was the enemy.[1] Doubtless the enemy was less formidable here than in Britain or France, but it remains true

---

[9] Both these observations are from June 1740, the first month of his reign. See Max von Boehn: *Deutschland im achtzehnten Jahrhundert,* "Die Aufklärung" (1922), 155.

[1] Erich Schmidt: *Lessing: Geschichte seines Lebens und seiner Schriften,* 2 vols. (2nd edn., 1899), I, 11.

that the pastorate, beset by want, degraded by dependence, distracted by outside activities and theological squabbles, offered unimpressive resistance to the progress of religious indifference. The great majority of pastors wasted their sermons by parading abstruse learning, interpreting obscure biblical passages, and spinning out etymological quibbles. Anticlericalism was rife among religious men—indeed especially among them—since they were repelled by what they heard in their churches and tormented by their need for a pure Christianity. Looking back upon his early years, Goethe records the decline in church attendance, the failure of Protestantism to hold the imagination even of those eager to believe. The religion he got in church in his youth, he recalls, was "merely a sort of dry morality" whose teaching "could appeal neither to the soul nor the heart."[2] Subversive propaganda—first Bayle, then Voltaire—thus found ready hearers and some cautious imitators. The religious situation was hardly desperate—the *Aufklärer* themselves expended far less venom on "superstition" than did their Western brethren—but it was disheartening and confused. Lichtenberg amusingly epitomized this confusion when he thanked God "a thousand times" for "letting him grow up to be an atheist."[3]

As in England, German theologians made some attempts at religious renewal. Pietism, with its rebellion against words in behalf of the Word, appealed to the poor, to women, and to sensitive spirits—its flowering, rather like the emergence of Methodism in England, was a severe critique of official religion. At the other end of the spectrum was rationalist theology—Neologism, liberal Christianity, and on rare occasions outright Natural Religion. "Christian religion," Goethe recalled, "oscillated between its own historical positive character and a pure deism."[4] The liveliest and boldest minds, he added a little poetically, were like butterflies discarding the very chrysalis in which they had developed, while others, more modest and more faithful to tradition, grew like flowers to beautiful bloom without cutting off their roots. Thus historical criticism and Christian rationalism

---

[2] *Dichtung und Wahrheit*, in *Gedenkausgabe*, X, 50.
[3] Aphorism E 249. *Aphorismen, 1775–1779*, ed. Albert Leitzmann (1906), 70.
[4] *Dichtung und Wahrheit*, in *Gedenkausgabe*, X, 367.

advanced side by side with the deism of Reimarus and the humanist religion of Lessing, the man who made Reimarus famous.

The brave consistency of Reimarus, the critical passion of
Lessing, or the anticlerical bluntness of Nicolai were rare in
eighteenth-century Germany. Writers concealed from themselves and from others the drying up of their religious impulse by
a vague religiosity that sought to embrace worldliness and piety at
the same time. Sentimentality was the deism of the timid: at mid-
century poets like Christian Gellert and Wieland simpered about
God and divine morality in a manner to disgust firm Christians
and radical *Aufklärer* alike: "Wieland's muse," Nicolai noted
shrewdly and sardonically, "is a young lady who also wants
to play the bigot."[5] In the long run this was intolerable, and
responsible intellectuals searched for a new, more vigorous stand
in the universe. When it came, German Humanism bore the marks
of classical thought. Even Voss, in his popular idyl *Luise*, which
idealizes the life of a village pastor, called for an infusion of
"Greek spirit" to rescue the pastor from modern barbarism, with
its venality, vulgarity and emptiness. But whatever the solution,
throughout the eighteenth century religion was on the defensive.
Voltaire's wry remark to d'Alembert, "When pedants battle, the
philosophes triumph,"[6] was meant to apply to France, but it
applies with only slightly less force to the German states.

IV

Whatever its range of application, Voltaire's remark had been
made about France, and France was in fact the country where the
treason of the clerks was most patent. As in Protestant Europe, in
France too it seemed as if the cunning of history was luring the
clergy into suicidal conduct. The parallel must not be pushed too

---

[5] Quoted in Sengle: *Wieland*, 84. The full complexity of the
German situation is exhibited by Herder, the thinker who
preached a sentimental religion of humanity in which his-
toricism, poetry, piety, primitivism, and rationalism were
strangely woven together and touched with genius.
[6] November 13 (1756). *Correspondence*, XXX, 197.

far: while neither the wealth nor the power of the French church was as great as the philosophes claimed in their tendentious pamphlets—the church owned, not a third of the land (as Voltaire and others asserted), but about a tenth, and it lost perhaps as many political battles as it won—it remains true that the French ecclesiastical establishment was far richer and far more influential than its Protestant counterparts. It was in law the first estate, free from taxation and servile obligations, and it successfully resisted practically all attempts to curtail its privileges: in 1750 and 1751 the hierarchy induced Louis XV to withdraw the *vingtième*, a 5 per cent tax on its income, which it refused to pay on political as much as on financial grounds. Yet in France too the clergy marched incorrigibly, inexorably, on its self-destructive way, arousing powerful antagonists, striking at unimportant opponents, and blandly underestimating the real adversary. Prolonged, undignified, and painfully public squabbles about papal decrees or royal authority over the clergy only exhibited to a wide public, ready to believe the worst, the decay of clerical morale. The most spectacular, although in the long run not the most damaging, instance of this suicidal behavior was the expulsion of the Jesuits from France in the 1760's. "One cannot say of the Jesuits," d'Alembert observed drily, "that their death was as brilliant as their life."[7] And one cannot say of the French church as a whole that its conduct was as intelligent in adversity as it had been in prosperity.

Surveying the Jesuits' downfall, d'Alembert sensibly listed several causes, but he took pains to give the main credit to the progress of philosophy and to the anger of the philosophes. This was a superficial explanation. In fact the Jesuits were the victims of a cultural evolution of which the progress of philosophy was only a part. By the eighteenth century unbelievers and believers alike had lost the key to the symbolic language of medieval Christendom. It was not philosophes alone who despised the Gothic cathedrals: pious monks rebuilt their monasteries, and cathedral chapters their churches, in the Italian style, and in their rage for modernity they whitewashed the walls, ripped up medi-

---

[7] *Sur la destruction des Jésuites en France* (1766), *Œuvres*, II, 63.

eval tombs, and demolished medieval statuary. At Angers the canons of the Cathedral of St. Maurice tore down fifteenth-century statues, the old choir screen, and priceless inscriptions. They covered over wall paintings and auctioned off most of the magnificent tapestry. And if we may judge from the sequence of tapestries depicting the Apocalypse—the only survivors of this pious holocaust—the loss was enormous.[8] Even the Benedictines of St. Maur, steeped in medieval manuscripts and historians to the bone, were unable to read the language of cathedral sculpture. The learned Montfaucon faced such sculptures with more piety than, say, his contemporary Montesquieu, but with no more comprehension: to him they were statues of French kings and portrayals of historical events. And it was priests like these who taught the young philosophes in the schools.

This estrangement from the medieval tradition was accompanied by widespread loss of religious fervor throughout the population. In Toulouse the provincial *parlement* found it necessary to issue decrees prohibiting taverns from staying open during Mass—not once but three times, since, it would seem, the original prohibition had not been obeyed. Citizens were fined for failing to decorate their houses on *Fête-Dieu;* rigorists complained that Pyrrhonism was prevalent and that churches were places of assignation and irreverent behavior during Mass. Thus the very pageantry of Roman Catholicism was beginning to pall—and among provincials!

The higher clergy was largely indifferent to this secularization, the lower clergy largely powerless to stop it. The fashionable impiety of elegant society was only underlined, if rather ironically, by the ostentatious piety of such immoral men as King Louis XV. Monastic orders declined in numbers and relaxed in discipline.

---

[8] The rage for modernizing churches, and thus destroying not merely historical monuments but also traditional feeling, was international. It was widespread in England, and in the German states as well, where the philosophe Lichtenberg protested against it: "Doesn't the 'improvement' of our hymnal look a great deal like our whitewashing of old Gothic churches, which we disfigure in the process? We should keep them from collapsing, and see to it that the floors are clean. A whitewashed Westminster Abbey would be hideous" (Aphorism J 200. *Aphorismen, 1789–1793,* 40).

The brilliant rhetoric of printed sermons, the remarkable historical scholarship, and the high level of theological disputation that had ennobled the French church in the seventeenth century gave way in the eighteenth century to place-hunting and sheer survival. The wealth of the bishops and the splendor of their palaces stood in stark contrast to the poverty of the rural clergy—an old story, this, but one all the more conspicuous in an age of improved travel and all the more anachronistic in an age of almost untrammeled secular criticism. What religious fervor there was found expression in revivalist riots, such as the notorious outbursts of hysteria in the Paris cemetery of St. Médard at the grave of a Jansenist reputed for piety and miraculous good works.

The only rational policy the church found it possible to adopt in such an unfavorable climate was to turn modern, and it turned modern with a vengeance. Sermons and educational tracts continued to treat the traditional subjects, but they treated them in a new way, almost as if a philosophe were looking over their author's shoulder. The old simple stark faith was being replaced by a gentler version, appropriate to a public informed about scientific discoveries and striving for bourgeois comforts. The very props of religious emotion were weakened in the widespread appeal to reason and reasonableness. The confidence of the upper bourgeoisie, still believers but proud and often skeptical believers, was reflected in their rejection of "enthusiasm," or "fanaticism," which was religious behavior reserved for the masses. The fear of death, which priests had kept alive in an earlier age with lurid reminders of hell, was no longer the central theme of sermons; priests now gave edifying homilies on the good Christian life. The church prettified the image of God in the same way: it drove out the absolute monarch who did with man as He pleased, in favor of a constitutional ruler bound to save those Christians who had fulfilled their contractual obligations. Finally, priests less and less emphasized the rigorous Christian teaching of sin: the old grim story of Adam's Fall had become less persuasive, and even those who attended Mass without fail were no longer inclined to feel guilty simply because they were human.

The most effective French modernists were the Jesuits. Vigorous and accomplished classicists, excellent rhetoricians, they supported the revival of ancient classics and propagated the new erudition in their schools, their journals, and their polemics. The *Journal de Trévoux*, the book-review journal they published under august patronage from 1701 to 1762, printed full and judicious essays on theology and, increasingly as the century progressed, on natural science, arts, and letters. It was conspicuous for its openness to new ideas and its objectivity. The innumerable slanders, chiefly circulated by ungrateful philosophes who had studied in Jesuit schools—the reports that the Jesuits preached regicide, lusted for power, neglected piety, and almost all practiced pederasty—were not merely malicious but largely untrue. The Jesuits of eighteenth-century France were suave and elegant; they bent with the winds of doctrine. But they were not irreverent or secular men; nor, as their conduct at mid-century proves, were they especially clever. Their history in the age of the Enlightenment shows that the treason of the clerks was forced upon them: intent on prolonging the time-honored compromise between classical learning and Christian piety, the Jesuits sought to maintain what was no longer tenable.

The fratricidal battles among Christians which made France such a hospitable theatre of operations for philosophes were staged through the rest of Catholic Europe as well: no one could question the piety of the Empress Maria Theresa or Charles III of Spain, but they too found it necessary to restrain the clergy and confirm, no matter how obliquely, the charges made by unappeasable unbelievers. In Lombardy and Tuscany the attack on clerical wealth and ignorance was led, or at least vigorously supported, by modern Catholics and by priests of advanced opinions. By the 1760's, when the Enlightenment was on the offensive everywhere and laments about atheism had multiplied all over Europe, frightened orthodoxy responded in panic and with ill-conceived counterattacks. Some of the celebrated cases that aroused Voltaire and through Voltaire the civilized world were signs of clerical weakness, not of clerical strength: the shocking execution of Calas in 1762 and the even more shocking execution of La Barre in 1766 were far from typical in a century where the pious were becoming liberal in their piety and relatively tolerant of the opposition —they were symptoms of hysteria. Thus even in its response to impiety the church furthered the cause of the Enlightenment.

In consequence the confrontations of Christians and philosophes often have the unreal aspect of a contest decided in advance. Let one such confrontation stand for many—James Boswell's encounter with the dying Hume. David Hume had had much time to prepare himself for death, for his decline was gradual and he retained his mental vigor to the end. His health had begun to fail in 1772, and by 1775, after he had shrunk from genial corpulence to frail emaciation, it was clear that he did not have much longer to live. His last months were cheered by his loving friends and by reading in Lucretius and Lucian, the two most implacable enemies of religion—one the fiercest, the other the wittiest—that antiquity had produced. William Cullen, one of a battery of distinguished physicians attending Hume in his last illness, reported that Hume jovially found only one regret at leaving this world: he "thought he might say he had been very busily employed in making his countrymen wiser and particularly in delivering them from the Christian superstition, but that he had not yet completed that great work."[9] Adam Smith, who saw him often, recalled that Hume had been reading Lucian's *Dialogues of the Dead;* in one of these dialogues a man who had recently died tries to persuade Charon that he is not yet ready to enter his boat to Hades. Hume amused himself by inventing a number of excuses to Charon that Lucian had failed to think of, but none of these, he cheerfully conceded, was convincing, and he must therefore die content. When Colonel Edmonstoune, an old friend, went home after bidding Hume a tearful farewell, he sent Hume the Epicurean verses which Chaulieu had addressed to a friend shortly before his own death. It was the most fitting gift in Edmonstoune's possession.

Hume's good nature and graceful acceptance of his imminent dissolution withstood even the tasteless intrusion of James Boswell. On July 7, 1776, about seven weeks before Hume's death, "being too late for Church," Boswell went to see the dying man. "He was lean," Boswell reports, "ghastly, and quite of an earthy appearance." This did not stop the omnivorous interviewer: "I know not how I contrived to get the subject of Immortality introduced. He said he never had entertained any belief in Religion since he

---

[9] Dr. Cullen to Dr. Hunter, September 17, 1776; quoted in Mossner: *Life of Hume,* 601.

began to read Locke and Clarke," and added "flatly" that "the Morality of every Religion was bad, and, I really thought, was not jocular when he said 'that when he heard a man was religious, he concluded he was a rascal, though he had known some instances of very good men being religious.'" Undeterred by Hume's appearance, Boswell then asked whether "it was not possible that there might be a future state. He answered It was possible that a piece of coal put upon the fire would not burn; and he added that it was a most unreasonable fancy that he should exist for ever." None of this was enough. "I asked him if the thought of Annihilation never gave him any uneasiness. He said not the least; no more than the thought that he had not been, as Lucretius observes." Boswell was dismayed, and "felt a degree of horrour, mixed with a sort of wild, strange, hurrying recollection of My excellent Mother's pious instructions, of Dr. Johnson's noble lessons, and of my religious sentiments and affections during the course of my life." The Christian was on the defensive, and grave doubts assailed him. Perhaps to dispel them—he does not tell us—Boswell then sought refuge in an argument that Hume would certainly have been too charitable to use: " 'But,' said I, 'would it not be agreable to have hopes of seeing our friends again?' and I mentioned three Men lately deceased, for whom I knew he had a high value." Hume "owned it would be agreable, but added that none of them entertained such a notion. I believe he said, such a foolish, or such an absurd, notion; for he was indecently and impolitely positive in incredulity." The interview then shifted to other topics; at the end Hume "said he had no pain, but was wasting away. I left him with impressions that disturbed me for some time."[1] The Christian outlived the pagan, but the pagan, sustained by the firmness of his incredulity, had won the debate. Not long after, as Gibbon notes with majestic approval, Hume died at Edinburgh, "the death of a philosopher."[2]

---

[1] See *Dialogues Concerning Natural Religion*, ed. N. K. Smith, 76-9.
[2] *Autobiography*, 177.

CHAPTER SEVEN

Beyond the Holy Circle

GIBBON, who had an apt phrase for most situations, also had a phrase for the encounter between Enlightenment and Christianity, their intimate association and inescapable enmity. He records in his *Autobiography* that as he was studying the nature of the gods, his inquiries led him to Beausobre's *Histoire critique du Manichéisme*, which "discusses many deep questions of pagan and Christian theology," and "from this rich treasury of facts and opinions I deduced my own consequences, beyond the holy circle of the author."[1] The critical reader stepping beyond the holy circle—no image can evoke more strikingly than this the philosophes' carefree, shameless utilization of pious learning for impious purposes, their distance from even the most rationalistic Christianity, their disenchanted modern philosophy.

I have said it before: the philosophes paid a price for fraternizing with the Christian enemy. But the Christians paid a far heavier price—it was the defender, not the aggressor, who was paralyzed by his concessions. Swift complained more than once that the clergy he knew best—the clergy of the Anglican church—found it hard to tell its enemies from its friends. The philosophes were less confused: Voltaire found it easy as well as amusing to praise the pacifism of the Quakers and the rationality of the Unitarians, and to claim these Christian virtues as anticipations of true philosophy. Swift himself discovered, much to his rage, that he was being placed in the camp of unbelief: many of his readers who enjoyed his *Tale of a Tub* still regretted it as a blow to religious certitude—as no doubt it was to some. Clerical reformers, Puritan critics of Anglicanism or Roman Catholic critics of stupid credulity, all wanted to restore the primitive church, or worthy re-

---

[1] *Autobiography*, 135–6.

ligiosity; they wanted to purify, not to destroy Christianity. But as they retreated before the Enlightenment, their careful work fell into the hands of the adversary. The battlefields of history are strewn with unintended consequences; the appropriation of Christian labors for secular purposes is not the least of these.

I. THE ABUSE OF LEARNING

I

OF ALL THE CHRISTIAN SPOILS the ones most consistently useful to the philosophes were the methods and the results of Christian erudition. In the latter half of the seventeenth century and early in the eighteenth an army of scholarly theologians employed the delicate and potent critical instruments developed in the Renaissance to advance the historical study and demonstrate the historical truth of the Christian religion. Learned Benedictines, Jesuits, and Anglicans refined the canons of criticism, radically improved paleography, developed numismatics, gathered vast collections of documents, and wrote authoritative monographs. These historians confronted their task with absolute honesty and devout industry—an industry never surpassed and rarely matched by the philosophes, who, for their part, worked hard enough—and piously pursued historical truth through the jungle of illegible documents, tangled chronology, and expert falsifications. Only a few of them bothered with secular history: Muratori—"the learned Muratori," Gibbon called him appreciatively—who founded the study of medieval Italian history with his exhaustive compilation of documents, did not let his priestly vocation interfere with his emancipated verdicts on the Italian past; and in Germany Johann Jakob Brucker, Lutheran pastor though he was, placed secular thinkers in the center of the stage in his history of philosophy. But their fellows elsewhere put their erudition quite directly into the service of their sect. Generations of indefatigable and contentious English scholars devoted their lives to lightening up the obscurities of medieval ecclesiastical history in order to answer, as one of them put it, "that never ending question, 'Where was your church before Luther?'"[2] Across the Channel, in Flanders and in Paris, monkish antiquarians expended their collective energies and lavish financial resources to establish a reliable calendar of saints, a sensible account of clerical life, and a credible martyrology—all to purify Catholic history from the dross of legend gathered through superstition or mendacity. It must be said of these scholars, of giants like Mabillon or Montfaucon, that they loved the past for its own sake just as they loved the truth for its own sake, but with them love of truth and love of history merged insensibly into love of God.

The philosophes were rather ambivalent about this erudition. As urbane men of letters they professed to have little respect for what they liked to call plodding pedantry. The scholars sought salvation in humble detail; the philosophes feared it as a morass. During his visit to Paris, Gibbon noted that "the learning and language of Greece and Rome were neglected by a philosophic age. The guardian of those studies, the Academy of Inscriptions, was degraded to the lowest rank among the three royal societies of Paris; the new appellation of *Erudits* was contemptuously applied to the successors of Lipsius and Casaubon; and I was provoked to hear (see M. d'Alembert, *Discours préliminaire à l'Encyclopédie*) that the exercise of the memory, their sole merit, had been superseded by the nobler faculties of the imagination and the judgment."[3] This is a shrewd hit: Enlightenment historians, anxious to avoid petty detail for the sake of larger vistas, often sacrificed scrupulous citation to literary form, precision to elegance; Enlightenment classicists, hostile to what Diderot had denounced as "anticomania"—and, one suspects, just a little envious of wealthy amateur antiquarians like the comte de Caylus—cut themselves off from interesting antique pottery and some stimulating learned discussion. But Gibbon's criticism, which has been much quoted, is less than wholly fair. Even d'Alembert, who had aroused Gibbon's indignation, regretted that the old contempt for philosophy had been transferred in his time to antiquarian erudition. "It

[2] See D. C. Douglas: *English Scholars: 1660–1730* (2nd edn., 1951), 19.
[3] *Autobiography*, 123.

seems," he wrote, "that people look on antiquity as on an oracle that has said everything, and which it is useless to interrogate." Such disdain is absurd: to believe that men "can no longer draw any advantage from studying and reading the ancients is to be either ignorant or presumptuous."[4] The philosophes did not wholly contemn the scholarship of their pious predecessors and equally pious contemporaries; they used it—although for purposes that would have appalled the scholars.

As might be expected, Voltaire furnishes some splendid instances of philosophical piracy: Voltaire abused clerical learning with more zest and less scruple than most of his brethren—he had, in any event, more time and practice than they. His thefts were flagrant and systematic. In the mid-1730's and throughout most of the 1740's he lived at the chateau of Cirey in Champagne with the marquise du Châtelet, who was an avid collector of lovers, a talented mathematician, and a respectable linguist. There, at Cirey, in close collaboration with his formidable bluestocking, Voltaire perfected his understanding of Newton, conducted experiments in physics, and studied the Bible: it was at Cirey that he perfected the proofs and read the documents that he would use much later, in the 1760's and 1770's, against revealed religion. He assisted Mme du Châtelet as she put together her "Examen de la Genèse," a sizable manuscript which despite its modest title analyzes the Bible from beginning to end, from Genesis to Revelation. He read and reread Bayle's *Dictionnaire historique et critique*, the English deists, and the orthodox biblical commentaries of Dom Calmet. And it was Calmet above all, Calmet the unimpeachable Benedic-

---

[4] This in the very *Discours préliminaire* to which Gibbon later objected (see d'Alembert, *Mélanges*, I, 154–5). Gibbon himself, the public defender and open disciple of seventeenth-century antiquarians, also saw their limitations: they were not philosophers. "Often their defender," he wrote, "never their zealot, I cheerfully admit that their manners were coarse, their labors sometimes trifling; that their intellect, drowned in pedantic erudition, annotated what should have been felt; they compiled instead of thinking. They were enlightened enough to sense the usefulness of their research, but not rational enough, or civilized enough, to know that they might have been guided by the torch of philosophy"—they might have been, but they were not. *Essai sur l'étude de la littérature*, in *Miscellaneous Works*, IV, 18–19.

tine, who guided Voltaire and his mistress through the intricacies of the Old and New Testaments and supplied them with the most delightful, and most damaging, religious lore. Neither the "Examen de la Genèse" nor its belated offspring, the *Dictionnaire philosophique*, could have been written without Calmet.

Antoine Augustin Calmet was a believer made to be victimized in an age of Enlightenment: he was innocent, generous, and utterly single-minded. His clerical vocation and his patience for detail showed themselves early, and his long uneventful career—he was born in Lorraine in 1672 and died in Lorraine in 1757—was but a commentary on his uncomplicated qualities. He became a Benedictine at sixteen and devoted himself to writing. The inexhaustible resources of his order and the century's taste for long books made it easy for Calmet, even inevitable, to convert his years of study into a small library of learned volumes. Dom Calmet loved Lorraine and wrote its history; he published a treatise on vampires in which he attempted to distinguish reliable reports from superstitious tales, the real from the manufactured apparition. But above all he poured his energies, his patience, and his linguistic equipment into Scriptural exegis: his *Dictionnaire historique, critique, chronologique, géographique et littéral de la Bible*, a compact work of reference, ran to four volumes; the *Commentaire littéral sur tous les livres d'ancien et du nouveau Testament*, his major effort, ran to twenty-eight. Their very detail made these commentaries indispensable, and they were at Cirey as they were to be later at Ferney, well-thumbed and in daily use. In fact, when in September 1752 Voltaire began to write his *Dictionnaire philosophique* at the court of Frederick the Great, he could not do without them, and he asked a friend to send him Calmet's "Bible Dictionary, with all the volumes of his commentaries." This "vast collection of sacred nonsense," he added ungraciously, "is full of remarkable things."[5]

The remarkable things Voltaire found in Calmet were of two sorts—they included what Calmet was and what he knew. It was basic philosophic strategy to turn the *érudits'* apologetic writings against them to convict them of credulousness or callousness, but

---

[5] Voltaire to Countess Bentinck, September 29 (1752). *Correspondence*, XXI, 78.

to accept their scholarship when that scholarship implied—or could be twisted to imply—a criticism of Christianity. Let Calmet defend the conduct and career of King David, and he is an "imbecile"; but let him concede that the Psalms are obscure, and he is "more sensible than other monkish compilers." Let Calmet suggest that the Hebrews had a philosophical system, and he shows himself to be a man who "compiled much and never thought"; but let him discover that the original Hebrew Text of Genesis I: 1 reads *dii creaverunt* instead of *Deus creavit,* and he becomes a respectable authority proving that the biblical Jews were polytheists. Let Calmet pretend to know that the malady of Job was syphilis, and he can be sarcastically written off as a "profound philosopher"; but let him concede that the Wars of the Lord are cruel and sanguinary affairs, and he can be quoted with confidence and approval. At times Calmet yields two rewards in a single passage: when he reports that there are thirty-nine apocryphal gospels, all equally inspired, Voltaire and his mistress deride him for treating them as sacred and, at the same time, accepting his figure, ridicule the early Christians for their credulous simplicity.[6]

Calmet was not an imaginative critic; his observations are often naïve and usually transparently apologetic. But he was not the fool or bigot he appears to be from Voltaire's scattered references to him in his *Dictionnaire philosophique*—a book, be it noted, first published seven years after Calmet's death. He was merely unworldly; he even extended hospitality to Voltaire. Early in 1753, after Voltaire had quarreled with his royal protector, he left the Prussian court in disgrace. He had no place to go or to stay: his mistress was dead; he could not remain in Prussia; and he was not granted permission to return to Paris. Depressed, irritable, aimless, he wandered from elegant refuge to elegant refuge, and then late in the spring of 1754 he found a welcome at the abbey of Senones in Alsace, where Calmet was abbot. "Today, 23 June 1754," Voltaire recorded in his notebook, at ease in the Senones library, "dom Calmet, abbot of Senones, asked me what was new; I told him that madame de Pompadour's daughter had died. 'Who is madame de Pompadour?' he replied. *Felix errore*

---

[6] Ira O. Wade: *Voltaire and madame du Châtelet* (1941), 109–15.

suo."[7] Calmet was indeed happy in his error, but his error was not the error Voltaire had in mind. It was rather the mistaken assumption—an assumption that deserves sympathy and some admiration—that hospitality and Christian charity were appropriate modes of conduct toward a pagan bent on propagating his cause at all costs.

II

It must not be supposed that most Christians fell into Calmet's error: in France especially, alert and influential clerics deplored the progress of philosophy and attempted to check it. The career of Diderot's *Encyclopédie*, harassed, suspended, and in 1759 suppressed, reveals how venomous even urbane ecclesiastics could become once they grew alarmed at the spread of freethinking: the *Journal de Trévoux* hounded the *Encyclopédie* volume by volume, first with nagging pettiness, later with undisguised ferocity. But this, as I have said, was a time when Christians were too busy committing fratricide to pay serious attention to the real enemy: they drove the *Encyclopédie* underground without stopping its production and helplessly witnessed its clandestine sale while they concentrated on banishing the Jesuits.

Among the Jesuits' charges against the *Encyclopédie* was that of plagiarism, and while this accusation was unfounded in many of its details—most of the Encyclopedists scrupulously listed their sources of information—it was in substance just, in fact more justified than even the canny Jesuits suspected: the frank acknowledgment of dependence concealed far more effectively than outright plagiarism the abuse of pious erudition for the usual philosophic purposes. Diderot himself, editor-in-chief and indefatigable scribbler of articles on all subjects, was the most expert and most disingenuously candid of the Encyclopedists, and his most conspicuous victim was Johann Jakob Brucker.[8]

---

[7] *Notebooks*, 351.
[8] In his article "Philosophie," Diderot modestly suggests that the many articles on the history of philosophy can offer nothing more than summaries, and he sends those readers who want to study the subject thoroughly to "the excellent work pub-

Brucker was a scholar typical of his age, when Europe was being deluged with vast compilations marked by firm views and heated partisanship, by patient erudition and trustworthy information. Born in 1696—two years after Voltaire, seventeen years before Diderot—Brucker studied at Jena, where he came under the influence of the Pietist theologian Johann Franz Buddeus, one of Wolff's persecutors. Buddeus, like his disciple Brucker after him, was a felicitous blend of critical spirit, religious fideism, and philosophical eclecticism; he taught, as did Brucker, that since man's reason has severe limitations, no single philosophical or theological system can lay claim to the whole truth—and yet since it is God who has endowed man with his reason, it is man's duty to use that reason to the limit.

This theological position, rationalist yet severely pious, had many affinities with the new scientific temper; it was symptomatic of the evolution of Lutheran thought, which was groping toward a critical attitude to Christian evidence. Significantly Brucker warmly admired Bayle's work and strenuously defended Bayle's character: different as they were in their religious world views, both enjoyed ridiculing priestcraft and miraclemongers with ponderous wit and pointed invective; both, skeptical as they were of reason, were less inclined to criticize rationalists than enthusiasts. I have noted how much modern Protestants and philosophes had in common, and Brucker's writings on the history of philosophy bear witness to this familiar fact: when Brucker derides the "dark" Middle Ages, denounces the "perversions" of scholastic thought, proclaims the "revival of learning" as a rebirth of civilization, extols Newton, and praises philosophers who have discarded sectarianism and bigotry, he speaks like a member of the little flock. Yet he never belonged to it: philosophy was never more to him than an all too fallible auxiliary to faith. If Brucker, a deeply religious, erudite, lucid, polemical historian, supported the philosophes' campaign to change the general way of thinking, he did so without knowing it and against his best intentions.

As Diderot noted, Brucker brought out his history of philos-

_____

lished by M. Brucker, first in German, and then in Latin, the *Historia critica philosophiae, a mundi incunabulis ad nostram usque aetatem deducta.*" There they will find "plenty to satisfy them." *Œuvres,* XVI, 280.

ophy, a work both large and great, first in German and then (presumably since few civilized Europeans had mastered that language in his time) in Latin. The *Historia* was a distinguished performance: orderly in presentation, deft in analysis, critical in mood, and richly informed with historical sense. Its last volume appeared in 1744—it was a year or so later that Diderot signed an agreement with a group of French publishers to edit an ambitious encyclopedia.

Diderot found the *Encyclopédie* tiring but stimulating— what he had taken on as a chore became a vocation. He was compelled to negotiate with greedy publishers, appease temperamental contributors, answer ecclesiastical critics, deal with capricious government officials, and read endless pages of proofs. Nor was this all: as a writer of catholic interests and inexhaustible energies, Diderot fed those interests and employed those energies by writing many of the articles himself. His frenetic activity had predictable consequences; harassed by church and state, busier than even he enjoyed being, Diderot often took the easy way out— the way of encyclopedists both before and after him: he copied from authorities he considered trustworthy or found congenial. Anecdotes, sentences, sometimes whole pages from Bayle's *Dictionnaire*, Basnage's *Histoire des juifs,* and most often Brucker's *Historia critica philosophiae* appear in the *Encyclopédie* over Diderot's name.

Much of this was as it should be: an encyclopedia is not a learned journal. Diderot was well-read in contemporary literature and knew, as all French schoolboys knew, the French and Latin classics. But there were limits to his learning, as there were to his time. Therefore he would follow Brucker page by page and point by point when he agreed with him (as he did on eclecticism) or needed some anecdotes (as he did for Machiavelli) or wanted a firm pattern imposed on a large subject (as he did in Greek philosophy) or was ignorant of a subject he wanted to include in the *Encyclopédie* (as he did with the German academician Christian Thomasius, whom Brucker much admired as the founder of the German Enlightenment and whom Diderot had probably never heard of and had certainly never read). And yet, even when Diderot was simply translating, he could not help himself: he would lighten the tone, subtly introduce a phrase that would serve the cause of anticlericalism, or omit material that might reflect discredit on his favorite philosophers. Diderot transcribed much of Brucker's essay on Epicureanism, but where Brucker is the accurate and dry reporter, Diderot is the passionate advocate; again, Diderot transferred long passages from Brucker's essay on Stoicism directly into the *Encyclopédie,* but here he argues with the man he is copying. Brucker had cold aversion for the Stoics; their good reputation, he suggested, rested on a superficial similarity of their doctrines to that of Christianity and on direct borrowings from Christian writers. Brucker's Stoics are contemptible hairsplitters, eclectics in the pernicious sense of that word, empty-headed compilers, and, in their advocacy of apathy, hypocrites. Clearly this was a verdict that Diderot could not sustain; he was, after all, in his own independent manner a latter-day Stoic and an articulate admirer of Roman Stoicism, which had tried to foster a sense of public obligation rather than apathy. Therefore Diderot offers sympathetic if slightly ironical portraits of the early Stoics, omits Brucker's cruel story that Chrysippus either laughed or drank himself to death, defends the Stoic doctrine against its critics—that is to say, Brucker—and criticizes it only to criticize, slyly, Christian ethics in turn: the Stoics, he writes, have been reproached with "bringing scholastic complications into polite society; it has been argued that they misunderstood the forces of nature, that their ethics were impractical, and that they inspired enthusiasm instead of wisdom. That may be; but then, what enthusiasm! It sacrifices us to virtue, and can keep our minds in a posture so tranquil and so firm, that the keenest pains will not wring from us a sigh, a tear! . . . Ordinary philosophers are men of flesh like others: the Stoic is a man of iron; one can break him, but not make him complain. . . . Christian morality is a mitigated Zenonism, and is consequently in more general use; still the number of those who rigorously conform to it is not large."[9] And

---

[9] "Stoïcisme," *Œuvres,* XVII, 208. In his haste and occasional uncertainty Diderot sometimes reproduces Brucker's sentiments which he himself was not sure he shared. Thus he gives only cursory treatment to Roman Stoicism (about which he writes with great warmth elsewhere) and he concludes his article with a summary typical of Brucker: The Romans "invented nothing" in philosophy: they "spent their time studying what the Greeks had discovered," so that "in philosophy, the masters of the world were nothing but schoolboys." "Romains (Philosophie des Étrusques et des Romains)," *Œuvres,* XVII, 34.

thus, as so often, the philosophe wins both ways: if there is a fault in pagan philosophy, Christianity shares in it; but in its virtues Christianity has no part. Diderot was Brucker's translator, but he was at once better and worse than that: the old Italian saying *traduttore, traditore* applies in a rather peculiar sense to the pagan Encyclopedist transcribing pages from his Christian authority.

III

All the men of the Enlightenment were cuckoos in the Christian nest; none more discriminating than Gibbon. Gibbon was a philosophe, delighted to participate in the offensive against the Christian religion in his own time by chronicling the emergence of Christianity in the Rome of antiquity. But Gibbon was a philosophe with a difference: he took pride in reconciling within himself two warring factions. He was the admirer of the *érudit* Mabillon and he was the disciple of the philosophe Montesquieu, the heir of Tillemont as he was (much as he disliked to admit it) the follower of Voltaire.

Gibbon was therefore exceptionally well placed to exploit Christian scholarship, and he exploited it with his characteristic respect for learning mixed with his equally characteristic irony: he conducted his forays with almost courtly elegance, diverted from objectivity only by his feline malice and his unrelieved disdain for religion. His *Autobiography* and the footnotes of his *Decline and Fall of the Roman Empire* teem with tart though ample acknowledgments. His victim Beausobre, whose *History of Manicheanism* had permitted Gibbon to step beyond the holy circle, a learned Huguenot who had left France after the revocation of the Edict of Nantes and became a prominent preacher in Berlin—Beausobre taught Gibbon the intricate history of the Gnostics and other heretical sects, and through his exceptional candor and empathy permitted Gibbon to write disparaging but well-informed paragraphs about early Christian idolatry. Beausobre, Gibbon remarked suavely, is "a protestant, but a philos-

opher," and that "but" bears a large burden of significance—it is
as revealing as it is impudent.[1]

Gibbon had other guides, religious but somehow philosophical, and he consumed their offerings with his scholarly gluttony.
We can still feel—almost taste—the passion behind Gibbon's
cadenced prose, as he recalls the day he began to build his fine
private library with the celebrated *Mémoires* of the Academy of
Inscriptions: "I cannot forget the joy with which I exchanged a
bank note of twenty pounds for the twenty volumes of the
Memoirs," nor "would it have been easy, by any other expenditure
of the same sum, to have procured so large and lasting a fund of
rational amusement."[2] As Gibbon well says—he always says things
well—the *Mémoires* were distinguished by "researches which
combined justness of insight, amenity, and erudition" with "that
which only yields to discoveries: a modest and wholesome ignorance"[3]—a combination of qualities of which, it may be confessed,
the former were more conspicuous in Gibbon's writings than the
latter.

When Gibbon came to write the *Decline and Fall of the
Roman Empire*, he wrote it with some learned volumes always
by his side, above all Tillemont, the seventeenth-century Jansenist,
the scrupulous historian of the early church. Tillemont provided
Gibbon with precise, copious, reliable information whose want he
felt sadly in the later chapters. It has often been said—not without
spite, but not without justification—that after the sixth century,
where Tillemont's ecclesiastical history breaks off, Gibbon's masterpiece shows marked signs of deterioration. It is true: uncertainty
takes the place of sure-footed knowledge, and prejudices swamp
detachment. Gibbon himself sensed something of this: he adverts,

---

[1] *Decline and Fall of the Roman Empire*, III, 214 *n*. He adds
that Beausobre "spins with incomparable art the systematic
thread of opinion, and transforms himself by turns into the
person of a saint, a sage, or an heretic. Yet his refinement is
sometimes excessive; he betrays an amiable partiality in favour
of the weaker side; and while he guards against calumny, he
does not allow sufficient scope for superstition and fanaticism.
A copious table of contents will direct the reader to any point
that he wishes to examine"—hardly a heated tribute (V, 97).
[2] *Autobiography*, 121.
[3] Ibid.

with an enthusiasm rare for him, to Tillemont's "inimitable accuracy" which "almost assumes the character of genius" and bids farewell to his Christian mentor with a tribute almost, but not quite, unmarred by his tendentiousness: "And here," he writes in the forty-seventh chapter, which recounts the troubled evolution of the Incarnation among the early Christians, "here I must take leave for ever from that incomparable guide—whose bigotry is overbalanced by the merits of erudition, diligence, veracity, and scrupulous minuteness."[4]

Nor did Gibbon neglect the great Benedictines Mabillon and Montfaucon, those brilliant pioneers of historical method and documentary criticism. Gibbon knew and admired Mabillon's *De re diplomatica* of 1681, whose statement of the principles governing the verification of documents has never been surpassed; he knew and used Montfaucon's great editions of the Greek Fathers. But as he learned and admired and adopted facts and interpretations from devout scholars, his antireligious spleen gave him no rest: "The most authentic information of St. Bernard must be drawn from his own writings," Gibbon notes, "published in a correct edition by Père Mabillon, and reprinted at Venice 1750, in six volumes in folio. Whatever friendship could recollect or superstition could add, is contained in the two lives, by his disciples, in the sixth volume: whatever learning or criticism could ascertain, may be found in the prefaces of the Benedictine editor."[5] There is something frigid about this sarcasm, a compulsive repetitiveness and automatic malice, that weaken its force for the modern reader. But it is also a reminder that the philosophes were missionaries, exceptional in being witty, typical in being humorless, and that for the sake of their calling they were ready to exploit the best the enemy had to offer, without mercy and without gratitude.

---

[4] *Decline and Fall of the Roman Empire*, V, 132 *n*.
[5] Ibid., VI, 332 *n*.

2 · THE MISSION OF LUCRETIUS

I

IN THEIR EARNEST RANCOR against religion the philosophes resembled no one quite so much as Lucretius, and it was fitting that Lucretius should provide them with their favorite tag: *tantum religio potuit suadere malorum.* Montesquieu quoted the line, and so did Holbach: the first generation of philosophes, like the last, was confident that it had been called by history to expose, and if possible eradicate, those evils.

That confidence, as we know, found more and more strident expression as the century went on. In the fashion of imperialists the spokesmen of the Enlightenment grew more radical and expanded their program: the more they got, the more they wanted. Polemical victories turned out to be not a reason for accommodation but for war to the end. In 1715, when Louis XIV died, the most imaginative French anticlericals confined themselves to private impiety and calls for reforms within the Church: their ideal was a kind of Anglicanism—a reasonable, respectable established church with little political power, no passion for repressing the free commerce of ideas, and no religious fervor. In 1788, when Louis XVI convoked the Estates General, the surviving philosophes were asking for complete disestablishment, a laic state. By that time, and even before, the audacious but playful blasphemies of Epicurean aristocrats had given way to the aggressive and humorless militancy of writers like Holbach and Diderot. Christianity, Diderot told his friends and family at Langres in a relatively early letter, serves its God by murder, "fire and sword in hand," and it recruits its servants—monks and nuns—from sick spirits seething with resentment.[6] Ten years later he told Damilaville, just back from a visit to Voltaire, a fanciful and shocking fable about the origins of religion: a misanthrope, having retired

---

[6] Diderot to his family and friends at Langres (January 6, 1755). *Correspondance,* I, 175–6.

to a cave to meditate vengeance on mankind, emerged to shout the word "God, God!" and from that day on, once that "abominable name" had been pronounced, men began "to argue, to hate each other, and to cut one anothers' throats."[7] Of all the vicious institutions perpetuating that abominable name, Christianity was surely the worst, but as time went by Diderot expressed some confidence that its days might be numbered. "It is raining bombs in the house of the Lord," he told Sophie Volland in 1768; there was hope that "the great prostitute of Babylon" might soon give way to the "reign of Anti-Christ."[8] Still, while men were living in a time heady with promise, the danger was not over: Diderot feared "the last convulsive movements of a wild beast wounded unto death."[9]

This was radical talk, but it had its parallels, if perhaps in somewhat milder tones, in other countries. In the German states the first overt though cautious defiance of orthodoxy came at the beginning of the eighteenth century, with the diffusion of historical criticism, rationalist metaphysics, and English deism. By the 1770's, when Lessing the theologian was at his most embattled, natural religion appeared as a serious competitor to Christianity, at least among intellectuals, and *Aufklärer* like Basedow and Wieland infuriated their pious contemporaries with their little didactic essays exposing superstitions and defending philosophy. In the Italian states anticlerical propaganda—which was taken by the Church, not without good grounds, as a form of anti-Christian, or at least heretical anti-Catholic, propaganda—reached heights of furious invective and was viciously repressed by the authorities. The gifted Neapolitan historian Pietro Giannone subjected the history of the Roman Church to unsparing criticism: in his vast *Istoria Civile del Regno di Napoli*, first published in 1723, he assailed the Inquisition, the wealth of the clergy, the worldliness of religious orders, the Index, the papal power of excommunication, and contrasted the corruption of the modern Church with the purity of apostolic times. He was forced into exile and led a wandering life until he was arrested in 1736 on Sardinian territory

---

[7] (September 12, 1765). Ibid., V, 117–18.
[8] (November 22, 1768). Ibid., VIII, 234–7.
[9] Diderot to David Hume, February 22, 1768. Ibid., VIII, 17.

—ironically on Easter Sunday, while he was taking communion—
and kept in prison until his death in 1748. In the north Beccaria
warmly, if privately, applauded d'Alembert's book against the
Jesuits: "The philosophers," he wrote to d'Alembert, "see the
wrong the Jesuits have done purely from the side of humanity
and science."[1] Such sentiments were held only by a small minority
—when Leopold of Tuscany abolished religious fraternities and
closed roadside shrines, he was faced with a popular revolt—but
the minority was growing in numbers and in audacity. In Britain,
finally, religious criticism passed from the deists into the hands
of Hume, Bentham, and other utilitarians—nearly all of them
uncompromising, outspoken secularists.

While the variations among the philosophes are far from
negligible, they only orchestrate a single passion that bound the
little flock together, the passion to cure the spiritual malady that
is religion, the germ of ignorance, barbarity, hypocrisy, filth, and
the basest self-hatred.[2] It is true that just as they disagreed on their
diagnoses, the philosophes disagreed on their prescriptions for
health: the atheists reduced the simple doctrines of natural religion to a mere expressive metaphor for the majesty of nature,
and the skeptics doubted that the truth of natural religion could
be reliably established. But both groups conceded to the deists
that natural religion alone—a religion without miracles, priestly
hierarchies, ritual, divine saviors, original sin, chosen people, and
providential history—was tolerable and intellectually respectable.
All other religions deserved to be extirpated: this was the meaning
of Voltaire's slogan—which was also the slogan of the others—
Ecrasez l'infâme.

---

[1] Beccaria to d'Alembert, August 24, 1765. *Illuministi Italiani,*
III, 199.
[2] There were some exceptional philosophes, notably Montesquieu, Turgot, and Lessing, who assigned to Christianity a
privileged position among religions, largely for its historical
role. But even they shared the majority view that revealed
religion had lost all its vitality, and remained a harmful survival, in the eighteenth century. —I shall return to the philosophes' use of medical metaphors in volume II of this essay.

II

The roots of this splenetic program are buried deeply within Christian civilization itself. It was an anticlerical program, angrily so, and skeptical, but it was more than anticlericalism or skepticism. To lampoon the clergy, to lament its corruption, its worldliness and deviations from its true vocation, had been a favorite occupation of educated and often uneducated men for centuries. Such criticism was at times the inspired lament of saintly men: through history there have been great Christians who were anticlerical and who were great Christians precisely because they were anticlerical. At other times this sort of criticism was merely scurrilous gossip, resentment against a privileged literate clerisy. But whatever it was, it was far from dangerous to religion or even to the clerical establishment: it served to discharge hostilities and occasionally induced ecclesiastics to reform themselves. In the same way skepticism about miracles or other proofs for Christianity was in itself relatively innocuous: it was confined to a narrow circle of emancipated spirits. Anticlericalism and skepticism became, as it were, political only as they joined forces with a naturalistic world view, a secular ethical system, and above all a triumphant scientific method. It was not Bayle or Erasmus singly or together but Bayle and Erasmus allied with Newton and Locke that created the atmosphere hospitable to the Enlightenment's Lucretian mission. The treason of the clerks did the rest.

The first men in modern times to set out on this mission were the English deists. Today their reputation is not high: they lie unread and are in fact for the most part unreadable. Indeed, when Burke contemptuously wrote their epitaph at the end of the eighteenth century, their vogue had long passed. But while their intellectual limitations are evident and their defeats at the hands of Bishop Butler and David Hume were devastating, their historical significance was considerable: they redrew the religious map of Europe. They were acute if not profound thinkers, equipped with a shrewd perception of their opponents' weaknesses; besides, whatever the shortcomings of their central principle—their watchmaker God who had endowed the world at the beginning of time with ethical laws that every individual can discover for himself through the use of his unaided reason—theirs was a philosophy emotionally appealing and logically persuasive. Goethe, who witnessed the deist phase of German thought, rightly suggested that in an atmosphere saturated with Newtonian science and the cult of common sense, deism was a perfectly sensible religion to adopt. The deists came at the right historic moment with the right arguments; they faded not mainly because they were bested in debate but because their teachings and their criticisms had become commonplace—that is to say, widely accepted.

The English deists were a true school of thought, a loosely joined family of intellectuals who sounded much like one another. A few among them, like Thomas Woolston, were eccentrics to the point of clinical insanity; more were rather like Anthony Collins, who was a respectable metaphysician and sober gentleman. But all of them were ruthless controversialists in an age of ruthless controversy, and while they refined their arguments as time passed, their basic position remained the same for more than half a century.

The real strength of this position, powerful enough to sting scholars like Bentley and satirists like Swift, lay in that happy conjunction of destructive and positive motives that also marks the philosophes' writings.[3] With few exceptions, of whom Woolston was probably the most extreme, the deists never ceased to claim that their crusades against miracles or priestcraft were undertaken solely for the sake of a pure, a natural Christianity: the deist Thomas Morgan, among others, went so far as to call his doctrine a Christian deism. To be sure (and here too they anticipated the philosophes) many of the deists were prudential liars, skillful evaders of the authorities. They had some reason to be: John Toland was unwelcome in most polite society across Europe, while Thomas Woolston, unable to pay an exorbitant fine for blasphemy, died in custody. Both men were unconventional, with no capacity for self-restraint, but they were perse-

---

[3] For a brief critique of Leslie Stephen's analysis of the English deists, in his *English Thought in the Eighteenth Century*, see the Bibliographical Essay, below, p. 550.

cuted for their views, not for their character: Anglican divines as
unbalanced as they continued to hold college fellowships or lucrative livings. It is true that their self-proclaimed championship of
a Christianity without revelation was at best self-contradictory
and for the most part an Aesopian subterfuge. But whether they
were prudent pagans or illogical Christians, the deists were animated not merely by spleen but by idealism as well. Like Voltaire,
their most famous admirer on the continent, they destroyed in
order to build.

While the deists observed a certain division of labor, they
all tended to scatter their shots across the broad front of revealed
religion. Each of their targets—the logic, ethics, and social consequences of Christianity—was equally inviting, but it was the
first that figured in deist strategy as decisive. Christian asceticism
could be discarded, Christian conduct amended, but Christianity
was absolutely, certainly true, or it was false; it was divine, or it
was nothing. For the believer down to the middle of the eighteenth
century, probability was not enough, and when Bishop Butler
argued in his refutation of deism, *The Analogy of Religion*, that
Christianity, like everything else in this world, rested on probabilities, he was not merely cutting the ground from under deist
objections, he was paying tribute to the power of the deist
argument.

John Toland, Locke's unwelcome disciple, was the first to
develop the logical argument fully and so persuasively that the
later deists, Collins, Woolston, Tindal, Middleton, and the others,
often turned to his work in search of arguments and proofs.
Toland's *Christianity Not Mysterious* rests on a simple rationalist
proposition: the only religion worthy of that name is a reasonable
religion. Now, in its inception Christianity had been just such a
religion: "There is nothing in the Gospel contrary to reason, nor
above it."[4] This claim is reminiscent of the Christian rationalists of
the seventeenth century; Locke had argued that revelation is
reason expanded, a divine support of fallible humans which, far
from contradicting reason, enhances its potency and enables men

---

[4] Toland, *Christianity Not Mysterious, Or a Treatise Shewing,
That There Is nothing in the Gospel Contrary to Reason, nor
ABOVE it* ... (1696).

to grasp the mysteries of the faith. But this resemblance is deceptive: the reasoning of Locke and Toland was more divergent than their rhetoric. For Toland "reason" meant what it meant in ordinary speech: what seems irrational to sensible, self-critical, educated men must in fact be irrational. It follows—and Toland was not afraid to draw this consequence—that since Christianity is at bottom reasonable, its proofs must be and appear to be reasonable also. The mysteries that envelop it cannot be part of the divine plan or proof of man's weak understanding; they must be deliberate mystifications. Christianity, Toland argued, has been tampered with: without the "Pretense" of mystery, "we should never hear of the *Transubstantiation*, and other ridiculous Fables of the Church of *Rome;* nor of any of the *Eastern Ordures*, almost all receiv'd into this *Western Sink.*"[5] It was a favorite polemical tactic in Protestant countries to attack all revealed religion indirectly by dwelling on the supposed absurdities of Roman Catholicism, but this was a device that Toland disdained. He included all Trinitarian doctrines, the Lutheran teaching of impanation, and even Arian speculation among the Eastern Ordures: converted Jews and superstitious Gentiles had introduced mysteries into Christian worship to its permanent damage.

From a critique of mysteries to a critique of the documents that recorded and the clerics who retailed them was only one short step. In 1698 in his *Life of John Milton* and a year later in *Amyntor* Toland raised doubts about the authenticity of the canonical gospels. He had already suggested in *Christianity Not Mysterious* that the clerisy kept nonsensical mysteries alive so "that we might constantly depend upon them for the Explication."[6] Men are born superstitious, or made superstitious by their nurses, and kept so by the priestly caste greedy for power. Thus Toland combined a straightforward rationalism with a naturalistic reading of the Bible and traditional anticlericalism to repudiate all historical forms of Christianity except the primitive—and largely imaginary—teaching of the man Jesus.

Anthony Collins, unlike Toland a Lockian whom his master was glad to acknowledge, added little to this line of reasoning: he

---

[5] Ibid., 25.
[6] Ibid., 26.

denounces priests for falsifying sacred documents, urges men to exercise their reason freely and repudiate improbable tales of divine intervention, maliciously calls attention to the unending quarrels among theologians on all points, and asks that the Bible be read as any other book—and in all this he sounds like Toland. It is only when he considers the authority of prophecies that he strikes out on his own.

As Christian apologists had understood since the beginnings of modern criticism, the status of the Old Testament prophecies was of critical importance. To the scandal of many pious contemporaries Locke had insisted that a good Christian need believe only that Christ is the Jewish Messiah as foretold by the prophets of the Old Testament. This is all he needs to believe, but he must believe that. Collins, far from repudiating this argument, made it his own: the proof of Christianity lies in the literal fulfillment of the prophecies; the divine authority of the New Testament depends on the divine truths contained in the Old. But, Collins adds, it can be shown that these prophecies did not literally come true. What, then, remains? For centuries Christian apologists had argued that the prophecies were fulfilled through the life of Christ in an allegorical rather than a literal sense. But to employ the canon of allegory, Collins comments, is to open the floodgates of fancy; almost any event whatever may be said to have been foretold in the opaque, elliptical pronouncements of the prophets. Thus Collins's logic makes what he calls "the difficulties against Christianity" invincible: the believer who rests his belief on the literal fulfillment of prophecies stands exposed as naïve; the believer who depends on allegory is a sophist. Here was a simple but telling argument in an age thirsting for reliable proofs and bewildered by the cacophony of controversy.

Collins first employed this argument in 1724, in his *Discourse of the Grounds and Reasons of the Christian Religion;* it was taken beyond the bounds of common sense and good taste in Woolston's six *Discourses on the Miracles of Our Saviour*, published between 1727 and 1729: the prophecies had foretold the central miracle of the Christian religion, the Incarnation, and Collins had shown these prophecies to be unintelligible or unfulfilled; Woolston now proceeded to argue with some cogency but extreme heat that Collins's critique held true of all the miracles reported in the

New Testament—they are allegories, that is to say, stories. Some of them are delightful, a few point a moral, but most of them are insidious lies. The miracles supposedly performed by Jesus are ludicrous romances; the Virgin, far from being divinely pure, was human and fallible; and the Resurrection is plainly "the most notorious and monstrous Imposture, that ever was put upon mankind."[7] Voltaire—who enjoyed Woolston's polemics, borrowed some of Woolston's arguments, but refined his language—recalled late in life that "no one before him had taken boldness and offensiveness this far. He treated the miracles and the Resurrection of our Saviour as puerile and extravagant stories. He said that when Jesus Christ converted water into wine for the guests who were already drunk, he must have been making punch."[8] Indeed, speaking through the transparent disguise of a rabbi, Woolston offered a drastic remedy: the only consequence that sensible Christian divines could draw from a careful examination of the New Testament was to "give up their *Religion* as well as their *Church*."[9]

This was shocking talk, but there were other deists, notably Tindal, who came to similar conclusions in somewhat less extravagant language. In his *Christianity as Old as Creation* (published in 1730, the year that Woolston went to prison for blasphemy) Tindal combined a virulent anticlericalism and scornful skepticism of the Bible with a warm, generous confidence in the natural religion of reason, inscribed in the hearts of humanity and accessible to men of the highest as well as those of the meanest understanding. Priests, far from realizing the purposes of natural religion, have perverted it: "Priests, on the pretence of the good of the Church" work the people up "to Tumults, Mutiny, Sedition and Rebellion"; and a close look at "Ecclesiastical History" will show that the clergy have allied themselves with the secular power: "The worst of princes have been most sure of their As-

---

[7] *A Sixth Discourse on the Miracles of our Saviour* (1729), in John Martin Creed and John S. Boys Smith, eds., *Religious Thought in the Eighteenth Century* (1934), 66.
[8] "Lettres à S. A. Monseigneur de Prince de *****, sur Rabelais et sur d'autres auteurs qui ont mal parlé de la religion chrétienne," (1767), *Œuvres*, XXVI, 485.
[9] *A Sixth Discourse*, in Creed and Boys Smith, *Religious Thought*, 67.

sistance even in carrying on the vilest Designs."[1] Nothing but
reasoning can improve reason; no man but moral man, free to
criticize and exercise his mind without constraint, can discover
the laws that the Divinity has laid down and is following Himself.
"The primitive Christians believed, there was an exact Agreement
between *Natural* and *Reveal'd* Religion; and that the Excellency
of the Latter, did consist in being a Republication of the Former"
—and the primitive Christians were right.[2] Long after this kind of
faith in universal rational nature and this equation of religion
with morality had faded, Tindal's ideal of the autonomous man
and his criticisms of revealed religions and their keepers retained
their vitality for his many readers.

III

By the early 1730's most of the leading deists had done their
work; what followed was largely the effort of epigones. Conyers
Middleton's *Free Inquiry*, which put the argument against miracles on a historical basis, was a late fruit: it came out in 1748,
the year David Hume entered theological controversy with his
celebrated essay on miracles. Besides, Middleton's intelligent historical argumentation was as much a weapon against as a weapon
for the deist cause. But while deism decorously decayed in England and theological polemicists lost readers to the novelists, it
found a ready hearing on the Continent. German culture, still
unformed and unsure, was particularly open to foreign influences,
and many educated Germans seasoned Wolff's popular but relatively tame Christian rationalism with a vigorous dash of English
deism. Christlob Mylius, the adventurous journalist who deeply
impressed the young Lessing, publicly praised "the learned Toland" and the "searching Woolston."[3] A German version of Tindal's *Christianity as Old as the Creation* became available in 1741,
and other deist writings followed—some of them translated by
liberal theologians like Spalding. Readers too impatient to wade

---

[1] *Christianity as Old as the Creation* (1730; edn. 1732), 254.
[2] Ibid., 387.
[3] Schmidt, *Lessing*, I, 63.

through long exposition and involved argumentation turned to the popular periodicals, which were printing appreciative reviews and generous excerpts from radical English literature. The English deists came to enjoy a popularity in the German states that enraged the orthodox and alarmed the authorities.

Characteristically the man who kept the deist cause alive in Germany was Lessing, who thrived on controversy and cherished debate as the lifeblood of culture. When he published fragments from Reimarus's *Apologie,* the notorious *Wolfenbüttel Fragments,* between 1774 and 1778, he aroused a storm of protests. Each of the fragments, taken alone, was both radical and familiar, but placed together they amounted to a scandal, and the sixth fragment, which questioned the historicity of the Resurrection, called forth passionate rebuttals and plunged Lessing into the most sustained and most acrimonious dispute of his life. It kept him busy, but he must have enjoyed it, for in 1778, harassed by persistent, vociferous critics, he brought out "Vom Zwecke Jesu and seiner Jünger," the last, longest, and most inflammatory of Reimarus's fragments that Lessing was to publish. "Vom Zwecke Jesu" portrays Jesus as a traditional Jew, persuaded that he is the Jewish Messiah foretold in the Old Testament, divinely called to found an earthly kingdom: he is the charismatic national leader who cares for his people alone. At first his followers, as fanatical a group of disciples as Jesus was a leader, believed in this circumscribed mission, but after his death they universalized his program, translated the earthly into a heavenly kingdom, and revised the story of Jesus's life to fit their altered purposes. Much of the gospels, in other words, consists of tactical interpolations and downright falsifications, and thus historical Christianity is a gigantic deception.

This was more than the authorities could tolerate: the liberal theologian Semler, by no means averse to a critical reading of Scripture as long as it was reverent, was stung to reply to these fragments because (as he reported in 1779) scholars and statesmen, and even solid bourgeois, read them with amazement, and young men were thrown into crises of doubt. The duke of Brunswick withdrew the privilege under which Lessing had published Reimarus's fragments and his own theological writings, and subjected him to the censor. Lessing, in turn, half dismayed and half relieved, returned to his old passion, the theatre, and wrote *Nathan der Weise*. The play is a symbol of victory in defeat: the publication of Reimarus's fragments was discontinued, Lessing the speculative theologian was silenced, but the deist message in its most constructive form was restated triumphantly in a play that all Germans read, most Germans praised—and very few Germans heeded.

IV

While in Protestant Germany the inroads of English deism were significant but in the long run ephemeral, in France they left a lasting impress. Collins's *Discourse on Freethinking* was translated into French in 1714, the year after its publication, and went into a second French edition three years later. It was only the first in a steady succession. In France, it seemed, English writers appeared more radical than they were at home: Pope's most deist poems were also his most widely read and most frequently imitated; Locke's tentative remark that it might be possible for a material being to be endowed with thought had a long and vigorous career among French freethinkers, who took it as an invitation to materialism;[4] and Newton, who was intensely pious though scarcely orthodox in his Christianity, was quoted in libertine circles as holding that "J.-C. was a man, not God's son, who hath given us a very good Morale."[5] Thus Pope's civilized religiosity, Locke's cautious metaphysical guesses, and Newton's earnest Christian inquiries were grouped with Collins's open radicalism to supply fuel for French deists.

---

[4] ". . . possibly [we] shall never be able to know whether any mere material being thinks or no," *Essay Concerning Human Understanding*, Book IV, chapter 3. This sentence had caused some controversy in England, but it was in France that it really blossomed. It was quoted, and exploited, by Voltaire in his widely read *Lettres philosophiques*, and by other even more radical writers after him.

[5] This remark was recorded by Antoine-Robert Pérelle, Councillor to the Grand Conseil, who was in touch with French and British libertines, in his journal of April 1718. E. R. Briggs, "L'incrédulité et la pensée anglaise en France au début du XVIIIe siècle," *Revue d'histoire littéraire de la France*, XLI (1934), 511.

All this activity is not surprising. As the intellectual ties between England and France were close, the prestige of English philosophers was high. The fashion of deism was a daughter of Anglomania. Besides, French readers greeted the English deists with pleased recognition: Toland and Woolston were popular in France largely because their religious thought had sturdy French parallels. But imported or indigenous, deism provided an influential and growing public with a satisfying theory of nature and a splendid sanctuary for wry and respectable impiety: it permitted skeptics to harass their devout contemporaries with insincere professions of allegiance to "true Christianity" as distinguished from "mere superstition." Many of the radicals who ended up as materialists reached their final position after a deist phase and, as Diderot's career shows, never wholly discarded deist rhetoric. And some materialists, like Holbach, found it useful to translate and paraphrase Trenchard, Toland, and Woolston as late as the 1760's.

French deists therefore had a widely ramified pedigree. Montesquieu—one of them for all his sociological relativism and lingering respect for Christianity—exemplifies this eclectic heritage: his sardonic sallies against the clergy, enthusiastic worship of an Architect-Creator, contempt for papist mystifications, disdain for all ritual, and respect for ethical speculation reflect wide reading and some disenchanting experience. It was not his encounter with Toland's *Letters to Serena* or his association with deist circles during his visit to England that made him a deist. Quite the contrary: Montesquieu studied and frequented English deists because he found them congenial. His first guides to natural religion were Cicero, Bayle and Plato, Fréret's bold scholarly excursions into the history and chronology of religion, and the provocative impious conversation of Fréret's patron, the comte de Boulainvilliers.

There was much of this conversation in France during the last years of Louis XIV and after, and much of it was nourished by a busy industry of clandestine writings. Scores of treatises, poems, and secular catechisms circulated from hand to hand, usually unprinted and for many years unprintable. Some were scurrilous slanders of Jesus; others concentrated on the crimes of the biblical Jews; still others summarized the ideas of Italian

Socinians or offered Spinoza's rationalist reading of the Bible as a model for reasonable men. A few of these manuscripts speculated about materialism or the souls of animals; a few suggested heterodox chronologies based on the supposition that Adam was not the first of men; but all of them were grimly anticlerical and all questioned the miracles. The sheer volume of these polemics —but that alone—is impressive; they leave a somewhat unpleasant aftertaste of coarseness and monotony, for they play endless variations on the two themes so familiar from deist diatribes: they excoriate the wickedness of priests and the incredibility of the Bible, and they glorify the Eternal Legislator, Who has endowed the universe with unalterable laws. "Reason and conscience are perfectly adequate for man's conduct"—this phrase, from an anonymous manuscript, Le militaire philosophe, which Voltaire highly esteemed for its logic and eloquence, might be found in all the others.[6]

But while most of these productions were derivative and crude, it was their very crudity, their very repetitiveness, coupled with the piquant secrecy which surrounded their production and facilitated their diffusion, that gave them a certain power in French society. All the tricks later used by Voltaire and Holbach were used in these writings, with such effect that many of their authors, unknown in their day, remain unknown or at least uncertain in ours. The comte de Boulainvilliers seems—one must say "seems," for the facts are impossible to establish firmly—to have been the center of a small coterie of freethinkers. What is more certain is that he wrote some treatises against revealed religion, including the Traité des trois imposteurs, first published in 1719 and widely disseminated, rarely as a printed book, more often as a manuscript. There were many like him, some, like Fréret, in respectable posts, who retained these posts by keeping their speculations secret.

The philosophes who read, memorized, distributed, and occasionally added to this literature were thus not lonely innovators. Rather they were gifted popularizers who used their literary

---

[6] Wade: Clandestine Organization and Diffusion of Philosophic Ideas in France, 55.

talents to say what had been said before but not so well. Their atmosphere was saturated with rationalist propaganda. Montesquieu's *Lettres persanes* and Voltaire's *Lettres philosophiques*, the two most distinguished radical books published before 1740, found such a receptive public precisely because the ideas they expressed so wittily were so familiar. Indeed, when in the 1760's Voltaire mounted his great campaign to *écraser l'infâme*, he invented nothing. He merely brought out into the open a battle that had been fought underground for more than half a century.

Voltaire's career as a publicist had its real beginning in 1718 with *Œdipe*, his first tragedy; it ended sixty years later, in 1778, the year of his death, when he returned to Paris in triumph, the symbol of an irresistible cause. It was not only long, this career, but also glorious, and it vividly reflects both the evolution of religious controversy in eighteenth-century France and the tenacious hold of deism on one of the century's liveliest minds. Voltaire began with the advance guard and ended up as an anachronism—at least among the radicals. As a precocious young man, all wit and intelligence, he was coopted into a precious society of wealthy gourmands, brilliant talkers, and homosexuals, who took impiety for granted—it was the mark of membership, not of independent thought. In this elegant and decadent environment Voltaire practiced the higher criticism on a low level: he learned obscene jokes about the Virgin and unprintable deist poems like the *Moïsade,* in which (in familiar style) a personified Good Sense scores rhetorical victories over doctrinaire believers and mystery-mongering priests.

But the wit turned philosopher. Before long Voltaire translated the irresponsible rationalism of his circle into a serious world view. His earliest successes, ostensibly remote from theological concerns, are the work of a deist whose rationalist religion is more than a game. Voltaire's version of Sophocles's *Oedipus,* which made him the rival of Corneille and Racine in the eyes of a public parched for good plays, pointedly depicts God as a kind of metaphysical villain, a cruel, despotic, and implacable being: Oedipus and Jocasta have committed incest and parricide, yet they remain virtuous, for their crimes are the crimes of the gods:

Inceste et parricide, et pourtant vertueux,
Impitoyable dieux, mes crimes sont les vôtres,
Et vous m'en punissez![7]

Voltaire's coterie was gratified by the philosophy of his tragedy, and so, it seems, were his old teachers, the Jesuits, who were at the time embroiled in a fierce struggle against the Augustinian theology of Jansenism. They were not gratified for long: in the *Henriade*, the epic poem he completed in the early 1720's, Voltaire turned on them to give vent to his principled anticlericalism. The *Henriade* is not primarily a work of propaganda; it is Voltaire's ambitious literary effort to become the Vergil of France. But deism keeps breaking in: the poem is both a hymn to Henri IV, who is shown to be France's greatest king, for being its most tolerant, and a tirade against religious fanaticism, against the assassins of St. Bartholomew's Day and the blood-thirsty papacy. It is a frigid poem, labored and rather mechanical, and it has not survived the passing of time and changes in taste, but it achieves a certain dramatic force in the polemical passages, in which Voltaire states in preliminary but articulate form the deist criticisms that will be his passionate theme in the 1760's.

Je ne décide point entre Genève et Rome,

Voltaire has Henri exclaim, which is to say that all positive religions are at bottom alike.[8] Forty years later he would specify what he here only implies: in tendency, at least, all religions are equally bad.

This was heresy, but Voltaire escaped censure by clothing his formulations in mythological or historical dress, attributing his opinions to pagans or Protestants, and ceaselessly parading his own piety. But as is evident from his *Épitre à Uranie*, written in 1722 and not published until the 1730's, Voltaire was no longer a Christian in the 1720's, not even a Christian deist. As I have

---

[7] *Œuvres*, II, 107–8. Diderot later said the same thing: "When it's a question of indicting the gods or man, I give the preference to the gods." Diderot to Sophie Volland (October 14–15, 1760). *Correspondance*, III, 135.

[8] Chant II, line 5. *Œuvres*, VIII, 66.

said earlier, in the *Épitre* he poses as a modern Lucretius who defies a cruel God and all His horrible mysteries and explicitly abandons Christianity so that he may be free to love the deist deity:

Je ne suis pas Chrétien, mais c'est pour t'aimer mieux.[9]

Then from 1726 to 1728 Voltaire was in England—part honored visitor, part exile—and there he interviewed Quakers, freely associated with men of letters, liberal aristocrats, and generous merchants, studied the English poets, attended the House of Commons, and was delighted to find his deism confirmed in his reading and in the very atmosphere. The *Lettres philosophiques*, his report on England, carefully prepared and brilliantly composed, is far more than a religious tract. It is a superb, if informal, piece of sociological analysis which exhibits British civilization as a complex configuration, the product of interacting cultural forces, including religion. It is a sympathetic account of British science, politics, philosophy, poetry, and social relations. It is a work of sly social criticism, which denigrates France by praising England. But it is also, one might say, a deist's book without being a deist book. On the surface Voltaire observes the proprieties: he is, after all, merely offering a travel report on a Protestant country. But the polemical intentions of the report are unmistakable. England is, if not precisely a deist's paradise, a country in which deism originated and now seems to be professed by the best people. The very pluralism which struck pious Frenchmen as the subversion of all social order seemed, at least in Voltaire's account, the cause of public felicity: "If there were only one religion in England, one would have to fear despotism; if there were two, they would cut each other's throats; but they have thirty, and they live happy and in peace."[1] Toleration, a relatively open society, and a mixed government with a powerful House of Commons—these institutions, historically and emotionally linked, have made England a leader in commerce, a pioneer in philosophy and science, and the cradle of dramatic and poetic genius.

---

[9] *Épitre à Uranie*, ed. Wade, *PMLA* (1932), IIII.
[1] *Lettres philosophiques*, VIe Lettre, I, 74.

This analysis was disturbing without being actionable. But it was buttressed by details which are more tendentious than precise and which are manifestly designed to advance the deist cause. Deism appears obliquely in the Seventh Letter, which describes briefly but with ill-concealed approval the "little sect" of Unitarians, a sect that seems to include giants like Newton and Locke. Deism appears more openly in the four letters devoted to the Quakers, strategically placed at the beginning of the book. Voltaire had real affection for the Quakers, mixed with wry amusement at their quaint speech and singular customs. But in the *Lettres philosophiques* he placed his amusement as a screen before his affection to make his account appear more innocuous than it was. Voltaire's Quakers are idealized beings, primitive Christians in the modern world: they live modestly and always speak the truth, tolerate the opinions of others, have no priests, confine their religious ceremonial to a simple prayer at meals, refuse to practice meaningless rituals like baptism or communion, reject all "Jewish ceremonies" in general, and believe that Jesus was the first Quaker, the teacher of a simple rational religion whose teachings were later corrupted. They are men, in a word, whom a Tindal would not criticize.

This is deist propaganda disguised as a report on an eccentric sect. But in the last Letter, Voltaire the deist speaks in his own voice, even if softly. The *Lettres philosophiques* had been published in English, incomplete, in 1733, and aroused some criticism. Voltaire, often easily frightened, for once was not afraid. "If I displease those madmen, the Jansenists," he told a friend that year, "I'll have on my side those buggers, the Reverend Fathers,"[2] and he added a Letter against Pascal, the arch-Jansenist—that famous last Letter—partly to please the Reverend Fathers, partly to please himself. It turned out that his estimate of the Jesuits was as wrong as it was inelegant; while the government seized the French edition in June 1734 and had it publicly burned as "scandalous, contrary to religion, good morals, and the respect due to authority,"[3] the Jesuits were not appeased; whatever their distaste for Pascal, the general tenor of the *Lettres philosophiques* deeply disturbed

[2] Voltaire to Cideville (July 14, 1733). *Correspondence*, III, 104.
[3] Peter Gay: *Voltaire's Politics: The Poet as Realist* (1959), 67.

them. Voltaire, said the reviewer in the *Journal de Trévoux*, had acted the "deist with the Quakers."[4]

The Jesuit who wrote these words was severe and perceptive, but the censor who refused to pass Voltaire's remarks on Pascal was more perceptive than he; for here, in the first encounter of the thoughtful worldling with the eloquent, austere Augustinian— the beginning of what was to become a lifelong preoccupation— Voltaire alludes more than once to the central issue, the nature of man, which defines the radical incompatibility of deism and Christianity. Posing in his favorite role, the champion, Voltaire undertook to defend man against this "sublime misanthrope." Pascal, he charged, had employed his undeniable talents to depict man as more miserable and more evil than he is. Many men in fact are happy, many are decent. Admittedly man's nature is mixed; it contains "good and evil, pleasure and pain," heady passions and cautious reason. But this does not make man an enigma, a religious puzzle to be solved only by submission to God. Man's contradictions arise in nature, and they must be understood and controlled through the science of man. Pascal's laments on the human condition may be eloquent, but they paralyze the will, make men revel in their wretchedness and face the world in despairing passivity. "Man is made for action, as fire tends upwards and the stone downwards." Indeed, Pascal's very metaphors, though moving, are misleading: man is not, as Pascal says, a bewildered castaway on a desert island—London and Paris, Voltaire counters in deliberate naïveté, in conscious refusal to take Pascal's anthropology seriously, "in no way resemble a desert island; they are well populated, opulent, civilized; men are as happy there as it is compatible with human nature to be." Nor is man a galley slave: Voltaire accepts man's nature, including his limitations and his vices. Even selfishness has its value: it lies at the bottom of all effort.

It is pointless to try to decide this debate: while Voltaire had great respect for the sublime misanthrope and even shared some of his misanthropy, the gulf dividing Pascal and Voltaire was unbridgable: the first accepted, as central, man's fall from Grace; the second vehemently rejected it in the name of human autonomy. But despite all this, for the sake of safety and propaganda, Voltaire

---

[4] René Pomeau: *La religion de Voltaire*, 136.

was ready to fight Pascal on his own ground, to show him not merely a misanthrope but a bad Christian. Pascal's paradoxes and supposed proofs of Christianity are puerile, uncertain, metaphysical, and sometimes a little indecent: "Christianity teaches only this: simplicity, humanity, charity."[5] Voltaire had been educated by the Jesuits and knew as well as any man in France that Christianity taught more than such secular cosmopolitan morality. Belief in original sin could not be written off as misanthropy. But then to pre-empt the title of "true Christianity" for deism was itself a favorite deist trick.

Voltaire never changed. His tone gained in range, his information in depth, his tactics in suppleness; he confronted and overcame crises of philosophical doubt. But he was to remain the enthusiastic radical of the *Lettres philosophiques*. For a while, though, waiting for the uproar over the English Letters to die down, he said nothing. He retired to Cirey with his mistress, and, as we know, his years there were years of intensive study and literary experimentation. They were also years of caution: while his writings are deist in their philosophy, they are, all of them, reined in by prudence, a last shred of reserve. Voltaire worked quietly, husbanded his rage, and waited—he could afford to wait. Meanwhile he urbanely masked his anti-Christian fury as sincere anticlericalism.

It was not until much later, until around 1760, that Voltaire discarded all compromise and threw away much of his caution. A great deal had happened, both to the movement and to him. Radical writers were being persecuted, and hard-working Encyclopedists harassed; the tempo of the anti-Christian crusade had quickened. Voltaire was ready: after long wandering he was safely settled at Ferney, just a short ride away from Genevan territory. He was old, rich, world-famous, and almost, if not quite, immune from prosecution. He had mastered the grim Pyrrhonism induced by the Lisbon Earthquake and the outbreak of the Seven Years' War. And he did not like to see the leadership of the movement—*his* movement!—pass into younger hands. He reread the notes he had taken at Cirey twenty years before and resumed work on blasphemous pamphlets he had begun at the court of

---

[5] *Lettres philosophiques*, XXV⁰ Lettre, II, 184–226 *passim*.

Frederick the Great. Man was born for action—he had said that in the *Lettres philosophiques*—and now the time for action had come. Long before, in 1738, he had written to a friend, "I know how to hate because I know how to love."[6] In the 1760's he translated this to mean that destruction must precede construction: many ask, he wrote, what shall we put in the place of Christianity? "What! A ferocious animal has sucked the blood of my family; I tell you to get rid of that beast, and you ask me, What shall we put in its place!"[7] To get rid of the beast Voltaire made himself into the unofficial adviser to the underground army arrayed against it: he began to use the phrase *Écrasez l'infâme*, which gave the army a battle cry and rallied its morale; and he took charge of its tactics: he warned the brethren to conceal their hand, to write simply, to repeat the truth often, to lie if necessary, and to convict the enemy out of his own mouth. He had his reward: the little flock recognized his pre-eminence. In 1762 Diderot affectionately saluted him as his "sublime, honorable, and dear Anti-Christ."[8]

No epithet could have been more welcome: a mere glance at the torrent of pamphlets that poured out of Ferney in the last sixteen years of Voltaire's life reveals a distaste for Christianity amounting almost to an obsession. Interpreters who restrict *l'infâme* to intolerance or fanaticism or Roman Catholicism shrink from a conclusion that Voltaire himself drew, and drew innumerable times, in these frenetic years: "Every sensible man, every honorable man, must hold the Christian sect in horror."[9] This is the central message of Voltaire's last and most intensive campaign: he repeats it with endless variations, with blasphemies, playful absurdities, and sometimes obscenities. Nothing was safe: the Trinity, the chastity of the Virgin Mary, the body and blood of Christ in the Mass, all are cruelly lampooned to enforce a single point: "May this great God who is listening to me, this God who surely cannot have been born of a virgin, or have died on the

---

[6] Voltaire to Thieriot (December 10, 1738). *Correspondence*, VIII, 43.

[7] *Examen important de Milord Bolingbroke*, in *Œuvres*, XXVI, 299.

[8] (September 25, 1762). *Correspondance*, IV, 178.

[9] *Examen important de Milord Bolingbroke*, in *Œuvres*, XXVI, 298.

gallows, or be eaten in a piece of dough, or have inspired these books filled with contradictions, madness, and horror—may this God, creator of all the worlds, have pity on this sect of Christians who blaspheme him!"[1]

This is pure rage—there is no rage equal to the rage of the angry idealist—but it is not out of control. Voltaire varied his arguments enough to prevent monotony and repeated them enough to carry his point. He adopted disguise after disguise; dead materialists, imaginary Englishmen, respectable divines regularly appear as the authors of Voltaire's most outrageous productions. Sometimes—and this was the most deceptive disguise of all—he told the truth, as with his celebrated edition of the *Extrait des sentiments de Jean Meslier*.[2] He was always the writer, never so furious as to muddy his clarity. That is what made him so effective and such a plague to his enemies: he was elusive, mendacious, and always a pleasure to read.

But neither his style nor his tactics alone guaranteed his effectiveness; he secured his vast public also because he linked his bitter sarcasms, not merely strategically but quite sincerely, to a constructive program. "I conclude all my letters by saying *Écr. l'inf...*," he wrote to a friend in 1762, "as Cato always said, 'It is my opinion that Carthage must be destroyed.' "[3] But Carthage must die that Rome might live. And so Voltaire assailed intolerance in the name of tolerance, cruelty in the name of kindness, superstition in the name of science, revealed religion in the name of rational worship, a cruel in the name of a beneficent God.

---

[1] *Sermon des cinquante*, published in 1762 but written ten years before at the Prussian court. *Œuvres*, XXIV, 354–5.

[2] Jean Meslier (1664–1729) spent his life as a priest, evidently coerced into the priesthood by his parents, but down to 1711 quiet and conscientious in the performance of his duties. His last years were marked by violent quarrels with his superiors, but his fame rests on a voluminous manuscript, his Testament, which he put together in his last years, and which was discovered after his death. The Testament denounces all religions, including—and especially—Meslier's own, as a mixture of fraud and error. Voltaire's abstract, published in 1762, follows Meslier faithfully.

[3] Voltaire to Damilaville, July 26 (1762). *Correspondence*, IL, 138.

The *Dictionnaire philosophique* is the best-known product of Voltaire's duel with revealed religion; justly so, for it is also the most remarkable. It was conceived, appropriately enough, at the court of Frederick the Great in 1752: Frederick, far more cynical and in a sense far less religious than Voltaire, may even have suggested the alphabetical compendium to him. If not, he was certainly the first and most appreciative reader of the early articles. Armed with Calmet, exhilarated at starting a revolutionary enterprise at the age of fifty-eight, schooled in the higher criticism, Voltaire wrote articles on "Abraham," "Âme," "Athlée," and "Batême" in rapid succession. Then came years of nomadic instability and depression, but even in the dark fifties Voltaire remembered his *Dictionary*. He filled his notebooks with piquant anecdotes or scurrilous remarks that he would later incorporate into it; even when he was writing *Candide,* he obviously kept the *Dictionary* in mind: the parallels between his best story and his most famous polemic are close and frequent.

But all this was marking time; Voltaire did not resume concentrated work on his one-man *Encyclopédie* until 1762, when he was involved in the Calas case and wholly committed to action against *l'infâme.* He importuned correspondents to supply him with material; he told Damilaville, in Paris, to send him "*presto, presto*" a recently published *Dictionnaire des conciles:* "Theology," he wrote acidly, "amuses me; there we find man's insanity in all its plenitude."[4] Then in June 1764 the first edition of the *Dictionnaire philosophique* was published in Geneva, with a false London imprint. It was compact and explosive, its success predictable and, given Voltaire's talents and years of preparation, inevitable. And while he gloried in that success and worked on a second edition, he frantically denied any part in the devilish work: he proclaimed to anyone who would listen that he had not written it, that he had not even read all of it. The lie was too blatant to be believed—and Voltaire was too vain an author to have it believed: the book showed the master's touch on page after page. While those lucky enough to own a copy circulated it among their friends, and Voltaire supplied the demand with edition after

---

[4] December 26 (1762). Ibid., L, 199.

edition, the need for his mendacity was painfully confirmed by the actions of governments everywhere: Geneva, the United Provinces, France, and the Holy See all burned the book and longed (as Voltaire ruefully said) to burn the author. For five years, from 1764 to 1769, amid fits of panic and moments of elation Voltaire reprinted, revised, and enlarged the book, and its successive editions record the flexibility of his politics and the stability of his deism.

The *Dictionnaire philosophique* is an intensely personal creation: no one but Voltaire could have written those articles on Newtonian science, freedom of the will, literary criticism, and theology, and sustained the wit, the freshness throughout. But it is also a cultural symptom. Its often savage tone and its firm concentration on religious questions are a commentary on the eighteenth-century mind: for most literate men theological controversy was anything but tedious and far from academic. Voltaire, who was a rational man of letters and not a compulsive eccentric, knew what he was doing when he devoted more than half of the *Dictionnaire* to the Jews of the Bible, arguments over man's soul, the history of the church, and pleas for tolerance.

He also knew what he was doing as he struck his poses and deployed the rich resources of his style against the adversary: he knew that a reader who is amused is already half-converted. In the eighteenth century the cause of Christianity suffered not merely from internecine struggles but also from the dullness of its apologists. Voltaire was never dull—witty in his duplicity, outrageous in his anecdotes, often fierce and prophetic in his moral indignation: "While the style of Kings and Chronicles is divine, still, the actions reported in these histories are perhaps not so divine. David assassinates Uriah; Ishbosheth and Mephibosheth are assassinated; Absalom assassinates Amnon; Joab assassinates Absalom; Solomon assassinates Adonijah, his brother; Baasha assassinates Hadab; Zimri assassinates Elah; Omri assassinates Zimri; Ahab assassinates Naboth; Jehu assassinates Ahab and Joram; the inhabitants of Jerusalem assassinate Amaziah, son of Joash; Shallum, son of Jabesh, assassinates Zachariah, son of Jeroboam; Menahem assassinates Shallum, son of Jabesh; Pekah, son of Remaliah, assassinates Pekahiah, son of Menahem; Hoshea, son of

Elab, assassinates Pekah, son of Remaliah. I pass over in silence many other assassinations. It must be admitted that if the Holy Spirit wrote this history, he didn't choose a very edifying subject."[5]

The tone of this paragraph, with its simple language and deliberate, resounding repetitions, is mock biblical, but the ironic conclusion is genuine Voltaire. The *Dictionnaire philosophique* is, in fact, a show window of Voltairian irony. Irony permitted him to say one thing and mean something else, to say what he must say but could not say directly, to illuminate by reflected light and reveal by concealing. Voltaire poses—transparently, for transparency is of the essence of the ironic game—as a good Christian bewildered by the unending controversies of theologians, as a prosecutor who takes the biblical Jews and early Christians at their word and convicts them on the basis of their own testimony, as a beleaguered Catholic who deftly expounds and feebly refutes the "false" arguments of Unitarians and deists, as an intelligent ignoramus who cannot bring himself to believe that important matters like the soul (which geniuses like Locke and Newton conceded to be impenetrable mysteries) can be clear to mere priests, as a wide-eyed traveler in space and time who is surprised to discover the rationality of the Chinese and the humanity of the Roman Stoics and thus by implication the irrationality and inhumanity of modern Christians. He poses, finally, as a humanitarian outraged by offensive Christian pedants who deny moral stature to pagan thinkers, by fat ecclesiastics who impose Lent on the poor as they gorge themselves, by cruel judges who lightly condemn their victims to torture, and by inquisitors who burn heretics. This, too, is a role, for Voltaire was a writer who kept firm hold on himself and his moods, but as the outraged humanitarian he is playing himself.

The arguments of the *Dictionnaire philosophique* require less analysis than its tactics: they follow well-established models. Anyone who knew anything about the deists, English or French, recognized Voltaire's criticism and relished the new way in which

---

[5] "History of Jewish Kings and Chronicles," *Philosophical Dictionary*, I, 307.

familiar things were being said: The Old and New Testaments are alike a collection of childish absurdities and irreconcilable contradictions—hence the prophecies of the Jews and the claims of the Apostles are either primitive allegories or manifest deceptions. The morality of the "Chosen People," exemplified by the conduct of King David, is abhorrent, and the history of the Church is a sanguinary compilation of stupid wrangles ending in civil war and mass murder—hence the fathers of Christianity, and Christians through history, are with their conduct conclusive arguments against the Christian religion. Revealed religion is an infectious disease: "Fanaticism is to superstition what delirium is to fever and rage to anger."[6] The infection inevitably leads to virulent manifestations: "The superstitious man is ruled by the fanatic, and turns into one."[7] And Voltaire defines superstition broadly: "Almost everything that goes beyond the worship of a supreme Being, and the submission of one's heart to his eternal commands, is superstition."[8] And that "almost" was a last concession to prudence.

This, as everyone recognized, was critical deism, accompanied, as such doctrine usually was, by its corollary, a naturalistic religion: Voltaire earnestly urged his readers to remember that men are ignorant visitors on this globe who must tolerate each other and develop their capacity for generosity and justice—this is all the philosophical system, all the theology men need. What, someone asks in one of the dialogues in the *Dictionnaire*, what must we do to be able to look at ourselves without shame and revulsion? "Be just" is the answer. And what else? "Be just."[9] Voltaire had said as much, if less openly and less intensely, half a century before.

V

While Voltaire continued to bait *l'infâme* almost to the day of his death, by the middle of the 1760's he was engaged with

---

[6] "Fanaticism," ibid., I, 267.

[7] "Superstition," ibid., II, 475.

[8] Ibid., 473.

[9] "Chinese Catechism," ibid., I, 130.

another adversary—materialism. Voltaire did not treat Holbach and his circle as infamous: he regarded the materialists as misguided allies and conceded that a society of atheists could exist peacefully, provided all the citizens were philosophers. But a belief in God was essential, partly because an atheist king, like an atheist merchant or an atheist servant, would feel liberated from all constraints with disastrous consequences to himself and his society, but partly also because it was true. That is why Voltaire did not adopt the atheism increasingly fashionable in advanced intellectual circles when he was an old man: he believed in God. His religious feeling was anything but simple. All creeds, all ritual, did violence to it; it was held in check by his irrepressible irreverence and confused by his disdain for the capacities of the lower orders. But it was authentic; and in his last years he tried to define and delimit it, notably in his poem of 1769, "A l'auteur du livre des trois imposteurs," which contains the most famous and most misunderstood of his epigrams. For once his customary felicity of expression had unfortunate results:

Si Dieu n'existait pas, il faudrait l'inventer

means, to be sure, that social utility proclaims the existence of God —but then so do the heavens.[1]

Such philosophical enthusiasm for a Watchmaker God moved the materialists to derisive laughter and exposed Voltaire— Voltaire of all men!—to sarcastic reflections on his "timidity" and "bigotry." But while the relations of Voltaire and Holbach were sometimes strained, usually they were cordial enough, and the pleasure their disputes gave to the pious was short-lived. For despite their serious disagreements over cosmology and the foundations of ethics they were firmly on the same side in the most important issue that divided men in the eighteenth century. They were on the side of science against piety, criticism against myth. N. S. Bergier, canon of Notre Dame, one of the devout collaborators on the *Encyclopédie*, neatly characterized this affinity when he condemned Holbach's *Christianisme dévoilé* as a book

---

[1] "A l'auteur du livre des trois imposteurs," *Œuvres*, X, 403. See Peter Gay, *Voltaire's Politics*, 265-6.

whose author "might equally well be an atheist, a skeptic, a materialist, a fatalist, or a cynic; for the one thing that matters to him is that Christianity should perish."[2] He might have added "deist" to his list, for Voltaire's hostility to Christianity was as thoroughgoing as Holbach's and as patent.

As the two philosophes were alike in their spleen, they were alike also in their recognition that they were battling a well-entrenched opponent. Revealed religion, it seemed, was for all its weaknesses truly built on a rock: the rock of money, influence, pervasive habit. Its appeal to man's most mysterious and unappeasable longings for certainty, for purpose, for survival after death, was hard to answer. Voltaire and Holbach were both wealthy and tenacious men, and both spent much of their time and money on their destructive errand, because they judged that this was what they must do: it was an exhausting as well as expensive business to conquer the venerable fortress of religion, even though it was crumbling from age, stocked with rusty weapons, and manned by indifferent and sometimes treacherous troops.

Their alliance was underscored by their strategies. Holbach was much like Voltaire in his readiness to use almost any method to bring and keep his message before the public. He ransacked English literature and discovered much rewarding material in obscure deist pamphlets or neglected works by Collins, Hobbes, and Hume.[3] He rescued impious French manuscripts like *Le militaire philosophe* from perhaps deserved oblivion. He printed two posthumous books by his friend Nicolas Boulanger, *L'Antiquité dévoilée* and *Despotisme oriental*, which brought scientific if rather extravagant speculations to bear on geological and prehistorical records in their search for a natural origin of religion. He entertained, frequently and informally, both in Paris and at his country estate, and encouraged bold talk about the need for strangling the last king in the entrails of the last priest: talented and indefatigable radicals like Raynal, the brothers Naigeon, and Diderot debated the origins of religion, the wicked-

---

[2] Quoted in W. H. Wickwar, *Baron d'Holbach* (1935), 64.
[3] Interestingly enough, Holbach translated two essays that Hume himself had suppressed, one on suicide, the other on the immortality of the soul.

ness of priests, the most efficacious method for disseminating the truth. Their ponderous jokes and rather self-conscious nicknames for one another only show that they took themselves very seriously; their solemnity sometimes borders on the comical. Diderot, a great favorite and vigorous participant in what they liked to call the "synagogue," has left a detailed record of this sociability in his letters to his mistress, and these letters, charming and intimate as they are, lay bare the reason why the Holbachian clique felt it necessary to be so ferocious and so tireless in its impiety: the Christian "mythology," Diderot said, was more productive of crimes than any other.[4] While myth is the negation of rational civilization, criticism (the little group hoped) would be the nemesis of myth: it is well known, Diderot told Sophie Volland, that "religion retreats to the extent that philosophy advances."[5]

Not content with editing, translating, and commissioning propaganda from others, Holbach wrote a large number of polemics himself and disguised them in the approved manner as the productions of writers who had died some time before. In his *Christianisme dévoilé* Holbach appears as Boulanger, who had obligingly died in 1759 and who (it was said in his day and has been said since) did even more for the cause by dying than he had done for it in his lifetime. In the same manner Holbach palmed off his *Esprit de Judaïsme* on Collins and his main work, the *Système de la nature*, on Mirabaud, who had died in 1760, after long and rather suspicious association with scholars like Fréret. When Holbach told the truth, he did so with intent to deceive: in 1772 he published his *Bons-sens* and credited it with sly veracity to the "author of the *Système de la nature*."

It is not necessary to rehearse these writings at length; they all sound in long stretches as though they had been written by Collins or Hume or Voltaire—and in a certain sense, of course, they had. They belong to a prolific family of antireligious diatribes designed to unmask Christianity, trace the "sacred contagion" to its roots—fear and ignorance—ridicule with all possible brutality the figures of Jesus, Mary, and Paul, contrast the

---

[4] Diderot to Grimm (September 1763). *Correspondance*, IV, 260–1.

[5] (October 30, 1759). Ibid., II, 297.

virtues of common sense with the vices of enthusiasm and superstition, and construct a naturalistic philosophy based on the
recognition of the eternal laws of nature. Holbach's work proposes
a consistent, somewhat simplistic, and therefore rather tedious
naturalism which has, one might say, the virtues of its vices; in its
unrelieved seriousness and its courageous confrontation of a
world without God it is not without a certain austere grandeur.

It is notorious that the young Goethe and his fellow students
at Strasbourg were deeply repelled by the *Système de la nature*
and accused Holbach of draining the universe of warmth and
color. One can sympathize with this response: neither the conception nor the tone of the book yields much satisfaction to the poetic
sensibility.[6] But the philosophes themselves, even those critical of
Holbach's ideas, were less inclined than the *Stürmer und Dränger*
to cavil at the frigidity of Holbach's irreligion. They knew that it
concealed a missionary's zeal—they knew it because they shared
it—and that while Holbach lacked Lucretius' poetic powers, he
partook of his polemical passion. They were critical of something
else: his self-assurance. They opposed what he opposed, but while
they agreed with him about what was false, they were by no
means as certain as he was about what was true. After reading the
Système de la nature, d'Alembert told both Voltaire and Frederick
of Prussia that, after all, in metaphysical matters the only reasonable position had been expressed long ago in Montaigne's question,
Que scais-je? And David Hume, who liked Holbach and visited
him faithfully when he was in Paris, had his own private reservations. Gibbon recalled that the "philosophers and Encyclopedists"
of Paris were filled with "intolerant zeal," preached "atheism with
the bigotry of dogmatics," and even "laughed at the skepticism
of Hume."[7] The first time Hume dined at Holbach's, he expressed
some doubt that there were any real atheists in the world. "Look
around you," Holbach replied, "and count the guests." There
were eighteen at table. "Not bad," said Holbach. "I can show you

---

[6] The most lyrical passage in the book is a hymn to nature, but
that is sentimental rather than exalted, and, as we know today,
it was written by Diderot.
[7] *Autobiography*, 145.

fifteen atheists right off. The other three haven't yet made up their minds."[8] Hume was half amused, half annoyed at this dogmatism and thought Holbach in this respect as bad as the Jesuits, but there is no evidence that Hume was distressed. But then Hume was unique.

3. DAVID HUME: THE COMPLETE MODERN PAGAN

I

IN THE RANKS of the philosophic family David Hume occupies a prominent but rather elusive place. His skeptical detachment saved him from Holbach's dogmatism and Lessing's poetic visions; his benign temper, from d'Alembert's irritable sensitivity. He was at ease in his world, far more at ease than most of his fellow belligerents, and, ironically enough, it was precisely his good humor that isolated him—among earnest crusaders the calm cheerful captain is a lonely man.

But Hume was set apart also by the strenuous demands he made on his readers. He was an accomplished craftsman, an elegant and supremely self-conscious writer, a Scot who compiled a list of proscribed Scotticisms and whom Samuel Johnson described, not without a certain mistrust, as French in his style. But for all its verve and clarity his epistemology was extremely disturbing in its implications and therefore hard to assimilate. And his moral program was hard to put into practice precisely because it was on principle so undoctrinaire.

Despite the difficulty of his thought, however, despite the profusion of his output and the range of his interests, neither critic nor admirer—neither Christian nor unbeliever—had the

---

[8] This story has often been told and sounds like a typical eighteenth-century anecdote. But it happens to be true: Diderot, who was there, reports the incident in a letter to Sophie Volland (October 6, 1765). *Correspondance*, V, 133–4.

slightest hesitation in placing Hume among the most radical of radical philosophes. When Boswell and Johnson talked about Hume, they talked about him with an unphilosophical aversion that smacks almost of fear. Johnson liked to denigrate Hume as an unbeliever from petty motives; with uncharacteristic want of generosity he even denied him courage at the thought of death, thereby denying to an infidel what he, a Christian, desperately lacked. After Boswell told him of his interview with the dying Hume, Johnson sneered that Hume "had a vanity in being thought easy."[9] Johnson tried to dispose of Hume's essay on miracles (among Hume's works the one that troubled and threatened him most) in the same way: by blackening Hume's motives. "Hume, and other skeptical innovators," he said, a little inelegantly, "are vain men, and will gratify themselves at any expence. Truth will not afford sufficient food to their vanity; so they have betaken themselves to errour. Truth, Sir, is a cow which will yield such people no more milk, and so they are gone to milk the bull."[1] James Beattie, the Scottish common-sense philosopher whom Johnson much admired, scored points against Hume more extensively argued than Johnson's but no more telling. In his *Essay on the Nature and Immutability of Truth*, a bombastic and meretricious treatise, Beattie imagined he could demolish Hume by putting him in the company of such infidels as Hobbes and Spinoza. When Joshua Reynolds celebrated Beattie's treatise with an allegorical painting, inevitably entitled "The Triumph of Truth," he imitated the tactics of his hero: Reynolds portrays Beattie standing with his book under his arm and watching, with some complacency, as an avenging angel propels three demons to the nether regions. One of these demons is of course the cowering Voltaire, and one of his companions on the descent to hell is David Hume. The philosophes on the Continent and in Britain alike, including those who did not fully understand or wholly agree with Hume, did not think that these two infidels belonged in hell, but they did think that they belonged together. They admired Hume's

---

[9] Boswell, *Life of Johnson* (under September 16, 1777), III, 153.
[1] Ibid. (under July 21, 1763), I, 444.

writings, loved his person, and cherished him as a leader in the common cause.[2]

Not without reason: in his intellectual pedigree, in his intentions, and in his very world view Hume belongs with the philosophes, no matter how amiable his disposition, individual his argumentation, and unexpected his conclusions. Dr. John Gregory, a professor at the University of Edinburgh who professed to detest Hume's philosophy but to like the man, was sure that Hume did "not know & cannot feel the mischief his writings have done,"[3] but Gregory's affection beclouded his judgment. It is true that Hume had marked if grudging respect for man's ability to resist rational argument and had little confidence that the liberation from superstition was either continuous or inevitable. But if the mischief that his writings did was limited, that was not for want of trying. Hume devoted his best energies to elaborating his critique of religion in the hope that some men at least would listen and (I am convinced) to satisfy an irrepressible need of his own. We know that when he was dying, he lamented that he was leaving unfinished his task of freeing his countrymen from "the Christian superstition." But he seems always to have thought the attempt worthwhile. His good temper and his acceptance of the world seduced him neither into blandness nor passivity. When he was in Paris in 1765, he looked back across the Channel and observed that the English were "relapsing fast into the deepest Stupidity, Christianity & Ignorance."[4] This dismayed him, for while he did not expect much from the world, he could not bring himself to be complacent about stupidity or ignorance—that is to say, Christianity. When he wrote about religion, as he often did, he was as implacable as Holbach and as sardonic as Voltaire; his convictions and purposes were theirs, even though his techniques were largely his own.

---

[2] This is true even though Kant apparently never read the *Treatise*, while most of the French philosophes mainly knew Hume's essays against religion and his *History of England*. But these were certainly enough to place him.

[3] Mossner, *Life of Hume*, 580.

[4] Hume to the Rev. Hugh Blair and others, April 6, 1765. *Letters*, I, 498.

II

"There is only one relation to revealed truth: believing it"—thus Kierkegaard epitomized in one striking sentence the essential characteristic of the Christian, and many centuries of apologetic effort. For Hume, of course, the appropriate relation to what passed for revealed truth was not believing it, and his own critical task was to find the reasons why it was unbelievable. He was as ready as the deists and the materialists to retail stories about the crimes of priests and the follies perpetrated by superstitious men, but that was mainly for pleasure or to supply supporting evidence. In the main Hume was concerned with the logic of belief and with its causes rather than with its consequences.

The first and most controversial of Hume's dissections of religion was his essay on miracles: Samuel Johnson was justified in singling it out as Hume's most insidious production. It was also his most characteristic production—in the time and circumstances of its composition, in the manner of its final appearance, in its tone and method of argument.

Hume wrote the essay at a decisive time in his life. It was both symptom and agent of his liberation from his religious heritage, an act which, like many such acts, was an act of aggression. In the late 1730's, recovering from his nervous illness in agreeable retirement at La Flèche, as he walked, debated with the local Jesuits, and wrote his *Treatise of Human Nature*, he discovered an argument which he was confident would rob all reports of miracles of their weight. He wrote it down, cautiously showed it to a few friends, and then, after some reflection, deleted it from the *Treatise:* "I am at present castrating my work, that is, cutting off its nobler parts," he wrote in December 1737, fearful that his reasonings might give offense. He rationalized his prudence (which he himself called his "cowardice") with a characteristic excuse: "I was resolved not to be an enthusiast in philosophy, while I was blaming other enthusiasms."[5] It was only a decade

---

[5] Hume to Henry Home, December 2, 1737. Ibid., I, 25.

later that he felt bold enough to publish the essay as a chapter in his *Enquiry Concerning Human Understanding*.[6]

Its placement (whether its intended placement in the *Treatise* or its final placement in the *Enquiry*) also places it in Hume's philosophy. Hume had, after all, hit upon its argument while he was reasoning his way through severely technical problems involving the meaning of causality, the evidential force of moral assertions, the relation of mathematical to factual statements. And now he incorporated the essay not into a treatise on theology but into an enquiry into the conditions of knowledge. Clearly Hume's argument on miracles was intimately associated with his epistemology; it was an indispensable part of his total world view—the critical counterpart and destructive precondition for his secular philosophy.

The essay itself exhibits this association subtly but unmistakably: it is pervaded by the attitude that marks all his work—his moderate skepticism, his confident philosophical modesty. This very modesty reinforces his strategic position: seeking to prove little, he disproves much. Hume's point is not that reports of miracles can never be sincere. It is not even—despite his own unwavering incredulity—that they can never be true. It is rather that they can never be satisfactorily demonstrated.

Hume constructs this argument through an implicit and devastating syllogism: "A wise man" proportions "his belief to the evidence," that is, he will adhere to a creed only if the evidence for it is adequate. Now, Hume claims, as far as all "popular religions" are concerned (and his phrase is a transparent euphemism for all revealed religions) we "may establish it as a maxim, that no human testimony can have such force as to prove a miracle, and make it a just foundation for any such system of religion."[7] It follows—and Hume is delighted to draw the conclusion in a much-quoted sentence, a sentence that mimics the

---

[6] The book we now know under this title was first published in 1748 under the title *Philosophical Essays Concerning Human Understanding*. The essay on miracles forms chapter X; it is followed by the chapter on "A Particular Providence and of a Future State," which is intimately related to that chapter in theme and argumentation.

[7] *Works*, IV, 89, 105.

Christian fideist to perfection—it follows that "upon the whole, we may conclude, that the Christian Religion not only was at first attended with miracles, but even at this day cannot be believed by any reasonable person without one."[8] The logic of belief was rocky terrain, and it had earlier been explored by the deists and by skeptics like Bayle. Just which miracles to accept was a question that had long divided Protestants from Catholics and created noisy divisions within Protestant sects and among Catholic scholars: erudite theologians had for centuries attempted to sort out the true from the spurious miracle. But all Christians, from the most emancipated to the most superstitious, had insisted on treating at least one class of miracles as a class apart: the miracles of Jesus Christ were privileged evidence, immune from criticism. Now Hume held that these reports must be judged precisely like other historical reports: they are subject to criteria of credibility. In addition to advancing this subversive idea Hume was ready to supply the criteria: "No testimony," he wrote, "is sufficient to establish a miracle, unless the testimony be of such a kind, that its falsehood would be more miraculous, than the fact, which it endeavours to establish."[9]

It is clear that this maxim, which asks men to adopt the most naturalistic explanation compatible with the evidence, owed its persuasiveness in large part to the century in which it was conceived and the public to which it was addressed. This, after all, was the age of modern Christianity, when the natural sciences and their methods were rising in prestige and growing in popularity, and when educated Christians were expressing serious reservations about most tales of prodigies. Even Samuel Johnson subscribed to this part of Hume's case and warned against a blind, childlike credulity. This was the public Hume was trying to persuade when he defined a miracle, accurately but in shrewdly chosen words, as a "violation of the laws of nature."[1]

Hume recognized that his syllogism, damaging as it was, did

---

[8] Ibid., 108.
[9] Ibid., 94.
[1] Ibid., 93. In a footnote to this page, Hume is even more explicit: "A miracle may be accurately defined, *a transgression of a law of nature by a particular volition of the Deity, or by the interposition of some invisible agent.*"

no more than to make miracles appear implausible. Therefore, to convert implausibility to impossibility—or rather (to do justice to his mocking, triumphant modesty) into extreme improbability —Hume turned to psychology and history for supporting evidence. It is a pervasive trait of human nature, he said, to seek out the unusual and to indulge the agreeable passion "of surprize and wonder": thus psychology, by uncovering an all too human propensity, yielded reasons for the popularity of miracles while it undermined their credibility. History, the temporal arena of miracles, performed the same function in Hume's argument. Critically read, history discloses that miracles have been attested by few men of "good-sense, education, and learning" and have almost all been disputed by eyewitnesses. Besides, they have usually been reported among "ignorant and barbarous nations," and they have declined, perhaps not so strangely, in our time.[2] To the surprise of the Reverend William Adams, who had written a courteous refutation of Hume's essay—to his surprise, perhaps, but not to ours, for Hume's assault was deadly—Samuel Johnson was prepared to use all methods, elevated or mean, to discredit his formidable, seductive antagonist: "ADAMS. 'You would not jostle a chimney-sweeper.' JOHNSON. 'Yes, Sir, if it were necessary to jostle him *down*.' "[3] Whoever might later jostle Hume down—largely by taking seriously his ironic fideism and proclaiming the continuing miracle of Christian revelation—it is safe to say that it was not Samuel Johnson.

III

In the essay on miracles Hume had speculated on man's passion for "surprize and wonder"; in the "Natural History of

---

[2] Ibid., 94, 96.
[3] Boswell, *Life of Johnson* (under March 20, 1776), II, 443. Johnson believed that "Christian revelation" was proved not "by miracles alone, but as connected with prophecies." (Under September 22, 1777). Ibid., III, 188. But this thrust, designed to refute Hume, misses the point that Hume had explicitly extended his argument against miracles to the prophecies: "What we have said of miracles may be applied," Hume insists, "without any variation, to prophecies." *Works*, IV, 108.

Religion" he extended his psychological epigrams into a sustained indictment. He was entering an arena crowded with philosophes, all busy seeking the reasons why men believed in supernatural beings, in the efficacy of charms, prayers, and certain ritual actions. It was, after all, obvious—pleasantly obvious, for it provided the philosophes with agreeable employment—that most men in all ages had entertained religious beliefs. To a critical age this fact required explanation.

The philosophes were here, as so often, the quick-witted and enterprising disciples of classical antiquity. Poets like Euhemerus and Lucretius, philosophers like Plato and the Stoics, had offered some startling conjectures about the origin of myths, and these were enlisted in the eighteenth century, complete with modern psychological terminology, in the indictment of Christianity. Some—the Euhemerists—had speculated that the gods had originally been powerful heroes or beneficent kings apotheosized by their worshipful admirers to serve as models for all mankind; others argued that the gods were intelligences animating, and represented by, heavenly bodies. A third school, following the Stoics, interpreted the gods as allegories, personifications of virtues, vices, and moral lessons. And finally there was the psychological theory, which explained religion as the product of men's fears and hopes, as their desire for immortality, their longing to recapture childlike innocence, their dread of the unknown.

For obvious reasons the philosophes preferred the last of these schools of thought to the others: the psychological theory alone was, as it were, denominationally neutral, as critical of Christianity as of pagan cults. This was a psychological age, an age when philosophy had turned from metaphysics to epistemology, when men's motives were being scrutinized with new vigor and new methods. And besides, this theory offered the philosophes some scientific support for their stock villains—priests, who, in league with kings, imposed fables on the credulous masses for their power and profit. This imposture theory was a variant of the psychological theory with a rationalist touch: it explained the enthusiasm of the many but postulated at the same time the rationality of the few through the ages. This explanation of religion did not go unchallenged; its rivals had their supporters. But, usually accompanied by the imposture theory, it held the field in the Enlightenment. It had been articulately propounded by Bayle and Fontenelle and diffused throughout Europe by their readers. For disciples of Lucretius it was wholly appropriate: it was, of all theories, the one most devastating to accepted beliefs.

Hume's "Natural History of Religion" is an elegant representative of this dominant school of thought.[4] Its very title is provocative: to examine the "natural" history of religion is to treat the sacred as a social phenomenon like any other and to strip it of the privileged status on which its prestige depends. True, in the very first paragraph Hume disclaims any intention of questioning the foundation of religion "in reason"—that, he says, is secure and beyond cavil. He proposes to inquire solely into the "origin" of religion "in human nature." But to outraged clergymen this was a meaningless distinction, a transparent veil designed to cover—and to reveal—the most unmeasured impieties. After all, Hume had made it evident in other writings, and, subtly, in the *Natural History* itself, that he did not really believe religion to have any rational foundations at all. Besides, if religion could be traced to its origins in human nature, it was degraded into a product of fancy, a mere projection, and its claim to objective veracity was gone. Bishop Warburton, who dogged Hume for the right reasons but with inadequate weapons, detected Hume's intentions with a perception sharpened by dislike: the design of the *Natural History*, he wrote darkly, is "to establish *naturalism*, a species of atheism, instead of religion."[5] No reader of Hume's essay will be inclined to discount Warburton's suspicion.

Warburton's anger, matched by the anger of pious readers everywhere, was easy to understand. The essay, Warburton said in exasperation, taught Bolingbroke's atheism "without Bolingbroke's abusive language."[6] This, of course, was precisely Hume's strength: no philosophe was more skillful than he in clothing his passion against religion in the vocabulary of logic and supporting

---

[4] With his characteristic lack of dogmatism, Hume does not rely on the psychological theory alone, but also uses the Euhemerist theory.

[5] Mossner: *Life of Hume,* 325.

[6] Ibid.

it with judicious arguments—and in the process converting that passion into science. Hume's method in the "Natural History" is therefore as remarkable and as destructive as his conclusion. In his search for the roots of religion he combines induction with deduction, information supplied by the records of the past and the reports of travelers (history and rather rudimentary anthropology) with speculative psychology. His hypothetical history of man's intellectual development is thus imaginative but not fanciful, inventive but realistic.

As Hume interpreted the evidence, man's belief in an "invisible, intelligent power" was widely diffused but by no means universal—some nations had no religion, and each religious nation differed from its neighbor in its worship and pious sentiments. It followed (and this was, for Hume, a weighty consideration) that the religious emotion was founded in deep-rooted but merely "secondary" passions: men's fundamental instincts, the instincts that call forth self-love, sexual desire, love of offspring, were so uniform that they could not possibly be responsible for a phenomenon as varied as religion. Rather, Hume argued, religion arose "from a concern with regard to the events of life, and from the incessant hopes and fears, which actuate the human mind."[7] Confronted by a monstrous birth, the uncertainty of the seasons, by storms and a myriad of unexplained and seemingly inexplicable events, primitive man oriented himself in his world by inventing a large number of special, parochial deities: Hesiod had listed thirty thousand of them, and even they were not enough. Antiquity (Hume records in a footnote worthy of Gibbon) even produced a god of sneezing, and "the province of copulation, suitably to the importance and dignity of it, was divided among several deities."[8] To barbarians the ordinary was extraordinary and required extraordinary explanations: "The anxious concern for happiness, the dread of future misery, the terror of death, the thirst of revenge, the appetite for food and other necessaries" create hopes and, more significantly, arouse fears, and so "men scrutinize, with a trembling curiosity, the course of future causes,

---

[7] "Natural History of Religion," *Works,* IV, 315.
[8] Ibid., 315 *n.*

and examine the various and contrary events of human life. And in this disordered scene, with eyes still more disordered and astonished, they see the first obscure traces of divinity."[9]

The first religion of mankind, therefore, was inevitably polytheism; monotheism was a late invention, the fruit of abstract thinking. Precisely for the same reason the first gods were anthropomorphic, projections with the features and characters of men; while the theists' conception of a god liberated from his human limitations, pure, remote, and worthy to be worshipped by a rational man, was the reward of maturity and cultivation. "We may as reasonably imagine, that men inhabited palaces before huts and cottages, or studied geometry before agriculture; as assert that the Deity appeared to them a pure spirit, omniscient, omnipotent, and omnipresent, before he was apprehended to be a powerful, though limited being, with human passions and appetites, limbs and organs."[1]

The religions prevalent in modern times were thus the offspring of a long development, a development that Hume refused to call progress. In the first place, Hume considered the evolution of belief from polytheism to rigorous monotheism as neither straightforward nor inevitable: the history of religion, in fact, was the history of "flux and reflux." Men "have a natural tendency to rise from idolatry to theism, and to sink again from theism into idolatry."[2] Especially the "vulgar," the poor and the illiterate are incapable of the logical and ethical effort required to sustain monotheism, and they generally indulge in a covert idolatry. This is evident in all religions, but especially so in Roman Catholicism: with its saints, its Virgin Mary, its superstitious doctrine of the Real Presence—with all this, Catholicism was a polytheistic superstition masquerading as a monotheistic creed.[3] Besides, the advan-

---

[9] Ibid., 317.
[1] Ibid., 311.
[2] Ibid., 334.
[3] Hume was not above repeating blasphemous and scurrilous stories against things sacred to Roman Catholics: "One day, a priest, it is said, gave inadvertently, instead of the sacrament, a counter, which had by accident fallen among the holy wafers. The communicant waited patiently for some time, expecting it would dissolve on his tongue: But finding that it still remained

tages of monotheism were doubtful: polytheism was crude in its teachings but tolerant in its practice, while monotheism, for all the nobility of its theology, easily turned to persecution to enforce its claim to a monopoly of the truth. But both had unwholesome, odious social consequences: they produced degrading self-contempt or crime.

The consequence implied in Hume's sociology of religion was that all houses of faith were houses of infection and that a rational man must escape, after exposing, the squabbles of theologians. That, indeed, was Hume's celebrated conclusion, much quoted but worth quoting once again: "The whole is a riddle, an aenigma, an inexplicable mystery. Doubt, uncertainty, suspense of judgment appear the only result of our most accurate scrutiny, concerning this subject. But such is the frailty of human reason, and such the irresistible contagion of opinion, that even this deliberate doubt could scarcely be upheld; did we not enlarge our view, and opposing one species of superstition to another, set them a quarrelling; while we ourselves, during their fury and contention, happily make our escape into the calm, though obscure regions of philosophy."[4] Thus Hume, disciple of Cicero and Bayle, having made his case, took to his heels.

IV

What he left behind was an ambiguous legacy. In two strategically placed passages, one in the first paragraph, the other in the last section of the "Natural History," Hume professes to subscribe to the argument from design: "A purpose," he writes, "an intention, a design is evident in every thing"; and again, "the

---

entire, he took it off. *I wish,* cried he to the priest, *you have not committed some mistake: I wish you had not given me God the Father: He is so hard and tough there is no swallowing him.*" Ibid., 343. That this is an old anti-Catholic story is evident from Voltaire's English notebook where it is recorded, in English, with some additional piquant detail. See *Notebooks,* 36.
[4] *Works,* IV, 363.

whole frame of nature bespeaks an intelligent author."[5] These categorical pronouncements read like generous, even decisive concessions to the proponents of natural theology, whether of the Christian or the deist persuasion. But in fact Hume found these concessions easy to grant because they were empty; they were rhetorical flourishes, nothing more. Warburton, speaking for a whole school of divines who would not trust Hume in anything, found these sentences offensively tepid and suspiciously rare, and he denounced them as veils for atheism. And Voltaire, speaking for the deists, was disturbed by Hume's hypothetical history of religion: a "philosophical scholar," he wrote in his *Dictionnaire philosophique*, courteously but firmly, "one of the profoundest metaphysicians of our day offers some strong reasons for believing that polytheism was man's first religion"; but, he rejoined, "I dare think, on the contrary, that people began by acknowledging a single God, and that later human weakness led to the adoption of several."[6] As Voltaire recognized, Hume's supposition that polytheism was the primitive religion was a threat to the deists' rather complacent epistemology, which held that man recognized by instinct, or at least with ease, the traces of God in the glorious workings of nature.

Hume's "Natural History of Religion" thus offered formidable if largely implicit objections to the deist position. They were brought into the open by Hume's *Dialogues Concerning Natural Religion*, which demolished that position completely. To be sure, the demolition was an academic affair: the *Dialogues* was not published until 1779, three years after Hume's and one year after Voltaire's death. By that time deism was no longer fashionable even among philosophes, although the argument from design persisted, a stubborn, troublesome ghost, into the nineteenth century. Hume's *Dialogues* is therefore less a lethal weapon than a death certificate.

Whatever its final cultural meaning, the *Dialogues Concerning Natural Religion* was the book that Hume cherished most. It had a poignant history, as pathetic as that of a posthumous child.

[5] Ibid., 309, 361.
[6] "Religion," *Philosophical Dictionary*, II, 438.

Hume had largely completed the manuscript by 1751, revised it carefully, and circulated it among a few chosen friends, including Adam Smith. They urged him to suppress it, and reluctantly, comically proclaiming himself the victim of tyranny, Hume acceded. But he was too fond of the *Dialogues* to permit it to remain in permanent obscurity: in the last months of his life he took precise, almost pedantic measures to guarantee its publication after his death. His solicitude was appropriate to its object: the *Dialogues* is Hume's "Dictionnaire philosophique," the epitome of his life's work; his "Nathan der Weise," dramatizing his deepest convictions, a work of literary art impressive even to those who reject its conclusions; his "Neveu de Rameau," a conscious, free imitation of a favorite classic, Cicero's *De natura deorum*, which makes its point as forcibly by the resonances evoked by its borrowings as by its departures from the model. It is almost unique in the literature of theological disputation in its felicitous marriage of form and substance—a drama, cerebral but exciting.

Hume knew that it was a drama he was writing: in 1751 he asked a correspondent to supply him with arguments that would strengthen one of the protagonists whom, he feared, he had neglected. About ten years before, he had criticized his beloved Cicero for reserving the good speeches in his dialogues to representatives of his own point of view.[7] This was not a mistake Hume proposed to make.

He did not make it. Hume is Philo, described in a brief prologue as the representative of "careless skepticism," but the reader may well be unaware—in fact, most readers have been unaware—of this identity.[8] And the dialogue is a genuine con-

---

[7] "Of the Rise and Progress of the Arts and Sciences," *Works*, III, 188–9.

[8] I must confess that in view of Hume's perfectly explicit and perfectly consistent philosophy, and in view of numerous allusions to the *Dialogues* in his letters, the uncertainty over just who represents Hume is a mystery to me. In his fine critical edition of the *Dialogues*, Norman Kemp Smith lists a number of distinguished philosophers who have debated the question, but his own position is perfectly straightforward: "Philo, from start to finish, represents Hume; and . . . Cleanthes can be regarded as Hume's mouthpiece only in those passages in which he is explicitly agreeing with Philo, or in those other

frontation of ideas; Hume gave it life, provided it with tension and verisimilitude, by having his three protagonists shift alliances in accord with the requirements of the debate and by distributing intelligent, convincing arguments among his speakers. To be sure, Demea, who stands for "rigid inflexible orthodoxy," is less important than the other two, since Philo-Hume's real antagonist is Cleanthes, a man of "accurate philosophical turn," who upholds the claims of rationalist natural religion and defends the argument from design; and it is Cleanthes, who sounds rather like Bishop Butler or like Voltaire in his constructive religious phase, on whom Hume expended his most anxious literary care. But while Demea is largely a foil, he is not a fool: his main argument for religion—man's invincible ignorance and perpetual misery—is the pious version of Hume's skepticism, and Hume must have delighted in having a "rigid" Christian pronounce his own most skeptical reservations.

Philo, however, is Hume's favorite, and Hume endows Philo's speeches with so much energy and subtlety, so much wit, that any summary must do them violence. Philo sets his antagonists against one another: he compels Cleanthes, who deduces God from the glory of the world and the possibilities of man and who draws analogies that reduce the deity to little more than human stature, to contend against Demea, who proves God's existence from man's misery and who denies that any epithet applicable to man is applicable to His august majesty. But this sort of con-

---

passages in which, while refuting Demea, he is also being used to prepare the way for one or other of Philo's independent conclusions." *Hume's Dialogues Concerning Natural Religion,* 59. I find myself in complete agreement with this position, and want to add only that on occasion the fideist Demea speaks for Hume, in a caricatured version of Hume's skepticism. One reason for all the difficulties is doubtless the final statement in the work, made by Pamphilius, who acts as a sort of *rapporteur,* and who concludes: "I cannot but think, that Philo's principles are more probable than Demea's; but that those of Cleanthes approach still nearer to the truth." (*Dialogues,* 228). But this is not to be taken as a statement of Hume's own conclusion; it is an imitation of the last sentence of Cicero's *De natura deorum*—and, I think, a delicious bit of irony behind which the elusive David Hume escapes once again.

frontation, which suggests the inconclusiveness of all theological proofs of God, is, while cunning, also a very old technique, and consequently Philo is not content to depend on it alone. He does more: he deprecates the intuition to which Cleanthes appeals as a will-o'-the-wisp, an unreliable guide to religious truth; and he tries to demolish the popular argument from analogy. Analogy, he suggests reasonably enough, can never provide a strong proof for anything; little can be legitimately inferred from apparent, and even from real, similarities. Indeed, the particular analogy on which proponents of natural religion generally rest their case is exceptionally feeble: we may concede that a watch implies a watchmaker—and it does so only because we have no experience of a watch that was not produced by a human artificer—but this does not mean that the universe necessarily implies a creator. A watch is not unique; the universe is.[9] Besides, the universe re-

---

[9] In his essay on "A Particular Providence," Hume cogently criticizes the argument from analogy with a chain of reasoning worth recording here. (1) "When we infer any particular cause from an effect, we must proportion the one to the other, and can never be allowed to ascribe to the cause any qualities, but what are exactly sufficient to produce the effect. A body of ten ounces raised in any scale may serve as a proof, that the counter-balancing weight exceeds ten ounces; but can never afford a reason that it exceeds a hundred." (2) "In works of *human* art and contrivance, it is allowable to advance from the effect to the cause, and returning back from the cause, to form new inferences concerning the effect. . . . But what is the foundation of this method of reasoning? Plainly this; that man is a being, whom we know by experience, whose motives and designs we are acquainted with, and whose projects and inclinations have a certain connexion and coherence, according to the laws which nature has established for the government of such a creature." But "the Deity is known to us only by his productions, and is a single being in the universe, not comprehended under any species or genus, from whose experienced attributes or qualities we can by analogy, infer any attribute or quality to him." The famous deduction based on seeing a single footprint in the sand and inferring from it a man, does not work successfully with the Deity: "The print of a foot in the sand can only prove, when considered alone, that there was some figure adapted to it, by which it was produced: But the print of a human foot proves likewise, from our other experience, that there was probably another foot, which also left its impression, though effaced by time or other accidents." *Works,* IV, 112, 118–19.

sembles a watch or a house far less than it does an animal or a vegetable: Philo mischievously proposes that the Creator might be a vegetable rather than a craftsman. Nor is this all: if we observe the universe without our ordinary preconceptions, we may well conclude that the intelligence that created it was little better than an amateurish bungler who, for all we know, made and discarded other worlds before he settled on this one.[1]

Little, very little, remains of the "religious hypothesis" after this assault. No matter how rationally argued or energetically defended, it is unconvincing and probably untrue. "*To know God*," concludes Philo, significantly quoting Seneca, "*is to worship him. All other worship is indeed absurd, superstitious, and even impious.*"[2] A reasonable man can do no more than to give a philosopher's calm recognition to the possibility that "*the cause or causes of order in the universe probably bear some remote analogy to human intelligence*"; but nothing follows from that recognition except the pleasure of modest, rational assent to a sensible proposition.[3] It warrants no belief in extraordinary tales, justifies no prayer and no church, and does not even provide guidance to conduct. For Hume religion has lost all specificity and all authority; it is no more than a dim, meaningless, and unwelcome shadow on the face of reason.

V

Near the end of the *Dialogues Concerning Natural Religion*, the protagonist of orthodoxy, pleased up to that moment with Philo's critique of the argument from design, suddenly wakes up to the true import of the skeptic's line of reasoning: "Hold! Hold! cried Demea: Whither does your imagination hurry you? I joined in alliance with you, in order to prove the incomprehensible

---

[1] This imaginative speculation was a favorite with the philosophes: in his short story, *Songe de Platon*, Voltaire supposes that while God himself is perfect, he left the creation of this world to a lesser angel who made a poor job of it. Hence the presence, indeed prevalence, of evil.

[2] *Dialogues Concerning Natural Religion*, 226.

[3] Ibid., 227.

nature of the divine Being, and refute the principles of Cleanthes, who would measure every thing by a human rule and standard. But I now find you running into all the topics of the greatest libertines and infidels; and betraying that holy cause, which you seemingly espoused. Are you secretly, then, a more dangerous enemy than Cleanthes himself?"[4] Not long after this outburst Demea rather ostentatiously leaves the field, while Cleanthes and Philo—deist and skeptic, who are, significantly enough, close friends—stay to conclude the discussion.

It is a superbly dramatic and profoundly touching moment: it shows, perhaps more clearly than any other passage of his work that I know, why Hume was at the same time the most isolated and the most representative of philosophes: he was simply the purest, most modern specimen of the little flock. Demea's vehement rhetorical question is far from naïve: as we have seen over and over again, in the great combat, anti-Christian deist and secular skeptic were allies, champions of criticism in deadly combat with the mythopoeic mentality. Even the modern rationalist Christian—if that is whom Cleanthes represents—could be enlisted in the struggle against myth. But within the army of the Enlightenment it was true that Philo was indeed a more dangerous enemy to religion than Cleanthes; with all their secularism, all their incredulity, the deists retained some rhetorical and even some emotional connections with the "religious hypothesis." In Hume the last threads are torn; his philosophy embodies the dialectic of the Enlightenment at its most ruthless—it appeals to antiquity at its most disenchanted, its tension with Christianity is wholly unappeasable at all points, and it pursues modernity most courageously.

For David Hume was both courageous and modern; he understood the implications of his philosophy and did not shrink from them. He was so courageous that he did not have to insist on his courage; he followed his thinking where it led him, and he provided through his own life (and, Samuel Johnson to the contrary, in the face of death) a pagan ideal to which many aspired but which few realized. He was willing to live with uncertainty,

---

[4] Ibid., 212-13.

with no supernatural justifications, no complete explanations, no promise of permanent stability, with guides of merely probable validity; and what is more, he lived in his world without complaining, a cheerful Stoic. Hume, therefore, more decisively than many of his brethren in the Enlightenment, stands at the threshold of modernity and exhibits its risks and its possibilities. Without melodrama but with the sober eloquence one would expect from an accomplished classicist, Hume makes plain that since God is silent, man is his own master: he must live in a disenchanted world, submit everything to criticism, and make his own way.

BIBLIOGRAPHICAL
ESSAY

OVERTURE

The Enlightenment In Its World

GENERAL

I have designed this bibliographical essay to serve two purposes: to record my intellectual debts and to give reasons for my positions. This book, after all, ranges widely, through many centuries and many areas, and again and again I found myself compelled to choose among interpretations, to settle as best as I could controversies over the character of a man or the meaning of a movement. In this essay I indicate the grounds of my choices.

The literature on the Enlightenment (to say nothing of the literature on antiquity, the Middle Ages, and the Renaissance, with which I am especially concerned in the opening chapters) is so enormous and is growing so rapidly that it would be folly for me to attempt to supply a complete bibliography or even to list all the works I have consulted. I shall concentrate on the works I have found most useful, most stimulating, or most perverse. In this respect, as in others, this is a highly personal essay.

My greatest debt is to the writings of Ernst Cassirer both in philosophy and in intellectual history. His central distinction between critical and mythical thinking lies at the heart of my interpretation. Much of Cassirer's work is an elaboration of this distinction. He has stated it systematically in his *The Philosophy of Symbolic Forms*, 3 vols. (1923, 1925, 1929; tr. Ralph Manheim, 1953, 1955, 1957),[1] especially in Volume Two, *Mythical Think-*

---

[1] Since it took me a half dozen years and more to write this book, I have had occasion to use a number of works both in the original and in English translation. In this essay I have adopted the following convention with such works: if a translation is readily available I give the title in English but list first the original date of publication and then, after the name of the translator, the date of publication in translation.

ing. In *Language and Myth* (1925; tr. Susan Langer, 1946) Cassirer summarizes his argument in brief compass, while late in life, haunted by the spectre of totalitarianism, he turned in his *The Myth of the State* (1944) to the resurgence of mythical thinking in our time and to its origins. Among his articles on symbolic form perhaps the most important are "Der Begriff der symbolischen Form im Aufbau der Geisteswissenschaften," *Warburg Vorträge, 1921–1922* (1923), 11–39, and "Das Symbolproblem und seine Stellung im System der Philosophie," *Zeitschrift für Aesthetik und allgemeine Kunstwissenschaft,* XXI (1927), 295–312. Cassirer's writings on intellectual history, which range through all of Western history from the ancient Greeks on,[2] are stimulating and profound: they attempt to penetrate beyond the variety of an epoch, beyond its contradictions, to its intellectual core—and they generally succeed. Taken together, they form an impressive account of what I have called "the fortunes of criticism."

Cassirer's philosophical and historical achievement has been intensively examined in *The Philosophy of Ernst Cassirer,* ed. P. A. Schilpp (1949). Among the articles in that volume the most significant, for me at least, are: Carl H. Hamburg, "Cassirer's Conception of Philosophy," 73–119; Robert S. Hartmann, "Cassirer's Theory of Language and Myth," 379–400; Wilbur M. Urban, "Cassirer's Philosophy of Language," 401–41; and—an important critique—John Herman Randall, Jr., "Cassirer's Theory of History as Illustrated in His Treatment of Renaissance Thought," 689–728. Charles W. Hendel, one of the first in this country to cherish Cassirer as man and as philosopher, has an appreciative and helpful "Introduction to the Philosophy of Symbolic Forms," *Philosophy of Symbolic Forms,* I, *Language,* 1–65. While Cassirer's perception of cultural forms as approximating either the ideal type of myth or that of criticism can be traced back to the Critical philosophy of Kant, to some characteristically pregnant asides of Goethe, to Hegel's grasp of the coherence that underlies the surface confusions of culture, and to some

---

[2] See below, pp. 426, 438–9, 441, 445–6, 464, 509, 519, 522–3, 527, 533.

brilliant, maddeningly casual witticisms of Heine, that perception is of course implicit in many modern attempts to divide Western history into periods. And it was made explicit (though not given the philosophical and psychological grounding it received at the hands of Cassirer) by Lord Acton: "Two great principles divide the world, and contend for the mastery, antiquity and the Middle Ages. These are the two civilizations that have preceded us, the two elements of which our's is composed. All political as well as religious questions reduce themselves practically to this. This is the great dualism that runs through our society." (This note, written down around 1859, deserves to be read in full. It was first printed by Herbert Butterfield, *Man On His Past: The Study of the History of Historical Scholarship* [1955], 212–14.)

For a decisive part of his life Cassirer was associated with the Warburg Institute in Hamburg, and his publications in its series of *Vorträge* and *Studien* reflected his reading in the superb Warburg library (a unique collection of writings on primitive cultures, linguistics, and art history), and his publications in turn left their mark on his colleagues there. I have followed Cassirer, as it were, into the Warburg library, and my book, I think, shows this: I am greatly indebted to the scholarly and delightful monographs on intellectual history and art history by Erwin Panofsky, Fritz Saxl, Jean Seznec, and Aby Warburg himself.[3]

I owe a great debt of a similar kind to the writings of Erich Auerbach, with their penetrating analysis of the deeper meaning of style and their distinction—in many ways analogous to Cassirer's central distinction—between realistic and "figural" perceptions of reality. It was in 1954 that I first read Auerbach's

---

[3] I shall refer to these publications in their appropriate places below, especially in chapters II, IV, and V, since most of them deal with the transmission of classical ideas through the Middle Ages into the Renaissance. Panofsky's compact and difficult essay *Idea: Ein Beitrag zur Begriffsgeschichte der älteren Kunsttheorie* (2nd edn., 1960; an Eng. tr. is in preparation), which takes the Platonic concept of "Idea" from Plato to Dürer, embodies the contribution of the Warburg Institute to perfection. It is explicitly indebted to Cassirer's work. Cassirer's association with this Institute has been remembered in a short, moving reminiscence by Fritz Saxl, *Philosophy of Ernst Cassirer*, 47-51.

celebrated *Mimesis: The Representation of Reality in Western Literature* (1946; tr. Willard R. Trask, 1953), which moves with sovereign ease through Western literature from Homer to Virginia Woolf. It was a revelation to me, and I returned to it often while I was writing my own book. Auerbach's long essay "Figura" (1944), (tr. by Ralph Manheim in *Scenes from the Drama of European Literature: Six Essays*, 1959), is a superb analysis of the figural view.[4]

As the book makes clear, I trust, it is my conviction that it was the age of the Enlightenment, not the age of the Reformation and Renaissance, that may be called the first truly modern century. I was delighted to find support for this conviction in a persuasive essay by Johan Huizinga, "Naturbild und Geschichtsbild im achtzehnten Jahrhundert," *Parerga* (1945), and in the magisterial if still controversial work of Ernst Troeltsch, particularly his *The Social Teachings of the Christian Churches*, 2 vols. (1911; tr. Olive Wyon, 1931), especially chapter III, and his *Protestantism and Progress: A Historical Study of the Relation of Protestantism to the Modern World* (1906; tr. W. Montgomery, 1912).

The Enlightenment has not lacked interpreters or expositors. To my mind, the best remains Ernst Cassirer; his *The Philosophy of the Enlightenment* (1932; tr. F. C. A. Koelln and J. P. Pettegrove, 1951) is remarkable especially for its lucid presentation of the function of "reason" in the eighteenth century. Each page has its suggestive idea. Yet the critics of the book (including Alfred Cobban in various bibliographical references; Kingsley B. Price, "Cassirer and the Enlightenment," *Journal of the History of Ideas*, XVIII; 1 [January 1957], 101–12; and Herbert Dieckmann, "On Interpretations of the Eighteenth Century," *Modern Language Quarterly*, XV: 4 [December 1954], 295–311) have rightly objected that Cassirer sees the Enlightenment in too orderly a fashion and imposes on it a dialectical progression culminating in his beloved Kantian Critical Philosophy. In addition, and in consequence of this preference, I think, Cassirer undervalues the French materialists and the skeptical contribution of Hume. Still, the book remains a classic in its field.

---

[4] I shall return to Auerbach. See below, pp. 495, 501.

Fritz Valjavec, *Geschichte der abendländischen Aufklärung* (1961), follows a chronological arrangement; it ranges widely and is especially useful on the prehistory of the Enlightenment, but it suffers from excessive compression. I have already polemicized at some length (and with not much effect) against Becker's charming and still influential attempt to assimilate the Enlightenment to its medieval past (*The Heavenly City of the Eighteenth Century Philosophers* [1932]), in "Carl Becker's Heavenly City" (1957), reprinted in my *The Party of Humanity: Essays in the French Enlightenment* (1954). Furio Diaz, *Filosofia e politica nel settecento francese* (1962), concentrates on France; it is exhaustive and the best recent Italian study of the *siècle des lumières* that I have seen. Daniel Mornet, *La Pensée française au XVIIIe siècle* (10th edn., 1962), is, as might be expected, a thoroughly well informed but not very venturesome presentation. Louis Réau, *L'Europe française au siècle des lumières* (1938), has offered an interpretation popular chiefly in France for its insistence on French intellectual supremacy over Europe; there is something in it but, as I hope my book makes plain, not so much as Réau thinks. Werner Krauss, *Die französische Aufklärung im Spiegel der deutschen Literatur des 18ten Jahrhunderts* (1963), is a series of discrete (and, what with its Marxism, inevitably discreet) essays of some interest. Basil Willey's *The Eighteenth Century Background: Studies on the Idea of Nature in the Thought of the Period* (1940) does not claim to be a complete interpretation but concentrates, as its subtitle shows, on the conception of nature, and consequently it is helpful. Arthur O. Lovejoy's celebrated essays in the history of ideas have an analytical aim that differs from my own attempt to write what I have called "the social history of ideas," which, while it values ideas for their own sake, seeks to understand them in their social context. Still, I have found Lovejoy's work immensely useful to me; I am indebted especially to his *The Great Chain of Being: A Study of the History of an Idea* (1936), which explicates his method and aim in the opening chapter and exemplifies it in the others. Chapters VI to IX deal in illuminating fashion with the "chain of being" in the eighteenth century. Lester G. Crocker's massive and erudite attempt to convert the history of ethics in eighteenth-century France into a prologue to the Marquis de Sade and a prefiguration of "the crisis of our time" strikes me as modish, wildly unhistorical and, as the Marxists used to say, "objectively reactionary." See my review of Crocker's *An Age of Crisis: Man and World in Eighteenth Century Thought* (1959) in *The Journal of Modern History*, XXXIII: 2 (June 1961), 174–177. Crocker's second volume, *Nature and Culture: Ethical Thought in the French Enlightenment* (1963), seems to take at least passing notice of criticisms only to reject them; still, the book is more restrained and useful than the first.[5] Paul Hazard has written two famous books on the period, both distinguished by almost legendary erudition and disfigured by vivid writing. *La Crise de la conscience européenne, 1680–1715,* 3 vols. (1934), makes a strong but to my mind not wholly convincing case for a profound change in the "European mind" at the end of the seventeenth century, but convincing or not, the book is extremely informative. *La Pensée européenne au XVIIIe siècle: de Montesquieu à Lessing* (1946), is comprehensive and ambitious, but, as Herbert Dieckmann has observed in a telling criticism ("Religiöse and metaphysische Elemente im Denken der Aufklärung," *Wort und Text: Festschrift für Fritz Schalk,* ed. Harri Meier [1963], 334–354, esp. 340 *n.*), Hazard's scheme is a rather mechanical plotting of the curve of cultural development and does not genuinely unify its period.

Other general surveys include Alfred Cobban, *In Search of Humanity: The Role of the Enlightenment in Modern History* (1960), which, though brief (only the two central sections of the book deal with the thought of the Enlightenment itself), is always sensible, vigorous, and dependable. Preserved Smith, *A History of Modern Culture,* Volume II: *The Enlightenment, 1687–1776* (1934), may be conventional but is marked by Smith's customary intelligence. George R. Havens, *The Age of Ideas: From Reaction to Revolution in Eighteenth-Century France* (1955), is really a series of careful scholarly biographies of the major French philosophes; it is reliable but a little adulatory and

---

[5] At this point I gratefully record my agreement with John Weightman's short but impressive attack on the modern cult of de Sade in *The New York Review of Books,* V: 2 (August 26, 1965), 5–6, which appeared after I had completed this book and was compiling this bibliographical essay.

rather indifferent to the historical context in which the Enlightenment evolved. Herbert Dieckmann's articles are more far-reaching in their significance than their brevity might suggest. In addition to "Religiöse und metaphysische Elemente," just cited, I should especially note "Themes and Structure of the Enlightenment" in *Essays in Comparative Literature* (1961). Among the popular works attempting to make the Enlightenment palatable to the general public, one of the most unfortunate specimens I have encountered is Sir Harold Nicolson's collection of stale anecdotes and outdated opinions, *The Age of Reason: The Eighteenth Century in Reason and Violence* (1961).

Crocker is not the only one to see the Enlightenment as the cursed mother of our cursed time. Other specimens of this genre include Louis I. Bredvold's sulphurous essay *The Brave New World of the Enlightenment* (1961), which belongs to the literature of denunciation, not of analysis; it is interesting mainly as a symptom of what happens if a sound scholar (and we owe to Mr. Bredvold some excellent studies of Dryden and Augustan literature) yields to tendentiousness. More serious is the work of J. L. Talmon, who is now in process of writing a voluminous history of what he calls "totalitarian democracy." The first volume, *The Origins of Totalitarian Democracy* (1952), deals with the Enlightenment and ends with the French Revolution. It is deeply sincere and is animated by love of freedom and decency, but its account of the philosophes as ruthless phantasts depends ultimately on a misreading of enlightened thought and on the careful selection of quotations, and on the author's dismaying failure to examine the historical effect of ideas. Even I do not think the Enlightenment was perfect; but as I have said elsewhere, it deserves better than to be held responsible for ideas it did not hold and consequences it did not produce.

I. THE LITTLE FLOCK OF PHILOSOPHES

My collective portrait of the philosophic family in this section rests, of course, on the entirety of my reading, both in the philosophes' writings (especially their letters) and in books about them. I shall, therefore, once again make no attempt to be exhaustive. The most continuously revealing collection of philosophes' letters, which, as its editor proudly but justly proclaims, reflects not merely a lively mind but a whole century, is Theodore Besterman's edition of Voltaire's *Correspondence*, 103 volumes (1953–1965). Georges Roth's edition of Diderot's *Correspondance*, 12 volumes so far, down to 1773 (1955–) is less extensive but in its own lively way as rewarding as Besterman's edition. It is possible, for example, to draw a portrait of Damilaville, the hanger-on par excellence, by following him through the pages of this *Correspondance* (see especially III, 23, 53–54). David Hume's fine *Letters*, ed. J. Y. T. Greig, 2 vols. (1932), can be supplemented by *New Letters of David Hume*, ed. Raymond Klibansky and Ernest C. Mossner (1955). I should note that I owe the idea of "family" as I use it in this book to a suggestion in Wittgenstein's *Tractatus*.

The philosophes' sociability is inevitably a prominent theme in many of the biographies; while much work still needs to be done on the international network of advanced thinking, there are some special studies that deserve to be mentioned here. Henry Grey Graham, *Scottish Men of Letters in the Eighteenth Century* (1901), contains faithful sketches of leading figures like Adam Smith, David Hume, Adam Ferguson, and others. It should be supplemented by Gladys Bryson, *Man and Society: The Scottish Inquiry in the Eighteenth Century* (1945), which connects the history of ideas with the history of sociability in continuously interesting fashion. E. C. Mossner, *The Life of David Hume* (1954), is the standard biography—exhaustive, scholarly, filled with material not readily available elsewhere, filled with everything, in fact, but life. Mossner's earlier *The Forgotten Hume: Le bon David* (1943) lays some troublesome ghosts. Leaving aside a detailed bibliographical consideration of Hume until later (as I shall leave aside details on the others), the writings of Norman Kemp Smith on Hume are simply indispensable, here and elsewhere. His *The Philosophy of David Hume: A Critical Study of its Origins and Central Doctrines* (1941) and his critical edition of *Hume's Dialogues Concerning Natural Religion* (2nd edn., 1947), though technical, throw much light on the Scottish Enlightenment. For Ferguson, see Bryson, the biography by William C. Lehmann, *Adam Ferguson and the Beginnings of Modern Sociology* (1930), and Herta Helena Jogland, *Ursprünge und Grundlagen der Soziologie bei Adam Ferguson* (1959), which, though rather solemn, has some pages on social life. Adam Smith deserves a full modern biography; no one was more intelligent and more centrally placed than he. His *Theory of Moral Sentiments* (1759, 6th edn., 1790) and his *Lectures on Rhetoric and Belles Lettres*, ed. John M. Lothian (1963), display the breadth and depth of his classical erudition. John Rae, *Life of Adam Smith* (1895), is thorough and remains useful, but it is now old; W. R. Scott, *Adam Smith as Student and Professor* (1937), for one, supplies much new material and some new interpretation. Glenn R. Morrow, *The Ethical and Economic Theories of Adam Smith: A Study in the Social Philosophy of the Eighteenth Century* (1923) is indispensable; it delightfully disposes of the Germanic invention of an "Adam Smith problem," Smith's supposed inconsistency between *The Wealth of Nations* and the *Theory of Moral Sentiments*. C. R. Fay, *Adam Smith and the Scotland of his Day* (1956), should also be consulted; and see the suggestive essays by John Maurice Clark and others, *Adam Smith, 1776–1926* (1928), talks delivered on the sesquicentennial of *The Wealth of Nations*, and rich in material on the rest of Adam Smith's system. For Millar, consult the study by William C. Lehmann: *John Millar of Glasgow, 1735–1801: His Life and Thought and His Contribution to Sociological Analysis* (1960). There is a good biography of the father of the Scottish common-sense school, who helped to shape Hume's thought as well: W. R. Scott, *Francis Hutcheson: His Life, Teaching and Position in the History of Philosophy* (1900).

The English Enlightenment was far less well organized than its Scottish counterpart. Sir Leslie Stephen's majestic *English Thought in the Eighteenth Century*, 2 vols. (1876) is dated in many of its firmly expressed judgments, and it is primarily an analysis of ideas, but it throws light on the polemical situation. Stephen's charming essay, *English Literature and Society in the XVIIIth Century* (1907), addresses itself more directly to the social bearing of literature. The first chapter of Élie Halévy's

masterly *The Growth of Philosophic Radicalism*, 3 vols. (1901-4;
tr. Mary Morris, 1928), has some valuable hints on the evolution
of ideas. A. S. Turberville, ed., *Johnson's England: An Account
of the Life and Manners of his Age*, 2 vols. (1933), is a scattered
collection of essays on social history, but J. L. and Barbara Ham-
mond, "Poverty, Crime, Philanthropy," I, 300-35, and R. W.
Chapman, "Authors and Booksellers," II, 310-30, give information
on the social, intellectual and professional environment of advanced English thought. Similar information is conveyed attractively and in most useful detail in Alexandre Beljame, *Men of
Letters and the English Public in the XVIIIth Century* (2nd edn.,
1897; tr. E. O. Lorimer and corrected in some details with notes
by Bonamy Dobrée, 1948). Still, much of the book is out of date.
It may be supplemented and corrected by such recent studies as
A. S. Collins, *Authorship in the Days of Johnson* (1927); J. M.
Saunders, *The Profession of English Letters* (1964), especially
chapters VI and VII; and J. A. Cochrane, *Dr. Johnson's Printer:
The Life of William Strahan* (1964), which, for all its concentration on a single publisher, touches on many interesting men and
ideas.

   If there is no single comprehensive study on the "English
Enlightenment," as there are numerous studies on the French
siècle des lumières and the German *Aufklärung*, this may have a
simple cause: more than elsewhere the boundaries between rationalist Anglicanism, Arminian dissent, tepid Christianity, and
outright deism are so thin and so porous that it is nearly impossible to discern a distinct *grouping* of men, even if there is, as I
should insist there is, a distinct *set of ideas* that makes for an
identifiable anti-Christian English Enlightenment. Jeremy Bentham, the arch-philosophe, who took eighteenth-century radical
ideas into the nineteenth, remains the center of controversy. His
eccentricities of style and behavior, the doubtful consequences of
some of his reformist notions (especially in the light of our
century, deeply suspicious as it is of planners), make such controversy inevitable. For a powerfully argued case against Bentham,
resting its argument on Bentham's model prison, the Panopticon,
see Gertrude Himmelfarb, "The Haunted House of Jeremy Bentham," in *Ideas in History: Essays in Honor of Louis Gottschalk*

(1965), 199–238. For all the persuasiveness of that essay, I find Mary P. Mack, *Jeremy Bentham: An Odyssey of Ideas* (1963), a comprehensive analysis of his life and ideas down to 1792, more congenial to my own rather sympathetic view of Bentham: the eccentricities should be read as eccentricities, and in the context of their day, rather than as foreshadowings of modern totalitarian social engineering. C. W. Everett, *The Education of Jeremy Bentham* (1931), is favorable to Bentham, as is Élie Halévy's *Growth of Philosophic Radicalism*. Still, what we need is a full interpretation, setting the man and his ideas into his time. Meanwhile, we can glean a great deal about his beneficent, but also sometimes annoying, influence on English life from S. E. Finer, *The Life and Times of Sir Edwin Chadwick* (1952), an excellent study of a powerful Benthamite.

Gibbon has been well served, best by himself. His *Autobiography* (I have used the recent edition by Dero A. Saunders [1961]) is, in a word, indispensable. The best biography is by David M. Low: *Edward Gibbon, 1737–1794* (1937), which uses Gibbon's diaries to advantage and corrects many common errors, including the famous error introduced into history by Gibbon himself—the claim that his father, anxious over the survival of the patronymic, named all his sons "Edward." G. M. Young, *Gibbon* (1932), short and without apparatus, is graceful and says the essential things as well as anyone could say them. Gibbon's correspondence has been well edited by J. E. Norton: *Letters*, 3 vols. (1956). We also have excellent editions of his journals: by David M. Low, *Gibbon's Journal to January 23, 1763* (n.d., 1929), with a helpful introduction; and Georges A. Bonnard, *Gibbon's Journey from Geneva to Rome* (n. d., 1961).

The amicable and stimulating intellectual intercourse of French philosophes with one another and with congenial foreigners is reflected perhaps most vividly in Diderot's correspondence; fortunately for the historian, Diderot and his mistress Sophie Volland were often separated, and so Diderot would sit down after an evening of talk and reproduce it in his long letters to her. The international and indeed cosmopolitan quality of this company appears in the same source: thus (to give but one example), on October 6, 1765, Holbach had at dinner Diderot, David

Hume, the abbé Raynal, Horace Walpole, and Allan Ramsay (*Correspondance*, V, 137). Important as this intercourse was, it has received much anecdotal but not enough sociological attention. Elinor G. Barber, *The Bourgeoisie in 18th Century France* (1955), includes writers in her analysis of the social status and aspirations of the bourgeoisie; Lucien Brunel, *Les Philosophes et l'académie française au dix-huitième siècle* (1884), considers the philosophes in a sensitive area of their experience and struggle for power. The well-known essay by Marius Roustan, *Les Philosophes et la société française au XVIIIᵉ siècle* (1906), insists on the effectiveness of the philosophes in the age of Louis XV, revising earlier critiques like Charles Aubertin, *L'Esprit publique au XVIIIᵉ siécle* (1873), and Felix Rocquain, *L'Esprit révolutionnaire avant la révolution* (1878), which both claimed that the philosophes were either powerless or, if influential, a force for disruption. Joseph Delort, *Histoire de la détention des philosophes et des gens de lettres à la Bastille et à Vincennes*, 3 vols. (1829), though sometimes untrustworthy, presents abundant material toward an understanding of the radicals' fears. Far better is Maurice Pellisson, *Les Hommes de lettres au XVIIIᵉ siècle* (1911), which follows the philosophes through their relations with the crown, the aristocracy, publishers, and the book-buying public, in style, and with valuable documentation. Jacques Proust, *Diderot et l'Encyclopédie* (1962), has a superb set of chapters (I–IV) on the situation of the writer that goes far beyond Diderot himself. David T. Pottinger, *The French Book Trade in the Ancien Régime, 1500–1789* (1958), concentrates, as its title indicates, on the publishing industry, its successes and failures, its supporters, customers, and victims, but it is also extremely informative on styles of thinking and communication through three centuries. Douglas H. Gordon and Norman L. Torrey show in their *The Censoring of Diderot's Encyclopédie and the Re-established Text* (1947) what a writer might have to go through in the Old Regime, but also what a greedy and fearful publisher was ready to do to his authors for the sake of security and sales. Daniel Mornet, *Les Origines intellectuelles de la révolution française* (1947), is justly celebrated for its researches into eighteenth-century libraries, famous and obscure, designed to discover the evolution of philosophic thought, but its discrimination among ideas is relatively crude. Kingsley Martin, *French Liberal Thought in the Eighteenth Century: A Study of Political Ideas from Bayle to Condorcet* (1929), is an attractive conspectus, intelligent and well written, but not wholly satisfactory on any single thinker. Ira O. Wade, *The Clandestine Organization and Diffusion of Philosophic Ideas in France from 1700 to 1750* (1938), is a valuable catalogue with some fascinating quotations from little-known manuscripts. For the philosophes' relations with authority, and their humorlessness, see Pierre Grosclaude's lengthy biography of an admirable public servant, *Malesherbes: Témoin et interprète de son temps* (1961). Much incidental light is shed on the philosophes by the much-used, perhaps overused, journals of E.-J.-F. Barbier, *Journal historique et anecdotique du règne de Louis XV*, ed. A. de la Villegille, 4 vols. (1847–56), and Mathieu Marais, *Journal et mémoires sur la régence et le règne de Louis XV*, ed. M. de Lescure, 4 vols. (1863–8). Grimm's literary correspondence, which retailed gossip, book reviews, and political and social news all over Europe to select correspondents, is opinionated and limited but fascinating and, if used carefully, extremely useful; the best edition is by Maurice Tourneux, *Correspondance littéraire, philosophique et critique de Grimm, Diderot, etc.*, 16 volumes (1877–82). Finally I should make special mention of *Considérations sur les mœurs de ce siècle* (1750), a brilliant essay by Charles Pinot-Duclos, himself a philosophe and a first-rate observer of his society and his times.

While Gustave Desnoiresterres's exhaustive biography of Voltaire, *Voltaire et la société française au XVIIIᵉ siècle*, 8 vols. (1867–76), is now badly out of date, it is still a mine of information on the Old Regime. It should be read in conjunction with Gustave Lanson, *Voltaire* (1906), which, though sixty years old, is marvelous in its economy and its discrimination; it is even a prophetic book in its anticipation of later scholarship. Of the dozens of special studies devoted to placing Voltaire in his world, the most significant are Ira O. Wade, *Voltaire et madame du Châtelet* (1941) and *Studies on Voltaire, with Some Unpublished Papers of madame du Châtelet* (1947), which together have compelled a re-evaluation of Voltaire's Cirey period and recognition of his seriousness as a scholar in the midst of polite society. Paul Chaponnière, *Voltaire chez les Calvinistes* (2nd edn., 1936), does for Voltaire at Geneva what Wade does for Voltaire at Cirey: it shows him at work. In my own essays on Voltaire in *The Party of Humanity* I have tried to do the same thing: to show Voltaire the hard-headed intellectual, alert to his environment and practical in his ideas. My *Voltaire's Politics: The Poet as Realist* (1959) is a full-length study of his tough-minded political thought. Since that book contains an exhaustive bibliographical essay (pp. 355–95) I need not multiply bibliographical indications here.

Diderot studies are booming in France and even more so in the United States. The best biographical and analytical study, which carries his life down to 1759, is Arthur M. Wilson's *Diderot: the Testing Years* (1957), rich in wisdom and amply supplied with bibliographical information in the notes. It may now be supplemented by Proust's thorough *Diderot et l'Encyclopédie* and Herbert Dieckmann's sensitive reading, *Cinq leçons sur Diderot* (1959). A few years before, Dieckmann reported on his discovery of Diderot papers, in his *Inventaire du Fonds Vandeul, et inédits de Diderot* (1951), which has greatly enriched us. Among dozens of other books, some of which I shall refer to later, I want to single out Jean Thomas, *L'Humanisme de Diderot* (2nd edn., 1938). The standard biography of Montesquieu, detailed, filled with new material, wholly reliable if perhaps a little unadventurous in the realm of ideas, is Robert Shackleton, *Montesquieu: A Critical Biography* (1961). Franz Neumann's fine "Introduction" to Montesquieu's *Spirit of the Laws* (1945) discusses not merely Montesquieu's political ideas and environment but his views of life, death, love, and happiness. For Holbach, see Pierre Naville, *D'Holbach* (1943), and W. H. Wickwar, *Baron d'Holbach: A Prelude to the French Revolution* (1935), an economical, straightforward account well equipped with apt quotations. Ronald Grimsley has recently published an intelligent and quite straightforward biography of *Jean D'Alembert, 1717–83* (1962), which is certainly much the best thing in English. Léon Cahen's *Condorcet et la révolution française* (1904), old as it is, is preferable to J. Salwyn Shapiro's well-meaning, accurate, but extremely Whiggish *Condorcet and the Rise of Liberalism* (1934).

Douglas Dakin has done justice to Turgot in his *Turgot and the Ancien Regime in France* (1939), which fully surveys his life and gives adequate space to Turgot's career as an Intendant; its chapters on his philosophy deserve to be expanded. For the radical ex-Jesuit Raynal there is Hans Wolpe's discriminating *Raynal et sa machine de guerre* (1957), more the biography of Raynal's book than of his life. Vauvenargues, the delicate psychologist of the passions, is well studied in May Wallas, *Luc de Clapiers, marquis de Vauvenargues* (1928). The old biography of Helvétius by A. Keim, *Helvétius, sa vie et son oeuvre* (1907), remains useful; the recent study by D. W. Smith, *Helvétius: A Study in Persecution* (1965), retells the familiar but critical event in the French Enlightenment—the storm over Helvétius's *De l'Esprit*—in satisfactory detail. For La Mettrie, see R. Boissier, *La Mettrie, médecin, pamphlétaire et philosophe (1709-1751)* (1931), and Aram Vartanian's long "Introduction" to his critical edition of La Mettrie's *L'Homme machine: A Study in the Origins of an Idea* (1960). While Diderot's biographers necessarily mention him, Grimm needs more study; Edmond Scherer, *Melchior Grimm* (1887), is now very old-fashioned. The irascible sculptor Falconet, another friend of Diderot's, has had some interesting attention recently, most notably in Herbert Dieckmann and Jean Seznec's edition, *Diderot et Falconet correspondance* (1959), which introduces a fascinating exchange. It may be read in full scattered through Roth's edition of Diderot's *Correspondance*. See also Herbert Dieckmann and Jean Seznec, "The Horse of Marcus Aurelius: A Controversy between Diderot and Falconet," *Warburg Journal*, XV (1952), 198–228; and the thoughtful Columbia dissertation by Anne Betty Weinshenker, "The Writings of Falconet, *Sculpteur-Philosophe*" (1962), which will, I trust, be published. S. Lenel, *Un Homme de lettres au XVIIIe siècle: Marmontel* (1902), is now inadequate; a useful book could be written on him. Another, even more important philosophe who calls for further attention is Condillac. Georges Le Roy has provided his edition of the *Œuvres philosophiques* of Condillac, 3 vols. (1947–51), with a brief, well-informed introduction; he has also published a specialized monograph on *La Psychologie de Condillac* (1937). For Maupertuis we have the fine detailed biography and analysis by Pierre Brunet, *Maupertuis*, 2 vols. (1929), which can now be supplemented with M. L. Dufrency's long article, "Maupertuis et le progrès scientifique," *VS*, XXV (1963), 519–87. Another celebrated scientist-philosophe of the age, Buffon, has been surprisingly neglected. Jean Pivoteau has supplied his edition of Buffon's *Œuvres philosophiques* (1954) with a short introduction, and he appears, of course, in histories of biology. Fortunately Jacques Roger's massive *Les Sciences de la vie dans la pensée française du XVIIIᵉ siècle* (1963) makes Buffon one of the protagonists of his long, fascinating story. See also Otis Fellows, "Buffon's Place in the Enlightenment," *VS*, XXV (1963), 603–29. Pierre Brunet, *La vie et l'œuvre de Clairaut (1713–1765)* (1952) is a remarkable short essay on a philosophic scientist of great importance. Nancy Mitford's sprightly *Voltaire in Love* (1957) does better than its title would suggest; it gives some interesting insights into the scientific as well as amorous life of the French Enlightenment.

The literature on Rousseau, that transplanted but ever-loyal Genevan, rivals that on Voltaire. Despite F. C. Green, *Jean-Jacques Rousseau: A Study of His Life and Writings* (1955), we still need a good comprehensive biography of Rousseau in English; Green's book is sensitive and especially helpful on Rousseau's literary works but rather skimpy and old-fashioned on his political and educational ideas. There are some fine analyses, however, in biographical form: Charles William Hendel, *Jean-Jacques Rousseau, Moralist*, 2 vols. (1934), which treats Rousseau's moral ideas, especially his "Platonism," in chronological order; and Ronald Grimsley, *Jean-Jacques Rousseau: A Study in Self-Awareness* (1961), a penetrating, sometimes superbly revealing study of Rousseau's psychological development. Grimsley's book, although it reaches similar conclusions, was conceived and written largely independently of Jean Starobinski's brilliant *Jean-Jacques Rousseau: la transparence et l'obstacle* (1958), a book I have already advertised enthusiastically in my *The Party of Humanity*, 232–8, and which ought to be available in English. Jack Howard Broome's recent *Rousseau: A Study of His Thought* (1963) is in the modern tradition—an attempt to see the man and his work as a whole. Broome's Rousseau is primarily the artist. Ernst Cassirer,

The Question of Jean-Jacques Rousseau (1932; tr. Peter Gay, 1954), seeks to make sense of the whole man and to relate him to his writings—to discover, as Cassirer usually tried to do, an inner unity behind superficial contradictions. There are other good books on Rousseau, but I may refer the reader to my "Reading about Rousseau," *The Party of Humanity*, 211–61, a glorified bibliography in the shape of a speculative essay.

There has been a good deal of writing on the German Enlightenment, most of it, not surprisingly, by Germans but much of it marred by a Germanic infatuation with its *Klassiker*, especially Goethe and Schiller, who are supposed to have "overcome" the "shallow" *Aufklärung*. This easy verdict makes sense only if all sorts of shallow ideas are first collected and then taken as the exclusive and characteristic property of the *Aufklärer*. A wider view would suggest not merely the intellectual depths of the German Enlightenment but also the debt of Goethe to it; surely an *Aufklärung* that could boast, among others, a Lessing, Lichtenberg, and Kant is hardly shallow. There is an angry but justified assault on the prevailing Romantic condemnation of the Enlightenment in Hans Wolffheim, *Wielands Begriff der Humanität* (1949), which, in addition to serving its polemical purposes, serves to rescue Wieland from a variety of charges. Cassirer's *Philosophy of the Enlightenment* is happily free from the Romantic bias (there is, indeed, a mild reproof to that bias in the Preface), but the book, as I have noted, tends toward a different fault, an over-estimation of the German *Aufklärer* at the expense of the French and the British.

Among the valuable writings on the subject, Wilhelm Dilthey's magnificent essays continue to be pre-eminent; Dilthey had a special affection for the eighteenth century, and his writings move beyond their subject to a general point of view.[6] Hans M. Wolff, *Die Weltanschauung der deutschen Aufklärung in geschichtlicher Entwicklung* (2nd edn., 1963) is a splendid essay in social history which fills in the background for Wieland and Lessing. Karl Aner has examined theological figures of the period

---

[6] I shall advert to Dilthey's writing individually in their appropriate places; see below, pp. 441, 445, 452, 484, 522.

with impressive learning and, especially for a German dealing with this sensitive subject, remarkable lack of awe for the giants of the classical period. I have therefore leaned heavily on Aner's *Die Theologie der Lessingzeit* (1929). Cay Ludwig Georg Conrad, baron von Brockdorff, *Die deutsche Aufklärungsphilosophie* (1926), is a useful compendium, typical of several such. W. H. Bruford, *Germany in the Eighteenth Century: The Social Background of the Literary Revival* (1935), is with justice the standard work on the social framework of the age of the *Aufklärung*, but it is worth recording Bruford's debt (and my debt as well) to that remarkable pioneer in social history, Karl Biedermann, *Deutschland im achtzehnten Jahrhundert*, 2 vols. in 4 (1854–80). Bruford's recent *Culture and Society in Classical Weimar, 1775–1806* (1962) is well informed and interesting though hardly profound; it has a very useful appendix on "Culture and Related Ideas from Cicero to Herder" (pp. 432–40). Max von Boehn, *Deutschland im 18ten Jahrhundert*, 2 vols. (1921), is chatty and illustrated yet serious. Hajo Holborn's pages on the period in his *A History of Modern Germany, 1648–1840* (1964) are characteristic of this wide-ranging professional historian. But I am most deeply indebted to Holborn's masterly article "Der deutsche Idealismus in sozialgeschichtlicher Beleuchtung," *Historische Zeitschrift*, CLXXIV (1952), 359–84, which tracks the birth of the unpolitical German back to the eighteenth century. Albert Köster, *Die deutsche Literatur der Aufklärungszeit* (1925), is a thoughtful essay—balanced, well-written, economical. It seems that there are some useful books on the period after all.

The most comprehensive study of Lessing remains Erich Schmidt, *Lessing: Geschichte seines Lebens und seiner Schriften*, 2 vols. (4th edn., 1923); it is stodgy but comprehensive. (See the vigorous attack by the Marxist Franz Mehring, *Die Lessing-Legende: Zur Geschichte und Kritik des preussischen Despotismus und der klassischen Literatur* [1893], which long enjoyed wide popularity and which scores some shrewd hits.) Benno von Wiese, *Lessing: Dichtung, Aesthetik, Philosophie* (1931), is a suggestive essay; H. B. Garland, *Lessing: The Founder of Modern German Literature* (1937), is the best biography in English—which is, unfortunately, not saying a great deal. The most interesting interpretation of Lessing's life and place in the Enlightenment is Wilhelm Dilthey, "Gotthold Ephraim Lessing," in *Das Erlebnis und die Dichtung* (edn. 1912). Ernst Cassirer's *Kants Leben und Lehre* (1918) is characteristic of the biographer: it is thorough, penetrating, uncompromising; the best English life is by A. D. Lindsay (1934), a satisfying blend of biography and analysis. After a long eclipse Wieland is finally coming back into his own; Friedrich Sengle, *Christoph Martin Wieland* (1949), is a model biography: severely chronological and continuously interpretative, based on a complete grasp of the sources and a sympathetic understanding of Wieland's place in German culture. Georg Christoph Wolffheim's *Wielands Begriff der Humanität* is, as I have said, an excellent book. Another valuable appreciation is by Fritz Martini, "Wieland und das 18te Jahrhundert," in *Festschrift für Paul Kluckhohn und Hermann Schneider* (1948), 243–65. Lichtenberg has been intelligently interpreted in the Introduction to Franz H. Mautner and Henry Hatfield, ed., *The Lichtenberg Reader* (1959), and in J. P. Stern, *Lichtenberg: A Doctrine of Scattered Occasions* (1959), a felicitous mixture of biography, analysis, and collection of texts. Moses Mendelssohn, Lessing's friend, appears in all the Lessing biographies; there are several biographies and monographs devoted explicitly to him, none satisfactory. Much the best is by Moritz Brasch, in his edition of Moses Mendelssohn's *Schriften zur Philosophie, Aesthetik und Apologie*, 2 vols. (1880). Friedrich Nicolai, who has not had a good press, is valued, and for the right reasons, by Karl Aner, *Der Aufklärer, Friedrich Nicolai* (1912). If the Italian *illuministi* are being discovered, much of the credit must go to Franco Venturi's pioneering collection of documents and comprehensive monographs. See especially his *Les Aventures et la pensée d'un idéologue piémontais, Delmazzo Francesco Vasco* (1940), and *Illuministi Italiani*, Vol. III (1958), on the northern Italians and Vol. V (1962), on the southern Italians, both with valuable biographical notes and bibliographies. Franco Valsecchi, *L'Italia nel settecento dal 1714 al 1788* (1959), is an enormous history of eighteenth-century Italy. Mario Fubini has edited an interesting collection of essays, *La cultura illuminista in Italia* (1957). Beccaria, the most famous and the greatest of the *illuministi*, has been rather shockingly neglected, even in Italy. But see the pages in Marcello T. Maestro, *Voltaire and Beccaria as Reformers of Criminal Law* (1942), a typical dissertation—honest, correct, and unimaginative; Carlo Antonio Vianello, *La vita e l'opere di Cesare Beccaria* (1938), and the first essay in Coleman Phillipson, *Three Criminal Law Reformers: Beccaria, Bentham, Romilly* (1923). Since the enormous correspondence of the brothers Verri is now available in full, a good modern study of these Milanese *illuministi* would be most welcome. Another Italian philosophe in search of a good study is the international wit, classicist, economist, and humanitarian, the abbé Galiani. He has been appreciated best as an economist. Of the general studies devoted to his life (mostly in France) and ideas (mostly in French) the most satisfactory (or least unsatisfactory) is Luigi Magnotti, *L'Abbé Ferdinand Galiani, sa philanthropie et ses rapports avec la France* (1933). I have also found Eric W. Cochrane's analysis of *Tradition and Enlightenment in the Tuscan Academies, 1690–1800* (1961) quite useful.

The American Enlightenment has been rather on the sidelines in this book; it has a place in it, for the Enlightenment was a Western movement, but I did not wish to overload the book—or myself, for that matter—with material, and I have thus drawn my examples primarily from Europe. As historians—even European historians—know, American history is being abundantly studied and studied well. Louis B. Wright, *The Cultural Life of the American Colonies, 1607–1763* (1957), is strikingly successful in summarizing a vast amount of material in a small amount of space without sounding like a catalogue; the bibliographical essay is full and dependable. The leading American philosophes have been fortunate in their biographers. For Benjamin Franklin, see the authoritative biography by Carl Van Doren, *Benjamin Franklin* (1938), and the splendidly concise *Benjamin Franklin: A Biographical Sketch* (1946) by Carl Becker. John William Ward's provocative essay, "Who Was Benjamin Franklin?" *American Scholar*, XXXII (Autumn 1963), 541–53, does justice to the complexity of a man too long seen through the eyes of Max Weber and D. H. Lawrence as a depressing Philistine. The most significant biography of Jefferson, amidst a crowded array, is Dumas Malone's admiring but judicious and scholarly *Jefferson and His*

Time, 3 vols. so far (1948, 1951, 1962). I have also depended on Nathan Schachner, *Thomas Jefferson, A Biography* (1951). The papers of Franklin and Jefferson are now being sumptuously edited, the first by Leonard W. Labaree and others, the second by Julian P. Boyd and associates, and I have especially relied on the early volumes. The only recent study of James Logan, Quaker, bibliophile, statesman, and intellectual, is Frederick B. Tolles, *James Logan and the Culture of Provincial America* (1957), which does not exhaust its subject. Zoltàn Haraszti, *John Adams and the Prophets of Progress* (1952), offers a fascinating glimpse into the interaction of European and American thought—it collects Adams's crusty and perceptive marginalia on his copies of the writings of Rousseau, Voltaire, and other philosophes.

The international intellectual relations among the philosophes form a fascinating chapter in the history of ideas—they are, of course, discussed in many of the intellectual biographies I have already cited.[7] An important start in comparative literature was made long ago by J. Texte, *J.-J. Rousseau et les origines du cosmopolitisme littéraire* (1895), but his book should be supplemented by F. C. Green, *Minuet: A Critical Survey of French and English Literary Ideas in the Eighteenth Century* (1935). There are many books on the impact of England on the Continent. G. Zart, *Einfluss der englischen Philosophen seit Bacon auf die deutsche Philosophie des 18. Jahrhunderts* (1881), is mainly a list; clearly more work is desirable. Adam Ferguson's influence on the Continent is glancingly mentioned in Jogland, *Grundlagen der Soziologie bei Adam Ferguson;* while Robert P. Wolff has studied the important question of "Kant's Debt to Hume via Beattie," *JHI,* XXI: 1 (January–March 1960), 117–23. For the subtle penetration of Newtonian ideas into France, see the magisterial study by Pierre Brunet, *L'Introduction des théories de Newton en France au XVIIIe siècle* (1931). Unfortunately volume II, which was to take Newton in France beyond 1734, never appeared. Hélène Metzger's *Newton, Stahl, Boerhaave et la doctrine chimique* (1930) is excellent on the transmission of scientific

---

[7] For the influence on the Enlightenment of such seventeenth-cent. philosophers as Spinoza and Locke, see below, pp. 531–3.

ideas. R. L. Cru, *Diderot as a Disciple of English Thought* (1913), is a useful specialized monograph, as is Norman Torrey's informative *Voltaire and the English Deists* (1930). The question of Voltaire's debt to England—it is important, for Voltaire was the leading Anglomaniac on the Continent and a leading retailer of English ideas—remains undecided. John Morley's claim in his *Voltaire* (1872) that England turned Voltaire the poet into a philosopher can no longer be sustained. Fernand Baldensperger, "Voltaire Anglophile avant son séjour d'Angleterre," *Revue de littérature comparée*, IX (1929), 25–61, shows the beginnings of his Anglomania; Gabriel Bonno's scholarly *La Constitution britannique devant l'opinion française de la Paix d'Utrecht aux Lettres philosophiques* (1931), Edouard Sonet's sound but not very original *Voltaire et l'influence anglaise* (1926), and Sir Gavin de Beer's invaluable collection of reports, which any future biographer will have to consult ("Voltaire's British Visitors," *VS*, IV [1957], 7–136; "Supplement," *VS*, X [1959], 425–38, and [with André Michel Rousseau], "Supplement," *VS*, XVIII [1961], 237–62), show the persistence of that Anglomania. W. H. Barber, "Voltaire and Quakerism: Enlightenment and the Inner Light," *VS*, XXIV (1963), 81–109, sheds new light on Voltaire's affectionate, amused, but slightly contemptuous attitude toward the English and American Quakers. Edith Philips studies Voltaire and other observers of the Quakers in *The Good Quaker in French Legend* (1932). Norman Torrey's "Bolingbroke and Voltaire, a fictitious influence," *PMLA*, XLII (1927), 788–97, does not seem wholly convincing to me in the light of other biographical data. I have dealt with Voltaire's debt to England in my *Voltaire's Politics*, especially in chapter II (see also the Bibliographical Essay there, 366–72); Shackleton's *Montesquieu* deals briefly but authoritatively with Montesquieu's indebtedness to English ideas.

Shackleton raises another, equally interesting matter: the influence of French ideas abroad. Montesquieu, as he shows, had loyal disciples in Italy. In general the diffusion of French ideas in Italy is treated rather sketchily by Henri Bedarida and Paul Hazard, *L'Influence française en Italie au dix-huitième siècle* (1934). Ronald Grimsley demonstrates d'Alembert's influence on the Continent in his *D'Alembert*, while Gladys Bryson demonstrates it for Scotland in her *Man and Society*. Wolff's *Weltan-schauung der deutschen Aufklärung* has some excellent pages on English and French influence on German thought; the first of Ernst Cassirer's two essays collected in *Rousseau, Kant, Goethe* (tr. James Gutmann, Paul Oskar Kristeller, and John Hermann Randall, Jr., 1945), "Kant and Rousseau," seeks to show in much detail what is only hinted at in his *The Question of Jean-Jacques Rousseau;* for all the importance of his findings, some modifications and refinements seem possible. Roland Mortier, *Diderot en Allemagne (1750–1850)* (1954), is an exhaustive and indispensable analysis of Diderot's many followers—including Goethe—in Germany. H. A. Korff, *Voltaire im literarischen Deutschland im XVIIIten Jahrhundert*, 2 vols. (1918), has a magnificent subject and in general does it justice, but the force of his work is weakened by his prejudice against Voltaire. Harcourt Brown has an interesting essay on "Maupertuis *philosophe:* Enlightenment and the Berlin Academy," *VS*, XXIV (1963), 255–69. Dilthey's old essays on the derivative Prussian Enlightenment remain as fresh as ever; see especially his "Friedrich der Grosse und die deutsche Aufklärung" (1901), in *Gesammelte Schriften*, III (1927), 81–205. All the *Aufklärer* were Anglomaniacs, as their letters—or, with Lichtenberg, who actually visited England, their travel reports— prove. Lichtenberg's dependence on English ideas is discussed in Mautner and Hatfield, *Lichtenberg Reader*, and Stern, *Lichtenberg;* for Wieland, see, as always, Sengle's biography; for Lessing, in addition to the studies listed, see Curtis C. D. Vail, *Lessing's Relation to the English Language and Literature* (1936), a painstaking survey of Lessing's ability to read English and of the English works he read. (Alexandre Aronson, *Lessing et les classiques français* [1935], does a similar job for the French language and letters.) There are even two helpful articles on the English reading done by Lessing's father, which suggest the ease with which ideas traveled in the late seventeenth and early eighteenth centuries: L. M. Price, "English Theological Works in Pastor Lessing's Library," *The Journal of English and Germanic Philology*, LIII (1954), 76–80; and Curtis C. D. Vail, "Pastor Lessing's Knowledge of English," *Germanic Review*, XX (1945), 35–46. A powerful English influence on German thought was that of Shaftesbury, and it has been thoroughly studied. See, among others, Ernst Cassirer, "Shaftesbury und die Renaissance des Platonismus in England," *Warburg Vorträge, 1930–1931* (1932), 136–55, and Cassirer, "Schiller und Shaftesbury," *The Publications of the English Goethe Society*, N.S. XI (1935), 37–59. Shaftesbury's influence on France, an interesting subject, is examined in Dorothy B. Schlegel, *Shaftesbury and the French Deists* (1956).

The influence of the European Enlightenment on America remains a matter of sustained, even angry, controversy; it is connected, unfortunately but inevitably, with the whole vexed question of the American character. It is not, I trust, my professional deformation as a European historian that leads me to reject the exceptionalist thesis as stated most extravagantly by Daniel J. Boorstin, first in *The Genius of American Politics* (1953) and later in *The Americans: The Colonial Experience* (1958) and again in those extraordinary essays, at once anti-European and anti-intellectual, collected in *America and the Image of Europe: Reflections on American Thought* (1960). Louis Hartz divorces America from Europe, more reasonably and less cheerfully than Boorstin, in his influential *The Liberal Tradition in America* (1955). Clearly the question is (at least in reasonable hands) a matter of emphasis: there are some unique features of the American experience—properly located in space and time, since that experience changes—as there are features that the Americans have in common with their European mother cultures. In my view not even Bernard Bailyn's discriminating formulas in his article "Political Experience and Enlightenment Ideas in Eighteenth-Century America," *AHR*, LXVII: 2 (January 1962), 339–51, wholly explain the relationship. In any event, I am convinced that the American Enlightenment was not (as Boorstin puts it in a peculiarly unhappy phrase) a "myth" but a reality, and that it arose in close conjunction with European philosophical as well as political developments.[8] See Chinard's *Adams*, Van Doren's *Franklin*, and Malone's *Jefferson*—cited above—and a scattering of other writ-

---

[8] The subject is too complex to permit of an easy solution or to profit from a brief discussion. I hope to deal with aspects of it in a book on historians in colonial America which I am now finishing.

ings: Bernard Bailyn's excellent analysis of the Americans' reading of British radicals, in his "General Introduction: The Transforming Radicalism of the American Revolution," *Pamphlets of the American Revolution, 1750–1776* (1965), 3–202, and the many informative footnotes; and George Sensabaugh, *Milton in Early America* (1964). A revealing book of jottings is Gilbert Chinard, ed., *The Literary Bible of Thomas Jefferson: His Commonplace Book of Philosophers and Poets* (1928). Felix Gilbert, *To The Farewell Address: Ideas of Early American Foreign Policy* (1961), is a graceful analysis of American ideas in a Western context; Howard Mumford Jones, *O Strange New World: American Culture: The Formative Years* (1964), is fascinating and enormously learned; it certainly proves over and over again the Europeanness of American culture. Still, I find much of it unconvincing—its notion of "Machiavellianism" in America, in particular, is based on very tenuous evidence and on the forcing of words. Carl Becker's *The Declaration of Independence: A Study in the History of Political Ideas* (1922) is subtle and urbane, as all of Becker's work, and very much devoted to proving the dependence of American thinkers on European ideas. For a special article, see Alfred O. Aldridge, "Benjamin Franklin and the philosophes," *VS*, XXIV (1963), 43–65, which is a little sketchy but suggestive.

The tensions within the philosophic family centered around three issues: the relations of the German philosophes, notably Lessing, with the French, especially the troublesome Voltaire (here Schmidt, *Lessing*, and Korff, *Voltaire im literarischen Deutschland*, are both informative but partisan); the great project of the *Encyclopédie* which, what with official harassment and publishers' rascality, caused much anxiety and some mutual recriminations (here, in addition to the biographies of the leading actors and Smith's *Helvétius*, the most informative studies are Proust, *Diderot et l'Encyclopédie*, René Hubert, *Rousseau et l'Encyclopédie* [n.d., 1928], and Raymond Naves, *Voltaire et l'Encyclopédie* [1938]); and, most dramatically, the quarrel between Diderot and Rousseau. Green, *Rousseau*, is partial to Rousseau, although he has good cause for his partisanship; Wilson, *Diderot*, offers a judicious and authoritative account. That Diderot and his friends were deeply agitated over Rousseau and his possible revelations is proved by their doctoring of Mme d'Epinay's memoirs: see Georges Roth's revealing edition, *Histoire de madame de Montbrillant*, 3 vols. (1951). The notes appended to Rousseau's autobiographical writings in *Œuvres*, I, are invaluable for an independent judgment. I have essayed a brief explanation of the essential incompatibility between Rousseau and Diderot above on pages 195–6, which accepts but goes beyond Cassirer's explanation in his *Question of Jean-Jacques Rousseau*. Jean Fabre, "Deux Frères ennemis: Diderot et Jean-Jacques," *Diderot Studies*, III (1962), 155–213, is excellent. A later quarrel, that between Voltaire and Rousseau, is discussed in all the biographies. George R. Havens has carefully collected Voltaire's tart, amusing marginalia on Rousseau's writings, which display at once Voltaire's acuteness and obtuseness, his humaneness and his ruthlessness: *Voltaire's Marginalia on the Pages of Rousseau: A Comparative Study of Ideas* (1933). Still, as the letters of d'Alembert and Voltaire, or Hume's letters from Paris, show over and over again: the philosophes did think themselves a *petite troupe*, a real family.

The best study of the philosophes' opponents in France is the vigorous and original essay by R. R. Palmer, *Catholics and Unbelievers in Eighteenth-Century France* (1939), which gives the Jesuits their due for their tolerance and their modernity and criticizes the philosophes for their own intolerance. Palmer states this case briefly, with statistical support, in his important article "The French Jesuits in the Age of Enlightenment," *AHR*, XLV: 1 (October 1939), 44–58. John N. Pappas's dissertation on the Jesuit journal, *The journal de Trévoux and the philosophes*, *VS*, III (1957), supports Palmer's interpretation. The corrections are welcome and essential reading for naïve liberals, but Palmer somewhat exaggerates the persecuting spirit of Voltaire and his friends and underestimates the very real difficulties of radical writers in the Old Regime. Still, his interpretation replaces the earlier work by A. Monod, *De Pascal à Chateaubriand* (1916). Bernard N. Schilling, *Conservative England and the Case Against Voltaire* (1950), is objective and informative but a typical dissertation. Charles Nisard, *Les Ennemis de Voltaire* (1853), is now badly out of date; François Cornou's biography of Fréron, that talented antiphilosophic journalist, *Trente Années de luttes contre*

Voltaire et les philosophes du XVIIIe siècle, Élie Fréron (1922), is a useful rehabilitation but marred by special pleading as partisan as the most worshipful Whig ever was. The result of such scholarship can be seen in F. C. Green's essay "Voltaire's Greatest Enemy," *Eighteenth-Century France* (1931), 111–54, which can only be called malicious. Far more substantial is Rudolf Unger, *Hamann und die deutsche Aufklärung,* 2 vols. (2nd edn., 1925), a lengthy, impressive study. Sir Isaiah Berlin has long been interested in "the enemies of the Enlightenment" or its uncertain allies; he has finally put some of his lectures down on paper in a pair of essays on Herder (see, "J. G. Herder," *Encounter,* XXV: 1 [July 1965], 29–48, and XXV: 2 [August 1965], 42–51). Others, I trust, will follow.

2. APPEARANCES AND REALITIES

As I hope I have made clear, an understanding of the philosophes' perception of their world is central to an understanding of the Enlightenment. While that perception was partial and partisan, not all of it should be ascribed to "false consciousness": the philosophes took from their world what they needed and wanted to know, but they often saw that world with remarkable penetration, with cool, disenchanted eyes. Herbert Dieckmann, "Religiöse und metaphysische Elemente im Denken der Aufklärung," already cited, draws the significant distinction between the philosophes' aspirations toward critical empiricism and their practice.

The philosophes' pessimism—or often moderate optimism—will claim my attention again in the second volume of this work. Meanwhile, there is abundant evidence for their pessimism in the thoroughly documented monograph by Henry Vyverberg, *Historical Pessimism in the French Enlightenment* (1958).

While the eighteenth century was filled with good Christians who yet had what I call the "Enlightenment style," the most remarkable, most interesting, and in many ways most touching representative of the group is Samuel Johnson. The most obvious source for his opinions is the life by James Boswell, edited by G. B. Hill and revised by L. F. Powell with pious care and invaluable footnotes in six volumes (I–IV, 1934; V and VI, 1950). James L. Clifford's engaging and scholarly *Young Samuel Johnson* (1955) gives us Johnson before Boswell; Bertrand H. Bronson, *Johnson Agonistes* (1946), has an interesting view of the whole man. I found Walter Jackson Bate, *The Achievement of Samuel Johnson* (1955), useful as well. Donald J. Greene's rather fierce but to me convincing essay, *The Politics of Samuel Johnson* (1960), seeks to rescue his man from the clutches of the neo-Conservatives of our day. A similar task is performed with considerable discrimination and philosophical care by Robert Voitle in *Samuel Johnson The Moralist* (1961). Greene's and Voitle's Johnson is my Johnson: he is really too good to be exploited for political controversies of our time—and then on the wrong side. W. K. Wimsatt, Jr., studies *The Prose Style of Samuel Johnson* (1941) with great learning and urbanity.

Two other matters deserve to be mentioned. The word "Augustan" is often used rather loosely when it is applied to the eighteenth century. Consult the article by James William Johnson, "The Meaning of Augustan," *JHI*, XIX: 4 (October 1958), 507–22. As for the *Essai sur les études en Russie*, which I say in the text (p. 12) is "probably by Grimm": this was long attributed to Diderot and is printed in his *Œuvres*. I accept the reasoning of Pierre Oustinoff, "Notes on Diderot's Fortunes in Russia," *Diderot Studies*, I (1949), 121–42.

CHAPTER ONE

The Useful and Beloved Past

1. HEBREWS AND HELLENES

While Heine was not the first to draw the distinction between Hebrews and Hellenes, he was the wittiest, and Matthew Arnold took it from him rather than from the lesser German publicists, like Börne, who had originated it. The *locus classicus* is in Heine's critique of Ludwig Börne: "As in his pronouncements on Goethe, so also in his judgments of other authors, Börne betrayed his Nazarene narrowness. I say 'Nazarene,' to avoid either the expression 'Jewish' or 'Christian,' although I use both expressions as synonyms to designate not a faith but a character. 'Jews' and 'Christians' are for me quite close in meaning, in contrast to 'Hellenes,' a designation I use to characterize, in the same manner, an inborn as well as a learned spiritual orientation and style of thinking rather than a certain nation. That is to say: all men are either Jews or Hellenes, men with ascetic, iconoclastic, spiritual tendencies, or men whose nature it is to love life, to take pride in self-development, and to be realistic. Thus there were Hellenes in the families of German pastors, and Jews who had been born in Athens, and perhaps traced their ancestry back to Theseus" (*Heines Werke*, ed. Oskar Walzel et al., 10 vols. [1913], VIII, 360). This distinction also informs Heine's great essays, *Die Romantische Schule* and *Zur Geschichte der Religion und Philosophie in Deutschland*, both masterpieces of what I should call intuitive intellectual history.

The old canard, first propagated by the German Romantics, that the philosophes had no sense of history can no longer be sustained. I have already polemicized against it in behalf of Voltaire in *Voltaire's Politics* and more generally in behalf of the

French Enlightenment in *The Party of Humanity*, 273–4. An early and devastating assault against it was made by Wilhelm Dilthey in 1901: "Das achtzehnte Jahrhundert und die geschichtliche Welt," in *Gesammelte Schriften*, III (1927), 209–68; Cassirer accepted and restated Dilthey's view in his chapter on "The Conquest of the Historical World," in *The Philosophy of the Enlightenment*. One reason for the continuing popularity of that canard is the undoubted superiority of the school of Ranke to the school of Voltaire; another, the innate conservatism of the historical profession, reluctant to surrender cherished clichés; a third, the scholarly blessing it has received in Friedrich Meinecke's subtle, learned, and influential *Die Entstehung des Historismus*, 2 vols. (1936). In my *Voltaire's Politics* (p. 364) I said that Meinecke "supports and refines Dilthey's thesis," and indeed Meinecke supplies good evidence for the excellence of the historical work of the philosophes. But I now think, more strongly than I did then, that Meinecke's book rests on a confusion between a sober account of the rise of the historicist mentality and an extravagant claim that that mentality alone produces "true" history. *Die Entstehung des Historismus* still awaits its critic (I say this in spite of Walther Hofer's serious philosophical *Geschichtsschreibung und Weltanschauung: Betrachtungen zum Werk Friedrich Meineckes* [1950].)

J. B. Black, *The Art of History: A Study of Four Great Historians in the Eighteenth Century* (1926), is a civilized set of essays on Robertson, Hume, Voltaire, and Gibbon, which takes these historians seriously. A. Momigliano, "Ancient History and the Antiquarian," *Warburg Journal*, XIII (1950), 285–315, is indispensable for an understanding of new developments in eighteenth-century scholarship. R. L. Bach, *Die Entwicklung der französischen Geschichtsauffassung im 18ten Jahrhundert* (1932), is regrettably slight: its very defects show the need for detailed studies on the rise of secular historical consciousness in the age of the Enlightenment. René Hubert's *Les sciences sociales dans l'Encyclopédie: La philosophie de l'histoire et le problème des origines sociales* (1923) is masterly; fortunately it sees the "social sciences" within the framework of history. Nellie N. Schargo, *History in the Encyclopédie* (1947), helpfully supplements

Hubert's pioneering work at specific points; Eberhard Weis, *Geschichtsschreibung und Staatsauffassung in der französischen Enzyklopädie* (1956), is rather thin. Roland N. Stromberg, "History in the Eighteenth Century," *JHI*, XII: 3 (June 1951), 295–304, is sensible. The philosophes' awareness of different styles of thinking in different cultures is well discussed in the chapters on Turgot and Condorcet in Frank E. Manuel's lively, indeed slightly frenetic *The Prophets of Paris* (1962). I find myself in close agreement with H. R. Trevor-Roper, "The Historical Philosophy of the Enlightenment," *VS*, XXVII (1963), 1667–87.

Now for specific historians. Montesquieu is thoroughly appreciated in Shackleton and in Meinecke's *Historismus*. For Voltaire, see E. Bourgeois's Introduction to his edition of the *Siècle de Louis XIV* (1890), which, though old, remains helpful; René Pomeau stresses the, to his mind underrated, *Histoire de Russie sous Pierre le Grand* in the short Preface to his useful, if incomplete, edition of Voltaire's *Œuvres historiques* (edn. Pléiade, 1957). Pomeau has written another, longer Introduction to his splendid edition of the *Essai sur les mœurs*, 2 vols. (1963). See also G. P. Gooch, "Voltaire as Historian," in *Catherine the Great and Other Studies* (1954), and various essays by Paul Sakmann, especially "Die Probleme der historischen Methodik und der Geschichtsphilosophie bei Voltaire," *Historische Zeitschrift*, XCVII (1906), 327–79. Furio Diaz, *Voltaire Storico* (1958), is a long study, full of insight. J. B. Brumfitt, *Voltaire, Historian* (1958), is dependable and, for all its economy, a full survey which pays special attention to Voltaire's precursors. Brumfitt has continued his researches: see "History and Propaganda in Voltaire," *VS*, XXIV (1963), 271–87, and his critical edition of Voltaire's *Philosophie de l'histoire* in *VS*, XXVIII (1963). I also profited from Lionel Gossman's imaginative interpretation "Voltaire's *Charles XII:* History into Art," *VS*, XXV (1963), 691–720.

For Gibbon, see Young and Low, already cited, and the splendid article by A. Momigliano, "Gibbon's Contribution to Historical Method," *Historia*, II (1954), 450–63. G. Giarrizzo, *Edward Gibbon e la cultura europea del settecento* (1954), is as comprehensive as its title suggests. I also learned from the interesting articles by C. N. Cochrane, "The Mind of Edward Gibbon," *The University of Toronto Quarterly*, XII: 1 (October 1942), 1–17, and XII: 2 (January 1943), 146–66; and two informal but telling evocations of Gibbon by H. R. Trevor-Roper, "Edward Gibbon after 200 Years," *The Listener*, LXXII: 1856 (October 22, 1964), 617–19, and LXXII: 1857 (October 29, 1964), 657–9. Lewis Curtis, "Gibbon's Paradise Lost," *The Age of Johnson*, ed. Frederick W. Hilles (1949), 73–90, sees Gibbon as the aristocratic philosopher-educator.

For Hume, in addition to Black's chapter in *The Art of History*, see the thorough, if aggressive, study by G. Giarrizzo, *David Hume politico e storico* (1962), and the important reviews of that book by Duncan Forbes in *The Historical Journal*, VI: 2 (1962), 280–95, and H. R. Trevor-Roper in *History and Theory*, III: 3 (1964), 381–9. These books and reviews should finally dispose of the old criticism that Hume's historical activities were a "betrayal of his philosophical vocation," a criticism to which I objected in an article published in 1957 (see now *The Party of Humanity*, 204–5 n.).

For all his striking achievements and contemporary reputation William Robertson has been rather eclipsed by his three great contemporaries Hume, Gibbon, and Voltaire. Manfred Schlenke, "Kulturgeschichte oder politische Geschichte in der Geschichtsschreibung des 18. Jahrhunderts," *Archiv für Kulturgeschichte*, XXXVII (1955), 60–97, makes a beginning, in addition to the essay by Black and references by Bryson in *Man and Society*, at redressing the balance. Still, a full-scale assessment would be welcome. Another desideratum is a careful study of Condillac as historian.

The interest of the philosophes in the history of non-Western powers has long aroused the interest of scholars; the intellectual relations of China, especially, and Europe have been thoroughly explored. Among a large literature the best are Virgile Pinot, *La Chine et la formation de l'esprit philosophique en France, 1640–1740* (1932), which, as its title indicates, concentrates on the propagandistic uses to which the missionaries' reports were put by French radicals back home; Walter Engemann, *Voltaire und China* (1932), which concentrates on the philosophe most important in the diffusion of pseudo-Chinese ideas; and now Basil Guy,

The French Image of China Before and After Voltaire, VS, XXI (1963), which supersedes earlier studies and has among other virtues an exhaustive bibliography.

2. A CONGENIAL SENSE AND SPIRIT

There are obviously two ways of dealing with the transmission of classical literature and ideas: from the position of the donor and from the position of the recipient. Questions concerning this transmission, and their transformation, arise in several strategic moments in Western history: at the beginning of Christianity, in the Renaissance, in seventeenth-century classicism, and in the Enlightenment itself. For the sake of clarity, even though I have naturally found a number of books illuminating for all these moments, I shall here deal with works treating the classics from the standpoint of the eighteenth century.[1]

A valuable early account of the development of classical scholarship from its beginnings in antiquity itself down to the nineteenth century is J. E. Sandys, *A History of Classical Scholarship*, 3 vols. (1903–1908), which may now be supplemented by Karl Borinski, *Die Antike in Poetik und Kunsttheorie vom Ausgang des klassischen Altertums bis auf Goethe und Wilhelm von Humboldt*, 2 vols. (1914, 1924), which traces the impact of classical ideas on criticism in modern times; and by O. Gruppe, *Geschichte der klassischen Mythologie und Religionsgeschichte während des Mittelalters im Abendland und während der Neuzeit* (1921), which has much interesting material on the transmission of myths in art and literature. Three rather short but informative books by J. A. K. Thomson, closely related by their manner of treating their materials, *The Classical Background of English Literature* (1948), *Classical Influences on English Poetry* (1951), and *Classical Influences on English Prose* (1956), happily do not

---

[1] For other standpoints, see below, chap. II 471–80, IV 492–6, and V 511–15.

neglect the eighteenth century. Gilbert Highet, *The Classical Tradition: Greek and Roman Influences on Western Literature* (1949), has a long section on what it rather oddly calls the "Baroque," which includes the unbaroque eighteenth century. A book so packed with facts and, indeed, learning, could hardly help having some uses, but Highet's periodization is perverse, and his literary judgment is often unliterary. While he deals with the classics only in passing, I have found René Wellek, *A History of Modern Criticism*, Vol. I: *The Later Eighteenth Century* (1955), extraordinarily sensible and well-informed.

Classical learning in eighteenth-century England is well discussed by M. L. Clarke in his essay *Classical Education in Britain, 1500–1900* (1959) and in his more specialized *Greek Studies in England, 1700–1830* (1945), which includes chapters on Greek education in the schools and universities, the contribution of such scholars as Porson, and the development of knowledge about Greece through historical, literary, and archaeological research. Clarke has also written a good study on *Richard Porson: A Biographical Essay* (1937). Reuben A. Brower's *Alexander Pope: The Poetry of Allusion* (1959) offers a sensitive and discriminating analysis of Pope's classical borrowings, which, with precision and urbanity, sheds light on eighteenth-century culture as a whole. See also Aubrey Williams, "Pope and Horace: The Second Epistle of the Second Book," *Restoration and Eighteenth-Century Literature*, ed. Carroll Camden (1963), 309–21. The precise quality of David Hume's classicism deserves further study, beyond the attention I have given it in this essay. There are useful hints in Mossner, *Hume*, and in Norman Kemp Smith's admirable edition of the *Dialogues Concerning Natural Religion*. For Gibbon, see especially Momigliano's article cited above.

For eighteenth-century France, see the old but not obsolete history by abbé Augustin Sicard, *Les Études classiques avant la Révolution* (1887), one of those proverbial gold mines of information. Jean Seznec, *Essais sur Diderot et l'antiquité* (1957), sounds and looks like a highly specialized monograph on Diderot's attitude toward classical art in his salons; actually the book is a superb study of Diderot's character, in which the half conscious, half unconscious emulation of classical antiquity played a significant role. In company with Momigliano, Seznec's book offers a perceptive portrait of the relation of *philosophe* to antiquarian in eighteenth-century France. (I should add that I read Seznec at the right time, as I was beginning to formulate the dialectic which was to become the skeleton of my essay.) See also Joan Evans, *A History of the Society of Antiquaries* (1956). For Diderot's classicism see also the revealing pages in Wilson, *Diderot*, 18–19; H. Gillot, *Diderot, l'homme, ses idées philosophiques, esthétiques et littéraires* (1937), and Thomas, *L'Humanisme de Diderot*, a splendid essay. Raymond Trousson, "Diderot et l'Antiquité grecque," *Diderot Studies*, VI (1964), 215–47, is highly informative.[2] See also Eric M. Steel, *Diderot's Imagery: A Study of A Literary Personality* (1941).

Montesquieu's affinity for the classics is discussed in Shackleton, *Montesquieu* (especially 68–76 on the lost *Traité des devoirs;* 146–70 on the early essays on Rome and the *Considérations;* and 225–370 *passim* on the classicism of *L'Esprit des lois*). H. Roddier analyzes Montesquieu's classical education at the Oratorian *collège* at Juilly and its influence on his masterpiece, in "De la Composition de *l'Esprit des lois:* Montesquieu et les oratoriens de l'académie de Juilly," *Revue d'histoire littéraire de la France*, LII (1952), 439–50; while Robert Shackleton has tried to reconstruct the *Traité des devoirs* through *L'Esprit des lois* in "La Genèse de *l'Esprit des lois*" in the same issue, 425–38. Ernst Robert Curtius's brief excursus, "Montesquieu, Ovid, and Virgil," in *European Literature and the Latin Middle Ages*, is, of course, brilliant; M. W. Rombout has written an ambitious monograph, *La Conception stoïcienne du bonheur chez Montesquieu et chez quelques-uns de ses contemporains* (1958), which proves beyond doubt the impact of Stoic moral ideas on Montesquieu and much of the French Enlightenment in general. See also Lawrence L. Levin, *The Political Doctrine of Montesquieu's Esprit des lois* (1936), which has a good deal on Montesquieu's dependence on the ancients. Johann Albrecht von Rantzau, "Politische Wirkungen antiker Vorstellungen bei Montesquieu," *Antike und Abendland*, V (1956), 107–20, concentrates, as its title shows, on the relation of

---

[2] See below, pp. 471–2.

classical antiquity to Montesquieu's politics; while Roger B. Oake, "Montesquieu's Religious Ideas," *JHI*, XIV: 4 (October 1953), 548–60, rightly, I think, stresses Montesquieu's Stoicism in religion.

Voltaire's classicism, like Hume's, deserves further study. Concordance in hand, Alexis Pierron has convicted Voltaire of many slips in his classical quotations and shows that he was a rather mediocre scholar. But Pierron's *Voltaire et ses maîtres* (1866), though useful in this respect, misses the point of Voltaire's paganism. It can be partially corrected by Raymond Naves's survey of Voltaire's taste (including his classical tastes), *Le goût de Voltaire* (1938), and by René Pomeau, "Voltaire au collège," *Revue d'Histoire littéraire de la France*, LII (January–March 1952), 1–10. George R. Havens and Norman L. Torrey have published *Voltaire's Catalogue of His Library at Ferney* in *VS*, IX (1959), which thoroughly documents at least his passionate *purchasing* of the classics.[3] Rousseau's antiquarian nostalgia, already noticed by such perceptive friends as Diderot, has received much attention, not all of it sensible. (See my essay "Reading About Rousseau," *The Party of Humanity*, esp. pp. 242–244.) Certainly Rousseau did not wander about the world thinking himself the modern reincarnation of some Plutarchian Spartan hero. For a reasonable appraisal of his Spartanism, see F. C. Green, *Jean-Jacques Rousseau*, 5, which explicitly corrects André Oltamare's overdrawn, "Plutarque dans Rousseau," in *Mélanges d'histoire littéraire et philosophique offerts à M. Bernard Bouvier* (1920). More significant than Spartan myths were Roman Stoic educational ideas: G. Pire has exhaustively proved Seneca's influence on Rousseau, "De l'Influence de Sénèque sur les théories pédagogiques de Jean-Jacques Rousseau," *Annales de la Société Jean-Jacques Rousseau*, XXXIII (1953–5), 51–92, and more comprehensively in *Stoïcisme et pédagogie: De Zénon à Marc-Aurèle, de Sénèque à Montaigne et à J.-J. Rousseau* (1958). Earlier studies of this relationship, of some independent value, are

---

[3] For Voltaire's growing pessimism, both before and after the Lisbon earthquake, see below, p. 488. His cheerful Epicurean poem *Le mondain*, extolling worldliness, has been well edited by A. Morize: *L'Apologie du luxe au XVIIIe siècle: Le Mondain et ses sources* (1909).

L. Thomas, "Sénèque et J.-J. Rousseau," *Académie Royale de Belgique: Bulletin de la classe des lettres et des sciences morales et politiques et de la classe des Beaux Arts* (1900), 391–421; Léon Herrmann, "Jean-Jacques Rousseau, traducteur de Sénèque," *Annales de la Société Jean-Jacques Rousseau*, XIII (1920–1), 215–24; and K. S. Tchang, *Les Sources antiques des théories de J.-J. Rousseau sur l'éducation* (1919). Bertrand de Jouvenel has explored his Spartan pessimism in "Rousseau the Pessimistic Evolutionist," *Yale French Studies*, No. 28 (Fall–Winter, 1961–1962), 83–96. Rousseau's "Platonism" remains controversial: Hendel, *Jean-Jacques Rousseau Moralist*, considers it decisive; Albert Schinz (see *Annales de la société Jean-Jacques Rousseau*, XXIII [1934], 201–6), explicitly addressing himself to Hendel's thesis, considers it unimportant. Schinz, I think, has a point when it comes to specific borrowings, and he rightly emphasizes Rousseau's debt to sources other than Plato, but Hendel has caught the tone and spirit of Rousseau's philosophizing, that subtle style of thought that depends less on specific ideas than on some inner affinity.

Not unexpectedly the Germans have spent much energy tracing their eighteenth-century ideas to their *geliebten Alten*, as Goethe called them; they have been enthusiastic if not always well-informed classicists and *Humanisten* since the days of Schiller and Humboldt. Dilthey's "Lessing," in *Das Erlebnis und die Dichtung*, Sengle's *Wieland*, Aner's *Nicolai*, and Cassirer's *Kant* all have informative pages on the classical education and classical tastes of their subjects. Carl Justi, *Winckelmann und seine Zeitgenossen*, 3 vols. (5th edn., 1956), is an invaluable and exhaustive biography of Germany's greatest eighteenth-century classicist and, beyond that, a study of the dawning taste for Greece, which Winckelmann did so much to foster and direct. German classical education has often been surveyed but never better than by Friedrich Paulsen, *Das deutsche Bildungswesen in seiner geschichtlichen Entwicklung* (4th edn., 1920). C. L. Cholevius, *Geschichte der deutschen Poesie nach ihren antiken Elementen*, 2 vols. (1854, 1856), is now old but still valuable for its encyclopedic coverage of the material. Walther Rehm, *Griechenland und Goethezeit* (1936), is in many ways characteristic of Germanic myopia joined to Germanic thoroughness: to Rehm the Germans are Real, Profound Classicists, while foreigners are more likely to be shallow and second-rate. But this parochialism is partially corrected by immense learning.

This kind of ideological classicism (of which Dilthey and Cassirer and recent scholars like Sengle have, of course, never been guilty) has called forth a reaction from non-German scholars, often rather vituperative. E. M. Butler's celebrated *The Tyranny of Greece over Germany* (1935) is a vigorous onslaught against German infatuation with Greece from Winckelmann to Stefan George; it stresses its reactionary, stultifying, and indeed insane aspects at the expense of its often delightful results in imaginative literature. This corrective of German parochialism should itself be corrected with Humphry Trevelyan, *Goethe and the Greeks* (1941); Barker Fairley's magnificent biography *A Study of Goethe* (1947); Henry Hatfield's informative monograph *Winckelmann and his German Critics* (1943) and his splendidly balanced *Aesthetic Paganism in German Literature: From Winckelmann to the Death of Goethe* (1964).

The relation of the Italians to their ancients, though close, was subtle and calls for further research.

For all the inexhaustible, positively frightening outpouring of writings on American history, the analysis of classicism in the American Enlightenment has mainly been confined to the best biographies of the leading figures. Jefferson is an exception: Fiske Kimball studied Jefferson's Palladian taste as early as 1916 in *Thomas Jefferson, Architect*, an authoritative monograph. Gilbert Chinard, so often a pioneer in scholarship, discusses "Thomas Jefferson as a Classical Scholar" in *The American Scholar*, I (1932), 133–43; while Louis B. Wright has an interesting essay on "Thomas Jefferson and the Classics," in *Proceedings of the American Philosophical Society*, LXXXVII (1943–4), 223–33. Karl Lehmann summarizes this scholarship and adds to it in *Thomas Jefferson, American Humanist* (1947), a useful book, though a little adulatory. Richard Gummere has collected his important essays in *The American Colonial Mind and the Classical Tradition: Essays in Comparative Culture* (1963), which contains valuable information on a wide variety of American debts to the ancients;

I have borrowed from it freely. Louis B. Wright's well-informed *The First Gentlemen of Virginia* (1940) perhaps takes its subjects' learning a little too seriously. Robert Middlekauff, *Ancients and Axioms: Secondary Education in Eighteenth-Century New England* (1963), is among the few really good books on liberal education in early America. Howard Mumford Jones, *O Strange New World*, has a relevant chapter (VII) on "Roman Virtue."[4]

For political classicism in England, see the informative monograph by Z. S. Fink, *The Classical Republicans: An Essay in the Recovery of a Pattern of Thought in Seventeenth-Century England* (2nd edn., 1962).

3. THE SEARCH FOR PAGANISM: FROM IDENTIFICATION TO IDENTITY

Phrases like "identity crisis" and the "search for identity" have become perilous clichés, a peril of which I was aware when I used them as explanatory categories. I decided, however, that Erik H. Erikson's formulations, developed out of his psychoanalytic work with disturbed adolescents, applied quite precisely to the philosophes whom I was studying. Erikson's best-known statement of the identity crisis is in his *Childhood and Society* (2nd edn., 1964), and he has made a famous application of it in *Young Man Luther: A Study in Psychoanalysis and History* (1958). I have depended most heavily, however, on "Identity and the Life Cycle," a series of papers published in *Psychological Issues*, ed. George S. Klein, I: 1 (1959). Behind Erik Erikson stands Sigmund Freud, and beside him Heinz Hartmann. While this book is an essay in intellectual, not in psychoanalytical history, I trust I have been aware throughout of the nonrational components in the making of intellectual systems. In addition to the standard works of Freud to which (I trust it is not presump-

---

[4] The Puritans' attitude toward learning in general and the classics in particular belongs to the seventeenth century and hence to chap. V (see below, p. 517).

tuous to say) I am profoundly indebted, I have learned from my rather unsystematic reading in ego-psychology, which is the most fruitful development in psychoanalytical thought since the work of the master himself. Of Hartmann's work, I have probably derived most benefit from his stimulating *Psychoanalysis and Moral Values* (1960) and from some of the essays collected in his *Essays in Ego Psychology: Selected Problems in Psychoanalytical Theory* (1964), especially "Psychoanalysis and the Concept of Health" (1939), 1–18, "On Rational and Irrational Action" (1947), 37–68, and "Notes on the Reality Principle" (1956), 241–67. Brigid Brophy, *Mozart the Dramatist* (1964), is a wildly (and often impermissibly) speculative attempt to understand Mozart's operas and through the operas the age of the Enlightenment in psychoanalytical fashion; for all its dubious, rash generalizations I found it stimulating, and I agree with its central contention that the eighteenth century was not merely charming, rococo, but a deeply passionate age; I agree, also, that the Enlightenment is the great rebellion of the ego against irrational authority.

Alert readers acquainted with my critique of Becker's *Heavenly City* may wonder if my statement in the text that the philosophes abandoned only part of their Christian heritage and repressed the rest represents a modification of my original position. It does not. I still argue for discontinuity between Christianity and Enlightenment, a discontinuity especially radical when we judge ideas by their function, not by their origins. On the functional treatment of ideas—an important matter—see the splendid if brief remarks by Ernst Cassirer, "Some Remarks on the Question of the Originality of the Renaissance," *JHI*, IV: 1 (January 1943), 49–56.

In addition to Schmidt, Aner, and Dilthey see, for Lessing's theological evolution, Henry Chadwick's "Introduction" to his edition of *Lessing's Theological Writings* (1957) and Hans Leisegang, *Lessings Weltanschauung* (1931). Georges Pons's fine long study, *Gotthold Ephraim Lessing et le christianisme* (1964), came to my attention too late to be used in the text; I am glad to say that reading it did not compel me to redraw my map of Lessing's intellectual itinerary. For Reimarus, see David Friedrich

Strauss, *Hermann Samuel Reimarus und seine Schutzschrift für die vernünftigen Verehrer Gottes* (1862), a long essay with long quotations.

I have dealt with the theme of love and work, and formulated tentatively what I have called the philosophes' "philosophy of energy," in my "The Unity of the French Enlightenment," now in *The Party of Humanity*, 114–32; and I shall deal with this idea once more in the second volume of this present work. By far the best discussions of *anticomanie* that I have seen are in Seznec's *Diderot et l'antiquité* and Momigliano's article on "Ancient History and the Antiquarian."

CHAPTER TWO

The First Enlightenment

---

1. GREECE: FROM MYTH TO REASON

Ever since the literary rediscovery of Greece in the Renaissance and its emotional rediscovery in the second half of the eighteenth century, there have been admiring, indeed adulatory, books on the "Greek miracle." Modern scholarship, alert to the achievements of Greece's neighbors, has modified this adulation and complicated our perception of the ancient world. But as I read it, the unique contribution of the Greeks, the invention of sustained critical thinking, remains securely theirs. Ernst Cassirer makes out an impressive case for Greek philosophy in "Die Philosophie der Griechen von den Anfängen bis Platon," *Lehrbuch der Philosophie,* ed. Max Dessoir, 2 vols. (1925), I, 7–140; as well as in "Logos, Dike, Kosmos in der Entwicklung der griechischen Philosophie," *Göteborg Högskolas Arsskrift,* XLVII: 6 (1941). From a rather different philosophical perspective, the same case was made earlier by F. M. Cornford, first in *From Religion to Philosophy: A Study in the Origins of Western Speculation* (1912), once again in *Before and After Socrates* (1932), and finally, most subtly, in *Principium Sapientiae: The Origins of Greek Philosophical Thought* (published posthumously by W. K. C. Guthrie in 1952). The rise of thought from myth, of drama from ritual, was the theme of other English scholars, like Jane Harrison, closely associated with Cornford; see especially her *Prolegomena To the Study of Greek Religion* (3d edn., 1922). Another admirable and convincing advocate of the proposition that "European thinking begins with the Greeks" is Bruno Snell: *The Discovery of the Mind: The Greek Origins of European Thought* (1948; tr. T. G. Rosenmeyer, 1953).

Proof that the difference between Greek and Near Eastern styles of thinking was a difference in kind (or, rather, became a difference in kind) has also been offered by students of Egyptian, Babylonian, and ancient Jewish culture. I refer especially to the stimulating collection of essays, all by scholars at the Oriental Institute at The University of Chicago, *The Intellectual Adventure of Ancient Man*, ed. Henri Frankfort (1946), which bases itself quite explicitly on Cassirer's thought but buttresses its philosophical position with unsurpassed knowledge of ancient Near Eastern documents. Some of the contributors to this volume have written independent works of considerable literary merit and scholarly value. See especially Henri Frankfort, *Ancient Egyptian Religion: An Interpretation* (1948), *Kingship and the Gods: A Study of Ancient Near Eastern Religion as the Integration of Society and Nature* (1948), and *The Art and Architecture of the Ancient Orient* (1954). H. A. Groenewegen-Frankfort, *Arrest and Movement: An Essay on Space and Time in the Representational Art of the Ancient Near East* (1951), and John A. Wilson, *The Burden of Egypt* (1951), other representatives of this group, elegantly and eruditely support the claims of Greek supremacy. There has been, of course, dissent from this claim for Greek uniqueness: Edward Chiera, a distinguished Assyriologist, for example, makes no distinction between mythical and critical thinking in his *They Wrote on Clay* (1938) and simply claims every instance of curiosity or speculation for "philosophy." This will not do. Far more formidable is Otto Neugebauer, *The Exact Sciences in Antiquity*, (2nd edn., 1962), which demonstrates the advanced state of Babylonian mathematics. But as I have said, such studies as Neugebauer's compel us to refine but not to abandon the claims to Greek supremacy and primacy. William A. Irwin, "The Hebrews," in *The Intellectual Adventure of Ancient Man* (pp. 221–60) stresses Jewish rationality but goes, I think, beyond his evidence. Max Weber's important essays on ancient Judaism, in *Gesammelte Aufsätze zur Religionssoziologie*, 3 vols. (1920–1), III, see party struggle in ancient Israel between Jahwists and others and emphasize the tradition of law, but also the strength of the prophetic strain, Jewish worldly asceticism, and charisma; his essays thus permit the interpretation I have briefly offered in the text.

Among general interpretations of Greek culture, Werner Jaeger, *Paideia: The Ideals of Greek Culture*, 3 vols. (1936; tr. Gilbert Highet, 2d edn., 1945), offers a powerful analysis moving from Homer to Plato; it credits the Greeks with the invention of philosophy and the ideal of "culture." *Paideia* is, as some critics have noted, an essentially aristocratic view of Greek civilization, and this view appears not merely in what it argues but in when it stops. Historians of the Hellenistic age have protested against what they call this "purism" (see, most recently, Moses Hadas, *Hellenistic Culture: Fusion and Diffusion* [1959]), but Jaeger's work retains, at least for me, its authority. Related articles by Werner Jaeger, learned and persuasive, are "Die Griechische Staatsethik im Zeitalter des Plato" (1924), in *Humanistische Reden und Vorträge* (2nd edn., 1960), 87-102, and "Die Griechen und das philosophische Lebensideal" (1947), ibid., 222-39.

The classic analysis of Fustel de Coulanges, *The Ancient City: A Study of the Religion, Laws, and Institutions of Greece and Rome* (1864; tr. Willard Small, 1873), has been generally superseded, although it remains a fascinating *tour de force*, an attempt long before Max Weber to write history through the use of ideal types. Fustel may now be corrected with Gustave Glotz, *The Greek City and Its Institutions* (1928; tr. N. Mallison, 1929), which takes explicit issue with Fustel; and the brilliant treatise by Victor Ehrenberg, *The Greek State* (1932; tr. Ehrenberg and Harold Mattingly, 1960). H. Michell, *The Economics of Ancient Greece* (2nd edn., 1957), adds much information on a difficult subject, while A. Andrewes, *The Greek Tyrants* (1956), for all its brevity, helps to clarify some vexed questions of Greek rule. E. R. Dodds, *The Greeks and the Irrational* (1951), is a masterly essay by a venturesome but learned and absolutely secure classicist; it brings to bear modern psychoanalytical thought on Greek civilization and, while it greatly enriches our knowledge of the emotional basis of that civilization, stands—like all responsible psychoanalytical thought—in the service of a secular, reasonable interpretation. Léon Brunschvicg, *Le Progrès de la conscience dans la philosophie occidentale*, 2 vols. (2nd edn., 1952), a magnificent essay, begins with Socrates and his "discovery of practical reason." Georg Misch, *A History of Autobiography in Antiquity*, 2 vols. (3rd edn., 1949–50; tr. Misch and E. W. Dickes, 1950), sees the beginning of self-portrayal in Egypt and Babylon but the beginning of true individuality and self-awareness in Greece.

A major unsettled controversy—of special relevance to the philosophes—is the relation of Greek philosophy to action, of thought to practice. John Dewey complained long ago, perhaps excessively, that Greek philosophers were apt to denigrate the *vita activa* in favor of the *vita contemplativa*. Franz Boll's delightful essay *Vita Contemplativa* (1920), from which I have learned much, sets this controversy in its context. Cassirer, Cornford, and Jaeger all defend Greek thinkers against the charge that they disdained experimentation, and they offer persuasive evidence that there was less separation of head and hand than Dewey suggests. So does John Burnet in his "Experiment and Observation in Greek Science," in *Essays and Addresses* (1929), 253–64. The question touches on the nature of Greek science, and on that subject Marxists, Idealists, and Pragmatists continue to fight their battles. The best writer among the Marxists is Benjamin Farrington; see especially his *Greek Science* (edn. 1961); but see also the excellent and devastating critique by Ludwig Edelstein, "Recent Trends in the Interpretation of Ancient Science," *JHI*, XIII: 4 (October 1952), 573–604, and Momigliano's review of Farrington's *Science and Politics in the Ancient World* (1939) in the *Journal of Roman Studies*, XXXI (1941), 149–57, which strikes me as conclusive refutation. The most famous work on Greek science is George Sarton, *A History of Science: Ancient Science Through the Golden Age of Greece* (1952), a veritable encyclopedia, complete but pedestrian, reliable but undiscriminating. S. Sambursky's *The Physical World of the Greeks* (1954; tr. Merton Dagut, 1956), on the other hand, is concise, alive with ideas, and magnificently suggestive not merely in its chosen field but for the very nature of the scientific attitude, the relation of science to philosophy and of criticism to myth. Arthur J. Brock, ed., *Greek Medicine* (1929), is a valuable collection of documents illustrating the empirical turn of Greek science; and Erwin Schrödinger, *Nature and the Greeks* (1954), is a stimulating essay by a great scientist. I have also relied on Marshall Clagett, *Greek Science in Antiquity* (1957), unpretentious and dependable.

Another sensitive area, significant for establishing both the affinity of and distance between the first and second age of criticism is Greek religion. The general surveys by H. J. Rose, *Ancient Greek Religion* (1946), and W. K. C. Guthrie, *The Greeks and their Gods* (1950), are as graceful as they are informative. "Our Predecessors," chapter I of Guthrie's book, offers an account of earlier views of Greek religion back to the eighteenth century. Guthrie's *Orpheus and Greek Religion: A Study of the Orphic Movement* (2nd edn., 1952), which masters the latest scholarship, is of special relevance in view of the philosophes' interest in Orphism. Martin P. Nilsson, *Greek Folk Religion* (1940), moves into the countryside; it is a fine companion to Dodds's *Greeks and the Irrational*. The relation of philosophy and religion (much closer in the first than in the second age of criticism) is well discussed by Frederick C. Grant in the full introduction to his collection of texts, *Hellenistic Religions: The Age of Syncretism* (1953). A. D. Nock, *Conversion: The Old and the New in Religion from Alexander the Great to Augustine of Hippo* (1933), is an elegant and stimulating book, of great importance to this chapter. Equally important to me was R. Reitzenstein, *Die hellenistischen Mysterienreligionen nach ihren Grundlagen und Wirkungen* (2nd edn., 1920), which emphasizes the continuing power of religion in the most philosophical of ancients and emphasizes, too, like Nock, antique syncretism and toleration. A very valuable, extremely informative book is Paul Wendland, *Die hellenistisch-römische Kultur in ihren Beziehungen zu Judentum und Christentum* (2nd edn., 1912), especially chapter VI, pp. 106ff. A. J. Festugière rehabilitates the religious feeling of the much-maligned Epicureans in an important small essay, *Epicurus and His Gods* (1946; tr. C. W. Chilton, 1955).

For Greek literature, the vehicle of religious as well as secular culture, see, among many studies, C. M. Bowra, *Ancient Greek Literature* (1933), a rapid survey; H. D. F. Kitto, *Greek Tragedy: A Literary Survey* (3rd edn., 1961), which is authoritative. E. Norden's *Die antike Kunstprosa vom VI. Jahrhundert vor Christus bis in die Zeit der Renaissance*, 2 vols. (1898–1909), remains justly famous for its extensive, learned, acute comments on prose writers.

There is an enormous literature on the Greek philosophers, to whom the philosophes, as we know, did less than justice. See Jaeger and Cassirer cited above. The notion that philosophy begins in wonder is beautifully expressed in Plato's *Theaetetus* (155c; see Cassirer, *Mythical Thinking*, 78). I have profited from Eduard Zeller, *Outlines of the History of Greek Philosophy* (1883; 13th rev. edn., Wilhelm Nestle, tr. L. R. Palmer, 1931), which, though old, remains a good introduction. Paul Friedländer, *Plato: An Introduction* (2nd edn., 1954; tr. Hans Meyerhoff, 1958), is a profound examination of such themes as Socratic irony, which, although not in Platonic guise, had its role to play in the Enlightenment. On that subject see also J. A. K. Thomson's suggestive essay *Irony: An Historical Introduction* (1927). Among other books on Plato, I used A. E. Taylor, *Plato: The Man and His Work* (6th edn., 1952), to my advantage; Taylor's *Socrates* (1933) tells us what we can reliably know. As for the philosophes' Socrates, see the relevant pages in Seznec, *Diderot et l'antiquité*, pp. 1–22, and B. Boehm, *Sokrates im achtzehnten Jahrhundert: Studien zum Werdegang des modernen Persönlichkeitsbewusstseins* (1929). Alexandre Koyré, *Discovering Plato* (1945), is a brief lucid attempt to read the dialogues directly without crippling preconceptions. W. D. Ross, *Aristotle: A Complete Exposition of His Works and Thought* (5th edn., 1953) is a thorough, patient introduction to all his writings; it should be read in conjunction with Werner Jaeger's bold attempt to construct an evolution in Aristotle's ideas: *Aristotle: Fundamentals of the History of His Development* (1923; tr. Richard Robinson, 2nd edn., 1948). But see, on this last, John Burnet's appreciative though critical essay "Aristotle," in *Essays and Addresses* (1929), 277–99. For Greek education, which was deeply involved in Greek philosophical speculation, see the magnificent survey by H. I. Marrou, *A History of Education in Antiquity* (1948; tr. G. R. Lamb, 1956).

The Greek historians, especially Thucydides, were of great importance to the Enlightenment. Herodotus, whom they liked to dismiss as a credulous tourist and an avid maker of myths, is now being restored to his place as the "father of history." See J. B. Bury's now old but still vigorous *The Ancient Greek*

Historians (1909), chapter II; Aubrey de Sélingcourt's recent *The World of Herodotus* (1962); T. R. Glover's older, learned *Herodotus* (1924); and the persuasive article by A. Momigliano, "The Place of Herodotus in the History of Historiography," *History*, XLIII (February 1958), 1–13. The literature on Thucydides, already large, is growing. Ever since F. M. Cornford advanced his revolutionary thesis that Thucydides' *History* had followed the conventions of the Greek drama (*Thucydides Mythistoricus*, [1907]), the issue has been debated. Cornford's notions have been attacked, refined, and modified; they have not been wholly discarded. See John H. Finley, Jr., "Euripides and Thucydides," *Harvard Studies in Classical Philology*, IL (1938), 23–68; "The Origins of Thucydides' Style," ibid., L (1939), 35–84; "The Unity of Thucydides' History," ibid., Supplementary Volume I (1940), 255–98; and his general book, *Thucydides* (1942). Charles N. Cochrane has suggested, on the other hand, that Thucydides was writing genuinely "scientific" history: *Thucydides and the Science of History* (1929) holds that Thucydides was influenced by the Greek physicians, whose medical philosophy was basically critical and naturalistic. In an interesting article, "Spatium Historicum," *Durham University Journal*, XLII (1949–50), 89–104, W. von Leyden has suggested that Collingwood's strictures against the "present-mindedness" of antique historians are not wholly founded. And in a sensible, irenic article, "History and Tragedy," *Transactions of the American Philological Association*, LXXIII (1942), 25–53, B. L. Ullman argues that ancient history was a mixture of drama and science. I am not equipped to settle this argument, but it does seem to me that even proof of the reliance of historians on powerful neighbors, like rhetoric or tragedy, may detract from but does not disprove the critical temper of historians like Thucydides.

In many respects the Hellenistic age was more important for the Enlightenment than the great classical age. The great question that agitates historians today—did the Romans destroy a flourishing culture when they conquered Greece, or was that culture already decaying?—was apparently not a pressing question among historians in the eighteenth century. Moses Hadas offers a sympathetic interpretation in *Hellenistic Culture;* W. W. Tarn,

Hellenistic Civilization (3rd edn., 1952), is an authoritative survey of the culture as a whole. Equally authoritative is Tarn's *Alexander the Great* (1948), the study of a statesman whom the philosophes in the main, and mistakenly, denigrated as a mere military adventurer. M. Rostovtzeff, *Social and Economic History of the Hellenistic World*, 3 vols. (1941), is now a classic. But see A. Momigliano's skeptical critique, "Rostovtzeff's Twofold History of the Hellenistic World," *Journal of Hellenistic Studies*, LXIII (1943), 116–17. The most significant contributions of Hellenism to the Enlightenment were its philosophical systems and philosophical attitudes. The standard work on the Stoics is Max Pohlenz, *Die Stoa: Geschichte einer geistigen Bewegung*, 2 vols. (2nd edn., 1959), which has a brief section on its modern influence. The first four chapters of H. Vernon Arnold's *Roman Stoicism* (1911) consider its Greek origins in some detail. Gilbert Murray has an appreciative essay, "The Stoic Philosophy," in *Stoic, Christian and Humanist* (1940), 89–118. Fortunately my own introduction to Stoicism was Edwyn Bevan's brief but penetrating *Stoics and Skeptics* (1913), which remains rewarding reading. Emile Bréhier, *Chrysippe et l'ancien stoïcisme* (rev. edn., 1951), is important. Robert Mark Wenley traces Stoicism through the centuries in his *Stoicism and Its Influence* (n.d. [1924]). An important aspect of Stoic thought (which they did not invent but which they refined and transmitted) was natural law; see Felix Flückiger, *Geschichte des Naturrechts*, Vol. I: *Altertum und Frühmittelalter* (1954), especially chapters V, VII, and IX. I am also much indebted to S. Sambursky, *Physics of the Stoics* (1959), which illuminates wide areas of Stoic thought and makes its impact on the eighteenth century plausible. As for the Epicureans, in addition to Festugière, see N. W. De Witt, *Epicurus and His Philosophy* (1954).

For awareness of Greece in the period of the Enlightenment, see especially Nellie Schargo, *History in the Encyclopedia*, and René Hubert, *Les Sciences sociales*. For classical scholarship in general, see Sandys. Francis C. Haber, *The Age of the World* (1959), analyzes the rising skepticism concerning Archbishop Ussher's famous date for the creation. Frank Manuel, *The Eighteenth Century Confronts the Gods* (1959), is a valuable monograph on eighteenth-century scholarship face to face with antique theories of religion; it contains some important pages on the mysterious scholar Nicolas Fréret. For Fréret see also a detailed monograph by Renée Simon, *Nicolas Fréret, académicien*, in *VS*, XVII (1961). Seznec on *Diderot et l'antiquité* is valuable as always. The revival of Greek learning in France, largely due to the antiquarian enthusiasm of abbé Barthélemy, is treated in interesting detail in Maurice Badolle, *L'Abbé J. Barthélemy (1716–1795) et l'hellénisme en France dans la seconde moïtié du XVIIIe siècle* (1926). See also L. Bertrand, *La Fin du classicisme et le retour à l'antique dans la seconde moïtié du XVIIIe siècle* (1897); and see Justi on Winckelmann.

Seventeenth-century historiography deserves much further treatment. Bach, *Entwicklung der französischen Geschichtsauffassung*, has a short chapter on Bossuet. Adalbert Klempt, *Die Säkularisierung der universalhistorischen Auffassung: Zum Wandel des Geschichtsdenkens im 16. und 17. Jahrhundert* (1960), keeps less than its grandiose title promises: it concentrates on German scholarship; but it is not without its uses. Leonard Krieger's recent, severely analytical *The Politics of Discretion: Pufendorf and the Acceptance of Natural Law* (1965) has material on seventeenth-century historiography. Central to the argument in my book, however, is Erik Iversen, *The Myth of Egypt and Its Hieroglyphs* (1961), which contains amidst a wealth of information a fascinating account of the seventeenth-century Jesuit scholar and Egyptomaniac Athanasius Kircher and also useful notes on scholars like Montfaucon. Frank Manuel has studied the historical preoccupations of Newton in his informative *Isaac Newton, Historian* (1963). Finally, for Petrarch's great reversal of "Dark Ages," see the magisterial article by Theodor Mommsen, "Petrarch's Conception of the 'Dark Ages,'" *Speculum*, XVII (1942), 226–42. For the philosophes' knowledge (or relative ignorance) of the civilizations of the near East, and of prehistory, see, once again, Hubert, *Les Sciences sociales*, especially chapters I, II, IV, and V. See also Manuel, *The Eighteenth Century Confronts the Gods*, and J. Deshayes, "De l'Abbé Pluche au citoyen Depuis: à la recherche de la clef des fables," *VS*, XXIV (1963), 457–86. There is also much material in specialized studies on the philosophes and the Jews, especially Hanna Emmrich, *Das Judentum bei Voltaire* (1930), and Hermann Sänger, *Juden und altes Testament bei Diderot* (1933). What is still needed, though, is a general conspectus of the philosophes' view of the ancient world. The Humanists' attitude toward early cultures has been briefly examined by Karl H. Dannenfeldt, "The Renaissance and the Pre-Classical Civilizations," *JHI*, XIII: 4 (October 1952), 435–49.

I have found Glyn E. Daniel, *A Hundred Years of Archeology* (1950), and the rather old book by Adolf Michaelis, *A Century of Archaeological Discoveries* (2nd edn., 1908; tr. Bettina Kahnweiler, 1908), useful. M. L. Clarke, *Greek Studies in England*, has two short chapters on eighteenth-century English archeology in Greece (chs. XIII and XIV). John L. Myres, *Homer and His Critics*, ed. Dorothea Gray (1958), is an immensely helpful, concise and judicious survey of Homeric studies from antiquity through the Enlightenment, Wolf, Schliemann, Wilamowitz-Moellendorf, down to the recent discussion over the poems as part of the Greek oral tradition. H. L. Lorimer, *Homer and the Monuments* (1950), marshals all the archeology available, in superb detail, to argue for two Homers. C. M. Bowra, *Tradition and Design in the Iliad* (1930), though slightly older (which is of moment in this fast moving field), remains an attractive argument for a single mind behind the *Iliad*.

As the reader will recognize without difficulty, the section on mythical thinking depends heavily on Cassirer, especially volume II of *The Philosophy of Symbolic Forms, Mythical Thinking;* the books of the Frankfort group; and the powerful phenomenological survey by G. van der Leeuw, *Religion in Essence and Manifestation*, 2 vols. (1933; tr. J. E. Turner, 2nd edn., 1963).

2. THE ROMAN ENLIGHTENMENT

The Enlightenment's view of ancient Rome was largely if not wholly literary; it can be pieced together from the modern biographies of Roman poets, historians, and orators, which usually end with a few perfunctory pages on the influence of their subject in modern times. Perhaps most useful are the series of books written by the classicists who have taken the trouble to worry over the decline of the classics and have compiled series under such appealing titles as "Das Erbe der Alten" or "Our Debt to Greece and Rome."[1] One conclusion that emerges from these series is that the philosophes were relatively realistic about the failings of Roman antiquity. Caroline Robbins, *The Eighteenth-Century Commonwealthman* (1961), 185–210, has some interesting observations about Adam Smith's and Adam Ferguson's views on antique slavery.

The whole span of Roman literature is surveyed by H. J. Rose in his invaluable *A Handbook of Latin Literature* (2nd edn., 1949) and more briefly by Michael Grant in *Roman Literature* (edn., 1958). The whole span mattered to the philosophes, but the two Roman writers indispensable to them were Lucretius and Cicero. George Depue Hadzsits, *Lucretius and His Influence* (n.d., [1925]), is a characteristic specimen of the series "Our Debt to Greece and Rome,"[2] of which Hadzsits was general editor. Like the others in the series, it offers a short biography, discusses his intellectual debts, and his doctrines of nature and culture. It ends with several chapters on the career of Lucretius's manuscripts and reputation through the centuries to the twentieth century. Like practically all other commentators, Hadzsits argues that the philosophes on the whole rejected Lucretius's physics and metaphysics but found something admirable in his "anti-clericalism." C. A. Fusil has demonstrated this selective affinity in two important articles, "Lucrèce et les philosophes du XVIIIe siècle," *Revue d'histoire littéraire de la France*, XXXV (1928), 194–210, and "Lucrèce et les littérateurs, poètes, et artistes du XVIIIe siècle," ibid., XXXVII (1930), 161–76. Gustav R. Hocke, *Lukrez in Frankreich von der Renaissance bis zur Revolution* (1935), is

---

[1] For the fate of classical ideas in the Middle Ages and Renaissance, see below, Chs. IV and V. Here I shall confine myself to works dealing with individual authors and their posthumous reputation.
[2] I shall refer to this series from here on as "Our Debt."

especially valuable for the "rediscovery" of Lucretius in the sixteenth century, but his catalogue of writers, especially philosophes and the antiphilosophe Cardinal Polignac, who were somehow engaged with the Lucretian doctrine, is also of value. More recently Wolfgang Bernard Fleischmann has summarized our knowledge in "The Debt of the Enlightenment to Lucretius," *VS*, XXV (1963), 631–43. Fleischmann's *Lucretius and English Literature, 1680–1740* (1963) is a specialized informative monograph. See also Wolfgang Schmid, "Lukrez und der Wandel seines Bildes," *Antike und Abendland*, II (1946), 193–219, and Manuel, *The Eighteenth Century Confronts the Gods*, 145–6, 227. Historians of science have paid some attention to Epicureanism in seventeenth- and eighteenth-century thought. Charles C. Gillispie's few pages (96–100) in his *The Edge of Objectivity: An Essay in the History of Scientific Ideas* (1960) are distinguished for their moderation and good sense. For Lucretius's pessimism, to which I shall return in volume II, see the beautiful pages in George Santayana, *Three Philosophical Poets* (1910). Voltaire's somewhat mysterious Lucretian poem of 1722 has been authoritatively edited by Ira O. Wade: "Épitre à Uranie," *PMLA*, XLVII: 4 (December 1932), 1066–1112.

The literature on Lucretius is large, the literature on Cicero is overwhelming. Theodor Zielinski, *Cicero im Wandel der Jahrhunderte* (4th edn., 1929), is frequently cited with extreme respect for its vigor and its learning, but while the latter is encyclopedic, the former strikes me as excessive. Still, I have used it with profit. John C. Rolfe, *Cicero and His Influence* (1923), another representative of "Our Debt," is useful but a little skimpy on the eighteenth century. Günter Gawlick, "Cicero and the Enlightenment," *VS*, XXV (1963), 657–82 is much better; I owe it a pair of quotations.

In the great debate over Cicero's character, I cannot share (for all my admiration for him as a historian) Mommsen's contempt; I do not read that contempt as an early clue to German authoritarianism, but I think that Mommsen misjudged Rome's need for a Caesar and exaggerated the irrelevance of Cicero's political stance. (I was delighted to find support in an excellent book of essays edited by T. A. Dorey, *Cicero* [1965], which came too late to benefit the text of my book.) I have profited from A. Michel's enormous thesis, *Rhétorique et politique chez Cicéron: Essai sur les fondements philosophiques de l'art de persuader* (1960). See also Gaston Boissier, *Cicero and His Friends: A Study of Roman Society in the Time of Caesar* (10th edn., 1895; tr. Adnah David Jones, 1900); it is dated but remains attractive; if it is dated, that is because of the immensely patient and brilliantly synthetic work of Sir Ronald Syme: *The Roman Revolution* (1939), which evokes the political life from Julius Caesar to Caesar Augustus with Namierite detail and precision and has much to say about Cicero's political role and personal character. (But note the respectful criticisms of this masterpiece by Momigliano in his review in *Journal of Roman Studies*, XXX [1940], 75–80, which throws some doubt on the validity of Syme's severely biographical method.) My own close acquaintance with Cicero's writings began with a collection of his major works, including *De divinatione, De officiis, De natura deorum,* and *Brutus,* fluently translated by Hubert McNeill and intelligently introduced by Richard P. McKeon (1950). There is a splendid translation of *De republica,* with an important introduction: *On the Commonwealth,* translated and edited by George H. Sabine and Stanley B. Smith (1929). Cicero's influence on the Enlightenment cannot be understood unless we understand his fundamental philosophical position, his humanism, which the philosophes found extraordinarily congenial. A fundamental book on antique humanism is Max Schneidewin, *Die antike Humanität* (1897), but Richard Reitzenstein, *Werden und Wesen der Humanität im Altertum* (1907), goes much further—it is a brilliant essay. Werner Jaeger traces humanism back to the Greeks in his "Antike und Humanismus" (1925), in *Humanistische Vorträge,* 103–16. E. K. Rand's short article, "The Humanism of Cicero," *Proceedings of the American Philosophical Society,* LXXI (1932), 207–16, makes Reitzenstein available to an American public. Walter Rüegg, *Cicero und der Humanismus* (1946), is mainly concerned with the transmission of Ciceronian ideas into the Renaissance but has a useful chapter on the origins of the modern word "humanism" (he is also, incidentally, very critical of Mommsen's treatment of Cicero). H. A. K. Hunt's *The Humanism of Cicero* (1954) is a major contribution to the literature; it is a little stodgy but manages to sort out a coherent humanist program from Cicero's philosophical writings without forcing the evidence. But I have learned most from Hans Baron's magnificent essay *Cicero and the Roman Civic Spirit in the Middle Ages and the Early Renaissance* (1938), which, despite its limited subject announced in the title, throws a great deal of light on the cultural attitudes of antique and modern pagans.

For Caesar, see F. E. Adcock, *Caesar as Man of Letters* (1956), short, precise, discriminating, technical. See also Matthias Gelzer, *Caesar, Der Politiker und Staatsmann* (6th edn., 1960). Anyone interested in the gap between the philosophes' cool treatment of the man, on humanitarian grounds, and the frenzied admiration of modern authoritarians yearning for another Caesar, should read Friedrich Gundolf's frenetic *Caesar: Geschichte seines Ruhms* (1925). Syme, *Roman Revolution*, is indispensable, both for its own sake and as a corrective. Lily Ross Taylor has summarized the modern scholarship of Gelzer, Premerstein, and Syme and presented a persuasive portrait of *Party Politics in the Age of Caesar* (1949); while William Hardy Alexander favorably reconsiders Caesar as a stylist in his "Pure Well of Latin Undefiled," *University of Toronto Quarterly*, XII: 4 (July 1943), 415–25.

Inevitably the great Augustans have gathered an enormous literature about themselves. Syme, *Roman Revolution*, shows sympathy for their situation. Grant Showerman, *Horace and His Influence* (1922), takes Horace through the ages in the characteristic style of "Our Debt." Brower's *Pope* shows how much one intelligent, cultivated reader can do with the complex question of cultural transmission—of Horace and others. On Diderot's use of a Horatian satire in his *Le Neveu de Rameau*, see Ernst Robert Curtius's completely convincing argument, "Diderot and Horace," in *European Literature and the Latin Middle Ages* (1948; tr. Willard R. Trask, 1953), 573–83; despite this, Gilbert Highet insists, wrongly (*Juvenal, The Satirist* [1954], 217–18), that Diderot is adapting the Ninth Satire of Juvenal. L. P. Wilkinson, *Horace and His Lyric Poetry* (1946), is learned and urbane; Eduard Fraenkel, *Horace* (1957), which analyzes the poems one by one, is, in a word, magnificent. Vergil (to begin with the inevitable "Our

Debt") has been tracked through the centuries by John William Mackail in *Virgil and His Meaning to the World of Today* (1922). W. F. Jackson Knight, *Roman Vergil* (1944), is an excellent survey of Vergil's life and poetry; the last chapter, "Vergil and After" briefly takes him down to modern times.[3] There is a fine book on Ovid by L. P. Wilkinson, *Ovid Recalled* (1955), which unfortunately stops with the seventeenth century; E. K. Rand, *Ovid and His Influence* (1925), in the "Our Debt" series, however, has a useful catalogue. Seneca, as we know, had an odd career in the Enlightenment, as before; he was distrusted by Epicureans like La Mettrie, who even wrote an *Anti-Sénèque* (1750), and admired by such unorthodox Stoics as Diderot. Richard M. Gummere, *Seneca The Philosopher and his Modern Message* (1922), is one of the best volumes in the "Our Debt" series. There is one poet, little read today, who was very popular in the Enlightenment for his vigor and his libertarian sentiments— Lucan. See especially Walter Fischli, *Studien zum Fortleben der Pharsalia des M. Annaeus Lucanus* (1943-4), and the important article by Eduard Fränkel, "Lucan als Mittler des antiken Pathos," *Warburg Vorträge, 1924-1925* (1927), 229-57. The reasons why Lucan is little read today are cogently, if rather brutally, offered by his translator Robert Graves: *Pharsalia: Dramatic Episodes of the Civil Wars* (1957). I found Gilbert Highet's well-received *Juvenal, the Satirist* unsatisfactory, not merely for its unconvincing identification of *Le Neveu de Rameau* but mainly for its unpolitical acceptance of Juvenal's own often reactionary and usually hysterical judgments as though they were serious social history. On the other hand, part III has useful material on the survival of Juvenal in later centuries. James Sutherland, *English Satire* (1962), extensively discusses Juvenal's imitators in England. I am also indebted to Henry Nettleship, "Life and Poems of Juvenal," in *Lectures and Essays*, Second Series (1895), 117-44.

Among the historians the one most debated in and important for the Enlightenment is Tacitus—there is need for a good monograph here. Meanwhile, see the useful essays by Jürgen von

---

[3] For the miraculous Vergil of the Christian millennium, see below, p. 496.

Stackelberg: "Rousseau, d'Alembert et Diderot traducteurs de Tacite," *Studi Francesi*, No. 6 (September–December 1958), 395–407, and *Tacitus in der Romania: Studien zur literarischen Rezeption des Tacitus in Italien und Frankreich* (1960), especially chapter 13. For Gibbon's dependence, see the references in Young and Bond. M. L. W. Laistner, *The Greater Roman Historians* (1947), devotes two good chapters to him; Gaston Boissier, "Tacitus" in *Tacitus and other Roman Studies* (1904; tr. W. G. Hutchinson, 1906), remains most suggestive; Clarence W. Mendell, *Tacitus, The Man and His Work* (1957), is another sound volume. But clearly the book to read is Sir Ronald Syme, *Tacitus*, 2 vols. (1958), an exhaustive, definitive study of the man, his times, and his work, written in a chilling imitation of Tacitean prose appropriate to Tacitus's bleak time—and ours? I found Erich Auerbach's analysis of Tactitus's social posture (*Mimesis*, 33–60, passim) most illuminating. Other Roman historians are well treated in Laistner, *Greater Roman Historians;* Sir Ronald Syme, *Sallust* (1964), does much to restore Sallust's reputation. Like Tacitus, both Livy and Sallust survived into the eighteenth century, and here too there is room for further study. The same holds true for Plutarch. Rudolf Hirzel, *Plutarch* (1912), is still the best book available.

While the debt of Rome to Greece is stressed everywhere, its partial independence is stressed by Brower, *Pope*, especially chapter IV; and in Victor Ehrenberg, *Society and Civilization in Greece and Rome* (1964), a remarkable synthesis. Tarn, *Hellenistic Civilization*, offers some good political reasons why the captives overwhelmed the captors.

Roman religion, which gave philosophes like Montesquieu and Gibbon such rewarding material, is well if briefly discussed in H. J. Rose, *Ancient Roman Religion* (1948), while Cyril Bailey's *Phases in the Religion of Ancient Rome* (1932) moves in gratifying detail from myth and mystery religions to religious philosophy. Franz Cumont long made the mysteries his special interest; I found *After Life in Roman Paganism* (1922) especially rewarding. Roman philosophy, intimately connected with religion, is analyzed carefully in Arnold, *Roman Stoicism;* Nock, *Conversion* (which includes conversion to philosophy); Pohlenz,

Die Stoa. The edition of the philosophers I used was Whitney J.
Oates, *The Stoic and Epicurean Philosophers* (1940), which contains the complete extant writings of Epicurus, Epictetus,
Lucretius, and Marcus Aurelius. There are some sympathetic
pages on Roman philosophizing (63–91) in Bernard Groethuysen,
Anthropologie philosophique (1952). Marrou's *History of Educa-
tion in Antiquity* has a comprehensive set of chapters on Rome. S.
Sambursky, *The Physical World of Late Antiquity* (1962), is an
impressive synthetic study of late ancient science. For rhetoric, to
which the philosophes still responded, see among many treatises on
Cicero, Michel (cited above) and the excellent general history by
M. L. Clarke, *Rhetoric at Rome: A Historical Survey* (1953).
Harry Caplan, "The Decay of Eloquence at Rome in the First
Century," in *Studies in Speech and Drama in Honor of A. M.
Drummond* (1944), 295–325, is an interesting analysis of the
transition from republic to empire and its consequences for elo-
quence. Why the philosophes should continue to respond to an
antique art is suggested in the informative monograph by Wilbur
S. Howell, *Logic and Rhetoric in England, 1500–1700* (1956).

For politics and society in the empire, the time to which
Gibbon devoted his best years and which constitutes the all-
important transition from the first age of criticism to the second
age of belief, there is abundant material. Gilbert Murray's famous
little book *Five Stages of Greek Religion* (2nd edn., 1935) has a
celebrated chapter on "The Failure of Nerve" both in paganism
and through the coming of Christianity. While Murray's argument
has been much discussed and somewhat modified by later scholars,
I have depended on it here as a general guide. Wendland's
Hellenistisch-römische Kultur is valuable here; see also a short,
carefully discriminating, and immensely suggestive book by
Johannes Geffcken, *Der Ausgang des griechisch-römischen
Heidentums* (1920). M. Rostovtzeff, *A History of the Ancient
World*, Vol. II, *Rome* (1927; tr. J. D. Duff, 1928), deals with the
empire relatively briefly but authoritatively in chapters 13 to 25;
the last of these offers Rostovtzeff's own theories concerning the
decline and fall. His *The Social and Economic History of the
Roman Empire* (1926) is a much larger and still magnificent work,
although its concluding question (p. 487), "Is not every civiliza-

tion bound to decay as soon as it begins to penetrate the masses?" has struck recent researchers as more loaded than revealing. Samuel Dill's social histories, *Roman Society from Nero to Marcus Aurelius* (2nd edn., 1911) and *Roman Society in the Last Century of the Western Empire* (2nd edn., 1899), do not show their age; they are immensely rich in information and vigorous in judgment and happily do not neglect philosophy. T. R. Glover, *The Conflict of Religions in the Early Roman Empire* (1909), learnedly but dramatically confronts pagan and Christian, Celsus and Origen. Pierre de Labriolle's *La Réaction païenne: Étude sur la polémique antichrétienne du Ier au VIe siècle* (1948) is extremely useful. H. St. L. B. Moss, *The Birth of the Middle Ages, 395–814* (1935), is a very good survey, which, however, does not replace Ferdinand Lot's classic *The End of the Ancient World and the Beginnings of the Middle Ages* (1927; tr. Philip and Mariette Leon, 1931). A. S. L. Farquharson, *Marcus Aurelius: His Life and His World*, 2nd edn. ed. D. A. Rees (1952) is an excellent portrait of the philosophes' favorite emperor. Andrew Alföldi has made the late empire his specialty; above all see his *The Conversion of Constantine and Pagan Rome* (tr. Harold Mattingly, 1948). For Lucian, the disenchanted wit who has so often and so inescapably been compared to Voltaire, see the fine edition by H. W. and F. G. Fowler, 4 vols. (1905), and an amusing modern rendering of *Selected Satires* by Lionel Casson (1962). Francis G. Allinson's *Lucian: Satirist and Artist* (1926), in "Our Debt," has some helpful chapters on the survival of his satire; Julius Steinberger examines *Lukians Einfluss auf Wieland* (1902), while Ludwig Schenk lists modern French borrowings in his *Lukian und die französische Literatur im Zeitalter der Aufklärung* (1931). The major analysis is the exhaustive thesis by J. Bompaire, *Lucien écrivain: Imitation et création* (1958). J. A. K. Thomson, *Classical Influences on English Prose*, has some helpful pages.

Finally, a word on the persistence of Latin: see, for some careful discriminations, Curtius, *European Literature*, especially page 68; for toleration of Greek in the East, see Wendland, *Hellenistisch-römische Kultur*, 25–27.

CHAPTER THREE

The Climate of Criticism

1. CRITICISM AS PHILOSOPHY

While the authorship of *Le Philosophe* remains obscure, its meaning, I think, is relatively clear; Herbert Dieckmann has dealt authoritatively with both the obscurity and the clarity in his critical edition (1948). Filangieri's commitment to philosophy needs further study; meanwhile see the comments by Francesco de Sanctis, *History of Italian Literature*, 2 vols. (1870; often revised; tr. Joan Redfern, 1931), II, 831–2. Kant's claims for philosophy and his *Streit der Fakultäten* are well discussed in Cassirer, *Kant*, 417–24. Karl Jaspers has some relevant comments on Kant's pride in philosophizing in his chapter on Kant in *The Great Philosophers: The Foundations* (1957; tr. Ralph Manheim, ed. Hannah Arendt, 1962), 230–81. On Thomasius's rejection of metaphysical abstractions, see Wolff, *Weltanschauung der deutschen Aufklärung*, 27 ff. Whitehead's famous assertion that *"les philosophes* were not philosophers"* is in his influential *Science and the Modern World* (1925), 86. I have argued against Whitehead in my *The Party of Humanity*, 191–2n.

For philosophy as good sense, see the charming and lucidly written if not always profound volumes of F. L. Lucas, *The Search for Good Sense: Four Eighteenth-Century Characters: Johnson, Chesterfield, Boswell and Goldsmith* (1958) and *The Art of Living: Four Eighteenth-Century Minds: Hume, Horace Walpole, Burke, Benjamin Franklin* (1959). See also Frederick's lament to Voltaire of November 17, 1760, that fanatics are letting loose their fury on "the apostles of good sense" (Seznec, *Diderot et l'antiquité*, 5). I have dealt with the philosophes' (and especially Voltaire's) attack on metaphysics in *Voltaire's Politics*, 18–32, where I also deal with "philosophical modesty." Voltaire's most dramatic expressions of this "modesty" are in his *contes;* above all see Ira O. Wade, ed., *Voltaire's 'Micromégas'* (1950), a splendid critical edition. For Wieland's version of that modesty, see Sengle, *Wieland,* 168, 232, 314; and Friedrich Beissner, et al., *Wieland: Vier Biberacher Vorträge* (1954). Stern, *Lichtenberg,* 79–81, briefly analyzes Lichtenberg's empiricism and opposition to metaphysics. For Hume, in addition to the titles cited, D. F. Pears, "Hume's Empiricism and Modern Empiricism," *David Hume, A Symposium,* ed. D. F. Pears (1963), 11–30.[1] Turgot's criticism of Buffon's "metaphysics" is noted in Georg Misch, *Zur Entstehung des französischen Positivismus* (1900).

For fideism, see especially Louis I. Bredvold's remarkable essay *The Intellectual Milieu of John Dryden: Studies in Some Aspects of Seventeenth-Century Thought* (1934), which delivers more than its modest title promises. There are some illuminating passages on demystification in the seventeenth century in Hazard's *Crise de la conscience.* I find myself in agreement with Paul Tillich's argument (*Systematic Theology,* Vol. II [1957], passim) that in religion complete demythologization is impossible.

Antique religious policy, which so fascinated the philosophes, is analyzed in the volumes on ancient religion discussed before; on Plutarch, Glover's *Conflict of Religions* is especially revealing (pp. 75–112). For Montesquieu, see Shackleton, passim, but a further analysis seems needed. Tacitus's style has exercised all his commentators; the definitive discussion is in Syme, *Tacitus,* chapters XVII, XXI–XXVII, and Appendices 34, 37–60.

2. THE HOSPITABLE PANTHEON

In a sense, of course, all philosophical schools are eclectic; all, consciously or not, organize a diversity of earlier teachings into what they hope is a coherent system. What makes the eclecticism

---

[1] I shall return to Hume: see below, pp. 551–2.

of the Enlightenment so striking—and so important—is that it is overt, wholly unapologetic. In consequence I discovered I had to abandon an early hypothesis, namely, that the atheists in the eighteenth century derived from ancient Epicureans, and the deists from ancient Stoics. In fact both Epicureans and Stoics were already eclectics in Rome, and so what the philosophes learned was precisely this—eclecticism. All volumes on ancient religion and philosophy that I have cited have material on antique tolerance and syncretism. I have borrowed freely from some splendid pages in Nock, *Conversion*. William Dilthey has scattered some brilliant hints in his *Weltanschauungslehre*, in *Gesammelte Schriften*, VIII (1931), especially 3–14. Tarn, *Alexander*, and Hadas, *Hellenistic Culture*, strongly emphasize early political and social syncretism. Pohlenz, *Die Stoa*, parts II to IV, details the evolution of Stoicism from a strict doctrine to an eclectic collection of ideas. For Vergil's eclecticism (to give but one instance) see Jackson Knight, *Roman Vergil*, chapter I. There is no general treatment of eighteenth-century eclecticism, but there are hints in the books on Diderot; for philosophical eclecticism in America, see Gummere, *Colonial Mind and Classical Tradition*, viii, x, and 14.

The most informative book on the dialogue, which takes the form through the ages, is Rudolf Hirzel, *Der Dialog*, 2 vols. (1895), which is detailed and has many suggestive ideas. On medieval dialogue, which had its limited function, see Friedrich Heer, *The Medieval World: Europe 1100–1350* (1961; tr. Janet Sondheimer, 1962), 75–78, 87 ff; and Charles Homer Haskins's suggestive little book on *The Rise of Universities* (1923). There is some interesting work on the function of dialogue in the Enlightenment. Dieckmann, *Cinq leçons sur Diderot*, chapter I ("Diderot et son lecteur"), shows convincingly how Diderot visualized himself in debate with his reader. John W. Cosentini, *Fontenelle's Art of Dialogue* (1952), is technical; for Wieland as writer and reader of dialogues, see Sengle, *Wieland*, especially 63, 77, 267, 302, and 333. Kant's sense of dialogue is well analyzed as an inner openness to intellectual debate in A. C. Ewing, *A Commentary on Kant's Critique of Pure Reason* (1938), especially 8. On "The Dialogues of Voltaire" see the Columbia dissertation by F. A. Spear (1951). Hume's *Dialogues Concerning Natural Religion* have, as I have said, been beautifully edited by Norman Kemp Smith. Herbert Davis has an essay, fertile in suggestions, on "The Conversation of the Augustans," in R. F. Jones and others, *The Seventeenth Century* (1951), 181–97. But of course the best, most impressive sources at our command are Boswell's *Life of Johnson*, Voltaire's and Diderot's correspondence, and Goethe's various recorded conversations.

On what I call in the text "cross-cultural dialogues," see Geoffroy Atkinson, *The Extraordinary Voyage in French Literature Before 1700* (1920), *The Extraordinary Voyage in French Literature from 1700 to 1720* (1922), and *Le Sentiment de la nature et le retour à la vie simple (1690–1740)* (1960), as well as Gilbert Chinard's various studies, all learned and imaginative, especially *L'Amérique et le rêve exotique dans la littérature française au XVIIe et XVIIIe siècle* (1913).[2] See also Durand Echeverria's engaging analysis *Mirage in the West: A History of the French Image of American Society to 1815* (1957). For Montesquieu's *Lettres persanes* we have fine critical editions by Antoine Adam (1954) and Paul Vernière (1960); see G. L. van Roosbroeck, *Persian Letters Before Montesquieu* (1932); while Diderot's *Supplément au Voyage de Bougainville* has been edited by Gilbert Chinard (1935) and Herbert Dieckmann (1955). Diderot's *Le Neveu de Rameau* has excited much argument; I have already mentioned Curtius's classicizing interpretation (p. 477 above), which I accept. Curtius conveniently reviews the literature. There is an excellent critical edition by Jean Fabre (1950). See also James Doolittle, *Rameau's Nephew: A Study of Diderot's "Second Satire"* (1960).

For Voltaire at Cirey, see the various books by Ira O. Wade, each extremely useful. Diderot's share in Rousseau's work is analyzed, for the first *Discours*, in George R. Havens's critical edition of Rousseau's *Discours sur les sciences et les arts* (1946),

---

[2] The appropriate place for primitivism is Volume II, where I intend to give it some close attention; the whole subject has been put on a satisfactory scholarly basis by the writings of A. O. Lovejoy, George Boas, and their pupils.

and for the second *Discours*, see Havens, "Diderot, Rousseau, and the *Discours sur l'inégalité*," *Diderot Studies*, III (1961), 219–62. Diderot's share in Raynal's history of the two Indies is subtly analyzed in Wolpe's *Raynal*. English conversation appears in many social histories, very intelligently in Sutherland, *Preface to Eighteenth Century Poetry*. Weimar, in Bruford. For Parisian art criticism as a form of combative conversation, see Albert Dresdner, *Die Entstehung der Kunstkritik* (1915), a superb book.

3. THE PRIMACY OF MORAL REALISM

Practically all the secondary material for this section was used before in earlier sections. For general orientation—realism—see, above all, the writings of Auerbach. Diderot's practicality is stressed by Proust and other commentators. For the claims of the *vita contemplativa*, see Jaeger, *Aristotle*, Boll, and Friedlaender. For Rousseau's moral position, see especially Hendel and also Robert Derathé's important and bold analysis *Le Rationalisme de Jean-Jacques Rousseau* (1948). Cicero's statements on the *vita activa* receive the importance they deserve in Sabine and Smith's edition of Cicero's *Commonwealth*. Useful also is the careful analysis of three key words in Cicero, "Auctoritas, Dignitas, Otium," by J. P. V. D. Balsdon, *Classical Quarterly*, new series, X (1960), 43–50, which shows that Cicero uses the phrase *cum dignitate otium* only three times and that this condition, though desirable for elderly statesmen, is not the ideal way of life. For those ways of life, see the penetrating pages on the will in Cassirer, *Mythical Thinking* (especially pp. 157, 172, 194, 199, 212–20), and, as well, Erwin Panofsky's original and stimulating *Hercules am Scheidewege und andere antike Bildstoffe in der neueren Kunst* (1930). For philosophy as action in late Stoicism, see Farquharson, *Marcus Aurelius*, 53 f. And finally I always return with profit to the appropriate pages in John Dewey's *Human Nature and Conduct* (edn. 1930), especially the introduction and chapter I.

4. CANDIDE: THE EPICUREAN AS STOIC

Not surprisingly *Candide* has called forth a sizeable literature; it is too amusing to be forgotten, too puzzling to be left
alone. While much of that literature is respectable and suggestive,
I have relied mainly on a close reading of the book in the context
of Voltaire's work. My introduction to my translation of *Candide*
(1963) now strikes me as less than satisfactory; it has one merit:
it explores the hitherto neglected connections between *Candide*
and the *Dictionnaire philosophique*. There are several good editions: that by André Morize (1913) has an excellent introduction; so does the recent edition by René Pomeau (1959). O. R.
Taylor's school edition (1942) has some helpful notes. Ira O.
Wade's exhaustive, *Voltaire and 'Candide': A Study in the Fusion
of History, Art, and Philosophy* (1959), reproduces the facsimile
of an important early manuscript (the "La Vallière manuscript")
and analyses in the greatest detail the genesis, composition, and
publication of the little book, the problem of evil which it so
wittily tackles, its style, and finally its meaning. It is perhaps too
heavy a burden for *Candide* to bear. The second, revised edition
of W. F. Bottiglia, *Voltaire's 'Candide': Analysis of a Classic*, in
VS, VIIa (1964; 1st edn., 1959), is much superior to the first
and shows that thoughtful criticism is not irrelevant, at least to
some authors. I still find myself uneasy with the author's manner
of reviewing and restating practically all the opinions of all the
commentators on *Candide*, although I also find myself in agreement with Bottiglia's central thesis—that Voltaire was indeed a
practical man (that is, after all, the thesis of my own *Voltaire's
Politics*). But what *Candide* still needs is the kind of analysis that
a Spitzer or Auerbach might give it; these two great scholars
indeed occupied themselves with Voltaire's style, if only in passing (see Spitzer, "Einige Voltaire-Interpretationen," *Romanische
Stil- und Literaturstudien*, 2 vols. [1930], II, 211–43, and Auerbach, *Mimesis*, 401–13, both of which, as Bottiglia rightly complains, are a little condescending for all their learning).

Candide inescapably brings up the vexed issue of Voltaire's optimism. I shall return to this question in volume II. Meanwhile, I should note that I dissent from Theodore Besterman's portrait of an optimist turned pessimist by the Lisbon Earthquake (see "Voltaire et le désastre de Lisbonne: ou, la mort de l'optimisme," *VS*, II [1956], 7–24). Rita Falke has dealt with the same subject in "Eldorado: le meilleur des mondes possible," ibid., 25–41. Mina Waterman, *Voltaire, Pascal and Human Destiny* (1942), is a useful monograph; far more exciting and profound is J.-R. Carré, *Réflexions sur l'anti-Pascal de Voltaire* (1935). Carré has written another, equally impressive essay: *Consistance de Voltaire le philosophe* (1935), which actually takes Voltaire's thought seriously, a rare distinction—at least until recently—in the literature on Voltaire. It was probably first tried by Lanson, and by Georges Pellissier, *Voltaire Philosophe* (1908), a systematic analysis; and later most successfully by André Bellessort, *Essai sur Voltaire* (1925), a little book that has justly achieved a great reputation among students of Voltaire. Two articles by George R. Havens are important here: "Voltaire's Pessimistic Revision of the Conclusion of his 'Poème sur le désastre de Lisbonne,'" *Modern Language Notes*, XLIV (1929), 489–92, and "The Conclusion of Voltaire's 'Poème sur le désastre de Lisbonne,'" ibid., LVI (1941), 422–6. For Voltaire's merciless and doubtless unfair caricature of Leibniz, see Oscar A. Haac, "Voltaire and Leibniz: Two Aspects of Rationalism," *VS*, XXV (1963), 795–809; and above all W. H. Barber's thorough and reliable monograph, *Leibniz in France from Arnauld to Voltaire: A Study in French Reactions to Leibnizianism, 1670–1760* (1955), which treats *Candide* with satisfying detail.

CHAPTER FOUR

The Retreat From Reason

My interpretation of the Middle Ages—my very use of that old seventeenth-century term which historians since Ranke have deplored and employed—may strike some readers as downright reactionary, as the Whig interpretation unabashed and unrevised. But I am confident that the portrait of the medieval mentality I have drawn in this chapter captures its contours accurately and properly distinguishes it from the mentalities that preceded and succeeded it. With all my respect for Curtius's magnificent *European Literature and the Latin Middle Ages* (a masterly account of the migration of classical ideas and classical literary forms through the centuries as an arduous pilgrimage on a "crumbling Roman road"), my own reading of the literature and philosophy of the Middle Ages leads me to stress discontinuity rather than continuity.

The issue is extraordinarily complicated. The philosophes' own view of the Middle Ages cannot be sustained without serious revision—I trust I make that clear in the text. J. B. Bury's pronouncement *en philosophe* that the Middle Ages was a "millennium in which reason was enchained, thought was enslaved, and knowledge made no progress" (*A History of Freedom of Thought* [1913], 52) is certainly untenable. And for a long time now scholars have exposed and denounced it: there must be hundreds of textbooks and general cultural histories lamenting the Enlightenment's blindness to medieval achievements or the philosophes' vicious prejudices against a religious culture. Still, oddly enough, the Enlightenment's total view of the Middle Ages, with all *its* complexities, has never been fully studied, and I have been compelled to piece together my own account from a close reading of the sources. L. Varga, *Das Schlagwort vom "finsteren*

Mittelalter" (1932) is often cited with respect; but it is no more than a survey—and a superficial survey at that—of a tenacious cliché. Its reputation, I think, reflects not its own virtues but the scarcity of good studies in the field. Among the most useful monographs are Shelby T. McCloy, *Gibbon's Antagonism to Christianity* (1933), M. S. Libby, *The Attitude of Voltaire to Magic and the Sciences* (1935), and John E. Barker, *Diderot's Treatment of the Christian Religion in the "Encyclopédie"* (1941). See also Schargo, *History in the Encyclopédie*, 185 ff, for some welcome discriminating pages on the philosophes' view of the Middle Ages. René Lanson, *Le Goût du moyen âge en France au XVIIIᵉ siècle* (1926), makes a beginning, but it is slight. Robertson's "View of the State of Society in the Middle Ages," which serves as a general introduction to his *Charles V*, is perhaps the most generous treatment of medieval history by any Enlightenment historian of the eighteenth century; it is criticized by S. R. Maitland, *The Dark Ages* (3rd edn., 1853). H. Weisinger has a useful survey on "The Middle Ages and the Late Eighteenth-century Historians," *Philological Quarterly*, XXVII (January 1948), 63–79, while Paul Frankl has collected testimony on the Gothic in his substantial compendium *The Gothic: Literary Sources and Interpretations through Eight Centuries* (1959). There is to my knowledge no comprehensive study of the philosophes' shabby treatment of the Byzantine empire. But J. B. Bury, in his definitive edition of Gibbon's *Decline and Fall of the Roman Empire*, usually so sympathetic to Gibbon, finds it necessary to add explanatory and corrective footnotes to Gibbon's text on Byzantium. Gibbon himself, it should be added in all fairness, was aware that his account of Byzantium was less well informed than his account of earlier centuries.[1]

---

[1] In checking the philosophes' view of Byzantium, I found the following volumes most useful: Steven Runciman, *Byzantine Civilization* (1933), and Norman H. Baynes, *The Byzantine Empire* (edn. 1943), both popular but excellent treatments. *Byzantium: An Introduction to East Roman Civilization*, ed. Norman H. Baynes and H. St. L. B. Moss (1948), is a splendidly informative collection of essays by leading Byzantinists like Henri Grégoire, Charles Diehl, and others. It is fully equipped with maps, illustrations, and a comprehensive bibliography.

Since much of the philosophes' attitude toward the Middle Ages was political, the great debate on the origins of the French constitution is of central importance for an understanding of the whole question. Here the argument over Montesquieu and his theory of the Germanic origins of French institutions is of the highest importance. See Franz Neumann, "Introduction" to Montesquieu's *Spirit of the Laws*, my own treatment in *Voltaire's Politics* (to which I have appended a sizeable bibliography), and the convenient and judicious summary in Franklin L. Ford, *Robe and Sword: The Regrouping of the French Aristocracy after Louis XIV* (1953).

The eighteenth-century view of its medieval past was not merely political; it was literary, artistic, and scholarly as well. For the literary revival, see the attractive book by Arthur Johnston, *Enchanted Ground: The Study of Medieval Romance in the Eighteenth Century* (1964), which moves from Hurd and Percy down to Sir Walter Scott. David Douglas, *English Scholars, 1660–1730* (2nd edn., 1951), is a magnificent account of the passionate British antiquarians who made Great Britain's medieval world accessible. For the earlier antiquarians there is T. D. Kendrick, *British Antiquity* (1950). Continental pious historians also helped to revive interest in the Gothic world; see especially the revealing articles by David Knowles, "The Bollandists," in *Great Historical Enterprises and Problems in Monastic History* (1963), 1–32, and "The Maurists," ibid., 33–62.

The abundance of available material, then, is coupled with the lack of any comprehensive study of the Enlightenment's attitude toward the Middle Ages. To make matters worse, as I shall show in the following pages, there is a curious ambivalence often displayed by and, I think, inherent in the position of apologists for medieval philosophy.[2] And finally the search for clarity

---

[2] In addition to specialized monographs on the medieval mind, I used several general histories of the Middle Ages in the course of writing this chapter. Here I should mention only C. W. Prévité Orton, *The Shorter Cambridge Mediæval History*, 2 vols. (rev. edn., P. Grierson, 1952), a little breathless in spots but extremely valuable. R. W. Southern, *The Making of the Middle Ages* (1953), is a subtle and penetrating essay

has not been helped by historians who have discovered in medieval life a true "Renaissance" as distinct from a revival of culture. Charles Homer Haskins's charming and influential essay *The Renaissance of the Twelfth Century* (1927) is perhaps the greatest sinner here: it is full of valid information, but its central generalization, expressed in its title, simply does not work. Curtius has adopted it and offered some persuasive reasons for it in his *European Literature* (53n, 255); H. Liebeschütz, *Medieval Humanism in the Life and Writings of John of Salisbury* (1950), and G. Paré, A. Brunet, and P. Tremblay, *La Renaissance du XIIe siècle* (1933), have offered further evidence; but impressive as they are, these books do not prove the existence of a Renaissance. They do prove that the variety and cultivation of the twelfth century was greater than the philosophes were ready to admit.

1. THE ADULTERATION OF ANTIQUITY

On the transmission of ancient myths, literary forms, and philosophical ideas, see the various volumes in "Our Debt to

---

on Western medieval society in the twelfth and thirteenth centuries. Friedrich Heer, *The Medieval World: Europe, 1100–1350* (1961; tr. Janet Sondheimer, 1962), tries to delineate an "open" medieval society during this period; it is suggestive, indeed brilliant, but not wholly convincing. J. M. Wallace-Hadrill, *The Barbarian West: A. D. 400–1000—The Early Middle Ages* (2nd edn., 1962), is a brief survey of a neglected period. For England, see especially Sir Maurice Powicke, *Medieval England* (1931), and F. M. Stenton, *English Society in the Early Middle Ages* (1951), which are both popular history at its very best. F. M. Stenton, *The First Century of English Feudalism* (1932), is rightly regarded with the highest respect; V. H. H. Green, *The Later Plantagenets* (1955), authoritatively deals with the later period. For Germany, see G. Barraclough, *Origins of Modern Germany* (2nd edn., 1947). For France, see the standard volume by R. Fawtier, *The Capetian Kings of France* (1940; tr. L. Butler and R. J. Adams, 1960). The Crusades are lucidly narrated and analyzed in Steven Runciman, *History of the Crusades*, 3 vols. (1951–4).

Greece and Rome," already cited, as well as the books by Sandys, Gruppe, Borinski, and Thomson. My acquaintance with the monographs published by the Warburg Institute fortunately began with my reading of Study No. 11, Jean Seznec's *The Survival of the Pagan Gods* (1940; rev. edn. tr. Barbara F. Sessions, 1953), a charming and convincing account of the fate of classical mythology in medieval and Renaissance hands; the book introduced me to the problem and incidentally dramatized Cassirer's distinction between mythical and critical thought as it applied to the Christian millennium. Fritz Saxl, "Die Bibliothek Warburg und Ihr Ziel," *Warburg Vorträge, 1921–1922* (1923), 1–10, lays down the Warburg program and gives an instance of the survival of Venus. Adolph Goldschmidt, "Das Nachleben der antiken Formen im Mittelalter," ibid., 40–50, offers some other striking instances. A. Doren, "Fortuna im Mittelalter und in der Renaissance," *Warburg Vorträge, 1922–1923* (1924), 71–144, is a distinguished survey of the survival of a pagan idea. R. Klibansky, *The Continuity of the Platonic Tradition During the Middle Ages* (1939), is brief, more a program than a monograph, but essential. R. R. Bolgar, *The Classical Heritage and Its Beneficiaries* (1958) has already acquired a well-deserved reputation for its vigorous love of the classics and its careful exposition of the medieval use (or abuse) of the ancients. I have learned much from it, and I have borrowed from him some instances of medieval hysteria. Richard Newald, *Nachleben des antiken Geistes im Abendland bis zum Beginn des Humanismus* (1960), is a generously proportioned survey, evidently the fruit of a lifetime's work. Jean Adhémar, *Influences antiques dans l'art du moyen âge français* (1939), is a characteristic Warburg product—solid and searching.

For the Church Fathers and classical antiquity, see specifically E. K. Rand, *Founders of the Middle Ages* (1928), a graceful set of lectures which begins with the encounter of Christianity and pagan culture and ends with Dante. For that encounter, see standard histories of early Christianity such as H. Lietzmann, *The Beginnings of the Christian Church*, 2 vols. (1932; tr. B. L. Woolf, 1937–8), to supplement and correct Gibbon's justly famous—or notorious—chapters XV and XVI in the *Decline and Fall*; C. N. Cochrane's impressive, learned *Christianity and Classical Culture:*

A Study of Thought and Action from Augustus to Augustine
(rev. edn., 1944), which, in its sweeping survey, treats Christianity
as a vast critique of pagan thought; and Henry Osborn Taylor,
The Classical Heritage of the Middle Ages (1901), which, for all
its age, holds up well. Curtius, *European Literature*, has much valuable material, persuasively presented, scattered through it—on the
specific policies of the Church Fathers, see chapters I to III. For
the final compromise, hammered out by the fifth century, see the
comments by Ernst Troeltsch, *Gesammelte Schriften*, IV, 166 ff.

Amid a vast literature dealing with the origins of Christianity,
I have learned perhaps most from Rudolf Bultmann, *Primitive
Christianity in its Contemporary Setting* (1949; tr. R. H. Fuller,
1956), which stresses its syncretic character. So does Arthur
Darby Nock, *Early Gentile Christianity and Its Hellenistic Back-
ground* (enlarged edn., 1964)—brilliant, as is all his work.

This encounter of Christian and pagan culture was, of course,
most dramatic in the lives of representative Christians. Adolf
Deissmann, *Paul: A Study in Social and Religious History* (2nd
edn., 1925; tr. William E. Wilson, 1927), takes Paul through his
pilgrimage from Judaism to Christianity to his Apostolate; Karl
Ludwig Schmidt, "Der Apostel Paulus und die antike Welt,"
Warburg Vorträge, *1924–1925* (1927), 38–64, attempts to place
him firmly in his environment. I found Arthur Darby Nock, *St.
Paul* (1938), highly instructive. For St. Jerome, his classicism, his
dream, and his Christian learning, see especially Harold Hagendahl,
Latin Fathers and the Classics (1958), an excellent study. The
dream has often been reported; for a modern discussion, see
Bolgar, *Classical Heritage*, 51. Clearly, the commanding strategist
was Augustine, and on him the literature is large. Augustine's
ambivalence is beautifully captured and exhaustively analyzed in
H. I. Marrou's *Saint Augustin et la fin de la culture antique* (4th
edn., 1958) and in the first-rate article by R. Reitzenstein,
"Augustin als antiker und als mittelalterlicher Mensch," which was
very important to me.[3] *Saint Augustine* (1930), a collection of
essays by M. C. d'Arcy and others, is valuable; see especially
Christopher Dawson, "St. Augustine and His Age," 11–77, and

---

[3] See *Warburg Vorträge*, *1922–1923*, 24–65.

John-Baptist Reeves, "St. Augustine and Humanism," 121–51.
Étienne Gilson, *The Christian Philosophy of Saint Augustine*
(1931; tr. L. E. M. Lynch, 1960), is a full introduction. See also
Ernst Troeltsch, *Augustin, die christliche Antike, und das Mittel-
alter* (1915), and the important article by Theodor E. Mommsen,
"St. Augustine and the Christian Idea of Progress," *JHI*, XII: 3
(July 1951), 346–74.

Another figure of strategic importance for this chapter is
Dante. Among the works I consulted, I found the following most
instructive: Erich Auerbach, *Dante: Poet of the Secular World*
(1929; tr. Ralph Manheim, 1961), which, though brilliant in itself,
has been partially superseded by Auerbach's own articles "Figura"
and "St. Francis of Assisi in Dante's 'Commedia,'" in *Scenes from
the Drama of European Literature*, 77–98, and in the moving
chapter on the *Divine Comedy*, "Farinata and Cavalcante," in
Mimesis, 174–202. All these essays move from the minute consideration of Dante's stylistic habits to Dante's style of thinking.
Étienne Gilson, from whom I dissent in other matters, has an
impressive and persuasive study of *Dante the Philosopher* (1939;
tr. David Moore, 1949), which surveys the literature with a keen
eye for controversy. In addition I have admired and used A.
Renaudet, *Dante humaniste* (1952), Joseph A. Mazzeo's subtle
examination of the conception of hierarchy in his *Medieval Cultural Tradition in Dante's "Comedy"* (1960), the specialized but
allusive essay by A. P. d'Entrèves, *Dante as a Political Thinker*
(1952), and the thoughtful evocation by Irma Brandeis, *The
Ladder of Vision: A Study of Dante's Comedy* (1960). Santayana's
chapter on Dante in his *Three Philosophical Poets* is graceful,
suggestive, and prophetic in its understanding of the figural conception of reality. It is also refreshingly independent: "Dante was
medieval, and contrition, humility, and fear of the devil were
great virtues in those days; but the conclusion we must come to is
precisely that the virtues of those days were not the best virtues,
and that a poet who represents that time cannot be a fair nor an
ultimate spokesman for humanity" (p. 120)—a view with which I
agree. As a historian, I trust, I have not acted as a judge; but to the
degree that this book can claim to move beyond historical analysis
to a philosophical comprehension of the past, it decides between

the Christian millennium, with its ideal of dependence, and the Enlightenment, with its ideal of autonomy, in favor of autonomy.

All the books on Dante touch on Dante's conception of classical antiquity. But Eternal Rome is a special subject; it has been examined with learning and vigor by Charles T. Davis, *Dante and the Idea of Rome* (1957), which includes (Introduction and pp. 236–8) a survey of the literature on this subject. Percy Ernst Schramm's substantial *Kaiser, Rom und Renovatio*, 2 vols. (1929) studies the survival of the idea of Rome down to the twelfth century and includes significant documents. See also Kenneth J. Pratt, "Rome as Eternal," *JHI*, XXVI: 1 (January–March 1965), 25–44.

The survival of Dante into the Enlightenment needs further study. See Naves, *Goût de Voltaire* (1938); and there is Hermann Oelsner, *Dante in Frankreich bis zum Ende des XVIIIten Jahrhunderts* (1898), which has good material but could be redone.

The literature on the medieval misuse of ancient sources—from ignorance as much as from malice—is sizable. Curtius's excursuses, "Misunderstandings of Antiquity in the Middle Ages" and "The Ape as Metaphor" (*European Literature*, 405–6, 538–540), are amusing and instructive. Vergil's fate in medieval hands has been specially studied; J. H. Whitfield has dealt with the important subject of *Dante and Virgil* (1949); the old book by Domenico Comparetti, *Virgilio nel medio evo*, has recently been reissued in two volumes (1937–1946); it should be read in conjunction with the fascinating lengthy monograph by John W. Spargo, *Virgil the Necromancer, Studies in Virgilian Legend* (1934).

Ovid came to have an immense vogue in the Christian millennium. Seznec, *Survival of the Pagan Gods*, has some fine pages, especially on the *Ovide moralisé*. Seznec has relied on an informative article by Lester K. Born, "Ovid and Allegory," *Speculum*, IX (1934), 362–79—so have I. C. S. Lewis, *The Allegory of Love: A Study in Medieval Tradition* (1936), beautifully written and beautifully argued, examines the place of Ovid in the medieval religion of love and his many uses for the medieval mind. D. W. Robertson's magnum opus, *A Preface to Chaucer: Studies in Medieval Perspectives* (1962), has much that is instructive to say (among many other things) on the survival of Ovid into the fourteenth and fifteenth centuries. See also Fausto Ghisalberti, "Mediaeval Biographies of Ovid," *Warburg Journal*, IX (1946), 10–59 a very interesting article; and W. F. Schirmer, "Chaucer, Shakespeare und die Antike," *Warburg Vorträge*, *1930–1931* (1932), 83–102, which also has some revealing comments on Ovid.

On Cicero in the Middle Ages, Zielinski's book is much less useful than Baron's great essay.[4]

2. THE BETRAYAL OF CRITICISM

The question of the nature and position of medieval philosophy is raised again and again, not surprisingly, by sympathetic historians of medieval philosophy. I have enjoyed the spirited polemics against "modern misreadings" by F. C. Copleston, *Aquinas* (1955); Maurice de Wulf, *Scholasticism Old and New* (tr. P. Coffey, 1907) and *Philosophy and Civilization in the Middle Ages* (1922); and above all Étienne Gilson, *The Spirit of Mediaeval Philosophy* (tr. A. H. C. Downes, 1936), *Reason and Revelation in the Middle Ages* (1938), and "Concerning Christian Philosophy: The Distinctiveness of the Philosophic Order," in *Philosophy and History: The Ernst Cassirer Festschrift* (1936), 61–76. These defenses certainly make the contempt for medieval learning of the philosophes—and of modern secularists—appear shallow and uninformed, and to that extent they are successful. At the same time, their argument seems to me to reduce itself to this: there was serious speculation in the Middle Ages; it was independent and in some areas free, not merely from ecclesiastical control, but even from religious concerns. Still, in areas where philosophy and theology conflicted, philosophy gave way; still, for all its independence, philosophy was distinctly inferior to theology in rank and directed by theology in its most important

---

[4] See above, p. 477.

researches. And so, to put it realistically, this freedom did not really amount to much. After all, the cliché that philosophy is the handmaiden of theology was not invented by a philosophe but by a medieval Christian.

Among general works on Christian speculation, Paul Vignaux, *Philosophy in the Middle Ages: An Introduction* (3rd edn., 1958; tr. E. C. Hall, 1959), is outstanding for its clarity and sobriety; I have relied also, and heavily, on the magnificent general survey by Émile Bréhier, *La Philosophie du moyen âge* (new edn., 1949). Étienne Gilson, *History of Christian Philosophy in the Middle Ages* (2nd edn., 1952; Eng. tr., 1955), is an excellent survey. The relevant chapters (I–V) in M. H. Carré, *Phases of Thought in England* (1949), intelligently appreciate both neglected and remembered philosophers and are sensitive to the varieties of medieval thought. Martin Grabmann's writings are justly celebrated for their erudition; see especially his *Geschichte der scholastischen Methode*, 2 vols. (1909–11), and the essays collected in *Mittelalterliches Geistesleben*, Vol. II of *Abhandlungen zur Geschichte der Scholastik und Mystik*, 3 vols. (1936).

Among works on individual philosophers, I have relied on Karl Barth, *Anselm: Fides Quaerens Intellectum* (2nd edn., 1958; tr. Ian W. Robertson, 1960), which is difficult but rewarding; Étienne Gilson, *The Christian Philosophy of St. Thomas Aquinas* (1922; tr. L. K. Shook, 1956); and Martin Grabmann, *Thomas Aquinas* (5th edn., 1926; Eng. tr., 1928). For the important developments inherent in Occam's thought, see the impressive work by Georges de Lagarde, *La Naissance de l'esprit laïque au déclin du moyen âge*, 5 vols. (2nd and 3rd edn., 1956–63), and the stimulating essay by M. H. Carré, *Realists and Nominalists* (1946), which proves—at least to my satisfaction—that a vast distance separates the Occamists and modern science. For medieval science, see the judicious, well-informed, and sympathetic (and, through their very sympathy, weighty) studies by A. C. Crombie: *Robert Grosseteste and the Origins of Experimental Science: 1100–1700* (1953) and the even more comprehensive *Augustine to Galileo: The History of Science, A.D. 400–1650* (rev. edn., 1959), the latter with a magnificently full and discriminating bibliography. I do not think that Crombie would draw quite the conclusions I have drawn. Medieval man's sense of impotence before nature is briefly but powerfully discussed by Erwin Panofsky in his analysis of the term *creare* during the Middle Ages and the Renaissance in "Artist, Scientist, Genius: Notes on the 'Renaissance-Dämmerung,'" in *The Renaissance*, six essays by Wallace K. Ferguson and others (ed. 1962), 121–82 *passim*.

On medieval encyclopedias, those vague forerunners of Diderot's great enterprise, there are two remarkable articles, one by Adolph Goldschmidt, "Frühmittelalterliche illustrierte Encyklopädien," *Warburg Vorträge, 1923–1924* (1926), 215–26, and Fritz Saxl, "A Spiritual Encyclopedia of the Later Middle Ages," *Warburg Journal*, V (1942), 82–134.

On what passed for Platonism in the Middle Ages, see Paul Shorey, *Platonism, Ancient and Modern* (1938), which, though vulgar in tone, has some essential information. Very useful are two important articles by Ernst Hoffmann: "Platonismus und Mittelalter," *Warburg Vorträge, 1923–1924* (1926), 17–82, and "Platonism in Augustine's Philosophy of History," in *Philosophy and History: The Ernst Cassirer Festschrift*, 173–90.

3. THE REHABILITATION OF MYTH

My general argument that the Christian world view was mythopoeic, though often in a very refined sense, goes back once again to Cassirer's *Mythical Thinking*. I have also derived much instruction from writers who would not all, I think, agree with me. Ernst Bernheim, *Mittelalterliche Zeitanschauungen in ihrem Einfluss auf Politik und Geschichtsschreibung* (1918), takes its point of departure from Augustine's political-mythical thought. Heinrich von Eicken, *Geschichte und System der mittelalterlichen Weltanschauung* (4th edn., 1923), is a comprehensive survey with many revealing quotations. Michael Seidlmayer, *Currents of Medieval Thought, with Special Reference to Germany* (tr. D. Barker, 1960), is short and intelligent; Alois Dempf, *Die Hauptform mittelalterlicher Weltanschauung* (1925), though also short, is pious and pretentious—precisely the kind of *Geistesgeschichte* that this delicate subject does not need. In his *Social Teachings of the Christian Churches* (I, 249–50) and elsewhere Troeltsch properly insists that asceticism was matched by Christian worldliness. See also C. S. Lewis's informal and instructive *The Discarded Image: An Introduction to Medieval and Renaissance Literature* (1964), which analyzes the medieval "world picture" with admirable clarity. Many of these books have been helpful, but I have learned most, I think, from Marc Bloch's masterly *Feudal Society*, 2 vols. (1939–40; tr. L. A. Manyon, 1961). Bloch writes social history and properly embeds the medieval *Weltanschauung* in the social context; one can *see* medieval man face to face with time, space, history, authority.

Bloch's book makes it perfectly clear that medieval religion, philosophy, and politics are inextricably intertwined and illuminate one another. Fritz Kern, *Kingship and Law in the Middle Ages* (a monograph [1914] and a long article [1919], rev. by Kern and tr. S. B. Chrimes, 1939), has justly achieved the status of a minor classic. Otto von Gierke, *Political Theories of the Middle Age* (tr. F. W. Maitland, 1900, from *Das deutsche Genossenschafts-recht*, Vol. III), though older, remains important. So does J. N. Figgis, *Studies of Political Thought from Gerson to Grotius, 1414–1625* (2nd edn., 1916). The major work on the period remains R. W. and A. J. Carlyle, *A History of Medieval Political Theory in the West*, 6 vols. (1903–36). It may now be supplemented with Ewart Lewis, *Medieval Political Ideas*, 2 vols. (1954), which prints documents and commentaries. Ernst H. Kantorowicz, *The King's Two Bodies: A Study in Mediaeval Political Theology* (1957), is a fascinating series of essays, perhaps inadequately unified but still of major importance, directed quite explicitly (see Preface, p. ix) at elucidating what Ernst Cassirer had called "the myth of the state"; in the process it sheds much light on the mythmaking quality of medieval thinking.

Theory and practice were, of course, in constant tension and interaction. On feudal society, in addition to Bloch's great work see F. L. Ganshof, *Feudalism* (3rd edn., 1957; tr. Philip Grierson, 1961), economical but remarkably comprehensive and with a full bibliography; and Otto Hintze's famous article "Wesen und

Verbreitung des Feudalismus," *Sitzungsberichte der Preussischen Akademie der Wissenschaften, Philosophisch-historische Klasse* (1929), 321–47. See also Sidney Painter's essay *French Chivalry: Chivalric Ideas and Practices in Mediaeval France* (1940). Medieval economic and urban life have been illuminated in the rather controversial histories of Henri Pirenne. Pirenne's *Economic and Social History of Medieval Europe* (1933; tr. I. E. Clegg, 1936) and his *Medieval Cities* (tr. Frank D. Halsey, 1925) both contain his much argued-over account of the rise of towns. For implicit criticism, a good essay, and useful documents on urban life, see John H. Mundy and Peter Riesenberg, *The Medieval Town* (1958).

Medieval religious life has naturally produced a large literature. Nearly all the books I have cited so far touch on it. In addition I want to cite the magisterial writings of David Knowles, especially *The Religious Orders in England*, 3 vols. (1948–59), and *The English Mystical Tradition* (1961). Henry Charles Lea, *The Inquisition of the Middle Ages* (abridged by Margaret Nicholson from the original three-volume work, 1961), is hostile but completely scrupulous. The same may be said of the works of G. G. Coulton, which are the despair of those who prefer what they regard as medieval order over our modern disorder. Consistently critical in tone, deeply convinced that religion breeds—perhaps *is* —superstition, Coulton nevertheless commands his sources with sovereign control; even if his conclusions remain in doubt, the material he offers is invaluable. See especially his comprehensive work *Five Centuries of Religion*, 4 vols. (1923–50).

For medieval literature, see the remarkable collection of essays by Erich Auerbach, *Literary Language and Its Public in Late Latin Antiquity and in the Middle Ages* (1958; tr. Ralph Manheim, 1965), which, as always with Auerbach, moves from a most minute examination of texts to the whole medieval style of thought. For the literature of courtly love and the troubadours, see Lewis, *Allegory of Love;* and Jessie L. Weston's famous, now perhaps a little dated *From Ritual to Romance* (1920). Standard histories of literature, like volumes I and II of the *Oxford History of English Literature*, and general treatments, like Heer's *The Medieval World*, all have helpful bibliographies. Curtius, *Euro-*

pean Literature, is indispensable; it reads literature as the expression of a cosmic order.

One of the most revealing aspects of medieval thought was its manner of writing history. Bloch has some brilliant insights (*Feudal Society*, I, 72–5, 88–92). V. H. Galbraith, *Historical Research in Medieval England* (1951), is dry but reliable. There is much revealing material in two modern editions of the works of Otto of Freising; see C. C. Mierow's edition and translation of Otto's *The Two Cities* (1928) and *The Deeds of Frederick Barbarossa* (1953). Walther I. Brandt has translated and edited the early fourteenth-century historian Pierre Dubois, *The Recovery of the Holy Land* (1956). These last three titles are among other important medieval documents, scrupulously translated and intelligently edited, in the "Records of Civilization" series edited by the history department of Columbia University. Heer's chapter in his *Medieval World* (XI) is generous and perceptive. Amid a vast periodical literature I mention only Eva Matthews Sanford, who has shown in "The Study of Ancient History in the Middle Ages," *JHI*, V:1 (January 1944), 21–43, that medieval historians did know something of antiquity; Moriz Ritter, "Die christlich-mittelalterliche Geschichtsschreibung," *Historische Zeitschrift*, CVII (1911), 237–305, which is an excellent general survey; Herbert Grundmann, "Die Grundzüge der mittelalterlichen Geschichtsanschauungen," *Archiv für Kulturgeschichte*, XXIV (1934), 326–36; Johannes Spörl, "Wandel des Welt- und Geschichtsbildes im 12. Jahrhundert?" in *Geschichtsdenken und Geschichtsbild im Mittelalter*, ed. Walther Lammers (1961), 278–97; and H. Fuhrmann, "Die Fälschungen im Mittelalter," *Historische Zeitschrift*, CXCVII:3 (December 1963), 529–54, 580–601, a fascinating discussion of the medieval conception of truth.

Medieval art, a vast religious tapestry, is perhaps even more revealing than medieval history. Emile Mâle, *Religious Art in France of the Thirteenth Century* (3rd edn., 1928; tr. Dora Nussey, 1913), is a penetrating analysis which explicates the symbolic meaning of the cathedrals without falling into the trap of overinterpretation. Erwin Panofsky has shed much light on the medieval mentality in a series of magnificent monographs, a joy to read. See especially his *Early Netherlandish Painting: Its Origins and Character* (1953) and *Abbot Suger on the Abbey Church of St. Denis and its Art Treasures* (1946). In his *Gothic Architecture and Scholasticism* (edn., 1957), Panofsky attempts to bring together two aspects of medieval activity into one architectonic whole; for a persuasive critique of his argument see Otto von Simson, *The Gothic Cathedral* (1956), xx–xxi. Simson's book was of the greatest importance to me; I owe it many insights into the medieval view of the visible world as a vast symbol, or set of symbols, for the invisible world. I also owe it the dramatic story of the fire at Chartres.[5] G. G. Coulton, *Art and the Reformation* (1928), is perhaps less penetrating than these volumes but offers a great deal of useful material (esp. chapters I–XVI). Among general histories of art and architecture, I found Paul Frankl's *Gothic Architecture* (1962) and Geoffrey F. Webb's *Architecture in Britain: The Middle Ages* (1956) most illuminating. For Honnecourt's sketchbook, much exploited, see especially Kenneth Clark, *The Nude: A Study in Ideal Form* (1956), 11–12.

As scholars have shown over and over again (see the pages of the *Warburg Journal* and the Warburg *Studies*), Christianity is filled with motifs common to many religions: the virgin mother, the son as savior, the power of water, magical symbols like the cross, the potency of the Word—these all appear in non-Christian religions. Van der Leeuw, *Religion in Essence and Manifestation*, is especially rich in suggestions; see also Mircea Eliade, *Patterns in Comparative Religions* (1949; tr. Rosemary Sheed, 1958); F. Boll, *Sternglaube und Sterndeutung* (2nd edn., 1919); and the great works of Hermann Usener, which have permanently influenced research in comparative religion. See especially Usener's *Götternamen: Versuch einer Lehre von der religiösen Begriffsbildung* (2nd edn., 1929) and his collection of "minor" writings, *Kleine Schriften*, 4 vols. (1912–1914). Cassirer's *Mythical Thinking* (to mention this indispensable book once again) offers a masterly conspectus of research done up to the 1920's. While Freud's anthropology now is regarded as dated, his suggestions on the

---

[5] See above, pp. 252–3.

origins and meaning of religion remain (to use a much overused word just once, where it is appropriate) seminal.

For number mysticism, which informed literature and architecture as much as religious speculation, see the general survey by Vincent F. Hopper, *Medieval Number Symbolism* (1938), which brings together a good deal of material. Simson, *Gothic Cathedral*, abundantly demonstrates the invasion of architecture by sacred numbers (see esp. pp. 22–27, 243–4, and the striking mathematical appendix [by Ernst Levy] on "The Proportions of the South Tower of Chartres Cathedral"). Curtius (pp. 501–14) deals with the number mysticism of many medieval writers, including Dante; this is also a prominent theme in Gilson's *Dante the Philosopher*. See also von Eicken, *Mittelalterliche Weltanschauung* (p. 630), Gilson, *Reason and Revelation* (pp. 29–30), and the helpful and interesting essay by Tobias Dantzig, *Number: The Language of Science* (4th edn., 1954).

CHAPTER FIVE

The Era of Pagan Christianity

The period of European history that I have carved out in this chapter—between 1300 and 1700—dramatizes events and conjunctions in Western history that strike me as decisive: the deep rift within the Christian millennium, an increasing passion to rediscover and repossess classical pagan thought and culture in all its purity; the persistence of the Christian religion as an enormous emotional and political force; and the conflict between these two—Christianity and paganism—which found its characteristic expression in Renaissance humanism and seventeenth-century classicism.

The general historical orientation of this chapter depends upon familiar books on early modern history—books by Pieter Geyl, J. E. Neale, and others, which I need not cite separately. But I want to call special attention to the kind of experimental social history that takes it rise from the work of Marc Bloch and Lucien Febvre and is now concentrated in the circle around the *Annales*. Fernand Braudel's celebrated *La Méditerranée et le monde méditerranéen à l'époque de Philippe II* (1949) has become the model for other investigations. I am also indebted to Robert Mandrou, *Introduction à la France moderne (1500–1640): Essai de psychologie historique* (1961), a remarkable survey of the conditions of life—nutrition, lodging, anxiety, and exhilaration—of early modern Frenchmen, a book worthy of imitation. The relation of religion and politics, the needs of the spirit and the demands of authority, deserve further exploration; I cite here a pioneering article by Emanuel Chill, "Religion and Mendicity in Seventeenth-Century France," *International Review of Social History*, VII (1962), 400–25.

I. THE PURIFICATION OF THE SOURCES

Ever since Jacob Burckhardt "invented" the Renaissance in his masterpiece, *Die Kultur der Renaissance in Italien: Ein Versuch* (1860), the literature around his essay has grown until it has reached unmanageable proportions. We are fortunate in the splendid bibliographical essay by Federico Chabod, "The Concept of the Renaissance," in *Machiavelli and the Renaissance* (tr. David Moore, 1958),[1] which collects and classifies and evaluates writings on the Renaissance down to 1957; I have used it to great profit. Another effective aid is Wallace K. Ferguson's well-known *The Renaissance in Historical Thought: Five Centuries of Interpretation* (1948). The central question in the historiography of the Renaissance is: did the Renaissance exist? The debate continues. I find myself in wholehearted agreement with those recent scholars who, while refining and modifying Burckhardt, accept his major argument: I agree that there was a Renaissance, and only one Renaissance, and that it took place in the Renaissance. Perhaps the most significant confirmation of this position has come from the art historians, especially from Erwin Panofsky. After carefully examining conflicting claims Panofsky's masterly *Renaissance and Renascences in Western Art* (1960) concludes that "something rather decisive . . . must have happened between 1250 and 1550" (p. 40) and then proves it in considerable detail. Panofsky's earlier *Studies in Iconology: Humanistic Themes in the Art of the Renaissance* (1939) is exhilarating, learned, and convincing; it lifts intellectual history to a high level indeed. See also his splendid study *Albrecht Dürer* (3rd edn., 1948) and a host of articles, conveniently listed in the bibliography to *Renaissance and Renascences* (p. 222); a few of these have been intelligently collected in *Meaning in the Visual Arts* (1955). Another such paperback could be compiled with ease. All these writings subtly differ-

---

[1] I shall deal with Machiavelli and the northern Renaissance of the sixteenth century below, pp. 517–20.

entiate between what the Renaissance took from medieval and what it took from antique sources, what was old, apparently new, and actually new. Garrett Mattingly made an engaging plea for a return to tested—that is, Burckhardtian—verities in "Some Revisions of the Political History of the Renaissance," in *The Renaissance*, ed. Tinsley Helton (1961), 3–25. Mattingly's *Renaissance Diplomacy* (1955), probably his best book, is far more than diplomatic history; it shows the modern world at birth. Johan Huizinga's essays "The Problem of the Renaissance" (1920) and "Renaissance and Realism" (1929), reprinted in a collection of his papers, *Men and Ideas* (tr. James S. Holmes and Hans van Marle, 1959), 243–87, 288–309, are sensitive, discriminating, and filled with ideas. *Facets of the Renaissance* (edn. 1963) contains a thoroughly modern survey in stimulating essays by Wallace K. Ferguson, Garrett Mattingly, E. Harris Harbison, Myron P. Gilmore, and Paul Oskar Kristeller.

Among books published since Chabod brought his bibliography up to date, the most important are in political and social history. Gene A. Brucker's *Florentine Politics and Society, 1343–1387* (1962) is the first in what promises to be an indispensable series of volumes on Florence on the verge of the Renaissance; its careful analysis of currents and countercurrents in Florentine society will certainly supplement and probably replace Ferdinand Schevill's useful but somewhat old-fashioned *History of Florence from the Founding of the City through the Renaissance* (rev. edn., 1961). Felix Gilbert's economical *Machiavelli and Guicciardini: Politics and History in Sixteenth-Century Florence* (1965) deserves special attention. I read it after I had completed this chapter, but it helped to confirm my point that while Renaissance humanism in general was Christian, it had its radical non-Christian, wholly disillusioned wing as well.

With its magnificent compression Gilbert's *Machiavelli and Guicciardini* does not supersede a series of Gilbert's earlier essays on Renaissance Florence. See especially "Bernardo Rucellai and the Orti Oricellari: A Study on the Origin of Modern Political Thought," *Warburg Journal*, XII (1949), 101–31, and "Florentine Political Assumptions in the Period of Savonarola and Soderini," ibid., XX (1957), 187–214. In this analysis of Florentine political institutions, essential to an understanding of the thought of the later Renaissance and neglected by Schevill, Gilbert has of course not been alone. Gilbert pays tribute to such important contributions of Nicolai Rubinstein's as "The Beginnings of Political Thought in Florence: A Study in Mediaeval Historiography," *Warburg Journal,* V (1942), 198–227, and "Politics and Constitution in Florence at the End of the Fifteenth Century," in *Italian Renaissance Studies,* ed. E. F. Jacob (1960), 148–83. A pioneering essay in this field is Delio Cantimori, "Rhetoric and Politics in Italian Humanism," *Warburg Journal,* I (1937–8), 83–102, one of the first to point to the significance of the political conversations in the Rucellai gardens, the Orti Oricellari. *Italian Renaissance Studies,* just cited, a collection of posthumous tributes to Cecilia M. Ady, also has a remarkable essay on Renaissance politics: L. F. Marks, "The Financial Oligarchy in Florence under Lorenzo" (123–47). Miss Ady's own *Lorenzo dei Medici and Renaissance Italy* (1955), for all its brevity and popular intentions, is marvellously clear on the mixture of ruthlessness and mysticism in one Renaissance family.

In one way or another, of course, all these titles concern themselves with that significant but elusive class of Renaissance intellectuals, the Humanists. There has been some first-rate work on them in recent years, correcting the influential but extravagant theses of G. Toffanin (especially in *History of Humanism,* 3rd edn., [1943; tr. Elio Gianturco, 1954]) that Humanism was the ancestor of the Counter-Reformation, an expression of Catholic scholarship. Myron P. Gilmore's general survey *The World of Humanism, 1453–1517* (1952) is judicious and successful. Eugenio Garin, *Der italienische Humanismus* (tr. Giuseppe Zamboni, 1947), is a strikingly original survey of Humanism from its beginnings with Salutati and Bruni to its end almost two centuries later with Bruno and Campanella. I found its observations on the relations of *vita activa* to *vita contemplativa* especially illuminating. It includes a brief, discriminating bibliography. Paul Oskar Kristeller has made the Humanists his lifework; I have learned a great deal from his *The Classics and Renaissance Thought* (1955), which is small only in size, and from a considerable number of his informative articles conveniently collected in *Studies in Renais-*

sance Thought and Letters (1956). In his effort to rescue the Humanists from the vague enthusiasms of ill-informed researchers, Kristeller perhaps narrows his definition unduly, but his work has been an essential corrective, an impressive marshaling of new evidence, and a stimulus to further work. Lauro Martines, *The Social World of the Florentine Humanists* (1963), ably corrects misconceptions concerning the Humanists' "poverty" or their supposed "alienation"; the book is a little unpolished, but its documentation is complete and revealing. Hanna H. Gray, "Renaissance Humanism: The Pursuit of Eloquence," *JHI*, XXIV:4 (October–December 1963), 497–514, gives rhetoric the importance it deserves in Humanist thought. While historians of science like George Sarton and Lynn Thorndyke used to expend much time and energy "proving" that the Humanists hated science —and that therefore there was no Renaissance—Sarton in one of his last papers took back much of this and reached a rather more generous appreciation of Humanist thinking: "The Quest for Truth: Scientific Progress during the Renaissance," *The Renaissance: Six Essays* by Wallace K. Ferguson and others (1953), 55–76.

Kristeller was among the first to take the philosophy of the Renaissance seriously; see his *The Philosophy of Marsilio Ficino* (1943). Kristeller was preceded and doubtless inspired by Ernst Cassirer, whose *The Individual and The Cosmos in Renaissance Philosophy* (1927; tr. Mario Domandi, 1963) is a subtle, profound examination of the inner tensions of Renaissance thought, of surviving mysticism in the midst of disenchantment; it concentrates perhaps too much on Nicholas of Cusa, and its account of the retreat of the Florentine Humanists from politics under Lorenzo de' Medici is rather unpolitical (it should be read in conjunction with the relevant pages of Martines, *Social World of the Florentine Humanists*), but these flaws apart, the book is overwhelming in its insights and its careful attention to nuance. In his last years Cassirer returned to the Renaissance. See above all his "Giovanni Pico della Mirandola: A Study in the History of Renaissance Ideas," *JHI*, III:2, 3 (April, July, 1942), 123–44, 319–46. Cassirer, Kristeller, and John Herman Randall, Jr. have also edited a collection of texts, *The Renaissance Philosophy of*

Man (1948), with translations and introductions by various hands, making available at least portions of the philosophical writings of Petrarch, Valla, Ficino, Pico, Pomponazzi, and Vives—a serious and helpful volume. N. A. Robb, *Neoplatonism of the Italian Renaissance* (1935), concentrates on Ficino but deals with other thinkers and tells some engaging (and true) stories about the life of these Platonists. Edgar Wind, *Pagan Mysteries in the Renaissance* (1958), is the precipitate of decades of scholarship, conveniently synthesized; the book gives meaning to the vague term "Neoplatonism." Kristeller's various essays (just cited in their collected form, *Studies in Renaissance Thought and Letters*), especially "Humanism and Scholasticism in the Italian Renaissance" and "The Philosophy of Man in the Italian Renaissance" (handily reprinted in Kristeller, *Renaissance Thought: The Classic, Scholastic, and Humanist Strains* [1961], 92–119, 120–39), make the point, often overlooked, that the currents of ideas labeled "Platonism" and "Aristotelianism" were eclectic mixtures in the Renaissance which often barely concealed their dependence on Scholasticism. A recent and important collection of Kristeller's papers, *Renaissance Thought II: Papers on Humanism and the Arts* (1965), brings together his newer essays and addresses; see also Kristeller, *Eight Philosophers of the Italian Renaissance* (1964), a set of lectures excellent in their economy. Kristeller's "El mito del ateísmo renacentista y la tradición francesa del libre-pensamiento," *Notas y Estudios de Filosofía*, IV:13 (January–March 1953), 1–14, is an important essay which polemicizes against the fashion prevailing among French scholars to make Renaissance philosophers into atheists. One of the first scholars to insist on the religious character of Renaissance Humanism (without denying the Renaissance itself some novel characteristics) was Ernst Walser, whose essays had considerable influence. They were collected as *Gesammelte Studien zur Geistesgeschichte der Renaissance* (1932), and I found them extremely informative.

This kind of discriminating scholarship has modified Burckhardt's argument for a sharp break between medieval and Renaissance modes of thinking, even if it has not destroyed Burckhardt's central thesis that the Renaissance was essentially different from the Middle Ages. The questions of the bridge between the medieval and Renaissance world and of the "origins" of the Renaissance have occupied many of the writers I have listed, notably Walser and Garin. See B. L. Ullman, "Renaissance: The Word and the Underlying Concept," *Studies in Philology*, XLIX (1952), 105–18, and also a remarkable set of editions and essays by Konrad Burdach, above all *Vom Mittelalter zur Reformation* (1893) and, even more important, *Reformation, Renaissance, Humanismus* (2nd edn., 1926), a study, among other things, of the large words that historians use so easily. These works, along with the contentions of Henry Thode (notably in his *Franz von Assisi und die Anfänge der Kunst der Renaissance in Italien* [1885]) that the ideal of the Renaissance was born in the Franciscan reform movements of the thirteenth century, are important correctives, but their final emphasis seems to me misplaced.

The Renaissance view of history offers access to its view of life. Hans Baron, *The Crisis of the Early Italian Renaissance: Civic Humanism and Republican Liberty in an Age of Classicism and Tyranny*, 2 vols. (1955), stands out among the recent work on the Renaissance (which is generally of high quality) as a masterly examination of the historical and political ideas of Salutati, Bruni, and others; I could have cited it in other sections of this bibliography as well. One of its many contributions is the warning against an overreaction to the liberal simplification of the Renaissance: there *was* a pagan strand in it, and it was important. Rudolf von Albertini, *Das florentinische Staatsbewusstsein im Uebergang von der Republik zum Prinzipat* (1955), is a study of the political consciousness of Florentines in the age of Machiavelli; his chapters on the historians are illuminating. Myron P. Gilmore has collected two of his interesting essays on Renaissance historians, "The Renaissance Conception of the Lessons of History" and "Individualism in Renaissance Historians," in his *Humanists and Jurists* (1963). For Bruni, see, in addition to Baron, B. L. Ullman, "Leonardo Bruni and Humanistic Historiography," *Studies in the Italian Renaissance* (1958), 321–44. See also the excellent article by Hans Baron, "Das Erwachen des historischen Denkens im Humanismus des Quattrocento," *Historische Zeitschrift*, CXLVII (1933), 5–20. The Humanist historians made a determined effort to underline the distance of their own time from the Middle Ages.

Herbert Weisinger has examined this effort in "The Renaissance Theory of the Reaction against the Middle Ages as a Cause of the Renaissance," *Speculum*, XX (1945), 451–67, and "The Self-Awareness of the Renaissance as a Criterion of the Renaissance," *Papers of the Michigan Academy of Sciences, Arts and Letters*, XXIX (1943), 561–7. See also Wallace K. Ferguson's opening chapter of his *Renaissance in Historical Thought* and his "Humanist Views of the Renaissance," *American Historical Review*, XLV:1 (October 1939), 1–28. William von Leyden has analyzed the Humanists' use of the term "antiquity" in his "Antiquity and Authority: A Paradox in Renaissance Theory of History," *JHI*, XIX:4 (October 1958), 473–92.

If history is a useful clue to the mind of the Renaissance, art is indispensable. It is at this point that the writings of the Warburg circle, on which I have depended so heavily at all times, make their greatest contribution. In addition to the writings of Panofsky cited before, see the essays by Aby Warburg collected in his *Gesammelte Schriften*, above all (although each of them deserves citation): "Sandro Botticellis 'Geburt der Venus' und 'Frühling'" (1893), "Sandro Botticelli" (1898), "Francesco Sassettis letztwillige Verfügung" (1907), "Der Eintritt des antikisierenden Idealstils in der Malerei der Frührenaissance" (1914), "Kulturgeschichtliche Beiträge zum Quattrocento in Florenz" (1929), "Dürer und die Italienische Antike" (1905), and "Heidnisch-antike Weissagung in Wort und Bild zu Luthers Zeiten" (1920). These are the essays in which Warburg develops his influential conception of the "compromise formula" of the Renaissance mind. The work of Fritz Saxl is a notable working out of Warburg's conceptions. See the full bibliography attached to the collection of Saxl's work in England, *Lectures*, 2 vols. (1957), I, 359–62. The essays collected in *Lectures* show the mature Warburg scholar at his best; I do not find it possible—or necessary—to single out any particular lecture but commend them all to the attention of my readers. I gleaned the anecdote about Mantegna and his antique excursion from J. E. Sandys, *Harvard Lectures on the Revival of Learning* (1905), 47. There are some very interesting articles on the sociology and iconography of Renaissance art in *Italian Renaissance Studies*, notably E. H. Gombrich, "The Early Medici as

Patrons of Art" (279–311); Edgar Wind, "Maccabean Histories in the Sistine Ceiling" (312–27); Maurice Bowra, "Songs of Dance and Carnival" (328–53); John Sparrow, "Latin Verse of the High Renaissance" (354–409); and Cecil Grayson, "Lorenzo, Machiavelli and the Italian Language" (410–32); all of which, especially the first two and the last, I found amusing and revealing. Parenthetically, the sociology of the Renaissance could use further exploration. Alberto Tenenti has attempted to trace the most fundamental attitudes of Renaissance man toward life and death, both in art, in his *La vie et la mort à travers l'art du XV siècle* (1952), and in general, in his *Il Senso della morte e l'amore della vita nel Rinascimento* (1957), two pioneering works of real stature. Alfred von Martin's *Sociology of the Renaissance* (1932; tr. W. L. Luetkens, 1944) is an interesting sociological essay in the tradition of Max Weber.

For a general introduction to Renaissance art, see the judicious survey by Cecil Gould, *An Introduction to Italian Renaissance Painting* (1957). J. von Schlosser is the art historian's art historian. See above all his edition of *Lorenzo Ghibertis Denkwürdigkeiten* (1912) and his *Die Kunstliteratur: Ein Handbuch zur Quellenkunde der neueren Kunstgeschichte* (1924). Heinrich Wölfflin, *Classic Art: The Great Masters of the Italian Renaissance* (6th edn., 1914; tr. Peter and Linda Murray, 1952), a great work, continues to be most useful. Panofsky, *Idea*,[2] has some brilliant suggestions. Rudolf and Margot Wittkower, *Born Under Saturn: The Character and Conduct of Artists—A Documented History from Antiquity to the French Revolution* (1963), has a rich field in the Renaissance, but with its hostility to psychoanalysis it is less telling than their other work. Rudolf Wittkower, "Individualism in Art and Artists: A Renaissance Problem," *JHI*, XXII:3 (July–September 1961), 291–302, on the other hand, makes its point. Millard Meiss, *Painting in Florence and Siena after the Black Death: The Arts, Religion and Society in the Mid-Fourteenth Century* (1951), is a rather specialized monograph on a limited subject, but a model of its kind, the ideal fusion of art history with psychological and social history. As for Renaissance archi-

---

[2] See above, p. 425 *n.*

tecture, I have learned most from Rudolf Wittkower's acute *Architectural Principles in the Age of Humanism* (first pub. as Warburg Study No. 19 in 1949; 3rd edn., 1962), in which the history of art and the history of religion merge in a comprehensive perception of culture. The book contains an invaluable appendix (No. III) on the history of the study of proportions—a subject to which Panofsky also has paid close attention: see especially his *The Codex Huygens and Leonardo da Vinci's Art Theory* (Warburg Study No. 13, 1940); "The History of the Theory of Human Proportions as a Reflection of the History of Styles" (1921; Eng. tr. in *Meaning in the Visual Arts*, 55–107); and "Die Perspective als symbolische Form," *Warburg Vorträge, 1924–1925* (1927), 258–330, which in its very title reveals its debt to Ernst Cassirer. These architectural historians have done a great deal to rescue Renaissance architecture from Ruskin's assertion that it was wholly pagan and from Geoffrey Scott's notion (advanced in his charming essay, *The Architecture of Humanism: A Study in the History of Taste* [2nd edn., 1924] that it was wholly sensual and self-indulgent. Anthony Blunt has written a remarkable essay, economical in size but large in conception, on *Artistic Theory in Italy, 1450–1600* (1940), which begins with Alberti and ends with Mannerism and the artistic censoriousness of the Counter Reformation. For Alberti, see also the excellent article by Rudolf Wittkower, "Alberti's Approach to Antiquity in Architecture," *Warburg Journal*, IV (1940–1), 1–18.

The Enlightenment considered the Humanists' rediscovery of antiquity to be of central importance. It is discussed in most of the works already cited. G. Voigt published his *Die Wiederbelebung des classischen Altertums* (2nd edn., 1880) in 1859, a year before Burckhardt's masterpiece, which also finds a prominent place for this revival. There has been much since. See Bolgar, Seznec, and, among others, the brief essay by Douglas Bush, *Classical Influences in Renaissance Literature* (1952). For Petrarch, who rediscovered the ancients both literally and emotionally, see the fine essays by Theodor Mommsen: "Petrarch's Concept of the Dark Ages," cited before;[3] "Introduction" to *Petrarch, Sonnets and Songs*

---

[3] See above, p. 472.

(1946), and his edition of *Petrarch's Testament* (1957). P. de Nolhac, *Pétrarque et l'humanisme* (2nd edn., 1907) is very comprehensive, detailed especially in its tracing of Petrarch's use of such ancients as Cicero, and still useful. There is also an attractive essay by H. W. Eppelsheimer, *Petrarca* (1926). The standard life in English is Ernest Hatch Wilkins, *Life of Petrarch* (1961), careful, reliable, but unadventurous. For Poggio, see Ernest Walser, *Poggius Florentinus, Leben und Werke* (1914), a good book; but I think a modern biography of that great scholar-detective could still profitably be written.

2. ANCIENTS AND MODERNS: THE ANCIENTS

The main problem in specifying the relation of the Renaissance to the Enlightenment is the main problem of the Renaissance itself: its modernity. This problem in turn is complicated—and illuminated—by the relation of the Renaissance to the Reformation, which turns in large part on the related question of the modernity of the Reformation. In his justly influential writings (whose general conclusions on this point I accept even if I think them somewhat overstated at times) Ernst Troeltsch rejected the modernity of Luther, although he was disposed to grant the modern tendencies in Calvin. It was against this point of view, in such startling contradiction to prevailing modes of periodization, that Karl Holl launched his *The Cultural Significance of the Reformation* (1911; tr. Karl and Barbara Hertz and John H. Lichtblau, 1959), which, though it corrects some of Troeltsch's views, does not seem—at least to me—to affect Troeltsch's central argument. Renaissance and Reformation, though subtly related, appear in many essentials to be in opposition. The latter (to put it in terms of this book) sought to restore and purify myth; the former sought to transfigure or abandon it.

Among many general treatments of the Reformation, Owen Chadwick, *The Reformation* (1964), strikes me as outstanding for its judiciousness and independence. See also E. Harris Harbison's collection of excellent essays: *The Christian Scholar in the Age of the Reformation* (1956). One useful way of approaching these questions—which are of such importance to a proper understanding of the Enlightenment's relation to its Christian past—is to study individual Reformers. John Dillenberger has performed a notable service to those who do not read German in his enthusiastic anthology *Martin Luther: Selections from his Writings* (1961), which surveys in its introduction the vast literature on Luther. I do not share Dillenberger's distaste for Erik H. Erikson's psychoanalytical exploration *Young Man Luther* (1958), a notable attempt that deserves better than to be called by Dillenberger a "well-meaning book" (xiii *n*). Among biographies, Heinrich Boehmer, *Martin Luther: Road to Reformation* (1929; tr. John W. Doberstein and Theodore G. Tappert, 1946), is outstanding; it confines its attention to the period before 1522. Roland H. Bainton's well-known biography, *Here I Stand: A Life of Martin Luther* (1950), is popular but reliable; its bibliography is large and useful. See also Clyde L. Manschreck, *Melanchthon: The Quiet Reformer* (1958). For a general history of Germany in this period, Hajo Holborn, *A History of Modern Germany: The Reformation* (1959), especially parts I and II, is satisfactory.

Perhaps the best recent study of Calvin is François Wendel's *Calvin: Origins and Development of His Religious Thought* (1950; tr. Philip Mairet, 1963), which has a brief biography and then turns to Calvin's theology. Its bibliography is very comprehensive. J. Bohatec, *Budé und Calvin: Studien zur Gedankenwelt des französischen Frühhumanismus* (1950), is a significant attempt to link the world of Reformation with that of Humanism. Another famous attempt is A. Renaudet, *Préréforme et humanisme à Paris pendant les premières guerres d'Italie (1494–1517)* (2nd. edn., 1953). F. W. Kampschulte, *Johann Calvin, seine Kirche und sein Staat in Genf*, 2 vols. (1869–99), to which my teacher Franz Neumann first called my attention, remains despite its age most interesting. Marc-Edouard Chenevière, *La Pensée politique de Calvin* (1938) analyzes a significant aspect of Calvin's thought and influence. John T. McNeill, *The History and Character of Calvinism* (1954), is a useful general survey tracing the lines of Calvinist influence through the centuries. R. M. Kingdon, *Geneva and the Coming of the Wars of Religion in France* (1956), is a good monograph.

The Reformation in England continues to excite controversy. A. G. Dickens's *The English Reformation* (1964), a recent synthesis, is an authoritative and a beautiful book; it offers clues to more detailed study in its references. For the rise of the Puritans, to whom the philosophes owed much even if they refused to acknowledge their debt to these "fanatics," see especially William Haller, *The Rise of Puritanism* (1938), an impressive survey of the literature in which the Puritans reveled—their sermons. See also M. M. Knappen's informative *Tudor Puritanism* (1939). Alan Simpson, *Puritanism in Old and New England* (1955), is short in compass but comprehensive in scope and impressive in judgment. The literature on American Puritans is enormous; it is graced by the magnificent work of Perry Miller, which has been praised highly since his death but which still needs a thoroughgoing appraisal. Miller's great trilogy, *Orthodoxy in Massachusetts: 1630–1650* (1933), *The New England Mind: The Seventeenth Century* (1939), and—an authentic masterpiece—*The New England Mind: From Colony to Province* (1953), traces the Puritans' dependence on Scholasticism, the Renaissance, English literature of the seventeenth century, and shows the working out of English thinking under American conditions. If there is to be a criticism of this achievement, it is, I think, that it takes the Puritans more seriously as thinkers than it should; it seems to me doubtful that they were as deeply indebted to the Renaissance as Miller claims. Samuel Eliot Morison's valiant rescue of the reputation of the Puritan mind, especially in his *Puritan Pronaos* (1936) and in his volumes on the history of Harvard, is well done, but it suffers from the same defect: the Puritans demonstrably were not the narrow-minded, dour enemies of pleasure and intellect portrayed in the caricature of Mencken, but their intellectual achievements remain rather severely limited.

Another way of grasping the relation of the Enlightenment to the Renaissance-Reformation period is through the pagans of the Renaissance, notably Machiavelli, whom the philosophes much admired. In addition to *The Prince*, the *Discourses*, and the *History of Florence*, Machiavelli wrote some splendid letters, reveal-

ing plays, and an important "Dialogue on Language." These last
three have been translated and collected in a good edition by J.
R. Hale, *The Literary Works of Machiavelli* (1961). The best
recent biography is Roberto Ridolfi, *The Life of Niccolò Machiavelli* (1954; tr. Cecil Grayson, 1963), reliable on the events of his
life but marred by a certain innocence in the realm of ideas, by
dogmatism, and by contempt for other scholars. The meaning of
Machiavelli remains in dispute, as it has for four centuries. Recently the issue has narrowed down to the respective dating of
The Prince and the *Discourses*. It is more than a bibliographical
question: if *The Prince* came first, then Machiavelli underwent
what Hans Baron would call a growth into the "civic humanism"
of the *Discourses*. This is precisely what Baron has argued in "The
'Principe' and the Puzzle of the Date of the 'Discorsi,'" *Bibliothèque d'Humanisme et Renaissance*, XVIII (1956), 405–28, and
"Machiavelli: The Republican Citizen and the Author of the
'Prince,'" *English Historical Review*, LXXVI (April 1961),
217–53. J. H. Hexter has tried to date the first book of the *Discorsi*, which depends on Polybius: since Machiavelli did not know
Greek and since Polybius was not translated until 1515, Book I
must have been written then or later ("Seyssel, Machiavelli and
Polybius VI: The Mystery of the Missing Translation," *Studies
in the Renaissance*, III [1956], 75–96); this is not wholly convincing. Felix Gilbert's subtle and important articles have sought
to discern layers of composition and even a missing treatise: "The
Humanist Concept of the Prince and the 'Prince' of Machiavelli,"
Journal of Modern History, XI: 4 (December 1939), 449–83, and
"The Composition and Structure of Machiavelli's Discorsi," *JHI*,
XIV: 2 (April 1953), 136–56. The whole dispute was started by
a famous sentence in chapter II of *The Prince*, in which Machia-
velli writes that he will refrain from discussing republics, "since
I have already discussed them at length on an earlier occasion."
In several articles Federico Chabod has taken this to mean pre-
cisely what it says: that at least part of the *Discorsi* had been
completed by the time Machiavelli came to write *The Prince*.
Chabod's interpretation of Machiavelli goes beyond this to comprehend the man and the thinker. See "An Introduction to 'The
Prince,'" "'The Prince,'" and "Machiavelli's Method and Style,"

all reprinted in *Machiavelli and the Renaissance;* they are masterly. Gilbert's *Machiavelli and Guicciardini*, already cited and praised, has a revealing bibliographical essay concerning the present state of research (pp. 316–30). J. H. Whitfield, *Machiavelli* (1947), is an excellent general study with special sensitivity to Machiavelli's use of language. Ernst Cassirer seeks to rescue Machiavelli both from his enemies and from his uncritical admirers by treating him as a secular theoretician of political power, a rational scientist in rebellion against myth (*The Myth of the State* [1946], 116–62); his defense may not be successful in all detail, but I agree with it in general. Leonardo Olschki, *Machiavelli the Scientist* (1945), is a provocative essay which sees Machiavelli as part of a practical movement; F. Chiappelli, *Studi sul linguaggio del Machiavelli* (1952), is short but not useless. For Machiavelli's posthumous influence, see the recent survey by Felix Raab, *The English Face of Machiavelli: A Changing Interpretation, 1500–1700* (1964). Friedrich Meinecke's famous book *Die Idee der Staatsräson in der neueren Geschichte* (1924) opens with a perceptive chapter on Machiavelli and traces "Machiavellianism" (which was not precisely the same thing as Machiavelli's thought) through the centuries, including the eighteenth, with a long and subtle chapter on Frederick II of Prussia. E. Levi-Malvano, *Montesquieu e Machiavelli* (1912), is only a beginning. Two other books are helpful: J. R. Charbonnel, *La Pensée italienne en France et le courant libertin* (1919), and Albert Cherel, *La Pensée de Machiavel en France* (1935), but much more work could profitably be done. K. T. Butler's essay "Louis Machon's 'Apologie pour Machiavelle,' 1643 and 1668," *Warburg Journal*, III (1939–40), 208–27, is the beginning of such new work.

For the Enlightenment the most important figure of the northern Renaissance was Erasmus. Preserved Smith, *Erasmus: A Study of His Life, Ideals and Place in History* (1923), is thorough and reliable; Johan Huizinga, *Erasmus of Rotterdam* (1924; tr. F. Hopman, 1952), an admirable essay, is particularly interesting on Erasmus's compromise between Humanism and Christianity. See also Huizinga, "In Commemoration of Erasmus" (1936), in *Men and Ideas*, 310–26; and two essays by Myron Gilmore: "Fides et Eruditio: Erasmus and the Study of History" and "Erasmus and the Cause of Christian Humanism," both in *Humanists and Jurists*, 87–114, 115–45. J. A. K. Thomson, "Erasmus in England," *Warburg Vorträge, 1930–1931* (1932), 64–82, throws much light on the migration of ideas. On the origins of the Renaissance in England, see Roberto Weiss, *Humanism in England during the Fifteenth Century* (2nd edn., 1957). Fritz Caspari, *Humanism and the Social Order in England* (1954), links social to intellectual history. For Erasmus's friend More, R. W. Chambers's fine biography, *Thomas More* (1938), is especially recommended. See also J. H. Hexter's ingenious attempt—quite successful—to clarify the meaning of the *Utopia* in his *More's Utopia: The Biography of an Idea* (1952). A. Renaudet's *Érasme: Sa Pensée religieuse d'après sa correspondance, 1518–1521* (1926) and *Études Érasmiennes, 1521–1529* (1939) are important for an understanding of the northern Renaissance mind. There is one useful article on Erasmus in the Enlightenment: Werner Kaegi, "Erasmus im achtzehnten Jahrhundert," *Gedenkschrift zum 400. Todestage des Erasmus von Rotterdam* (1936), 205–27. For other northern figures, see the stimulating set of essays by Lewis Spitz, *The Religious Renaissance of the German Humanists* (1963). Rabelais has been much written about, never more provocatively than in Lucien Febvre's *Le Problème de l'incroyance au XVIe siècle, la religion de Rabelais* (1947), a characteristic effort, written with Febvre's usual excessive vitality, born, I think from the urge to communicate, but brilliantly suggestive and precise on the vexed question of the irreverent Christian. I also learned a great deal from William J. Bouwsma, *Concordia Mundi: The Career and Thought of Guillaume Postel (1510–1581)* (1957); Postel was an odd mixture of humanist and crank, mystic and historian—in a word, a typical sixteenth-century figure.

My feeling about Montaigne parallels that of the philosophes: the best thing to do is to read him directly. But I have profited from guides: Donald M. Frame's skillful essay, *Montaigne's Discovery of Man: The Humanization of a Humanist* (1955), bases itself mainly on two landmarks in the study of Montaigne: Fortunat Strowski's *Montaigne* (1906) and Pierre Villey's comprehensive *Les Sources et l'évolution des 'Essais' de Montaigne* (1906), both of which demonstrated the evolution of Montaigne's ideas through distinct stages; Frame pleads for a flexible, psychologically convincing interpretation of these stages. I am, however, less convinced by Frame's attempt to discover the true meaning of Montaigne's skepticism in "Did Montaigne Betray Sebond?" *Romanic Review*, XXXVIII (December 1947), 297–329. Paul Hensel has an interesting essay on "Montaigne und die Antike," *Warburg Vorträge, 1925–1926* (1928), 67–94. The indefatigable Gustave Lanson published a suggestive study, *Les 'Essais' de Montaigne* (1930), and there is a fine biography by Strowski, *Montaigne: Sa Vie publique et privée* (1938). For Montaigne's later influence, see especially M. Dréano, *La Renommée de Montaigne en France au XVIIIᵉ siècle* (1952), and the fascinating essay by Léon Brunschvig, *Descartes et Pascal, Lecteurs de Montaigne* (1944).

Pierre Bayle richly deserves further study. What we now have is an indispensable preliminary to that study: debate. The standard biography in English is by Howard Robinson, *Bayle the Skeptic* (1931), which sees him as a modern skeptic; the book includes numerous references to Bayle's posthumous influence. J. Delvolvé, *Religion critique et philosophie positive chez Pierre Bayle* (1906), though now old remains important for its comprehensive analysis and readiness to discover Bayle's "positive philosophy." Robinson's view has recently been challenged, especially in several (though by no means all) articles in *Pierre Bayle: Le Philosophe de Rotterdam*, ed. Paul Dibon (1959), which seek to place Bayle in the fideist-Protestant tradition—to the protest of several reviewers, including Robinson himself. The same attempt has been made by W. H. Barber in his intelligent essay "Pierre Bayle: Faith and Reason," in *The French Mind: Studies in Honour of Gustave Rudler*, ed. Will Moore et al. (1952), 109–25. See Herbert Dieckmann's critical review in *JHI*, XXII: 1 (January–March 1961), 131–6, and the article by Harry M. Bracken, "Bayle not a Sceptic?" ibid., XXV: 2 (April–June 1964), 169–80, which sees Bayle as a complex figure but a skeptic still. My own view is that while the Dibon group has compelled a reconsideration of that subtle and many-faceted attitude that is called skepticism, Bayle's place among the modern, irreligious skeptics, though somewhat altered, remains relatively secure. We may await the completion of Elizabeth Labrousse's massive biography now in progress; two volumes have so far appeared (1963, 1964). In addition we have her articles, "Les coulisses du Journal de Bayle," in Dibon, *Bayle*, 97–141, and "Obscurantisme et lumières chez Pierre Bayle," *VS*, XXVI (1963), 1037–48, and her *Inventaire critique de la correspondance de Bayle* (1961), all highly enlightening. There is some good work on Bayle's influence on the age of the Enlightenment. Erich Lichtenstein, *Gottscheds Ausgabe von Bayles Dictionnaire* (1915), shows the uses and abuses of Bayle in the early *Aufklärung;* R. Shackleton's "Bayle and Montesquieu," in Dibon, *Bayle*, 142–9, though short, is authoritative; while Richard H. Popkin adverts to Bayle's influence on Hume, ibid., 15–19. The best study of Bayle and Hume remains Norman Kemp Smith's excellent edition of Hume's *Dialogues Concerning Natural Religion*. C. Louise Thijssen-Schouten, "La Diffusion européenne des idées de Bayle," in Dibon, *Bayle*, 150–95, has numerous references but is disappointing. For Bayle and Winckelmann see Justi, *Winckelmann*, I, 129 ff; for Bayle and Wieland, see Sengle, *Wieland*, 20–21. When I published my *Voltaire's Politics* in 1959, I said that "there remains room for a good study of the impact of Montaigne, Naudé, Saint Evremond, Bayle on Voltaire" (p. 365)—the last of these has now been supplied by H. T. Mason, *Pierre Bayle and Voltaire* (1963), crisp and dependable. Diderot's dependence, and the harassment to which he was exposed by his printer for dealing sympathetically with Bayle's skepticism, is analyzed in Gordon and Torrey, *The Censoring of Diderot's Encyclopédie*.

For the revival of antique Stoicism, the work of Wilhelm Dilthey is of crucial importance: the essays collected in *Weltanschauung und Analyse des Menschen seit Renaissance und Reformation*, in *Gesammelte Schriften*, II (5th edn., 1957), remain unsurpassed. I am deeply in their debt in my analysis not merely of modern Stoicism but of the mind of sixteenth- and seventeenth-century Europe in general. L. Zanta, *La Renaissance du Stoïcisme au XVIe siècle* (1914), is a significant monograph but lacks Dilthey's profundity. Zanta has also edited the sixteenth-century French version by André de Rivaudeau of Epictetus's *Manual* (1914). Ernst Cassirer has some important comments on Neo-Stoicism in *The Myth of the State* (chapter XIII) as well as in his

Descartes: Lehre, Persönlichkeit, Wirkung (1939), especially 221 ff. I am indebted to Eugene F. Rice, Jr., *The Renaissance Idea of Wisdom* (1958), which culminates in Charron but deals generously with sixteenth-century classical ideas on the way. For Justus Lipsius, see Jason Lewis Saunders, *Justus Lipsius: The Philosophy of Renaissance Stoicism* (1956), thorough but plodding; it should be supplemented with R. Kirk's interesting edition of a sixteenth-century English translation of Lipsius's *Two Bookes of Constancie* (1939) and by an excellent article by Gerhard Oestreich, "Justus Lipsius als Theoretiker des neuzeitlichen Machtstaates," *Historische Zeitschrift*, CLXXXI: 1 (February 1956), 31–78. The significance of Stoicism for the lives of educated Elizabethans and their contemporaries is discussed by Hardin Craig, *The Enchanted Glass: The Elizabethan Mind in Literature* (1936), while George Williamson analyzes the anti-Ciceronian, Senecan style in literature and philosophy in Bacon and others: *The Senecan Amble* (1951). For Grotius, see Johan Huizinga, "Grotius and His Time," (1925) in *Men and Ideas*, 327–41, and the admirable pages in Cassirer, *Philosophy of the Enlightenment* (187, 237–43, 257–9), while Althusius is the subject of a deservedly famous monograph by Otto von Gierke: *Johannes Althusius und die Entwicklung der naturrechtlichen Staatstheorien* (3rd edn., 1913). Sections of volume IV of Gierke's difficult *Das deutsche Genossenschaftsrecht* have been translated by Ernest Barker under the title *Natural Law and the Theory of Society*, 2 vols. (1934), which takes the natural-law conception of the state through its classical century (the seventeenth) and through its decay in the Age of Enlightenment.

For Jean Bodin, see Roger Chauviré, *Jean Bodin, auteur de la République* (1914); and a sympathetic and comprehensive essay by George H. Sabine, "The Colloquium Heptaplomeres of Jean Bodin," in *Persecution and Liberty: Essays in Honor of George Lincoln Burr* (1931), 271–310, which succeeds in making sense of a complex thinker. I am indebted to Julian H. Franklin's short perceptive study *Jean Bodin and the Sixteenth-Century Revolution in the Methodology of Law and History* (1963), which places Bodin in the tradition, but also as the culmination of developments in sixteenth-century legal and historical thought.

The modern Epicureans deserve more study. Gassendi has

been appreciated in a collective set of lectures, *Pierre Gassendi: Sa Vie et son œuvre* (1955), which I have used profitably. The pages on "Gassend" in E. J. Dijksterhuis, *The Mechanization of the World Picture* (1950; tr. C. Dikshoorn, 1961), 425–33, are excellent. Hocke, *Lukrez in Frankreich*, has much material on the modern Epicureans in France; Thomas F. Mayo, *Epicurus in England* (1934), is useful for England. René Pintard, *Le Libertinage érudit dans la première moitié du XVIIᵉ siècle*, 2 vols. (1943), is a comprehensive and important treatment of a number of relatively minor thinkers; it is therefore indispensable for an understanding of modern paganism, but Kristeller has objected with some justice that the work rather exaggerates the alienation from Christian culture of the men it treats. There is a splendid edition of Saint Evremond's letters with a good introduction by John Hayward (1930). H. T. Barnwell's *Les Idées morales et critiques de Saint-Evremond* (1957) is a serious monograph for this witty *bon vivant;* it includes a full bibliography. J. S. Spink, *French Free-Thought From Gassendi to Voltaire* (1960), has collected a good deal of interesting material; I owe it a pair of quotations from seventeenth-century *bon vivants* and minor thinkers.

Finally, two special topics: printing and seventeenth-century classicism. For the first, see the relevant pages in Bolgar and the authoritative study by Lucien Febvre and H. J. Martin, *L'Apparition du livre* (1958). For the second, an elusive and fascinating subject, see Henri Peyre's orderly and useful essay in definition, *Le Classicisme français* (1942). René Bray, *La Formation de la doctrine classique en France* (1951), is a comprehensive, indeed massive survey of major importance. Antoine Adam's large scale *Histoire de la littérature française au XVIIᵉ siècle*, 5 vols. (1956), has much on classicism; I found Paul Bénichou, *Morales du grand siècle* (1948), a sophisticated Marxist reading of Corneille, Pascal, Racine, and Molière, immensely stimulating. I am similarly indebted to E. B. O. Borgerhoff, *The Freedom of French Classicism* (1950), which is shrewd, erudite, and informal. A. J. Krailsheimer, *Studies in Self-Interest from Descartes to La Bruyère* (1962), is a thoughtful and original account of the classical moralists. Leo Spitzer has a brilliant reading of Racine in "The 'Récit de Théramène," in *Linguistics and Literary History: Essays in*

Stylistics (1948), 87–134. For Poussin, see especially the revealing pages in Anthony Blunt, *Art and Architecture in France, 1500–1700* (2nd edn., 1957), 158–71. Jules Brody, "Platonisme et classicisme," *Saggi e ricerche di letteratura francese,* II (October 1961), 7–30, is an important essay. For the "Humanism" of seventeenth-century classical painting, see Panofsky, *Hercules am Scheidewege,* 139–41.

3. ANCIENTS AND MODERNS: THE MODERNS

The scientific revolution of the seventeenth century has long been the subject of intensive study and recently of intelligent synthesis. Dijksterhuis (Part IV, "The Evolution of Classical Science") is outstanding for its judiciousness and clarity. A. R. Hall, *The Scientific Revolution, 1500–1800: The Formation of the Modern Scientific Attitude* (1954), is the best general work I have encountered. For the evolution of the new cosmology down to Newton, see the lucid exposition by Thomas S. Kuhn, *The Copernican Revolution: Planetary Astronomy in the Development of Western Thought* (1957). Kuhn has also written a speculative essay, *The Structure of Scientific Revolutions* (1962), on innovation and conservatism in science, which I found most rewarding. Martha Ornstein, *The Role of Scientific Societies in the Seventeenth Century* (3rd edn., 1938), is the classic monograph on the subject; it beautifully conveys the atmosphere among leading scientists in an age of rapid change. The number of philosophical works seeking to assess the meaning of the revolution is large and growing steadily. I shall refer to some of them below; here I mention only Alexandre Koyré, *From the Closed World to the Infinite Universe* (1957), which moves from Nicholas of Cusa down to the debate between Newton and Leibniz—a most suggestive work.[4] Volume III of *A History of Technology,* "From

---

[4] For other books by Koyré, see below under Galileo and Descartes.

the Renaissance to the Industrial Revolution, c.1500–c.1750," ed. Charles Singer et al. (1957), contains an indispensable series of articles. Herbert Butterfield, *The Origins of Modern Science, 1300–1800* (1951), has many interesting observations on the relation of science to social thought.

In the analysis of the new scientific world view, specifically of the impact of science on literature and art, the writings of Marjorie Nicolson hold a special place. They, more than other books on this subject, have managed to discredit the Romantic charge that Galileo's primary and secondary qualities in particular and Newtonian science in general made the world bleak, colorless, and loveless. *Newton Demands the Muse* (1946); *Voyages to the Moon* (1948); *Science and Imagination*, a series of articles, mainly dealing with the impact of the telescope on the poetic mind, first collected under that title in 1956; *Mountain Gloom and Mountain Glory: The Development of the Aesthetics of the Infinite* (1959); and *The Breaking of the Circle: Studies in the Effect of the 'New Science' on Seventeenth-Century Poetry* (2nd edn., 1960)—all of these volumes repay careful study; each marshals impressive evidence for the impact of modernity on a society under pressure from natural philosophy. R. F. Jones has written many fine articles on the impact of Baconian science on seventeenth-century science; they have been collected, with a sheaf of tributes to Jones, in *The Seventeenth Century: Studies in the History of English Thought and Literature from Bacon to Pope* (1951). *Seventeenth-Century Science and the Arts*, ed. Hadley Howell Rhys (1961), in the Nicolson tradition, contains four interesting essays: "Seventeenth-Century Science and the Arts" by Stephen Toulmin (3–28), "Science and Literature" by Douglas Bush (29–62), "Science and Visual Art" by James S. Ackerman (63–90), and "Scientific Empiricism in Musical Thought" by Claude V. Palisca (91–137). On the minority view, that science was destroying traditional values, see Victor Harris, *All Coherence Gone* (1949), which begins but does not stop with Donne. Richard S. Westfall, *Science and Religion in Seventeenth-Century England* (1958), interestingly reports on the continuing alliance but also the rising tension between God and Nature. E. M. W. Tillyard, *The Elizabethan World Picture* (1943), and Theodore Spencer's brilliant

Shakespeare and the Nature of Man (2nd edn., 1955) deal with the mental world just preceding Bacon and Galileo and thus permit an assessment of the enormous destructive—and liberating —power of the scientific revolution, especially with regard to the idea of hierarchy. Much light on the relation of science to religion is shed by Walter Pagel in his *The Religious and Philosophical Aspects of van Helmont's Science and Medicine* (1944).

The meaning of Galileo's philosophy of nature has in recent decades circled around his "Platonism," a subject of central importance for this book. See especially Ernst Cassirer, "Galileo's Platonism," in *Studies and Essays in the History of Science, offered in Homage to George Sarton*, ed. Ashley Montagu (1946), 276–97, a moderate plea for Galileo's "modern" version of Platonism. Earlier, Cassirer had subjected Galileo's epistemology to searching examination in his "Wahrheitsbegriff und Wahrheitsproblem bei Galilei," *Scientia*, LXII (September–October 1937), 121–30, 185–93. Shortly before Cassirer published his essay on Galileo's Platonism, Alexandre Koyré had described Galileo's science as a triumph of Plato over Aristotle in two important articles: "Galileo and Plato," *JHI*, IV: 4 (October 1943), 400–28, and "Galileo and the Scientific Revolution of the Seventeenth Century," *The Philosophical Review*, LII: 4 (July 1943), 333–48. In the same issue of that journal Leonardo Olschki somewhat modifies Koyré's sweeping statements in a general survey of Galileo's scientific achievement: "Galileo's Philosophy of Science," (pp. 349–65). For that achievement, the magnificent analysis by Koyré, *Etudes Galiléennes*, 3 vols. (1939), remains indispensable. Gillispie's *Edge of Objectivity* has two lucid and sympathetic chapters (I and II) on Galileo, while Giorgio di Santillana reports on the celebrated muzzling of Galileo by the Church in his *The Crime of Galileo* (1955). Erwin Panofsky has explored Galileo's mind in a fascinating little book, *Galileo as a Critic of the Arts* (1954). Galileo's own writings are accessible in felicitous modern translations: Stillman Drake has edited some of the shorter writings under the title *Discoveries and Opinions of Galileo* (1957) as well as the decisive *Dialogue Concerning the Two World Systems, Ptolemaic and Copernican* (1953).

The debate over Galileo is interesting and of considerable

importance to this book, but it is relatively marginal to his whole
thought; the debate over Descartes, on the other hand, involves
his whole world view. In a series of important books Étienne
Gilson has stressed Descartes's ties to medieval thought—a paradoxical contention in view of Descartes's explicit, vehement repudiation of all Scholastic influence. See Gilson's *La Liberté chez
Descartes et la Théologie* (1913); *Études sur la rôle de la pensée
médiévale dans la formation du système cartésien* (1930); and
above all his exhaustive, erudite critical edition of Descartes's
Discours de la méthode (edn. 1947). The same view is taken in
an early book by Alexandre Koyré, *Descartes und die Scholastik*
(1923), and by some other commentators. These works compel a
cautious use of the word "modern," which has been applied all
too freely to Descartes, but they do not, I think, compel assent:
whatever the roots of Descartes' thought, its intention and function were radical. For this latter view, see especially the impressive
commentaries by Norman Kemp Smith, *New Studies in the
Philosophy of Descartes: Descartes as Pioneer* (1952), from which
I profited greatly; I am especially indebted to Smith's discussion of
Descartes' affinity to the Stoics (esp. 342–3n) and his practical
interest in medicine (ch. XIII, "Descartes as Pioneer"). Cassirer
has always been a champion of Descartes' modernity; see above
all his *Descartes*[5] as well as *Das Erkenntnisproblem in der Philosophie und Wissenschaft der neueren Zeit*, Vol. I (3rd edn.,
1922), Book III. For an interesting appreciation of "Cartesian
Freedom," see the essay by Jean-Paul Sartre in a collection of
Literary and Philosophical Essays (tr. Annette Michelson, 1962),
180–97. For Descartes' impact on the Enlightenment—still much
controverted—see Aram Vartanian, *Diderot and Descartes: A
Study of Scientific Naturalism in the Enlightenment* (1952), a
thorough, informative, and persuasive study which, however, does
not persuade me: while it seems plausible to argue that there was
more Cartesianism in eighteenth-century philosophy than the
philosophes were ready to admit, it is true (on Vartanian's own
showing) that they admitted it cheerfully, and true, too, that other
sources for their materialism were readily available. For the con-

---

[5] See above, p. 523.

vergence of Descartes and Bacon, of which I make much in the text, see Robert McRae, "The Unity of the Sciences: Bacon, Descartes and Leibniz," *JHI*, XVIII: 1 (January 1957), 27–48.

Francis Bacon, patron saint of the *Encyclopédie*, eludes his commentators—though there are many of them. He was too many-sided and too eccentric, the results of his scientific work are too uncertain, to permit of simple solutions. Benjamin Farrington, not surprisingly, sees him as *Francis Bacon: Philosopher of Industrial Science* (1949); for all its Marxist bent and all its casual composition, the book is useful. Historians of philosophy have often been unduly lighthearted about Bacon's achievement: see C. D. Broad, *The Philosophy of Francis Bacon* (1926), which regards Bacon as relatively unimportant to the history of science. F. H. Anderson, *The Philosophy of Francis Bacon* (1948), is much better: it is a sound general study, which also manages to bring order into the chronology of Bacon's writings. But by far the most impressive book on the Baconian revolution that I have encountered is R. F. Jones, *Ancients and Moderns: A Study of the Background of the Battle of the Books* (1936), a magisterial survey of the impact of Bacon's ideas on his world. Ornstein's *Scientific Societies* should also be read for confirmation of Bacon's immediate and enduring significance. Charles W. Lemmi, *The Classic Deities in Bacon* (1933), shows Bacon's utilization of ancient mythology. Robert E. Larson's attempt to turn Bacon into an ancient for all his modern rhetoric, "The Aristotelianism of Bacon's *Novum Organum*," *JHI*, XXIII: 4 (October–December, 1962), 435–50, strikes me as perverse.

L. T. More, *Isaac Newton: A Biography* (1934), full and judicious, has long been the standard life, but now that Newton's correspondence is being published in a magnificent edition by H. W. Turnbull and others, a definitive biography will soon be possible. (At the time I completed this book, in late 1965, three volumes, reaching to 1694, have appeared.) E. A. Burtt, *The Metaphysical Foundations of Modern Physical Science* (2nd edn., 1932), remains an authoritative exposition of the philosophical basis of Newtonianism; it is especially revealing in its insistence that Newton did not banish God from the universe but required Him to set it straight from time to time. For this all-important question of cosmology, the correspondence between Leibniz and Samuel Clarke, who acted as Newton's spokesman, is indispensable. *The Leibniz-Clarke Correspondence: Together with Extracts from Newton's 'Principia' and 'Opticks'* has recently (1956) been excellently re-edited by H. G. Alexander. H. S. Thayer's edition of *Newton's Philosophy of Nature: Selections from His Writings* (1953), though brief, is meaty; I have used it freely. Among a sizeable literature, the essays put together as the *Royal Society Newton Tercentenary Celebrations* (1947) are particularly interesting; the volume includes J. M. Keynes's famous "Newton, the Man," which seeks to turn Newton (wittily but, I think, unsuccessfully) into an alchemist. I. Bernard Cohen has examined with much success the experimental bearing of Newton's natural philosophy with special reference to its impact on American science. His *Franklin and Newton: An Inquiry into Speculative Newtonian Experimental Science and Franklin's Work in Electricity as an Example Thereof* (1956) is useful also for its meticulous study of the meaning of the key word "hypothesis" in Newton's thought. I have already referred to Frank Manuel's *Isaac Newton, Historian*, which illuminates Newton's versatility and complexity by studying his passionate concern with biblical chronology. For the diffusion of Newton's ideas in France (to which I shall devote some attention in the second volume of this essay), see the splendid monograph by Pierre Brunet, *L'Introduction des théories de Newton en France au XVIIIe siècle*, which I have already mentioned.

Fontenelle has fortunately been rescued from the all-too-simple appellation "Cartesian," almost singlehandedly, by Leonard M. Marsak in a series of impressive papers. See *Two Papers on Bernard de Fontenelle*, "Publications in the Humanities, No. 38" (Department of Humanities, Massachusetts Institute of Technology, 1959), and the comprehensive essay, "Bernard de Fontenelle: The Idea of Science in the French Enlightenment," *Transactions of the American Philosophical Society*, IL: 7 (December 1959), on which I have depended. J.-R. Carré, *La Philosophie de Fontenelle, ou le sourire de la raison* (1932), is an excellent study of Fontenelle's philosophical rationalism, but it does little with Fontenelle's scientific achievement and social environment. Robert Shackleton has edited Fontenelle's *Entretiens sur la pluralité des mondes* and *Digression sur les anciens et les modernes* (1955) with a full introduction.

The literature on Locke is very sizable, and with the gradual publication of the Lovelace collection of his papers, it is growing rapidly. For that collection, see P. Long, *A Summary Catalogue of the Lovelace Collection of the Papers of John Locke in the Bodleian Library* (1959). Peter Laslett has brought out a first-rate critical edition of the *Two Treatises of Government* (1960) with a comprehensive introduction which proves once and for all that the celebrated second *Treatise* was not written to defend the Glorious Revolution but to support the Exclusion of the future James II from the throne. John Lough has edited the revealing *Locke's Travels in France, as Related in His Journals, Correspondence and Other Papers* (1953), while W. von Leyden has edited Locke's equally revealing early *Essays on the Laws of Nature* (1954). While Maurice Cranston's *John Locke, a Biography* (1957) effectively uses the Lovelace papers, its treatment of Locke's ideas is too thin to be satisfactory; indeed, the aged H. R. Fox-Bourne, *Life of John Locke*, 2 vols. (1876), which prints many otherwise unavailable documents, retains its usefulness. I have published large sections of Locke's *Some Thoughts Concerning Education* (1964) with a brief introduction. While D. J. O'Connor's little *John Locke* (1952) provides an intelligent introduction to the man and his thought, the best general treatment is by Richard I. Aaron, *John Locke* (2nd edn., 1955), which stresses Locke's empiricism. James Gibson, *Locke's Theory of Knowledge and Its Historical Relations* (1917), is a technical analysis of Locke's epistemology, to be read in conjunction with Aaron's book. I learned much from Raymond Polin, *La Politique morale de John Locke* (1960), a stimulating study that brings to bear a trained philosopher's mind on one of the most influential minds of the seventeenth century. The idea of property has long interested commentators, and C. B. Macpherson's various articles, culminating in his *The Political Theory of Possessive Individualism: Hobbes to Locke* (1962), state the radical case with refreshing clarity. On Locke's educational theories, which were of crucial importance to the philosophes, see especially Pierre

Villey, *L'Influence de Montaigne sur les idées pédagogiques de Locke et de Rousseau* (1911), and Nina Reicyn, *La Pédagogie de John Locke* (1941). Locke's political thought must be reconsidered after Laslett's work, but J. W. Gough's sensible *John Locke's Political Philosophy* (1950) remains useful. John W. Yolton, *John Locke and the Way of Ideas* (1956), is an important study of Locke's radical reputation in England, while Gerd Buchdahl, *The Image of Newton and Locke in the Age of Reason* (1961), is mainly an anthology, and a short one, but not without its uses.

Hobbes, Leibniz and Spinoza occupy a somewhat less prominent place in this chapter; hence a few bibliographical references will be adequate. Among the outstanding commentaries on Hobbes, the most noteworthy are Ferdinand Tönnies, *Hobbes: Der Mann und Denker* (3rd edn., 1925); Raymond Polin, *Politique et philosophie chez Thomas Hobbes* (1952); Michael Oakeshott's long and brooding "Introduction" to Hobbes's *Leviathan* (1947), to my mind the best thing that Oakeshott has done; and John Plamenatz's splendid analytical chapter in his *Man and Society*, 2 vols. (1963), I, 116–54. Leo Strauss, *The Political Philosophy of Hobbes* (tr. Elsa Sinclair, 1936), is idiosyncratic but suggestive. In recent years there have been attempts to enlist Hobbes under the banner of religion; the most successful of these is Howard Warrender, *The Political Philosophy of Hobbes: His Theory of Obligation* (1957), but even that strikes me as forcing the argument. For Hobbes's reputation, a fascinating subject which should be but has rarely been pursued into the eighteenth century, see especially John Bowle, *Hobbes and His Critics: A Study in Seventeenth Century Constitutionalism* (1951), and Samuel I. Mintz, *The Hunting of Leviathan* (1963). One useful exploration is Leland Thielemann, "Diderot and Hobbes," *Diderot Studies*, II (1952), 221–78.

Stuart Hampshire, *Spinoza* (1951), is a splendid introduction; H. F. Hallett, *Benedict de Spinoza: The Elements of His Philosophy*, (1957) is, for all its engaging subtitle, highly demanding but rewarding; its bibliographical note is extremely helpful. Harry A. Wolfson's well-known *The Philosophy of Spinoza*, 2 vols. (1934) is a full-fledged commentary in the old tradition, dissecting each of Spinoza's ideas with delicate care. Cassirer's article "Spinoza's Stellung in der allgemeinen Geistesgeschichte," *Der Morgen*, VIII: 5 (1932), 325–48, is short but pregnant. Paul Vernière has written a remarkably full and attractive work on Spinoza's influence: *Spinoza et la pensée française avant la révolution*, 2 vols. (1954); it has a valuable chapter on Spinoza and the *philosophie des lumières* (Part II, chapter 3).

Ernst Cassirer made the philosophy of Leibniz one of his special concerns. One of his earliest works was *Leibniz' System in seinen wissenschaftlichen Grundlagen* (1902), a substantial monograph; he followed it with his edition of Leibniz's philosophical writings (1904, 1906, 1915) and devoted a chapter to him in *Das Erkenntnisproblem in der Philosophie und Wissenschaft der neueren Zeit*, Vol. II (1907; 3rd edn., 1922), Book V, chapter 2; and an important chapter—the first—in *Freiheit und Form: Studien zur deutschen Geistesgeschichte* (1916); stressed the significance of Leibniz for the Enlightenment in some important pages of his *Philosophy of the Enlightenment;* and returned to him once again near the end of his life with "Newton and Leibniz," *The Philosophical Review*, LII: 4 (July 1943), 366–91. Ruth Lydia Saw, *Leibniz* (1954), is a useful general introduction; a technical commentary of great merit is H. W. B. Joseph, *Lectures on the Philosophy of Leibniz*, ed. J. L. Austin (1949). R. W. Meyer has chosen to treat the important question of Leibniz the peacemaker in his *Leibnitz and the Seventeenth-Century Revolution* (1948; tr. J. P. Stern, 1952). Hans M. Wolff, *Leibniz: Allbeseelung und Skepsis* (1961), reconciles two aspects of Leibniz's thought, his metaphysics and his epistemology, in a subtle essay, while W. H. Barber's *Leibniz in France*, already cited, traces the impact of Leibniz's thought, real or distorted, down to *Candide*.

A word on rational theology in seventeenth-century England: see especially Ernst Cassirer, *The Platonic Renaissance in England*, Warburg Study No. 24 (1932; tr. James P. Pettegrove, 1953), a splendid monograph which does not, however, wholly replace John Tulloch's excellent, massive *Rational Theology and Christian Philosophy in England in the Seventeenth Century*, 2 vols. (1872), which devotes the whole second volume to the Cambridge Platonists. See also the excellent monograph by Rosalie L. Colie, *Light and Enlightenment: A Study of the Cambridge Platonists and The Dutch Arminians* (1957). While, then, much good work has been done on linking the seventeenth century to the eighteenth (and on separating them), much more, in the style of Vernière's study of Spinoza and Barber's study of Leibniz, needs to be done.

CHAPTER SIX

In Dubious Battle

I. THE CHRISTIAN COMPONENT

Much of the material used in this section has been used throughout the book and has therefore been cited before.[1] More work is needed, for the problem of just what and how much the Enlightenment owes to its religious environment is extremely complicated; it has never been fully explored. One reason for the complication is what I have called the fallacy of "spurious persistence" (in "Carl Becker's Heavenly City," now in *The Party of Humanity*, esp. pp. 190 ff). What, say, does Diderot mean with his all too familiar remark, "Posterity is to the philosopher what the other world is to the religious man"?[2] He may be suggesting no more than that these two distinct ideas have similar functions. There is no need to assume that the later idea is in any way derived from the earlier one, that the appeal to posterity is a conscious or unconscious translation of the belief in the immortality of the soul. True: changes in rhetorical styles sometimes mask the tenacious survival of an idea, but that survival must be demonstrated, not simply assumed. Even if the historian can show an authentic dependence of one idea on an earlier one, this does not entitle him to conclude that nothing, or little, has changed. Specifically, even if he can show that a secular idea has been deliberately substituted for a religious idea, there is nothing "mere" about this substitution, since its consequences may be of great historical import. While I have not fully mapped the de-

---

[1] For discussions of Lessing, his ideas, and his career, see above, pp. 440-1, 462.
[2] I shall return to this remark in volume II, in my chapter on progress.

pendence of the Enlightenment on Christianity, I am certain that
any such inquiry should be governed by the principles I have just
suggested and by my insistence in the text that ideas be judged
above all by their function.

For Young's *Night Thoughts* and other British exponents of
Christian common sense, see A. R. Humphreys, *The Augustan
World* (1954), chapter IV, "The Religious World," (he quotes
Young's lines on p. 176). See also Hoxie Neale Fairchild, *Religious
Trends in English Poetry*, 4 vols. (1939–49), especially Vols. I
and II. The transition from Latitudinarianism to deism in England
is well described in Yolton, *Locke and the Way of Ideas*. Richard
H. Cox, *Locke on War and Peace* (1960), an intelligent study
marred by an obsessive searching of texts for the truth "between
the lines" characteristic of most followers of Leo Strauss, has some
useful confirmation of Locke's affinity for antique paganism
(62–63). German modern Protestant thought is analyzed in masterly fashion by Aner, *Theologie der Lessingzeit*, which I have
singled out for praise before. Ernst Troeltsch has some thoughtful
observations on the relations of Calvinism to the Enlightenment
in *Gesammelte Schriften*, IV, 183–4. George L. Mosse has explored the relationship of Protestantism and Enlightenment in
two significant articles, which should set the pattern for further
work: "The Importance of Jacques Saurin in the History of
Casuistry and the Enlightenment," *Church History*, XXV: 3
(September 1956), 1–15, analyzes the ideas of an early eighteenth-
century Huguenot preacher; "Puritan Radicalism and the Enlightenment," ibid., XXIX: 4 (December 1960), 1–16, suggests
some interesting strands in the modernization and rationalization
of Puritan piety. In New England that piety underwent changes
worthy of close examination: Perry Miller has laid down the lines
of research and offered many cogent generalizations in his *The
New England Mind: From Colony to Province*. Some of his suggestions have been followed out by his pupil Conrad Wright, *The
Beginnings of Unitarianism in America* (1955), a most intelligent
monograph. See also Joseph Haroutunian, *Piety versus Moralism:
The Passing of the New England Theology* (1932), and Leonard
J. Trinterud, *The Forming of An American Tradition: A Re-
Examination of Colonial Presbyterianism* (1949). But the subtle

process of the "secularization" and "liberalization" of Puritanism deserves close study; it is striking that Leverett, Brattle, and Colman, the leaders of this movement in early eighteenth-century Boston and Cambridge, either have no or only antiquated biographies.

2. THE TREASON OF THE CLERKS

The Treason of the Clerks is the Christian component viewed from the other side. I have pieced it together both from the history of the eighteenth-century mind as it manifests itself in modern Christians and from the history of eighteenth-century churches. For the attack on "fanaticism" and "enthusiasm" on the part of Christians—the bridge of good sense—see Ronald A. Knox, *Enthusiasm: A Chapter in the History of Religion with Special Reference to the Seventeenth and Eighteenth Centuries* (1950), a work at once charming and serious and a major contribution to an understanding of the religious mind through the centuries—it is limited in its objectivity in only one respect, that of nearly always discovering the sensible center (between fanaticism on one side and cold ritualism on the other) in orthodox Roman Catholicism.

One excellent representative of the school of Christian good sense is Jonathan Swift. For purposes of this book I can leave aside the controversies over Swift's attitude toward man as revealed (or not revealed) in the celebrated fourth book of *Gulliver's Travels.* What is central here is his religious attitude, and on this among the most sensible books that I have found is Phillip Harth, *Swift and Anglican Rationalism: The Religious Background of 'A Tale of a Tub'* (1961), which places Swift quite properly in his Anglican environment and eschews interpretative extravagances. Among other good books on Swift, all of which shed light on Swift's religious views no matter how strongly they may disagree on whether to take a "hard" or a "soft" line on the fourth book of *Gulliver,* I merely list: Ricardo Quintana, *Swift: An Introduction* (1955) and his rather more extensive *The Mind and Art of*

Jonathan Swift (1936); the collection of short pieces and sets of
lectures by Herbert Davis, who has edited much of Swift:
Jonathan Swift: Essays on His Satire and Other Studies (1964);
Louis A. Landa, whose *Swift and the Church of Ireland* (1954)
examines a significant part of Swift's career; and Irvin Ehrenpreis,
Swift: The Man, His Works, and The Age, a proposed three-
volume biography of which Volume I, *Mr. Swift and His Contemporaries* (1962), takes him down to the "Tale of a Tub" and
the essays appended to it, of which he does not think much. See
Ehrenpreis's demurrer (p. 241) to James L. Clifford's appreciative
article on "Swift's *Mechanical Operation of the Spirit*," in *Pope
and His Contemporaries, Essays Presented to George Sherburn*,
ed. James L. Clifford and Louis A. Landa (1949), 135–46; Clifford,
I think, has the better of the argument: the worldly, even sexual
basis of celestial speculations is stated with brilliant insight in this
impudent little Swiftian satire. There is a good article by Clarence
M. Webster on "Swift and Some Earlier Satirists of Puritan
Enthusiasm," *PMLA*, XLVIII (December 1933), 1141–53. Bonamy
Dobrée, though often a little perverse, has some useful observations on Swift's reasonable religion in his *English Literature in the
Early Eighteenth Century, 1700–1740* (1959), 60–72, on which I
have drawn. I am indebted to Dobrée for citing a little-known
passage from Pope's Preface to the 1717 edition of his poems,
which demonstrates the intimate affinity of modern good sense
with the appeal to antiquity: "All that is left to us is to recommend
our productions by the imitation of the Ancients: and it will be
found true, that in every age, the highest character for sense and
learning has been obtain'd by those who have been most indebted
to them. For to say truth, whatever is very good sense must have
been common sense in all times" (ibid., p. 127).

One major reason for the widespread difficulty in compre-
hending—and even seeing—the oddly intimate and yet irreconcilable relation of Christianity and Enlightenment has been the
prevalent liberal cliché that sensible men must be irreligious (or
at least anti-Christian), while good Christians must be knaves or
fools. The philosophes knew better from personal experience even
if they had some trouble fitting reasonable Christians into their
theoretical schemes. For the twentieth-century historian one con-

venient way of studying the liberal Christian, the man who loved
science and worshipped God, believed in the regularity of nature
but credited at least some miracles, admired the ethical precepts of
the Stoics but wished above all to live a Christian moral life, is to
study such men as Albrecht von Haller and some of the leading
figures of Augustan literature, who each in his own way belonged
to this tribe for which, as I have said, the Whig view of history
has no understanding and no place.

For Haller, scientist, poet, celebrated physiologist, and theological controversialist, a modern Christian who suffered all his
life from spells of acedia and attacks of unbelief, all of which he
recorded in his moving diaries, see the long biography by L.
Hirzel, *Hallers Leben und Dichtungen* (1882), which serves as the
introduction to his critical edition of Haller's poems; an interesting monograph on Haller's classical tastes, Anna Ischer, *Albrecht
von Haller und das klassische Altertum* (1928); a useful article by
Howard Mumford Jones, "Albrecht von Haller and English
Philosophy," *PMLA*, XL (1925), 103–27; and Stephen d'Irsay,
*Albrecht von Haller: Eine Studie zur Geistesgeschichte der
Aufklärung* (1930), which, though frenetic in tone, has much that
is revealing about this complex and tormented personality.

For the English writers, Alan Dugald McKillop, *The Early
Masters of English Fiction* (1956), offers informative and percep-
tive essays on Defoe, Richardson, Fielding, Smollett, and Sterne.
For Defoe, the Nonconformist mind in action, see J. Sutherland,
Defoe (2nd edn., 1950), brief but authoritative; and Maximillian
E. Novak, *Defoe and the Nature of Man* (1963), which is an
interesting essay. William L. Payne has performed a service in
compiling *The Best of Defoe's 'Review'* (1951), an excellent
anthology. See also Ian Watt, "*Robinson Crusoe* as Myth," in
*Eighteenth-Century English Literature: Modern Essays in Criti-
cism*, ed. James L. Clifford (1959), 158–79. For Richardson, see
McKillop, *Samuel Richardson: Printer and Novelist* (1936); and
the relevant chapters (V–VII) in Ian Watt, *The Rise of the Novel*
(1959). Fielding, novelist, magistrate, and humanitarian, offers an
interesting subject of study; the very controversy over whether
his benevolence has primarily religious or secular roots suggests
the complex quality of the Age of Enlightenment. W. L. Cross,

The History of Henry Fielding (1918), is still basic; George Sherburn, "Fielding's Social Outlook," in Clifford's *Eighteenth-Century English Literature*, 251–73, has important material. One other writer, an influential Latitudinarian open to most of the modern currents of his age and easily deprecated in recent years, is Joseph Addison: Bonamy Dobrée's essay on Addison in his *Essays in Biography, 1680–1726* (1925) is an instance: cleverly—too cleverly—it makes Addison into the first Victorian, an appellation more catchy than appropriate. Another instance, though brilliant in its way, is "Addison" by C. S. Lewis, in Clifford's *Eighteenth-Century English Literature*, 144–57. Much the best, I think, is the long biography by Peter Smithers, *The Life of Joseph Addison* (1954), but we still need a full appraisal of Addison's civilized religiosity and his propaganda in behalf of cultivation. Among the poets Alexander Pope is most interesting and most elusive; in recent years he has been very popular. Since the critics began to seize on him, the literature has grown rapidly. The authoritative edition of his works, "The Twickenham Edition," ed. John Butt et al., 6 vols. (1939–61), is magnificently annotated. Pope's correspondence has been impeccably edited by George Sherburn, 5 vols. (1956). Geoffrey Tillotson's *Pope and Human Nature* (1958) has been equally important in the re-evaluation. Maynard Mack, "Wit and Poetry and Pope: Some Observations on His Imagery," in *Pope and His Contemporaries*, 20–40; Cleanth Brooks, in *The Well-Wrought Urn* (1947), chapter V, "The Case of Miss Arabella Fermor"; and W. K. Wimsatt in a series of essays, only some of which are explicitly addressed to the meaning of Pope (conveniently collected in *The Verbal Icon: Studies in the Meaning of Poetry* [1954]) have all pleaded with cogency and learning for the distinction between the poet Pope and his poetic creations—a point important not merely for his poetry but for an understanding of that subtle process of secularization in eighteenth-century Europe of which Pope was a witness and to which, I think, he contributed. The first serious protest against the abuse of the notion of "persona" that I have seen is by Irvin Ehrenpreis, "Personae," in *Restoration and Eighteenth-Century Literature: Essays in Honor of Alan Dugald McKillop*, ed. Carroll Camden (1963), 25–38; but I think that more can still be done. The poem central to an appraisal of Pope's real religious opinions is of course his *Essay on Man*, which many have read as a deist poem, a reading that runs afoul of Pope's declared Catholicism and of his violent, even vicious criticism of English deists in his *Dunciad*. For an appraisal of the debate, see Maynard Mack, ed., *An Essay on Man*, "The Twickenham Edition," Vol. III, part I (1950). Parenthetically, another fruitful area for the study of liberal, reasonable Christianity is in the American colonies, which produced such complex types as Thomas Jefferson, who began as a complete pagan and then reverted to a kind of ethical Christianity with Jesus as the supreme moral teacher. A book like Edmund S. Morgan's biography *The Gentle Puritan: A Life of Ezra Stiles, 1727–1795* (1962) tells us more about the religious complexion of the Enlightened West than more formal essays.

For the style of civilized sanity in England in general, see the two charming books by F. L. Lucas.[3] Sutherland, *Preface to Eighteenth Century Poetry*, 11–12, rightly stresses (and other historians have agreed) how much of this appeal to common sense was the desire to get away from—perhaps to shut out the very memory of—the violence of the seventeenth century. The philosophes had the highest regard for some of these modern Christians and made great demands on them: Gibbon was surprised and disgusted to find "Mr. Addison, an English gentleman" among the "herd of bigots" who write "superficial" apologetic tracts (*Decline and Fall of the Roman Empire*, V, 247 *n*).

As for the English Church, which participated in this development, see above all the splendid books by Norman Sykes, which have done a great deal to rescue the reputation of the eighteenth-century Anglican church from the charge of torpor and irreligion and have offered instead a nuanced portrait of a church politically involved and theologically progressive. *Church and State in England in the XVIIIth Century* (1934) is Sykes's masterpiece; but at least three other books of his deserve mention even in this truncated bibliography: *Edmund Gibson: Bishop of London, 1669–1748* (1926), *William Wake: Archbishop of Canterbury*, 2 vols. (1957), and *From Sheldon to Secker: Aspects of English*

---

[3] See above, p. 482.

Church History, 1660–1768 (1959), on which I have heavily relied. Sykes shows conclusively that the ecclesiastical politics often blamed on Walpole had deep seventeenth-century roots. Sykes has also compelled re-evaluation of Bishop Hoadly in a fine essay, "Benjamin Hoadly," in *Social and Political Ideas of Some English Thinkers of the Augustan Age*, ed. F. J. C. Hearnshaw (1928), chapter VI. The first results of this re-evaluation can be seen in Bernard Bailyn's "General Introduction" to *Pamphlets of the American Revolution*, pages 30–4. J. H. Plumb has used Sykes to good effect in *Sir Robert Walpole: The Making of A Statesman* (1956). To my knowledge the only modern study of the great, influential Archbishop Tillotson is Louis G. Locke's *Tillotson: A Study in Seventeenth-Century Literature* (1954), which is more concerned with his literary style and literary reputation than with his theological style—or were literature and theology here the same? See also the old but still useful J. H. Overton, *Life in the English Church, 1660–1714* (1885); and Overton and F. Relton, *The English Church, 1714–1800* (1906). W. Fraser Mitchell, *English Pulpit Oratory from Andrewes to Tillotson* (1932), is a vigorous analysis of changing styles of thinking through changing styles of rhetoric. M. G. Jones, *The Charity School Movement: A Study of Eighteenth Century Puritanism in Action* (1938), is a model monograph: complete, thoughtful, revealing. Its very presence calls attention to the need for further research on eighteenth-century English dissent, on which R. K. Webb's forthcoming work on Unitarianism should shed much light. Meanwhile, see Olive M. Griffiths, *Religion and Learning: A Study in English Presbyterian Thought* (1935). John Wesley's *Journal* and *Letters* are available in good modern editions, the former edited by N. Curnock, 8 vols. (1909–16), the latter by J. Telford, 8 vols. (1931). There are several good biographies of Wesley. James Laver, *Wesley* (1933), is brief and judicious; I owe it my account of the touching moment when Charles Wesley read Marcus Aurelius (p. 119). V. H. H. Green, *The Young Mr. Wesley* (1961), is a well-informed, illuminating analysis of Wesley down to his conversion. It proves, if proof be needed after the testy pages of Gibbon's *Autobiography*, how deeply Oxford had sunk into religious and intellectual lethargy in the early eighteenth century. For the social consequences, see Robert F. Wearmouth, *Methodism and the Common People of the Eighteenth Century* (1945).

There is much interesting testimony to the development of the modern German religious mood in Goethe's autobiography, which I have often cited in the text. See *Dichtung und Wahrheit*, in *Gedenkausgabe*, X, 302 f, 318 ff, 367, 536–7, 557. The standard authorities—Bruford, *Germany in the Eighteenth Century;* Wolff, *Weltanschauung der deutschen Aufklärung;* Biedermann, *Deutschland im achtzehnten Jahrhundert*, and once again Aner, *Theologie der Lessingzeit*—offer much evidence. A. L. Drummond, *German Protestantism since Luther* (1951), is a general survey but lacks depth. There is a short interesting article by Dagobert de Levie on "Patriotism and Clerical Office: Germany 1761–1773," *JHI*, XIV: 4 (October 1953), 622–7. Troeltsch's discriminating definition of "secularization" as the demotion of the church-centered life rather than the death of religion, to which I am indebted, is largely based on German sources (see *Protestantism and Progress, passim*). For the worldly concerns of Pietists, see F. Paulsen, *Geschichte des gelehrten Unterrichts* (edn. 1885), 382. Paul Drews, *Der evangelische Geistliche in der deutschen Vergangenheit*, Monographien zur deutschen Kulturgeschichte, Vol. XII (1905), is thin but has some material. Clearly much work needs to be done in eighteenth-century German social and religious history. For Lessing, in addition to the other authorities see also the remarkable essay by Eduard Zeller, "Lessing als Theolog," *Vorträge und Abhandlungen*, Zweite Sammlung (1877), 283–327. Sengle's fine *Wieland* again and again shows how hard the struggle for secularism was, and how confused. I owe the report on Handel's organ playing to Newman Flower, *George Frideric Handel, His Personality and His Times* (1948), 60–61. For the association of anti-Jewish with anti-Christian spleen in the German Enlightenment (or parts of it), see Stern, *Lichtenberg,* 240 ff. The relation of freemasonry to the Enlightenment has been much discussed, but what with the obscurity of masonic history, not much light has been shed so far. But see Pierre Grappin's short, helpful *mise au point* with a splendid bibliography, "Lumières et franc-maçonnerie en Allemagne au XVIIIe siècle," *Utopie et institutions au XVIIIe*

siècle: Le Pragmatisme des lumières, VIe section, "Congrès et colloques," IV (1963), 219–27. It will be obvious to the alert reader that I dissent from Ernst Cassirer's estimate of the German Enlightenment as basically religious (see *Philosophy of the Enlightenment*, chapter IV.)

In view of Frederick II's importance as a statesman, littérateur, and host to philosophes, his religion is a fascinating subject. Max von Boehn, *Deutschland im achtzehnten Jahrhundert*, "Die Aufklärung," is to the point; I owe it two quotations in the text. The best-known biography is by Reinhold Koser, *Geschichte Friedrichs des Grossen*, 4 vols. (4th and 5th edn., 1912), which is extremely well informed, rich in detail, but lacking in objective distance. Adolf Berney, *Friedrich der Grosse: Entwicklungs-geschichte eines Staatsmannes* (1934), traces Frederick's personal and intellectual evolution with admiration but happily without adulation. Werner Langer, *Friedrich der Grosse und die geistige Welt Frankreichs* (1932), studies his dependence on and rebellion against his French mentors convinced that the pupil was superior to his teachers, a not uncommon failing of German studies of *Friedrich der Einzige*. I have dealt with the relations between Frederick and Voltaire in *Voltaire's Politics*, chapter III. See also Eduard Zeller, *Friedrich der Grosse als Philosoph* (1886), and the fine essay by Wilhelm Dilthey, "Friedrich der Grosse und die deutsche Aufklärung," *Gesammelte Schriften*, III, 81–205. Gerhard Ritter, *Friedrich der Grosse: Ein Historisches Profil*, should be read both in the first edition of 1936, which adroitly seeks to assimilate Frederick to the *Führer*, and the third edition of 1954, which adroitly seeks to free Frederick from the charge that he had anything in common with those nasty Nazis. Perhaps it takes a Frenchman to see Frederick and his philosophy plain, though of course there is often a danger of excessive hostility. Above all, see Ernest Lavisse, *La Jeunesse du Grand Frédéric* (1891) and *Le Grand Frédéric avant l'avènement* (1893). Against Lavisse's judgment—*Non, il n'était pas bon*—Meinecke uttered a heartfelt protest: Lavisse, he wrote in *Die Idee der Staatsräson* (p. 353), grossly misjudged the king. Meinecke was subtler than Lavisse, but Lavisse saw his man clearly.

I know of no comprehensive social study of the Protestant

clergy in Europe. A number of national histories have revealing details. B. J. Hovde, *The Scandinavian Countries, 1720–1865: The Rise of the Middle Classes,* 2 vols. (1943), for instance, describes the energy with which Swedish and Danish clergymen exploited their flocks (I, 194 ff).

The French religious situation offers many striking instances of the treason of the clerks in the Catholic world. I am deeply indebted to Bernard Groethuysen's subtle analysis of the shift in religious rhetoric from a rather grim Augustinian emphasis on hell and damnation in seventeenth-century sermons to the bland modern emphasis on good Christian living in eighteenth-century sermons in his *Die Entstehung der bürgerlichen Welt- und Lebensanchauung in Frankreich,* 2 vols. (1927–30); this book is an excellent and pioneering work and unavailable in English, and R. R. Palmer's severe strictures on it (in his *Catholics and Unbelievers in Eighteenth Century France,* which is itself an excellent corrective to liberal misreadings of religious history) are too strong. The search for a compromise is depicted in Robert Mauzi's chapter on the "Chrétien honnête homme" in his *L'Idée du bonheur dans la littérature et la pensée française au XVIIIᵉ siècle* (1960). In a splendid book on Angers,[4] John McManners portrays a religious society just secular enough to give hearing to Enlightenment ideas, just pious enough to cause friction; it also rather comically shows the alliance of educated Christians with educated secularists (see esp. pp. 22, 24, 33 ff, 43–4). There are valuable insights into the decline of piety in Toulouse in David D. Bien's excellent *The Calas Affair: Persecution, Toleration, and Heresy in Eighteenth-Century Toulouse* (1960), especially chapter II, from which I have drawn my description in the text. Franklin L. Ford, *Strasbourg in Transition, 1648–1789* (1958), is illuminating on another kind of French town, where a Protestant German tradition came to be overlaid by a Catholic French tradition after the city was annexed in 1681 (see especially chapter V, "Catholics and Protestants"). The rage for modernity and the ignorance of scholarly clerics like Montfaucon is demonstrated in McManners' book; in Emile Mâle, *The Gothic Image* (vii, 20);

---

[4] *French Ecclesiastical Society under the Ancien Régime* (1960).

and in the interesting article by Jacques Vanuxem, "The Theories of Mabillon and Montfaucon on French Sculpture of the
Twelfth Century," *Warburg Journal*, XX (January 1957), 45–58.
L. Cahen has chronicled the political battles of the French Church
in *Les Querelles religieuses et parlementaires sous Louis XV*
(1913); E. Préclin and E. Jarry have written an excellent general
survey that centers on France but covers all, of Catholic Europe,
Les Luttes politiques et doctrinales aux XVIIe et XVIIIe siècles, 2
vols. (1955–6), which forms Volumes XIX, Part I, and XIX, Part
II, of the general "Histoire de l'Église depuis les origines jusqu'à
nos jours," ed. Augustin Fliche and Victor Martin. Préclin has
also written a monumental and powerful study of French
Jansenists in the age of the Enlightenment: *Les Jansenistes du
XVIIIe siècle et la Constitution civile du clergé* (1928). Henri
Brémond, *Histoire littéraire du sentiment religieux*, 12 vols.
(1929–36), can be read selectively; it is a mine of information even
for those who do not share its pious orientation.

I have compiled my account of d'Alembert's Genevan visit
and its disastrous consequences from obvious sources: Grimsley's
biography of d'Alembert, the biographies of Rousseau and
Voltaire, and their correspondence, mentioned before. In addition,
I have used F. Fuchs's excellent critical edition of J.-J. Rousseau,
Lettre à d'Alembert sur les spectacles (1948). I have dealt briefly
with the decay of Calvinist severity in Calvin's city in *Voltaire's
Politics*, chapter IV.

CHAPTER SEVEN

Beyond the Holy Circle

---

1. THE ABUSE OF LEARNING

For the learning which the philosophes abused, see Douglas's splendid *English Scholars*; Momigliano's many articles, already cited;[1] H. Bresslau, *Handbuch der Urkundenlehre für Deutschland und Italien*, 2 vols. (2nd edn., 1912–31); and an interesting monograph by Emil Clemens Scherer, *Geschichte und Kirchengeschichte an den deutschen Universitäten* (1927), especially parts II and III. For the tension between philosophes and *érudits*, see especially Momigliano and Seznec, *Diderot et l'antiquité*, passim.

Calmet deserves a modern study. Meanwhile, see A. Digot, *Notice biographique et littéraire sur Dom Augustin Calmet* (1860); and useful biographical articles by Ph. Schmitz in Baudrillart, *Dictionnaire d'histoire et de géographie ecclésiastiques*, II, 450–3; and the unsigned article in Hoefer's *Nouvelle Biographie générale*, VIII, 238–42. My indispensable source for Voltaire's— and Mme du Châtelet's—exploitation of Calmet's scholarly writings is Wade, *Voltaire and madame du Châtelet*, which summarizes and quotes from Mme du Châtelet's *Examen de la Genèse* at great length.

Like Calmet, Brucker has been rather neglected. Historians of philosophy have recognized him as a father—or rather precursor —of a genre that reached self-conscious maturity with Hegel (see, for instance, Wilhelm Windelband, *Lehrbuch der Geschichte der Philosophie* [4th edn., 1907], 8), but the only book specifically devoted to him is Karl Alt's skimpy *Jakob Brucker, ein Schulmeister des 18. Jahrhunderts* (1926), which summarizes his life,

---

[1] See above, pp. 452, 453, 467, 470, 471.

lists and dates his publications, but offers no interpretation. For
contemporary interest in Brucker, see Goethe, *Dichtung und
Wahrheit*, 246; see also the reception accorded Brucker's great
Historia by the French Jesuits: in 1754 (ten years late!) their
journal, *Mémoires pour servir à l'histoire des sciences et des arts*
(popularly known as the *Journal de Trévoux*), gave it a respectful
and extensive review (pp. 455–77, 603–26, 1777–1801) and praised
its moderation and erudition. In 1792 William Enfield, a well-
known Protestant cleric and publicist, brought out a shortened
version of the 1756 edition of the *Historia*, which he called "a vast
magazine of important facts, collected with indefatigable industry,
digested with admirable perspicuity of method and written with
every appearance of candour and impartiality" (p. iv), high but
by no means unmerited praise. Diderot's borrowings from Brucker
were noted as early as 1774, when a German reviewer commented
on them rather acidulously (see Mortier, *Diderot en Allemagne*,
354–5). Lord Morley, Diderot's nineteenth-century biographer,
noted it also: *Diderot and the Encyclopaedists*, 2 vols. (1878), I,
217 ff. Diderot himself, as I suggest in the text, tried to blunt any
possible charges of plagiarism by mentioning his reliance on
Brucker (as at the end of the article "Chinois," for one), so that
Arthur Wilson can properly say in his *Diderot* (p. 216) that
"Diderot freely borrowed from a recent history of philosophy
written in Latin by a German named Brucker, a fact which
Diderot did not attempt to conceal." True, but his admission concealed the extent of his borrowings. There are some comments on
the subject in Barker, *Diderot's Treatment of the Christian
Religion*, while Proust has an excellent pair of chapters (VII and
VIII) and an invaluable appendix (IX) which lists the sources of
many of Diderot's articles in the *Encyclopédie*, and in this list
Brucker necessarily appears often. The analysis of the particular
use to which Diderot put Brucker, however, is mine.

Since Gibbon trumpeted his learning with engaging frank-
ness, the best sources of information on his borrowings are his
Autobiography and the footnotes in *The Decline and Fall of the
Roman Empire*. Geoffrey Keynes's *The Library of Edward
Gibbon: A Catalogue of His Books* (1940), confirms Gibbon's
scholarly voracity. See also the observations in Giarrizzo, *Edward

Gibbon e la cultura Europea (passim), and some brilliant pages in Young, *Gibbon* (68–78). As for the scholars he used most prominently: Mabillon is well summarized in M. D. Knowles, "Jean Mabillon," *Journal of Ecclesiastical History*, X:2 (1959), 153–73; E. de Broglie, *Mabillon et la Société de l'Abbaye de Saint-Germain-des-Prés à la fin du dix-septième siècle*, 2 vols. (1888); the useful collective volume of essays *Mélanges et documents publiés à l'occasion du 2ᵉ centenaire de la mort de Mabillon* (1908), which includes a most helpful analysis of *De re diplomatica;* and Gall Heer, *Johannes Mabillon und die Schweizer Benediktiner: Ein Beitrag zur Geschichte der historischen Quellenforschung im 17. und 18. Jahrhundert* (1938), a revealing glimpse of pious learning. For Le Nain de Tillemont, see the detailed treatment by C. A. Sainte-Beuve, *Port-Royale*, 10 vols. (edn. 1926–32), esp. Vol. V. For Du Cange, see H. Hardouin, *Essai sur la vie et sur les ouvrages de Ducange* (1849). There is no modern work on Isaac de Beausobre, the Huguenot divine whose history of the Manicheans allowed Gibbon to step beyond the holy circle.

I owe the observation that Swift's *Tale of a Tub* struck at least one reader as conducive to irreligion to a quotation from the *Diary* of Dudley Rider, a distinguished jurist and judge (quoted in Dobrée, *English Literature in the Early Eighteenth Century*, 363).

2. THE MISSION OF LUCRETIUS

The material for this section is familiar. That religion was the necessary enemy of philosophy was commonly assumed by all the philosophes. Diderot puts it most vehemently in his intimate correspondence: as philosophy gains, religion recedes (*Correspondance*, II, 297–305); Christianity is a "mythology" and the mother of crime, (IV, 260–1); and in all respects, true "philosophy" is opposed to Christianity (IV, 176–7). The same position may be drawn from thousands of other sources; even when d'Alembert is being most reasonable and circumspect (as in his "De l'abus de la critique en matière de religion," *Mélanges*, IV,

323–80), the enmity seems inescapable, almost tragic. And yet to complicate things, see Diderot in good-natured dispute with père Berthier (*Correspondance*, I, 137).

I have spoken of deism before.[2] What is needed above all is a set of reliable biographies of the leading deists. A. Lantoine, *Un Précurseur de la franc-maçonnerie: John Toland, 1670–1722* (1927), is an exceptional book in an open field. The classic study of the English deists is Leslie Stephen's great *English Thought in the Eighteenth Century*. Stephen, however, underestimated both the deists' philosophical acumen and their influence; moreover, his distinction between critical and constructive deism, which has received almost universal acceptance, separates the very modes of thinking which, conjoined, gave the deists their strength. Roland N. Stromberg, *Religious Liberalism in Eighteenth-Century England* (1954), and Ernest C. Mossner, *Bishop Butler and the Age of Reason: A Study in the History of Thought* (1936), help to bring the analysis of deism up to date. Arthur O. Lovejoy's well known essay "The Parallel of Deism and Classicism," in *Essays in the History of Ideas*, 78–98, is extremely suggestive and repays close study (I had the good fortune of hearing a point-by-point rebuttal of this essay by Professor Stromberg at a meeting of a University Seminar at Columbia University; clearly Lovejoy overstressed some parallels, overlooked others, and neglected some significant differences). For the importation of deism into France, see Torrey, *Voltaire and the English Deists;* and E. R. Briggs, "L'Incrédulité et la pensée anglaise en France au début du XVIIIᵉ siècle," *Revue d'histoire littéraire de la France*, XLI (1934), 497–538. On deism in Germany (which Goethe thought a natural kind of religion for educated men to adopt [*Dichtung und Wahrheit*, 154]), see Hermann Hettner, *Geschichte der deutschen Literatur im achtzehnten Jahrhundert*, 4 vols. (4th edn., 1893–4). For Reimarus, see the essay by Strauss.[3]

For the aggressive deist and atheist line, cherished by Holbach and Hume and Voltaire, that religion is a disease, see the relevant pages in Manuel, *The Eighteenth Century Confronts the*

---

[2] See above, pp. 374–96.
[3] See above, pp. 462–3.

Gods, 34–40, 70 ff, 228 ff. For Voltaire's religion, Pomeau, *Religion de Voltaire*, is, once again, indispensable. I have summarized the various meanings imputed to *écrasez l'infâme*—merely against fanaticism, merely against Catholicism, against all organized supernatural religions, an expression of atheism—and come out for the third of these in my *Voltaire's Politics*, chapter V. For Meslier, see Andrew R. Morehouse, *Voltaire and Jean Meslier* (1936). For Voltaire's tactics and strategies, transparent but very interesting, see my analysis of his *Dictionnaire philosophique* (now in *The Party of Humanity*, 7–54), but more can be done.

I should say the same about materialism, although we have good scholarly work by Vartanian on La Mettrie and reliable books by Wickwar and Naville on Holbach.[4] Frederick Albert Lange, *The History of Materialism and Criticism of its Present Importance*, 3 vols. in 1 (1865; tr. E. C. Thomas, edn. 1950), has by no means lost its value. See also the extremely interesting essay by E. A. Gellner, "French Eighteenth-Century Materialism," in *A Critical History of Western Philosophy*, ed. D. J. O'Connor (1964), 277–95, which raises some fundamental issues and seeks to contrast the philosophy of the Enlightenment with the philosophical temper of our own day.

3. DAVID HUME: THE COMPLETE MODERN PAGAN

As I have said before, the books on Hume by Norman Kemp Smith, Passmore, and Mossner are indispensable. Each of these interpretations emphasizes the positive intent of Hume's philosophy and refutes the widespread notion that Hume was "merely" a "destructive" skeptic. Special studies, like Giarrizzo's book on Hume as a historian, add important insights.[5] There is also a large and meritorious technical literature. See Ralph Church, *Hume's Theory of the Understanding* (1935); H. H. Price, *Hume's Theory*

---

[4] See above, pp. 398–401.
[5] See above, p. 454.

of the External World (1940); and Anthony Flew, *Hume's Philosophy of Belief: A Study of His First Inquiry* (1961). A symposium held at Edinburgh, *Hume and Present Day Problems* (1939), with contributions by Norman Kemp Smith, J. L. Austin, C. A. Mace, and others, is valuable. Eugene Rotwein has felicitously edited David Hume's *Writings on Economics* (1955) and provided it with a full introduction that deals perspicaciously with Hume's psychology. John Vladimir Price, "Skeptics in Cicero and Hume," *JHI,* XXV: 1 (January–March 1964), 97–106, though helpful in connecting Philo with Cotta, adds little to what we know. I was delighted to read Stuart Hampshire's brief appraisal of Hume, "Hume's Place in Philosophy," in *David Hume: A Symposium,* 1–10, which accords precisely with my own estimate —an estimate I have arrived at after years of close and affectionate concern with Hume's work. Hume, writes Hampshire, "defined one consistent, and within its own terms, irrefutable, attitude to politics, to the problems of society, to religion; an attitude which is supremely confident and clear, that of the perfect secular mind, which can accept, and submit itself to, the natural order, the facts of human nature, without anxiety, and therefore without a demand for ultimate solutions, for a guarantee that justice is somehow built into the nature of things. This philosophical attitude, because it is consistent and sincere, has its fitting style: that of irony . . ." (pp. 9–10). The demands and the possibilities of modern paganism have rarely been stated better than this.

Bibliography of
Works Frequently Cited

THE WRITINGS of the philosophes are in a curious bibliographical limbo. While, as I said in the Preface, there is much valuable scholarly activity, the complete works of some philosophes—like Hume—are not available at all; the works of others—like Voltaire —are outdated and are now being superseded piecemeal by critical editions of their major writings and their correspondence. The works of still others—like Rousseau—are, fortunately, now being collected in authoritative editions, but these editions are incomplete. As a result, I have been compelled to cite from a variety of editions; I list the most important of these below, together with short titles wherever sensible. Other editions will be identified directly in the footnotes.

Jean Le Rond d'Alembert: *Mélanges de littérature, d'histoire, et de la philosophie*, 5 vols. (1757). Cited as *Mélanges*.
———: *Œuvres complètes*, 5 vols. (1821–22). Cited as *Œuvres*.
Francis Bacon: *Works*, ed. James Spedding, R. L. Ellis, and D. D. Heath, 14 vols. (1857–74), which contain the Latin writings (vols. I–III), English translations and English writings (vols. IV–VII), the correspondence and a biography by Spedding (vols. VIII–XIV).
James Boswell: *Boswell's Life of Johnson, Together with Boswell's Journal of a Tour to the Hebrides and Johnson's Diary of a Journey into North Wales,* ed. George Birkbeck Hill, rev. by L. F. Powell, 6 vols. (1934–50). Cited as *Life of Johnson*.
Étienne Bonnot, abbé de Condillac: *Œuvres philosophiques*, ed. Georges Le Roy, 3 vols. (1947–51). Cited as *Œuvres*.
Marie-Jean-Antoine-Nicolas Caritat, marquis de Condorcet:

Œuvres, eds. A. Condorcet O'Connor and M. F. Arago, 12 vols.
(1847). (I have abbreviated the long title of Condorcet's
Esquisse d'un tableau historique des progrès de l'esprit humain,
as *Esquisse*).

Denis Diderot: *Correspondance*, ed. Georges Roth, 12 vols., so
far, down to 1773 (1955–).

————: *Œuvres complètes*, eds. Jules Assézat and Maurice
Tourneux, 20 vols. (1875–7). Cited as *Œuvres*.

————: *Œuvres esthétiques*, ed. Paul Vernière (1959).

————: *Œuvres politiques*, ed. Paul Vernière (1963).

————: *Œuvres romanesques*, ed. Henri Bénac (1951).

————: *Salons*, ed. Jean Seznec and Jean Adhémar, 3 vols. so far
(1957–). Vol. I (1957) covers the salons of 1759, 1761, and
1763; vol. II (1960), the salon of 1765; vol. III (1963), the salon
of 1767.

The Encyclopédie of Diderot and d'Alembert: Selected Articles
[in French], ed. John Lough (1954). Cited as *The Encyclopédie*.

Edward Gibbon: *Autobiography*, ed. Dero A. Saunders (1961).

————: *The History of the Decline and Fall of the Roman Empire*,
ed. J. B. Bury, 7 vols. (1896–1902). Cited as *Decline and Fall of
the Roman Empire*.

————: *Miscellaneous Works of Edward Gibbon, Esq., with
Memoirs of his Life and Writings, Composed by Himself:
Illustrated from His Letters, with Occasional Notes and Narra-
tive*, ed. John, Lord Sheffield, 5 vols. (2nd edn., 1814). Cited as
Miscellaneous Works.

Johann Wolfgang Goethe: *Gedenkausgabe der Werke, Briefe,
und Gespräche*, ed. Ernst Beutler, 24 vols. (1949). Cited as
Gedenkausgabe.

Friedrich Melchior Grimm: *Correspondance littéraire, philosophique et critique par Grimm, Diderot, Raynal, etc.*, ed. Maurice
Tourneux, 16 vols. (1877–82). Cited as *Correspondance
littéraire*.

David Hume: *Dialogues Concerning Natural Religion*, ed. Norman Kemp Smith (2nd edn., 1947). Cited as *Dialogues*.

————: *The Letters of David Hume*, ed. J. Y. T. Greig, 2 vols.
(1932). Cited as *Letters*.

————: *New Letters of David Hume*, ed. Raymond Klibansky and Ernest C. Mossner (1954). Cited as *New Letters*.

————: *The Philosophical Works of David Hume*, ed. T. H. Green and T. H. Grose, 4 vols. (1882 edn.). Cited as *Works*.

Immanuel Kant: *Immanuel Kants Werke*, ed. Ernst Cassirer, with Hermann Cohen, *et al.*, 11 vols. (vol. XI is Cassirer's *Kants Leben und Lehre*), (1912–22). Cited as *Werke*.

Gotthold Ephraim Lessing: *Sämmtliche Schriften*, ed. Karl Lachmann and Franz Muncker, 23 vols. (1886–1924). Cited as *Schriften*.

Charles de Secondat, baron de Montesquieu: *Œuvres complètes*, ed. André Masson, 3 vols. (1950–5). Cited as *Œuvres*.

Jean-Jacques Rousseau: *Œuvres complètes*, ed. Bernard Gagnebin, Marcel Raymond, et al., 3 vols., so far (1959–). Cited as *Œuvres*.

Anne-Robert-Jacques Turgot, baron de l'Aulne: *Œuvres de Turgot et documents le concernant*, ed. G. Schelle, 5 vols. (1913–23). Cited as *Œuvres*.

Voltaire (François-Marie Arouet): *Voltaire's Correspondence*, ed. Theodore Besterman, 103 vols. (1953–65). Cited as *Correspondence*.

————: *Lettres philosophiques*, ed. Gustave Lanson, 2 vols. (1909).

————: *Voltaire's Notebooks*, ed. Theodore Besterman, 2 vols., continuously paginated (1952). Cited as *Notebooks*.

————: *Œuvres complètes*, ed. Louis Moland, 52 vols. (1877–85). Cited as *Œuvres*.

————: *Œuvres historiques*, ed. René Pomeau (1957).

————: *Philosophical Dictionary*, ed. and tr. Peter Gay, 2 vols., continuously paginated (1962).

Christoph Martin Wieland: *Sämmtliche Werke*, ed. J. G. Gruber, 50 vols. (Vol. L is a biography of Wieland by Gruber), (1824–7). Cited as *Werke*.

INDEX

Aaron, Richard I., 305
Abelard, Pierre, 171, 217, 225, 231–2
Academics, 126, 190, 316 *n.*
Adam, Charles, 311 *n.*
Adams, Rev. William, 407
Addison, Joseph, 39, 41, 211
Agesilas, 47
Agricola, Gnaeus Julius, 111
Ainsworth, Michael, 30, 327 *n.*
Alcibiades, 47, 286
Alembert, Jean Le Rond d': and his contemporaries, 5, 10, 13, 16, 18, 23 *n*, 140–1, 147, 183, 351, 360, 400; writings of, 11, 14, 143; born, 17; way of life, 25–6; quoted, 36, 43–4, 318, 319; schooling, 45–6; and other writers, 49 *n.*, 310, 315, 335; and classical writers, 81, 276 *n.*, 360–1; on history, 121, 277 *n.;* on metaphysics, 138; philosophy of, 134, 139, 401; on criticism, 141–2; on Humanists, 257–8, 262–3; and his time, 319; and religion, 324; and Geneva article, 336–8; on Jesuits, 352, 372
Alexander, 163–4
Alfieri, Comte Vittorio, 47, 192
Alfonso V, 273
allegory, use of, 222–4, 239–40, 282, 378–9
Amyot, Jacques, 281
Anacreon, 48
Aner, Karl, 45 *n.*, 331 *n.*
Anglomania, 12, 383
anticlericalism, 17, 149, 350, 371, 372, 374, 379, 384, 386, 390
Antonines, 115, 118
Apulius, 164
Argenson, René Louis de Voyer d', marquis d', 41

Aristotle: and philosophes, 44 *n.*, 82, 105; and his time, 85, 213, 218, 315; philosophy of, 194–5, 196, 230, 231; Christians on, 219, 225, 232–3, 244; saints on, 232; and Humanists, 263, 267; translations of, 281; as subject, 306
Aristotelians, 196, 247, 268
Arians, 320
Arminianism, 299, 325, 326
Arminius, Jacobus, 299
Arrian, 151 *n.*
Asser, 244
Atticus, Titus Pomponius, 260
Aubrey, John, 44 *n.*
Auerbach, Erich, 239
Aufklärer: characteristics of, 4, 21; and philosophes, 16, 62, 325, 326, 335; and Bayle, 291; and religion, 350, 351; writings of, 372
Aufklärung, 21, 328
Augustus, Caesar: reign of, 97–8, 110, 111, 112, 122, 124, 125, 155, 159, 161, 215, 223; and philosophes, 154, 158 *n.*
Aurelius, Marcus: *see* Marcus Aurelius
Averroës, 273
Averroists, 233, 247
Bacon, Francis: and philosophes, 11, 227 *n.*, 322; quoted, 35 *n.*, 144, 286–7; philosophy of, 135, 148, 182, 310–13; and other writers, 161 *n.*, 287 *n.*, 315, 320, 321; and Scholastics, 181; on nature, 186

Bacon, Roger, 233, 247, 248
Baillie, J. B., 37 *n.*
Barbier, Antoine, 26

Barthélemy, abbé Jean Jacques, 64 *n*., 84

Baron, Hans, 259 *n*.

Basnage, Jacques, 366

Basedow, Johann Bernhard, 372

Bayle, Pierre: and philosophes, 17, 283, 284, 335, 383, 412; writings of, 62, 286 *n*., 290–2, 293–4, 309, 406; and classical writers, 152; and Humanists, 277; influence of, 291–2, 294, 295, 350, 374; and other writers, 306, 331, 361, 365, 366, 409

Beatrice: *see* Portinari, Beatrice

Beattie, James, 402

Beausobre, 358, 368

Beccaria, Cesare Bonesana, marchese di, 7 *n*., 10, 11 *n*., 12, 15, 17, 129, 138 *n*., 176, 373

Bekker, Balthasar, 145

Benedictines, 76, 353, 359, 370

Bennett, Charles H., 22 *n*.

Bentham, Jeremy, 11, 53, 120, 142, 170, 171, 373

Bentinck, Countess, 362 *n*.

Bentley, Richard, 316, 375

Bergerac, Cyrano de: *see* Cyrano de Bergerac

Bergier, N. S., 397

Berkeley, George, 22, 133

Bernis, Cardinal François Joachim de Pierre de, 339

Berthier, père, 24

Blackstone, Sir William, 142

Blair, Rev. Hugh, 9 *n*., 20 *n*., 342 *n*., 403 *n*.

Bletterie, abbé de la, 320

Bloch, Marc, 244 *n*., 245

Blumenfeld, Hélaine, 70 *n*.

Boccaccio, Giovanni, 257, 262, 264, 278

Bodin, Jean, 283, 298, 300, 303

Boehn, Max von, 349 *n*.

Boerhaave, Hermann, 31, 330

Boethius, 235

Bolingbroke, Henry St. John, 55, 409

Bonnard, Georges A., 58 *n*.

Bornmüller, Franz, 69 *n*.

Bossuet, Jacques-Bénigne, 34, 75–8

Boswell, James: and his contemporaries, 21, 133; and Johnson, 22, 147 *n*., 293, 402; and other writers, 42 *n*.; writings of, 177, 401 *n*.; on religion, 340; at Hume's deathbed, 356, 402.

Botticelli, Sandro, 276

Boucher, François, 8

Boulainvilliers, Henri de, comte de Saint-Saire, 383, 384

Boulanger, Nicolas-Antoine, 19, 398

Boyle, Robert, 306, 310, 316, 318

Boys Smith, John S., 379 *n*.

Bracciolini, Poggio: *see* Poggio Bracciolini

Briggs, E. R., 382 *n*.

Brucker, Johann Jakob: writings of, 75, 81 *n*., 161 *n*., 227 *n*.; 359, 365–6; and other writers, 160, 366, 367; influence of, 286 *n*.; life of, 364–5

Brunelleschi, Filippo, 275

Bruni, Leonardo, 171, 259, 260, 261, 263

Bruno, Giordano, 161 *n*.

Brunswick, Duke of, 381

Brutus, Marcus Junius, 45 *n*., 47, 214, 264

Bryson, Gladys, 34 *n*., 134 *n*., 342 *n*.

Buddeus, Johann Franz, 365

Buffon, Georges-Louis Leclerc de, 10, 14, 16, 17, 19, 25, 88, 89, 136, 191

Burckhardt, Jakob, 266, 276

Burke, Edmund, 374

Burnet, Thomas, 78

Butler, Bishop Joseph, 24, 339, 374, 376, 415

Caesar, Julius, 35, 47, 57, 96, 107, 108, 109, 110, 167, 286

Calas, Jean, 179

Calas family, 187, 393

Caligula, 111, 112, 281

Calmet, Dom Antoine Augustin, 361–4, 393

Calvin, John, 211, 280, 322, 337

Canaan, Edwin, 129 *n.*

Carneades, 43

Carroll, William, 327 *n.*

Casaubon, Isaac, 360

Cassirer, Ernst, 131, 186 *n.*, 265 *n.*, 267 *n.*, 328 *n.*

Cassius Longius, Gaius, 214

Catherine of Russia: *see* Catherine the Great

Catherine the Great, 11, 32, 48, 94, 98, 197

Cato, 47, 112, 392

Catullus, Gaius Valerius, 98, 108, 109–10, 121, 262

Caylus, Anne Claude Philippe de Tubières, comte de, 360

Celsus, 125

Champailler, Yvonne, 76 *n.*

Charlemagne, 76, 218, 219–20, 244

Charles of Burgundy, 245 *n.*

Charles II, 314–15

Charles III of Spain, 355

Charron, Pierre, 303

Châtelet, Gabrielle-Émilie Le Tonnelier de Breteuil, marquise du, 176, 361

Chaulieu, abbé de, 307, 356

Chesterfield, Philip Dormer Stanhope, Earl of, 41, 144 *n.*, 177, 191 *n.*

Cheyne, Dr. George, 64 *n.*

Chinard, Gilbert, 55*n.*

Christ: philosophes on, 7, 217, 301 *n.*, 307, 333, 336, 338, 381, 388; teachings of, 55, 169, 171, 332, 377; as subject, 62; coming of, 76, 208, 215, 216, 222, 228; saints on, 231, 232; Dante on, 235; early Christians on, 240, 241; and Humanists, 274; in art, 276; reincarnation of, 300, 379; as Jewish Messiah, 378; miracles of, 379, 406; slander against, 383, 399

Christianity: and philosophes, 8, 35, 37, 44, 51, 60–2, 68, 136, 149, 168, 169, 170, 203, 210–11, 286, 323, 327, 332, 337, 371–2, 373 *n.*, 389–91, 406; and Enlightenment, 18, 59, 268, 418; and paganism, 207, 211, 220, 315 *n.*, 317, 324, 368; origins of, 207–9, 212–13; and ancients, 216, 223; and Dante, 236; early views on, 241, 248, 314, 300; and numerical thinking, 250–2; and Stoicism, 264, 302–3; and Humanists, 274; in Reformation, 280, 282; and art, 282; campaign against, 296, 323 *n.*, 374, 399, 408; campaign for, 316; as subject, 321; in seventeenth century, 326, 330; and science, 338; in eighteenth century, 339, 342, 345, 350, 367, 394, 406; and deists, 375–83

Chrysippus, 367

Chrytäus, David, 301

Church Fathers: on classical writers, 101, 264, 274, 304; and philosophes, 215, 216, 324, 331; on religion, 220, 339; on philosophy, 229; writings of, 281 *n.*; and Stoicism, 302–3

Cicero: and philosophes, 32, 47, 50, 51, 53, 55, 56, 57, 62, 63, 64, 66, 67, 69, 105–9, 126, 129, 150, 151, 152, 153, 159, 162, 183, 192, 203, 259, 293, 313, 383, 412, 414, 415 *n.*; and his contemporaries, 35, 83, 98, 99, 105, 123, 128, 317, 318; writings of, 85, 125, 178, 194–5; life of, 96, 164, 191–2; death of, 110; on myths, 154; on religion, 155–6; and Stoicism, 165, 296; philosophy of, 189–90, 270; St. Jerome's study of, 219; and Christians, 224–5, 363; and other writers, 235, 388, 303, 316 *n.*; admiration of, 259–63, 271; and Humanists, 267, 273; translations of, 281, 299; influence of, 298, 299; on Epicureans, 304

Cideville, de, 52, 337 *n.*, 388 *n.*

Clark, Sir Kenneth, 221

Clarke, Samuel, 316, 320, 326, 357

Claudius, 112

Clephane, John, 254

Cochrane, Charles N., 216 n.

Colbert, Jean Baptiste, 282

Coleridge, Samuel Taylor, 288

Collins, Anthony, 326, 375, 376–9, 382, 398, 399

Columella, Lucius Junius, 67

Commodus, Lucius Aelius, 115

Condillac, Étienne Bonnot de, 17, 79 n., 88, 136, 139–41, 196, 227, 246, 306, 320

Condorcet, Marie Jean Antoine Nicholas de Caritat, marquis de: and his time, 34–5, 36; on history, 73, 78, 82, 121, 209, 246, 280–1; and Stoicism, 165; influence of, 181, 257; on Christianity, 210, 212; on Dante, 214; on Scholasticism, 227

Conrad of Hirsau, 220

Constantine, 35 n., 76, 222, 273

Conway, Henry Seymour, 106 n.

Coornhert, Dirck, 299

Copernicus, Nicolaus, 279

Copley, Sir Godfrey, 345 n.

Corneille, Pierre, 11, 385

Cosimo, Piero di: see Piero di Cosimo

Counter-Reformation, 296

Coverley, Sir Roger de, 344

Cowley, Abraham, 315, 321

Crates of Thebes, 164

Crébillon (Prosper Jolyot), 106

Creed, John Martin, 379 n.

Créqui, Maréchal de, 287 n.

criticism: and philosophes, 17, 18, 34, 121–2, 126, 127, 141–5, 149, 172, 236; relation to philosophy, 130–1, 304; and Middle Ages, 237

Cullen, Dr. William, 356

Curchod, Suzanne, 117

Curtius, Ernst Robert, 70 n., 220 n., 226 n.

Cyrano de Bergerac, 307

Cyrus the Younger, 77

Dacier, André, 51

d'Alembert: see Alembert, Jean Le Rond d'

Dalrymple, Sir David, Lord Hailes, 323 n.

Damian, St. Peter, 200, 217, 233

Damilaville, Étienne-Noël, 19, 103 n., 371, 392 n., 393

Dante: and philosophes, 23, 271 n.; as poet of Middle Ages, 212–14; and Vergil, 213–15, 218, 220–1, 236; and classical writers, 224; writings of, 238, 239, 269; use of philosophy, 235–6; on religion, 241; on astrology, 248; on numbers, 251–3; as subject, 260; and Humanists, 264; and Epicureans, 304

Darwin, Charles, 89

Daubenton, Louis Jean Marie, 19

David (King), 363, 396

David, Gerard, 48

Davis, Herbert, 339 n.

Davus, 173–4

deists: English, 374–82; German, 382–3; French, 383–5; Voltaire and, 385–96, 398, 413

Demosthenes, 213

Denis, Madame, 69

Descartes, René: philosophy of, 12, 139, 148, 182, 310, 311, 313, 320; and his contemporaries, 17, 43 n., 181, 283 n.; on metaphysics, 186; on Scholasticism, 227 n.; and Stoicism, 303; and Galileo, 318

Dick, Hugh G., 144 n.

dialogue: ancient, 171–2; philosophes and, 172–4, 175–8; Diderot quoted, 174–5; Candide as, 199–200; Stoics use of, 301 n–2 n.

Diderot, Denis: letters to Sophie Volland, 5, 7, 48, 64, 162, 176, 180 n., 187, 188, 340, 341, 372, 386 n., 399, 401 n.; and Encyclopédie, 6, 39–40, 80, 81, 103, 127, 149, 182–3, 227, 229, 307, 364, 365–8; personality of, 8, 9, 47–8; influence of, 10; early life, 11;

writings of, 12, 14, 16, 32, 66, 85, 172, 179, 181, 197, 214, 309, 400 *n.*; and his contemporaries, 13, 14, 15, 25, 26, 141, 176–81, 197, 336, 337, 365, 391, 398–9; born, 17; and classical writers, 18, 45 *n.*, 47–50, 70–1, 72–3, 74, 75, 77–8, 79–81, 105, 109, 113, 117, 128–9, 151, 155–6, 159, 162, 164, 188–9, 226 *n.*, 264, 275; quoted, 20, 43, 70, 146, 185, 197, 206; on history, 59, 94, 168, 210; atheism of, 63–4; philosophy of, 100, 103, 136, 187–9, 267, 268 *n.*, 290; on criticism, 142; on miracles, 146, 147, 148; on eclectics, 160–1; and religion, 169, 180, 323 *n.*, 342, 371–2,383; dialogue of, 173–6; and Voltaire, 188; quarrel with Rousseau, 195–6; and other writers, 286, 287 *n.*, 288, 289–90, 294, 295, 301, 301 *n.*, 305 *n.*, 306, 308; on Epicureans, 307; on Stoicism, 367

Diderot, Denise, 64 *n.*
Dieckmann, Herbert, 49 *n.*, 128 *n.*
Dilthey, Wilhelm, 86, 297, 298, 299
Diogenes, 43, 48, 49 *n.*, 164
Domitian, 111, 113, 114, 115
Donatello, 275, 276
Donne, John, 314
Douglas, D. C., 360 *n.*
Dryden, John, 315, 316 *n.*
Dubos, Jean Baptiste, 209
Duclos, Charles Pinot, 6, 19, 25
Dufour, Theophile, 68 *n.*
du Parc, 179 *n.*
Durandus, Gulielmus, 240
Dürer, Albrecht, 267, 267 *n.*-8 *n.*
Du Vair, Guillaume, 301, 303

Eberhard, J. A., 332
eclecticism: and philosophes, 160, 170, 283; defined, 163; and Stoicism, 164–5; in philosophy, 165–6, 267, 272; *Candide* as, 200
eclectics, 94, 160–1, 162–3, 202
Edmonstoune, Col. James, 356
Edwards, Jonathan, 75

Einhard, 244
Eliot, T. S., 269
Elizabeth I, 147
Elliot, Gilbert, 66, 67 *n.*
Empiricus, Sextus, 154
Epicharmus, 291
Epictetus, 54, 55, 120, 165, 288, 296
Epicureanism: and philosophes, 99, 268, 296; background of, 304–8; and other writers, 367
Epicureans: and philosophes, 42, 54, 55, 94, 104, 126, 172, 281; philosophy of, 100, 102, 154, 292 *n.*, 317–18; and Stoicism, 165, 202; ancients as, 188, 190; and Christianity, 274, 296; writings of, 283; ancient attitude toward, 304; seventeenth-century, 307, 314
Epicurus: and philosophes, 42, 43, 52, 122; and Christians, 104; and his contemporaries, 163, defended by Gassendi, 305; as subject, 306; admiration of, 307
Erasmus, 257, 260, 264, 266, 269, 270, 274–5, 281, 282, 374
Euhemerus, 408
Euler, Leonhard, 23, 338
Euripedes, 48, 282

Falconet, Étienne Maurice, 48 *n.*, 70 *n.*, 105 *n.*, 132
Farrar, Austin, 319 *n.*
Fassó, Luigi, 47 *n.*
Ferguson, Adam: influence of, 11; and his contemporaries, 15, 147 *n.*; writings of, 34, 95; early life, 54; and classical writers, 85; quoted, 134 *n.*
Ficino, Marsilio, 265, 266–7, 272
Filangieri, Gaetano, 10, 129–30
Fink, Z. S., 44 *n.*
Fischli, Walter, 113 *n.*
Fitz-James, Monseigneur de, 50
Fleury, Claude, 75
Fontenelle, Bernard Le Bovier de, 12, 53, 86, 317–18, 409
Foote, Samuel, 340
Forbes, Sir William, 42 *n.*

Fowler, H. W. and F. G., 151 *n.*

Frankfort, Henri, 92

Franklin, Benjamin, 8, 14, 17, 40,

Frederick II: *see* Frederick of Prussia

Frederick the Great: *see* Frederick of Prussia

Frederick of Prussia: and philosophes, 11, 25, 43, 98, 115, 198, 285, 362, 391, 393, 400; reign of, 99; and classical writers, 102, 120; and religion, 209, 348-9; and Bayle, 293

Fréret, Nicolas, 85, 383, 384, 399

Fréron, Élie, 6

Freud, Sigmund, 122

Froissart, Jean, 245 *n.*

Frontinus, Sextus Julius, 111

Fulgentius, Fabius Planciades, 222

Galiani, Abbé Fernando, 14, 15, 19, 49

Galileo, 83, 228, 247, 250, 279, 299, 309, 310, 314, 318

Gassendi, Pierre, 305-8, 309

Gay, Peter, 388 *n.*, 397 *n.*

Gellert, Christian Fürchtegott, 351

George I, 344

Ghiberti, Lorenzo, 221

Ghirlandaio, 276

Giannone, Pietro, 11, 372-3

Gibbon, Edward: and his contemporaries, 11, 357, 400; quoted, 13, 70, 73, 87, 115, 143, 278; on decline and fall of Rome, 15, 94, 95, 96, 111, 118, 119-20, 207, 213, 215, 369-70; influence of, 38, 180-1; early life, 55-6; on his discovery of Rome, 57-8, 271; and religion, 60, 156-7, 211, 326, 358, 359; and classical writers, 85, 114, 117, 123, 126, 151-2, 154, 157-9, 189, 222, 361 *n.*; and other writers, 106, 292, 300, 300 *n.*, 320, 368-9; 410; on criticism, 131, 150; irony of, 153; on history, 209, 210-11, 218, 277

Gilbert, D. L., 47 *n.*

Gilson, Étienne, 217 *n.*

Giotto, 35 *n.*, 257

Giulini, Alessandro, 71 *n.*

Glanvill, Joseph, 316, 325

Glover, T. R., 154 *n.*

God: philosophes on, 7, 25, 61-2, 76, 122, 142, 173, 180, 182, 203, 254, 332, 335, 351, 387, 389, 390-1, 397, 415-16, 417 *n.*, 419; Christians on, 145, 233, 235, 238, 239-41, 250; early views on, 208, 229, 240, 242-3, 248, 252, 272, 305, 309-10; saints on, 217, 230, 231, 234; in art, 276; seventeenth-century views on, 315, 327; eighteenth-century views on, 345, 354; and deists, 374-5

Goethe, Johann Wolfgang von, 16, 62, 63, 145, 177, 179, 350, 375, 400

Goldsmith, Oliver, 42

Gottsched, Johann Christoph, 293

Grabmann, Martin, 230 *n.*

Gracchi, 47

Graham, Henry Gray, 54 *n.*

Gray, Thomas, 6

Greek Miracle, 78, 86

Green, F. C., 6 *n.*

Gregory, Dr. John, 403

Greppi, Emanuele, 71 *n.*

Grimm, Baron Friedrich Melchior von, 12, 19, 48, 49, 98, 104-5, 399 *n.*

Grimsley, Ronald, 46 *n.*

Grosseteste, Robert, 247, 248

Grotius, Hugo, 299-300, 320

Guicciardini, Francesco, 278, 298

Gummere, Richard M., 39 *n.*, 40 *n.*

Hadrian, 115

Hagedorn, Friedrich von, 12

Haller, Albrecht von, 22, 23

Handel, George Frederick, 348 *n.*

Harrington, James, 44 *n.*, 283

Hartley, David, 23, 340

Hatfield, Henry, 142 *n.*

Hayward, John, 287 n.

Hazard, Paul, 291 n.

Hegel, Georg Wilhelm Friedrich, 37, 237

Heine, Heinrich, 33

Helmont, Jan Baptista van, 316

Héloïse, 232

Helvétius, Claude, 6, 10, 11, 17, 54, 136, 340

Henri IV, 60, 386

Henry VIII, 280

Herbert, Edward, Baron of Cherbury, 303

Hercules, 76

Herder, Johann Gottfried von, 87, 177, 349, 351 n.

Herodotus, 74 n., 77 n., 85, 123

Herrad, abbess of Hohenburg, 229

Hesiod, 410

Hildesheim, abbot of, 220

Hippocrates, 31

Hoadly, Benjamin, 344

Hobbes, Thomas, 17, 43 n., 44 n-5 n., 99, 161 n., 314, 316, 349, 398, 402

Hocke, Gustav R., 105 n.

Holbach, Paul-Henri, baron d': and his contemporaries, 7, 15, 17, 19, 49, 173, 176, 397, 398–401; philosophy of, 12, 144–5, 184, 400; quoted, 54; on history, 89; and classical writers, 108, 190, 371; antireligion, 103, 105, 181, 318; on criticism, 150; writings of, 176, 384, 399–400; and other writers, 291, 306, 383, 403

Home, Henry: *see* Kames, Henry Home, Lord

Homer: and philosophes, 31, 45, 48, 49, 54, 86, 226 n., 323; and his contemporaries, 123; influence of, 213, 288; Dante on, 224; writings of, 304

Honnecourt, 238–9

Horace: and philosophes, 9 n., 39, 40, 42, 46, 48, 49, 50, 57, 62, 63, 67, 69, 70, 96, 110, 162–3, 187; writings of, 83, 96, 173–4, 226 n., 282; philosophy of, 85, 125, 163; and his contemporaries, 97, 120; life of, 164; and Stoicism, 165; and Christians, 223–4; and Humanists, 267; translations of, 281; Montaigne on, 288

Hrabanus, Maurus, 219–20, 221, 228

Hubert, René, 73 n.

Huizinga, Johan, 244 n.

Humanism, 10, 73, 107, 108, 280, 301, 351

Humanists: rediscovery of antiquity, 74, 261–8, 278; characteristics of, 226, 258, 268 n., 269, 282; Christian, 257, 260; philosophes on, 257–8; and classical writers, 271, 305; early, 273; late, 274–5, 314; on art, 277; and printing, 280–1; and religion, 297

Humboldt, Baron Wilhelm von, 239

Hume, David: and his contemporaries, 5, 8, 11, 15, 16, 372, 400–1; quoted, 9, 25–6, 34, 36, 64, 65–7, 69, 73, 74, 177, 206, 254, 319–20, 323, 416 n.; writings of, 10, 67, 145, 181, 190, 192, 263, 399; influence of, 13, 14, 22, 35, 329; born, 17; on Enlightenment, 20; on history, 32–3, 86, 89, 94, 121, 210; influence of, 38; paganism of, 64–7; philosophy of, 85, 129, 132, 134–5, 136, 143, 149, 283, 292 n., 405–7; on metaphysics, 136, 137–9; on miracles, 146, 147, 148, 404–7; on criticism, 150, 152–3; irony of, 153; on eclectics, 161; and religion, 169, 325, 326, 330, 341–2, 373, 374, 380, 407–19; dialogue of, 173; on Scholasticism, 227; and other writers, 285, 291–2, 318, 398; death of, 356–7; career of, 401–3

Hunter, Dr. John, 356 n.

Hutcheson, Francis, 65, 66

illuministi, 55, 70–1, 129
Inquisition, 32, 198
Isidore of Seville, 229

James II, 343
Jansenists, 26, 281, 354, 388
Jefferson, Thomas, 11, 17, 55, 83, 105
Jerusalem, J. F. W., 330
Jesuits: philosophes' attitude toward, 22, 24, 200, 202, 372, 401; banishment of, 26; and *illuministi,* 55; writings of, 76, 104, 359; use of pagan writings, 282; and Bayle, 294; teachings of, 326; expulsion from France, 352–3; eighteenth-century, 354–5; on *Encyclopédie,* 364; and Voltaire, 386, 388–9, 390; and Hume, 404
Joachim of Floris, 335
Jogland, Herta Helena, 54 *n.*
John of Salisbury, 217, 222, 225, 243
Johnson, Samuel: and his contemporaries, 21, 401, 404, 406, 418; and Boswell, 22, 147 *n.,* 357, 402; quoted, 39, 42, 402; writings of, 40; on witchcraft, 147 *n.,* and Bayle, 293; and Grotius, 300; and religion, 338, 340, 344, 346, 407
Judaism, ancient, 93, 153
Judas, 214
Julian, 320, 323
Justi, Carl, 46 *n.*
Justin Martyr, 220
Juvenal, 40, 98, 116–17, 125, 153–4, 167

Kaegi, Werner, 275 *n.*
Kames, Henry Home, Lord, 15, 128 *n.,* 341, 404 *n.*
Kant, Immanuel: on Enlightenment, 3, 20–1, 27, 33, 39; writings of, 10, 145, 197; and his contemporaries, 11, 13, 14, 15, 17, 19, 141–2, 176; schooling, 45; and classical writers, 73, 74 *n.,* 120; on history, 87, 89; philosophy of,

108, 130, 131–2, 134, 143, 180, 231, 235, 258; on metaphysics, 136–7; and religion, 329–30
Kepler, Johannes, 250
Ker, W. P., 315 *n.*
Kierkegaard, Sören Aabye, 404
King, C. W., 153 *n.*
Kircher, Athanasius, 77, 98
Kirk, Rudolf, 301 *n.*
Klopstock, Friedrich, 12

La Barre, Chevalier de, 355
La Condamine, Charles Marie de, 340
Lactantius, Firmianus, 273
Lagrange-Chancel, Joseph de, 54, 104
Lambert von Hersfeld, 229
Lambin, Denis, 304
La Mettrie, Julien Offroy de, 8–9, 89, 103, 162, 306
La Mothe le Vayer, François de, 306–7
Lampridius, Aelius, 67
Landriani, Gerardo, 261
Languis, 301–2
Le Cati, 135 *n.*
Le Clerc, Jean, 11
l'Église, Baron Blot de, 307
Leibniz, Baron Gottfried Wilhelm von, 52, 135, 139, 161 *n.,* 203, 305, 316, 319, 329, 331, 334–5
Leitzmann, Albert, 4 *n.,* 350 *n.*
l'Enclos, Ninon de, 307, 308
Leopold II, 373
Leslie, Charles, 346
Lessing, Gotthold: and his contemporaries, 5, 11, 17, 19; writings of, 10, 12, 16, 26, 173–4, 176, 179, 181, 197, 214, 298; influence of, 14, 38; quoted, 30; religion of, 60–2; and classical writers, 68, 84–5, 94, 114; philosophy of, 131, 149, 182, 331–5, 401; on history, 210; and other writers, 283, 291, 295, 380; and religion, 330, 351, 372, 373 *n.,* 381–2; early life, 348 *n.,* 349

Lessing, Karl, 330 n., 332 n.
Lichtenberg, Georg Christoph, 12, 14, 20, 135, 142, 197, 206, 350, 352
Lipsius, Justus, 264, 284, 300–3, 309, 360
Livy, 44 n., 85, 97, 110, 122, 164, 218, 281, 283
Locke, John: and Enlightenment, 11, 135, 256, 320–1; writings of, 17, 139, 235, 327, 382; quoted, 70; and philosophes, 84, 322; and his contemporaries, 138, 176; and classical writers [...] it- [...] nd

[...], [...], 209, 350, 357, 371, 387, 400, 409; and his time, 98–104, 108, 110; writings of, 190, 408, 409; and Humanists, 262, 263; and Epicureans, 304–5
Luther, Martin, 280, 322, 360
Lyell, Sir Charles, 89
Lysippus, 221

Mabillon, Jean, 360, 368, 370
Mably, abbé de, 18
McCloy, Shelby T., 320 n.
Machiavelli, Niccolò: and classical writers, 44 n., 281, 283; influence of, 55; as pagan, 74, 195; style of, 257, 309; writings of, 269, 278, 279, 302; and philosophes, 284–6; and other writers, 366

Machiavellianism, 285, 286
Mack, Mrs. Mary P., 54 n.
McManners, John, 141 n.
Maecenas, 111
Magee, William, 22
Magnus, Albertus, 225
Mahomet, 346
Mâle, Émile, 182 n.
Malebranche, Nicolas de, 139
Malesherbes, Chrétien, 6, 26, 141
Malherbe, François de, 276 n.
Manetti, Giannozzo, 273
Mann, Horace, 16 n.; 84 n.
Mann, Sir Horace, 253
Mantegna, Andrea, 275
Manuel, Frank, 77 n.
Manutius, Aldus, 281
Manuzzi, Aldo, 304
Marche, Olivier de la, 245 n.
Marcus Aurelius: and philosopher, 47, 50, 120, 124; writings of, 108, 109; time of, 125; and Stoicism, 165, 288, 296; philosophy of, 196; and Wesley, 347
Margaret of York, 245 n.
Maria Theresa, 355
Marmontel, Jean-François, 18, 63, 112–13, 191 n.
Marsak, Leonard M., 317 n.
Martial, 98, 114–15, 164, 186
Masaccio, 275
Mather, Cotton, 338
Maupeou, René Nicolas Charles Augustin de, 26
Maupertuis, Pierre Louis Moreau de, 14
Maury, Rev. James, 55
Mautner, Franz, 142 n.
Mayo, Thomas F., 306 n.
Medici, Cosimo de', 270
Medici, Lorenzo de', 257, 272
Medici, the, 267, 276, 277, 286
Melior, Cardinal, 253
Memmius, 100, 104
Mendelssohn, Moses, 11, 19, 30, 176
Meslier, Jean, 392 n.
Messalina, Valeria, 111

metaphor, early Christians' use of, 239–40, 242

metaphysics, 17, 23, 132–41, 136, 181, 186, 208, 228

Michelangelo, 276, 282

Michelet, Jules, 277

Middleton, Conyers, 40, 106, 259, 376, 380

Middle Ages: religion during, 208–9, 242; Enlightenment view of, 209–12, 257; and Dante, 213, 215; Christians during, 219; writers during, 225–6; philosophes on, 227, 233, 246; characteristics of, 237, 240, 246–7, 248–9, 251, 269, 276; and classical writers, 262, 288; and other writers, 365

Millar, Andrew, 254

Milton, John, 44 n.

Mirabeau, Victor Riqueti, marquis de, 46

miracles, 146–59, 384, 404, 406

Molière, 281, 307

Mommsen, Theodor, 97

Monboddo, Lord James Burnett, 77 n.

Montague, F. C., 142 n.

Montaigne, Michel Eyquem de, 42, 281, 284, 287–90, 300, 303, 400

Montamy, M. de, 341

Montesquieu, Charles de Secondat, baron de: and his contemporaries, 10, 11, 22, 26, 136, 317; philosophy of, 12, 180 n.; writings of, 16, 172, 385; born, 17; and classical writers, 18, 50–1, 83, 86, 105, 117, 120, 126, 162, 259, 371; on history, 34, 75, 95, 96, 119, 121, 154–5, 168, 169; influence of, 38; quoted, 87; on criticism, 150; and other writers, 285, 291, 295, 298, 300–1; and religion, 352, 373 n., 383

Montfaucon, Bernard de, 352, 360, 370

Morellet, abbé André, 10, 11 n.

Morgan, Thomas, 375

Moses, 48, 74, 76, 220, 307, 315, 321

Mossner, Ernest C., 13 n., 291 n., 326 n., 356 n., 403 n., 409 n.

Mozart, Wolfgang Amadeus, 22

Muratori, Lodovico Antonio, 359

Mure, Elizabeth, 342

Murray, Gilbert, 107 n., 118

Mylius, Christlob, 380

mythical thinking, 90–4, 100, 118, 123–5, 185–6, 237–8, 242, 250–2

Nachod, Hans, 267 n.

Naigeon brothers, 70, 348

Naville, Pierre, 54 n.

Neologians, 330, 331, 332, 348, 350

Neoplatonists, 83, 232, 242, 250, 266, 276

Nero, 67, 110, 111, 112–13

Nerva, 110–11, 115

Newton, Sir Isaac: influence of, 11, 14, 17, 320, 374; and his contemporaries, 12, 31, 32; and philosophes, 74 n., 136, 143, 322; and classical writers, 77 n., Pope on, 103; science of, 121, 135, 139, 199, 310, 316; and other writers, 305, 306, 316, 320, 361, 365; and his time, 309; writings of, 314; and religion, 382, 388, 395

Niccoli, Niccolò, 264

Nicolai, Christoph, 16

Nicolai, Friedrich, 45, 351

Nicolas V, 274

Nicolaus of Cusa, 239, 240, 272, 274

Nietzsche, Friedrich Wilhelm, 270

Noah, 76

North, Sir Thomas, 281

Norton, J. E., 56 n.

Numa, 155

Occam, William of, 235

Oestreich, Gerhard, 301 n.

Oglethorpe, James Edward, 39

Olivet, abbé d', 64 n.

Origen, 169, 219, 241

Orléans, Duc Louis Philippe d', 341

Oswald, James, 341 *n.*

Otloh of St. Emmeram, 219

Otto of Freising, 244

Ovid: and philosophes, 40, 43, 50, 110; and his contemporaries, 97; on religion, 153–4; origin of, 164; and Christians, 219, 222–3, 248, 305; Dante on, 224; and Humanists, 264; translations of, 281; as subject, 282, 288

Paganism: and philosophes, 8–9, 26, 46, 48, 51, 55, 60, 62–3; ancient, 170; and Christianity, 207, 216, 217–18, 220, 224, 256–7, 282, 368

Palissot de Montenoy, Charles, 6, 10

Panaetius, 50, 165

Panofsky, Erwin, 242 *n.*, 267 *n.*

Parma, Prince of, 227

Pascal, Blaise, 75, 174, 283, 314, 320, 388–90

Patrick, Simon, 315

Patrizzi, Francesco, 265

Pausanias, 49, 85

Pelopidas, 47

Pepi II, 92

Percy, Thomas, 211

Pérelle, Antoine-Robert, 382 *n.*

Pericles, 35

Peripatetics, 194

Persius, 49, 113

Petrarch: writings of, 71, 265, 268 *n.*, 270, 278; time of, 256, 257; on Cicero, 260–1; and his contemporaries, 263, 278; and classical writers, 267; death of, 269; life of, 270–2; and Humanists, 274, 275

Petronius, 113, 125, 162

Pharaohs, 79

Pico della Mirandola, Giovanni, 268, 272–3, 279, 298

Piero di Cosimo, 304

Pietiests, 62, 291, 326, 328–9, 348, 350

Pilate, Pontius, 143

Plan, Pierre-Paul, 68 *n.*

Planck, Gottlieb Jakob, 331

Plato: and philosophes, 48, 62, 68, 83, 121–2, 135, 383; philosophy of, 52, 77, 80, 148, 193–5, 230, 276, 409; and Scholastics, 82; antireligion, 102; and his time, 135, 171, 213; and his contemporaries, 144; life of, 192; Christians on, 219, 229, 232, 244; writings of, 226 *n.*, 281; and Humanists, 263, 271, 272–3; and other writers, 309, 310, 316 *n.;* and Cambridge Platonists, 314

Platonism, 208, 216, 247, 272, 310

Platonists, 83, 172, 196, 232, 257, 268, 283, 314, 325

Plautus, 56, 59

Pliny the Elder, 65, 85, 98, 107, 123, 124

Pliny the Younger, 115–16, 123–4, 187

Plotinus, 272

Plutarch: and philosophes, 46, 47, 51, 64, 67, 292; writings of, 85, 120, 123, 125, 126; on religion, 152–4; philosophy of, 166, 243; origin of, 164; translations of, 281; influence of, 284

Poggio Bracciolini, Giovanni, 261, 262

Pohlenz, Max, 301 *n.*

Polignac, Cardinal de, 104

Politian, 276

Polybius, 154, 281, 283, 296, 301

Pomeau, René, 339 *n.*, 389 *n.*

Pompadour, Mme de, 363

Pompey, 112, 286

Pope, Alexander, 22, 40, 103, 114, 186; writings of, 382

Pope Gregory, 217

Pope Gregory VII, 217

Pope Innocent III, 273

Porten, Catherine, 56 *n.*

Portinari, Beatrice, 236, 251

Posidonius, 165

Pottle, Frederick A., 22 *n.*, 340 *n.*

Pougens, C., 46 *n.*

Poussin, Nicolas, 282
Priestley, Joseph, 23
Prophets, 48
Proust, Marcel, 286 *n*.
Pyrrho, 284, 290, 307
Pyrrhonism, 291 *n*., 293, 353, 390
Pyrrhonists, 289, 290, 292 *n*.
Pythagoras, 77

Quintilian, 113–14, 125, 164, 178, 262

Rabelais, François, 262, 265
Rae, John, 22 *n*.
Racine, Jean Baptiste, 11, 281, 282, 385
Ramses II, 92
Ramses III, 92
Rand, Benjamin, 11 *n*.
Raphael, 257, 276
Raynal, Guillaume, 15, 18, 63, 145, 176, 398
realism, 178–80, 184–5, 186, 196–7, 238–9, 284
Reformation, 275, 280, 296
Reformers, 280
Reimarus, Herman Samuel, 61–2, 351, 381–2
Renaissance: and philosophes, 17, 55, 261, 277, 279; time of, 74, 75, 95, 113, 244, 245, 255, 257–60, 268, 269; pagan thought during, 220; and classical writers, 259–61, 264; characteristics of, 263, 264, 265, 266, 267, 269, 270, 276, 277, 278, 280, 302; and Humanists, 263, 265, 274; artists of, 275–6; Christianity during, 314, 359
Restoration, 315, 343
Revett, 84
Reynolds, Sir Joshua, 402
Ridolfi, 286 *n*.
Rienzi, Cola di, 269
Robertson, William, 15, 19, 227–8, 232, 258
Rollin, Charles, 75
Rousseau, Jean-Jacques: philosophy

of, 5, 112, 166, 179, 180, 245–6; and his contemporaries, 7, 11, 13, 26, 48 *n*., 322, 336; life of, 8, 15, writings of, 16, 128 *n*., 176; born, 17; attitude toward civilization, 25, 271; quoted, 36; and classical writers, 45 *n*., 46, 47, 77 *n*., 82–3, 196, 226 *n*., 281; deism of, 67–8; on history, 88, 208; on criticism, 150; quarrel with Diderot, 195–6; and other writers, 285, 291, 300 *n*.
Rupelmonde, Mme de, 104

Sack, A. F. W., 330
Sade, Comte Donatien Alphonse François de, marquis de, 25
Sahure, 92
St. Ambrose, 224
St. Anselm, 171, 231, 250
St. Augustine: and philosophes, 32; writings of, 83, 211, 270, 282; time of, 217; on antiquity, 218, 225; and other writers, 219; and paganism, 220; and classics, 220–1, 229–31; philosophy of, 235, 241, 242, 266; as subject, 272
St. Bernard of Clairvaux, 210–11, 217, 370
Saint-Évremond, Charles de Marguetel de Saint-Denis, Seigneur de, 287 *n*., 308
St. Jerome, 218–19, 224–5, 274, 282
St. John, 251
St. Paul, 169, 216–17, 232, 273, 301 *n*., 399
St. Prosper, 46
St. Thomas, 273
St. Thomas Aquinas, 171, 182, 211, 225, 233–4, 237, 243, 248, 250, 282
Sallust, 56
Salutati, Coluccio, 260–1
Savonarola, Girolamo, 273, 276
Scaevola, Gauius Mucius, 46
Schmidt, Erich, 349 *n*., 380 *n*.
Scholasticism, 23, 226–7, 268 *n*., 273, 298

Scholastics: and clasical writers, 82, 225; critics of, 72, 316, 321; and philosophes, 181–2, 183, 209, 227, 324; characteristics of, 228, 231, 232, 233, 250; on Cicero, 260; and Humanists, 267, 278

Scipio Africanus, 107, 192, 196, 224, 260, 302 *n.*

Semler, Johann Salomo, 381

Seneca: and philosophes, 18, 32, 43, 48, 51, 54, 55, 64, 117, 128, 142 *n.*, 151, 159, 162, 301 *n.*, 417; life of, 112, 192; writings of, 124; quoted, 108, 196, origin of, 164; and Stoicism, 165, 188, 264, 289, 296; and Christians, 208, 220; and Humanists, 267, 281; and other writers, 288, 302, 303; translations of, 299, 301; influence of, 299; attitude toward, 308; time of, 319

Sengle, Friedrich, 63, 136 *n.*, 275 *n.*, 351 *n.*

Servetus, 337

Seznec, Jean, 49 *n.*, 70 *n.*, 134 *n.*

Shaftesbury, Anthony Ashley Cooper, Earl of, 11, 30, 41, 64, 144, 150, 177, 327, 330

Shakespeare, William, 12, 243–4, 285, 322

Sharp, Archbishop, 345–6

Silvestris, Bernard, 222

Skeptics, 126, 296, 308, 325

Smith, Adam, 11, 14, 15, 54, 129, 134, 172, 181, 356, 414

Smith, N. K., 357 *n.*, 414 *n.*

Smollett, Tobias George, 188 *n.*

Society of the Dilettanti, 84–5

Socinians, 317, 320, 324, 329, 331, 337, 384

Socrates: and philosophes, 43, 48, 286; philosophy of, 81–2, 170; time of, 125; on himself, 144; Christians on, 219, 244; influence of, 288, 316 *n.*

Solon, 79

Sonnenfels, Freiherr von, 19

Sophocles, 69, 282, 385

Spalding, J. J., 330, 380

Spink, J. S., 307 *n.*

Spinoza, Baruch, 62, 139, 176, 283, 285, 293, 303, 331, 384, 402

Sprat, Thomas, 315

Statius, 114, 215

Stephens, Leslie, 375 *n.*

Stern, J. P., 135 *n.*

Stewart, Dugald, 34 *n.*, 54

Stoicism: and philosophes, 50, 174, 313, 326; and ancients, 112, 189; and eclecticism, 164–5; and Christianity, 216, 264, 296, 298, 303–4; Roman, 268; popularity of, 301; of later writers, 302–3; Epicureans on, 304; other writers on, 367

Stoics: and philosophes, 13, 32, 41, 50, 54, 83, 94, 172, 324, 419; philosophy of, 107, 123, 129, 154, 164–5, 166, 194, 202, 240, 292 *n.*, 317, 395, 408; ancients as, 113, 125, 163, 165–6, 188, 190; Christian, 170, 257, 320, 325; and other writers, 367

Strabo, 67, 152

Stradling, Sir John, 301 *n.*

Stromberg, Roland, 325 *n.*

Stuart, Gilbert Charles, 84

Suetonius, 111, 116, 124

superstition: and philosophes, 4, 51, 83–4, 125, 152–3, 185, 190, 237; and ancients, 80, 150, 155; and Christianity, 237

Sutherland, James, 42 *n.*, 345 *n.*

Swedenborg, 137

Swift, Jonathan, 39, 133, 142, 162, 325, 339, 358, 375

Sykes, Norman, 315 *n.*, 345 *n.*, 346 *n.*

symbols, early Christians' use of, 239–42, 249–53

Syme, Sir Ronald, 158 *n.*

Tacitus: pholosophy of, 32, 125; and philosophes, 49, 57, 67, 117, 157, 283, 285; and his contemporaries, 98, 111, 113, 116–17, 118; writings of, 126, 281; on religion,

157; style of, 157–9; and Humanists, 262; and Stoics, 300

Tannery, Paul, 311 *n.*

Tasso, Torquato, 31, 67

Terence, 48, 49, 57, 69, 128

Tertullian, 216 *n.*, 217

Terentia, 156

Thales, 72, 73

Thayer, H. S., 316 *n.*

Theophrastus, 69

Thomasius, Christian, 132, 301, 328, 366

Thucydides, 74, 76

Tiberius, 118

Tillemont, Sébastien Le Nain de, 368–70

Tillotson, Archbishop John, 61, 326, 344, 345 *n.*, 346

Timoleon, 17

Tindal, Matthew, 327, 376, 379–80, 388

Toland, John, 145, 327, 375, 376–7, 380, 383

Toynbee, Mrs. Paget, 7 *n.*

Trajan, 98, 115, 281

Trenchard, 383

Tressan, Comte de, 284 *n.*

Tronchin, Dr. Théodore, 337

Tudors, 279

Tullius, 219

Tully: *see* Cicero

Turgot, Anne Robert Jacques: and contemporaries, 13, 17, 136; and religion, 25, 373 *n.*; influence of, 38; and classical writers, 39, 195; writings of, 77 *n.*; on history, 121 209

Tuthomsis III, 92

Ussher, Archbishop James, 89

Utilitarians, 150, 373

Uz, Johann Peter, 275 *n...*.

Valla, Lorenzo, 265, 273–4

Varro, 152, 154, 219, 229

Vasari, Giorgio, 35 *n.*, 265, 275, 278

Vauvenargues, Luc de Clapiers, marquis de, 46

Vergil: and philosophes, 9 *n.*, 46, 48, 49, 50, 54, 57, 62, 69, 217, 386; and his contemporaries, 97, 98, 99, 112, 120; Voltaire on, 97–8; writings of, 116, 215, 282; origin of, 164; use by Church Fathers, 208; Dante on, 213–15, 218, 221–2, 224, 236; and Christians, 222, 223; and Humanists, 263; translations of, 281; Montaigne on, 288

Verri, Alessandro, 71

Verri, Pietro, 71 *n.*

Velat, abbé, 76 *n.*

Villard de Honnecourt, 238

Vincent of Beauvais, 182, 233, 248

Virgin Mary, 252–3, 275, 276, 379, 391, 399, 411

Voltaire: and his contemporaries, 5, 13, 14–15, 18, 19, 20, 21, 26, 48 *n.*, 62, 68, 69, 98, 103, 127, 138, 141–2, 174, 187, 188, 308, 368, 371, 385–6, 400, 402; philosophy of, 6, 7, 11, 12, 132, 136, 143, 144, 172, 180, 182, 247, 258, 318, 373; life of, 9, 25; writings of, 10, 16, 145, 176, 181, 191 *n.*, 197–203, 270, 283, 384, 385–6, 393–6, 399, 412, 417 *n.*; influence of, 17, 350; on Jesuits, 24; on clergy tax, 26; quoted, 30, 31, 43, 52, 53, 54, 73–4, 108, 122–3, 125, 133 *n.*, 168, 228, 351, 394–5; on eighteenth century, 33, 41, 168, 179, 181; on history, 34, 35, 74, 75, 77 *n.*, 79, 85, 89, 93, 167, 209, 210, 266, 273 *n.*, 277 *n.*, 280; and classical writers, 43, 47, 51–2, 55, 73–4, 80, 83, 97–8, 102, 103–4, 105, 106, 109, 112, 114, 116, 117–18, 191, 216, 222, 226–7, 259, 271 *n.*, 274, 281, 282; early life, 64; on Epicureanism, 99; on metaphysics, 135; on miracles, 147, 148; irony of, 153; on religion, 168–71, 203, 209, 254–5, 324, 326, 329, 335, 348, 352, 354, 358, 376, 386–9, 415; and other writers, 213, 214, 274–5, 283, 285–6, 289, 291, 293, 295, 301, 302 *n.*, 305, 306, 307, 315, 316–17, 320, 321, 323, 379, 382 *n.*, 384, 403; and Geneva article, 336–8; later life, 361–2; collaboration with mistress, 361–4; career of, 385; and deism, 387–96, 413; and Holbach, 397–8

Volland, Sophie, 5, 7, 9, 48, 64, 162, 176, 180 *n.*, 187, 188, 340, 341, 372, 386 *n.*, 399, 401 *n.*

Voss, Johann Heinrich, 351

Wade, Ira O., 104 *n.*, 324 *n.*, 384 *n.*, 387 *n.*

Walpole, Horace: and his contemporaries, 6–7, 10, 15, 26 *n.*; quoted, 16, 106; on his time, 41, 84, 253–4; and religion, 343, 344, 349

Warburg, Aby, 259, 270

Warburton, Bishop William, 409, 413

Warren, Mme de, 68

Weinshenker, Anne Betty, 132 *n.*

Wesley, Charles, 39, 347

Wesley, John, 254, 300, 346–7

Whitefield, George, 254, 346

Whitehead, Alfred North, 310

Wickwar, W. H., 398 *n.*

Wieland, Christoph; and his contemporaries, 5, 11, 17, 135–6, 177; quoted, 13; and classical writers, 39, 63, 83, 120, 159, 172, 275 *n.*; paganism of, 62–3; philosophy of, 70; writings of, 143–4, 179, 275; and predecessors, 283, 291; and religion, 351, 372

Wilkes, John, 54

Wilson, John A., 91

Winckelmann, Johann Joachim, 46, 77 *n.*, 84, 120, 293

Wittkower, Rudolf, 276

Wolff, Baron Christian von, 62, 301, 328–30, 331, 365, 380

Wolff, Hans M., 132 *n.*

Woolston, Thomas, 375, 376, 378–9, 380, 383

Xenophon, 62, 74, 76, 189

Yolton, John W., 327 *n.*

Young, G. M., 117 *n.*, 326

Yvon, abbé, 73

Zeno, 43, 164

Zoroaster, 74

A NOTE ABOUT THE AUTHOR

PETER GAY was born in Berlin, Germany, in 1923 and came to the United States as a young man. A graduate of the University of Denver, he took his M.A. and Ph.D. degrees at Columbia University and joined the Columbia faculty in 1947 as a part-time lecturer in government. He later became assistant professor of government; in 1955 he decided to switch to the department of history at Columbia. In 1962 he was made full professor of history. Regarded as one of the leading authorities on the intellectual history of eighteenth-century Europe, Professor Gay has published many articles and several books, including *The Party of Humanity: Essays in the French Enlightenment, The Dilemma of Democratic Socialism,* and *Voltaire's Politics.* He has also translated Voltaire's *Philosophical Dictionary* and *Candide.*

judicious 114

authoritarian dogma + ecstatic
    experiences 119

"pitiless legalism of Calvin" 211

Voltaire on the LisS 254, 255

philosophical theologian =
    strange centaur (Gibbon) 320

English Church in XVIII C. 343

Benjamin Hoadly 344
